THE BURDENS OF BROTHERHOOD

THE BURDENS OF
BROTHERHOOD

Jews and Muslims from
North Africa to France

Ethan B. Katz

Harvard University Press

Cambridge, Massachusetts
London, England
2015

First printing

Library of Congress Cataloging-in-Publication Data

Katz, Ethan, author.
The burdens of brotherhood : Jews and Muslims from North Africa to France /
Ethan B. Katz.
pages cm
Includes bibliographical references and index.
ISBN 978-0-674-08868-9 (alk. paper)
1. Jews—France—Social conditions—20th century. 2. Jews—France—Social
conditions—21st century. 3. Muslims—France—Social conditions—20th century.
4. Muslims—France—Social conditions—21st century. 5. Jews—Cultural
assimilation—France. 6. Muslims—Cultural assimilation—France.
7. Social integration—France. 8. France—Ethnic relations. I. Title.
DS135.F83K378 2015
305.892'4044—dc23
2015010848

For Allan Katz and Nancy Cohn—
loving, nurturing parents and citizens of the world

CONTENTS

THE BURDENS OF
BROTHERHOOD

INTRODUCTION

The Jewish-Muslim Question in Modern France

On August 28, 1961, as the French-Algerian War neared its bitter end, two Algerian Jews who had recently arrived in the French port city of Marseille went looking for help in the same unlikely destination. Both men needed a place to live for their large families and a job to support them. Simon Zouaghi was married with seven children and had run a butcher shop in Constantine; he left Algeria due to a growing sense of insecurity about its future. For Martin Mardochée Benisti, a husband and father of four who worked as a cook in Constantine, threats to him or his family precipitated his departure. Neither man could bring much with him in the way of resources when he crossed the Mediterranean to France.[1]

Zouaghi, Benisti, and their families were part of a growing stream of Jews and colonial settlers leaving Algeria for the French mainland in the face of continuing violence and the increasing likelihood that Algeria would soon become independent. For many Jewish emigrants, the rise of the National Liberation Front (FLN) independence movement, in which Islam played a growing role, and uncertainty about whether Jews would be welcome in a free Algeria, became key factors in the decision to leave. On this day, Zouaghi and Benisti both chose to try their luck at Marseille's government office for the Service of Muslim Affairs (SAM).

Odd as the choice may sound for Algerian Jews to seek help at an agency for Muslims, Zouaghi and Benisti were far from alone. Between July 1961 and May 1962, approximately one thousand recently arrived Algerian Jews showed up at Marseille's SAM office to ask for assistance. These Jews were more than 40 percent—a rather disproportionate number—of the twenty-three hundred non-Muslims who stepped through the office's doors and registered during these chaotic eleven months.[2] The

1

Jews who came here hailed from cities and small towns across Algeria; professionally, most were small shopkeepers, artisans, or of other modest backgrounds. Nearly all cited the ongoing events in Algeria as their cause for departure.

During the same period, thousands of Jews from Algeria looked to other sources for help. These included the social services arm of the French Jewish community, Catholic and Protestant charities, the French Red Cross, the government minister of public health and population, and the recently established office of the secretary of state for *rapatriés* (the "repatriated" from France's colonies and former colonies); a few even wrote directly to President Charles de Gaulle. Charitable organizations and government agencies found themselves overwhelmed as the trickle of immigrants from Algeria became a flood of over 1 million people.[3] Thus, at some level, we can see those Jews who walked into the SAM as simply a few among many who desperately sought aid wherever they might find it. And yet the question persists: With so many possible places to turn, why were Jews, seemingly fleeing from their Muslim neighbors, more willing than most other new immigrants to try their luck at a government office designated specifically for Muslims?

Indeed, in the context of France's Jewish-Muslim crisis of the twenty-first century, this episode defies a host of common assumptions. It has become conventional wisdom to see Jewish and Muslim lives as strictly separated, if not violently opposed due to the impact of the Israeli-Arab conflict. We often assume that the histories of Jews in modern Europe and Muslims in North Africa have little to do with each other; we think of Jews as long integrated within France and Muslims as perpetually excluded. Likewise, this story does not fit the sharp dichotomies through which we tend more broadly to understand the history of France and of Jews and Muslims in the modern world. These dichotomies include assimilation and difference; powerful and powerless; privileged and underprivileged; colonizer and colonized; secular and religious; citizen and foreigner. In the French Mediterranean of autumn 1961, today's assumptions were hardly the norm; what appears in hindsight as clearly defined was rather more fluid at the time.

Although it remains difficult to interpret the choices of the one thousand Jews who entered the SAM office, it is evident that their decision was emblematic of a moment—crucial to the history this book recounts—of transition and deep uncertainty. The legal, national, and ethnic status of all those from Algeria remained in flux; for many Jews and Muslims, complex and multiple allegiances existed. The socioeconomic background of most Jews who came to the SAM was not incidental. Among Algerian Jews, who had been French citizens for most of the previous ninety years, those of modest background were the most likely to continue to follow traditional Algerian customs, speak a Jewish dialect of Arabic, and maintain personal and professional ties to their Muslim neighbors.[4] The registration of these Jews at the SAM possibly reflected the recommendation of Muslim fellow arrivals from Algeria; at the very least, it indicated how entangled the lives of thousands of Jews and Muslims had long been on both sides of the French Mediterranean. Furthermore, the choice suggested that in spite of the current challenges, some degree of comfort endured among many Jews with regard to peoples and things called "Muslim." Jews from Algeria appeared as likely to feel affinity for Muslims as for European settlers. Perhaps most important, ethnoreligious labels, although surely significant, did not determine everything; Jews and Muslims could understand themselves and one another in myriad ways.

The document that informs us about these Jews having entered a space designated for Muslims also reveals a great deal about the insecurity of this moment for the French state. The names listed in this registry are placed under the heading of "French coming from Algeria received at the Service of Muslim Affairs." This phrase implied that Frenchness set apart Jews and colonists from the main group served at this office: Muslims. Of course, Muslims from Algeria were French too. In fact they continued to enjoy the fully equal legal rights as French citizens that they had acquired only three years earlier, with the 1958 Constitution of the Fifth Republic. Nevertheless, by late 1961, government memos that reaffirmed those rights had also begun to separate "Muslims" and "Europeans" of Algeria into two discrete categories.[5] The title scrawled at the top of this list thus constituted one government administrator's attempt, fraught with anxiety about the future, to assign clarity where little in fact existed. As is so often the case with sources that illumine the complex history of Jews and Muslims in France, this document has a multilayered meaning. The list's heading carries the veneer of hardened ethnic categories that are by now familiar to us; in fact, however, the author has imposed the very boundaries between groups that he or she claims merely to describe. Such a realization points us toward a far less familiar and more pliable reality that demands our attention.[6]

Rethinking the Jewish-Muslim Question

This book offers a history of Jewish-Muslim relations—social, political, and cultural—in metropolitan France, from the Great War to the present. How has it come to be the case that relationships in France between "Jewish" and "Muslim" individuals and groups are commonly reduced to "Jewish-Muslim relations" and linked automatically to transnational webs of ethnoreligious solidarity and conflict? Why do we assume that actors and observers imagine their interactions as principally between Jews and Muslims? What is gained or lost by understanding relations in these ways and projecting this framework onto the past?[7] How could such relationships be understood differently depending on their time, place, and articulation?

To answer these questions, we have to begin by thinking ourselves back into a series of moments in modern France where relations between Jewish and Muslim individuals and groups were not necessarily conceived by either participants or observers as "Jewish-Muslim interactions." As this book undertakes such an effort, it advances three principal arguments. First, historically, what we now call Jewish-Muslim relations in France were neither inevitably ethnoreligious nor necessarily oppositional. Rather, Jews and Muslims in France interacted on a wide range of terms. I use the phrase *terms of interaction* to explore the various categories and milieux through which Jews and Muslims defined, perceived, and related to each other. Many Jews and Muslims inhabited the same or adjacent locales; enjoyed common culinary and musical traditions; faced similar or divergent paths to integration as new arrivals in France; participated as allies or opponents in local, national, and international conflicts; patronized the same cafés and grocery stores; and interacted on more intimate terms as neighbors, friends, and occasionally even lovers and family members. This book first traces, from World War I until the era of decolonization, the opening of a rich, complex tapestry of possible terms of Jewish-Muslim interaction. Next, focusing on the second half of the twentieth century, I analyze how relations between Muslims and Jews became defined increasingly by potentially conflicting ethnoreligious categories. However, even in this context, Jews and Muslims continued to interact in a multiplicity of ways that far escape the narrow framing of their relationships as encounters between Jews and Muslims.

As such I argue further that both the primacy and the very meaning of Jewish and Muslim ethnoreligious identities are best understood as highly *situational*; only at specific historical moments, particularly in the post-colonial period, did they become perceived as *definitional,* or overriding and singular. "Jewish" and "Muslim" have been highly amorphous, contingent, ever-shifting categories in modern France, constructed both from outside and within. As used here, these categories can include any individual or group self-understood or identified by external forces as Jewish or Muslim. Particularly in their modern incarnations, Judaism, Islam, Jewishness, and Muslimness have carried a multiplicity of meanings and practices rather than a single definition. In France, these categories could reflect everything from religious observances, to social networks, to racial stereotypes.

Therefore, when I speak throughout this book of Jewish-Muslim relations, or of Jewish-Muslim conflict and coexistence, I do so not as an acceptance of fixed categories or binaries, but in order to acknowledge that the ethnoreligious categories of Jew and Muslim had real and often crucial significance for Jews and Muslims themselves, as well as for the French state and broader society. Moreover, we necessarily write in the discernible terms of our time, even when we question the assumptions behind them. I contend that the best way to complicate the framework of "Jewish-Muslim relations" and reformulate our understanding of these relations is not to disregard the terminology altogether; rather, it is to show how such relations entailed many different types of self-understandings and interactions.

As for the third major argument, this book maintains that Jews and Muslims in France did not conceive of one another in a primordial manner divorced from the wider context of what Gary Wilder has termed the "French imperial nation-state."[8] Rather, their interactions were always what I call triangular, with France as the third party. That is, Jews and Muslims related to one another through their respective relationships to the French state and society and to definitions of French national and imperial belonging. Thus competing understandings and institutional manifestations of "Frenchness" inflected how Jews and Muslims saw one another and framed their every interaction. To a significant extent, the reverse was also true: Jews and Muslims often appraised their relationship to France through their relations with one another.

In the process, these two so-called marginal groups did much not only to illuminate but also to define the meaning of French nationhood, empire, and citizenship. In part, I contend that Jews and Muslims have helped to shape and reveal the possibilities and paradoxes of modern France as a Mediterranean space—at the level of politics, religion, demography, culture, collective memory, and even sensory experience. This has occurred through a range of ever-evolving Jewish and Muslim mobilities, encounters, and transnational connections, characterized at certain times by remarkable fluidity and at others by brutal division.

New Histories of Jews, Muslims, and France

The Burdens of Brotherhood focuses in large part on daily encounters and mutual perceptions between ordinary Jews and Muslims. I concentrate principally on two spheres of interaction: politics and sociocultural settings. Political interactions ranged from rallies or meetings in which Jewish and Muslim activists participated side by side, to competing stories in the press, to violent confrontations or joint combat in the context of national or international conflict. Until the late twentieth century, political relations occurred mainly between Ashkenazic Jews, particularly of the Left, and North African Muslims; here encounters were driven primarily by competing or common Jewish and Muslim claims to individual or collective rights. Sociocultural interactions, by contrast, were largely a product of the migration of hundreds of thousands of Jews and millions of Muslims from Algeria, Morocco, and Tunisia to France in the course of the twentieth century. Members of the two communities often settled in adjacent quarters in and around Paris, Marseille, and other cities. By the 1990s, the strong majority of the country's Jews and Muslims were of North African descent. Thus sociocultural encounters occurred primarily around common North African heritage and customs in neighborhoods, cafés, and food markets. Such overlapping culture sometimes extended to more structured events, such as musical soirées, sporting contests, and occasionally religious rituals.

To date, the lived interactions of ordinary Jews and Muslims in France have been almost entirely overlooked in both collective memory and scholarship. A complex history of varied encounters risks being lost in the powerful current of contemporary events. Since the early twenty-first century, a visible breakdown in relations between France's Jews and Muslims has occurred. With half a million Jews and 4 to 6 million Muslims, France is home to the largest Jewish and Muslim populations in Western Europe.[9] France has been the site of some of the most persistent—and lethal—antisemitic attacks in Europe in recent years; many of the perpetrators of such attacks have been Muslim. Commentators have thus frequently treated France as a microcosm for the larger challenges of Muslim integration and renewed antisemitism facing Europe.

Current conditions have also helped to spur the beginnings of a scholarship that examines Jews and Muslims in France together.[10] With occasional exception, however, books that treat both groups are oriented toward the present, focus much more heavily on one group than the other, or emphasize conflict far more than coexistence.[11] More broadly, relational or comparative studies of minorities in France remain rare.[12] Instead, scholars have typically examined one group in isolation from other minorities; for Muslims and Jews this has meant treating one or the other as inherently singular and examining that group's relationship to the French state and larger French society.

Placing Jews and Muslims within a single story has a number of important consequences. It brings greater nuance and precision to the two groups' respective paths and positions in France and shows how deeply interwoven they have been. This book's historical approach to Jews, Muslims, and their relations in France seeks as well to transcend contemporary polemics around Muslim-Jewish conflict, competing histories of suffering, and antisemitism and Islamophobia. Equally important, such a framework problematizes conventional narratives of modern France itself.

Many of the greatest challenges and opportunities for writing Jews and Muslims in France into one another's histories lie in the specifically colonial nature of this history. Colonialism has, until quite recently, been a decidedly problematic subject for both scholarly and popular understandings of modern French history, modern Jewish history, and the history of Muslims in Europe. This book seeks to build on new approaches in each of these fields. In the first instance, historians on both sides of the Atlantic have moved increasingly away from an older model that sharply distinguished the history of modern France, understood as that of a universal, democratic republic, from the history of the French colonial empire. Recently a number of scholars have insisted as well on the need to treat the empire not as an exception or separate dark side to France's egalitarian republic, but rather as inextricably linked to mainland France. Most now agree that metropole and colony each must be understood as sites of both universal and exclusionary practices and ideologies, at once places of liberal progress and brutal oppression.[13]

In modern Jewish history, a previous model that centered, especially in France, on a linear process of emancipation and assimilation at the

expense of public Jewish identities has been supplanted by work that illuminates greater complexity in many French Jews' personal and public
expressions of Jewishness, ways of achieving Jewish agency, and paths
to modernity.[14] Such developments have helped to open the way for a
growing interest in Jews and colonialism. This topic was previously neglected for several reasons: historical and contemporary polemics around
Zionism's relationship to colonialism; an avoidance of the topic of "Jewish
power" due to antisemitic stereotypes; a long-standing scholarly bias
toward European Jewry at the expense of Jews in much of the colonized
world; and a seeming blindness among both Jewish and colonial historians
to Jews' presence in colonial history, due in part to the way that Jews did
not fit many of the categories basic to the rhetoric and systems of colonialism. Recently, however, particularly in the case of colonial North
Africa, historians have begun to explore Jewish history and colonial history as important sites for one another.[15]

Because within French history Jews were long categorized as belonging
to the republic and Muslims to the empire, bringing their deeply interwoven stories together has major implications. The history of Jewish-
Muslim relations in France unfolded between and within metropole and
colony. A series of developments that have defined this history in metropolitan France—waves of migration; shifting state policies of citizenship;
neighborhood settlement patterns; discourses of assimilation, pluralism,
and Otherness; and violence and its legacies, to name but a few—have
carried distinctly colonial dimensions, particularly in connection to French
Algeria. By engaging Jewish history with colonial history, my study suggests that France's Jews were made as much by Jewish imperial projects in
the Francophone world and Jewish participation in French colonialism as
Jews in the French colonies were shaped by the experience of metropolitan Jewry.[16] Moreover, such an approach begins to correct an imbalance
in historical scholarship on French Jewry whereby Ashkenazic Jews have
received far more attention than North African Jewish immigrants and
their descendants.[17]

Along related lines, cross-national and comparative discussions of
Muslims in Europe have largely underestimated the distinctively colonial
dimensions of the French case; they have almost ignored altogether the
longevity and interconnectedness of France's histories of Muslims in
colony and metropole.[18] In the case of Muslims in French history by contrast, colonialism has been central to the work of a number of French
and American scholars. Recent studies of Muslim political and social life

during colonial and postcolonial migrations have shown the precise challenges posed to Muslim integration in France. Frequently, however, this scholarship risks painting a unidirectional picture in which Muslims have done little to fashion what it means to be Muslim and French; instead their existence too often appears one of static inequality structured almost solely (and entirely negatively) by the French nation-state and its terms of citizenship.[19] Because this book shows Muslims operating in relation to not only the French state and broader society but also in relation—and comparison—to another minority ethnicity, it begins to illuminate a range of Muslim positions between subjugation and resistance.

Sources and Methodologies

Writing the history of Muslim-Jewish relations in France necessitates searching for Jews and Muslims in a host of unlikely, uncategorizable, and previously unknown places. Much of the printed record of Muslim-Jewish encounters in France appears in government reports and memos, but as suggested by the story at the start of this Introduction, these documents must be examined with tremendous care. In part, this requires us at once to trace and deconstruct a series of classifications recorded in the archives of the colonial state and too often mimicked rather than interrogated by historians.[20] Such groupings long assigned Jews and Muslims to falsely dichotomous positions that rendered nearly invisible the greater fluidities of daily existence and interaction.[21]

In seeking to draw out the rich complexity of Muslim-Jewish encounters, I have attempted whenever possible to bring diverse sources into conversation with one another. This book draws on not only state but also community, associational, and private archives; numerous press sources; more than thirty-five oral interviews; and memoirs, novels, and films. In order to weigh diverse Jewish and Muslim perspectives on the same events and issues, I have combed various internal sources, including periodicals, pamphlets, meeting minutes, and correspondence of an array of movements and institutions in which Jews, Muslims, or members of both populations participated. Mindful of the importance of Jewish-Muslim mutual perceptions, I have used the same materials to probe the two groups' representations of one another. When examining such documents produced by nonstate actors, I have searched for narratives, dissonances, and gaps that echo, transpose, contest, or depart from those contained in French state sources.

Maximizing all of these sources becomes far more possible with the help of oral interviews. Where the archival records of the state discuss Muslims and Jews, the preeminent concern is conflict. Even internal Jewish and Muslim sources share this focus to a significant degree. Certain state sources like census records or surveillance reports on cafés offer useful information about the proximate social geography of many Jews and Muslims, but such materials do not in themselves illuminate actual Jewish-Muslim encounters. In this context, oral histories serve at least two critical purposes. First, they provide records of relationships between individuals in shared spaces that otherwise remain inaccessible to historians. Oral histories offer access to the social world of interior locations—such as homes, cafés, food markets, and athletic clubhouses—that tend to leave no written trace. The latter point is particularly pertinent for those like most Jews and Muslims in twentieth-century France: ordinary people from modest backgrounds of little fame, and therefore unlikely to compose autobiographies or preserve letters or diaries. Second, here oral histories become competing narratives that frequently challenge the rigid boundaries that have so defined state documents.[22] Indeed, many of my interviewees explicitly questioned assumed divides of Jew and Muslim, or undermined their own generalizations about mutual hostility with anecdotes of warm relations.[23] Thus oral histories prove critical to reading written documents in a manner that registers both the simultaneous power of ethnoreligious categories and history's more multivalent, often fluid lived experiences, identities, and encounters.

Oral histories of course pose challenges of personal subjectivity and the unreliability of memory over time, but careful historians can often account for these at least as well as the pitfalls of written sources. I have generally used oral histories to illuminate social and cultural settings, important political movements, or crucial historical moments rather than to verify precise facts. Whenever possible, I have placed oral histories alongside written documents that ground their social context. Moreover, I have sought to speak to multiple members of the same neighborhood, association, or social or political group in order to find what was common and divergent in their recollections.[24] Finally, as with written sources, I have analyzed oral accounts as much for their narrative arc and the assumptions they reveal as for their detailed portraits of a given space, organization or set of relationships.[25]

The breadth of sources used in this book is part of an effort to combine top-down and bottom-up approaches to history. The same goal informs my attention to local specificity. I examine and compare Jews and Muslims in three cities: Paris, Marseille, and Strasbourg. All three were home to large numbers of Jews and Muslims by the early twenty-first century and have been important historical sites for one or both populations, but they have as many differences as similarities. Paris, imperial capital and metropolis, has long been home to a plurality, often a majority, of France's Jews and Muslims. It has been as well a leading hub for political activists from across France, Europe, and the Mediterranean. Since the turn of the twentieth century, Marseille, a large port city on France's southern coast, has been a magnet for immigrants. Today, 80,000 Jews and 200,000 Muslims, many sharing North African heritage, live in Marseille. Along with the city's geography, many newcomers from southern Europe, the Levant, and North Africa have given it a distinctly Mediterranean air. Strasbourg, home to sizable Jewish and Muslim communities, is the largest city in Alsace, where a majority of French Jews lived until the late nineteenth century. Because it was part of Germany in 1905 when France instituted its law of separation between church and state, Alsace has never been subject to a strict official secularism. The state pays the salaries of priests, pastors, and rabbis (and a debate took place in the early twenty-first century about whether to add imams to this list), and religious instruction occurs in schools. This unusual religious environment, along with Strasbourg's large traditional Ashkenazic Jewish community, and sizable numbers of Jewish and Muslim Moroccan immigrants and Algerian and Turkish Muslims, has made the city a unique backdrop for Jewish-Muslim relations. In the course of this book, comparisons between Paris, Marseille, and Strasbourg repeatedly illustrate how urban settings, geography, local politics, and population sizes have affected Jewish-Muslim relations in modern France.

Situational Ethnicity

To date, scholars of Jewish-Muslim relations have frequently emphasized either a long-standing history of Muslim antisemitism or painted an idealized picture of Muslim-Jewish coexistence suddenly shattered by colonialism (and Jewish cooperation therein) or the Zionist-Arab conflict.[26] Both outlooks assume that interactions between members of the two populations should automatically be categorized as encounters between Jews and Muslims, understood as bounded ethnoreligious groups with potentially conflicting loyalties. This study operates from a different premise: that if we set aside such a dichotomous framework and ask after the actual dynamics and catalysts in Jewish-Muslim relations, we can learn a great deal more about various levels of interaction and underlying factors.[27] Time and again, the history of Muslims and Jews in France reminds us that members of competing ethnoreligious groups have relationships that are multifaceted in nature—dictated on the one hand by individual, everyday encounters and mutual interests and linked on the other hand to perceptions of deeply rooted collective differences.[28]

In order to bring greater clarity to this paradox, this book draws on the concept of situational ethnicity.[29] Situational ethnicity highlights the manner in which, very often, ethnic identity, allegiance, organization, and status are not fixed but constructed and negotiated, among both intra-group and external forces, and often in opposition to other ethnic groups.[30] The notion of situational ethnicity means, furthermore, that for groups and individuals, ethnic attachments and identifications are neither inevitably central nor singularly defined; rather, they emerge in particular contexts and varying forms. Within the family and a cultural association, for example, ethnicity may become central, but in other contexts, affiliations such as class, gender, profession, political leaning, or nation may be far more pronounced.[31] Because situational ethnicity illuminates how changing contexts frequently shift the meaning of ethnic identities, boundaries, and relations, it provides an invaluable framework with which to think through Jewish-Muslim encounters in modern France.

Consider, for instance, the case of the famous Algerian Muslim musician and playwright Mahieddine Bachetarzi and his orchestra and acting troupe El Moutribia. Many, and at times most, of the performers in El Moutribia were Jews like Lili Labassi and Salim Hallali. Each year on tours to France, Jews and Muslims of the group performed together before crowds of mostly Muslim workers in "North African" cafés. In such a context, musicians and audience members alike appeared as Algerian natives of French nationality enjoying shared music and culture. Yet differences in legal status meant that during the same tours, ethnicity suddenly became attached to citizenship and the ability to travel freely for Jewish performers, and to subject status and severe travel restrictions for Muslims. In August 1934, following Jewish-Muslim riots in Constantine, many of the same Muslims who had cheered Bachetarzi's performers were participating in Algerian nationalist meetings where Muslimness was emphasized as an oppositional identity and Jews were described as accom-

plices to the crimes of French colonialism. These Muslims briefly boy-
cotted El-Moutribia's performances in Paris. Two years later the Jewish
members of the group had their ethnicity reinforced more positively as
the context changed yet again. Now they listened to the thunderous cheers
from audiences for the name of Léon Blum, leader of the Socialist Party,
a proud Jew, and the new prime minister in the Popular Front government that inspired hope for greater equality among many Muslims.[32]

Such multileveled and shifting Jewish and Muslim identifications and
statuses can begin to help us to rethink larger assumptions about minorities in modern France. Despite their richly illuminating potential,
approaches along the lines of situational ethnicity have scarcely been
applied to French history.[33] The absence is hardly coincidental. Too often
French historians have accepted relatively uncritically the rhetoric of a
republican ideology that sought to relegate differences—of ethnicity, religion, locality, culture, and even gender—to the private sphere as the
price of inclusion.[34] This ideology insisted on the capacity and necessity
of all members of society to be "French first" in public. Since the mid-
1990s, scholars have done much to highlight how republican principles
were hardly applied equally or without inherent exclusions. A common
set of republican impulses, they have shown, simultaneously formulated
the aspirations and rhetoric of universalism *and* produced the scientific
urge to classify and demarcate categories of particularity. But in the process, these more critical histories risk simply reinforcing in negative
terms the enormous explanatory power assigned to French citizenship's
assimilatory logic and emphasis on sameness.[35] Most historians have
continued to assume that multifaceted statuses or identities, nearly impossible in public and steadily eroded even in private, were fleeting and
could hardly define social, cultural, or political relations in modern France.

In fact, such a stark conception of Frenchness was never uncontested,
and it did not translate unambiguously into concrete policy or social reality. Even as many ideologues of French republicanism insisted in
theory on the power of its national project to erase all public traces of
difference, the practice of "Frenchification" under the republic often took
more pragmatic forms. Moreover, recent scholarship has shown how for
many citizens and subjects of France, regional, religious, immigrant, and
even colonial particularities often functioned not as oppositions or
insurmountable obstacles to full acceptance, but rather as means of
attempting to mediate one's integration and membership in the French
nation. In the process, by identifying oneself in such a multifaceted

manner, various groups expanded the possible meanings of Frenchness. Examples of pragmatic, malleable forms of being French that could accommodate difference range from republican schools that taught specific loyalty to one's village as a locally rooted love for the Fatherland; to the ambiguous status of *métis* (of "mixed-race" heritage) citizens across the empire; to the space that opened in interwar Paris for the negritude movement of black Africans for cultural revival.[36]

In settings that range from administrative offices to concert stages, from meeting halls to cafés, the Jews and Muslims examined here enable us to ascertain better that France was never absolutist in either its assimilationist policies or its secularism; instead, it was assimilated as much by its minorities as vice versa and accommodated difference far more often in republican and imperial practice than it did in Jacobin theory. Jews and Muslims played an active role in this story. Whether as loyal French soldiers with particular ritualistic religious demands during World War I or as activists seeking to combine their Jewish or Muslim ethnoreligious identity with claims on the republic during the French-Algerian War, both Jews and Muslims used the language of liberty, fraternity, and equality for their own purposes, testing and contesting republican assumptions and practices. At times, such appropriation rendered France more inclusive, and at other times it offered terms in which to resist France's exclusionary tendencies.

In light of recent scholarship, then, the history of Jews and Muslims points us toward a new framework for the history of inclusion and exclusion in France across the great expanse of the twentieth century. Between 1914 and 1962, France might best be understood as, often self-consciously, all at once a multiethnic empire and a multiconfessional republican nation-state.[37] Postcolonial France may be seen as a place where difference defined status and identification more starkly than under the empire, and the meaning of Frenchness was hotly contested around questions of uniformity and diversity.

Burdens of Brotherhood: Colonial, Religious, Transnational, and Racial

This book's central arguments—regarding the wide-ranging terms of Jewish-Muslim interaction, Jewish and Muslim ethnicity as situational, and the centrality of the French state and notions of Frenchness to Jewish-Muslim relations—find their precision in the three underlying components of identification and status that long defined Jews' and Muslims' respective positions in France and in relation to one another: the place of each group as North African natives under French colonial rule, Jews' and Muslims' positions as religious minorities in an at once officially secular and majority Catholic country, and the complex political and cultural attachments of members of both groups to transnational movements and entities. A fourth element, race, frequently overlapped in important ways with the preceding three factors, though it was less pronounced. These factors affected Jews and Muslims in ways that were often parallel and interrelated but almost never equivalent.

Along each of these four lines of status and identity, both groups occupied a persistently uncertain position in modern France. That is, Jews and Muslims, albeit to varying degrees, were considered ever in the process of becoming fully French, ever "almost French." This reflected the way that Muslims and Jews found themselves persistently in the crosshairs of a basic paradox of French universalism, one closely linked to the simultaneous impulses of the republic to assimilate and accommodate difference.

I use the term *burdens* here because this word best reflects the widespread conception since the French Revolution of the proper citizen of the republic as an abstract, independent individual. According to this conception, any non-"French" elements of one's background acted as a hindrance to a fully and singularly French public self and had to be overcome.[38] And yet when the state granted greater inclusion to Jews or to Muslims, it did so in a manner that marked them as a distinctive ethnoreligious group, from the Crémieux Decree of 1870 that instantly made Algerian Jews into French citizens en masse, to the creation of a new legal category, French Muslims from Algeria, after World War II. Thus, at the moments of greatest exclusion for the two groups—Vichy and the German Occupation for Jews, the end of the Algerian War for Muslims—they did not become designated as different; rather that designation took on new meaning.[39]

Such persistent marking anchored itself in the four components of the colonial, the religious, the transnational, and the racial. Jews and Muslims were, of course, not alone as minority groups in France who appeared "encumbered" by other attachments in their effort to attain full Frenchness. Colonial migrants from across the empire, immigrants from other parts of Europe, asylum seekers fleeing persecution, Roma lacking a permanent address, and Protestants as a sizable religious minority—to name but a few examples—all faced the uncertainties of French policy, conceived strategies of integration and negotiation, and had to prove their worthiness of acceptance in France. What made Jews' and Muslims' (however distinct) positions uniquely burdened in modern France was the combination of each of these four elements in shaping their status and identity. Moreover, Jews and Muslims experienced persistent uncertainty along each of these lines, making their path to belonging in France, more than for most other groups, a matter of recurrent debate and renegotiation.

Most Jews and Muslims in colonial North Africa long occupied positions between total subjugation and full acceptance as equal French citizens. In Algeria, with the important exception of the Vichy period, Jews were generally far closer to that equality than Muslims. Nearly all Jews of Algeria received legal equality in 1870, almost ninety years before Muslims in Algeria were granted full rights as citizens. To a lesser extent, this divide existed as well in Tunisia; though Jews never received citizenship en masse there, they took far greater advantage than Muslims did of measures like the 1923 Morinaud Law that enabled many more residents to apply for French citizenship. Moroccan Jews, by contrast, actually became disempowered in many respects under French rule: rarely could they become French citizens, and unlike in Algeria or Tunisia, they remained *dhimmis,* subjects of the Moroccan sultan with inferior status to Muslims under Islamic law. In fact, due to colonial reforms of the court system, they had fewer options for legal redress than prior to the protectorate.[40] It is the combination of proximity and distance in the two groups' colonial statuses that makes their histories so revealing when taken together. Through the rights they acquired and were denied, and through their various postures of integration, hybridity, and resistance to French language, culture, and nationality, Jews and Muslims exemplified the tensions within France's colonial policies and practices: between assimilation and differentiation, between equality and exclusion, between unity and division.

Religiously, many Christian French nationalists, and more than a few Jews and Muslims, understood Judaism and Islam as total systems of law and practice that pervaded every area of life in a manner incompatible with republican *laïcité,* or public secularism. Thus civic and religious leaders by turns demanded that Jews and Muslims secularize to fit into the republic and denied that adherents of one faith or the other had the capacity or obligation to do so. Given the enduring importance of the

Catholic Church in French culture, meanwhile, at particular moments, the Jewish and Muslim relationship to a Catholic-led national "sacred unity" became a key barometer for the level of acceptance of Judaism and Islam as non-Christian faiths.[41]

Within emerging transnational spaces, Jews and Muslims sought to negotiate growing allegiances to entities and movements beyond France, principally Jewish, North African, and Middle Eastern nationalisms. In time, with the termination of the Palestine Mandate, Israeli independence, and decolonization in North Africa, these ties became relationships to nation-states outside of France. Such extra-French attachments conflicted with conventional perceptions of singular public devotion to the republic.

When widespread French notions of Jewish or Muslim difference along the lines of the first three categories ossified, they could morph rapidly into fixed racial definitions. Racial ideas at times treated Jews and Muslims as at least possibly fully "European" or "white," while in other moments darkening one or both groups' presumed racial character. Yet the assimilationist thrust of France's civilizing mission meant that even racial difference was not necessarily seen as immutable. In the 1930s, for example, a French colonel commanding the Second Regiment of the black African *tirailleurs sénégalais* described how one of his typical soldiers became rapidly Frenchified: "Washed in the soap of Marseille, rid of his parasites, closely shaven, our half-savage of the day before has hardly put on his shorts and his short khaki vest, with the broad red flannel belt and the scarlet *chéchia*, when he is transformed. Physically transformed, but also morally transformed. . . . [He becomes] a new soul in a new uniform."[42]

In the context of the more malleable strands of the republican tradition, Jews' and Muslims' uncertain colonial, religious, transnational, and even racial positions were not merely burdensome obstacles. Likewise, these components were not always mutually exclusive from the two groups' capacity for what the French call *fraternité,* or the "brotherhood" of the French nation. Indeed, these burdens also constituted the terms in which Jews and Muslims frequently made claims on the French state and by which they tested and expanded the meaning of brotherhood.

Furthermore, members of the two populations brought colonial, religious, transnational, or racial dimensions of status and identity into their efforts to find common ground with each other, to affirm a different kind of Jewish-Muslim brotherhood. On the one hand, these so-called burdens led to numerous dichotomies that divided Jews and Muslims: many members of the two populations became situated as French Jewish citizens and Muslim French subjects; as followers of Judaism and Islam with conflicting narratives, texts, and doctrines; as supporters of Zionism and Palestinian Arab nationalism in the Middle East conflict; and on opposite sides of the boundaries between "white" and "nonwhite" in French racial conceptions. On the other hand, these attachments hardly prevented and sometimes facilitated relations between Jews and Muslims from the Maghreb (North Africa). Members of the two populations became drawn together by familiarity with one another's religious customs and holy sites, folk stories and songs. Many shared an awareness of how the two group's everyday lives had long overlapped in North Africa.

Appreciating the many-sided burdens of Jewish-Muslim brotherhood enables us to analyze more fully cases like the riot that erupted in the Belleville section of Paris in June 1968 after a bet over a game of cards between a Jew and a Muslim in a café went sour. Here was a longtime shared activity and space of Mediterranean culture in a neighborhood inhabited by large numbers of postcolonial immigrants Muslim and Jewish. Yet a disagreement over cards soon became the spark for Muslim-Jewish riots. Among participants and observers alike, the violence, occurring near the one-year anniversary of the 1967 Arab-Israeli War, rapidly became linked to both the divergent political and social implications of decolonization for many Jews and Muslims and their presumed opposing allegiances in the Middle East conflict. Two communal leaders—one religious, Belleville rabbi Emmanuel Chouchena, and the other political, Tunisian ambassador Mohamed Masmoudi—helped to deescalate tensions by walking around Belleville together, offering an effective example of Jewish-Muslim fraternity.[43]

For all of their parallels, Jewish and Muslim burdens were almost never equivalent in their importance for members of the two populations. Crucial differences in their respective positions often created asymmetrical power dynamics and fostered tensions between the two groups. Jews in French North Africa, and often in metropolitan France, corresponded to the well-known Tunisian Jewish author Albert Memmi's articulation of his experience knowing and identifying as much with the colonizer as the colonized.[44] While only in Algeria did most Jews enjoy equal French citizenship, tens of thousands of Jews in Tunisia and Morocco benefited significantly from the schools of the Paris-based Alliance israélite universelle, which saw itself as spreading French civilization, language, culture, and secularism to Jews of the Francophone world and beyond.

The relative advantages of such a position for Jews in relation to Muslims often continued well after the end of colonial rule. The majority of North African Jews who migrated to France in the twentieth century were French citizens; most at least had been educated in French schools and spoke French. Few Muslim immigrants from North Africa shared any of these characteristics basic to adaptation. These differences played a major role in many Jews' ability to move into middle-class professions and better neighborhoods fairly quickly, while most Muslims, typically working as seasonal laborers for meager wages, languished in dingy, run-down neighborhoods with high rates of crime and unemployment. Moreover, given the long-standing place of the family as both building block and metaphor for the French nation, Jews benefited from arriving largely as families, whereas most Muslims came as individual male laborers.[45] The relative absence of Muslim family life on metropolitan French soil reinforced ubiquitous images of Muslim sexual or family abnormality.[46] Likewise, religiously, Jews enjoyed the vestiges of Judaism having been a religion officially recognized, subsidized, and supervised by the state in the nineteenth century, as well as full autonomy under the 1905 separation law. Not only had the state never created recognized Muslim interlocutors or helped fund Muslim religious institutions; in both colony and metropole, Muslim establishments never escaped state oversight.[47] During decolonization, a well-established Jewish community mobilized massive resources to welcome its North African coreligionists. No comparable Muslim communal structure stood prepared to help integrate new arrivals.

Transnational Jewish and Muslim attachments were the most fiercely contested between the two communities. French foreign policy in the Middle East—from the country's early support for Israel to its recognition of the Palestinian Liberation Organization in the 1970s—was rarely understood as evenhanded. Moreover, visible attachments to transnational movements and entities such as Zionism, anticolonialism, and Palestinian Arab nationalism have carried differently weighted meanings in France depending on time, place, and context.

Finally, while Jewish or Muslim status has become racialized, the two groups have rarely been seen as racially equal. Although racial thinkers and state actors defined French Jews as "white" more often than they did

Muslims, antisemitism repeatedly resurfaced, from the horrors of Vichy to the rise of the Front national. Muslims, meanwhile, saw their religious status racialized from early on by the French state. This situation, in part based on the alleged centrality of physical needs in Islamic religious practices—and therefore the difference assigned to Muslim bodies—proved remarkably difficult to overcome in twentieth-century France.[48]

Evolving Histories of Coexistence and Conflict

Thinking our way out of the binaries of the present and into a richer tapestry of Jewish-Muslim relations entails focusing closely on several critical junctures of history. Ultimately this is not a book about France's current Muslim-Jewish crisis but rather the long evolution in relations that preceded it. In the course of the twentieth century, notions of ethnoreligious identity among both France's Muslim and Jewish populations underwent a series of shifts. During a period that largely coincided with the last several decades of the French empire, Jewish and Muslim identifications and interactions were highly contingent and fluid; both coexistence and conflict unfolded within a rich tapestry of relationships among Jews, Muslims, and the French state. In the mid-1960s, this began to change: notions of Jewishness and Muslimness in France became more tightly connected to new political engagements that often drew sharp dichotomies and made widely encompassing demands on their followers. At the local level, Jewish-Muslim encounters, increasingly understood through the lens of wider national and international struggles, began to occur less in fluid spaces and relied more on clearly demarcated boundary lines.

Both specifically French and international forces drove this politicization. In the first instance, the loss of France's empire created new challenges for notions of a French "civilizing mission," engendering both the difficulties and possibilities of a multicultural republic. Following the massive postcolonial migrations, meanwhile, a majority of Muslims and Jews took divergent paths in their economic opportunities, social geography, and legal standing. During the same period, a series of movements beyond French shores, in the Middle East and the postcolonial world, were reshaping Jewish and Muslim politics in France and across the rest of the globe. These included Zionism, particularly in its more right-wing and religious variants, Palestinian nationalism, and several strains of both left-wing internationalism and Islamism. And yet in spite of the oppositional impact of such developments, Jewish-Muslim relations remained contingent on shifting contexts, and coexistence continued in certain shared spaces of cultural interaction and daily life. At this writing, the history of Jewish-Muslim entanglement in France has no known ending; its beginning can clearly be found in the French lines during World War I.

1

JEWISH, MUSLIM, AND POSSIBLY FRENCH

In late March 1917, while the stalemate of World War I along the western front continued, the Jewish holiday of Passover approached. For several days two French soldiers, one Jewish and the other Muslim, found themselves side by side in the same trench. One evening, during a pause in the fighting, the two spoke about the upcoming religious occasion and their respective faiths. Habib, the Jewish soldier, turned to his Muslim comrade, Rahmoun Hadj Hattab, and told him, "Passover, the holiday that we are about to celebrate as Jews, reminds us of the extraordinary power of God in human affairs, but it also shows us that God only helps us if we help ourselves to the fullest of our capacity."[1] He argued that although God had delivered the people of Israel from the hand of its enemies, the Exodus could never have occurred without Moses and Aaron repeatedly appearing before Pharaoh and eventually convincing the Jewish people to follow them out of Egypt. "If I have one reproach to address to Islam," he remarked, "whose faith is otherwise in such perfect agreement with ours [as Jews], it is the fact that [Islam] exalts the feeling of dependence and of submission to divine will, to the detriment of the human energy that is called upon to react constantly against evil."

Rahmoun objected immediately. He deemed his own faith a "daughter" of Judaism and said that Habib should not misjudge the teachings of Islam based on a few of its followers. The Muslim soldier then sought to illustrate his point by recounting a story from Islamic tradition.[2] In the story, Moses became gravely ill during the Israelites' journey in the desert but refused to call a doctor. Using an Arabic phrase, Rahmoun quoted Moses's rationale: Moses said "Hattabib raani," or "The Doctor [God] saw me," and claimed, "That suffices. I am in his hands."[3] Rahmoun explained to Habib that finally, with Moses's condition worsening, "a voice—what you call a *bath kol*—made itself heard and declared, 'Oh Moses, my servant, to what point will you refuse to grant me the glory of calling a man of science? Are you trying to stifle an art that I created and thanks to which human suffering can be relieved and healed?' Moses understood the reproach from the Almighty and in his love for God called the doctor whose wise care promptly restored his health." After concluding his story, Rahmoun exclaimed to his friend, "You see, our religions profess the same doctrine. Faith should not prevent action; rather it should inspire and support it." Habib agreed, and found that their discussion had strengthened his own belief in God's guiding presence.

It is difficult to know if this conversation, detailed in the pages of the popular Jewish weekly *L'Univers israélite,* took place as reported.[4] Yet as both a possible encounter and a compelling story, the account illuminates crucial aspects of early Jewish-Muslim relations in France. Habib and Rahmoun noted with pride and respect each other's common membership in Abrahamic, monotheistic faiths. Moreover, the story includes signs of mutual religious and cultural knowledge: Rahmoun's reference to the Hebrew expression *bath kol,* or heavenly voice, as well as his choice to recount a Muslim tradition about Moses, the central figure in the Passover story and arguably in all of Jewish tradition, and Habib's use and translation of Arabic, as well as his apparent acquaintance with certain Muslim sources. The two men spoke of each other's faiths as deeply and explicitly interconnected. For numerous North African Jews and Muslims whose communities had lived together for centuries, such mutual knowledge and respect was indeed common. It was part of a shared North African linguistic, cultural, and religious heritage that soldiers like Habib and Rahmoun brought with them to the metropole.[5]

The warm tenor of their conversation also suggested bonds of French solidarity forged in combat. Habib described Rahmoun as a friend, a brave soldier for France, and a devout Muslim. Such words, and the appearance of this story in traditional French Jewry's leading organ, resonated with France's wartime *union sacrée,* or patriotic "sacred union" joining people of all faiths. Furthermore, by featuring Habib's account, the *Univers israélite* expressed the Jewish community's commitment to the ideal of the republic as a bridge between Jews and Muslims. As an interfaith tale of two soldiers fighting together under the tricolor flag, the story implied that such a cordial discussion of theology was made possible by the republican value of *laïcité* (French public secularism), which fostered the common understanding that Frenchness, not religion, served as both soldiers' primary source of identity. In a related vein, the army appears here as the school of the fatherland that could help France to complete the dissemination of republican values to its Muslim colonial subjects.[6] In this framework, Habib plays a key role in helping the French to spread civilization among North African natives. His initial emphasis on the contrast between an active human role in Judaism and Islam's passivity implies a distinction between (colonial and Jewish) modernity and (Muslim and native) primitiveness. Yet the central place that Habib gives to medicine in his rendering of the Muslim version of the story may allude to the achievements of medieval Islamic science.[7] Thus Habib's story evokes the glorious past of Islamic civilization as a hope for its modernization, led by the guiding hand of France, including its Jews.

Habib and Rahmoun's tale demands our attention for a number of reasons, but none more so than its timing. Even three years earlier, such a conversation in metropolitan France would have been nearly unimaginable.[8] World War I was the foundational event for Jewish-Muslim relations in modern metropolitan France. Since the French Revolution, the French state had linked military service to citizenship, and the Third Republic used universal military conscription for men to make the army an instrument in its mission of nation building. World War I both tested and accelerated that mission. Though constantly termed by the French "a war to save civilization," World War I exposed fundamental questions about the cherished civilizational values of freedom, equality, and brotherhood that the country purported to defend. In particular, the war measured France's capacity to extend the assimilationist logic of republican nationalism to those living in its empire.[9] Through an influx of foreigners and colonial subjects into the metropole, the war also ushered in a new era of unprecedented population movement and interethnic and interreligious contact in France, further testing the republic's ability to "make Frenchmen."

It is impossible to understand the history of Jewish-Muslim relations in France if we fail to place the French state at the heart of the story. The circumstances of World War I and its aftermath enabled the state to play a pivotal role in defining the terms of early Jewish-Muslim interactions in the metropole. Likewise, Jews and Muslims themselves perceived and articulated their initial relations principally through the lens of each group's relationship to the French nation. Thus from their inception, interactions between Jews and Muslims in France were not a binary but a decidedly triangular affair.

The war and its aftermath brought to the surface three components of status and identification—colonial, religious, and transnational—that have defined Jews' and Muslims' relations with one another and the French nation ever since. A fourth element, race, though more ambiguous and often less central, already overlapped in important ways with the preceding three factors. The war highlighted the combination of these components and the manner in which they created unique burdens for Jews and Muslims in modern French history.

In each instance, the developments of the period placed Jews and Muslims in an uncertain position whereby they appeared ever in the process of becoming fully French, that is, they were perpetually "almost French." Jews' and Muslims' particular burdens, and the uncertainties these factors created in each group's status, proved crucial to their relations. Just as important as the parallels in the two groups' positions were the frequent distinctions between them. Colonially, the service of Jews and Muslims from North Africa together in the French forces often reinforced their culture as longtime natives of the Maghreb. At the same time, experiences on the battle and home fronts often underscored legal differences between the two groups. Most notably, Algerian Jews were citizens, whereas Algerian Muslims merely held French nationality.[10] Religiously, the war strengthened republican *laïcité* by enabling all soldiers to relate to one another as French first. Yet the French state and various religious groups repeatedly highlighted the war not as a moment of religious neutrality but of ecumenical sacred unity. In this context, the period showed the parallels between Jews and Muslims as non-Christian religious minorities with distinctive ritual practices, but also highlighted the sharp contrast between the more accepted position of French republican Judaism and the ambiguous, ceaselessly debated status of Islam.[11]

The war and its aftermath led to the emergence of a third problematic component of identity and status: growing transnational allegiances. Two pivotal events, the Russian Revolution of 1917 and the remaking of the Middle East, galvanized communism, Zionism, Arab nationalism, and, in time, anticolonialism. During the interwar era, particularly in light of large-scale migrations of Muslims and Jews, these transnational movements would play an increasingly important role in Jewish and Muslim politics in France. Finally, although questions of race were avoided in official French discourse, they were already ubiquitous in cultural, intellectual, and political discussions in wartime France, complicating the relative standing and interactions of Jews and Muslims.[12]

The respective positions of Jews and Muslims were rarely equal, but they were also hardly fixed. On the one hand, they rested on the dichotomies of French imperial nationhood: colonial subject versus French citizen, visible religious minority versus culturally Catholic or legally secular "French," transnational activist versus French nationalist, and nonwhite versus white. These oppositions often took legal form, could produce their own social realities, and made their way into many archival documents. On the other hand, for these very reasons, such polarized understandings have too often overwhelmed our perception of a more fluid historical moment. During World War I, Jews and Muslims repeatedly asserted ambiguous identifications and statuses that did not fit neatly into official binaries. Both groups highlighted the deep anxieties, contrasting voices, and contradictions of French metropolitan and colonial governance.[13] Jews' and Muslims' in-between stations along colonial, religious, transnational, and even racial lines opened avenues for a broad range of interactions with both the French nation-state and one another. In the process, Jews' and Muslims' multiple attachments, along with their patriotic acts and words, emblematized a moment of unprecedented fluidity in the definition of belonging in modern France.

Jewish and Muslim Experiences of World War I

From 1914 to 1918, over 800,000 imperial subjects came to France to fight on the battlefield or work on the home front. They arrived in large numbers not only from the Maghreb but also from Indochina, Madagascar, and West Africa. Still, nearly 400,000 North African Muslims, comprising 260,000 soldiers and over 130,000 laborers, made up a strong plurality of colonial soldiers and laborers.[14] Unlike European migrants, the colonial newcomers would all be regarded, to varying degrees, as people of color.[15] Meanwhile, 38,000 Jews from France and North Africa fought for the French armed forces, and 85,000 Jewish civilians resided in the metropole.[16]

During the war, Jews and Muslims related to Frenchness in simultaneously different and parallel fashions. Many members of both groups saw the war as an opportunity to further or complete their integration into the French nation. For Jews, however, such an endeavor proved simpler than for Muslims. On the eve of the war, France's Jewish community, numbering approximately 110,000, consisted of individuals whose families had lived in the country for centuries, along with sizable numbers of recent immigrants from Eastern Europe, the Levant, and North Africa. The Jews of France had a long-established and centralized communal structure. Increasingly bourgeois, much of metropolitan French Jewry had integrated successfully into France's economy, society, and politics. In addition, with the Crémieux Decree of October 1870, nearly all of Algeria's 37,000 Jews had gained French citizenship.[17] Subsequently, growing numbers of Jews became culturally French. For some, this meant abandoning North African traditions. Others maintained many of the long-standing Algerian customs that tied them to their Muslim neighbors, but often in a more private manner centered on the home and family.[18]

World War I began only eight years after the official end of the Dreyfus affair (1894–1906). Thus the war broke out at a moment ripe for the reassertion of Jewish civic participation in France. French Jews—from those who rushed to join the National Guard at the start of the French Revolution to the representatives to Napoleon's Assembly of Notables who connected Jews' "love of country" to their service in the revolutionary wars—had long seized on the broader connection between citizenship and military service as a means to further their integration.[19] The Dreyfus affair had thrown such a linkage into question. Dreyfus, a Jew who had risen to the General Staff of the French military, was a symbol of Jewish integration; suddenly, he found himself falsely convicted as a traitor, publicly humiliated in the courtyard of the École militaire, and shipped to the penal colony of Devil's Island. The affair's rampant, often racial, antisemitism in both the mainland and Algeria had marked Jews with difference and provoked a rebirth of Jewish consciousness among segments of the community. Much of the community leadership, however, saw the ultimate exoneration of Dreyfus as proof of the republic's capacity to protect its Jews.

In this context, the war carried two distinct meanings for native French Jews: an opportunity to prove Jewish patriotism for France and a cause aligned with the revolutionary and republican tradition.[20] Likewise, in the shadow of both emancipation and Dreyfus, Algerian Jews perceived the war as their first great opportunity to sacrifice themselves on behalf of France. Immigrant Jews from Eastern Europe and the Ottoman Empire idealized France as a beacon of liberty. On August 3, 1914, Jewish immigrant organizations posted signs all over Paris in French and Yiddish:

"France, the country of liberty, equality, and fraternity . . . France, where we have found, we and our families, for many years, a refuge and a shelter, is in danger! . . . [O]ur most sacred duty is to put ourselves at once at the disposal of that great and noble nation in order to participate in her defense."[21] Ottoman Jewish immigrants, despite the obstacles posed by Istanbul's participation on the side of the Central Powers, sought to enroll in the French armies. By war's end, approximately eighty-five hundred Jewish noncitizens had volunteered for service.[22] Thus the war united the diverse strands of French Jewry around shared ideals.

The French Jewish community often invoked its patriotic service as a way to battle discrimination and defend its loyalty. Both fixtures of the Jewish press, *Archives israélites,* the mouthpiece of acculturated, republican Judaism, and the more traditionalist *L'Univers israélite,* expended considerable ink on Jews' sacrifice for France.[23] Each issue of both weeklies included accounts and lists documenting Jewish soldiers' heroism. At the same time, they cited troubling instances of antisemitism. Indeed, even amid the constant rhetoric of national unity, many French figures and groups that had propagated antisemitism in the years preceding the war did not halt their efforts. A wave of accusations in summer 1915 claiming that France's Russian Jewish immigrants had been evading military service led some not to enlist or even to flee the country. In the course of the war, more than 150 publications appeared in France attacking such alleged subversive forces as Jewish German spies or the Jewish-Masonic conspiracy. In this context, the Jewish press repeatedly linked Jewish soldiers' service to full acceptance and equality in French society.[24]

For the Algerian Muslims who would make up the majority of France's Muslim soldiers and laborers during World War I, the early period of the Third Republic had created a far more negative relationship with the French state. The war followed four decades marked by the Mokrani revolt of 1871, a fierce if brief guerilla uprising in northern Algeria, the brutal discrimination of the *code de l'indigénat* ("native's code") instituted in 1881, and the gradual emergence of cultural resistance, which coalesced around Islamic heritage and the memory of Ottoman rule. In this context, in the years preceding the war, most Muslims resisted even well-meaning efforts by certain liberal French colonialists and Algerian Muslim notables to enable them to "become French." Several proposals that advocated Muslims' participation in the army as a civic entry ticket to French society faced stiff opposition. In contrast to their Jewish counterparts, most Muslims feared that military service would not improve their status but would instead bring the irreversible loss of their religious and ethnic identity through acculturation, citizenship, or both.[25]

It should be no surprise then that World War I elicited mixed reactions from the Algerian Muslims called on to serve as soldiers in the trenches or as laborers on the home front.[26] French recruitment propaganda drew parallels between the battle against Germany and that of the Middle East Arabs against the Ottomans, and suggested that Muslim soldiers would earn civic equality. In 1914, War Minister André Millerand even went so far as to promise a Muslim cleric (visiting troops in the mainland) that Algerians fought for "not only their adoptive fatherland but also the patrimony of liberty they won nearly a century ago and which will not cease henceforth to increase."[27] Over the next four years, French officials debated the question of naturalization for Muslim soldiers, particularly those of Algeria. At the heart of many of these discussions was the issue of whether these soldiers could at once retain their *statut personnel musulman* (Muslim personal status) and become full French citizens.[28] Even as major reform appeared imminent, Muslim enthusiasm for the war effort was far from universal. Some Muslims refused to serve, citing the brutalities and injustices of the colonial system. Other factors dampened the morale of those Muslims who fought for France. These included family members' fears about losing their sons' agricultural labor, the cold weather in Europe, and enemy propaganda alleging the impending arrival of a German-chosen Algerian sultan and comparing German treatment of Muslims favorably to that of the French.[29] Reflecting the contradictions of their position in France, Muslim soldiers were kept under tight state surveillance from their sleeping quarters to the battlefield itself.[30]

The early months of the war witnessed widespread problems among North African Muslim soldiers: maladjustment, panic in battle, massive casualties, and frequent disobedience (including self-mutilation to escape combat). Yet throughout the war, Muslim soldiers, with few exceptions, remained loyal. Despite regular calls from the Ottoman sultan to join a jihad, or Muslim holy war, Muslim soldiers taken prisoner by the Central Powers rarely agreed to fight on the Turkish side. In the war's first two years, as Muslim combatants gradually adapted to the climate, the food, and the realities of modern warfare, their morale and performance improved. Only one Muslim unit participated in the mutinies of May and June 1917; officers by then had developed such confidence in Muslim soldiers that they used some North African regiments for the surveillance of French units with suspect loyalty.[31] Despite occasional hostility, colonial soldiers' participation on the front lines brought them newfound appreciation and a warm welcome from the French population.

Although there were considerable disparities in the war's meaning for Jews and Muslims, the two groups related to the French state in similar ways. In the process, each group revealed the paradoxical nature of its difference in France. Newspapers such as the Muslim weekly *L'Islam* of the assimilationist Young Algerians movement, and the indigénophile weekly *El Akhbar,* edited by the colonial liberal Victor Barrucand, had previously sought greater integration for Algeria's Muslims, but to little avail.[32] Now, with the war on, they seized the opportunity, emphasizing the ties between France and its North African subjects in a manner analogous to the appeals among France's Jewish immigrants. On August 4, 1914, the editorial in *L'Islam* declared: "In the face of the terrible dangers that threaten France, our dear adoptive Fatherland, cradle of all liberties, our duty as loyal Muslims, profoundly attached to the republican institutions is utterly clear. . . . For God, for our homes, for our welfare, finally for our Fatherland." Referring to "the generous France, the valiant France of '89," the author echoed the Jewish press's frequent theme of France as the land of revolution and liberty.[33] These organs extolled the patriotic sacrifice of North African Muslims specifically as at once affirming and cementing their place in France's national family. Thus, just as Jews continued their long-standing effort to demonstrate that *as Jews* they were good patriots, Muslims and their allies emphasized their devotion to France *as Muslims*. In this manner, both Jews' and Muslims' attempts to show their love for France repeatedly highlighted supranational ethnoreligious loyalties.[34]

The war experience regularly reminded Jews and Muslims of the religious dimension of their identity and status in France. As minorities in a country that remained deeply Catholic, members of the two groups faced common challenges. In June 1915, among one North African unit, Jews and Muslims alike found themselves in the unusual situation of being bestowed with the consecration of the Sacred Heart in a church in the Belgian town of Westvleteren. A French official in attendance recorded the discomfort of a number of Muslim soldiers.[35] Similarly, during the war's first year, French authorities mistakenly placed crosses on the gravestones of many Jewish and Muslim soldiers. Once the government realized its error, it emphasized that Muslim graves should take the shape of a rectangular bottom with a pointed circle on top, bear the insignia of a Muslim crescent with a star inside, and face toward Mecca; the authorities also gave precise instructions about the need for a Muslim to be present to take the profession of faith, as well as how to wash the body in hot water and wrap it in white in preparation for the burial (Figure 1.1). They told Jewish chaplains to replace mistaken crosses with the tablets of the Ten Commandments and to perform the funerary rites "in accordance with Jewish law."[36]

The challenge of burial practices pointed to Jews' and Muslims' commonality as religious minorities with particular ritual needs, but also to important differences between the two communities and their practices in the eyes of the French state. The respective statuses of Judaism and Islam were hardly equivalent. Every French army corps, and each division with a significant number of Jewish soldiers, included a rabbi.[37] In addition, it seems that Jewish soldiers who desired kosher food could rely on the support of the organized Jewish community.[38] Rabbis helped to ensure proper burial practices and grave markings, and distributed a "soldier's prayer-book" and gathered Jews for prayer when possible.[39]

For Muslims, whose religious life was widely perceived to be more demanding on their bodies, daily rhythms, and *mentalités* and who lacked established community institutions in the mainland, the state played a more direct role in addressing religious demands.[40] Early in the war, the presence of Islamic clerics was less regular and organized than that of their Jewish counterparts. In time, the French military brought sizable numbers of imams, *talaba* (madrasa-educated scholars), and notables from Islamic brotherhoods for regular visits to majority-Muslim regiments. The army also distributed copies of the Quran. The French command took responsibility for supplying halal meat and respecting other culinary customs; officers frequently admonished suppliers for distributing food containing pork, and the army compiled a cookbook of Algerian recipes for the leaders of colonial units. Some French commanders even fasted on Ramadan to show solidarity with their Muslim troops.[41]

This focus of the French state on supporting Islamic ritual life in part reflected the widespread fear that the call to jihad of the Ottoman sultan would prompt mass defections to the enemy. In fact, however, among Muslim soldiers, the importance and meaning of religious belief and practice varied tremendously. Islam proved to be one contingent and highly variable component in a multifaceted set of identifications, interests, and

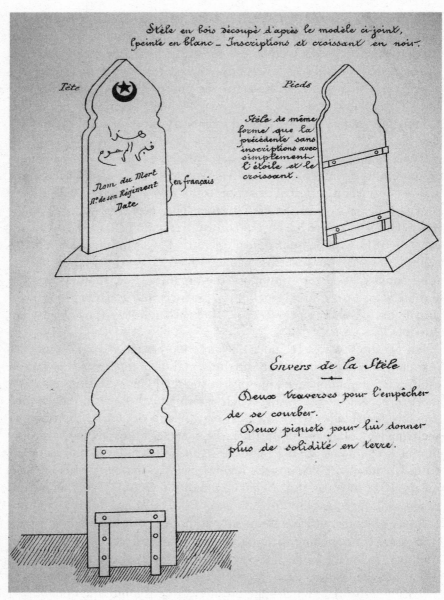

Figure 1.1. Instructions from the French government for the proper construction, inscription, and placement of the tombs of Muslim soldiers, April 1915. (Archives Nationales d'Outre-Mer, FR ANOM, 81 F 834.)

allegiances that together determined the loyalty and morale of a given Muslim soldier.[42]

Nevertheless, French officials often worried that Islam exercised such an all-encompassing power over its believers that it undermined Muslim soldiers' fitness for French citizenship. In a typical remark at a meeting of the Interministerial Commission on Muslim Affairs in January 1916, the representative of the colonial administration in Algeria, Octave Depont, declared that Islam would need years to develop the proper separation between state and religious law. He sought to support his point through the example of Jews, who had been able "to separate Hebraic law from the religion" only over a period of centuries. Such a comment revealed much about the relative levels of acceptance of Judaism and Islam, respectively, in early twentieth-century France. Moreover, for many officials, some Islamic customs appeared antithetical to full assimilation to the French nation. For example, debates about naturalization for Muslim soldiers focused in particular on polygamy, which, though rarely practiced in Algeria, proved for many the alleged incompatibility of Islam and Frenchness. Many Muslims, meanwhile, saw Islamic law as an essential component of their religious identity and did not wish to become French.[43]

Crossing the Mediterranean: Jews and Muslims in the African Army

Even as they framed much of the war's meaning in terms of their own community's relationship to the French nation-state, Jews and Muslims also began to define their relationship to one another. Members of the two groups served together in a number of settings. Over the course of the war, significant numbers of native French Jews and Jews of the Foreign Legion fought alongside Muslims.[44] In addition, Algerian Jews formed a small presence in La Coloniale, the force organized around all of France's overseas possessions outside of the Maghreb; La coloniale's West African soldiers included a sizable number of black African Muslims.[45] But by far the closest and most regular interactions were those between North African Jews and Muslims in the so-called African Army, the North African–based French forces that fought in the Hexagon (mainland France), Africa, and the Near East.[46]

Jewish-Muslim relations in the African Army at once reflected and actualized the similarities and differences in the two groups' respective colonial and religious statuses. Through their service, Algerian Jews hoped to complete their integration into the French nation and the French Jewish community. At the same time, they strengthened their ties with their Muslim brethren in arms.[47] Many Algerian Muslim soldiers perceived the existence of two Frances, one a brutal colonizer and the other a republican liberator. These Muslims often identified their service with the latter, democratic France and its fight against the "barbaric" German enemy. During the war, many Muslims received a political education. In metropolitan France, they tasted the benefits of republican democracy; in the army and the cities of the Hexagon, they received more equal treatment than they ever had in the colony. Many hoped that the end of the war would bring the egalitarian ideal to Algerian soil. The experience of fighting far from home, however, also underlined their differences from their French brothers (including many Jews) in the trenches, sparking a more distinctly Algerian identity.[48]

Muslims and Jews in the African Army had ample opportunity to interact with one another. On the eve of the war, Algerian and Tunisian battalions were organized in nine *tirailleur* and four *Spahi,* or cavalry regiments. Arriving in France in August 1914 as their own brigade, the Moroccans formed their own tirailleur regiment in December of that year.[49] Most Muslims served in the tirailleurs, a term literally meaning "sharpshooters" but used to designate infantry units of colonial subjects, whereas most Jews served in the *Zouaves* and *infanterie légère,* that is, the "European" North African infantry units. Yet many units included both Muslims and Jews.

In the Algerian-Tunisian tirailleurs, for example, most officers were French, and French citizens from North Africa made up roughly 20 to 30 percent of the soldiers.[50] The latter group included a number of Algerian Jews and occasional Jewish volunteers from Morocco and Tunisia.[51] A few Algerian Jews also served in the Moroccan tirailleurs, and a handful joined the largely Muslim Spahis. Beginning in spring 1915, many Jews and Muslims served together in four mixed tirailleur-Zouave regiments, three consisting of two or three battalions of tirailleurs and one of Zouaves, and the fourth made up of three Zouave battalions and one tirailleurs battalion.[52] Each division of the African Army included roughly equal numbers of Zouaves and tirailleurs, and the two groups often went into battle side by side.[53] Muslims and Jews were also together in the artillery and the Chasseurs d'afrique, or "European" cavalry forces. Jews were among the French citizens who made up a majority in these units, while Muslims also formed a sizable contingent.[54]

Although it is difficult to determine the exact number of North African Jews and Muslims who served in such close proximity, we may glean indications from an incomplete honor book published in 1919 by the Algerian Jewish community to recognize its decorated and deceased veterans.[55] Of the approximately 1,450 Algerian Jewish soldiers for whom the citation in the *Livre d'or,* or honor book, of Algerian Jews indicates their unit, 90, or 6.2 percent, served in a regiment with mostly Muslim comrades. This figure includes tirailleurs, mixed tirailleur-Zouave units, interpreters, and the smaller numbers of Jews in the Spahis and North African laborers. Another 85, or 5.9 percent, served with significant numbers of Muslim comrades in either the artillery regiments or Chasseurs d'afrique cavalry units.[56] If these numbers are representative, then altogether, among the more than 13,000 Algerian Jewish soldiers who fought for France, over 1,500, or 12 percent, served with Muslims in the same regiment. With Jews in nearly all tirailleur and mixed Zouave-tirailleur units, a far higher proportion of the 260,000 North African Muslims who fought for France served in a regiment that included Jews.[57] Despite their differences in status, elements like common language, similar prayer melodies, a shared desire for Arabic coffee, and divisional festivals with a North African flavor underscored the commonalities in these soldiers' colonial and religious identities.[58]

The organizing arrangements and terminology of these units reflected the colonial, religious, and racial boundaries that helped to shape the terms of Jewish-Muslim interaction in the French forces. French officials had long believed the black African tirailleur sénégalais to be the most warrior-like of their colonial soldiers.[59] Among North Africans, they regarded Moroccans as the fiercest fighters, followed by Algerians, also considered good soldiers, with the battlefield abilities and tendencies of Tunisians in greater doubt. The tirailleur-Zouave regiments were dubbed mixed due to their inclusion of not only French citizens and subjects, but also so-called whites and nonwhites. Despite enduring antisemitism, Algerian Jews were part of the white forces, employed—in both mixed regiments and the composition of divisions and larger battlefield forces—in order to balance and monitor nonwhite imperial soldiers.[60] Like other white French citizens, many Algerian Jews served in positions considered skilled or specialized: as interpreters, medical personnel, engineers, and signalers.[61] In contrast, French officials perceived most of the *troupes indigènes* as racially ill suited to such tasks and used them largely as shock troops.[62] In artillery units of the African Army, Jews were among the French who made up most of the cadres and the gun teams; they served alongside Muslims, the latter often responsible for the more menial jobs of handling ammunition, transport, and, in the mountain regiments, mules. Still, because of their ambiguous legal status and their often lighter skin color, North African, particularly Algerian, Muslims remained more racially malleable than black Africans.[63] Though he opposed extending citizenship to them, Algeria's governor-general Charles Lutaud declared in 1916 that Algerian Muslims were "perfectible whites" like all Frenchmen.[64] From early in the war Jews' and Muslims' positions and relations were repeatedly articulated not only in colonial or religious but also racial terms.

Even as they navigated racial stereotypes and legal distinctions, the majority of Muslims and Jews in the same units served as relative equals: ordinary soldiers without rank. Here, unlike in the metropolitan armies, few Jews were officers and the French military systematically kept most Muslims from gaining promotions.[65] Given their frequent similarity in military status, Jews and Muslims in the same regiment regularly had to encourage, protect, or assist one another amid the chaos and brutality of total war, a context where interethnic differences hardly mattered. While surviving Muslim sources of this sort of interaction are quite limited, Jewish publications from during and immediately following the war illuminate how Jews in the tirailleurs or mixed regiments received numerous citations for rallying or protecting Muslim comrades under enemy fire.

The Algerian Jewish *Livre d'or* proves particularly insightful of both the experience on the battlefield and its communal renderings.[66] This three-hundred-page book was created in significant part to tout the French patriotism and national belonging of Algerian Jews. It is unremarkable that the book barely mentions the more subjugated and stigmatized Algerian Muslim fellow soldiers. Yet if read carefully, the honor book contains crucial evidence of multifaceted Jewish-Muslim interactions in the trenches. During the war's opening phase, for example, on September 16, 1914, Samuel Timsit, a Jewish medical major in the Fifth Regiment of the Algerian tirailleurs, under surprise attack at 100 meters from enemy lines, brought all of the wounded he could possibly gather to a nearby ambulance. In July 1916, Raymond-Rahmime Parenté, a

Jewish medical corporal in the Fourth Regiment of the tirailleurs de marche, tended continuously to the wounded of his unit amid an artillery barrage.[67] On the offensive of August 20, 1917, he was in the first wave of a group sent out to sweep the trenches. Facing constant fire, he orchestrated the evacuation of the wounded by newly captured German soldiers.[68] In instances like these, the honor book declines to mention the obvious: Muslims constituted the vast majority of the troops being rallied or cared for by the Jewish soldier described.

Similarly, Muslims' letters from the war's early battles only rarely took notice of the religious confession of the writer's fellow soldiers. In late 1914, Farhiat ben Salah wrote from his hospital bed in Chateau-Gontier with words that expressed the indiscriminate nature of the carnage: "The war is terrible, creatures are mowed down like corn at harvest time, we fight day and night. . . . The people of the country and the whole population, you can put them in a great bathtub. No one can escape the danger without complete ruin. . . . The real situation is impossible to describe."[69] Such examples suggest that for North African Jews and Muslims, that which they shared—the commonality of the French colors, daily combat together, and linguistic and cultural elements—helped to facilitate cooperation and coexistence. Moreover, fighting side by side appeared to render group boundaries, if not invisible, highly permeable.

North African Jewish and Muslim soldiers' new sense of French brotherhood found occasional expression in the words of communal leaders. On March 12, 1916, at a memorial service for deceased soldiers inside an Algiers synagogue, Grand Rabbi L. Fridman, himself a military chaplain, framed the issue in striking terms: "My brothers and sisters, how proud you can feel of those whom you mourn. . . . I myself saw from your sons, how, bloody and mutilated, they sought to return again to the battle, to the danger, to death!"[70] Hinting at French and Algerian Jewry's optimism regarding the impact of France's "civilizing mission" in Algeria, he exclaimed with condescension, "How many times I heard with an unspeakable emotion their valorous officers tell me: 'Oh, what brave little soldiers our Africans!'" In its simultaneously infantilizing and effusive tone, Fridman's rhetoric echoed numerous statements by French officials about the colonial subjects fighting in the French war effort.[71]

As he continued, Fridman emphasized the sacrifice of those of all ethnicities, paraphrasing a biblical passage to imply that a single God was another element they shared: "Yes, my brothers, what brave little soldiers! And how you can be proud of your children! Algerians and Tunisians,

Christians and Protestants, Muslims and *israélites,* all our soldiers of Africa have nobly done their duty and our well-loved France can say with the prophet Isaiah, 'This is certainly my people. They are my sons. They are all worthy of me.'" Fridman envisioned the memory of shared combat as a new beginning for French unity: "And well, my brothers, will it not be the duty of every Frenchman to finally make a clean slate from all the prejudices which have often so sadly divided us? . . . After this mighty struggle, unique in history, where all the children of France have shed their blood so generously for the Fatherland, will we forget that for this Fatherland we have all given what we hold most dear in the world: our children? . . . No, my brothers, we will not forget." Fridman concluded by forecasting the war's haunting power for French and colonial society, but did so in a hopeful fashion. "Even if misfortune wanted that it would be otherwise," he promised, "our beloved who have died would rise from their graves in order to remind us . . . that we must consider all of us, from here on, as children of a single family [with] only a single ambition: the grandeur and prosperity of our beloved France."

In this powerful speech, the rabbi had drawn together several themes. As he invoked a quotation from the Jewish prophet Isaiah to articulate the sentiments of "our well-loved France," he echoed long-standing connections drawn by Jewish leaders between the values of the Hebrew Bible and those of modern France. As he translated the verse in a rather loose, almost Midrashic fashion, he further sacralized the nation and the war effort by turning the biblical phrasing—replacing God, the original speaker, with France itself.[72] Coupled with Fridman's mention of the resurrection of dead soldiers, such rhetoric heightened the message of a sacred duty, for all of France, to remember this moment of unity and shared sacrifice. And yet even within his tribute to unified service for the fatherland, Fridman emphasized colonial (the mainland and Africa), ethnic (Algerian and Tunisian), and religious ("Christian" and Protestant, Jewish, and Muslim) differences.

Fridman's optimistic assessments of interconfessional sacred unity were hardly shared by everyone. Other Jewish leaders and French state actors harbored negative ideas about both Jews and Muslims, and saw conflict between the two groups as inevitable. In February 1915, for instance, the internationalist French Jewish organization the Alliance israélite universelle (AIU) learned of the case of one Jewish soldier named Chemoul, an expert in Arabic language and Islamic law, who had volunteered and been assigned for duty as the new interpreter in the Eighth Regiment of the tirailleurs.[73] The regiment's colonel, however, upon meeting Chemoul and learning he was Jewish, told him that there was no place for Jews in his company. When they received Chemoul's letter reporting this incident, the officials of the AIU chose not to offer assistance. Rather, the organization's representative concluded that the supervising officer "may not have overstepped his authority," since he "would be able to justify his decision by the fact that animosity prevails between Arabs and *israélites* and by his desire to avoid any incident that this situation might have been able to provoke. It is therefore preferable not to protest officially against the conduct of the colonel of the 8th tirailleurs."[74]

These words suggest that many state actors and AIU leaders shared the assumption that if Jews and Muslims were forced to serve in close proximity, tensions or even altercations would likely result. Two months after the incident with Chermoul, an AIU official reported that early in the war, many Jews had been subofficers in the tirailleurs but had been reassigned to other units. He surmised that the reason was that "Arabs" refused to follow orders from Jews.[75]

Parallel assumptions about Jewish-Muslim hostility seemed to inform the brief references to Jews in the widely disseminated pamphlet of Algerian deserter Boukabouya Rabah that appeared in 1915. Financed by the Germans and the Ottomans, this book decried France for its treatment of Muslims in the army, emphasized the lack of attention to Muslim ritual and pastoral needs, and extolled the Germans as far superior to the French in a range of areas. On three occasions, Boukabouya grouped Jews with Maltese, Italians, and Spanish as "neo-French," claiming these four groups were tightly monitoring Muslims on the field of battle with orders to kill those who hesitated to fight and that they were constantly replacing Muslims in officer positions as the French army sought to reduce the latter to a minimum. Such references lumped Jews in the opposing camp of Muslims, categorizing them with those groups whose members had historically been the most inclined toward colonial racism (and antisemitism) among the settler classes in Algeria.[76]

While revealing of the cultural assumptions of certain Algerian Muslims about Jews as colonialist oppressors, these references appear to have been rather exceptional. These were the only three mentions of Jews, two of them buried in footnotes, in a booklet that ran forty pages long.[77] Echoing this relative disinterest is a sample of letters from late 1914 by

Muslims in tirailleur units that included Jews, read by the French censors specifically with an eye toward negative attitudes or low morale. These letters discussed a host of issues—complaints about massive casualties; problems of food, equipment, and ammunition; and expressions of Muslims' particular interest in the Ottoman position in the war—yet they made no mention of Jews.

As suggested by both the words of Chemoul's would-be colonel and the AIU response to Chemoul's complaint, the greatest concerns about Jewish-Muslim proximity in the French army often came from the state. These reservations were particularly pronounced in the case of Tunisia, where they derived as much from crude antisemitism as from stereotypes about Muslim hostility toward Jews. In autumn 1916, Minister of War Pierre Roques wrote to the resident-general of Tunisia, suggesting that in an effort to maximize the recruitment class of native troops for 1917, perhaps it would make sense to add a call to arms of all Tunisian Jews (originally not included in the military recruitment law in Tunisia). In his lengthy, revealing reply, marked "confidential," Resident-General Gabriel Alapetite unleashed a screed against Tunisian Jewry and summarily rejected the minister's suggestion.[78]

Alapetite insisted that the situations of Tunisian and Algerian Jews were dramatically different. In a manner highly indicative of the capacity of wartime service to push the boundaries of Frenchness, Alapetite assumed that conscription among Tunisian Jews would translate into granting them citizenship en masse, an act he viewed as a costly provocation to Muslims: "We must choose: if we orient ourselves . . . toward an extension of the Crémieux Decree to [Tunisia], this would be to accept the obligation going forward of containing the Muslim population only by force; this would be exchanging the faithfulness of important and proven [Muslim] military contingents for a [Jewish] secondary force that all of the current data permits us to consider as mediocre in every regard." Alapetite described Jews as clannish and utterly disinterested in integration, the French cause, or any greater good; he characterized their conduct since the start of the war as ungenerous and exploitative, even "parasitic," to the potential "ruin" of many Muslims. In this context, he foresaw grave dangers in giving them a path to citizenship, claiming, "Until the present, political power has escaped the Jews in Tunisia, it is the only force that they lack. They know well that if they have it, the enslavement of the Muslim natives won't be long in coming." Deeply concerned about how

Tunisian society would be disrupted by Jews serving en masse and implying that Jews were cowardly soldiers, Alapetite explained that until this point, Muslims had made sacrifices and submitted to France's military demands, but "that is on the condition that the *ISRAÉLITEs* do not mix with them and do not spread here the cry of run-for-your-lives." According to the resident-general, since the start of the war, Muslims had already experienced numerous attacks by Algerian Jewish soldiers stationed in Bizerte and Tunis, who "adorned with the French uniform and armed with a bayonet or a revolver [cannot] resist the desire to strike Muslims."[79]

Alapetite's document, remarkable in displaying openly such virulent antisemitism from a high-level colonial official, encapsulated a wider culture in which the French administration in Tunisia repeatedly expressed profound misgivings about Jewish conduct, and specifically the volatility of Jewish-Muslim interchanges. In December 1916, Simon Journo, a Jewish soldier home on leave, was incarcerated for the murder of a Muslim. The official who wrote up the report concluded by citing "the frequency and gravity of disorders of which the *israélite* soldiers are at fault, and of which the Tunisian Muslim *indigènes* are nearly always victims."[80] Yet it was Muslim attacks on Jews that would exacerbate fears about Jewish-Muslim contact in wartime Tunisia. The apparent cause was resentment of Jews for allegedly shirking their patriotic duty—a charge not only leveled by the likes of Alapetite but also made frequently in the French colonial press. In August 1917, a number of Muslim tirailleurs home on leave attacked Jewish shops in several towns, supported by the chanting of onlookers. Large-scale anti-Jewish attacks occurred again during the celebrations that followed the armistice in November 1918.[81] In the intervening period, even as French officials repeatedly sought to take measures to separate Jews and Muslims in Tunisia, civilian and military alike, numerous small altercations between members of the two groups were reported.[82]

The state's triangular role in Jewish-Muslim relations could take surprising turns. Whatever French officials' broader concerns about Jewish-Muslim tension within the French forces, in at least one area, fears of conflict became wholly trumped by military necessity. Due to their native knowledge of Arabic, alongside their French education and more frequent contact with Europeans and Western culture, Algerian Jews had long constituted a high percentage of the lower-ranking military interpreters; these men played a critical role as intermediaries between French personnel and Muslim soldiers.[83] As one report from Tunisia explained, "Placed in immediate and permanent contact with the *indigène*, [the interpreter] visits a unit each day, speaks with the tirailleurs, receives their requests . . . records them, studies them, and transmits them, in the name of the head of the corps, to the Résidence Générale of France in Tunis."[84]

Not just facile translators of one language to another, interpreters played numerous other roles for the men in the regiments. Muslims often turned to interpreters to confide private matters or receive personal guidance or support. Interpreters periodically intervened to increase rations of traditional North African cuisine like dates and couscous. They placed orders with the French command for more copies of the Quran, sought to curb proselytizing by clerics of other faiths, and helped to ensure proper burial practices. Away from the battlefield, interpreters visited wounded Muslim soldiers in the hospital, helping them to feel more at home and inquiring into their needs (Figure 1.2). In February 1915, one interpreter wrote a report from the military hospital in Pouges-les-Eaux, in the department of Nièvre in the region of Bourgogne. He explained that the preferred gifts for the Tunisian Muslim soldiers in his hospital were tobacco, cigarette paper, letter-writing paper, and fruits and other sweets, adding that "the majority" of the soldiers expressed a desire as well for Arabic-language newspapers.[85]

Interpreters did more than attend to needs; they also constantly monitored and sought to influence Muslim morale and loyalty. The same interpreter writing from Pouges-les-Eaux reported, in a paternalistic yet satisfied tone, that the Muslim soldiers in treatment there "behave themselves very well," and he mentioned their "naturally sweet and placid character."[86] Empowered by their skill despite their generally low-ranking status, interpreters assessed the attitudes of Muslims by listening in on their conversations and reading their private correspondence, and they worked with commanding officers to assign punishment or reward accordingly. In November 1914, with the Entente officially at war against the Ottomans and the sultan having called for jihad against France and its allies, French authorities became even more concerned about Muslim loyalties, and interpreters disseminated pro-French propaganda among Muslim soldiers. The invasion of the Dardanelles in spring 1915 prompted another wave of French concern about Muslim international solidarity exceeding devotion to France. Even as most Muslim soldiers proved as steadfast as any others in their loyalty, French fears and preoccupations

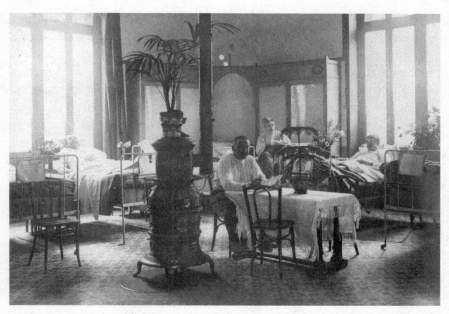

Figure 1.2. Soldiers recuperating in the "Pavilion of Tunisia" at the "jardin colonial" military hospital in Nogent-sur-Marne on the eastern outskirts of Paris, ca. 1915. Such hospitals were frequent sites for interactions between military interpreters and colonial soldiers. (Archives Diplomatiques, MAE, CADN, Protectorat Tunisie, 1TU/125/22.)

with the surveillance and propaganda work of the interpreters and others persisted throughout the war.[87]

Interpreters, charged with monitoring attitudes, sentiments, and emotions, even relayed detailed accounts of Muslim soldiers' sexual relations. Since the nineteenth century, so-called proper sexual behavior had been central to bourgeois norms. Moreover, sexual encounters between the colonized and the French had long been a source of anxiety. Cases of "white" colonizing men sleeping or cohabiting with "colored" colonized women were perceived as conquests of a sort; but French state and society saw the reverse relationship, of the "colored" colonial soldier and the "white" native French woman, as threatening. The latter sexual encounters undermined assumptions about European racial superiority and could "pollute" the nation. French officials also worried that relationships between colonized men and "white" women (and frequent reporting about such relationships in the colonies via thousands of revealing letters and photographs) would lead colonial subjects to regard European women in a manner that could weaken French rule. Thus the interpreter's duty to monitor the Muslim soldier's sexual activity carried particular importance. For Jews, as frequently selected interpreters, it signaled the degree to which, whatever the challenges they faced, they were marked as capable of attaining and monitoring standards of "normal" civic behavior in a manner that set them apart from most Muslims.[88]

The power dynamics of the relationship between Jewish interpreters and Muslim fellow soldiers illustrate well how, for all of the commonalities and shared experiences that seemed to marginalize group differences, Jewish-Muslim religious, legal, and racial distinctions never disappeared. Muslims and Jews were not altogether equal, it appears, in the danger they faced on the battlefield. Given their overexposure as shock troops, the mostly Muslim tirailleurs had the highest mortality rate of all the French forces from Algeria. Among Muslims mobilized in Algeria, one of every 4.32 died in combat, whereas the number for "Europeans" (that is, French citizens) mobilized in Algeria was one in 5.46. Such circumstances lent validity to rumors, widely circulated in Algeria, that French officers were most ready to let Muslims die and therefore often sent their units first into the breach.[89] Particularly during the first year and a half of the war, Algerian Muslims faced much greater obstacles than their French colleagues to gaining leave to visit their families. A song popular in Algeria during this period exclaimed: "If you're a Christian or Jewish mother, you will see your son, you will touch him, and will embrace him. If you're a Muslim mother, you will not see your son, or touch him, or embrace him."[90]

Throughout the war, French officials repeatedly reprised the state's dual role as unifier and divider with respect to Muslims and Jews. At times, this took the form of struggling—in the face of the growing multiplicity of identities, allegiances, and statuses engendered by the war's events—to maintain a rhetoric that clearly distinguished between belonging and exclusion: of citizen versus subject, French versus foreign, civilized versus not yet civilized, and white versus nonwhite. This was exemplified by a ceremony that took place on March 1, 1915, at the hospital of the girls' school in Le Mans to honor the Jewish Zouave Youda ben Bourak (Figure 1.3). When wounded by enemy fire, Bourak had exclaimed, "My flesh means nothing! *Vive la France!*" Before two hundred mostly North African soldiers at the hospital, General Leguay, former division commander in Constantine, awarded Bourak the Military Medal and cited him as "the most beautiful example of patriotism and self-sacrifice to his

Figure 1.3. The Jewish zouave Youda ben Bourak proudly stands with his medals, as pictured in *L'Univers israélite*, April 16, 1915. (Bibliothèque Nationale de France.)

comrades who surrounded him." "I am happy," continued Leguay, "to have been delegated for this ceremony and to award an *israélite* the medal of the brave. Your co-religionists must know well that you are honored with this distinction." The general then switched from French to Arabic to extol the many Muslims present: "Look, you others, Arabs, what a Jew has done; you must be brave like him and imitate him."[91] Leguay's words and manner of speaking reflected the struggle to define the place of Algeria's Jews and Muslims and the persistent ambiguities raised by the war experience for the two groups' relations with each other and with the French state.

By pointing to Bourak as a model specifically for both Jews and Muslims, Leguay suggested that the French military still in some manner classified the two groups separately from other French soldiers. According to this logic, Algerian Muslim natives should emulate their fellow natives. Yet the phrase "you others, Arabs" separated Algerian Jews like Bourak from their Muslim counterparts along colonial and racial lines. By addressing Bourak and the French officials in French and the Muslims in Arabic, Leguay highlighted cultural and linguistic divisions between many Jews and Muslims.[92] Furthermore, in his condescending words to the Muslims, he suggested that these unemancipated indigenous Algerians might follow the example of their more enlightened and Frenchified Jewish (erstwhile) brethren.

In addition, Leguay's rhetorical focus here on Arabs seems hardly accidental. Since the nineteenth century, the French military had developed racial perceptions that saw Kabyles, the largely sedentary, mostly Berber populations of the northern mountainous region of Kabylia, in more favorable terms than the more itinerant Arabs who lived largely in the lowland plains. According to this mythical dichotomy, Kabyles were less fervently religious than Arabs, more European, and, some claimed, even racially white. Moreover, the experience of French officers in battle against both groups had led the military to consider Arabs less skillful and disciplined as fighters than Kabyles.[93]

The contradictions of his speech notwithstanding, Leguay framed ben Bourak as a perfect example for the narrative of France and its military as great nation builder and assimilator. French and Algerian Jews saw their young hero as a model for the active roles that their communities could play in the construction of the French imperial nation. Soon after the ceremony at Le Mans, an AIU official depicted in a letter the soldier's veritable transformation at the army's hands: "He is an *israélite* from the south of Algeria, dressed like an *indigène,* mumbling barely two words of French. When he presents himself [for service], his appearance and his fright express a total physical and moral wreck . . . [reminding] me of the most unfortunate Jews of the Moroccan mellahs. You can imagine the easy jokes about this 'flea-ridden future defender of the *Patrie.*' Five months later, the newspapers publish the story of his exploits." French and Algerian Jewish publications repeated with evident pride the story of Youda ben Bourak's bravery and Leguay's words.[94]

At such moments, Jews seemed to appreciate how their wartime service alongside North African Muslims could affirm their own unimpeachable French civic credentials. Such an outlook was contiguous with a notion developed by both French and Algerian Jewry across the nineteenth century that Algerian Jews were more prepared than Muslims to participate in the civilizing mission. That is, Jews were more connected than Muslims to French culture and values and, particularly with regard to family and gender norms, readier to shed outmoded religious customs and laws.[95] This context helps us to appreciate better the impetus behind an agitated letter from an Algerian Jew that appeared in September 1916 in *L'Univers israélite.* "Since the *israélites* of France have discovered that their Algerian coreligionists are fighting well and in large numbers," began the writer, "they speak regularly, regarding us, of the 'brave regiments of zouaves and tirailleurs.' This irritates us to no end." He implored the newspaper: "Would you please say that the regiments of native tirailleurs are recruited, as their name indicates, among the Muslim natives. The Algerian *israélites* only serve there by exception and in small number (there are even corps that do not accept them on principle). They form, with other French of Algeria, the contingent of the zouave regiments and that brings them glory enough. Therefore, note the distinction, I beg of you. This will bring pleasure to our good friends the 'tiraillous,' and to us as well."[96] The writer of this letter appeared exasperated at the categorization of himself and other Algerian Jewish Zouaves as "Zouaves and tirailleurs." Particularly with his use of the patronizing term tiraillous, he sought to clarify that the Jews were part of the body of the "French of Algeria," and thereby very different from the "Muslim natives." In speaking of how the tirailleurs would themselves appreciate a clearer distinction, he also hinted once more at assumptions about Muslim innate hostility toward Jews.

All at once, this letter writer stakes a claim to being Jewish, French, emancipated, and white instead of Muslim, indigenous, subjected, and nonwhite. The racial element is less explicit, but it resonates in the wider context: along with the racialized arrangements of the French military, exoticized representations of black African and North African tirailleurs regularly appeared in the French press. The arrival of so many French colonial subjects in the metropole created a sense of peril around French European racial identity. Stories of illicit sexual acts by North African men with French women led to violence and to French policies designed to isolate Muslim soldiers and laborers from their French hosts.[97]

Colonial and racial elements found further reflection in French Jewish communal discourses about Algerian Jews. The anonymous letter writer sought to counter a number of discussions from Jewish figures and press outlets that implicitly grouped together Algerian Jews and Muslims.[98] He first bristled at a longtime ignorance, inattention, and condescension on the part of native French Jews regarding their cohorts in Algeria. Indeed, in an article of autumn 1915, the editors of *Archives israélites* described Algerian Jewish soldiers thus: "Everywhere [they] fight like lions, showing a masculine courage, a warlike spirit that one would not have expected on the part of these Jews who entered late into the French polity and in whom the spirit of even the Maccabees appears to revive itself."[99] Such depictions connected in part to long-standing Jewish efforts to underscore Jews' militaristic toughness: since the nineteenth century, European Jewish leaders had often used the term *new Maccabees* to emphasize the strength and fervor of Jewish soldiers, and Zionists had adapted the reference for their purposes.[100] Yet particularly juxtaposed to a mention of Algerian Jews' recent acquisition of French citizenship, words like *lions* and *warlike* also present an unmistakably colonialist image of the Algerian Jews as African or Arab warriors. Echoing some of Rabbi Fridman's words, these accounts set French Jews of the metropolitan, largely Ashkenazic, republican tradition apart from their (newly integrating) Algerian counterparts. Such a combination of terms, while suggesting that French Jewry could help to elevate the status of its Algerian coreligionists, also placed distance between the Jewish populations of the metropole and the colony, thereby guarding the former's French credentials.

The Home Front: Jews, Muslims, and the *Union Sacrée*

The importance of Jews' and Muslims' respective colonial and religious statuses and identities extended beyond the battlefield, defining early Jewish-Muslim representations and daily interactions on the home front.

In this respect, France's *union sacrée* became a key barometer for the parallels and contrasts in the two groups' positions. At the outbreak of the war in August 1914, French leaders called for a "sacred union." Coined to describe the newly formed national unity government, the phrase soon took on broader connotations. Monarchist and socialist members of parliament shook hands; feminists put on hold their demands for women's right to vote and devoted their energies to the war effort; Catholic clerics made temporary peace with their long-standing opponents, the teachers of the republican schools. In this context, discussions of the multiple confessional groups serving under the French colors gave Jews—and France's other historically persecuted religious minority, Protestants—significant attention; in addition, the Jewish and Protestant press and institutions regularly highlighted their respective communities' sizable participation in the *union sacrée*.[101] Yet Catholic, Protestant, secular, and indeed Jewish representations of the *union sacrée* almost invariably failed to account for the huge Muslim contingent among the French troops. Here we find another telling silence in the archives, both obscuring and drawing out complex realities about French nationhood and Jewish-Muslim relations during the war.

Maurice Barrès's series of articles on the *union sacrée,* published in the popular *L'Écho de Paris* in October 1916 and later compiled in the 1917 volume, *Les diverses familles spirituelles de la France,* provides an instructive example of this silence.[102] Barrès, an avowed Catholic, had been a leading anti-Dreyfusard. As a deputy in parliament and celebrated writer, he advocated an ethnic, exclusivist French nationalism. In his discussion, however, of France's "diverse spiritual families," he described "traditionalists," Protestants, socialists, and Jews as the four elements making up the national greatness of France. He gave particular attention to Rabbi Abraham Bloch, who was fatally wounded in the winter of 1914 while placing a crucifix on a dying Christian soldier and thus became a symbol of the *union sacrée*. Barrès made no mention of the far larger number of Muslims fighting for France.

Jews responded with great pride to Barrès's account. His praise for France's Jews as one of the country's integral "spiritual families" and his celebration of a mythical scene that fused Jew and Christian on the battlefield marked a kind of watershed. These words appeared to turn the page on long-standing enmity between Jews and Catholics across the nineteenth century, particularly during the Dreyfus affair. The healing effort, moreover, came from both sides. The Jewish press had spilled ample ink valorizing the heroism of Rabbi Bloch's final moments and celebrating the broader Jewish participation in the *union sacrée*. Thus, whereas throughout the nineteenth century, French Jews had repeatedly used anticlerical attacks on the Catholic Church as a way to solidify their own credentials as modern, liberal French citizens, World War I witnessed a reshuffling, at least briefly, of interreligious relationships.[103] In 1905, landmark legislation separating church and state had resolved a decades-long struggle between clericalists and secularists. The law eliminated official status and most state funding for religious groups, but also gave the three previously recognized religions—Catholicism, Protestantism, and Judaism—newfound independence from public oversight. Ten years on, the law appeared to constitute a truce that had paved the way for the emergence of Jewish and Christian public religious identities as mutually agreeable rather than hostile. In another event hailed as an example of wartime sacred unity, on at least one occasion, Barrès and his former Jewish Dreyfusard nemesis, Joseph Reinach, toured the trenches together in support of French soldiers.[104]

Jews, as we have seen, had found in Muslims a new religious group vis-à-vis which they could strategically position themselves for integrationist motives. Just as Jews noted triumphantly their inclusion in Barrès's account, those writing on behalf of France's Muslims protested their conspicuous absence. In a cover story of June 1, 1917, in *El Akhbar,* Victor Barrucand, who had begun his own career as an ardently Dreyfusard journalist, exclaimed, "Maurice Barrès has forgotten only one group in his composition: he says nothing of Islam and the French Muslims. . . . Like all of us, he knows, meanwhile, in what an exemplary manner the French Muslims . . . of Africa have understood their duty toward the mother country, and he certainly would not be the last to recognize what we owe them. Why then has he separated them from the spiritual families of France?"[105] Barrucand asserted that Barrès's attention to Algeria's Jews made "his grave silence regarding Muslims even more insulting." Barrès responded to his attack with a letter to *El Akhbar* in which he apologized and promised to research Muslim soldiers' contributions in order to rectify his mistake.[106] It was no accident that Barrucand mentioned Barrès's praise for Algeria's Jews as a point of comparison. While both Jews and Muslims repeatedly highlighted their service to prove their Frenchness, one did so as a statement of affirmation, the other as a plea for equal rights. *El Akhbar's* editor implicitly asked how anyone could extol a smaller group of relative privilege while ignoring one of greater sacrifice and lesser status. Barrucand had originally been sent to Algeria by France's major civil liberties organization, the League of the Rights of Man (LDH), specifically to fight against a wave of settler antisemitism. Now he was focused on a different case of discrimination. His recognition of diverse groups fighting for common cause implied a more expansive version of the *union sacrée* than that generally found in public discourse during the war.[107]

By and large, the French Jewish community also remained silent about Muslims in discussions of the *union sacrée*. To be sure, exceptions appeared, most notably from Homel Meiss, the chief rabbi of Marseille, who declared in a 1919 message on the theme of peace: "The Fatherland should be one and indivisible, because—we cannot repeat it often enough—there were no Catholics, there were no Protestants, there were no Jews, there were no Muslims, on the battlefields of the Marne, the Meuse, Flanders, and the Dardanelles, but uniquely 'soldiers' of France who superbly did their duty."[108] Moreover, in multiple wartime discussions of ecumenism or sacred unity, Meiss included Muslims alongside Jews and Christians.[109] Perhaps this owed to his service in France's Mediterranean port, where Muslims, as well as Jews from majority Muslim lands, disembarked, passed through, and settled in significant numbers from an early date. More typically, celebrations of the *union sacrée* in the Jewish press and rabbinical writings and speeches cited Jews, Catholics, and Protestants while ignoring Muslims.[110] Thus organized French Jewry echoed the assumption of leading nationalists like Barrès: Muslims, though fighting in greater numbers than Jews or Protestants, were hardly vital to the *union sacrée* and needed only occasional mention.[111]

One reason for Muslims' relative absence from conceptions of the *union sacrée* was likely the inability of much of the French state and society to imagine them as a fully equal part of the nation. This hierarchy could be seen as well in the treatment Muslims received as migrant workers in the metropole. Despite their sizable numbers, Muslim wartime laborers were largely hidden, deliberately isolated from the rest of the French population, including Jews. Muslims who came as workers were employed in a variety of public and private enterprises: munitions factories, supply workshops, lumber yards, storage and engineering centers, agriculture, transports, mines, gas factories, and landscaping.[112] Through the Colonial Labor Organization Service (SOTC) of the War Ministry, the French government tried to manage colonial laborers' every move. The SOTC categorized workers by nationality and assigned their employment, housing, food, and transport, separating them as much as possible from the native French population.[113] From the time they arrived in Marseille, they received special uniforms; they were typically housed three or four in a single room and considered "undesirable neighbors."[114] Similar to their military counterparts, these North African Muslim migrants commonly were tasked with the most challenging of duties, and they struggled to adjust to the many new conditions of metropolitan life, including the colder climate. One typical report from 1917 on North African workers in Lyon declared: "Given the average age of these youths, it is impossible to ask for [the assigned] 10 hours of work, usually very heavy work, in one day. This loading work is difficult, exhausting, the shells are very heavy for these young arms, the nights are cold and their lungs are used to the hot dry air of Algeria and Morocco." These Muslim workers also earned substantially lower salaries than French workers.[115]

Under such circumstances, it is hardly surprising that Muslim workers had less frequent contact with Jews than their military counterparts, and little documentation exists regarding relations. Yet their isolation was hardly absolute. Algerian Muslims concentrated residentially and socially in neighborhoods of, among others, Paris's 12th, 13th, 15th, 18th, 19th, and 20th arrondissements. Each of these quarters, particularly the last, housed sizable numbers of Jewish immigrants. In the 11th arrondissement, a smaller, more elite Muslim population lived alongside most of Paris's Ottoman Jewish immigrants. Neighborhoods overlapped similarly in the port city of Marseille. Illustrating the potential for interaction, Muslims looking for halal meat regularly entered kosher butchers' shops. Given that many Muslims have long considered kosher meat permissible under Islamic law, since the nineteenth century, a number of North African Muslim travelers had sought out kosher butchers when visiting Europe. In wartime France, many observant Muslims naturally turned to Jewish slaughterhouses for their meat.[116]

Indeed, on a small scale, Jews and Muslims began to enter each other's sociocultural, political, and even religious spaces. On Monday, July 31, 1916, in Paris's 2nd arrondissement, a celebration was held for the Muslim holiday of Aïd el-Fitr.[117] The event took place in the piano store and residence of Eugène Tenoudji, a forty-two-year-old Jew originally from Constantine, Algeria.[118] Tenoudji provided the space to Ammou Missoum Chekroum, a thirty-year-old Algerian Muslim who had come to France shortly before the war. The owner of a cafeteria, who went by "Chérif," claimed a religious background and helped to organize groups and events for wounded Muslim soldiers, Chekroum was well liked by many of his Muslim comrades. Yet the previous year he had come to the attention of French police for being "of doubtful morality, lazy and devoid of scruples."[119] The authorities alleged at various points that Chekroum was an imposter, with no actual religious training or authority; had two French mistresses; or had even converted to Protestantism. The concern that Parisian police revealed regarding Chekroum's event also reflected their hostility toward any Islamic religious gatherings that occurred outside official spaces or did not fit official preconceptions of Muslim practices.[120] Whereas state-sponsored wartime Muslim observances and worship sites often met a tepid response, Chekroum's event, which violated the municipal ordinance that designated August 1 as the only day for the observance of Aïd el-Fitr, stirred considerable interest among many Muslim soldiers in Paris.[121]

Early Monday morning, as many as seven or eight hundred Muslims arrived at Tenoudji's piano-shop-turned-mosque for the holiday's traditional morning prayers.[122] They then returned that afternoon for Arabic coffee and mint tea, when French military veteran Jehan Soudan de Pierrefitte addressed the gathering: "As a former cavalry officer and a practicing Catholic, I come to salute you, you who have fought for your mother France, and to tell you that in the French army, there are soldiers of all religions who respect and love each other and who fight for the same cause, which is that of France and of Justice."[123] Chekroum and a number of those around him decided to give the meeting place the name of "zaouïa of the brave."[124] They hung both the French tricolor and a green Muslim flag from the balcony. On learning of these events that flouted their orders for the date of the holiday's observance, French police quickly intervened, and despite Tenoudji's best efforts, they ordered the establishment closed. As was often the case, a gathering of colonial immigrants had aroused considerable apprehension.[125]

This unusual episode illustrates vividly how the war placed Jews' and Muslims' uncertain colonial and religious positions at the heart of their relations in the metropole. It also displays the manner in which reports of the Paris police on North African Muslims already crafted Islamophobic narratives of anti-French defiance about individuals like Chekroum, while revealing beneath the surface a rather different reality of interconfessional relations and multifaceted identities. For Tenoudji, the holiday, with its food and drink of the Maghreb and its Muslim religious fervor, undoubtedly recalled experiences in Constantine. Both men were likely reminded of an ambiance in which Jews and Muslims at times mingled in one another's cultural and ritual spaces, coming together in cafés and sometimes at each other's life cycle or holiday celebrations. Simultaneously Tenoudji acted as a kind of bridge who could help to bring Muslims closer to Frenchness. The pairing of French and Muslim flags in public asserted the possibility of a multifaceted civic identity. Noting at once his Catholicism and the army's *laïcité*, Pierrefitte appeared uniquely positioned to affirm the compatibility of France and Islam. At the same time, the police's decision to break up the gathering, shortly after the Islamic flag appeared on the balcony, signaled that Algerian Muslims' religion still restricted their ability to gain full acceptance as French.

Just as Tenoudji's more secure place in Paris's urban fabric enabled him to open his business for Chekroum's religious event, some French Jews were in a position to try to assist Muslims in larger ways. In the course of the war, a few major French Jewish figures directly promoted the political rights of Muslims. The most prominent was Joseph Reinach. Reinach was a classic case of what Pierre Birnbaum has termed "state Jews," who made devotion to the republic much of their life's work and rose to eminent positions within the state apparatus.[126] Born in 1856, Reinach grew up in an Alsatian Jewish family deeply committed to the ideals of the Revolution. Rising quickly in politics, Reinach befriended many of the architects of the Third Republic, serving by age twenty-five as chief of staff to Léon Gambetta at the Ministry of Foreign Affairs, and in the 1880s was elected to a seat in the Assemblée nationale. There, he quickly took an interest in promoting French imperial expansion, extolling the "civilizing mission" as both in the French national interest and vital to the spread of human freedom. He later became a leading Dreyfusard, publishing numerous pamphlets and working furiously behind the scenes during the affair. While avowedly assimilationist, Reinach remained proudly Jewish, having a Jewish wedding and serving as secretary of the AIU in the mid-1880s. Due to his central role in the affair, he was subjected to repeated, vicious antisemitic attacks.

In May 1916, Reinach published an article in *Le Figaro* advocating greater equality for France's Muslim subjects. He declared:

Muslims of Asia and Africa, fighting in the English and Russian armies as in ours, mixing their heroic blood with ours, have acquired great rights, from the Ganges to the Volga, and from the Persian Gulf to the Atlantic. Oppressions, which have always been detestable, would be tomorrow frightfully ungrateful. Whoever has shed with us his blood has the right to our liberty and our justice. [Whether] bureaucratic or military, parliamentary or electoral, we must break all resistance [and] produce a vast reform in the status of the Muslim *indigènes*.[127]

Reinach's words here argued for a new chapter in the long-standing connection between French military service and citizenship. Yet his vision went even further, for it situated World War I as a broader turning point in the history of colonial empires, whereby the service of various colonized peoples could transform their relationship to their mother country. The editors of *El Akhbar* reprinted the article in part and saluted Reinach's courage.[128] Reinach responded with a brief letter praising the newspaper's longtime advocacy for Muslim rights, concluding, "Always and everywhere, we must be firm about the principles of modern France."[129]

Reinach recalled an earlier close companion of Gambetta and prominent AIU member, Adolphe Crémieux, and the latter's famous decree emancipating Algerian Jewry. In discussing the wartime service of their Algerian coreligionists, French Jews often invoked the decree with pride. Muslims and their allies like Victor Barrucand, in contrast, increasingly saw the act as an emblem of colonial injustice and inequality. For France's Muslims, Crémieux and Reinach thus represented two faces of the state Jew's power to affect Muslims and their relations with Jews: Crémieux as threatening, Reinach as benevolent. Both faces would repeatedly reappear in the decades to come.[130]

Not long after Reinach's exchange with *El Akhbar,* the LDH took a position as an organization supporting French citizenship for Algeria's Muslims. Founded in part by Reinach and other Jews during the Dreyfus affair, the LDH had grown to eighty thousand members by 1910. Liberal, largely middle-class Jews remained a sizable contingent, constituting 10 to 12 percent of those on the league's central committee between 1898 and 1940.[131] During the years before the war, the LDH had become a leading voice for reform and Muslim rights in Algeria. In November 1917, the league recommended that all Algerian Muslims who fought for France in World War I and applied for French citizenship should be granted their request without having to forfeit their personal status as Muslims.[132]

At the meeting where this position gained unanimous approval, Edmond Zadoc-Kahn, son of France's famous former chief rabbi, Zadoc

Kahn, applauded the decision. During the affair, his father had quietly urged Jewish leaders to defend Dreyfus and had himself become the victim of virulent antisemitism. Now, his son publicly exclaimed, "I believe that I can affirm that the French *israélites* will come with great satisfaction to confer civic rights to the indigenous Algerians who fight so valiantly for France." In response, a writer for *L'Univers israélite* urged the league to go further. Arguing that all Muslim soldiers should automatically gain citizenship with or without an application, he asked, "Isn't it the equitable complement to the Crémieux Decree? We think so and do not hesitate to say it." In closing, this writer in effect envisioned an expanded *union sacrée* of the future, speaking of the unity "between all the children of Algeria: Christian colonists, Muslim *indigènes,* and *israélites.*"[133] These words elicited enthusiastic responses from both Jewish and Muslim readers. An anonymous Muslim leader addressed a glowing letter to the journal, in which he spoke of his longtime desire for interethnic "rapprochement" and promised: "We will never forget, we Muslims, the liberal and patriotic attitude of Monsieur Zadoc-Kahn and of your estimable newspaper."[134]

These words and actions on behalf of Algerian Muslims pointed to the parallels between Muslims' current challenges in France and those that Jews had faced historically. The presence of these particular leading French Jewish individuals and groups—like that of Victor Barrucand—implicitly connected the current cause to the last great struggle of both republican Judaism and the republic itself: the defense of Dreyfus. Now, at the moment when Algerian Muslims fought for the fatherland, prominent Jews spoke from their position of relative security and empathy to promote Muslim rights. These Jews' activism underscored the idealistic components of much of French Jewry's commitment to the colonial republican vision. Just as the courage of Jews and Muslims on the battlefield made an implicit case for each group's full acceptance in a more multiethnic French citizenry, by the war's end, several leading French Jews had explicitly offered a more inclusive vision of what it could mean to be French.

Transnational Stirrings: Zionism and Arab Nationalism in Paris

During the war, Jewish-Muslim political encounters began to take on international dimensions, occasionally in connection with the question of Palestine. The end of the Ottoman Empire, the Balfour Declaration, and the eventual creation of the mandate system in the Middle East made World War I a critical turning point in the history of Zionism and Arab nationalism.[135] While adding another layer to the complex identities and allegiances of thousands of Jews and Muslims in France, such developments did not necessarily lead to greater conflict between the two groups. Amicable engagements among a small number of Jews and Muslims regarding the Middle East were not entirely new to France. Already on the war's eve, in summer 1913, Paris was the site of the "First Arab Congress," where Lebanese, Syrian, and Zionist representatives all took part, and several Zionist and Arab activists sought to achieve entente.[136]

Wartime encounters between Jews, Muslims, and frequently Christians around such topics continued to be fluid and even positive. By the spring of 1915, a thirty-seven-year-old Jewish doctor named Charles Zalta from Damascus, born to Iranian parents but later naturalized French, had garnered notice from Paris police for his role in the movement for Syrian autonomy or independence. French authorities suspected that around Zalta, a group of Christian, Muslim, and Jewish activists, working in the Syrian, Lebanese, and Zionist movements, operated in overlapping circles; rivalries existed among them, but so too did a sense of mutually aligned interests.[137] By November 1916, when about five hundred Zionists gathered at a meeting in Paris, a substantial Arab revolt, aided by the French and British, was well underway. The prospect that Palestine and much of the Middle East would be "liberated" soon from the Ottoman Empire appeared increasingly likely. At this meeting, one of the speakers was an Arab Muslim who had grown up in the Jerusalem area and sought to convey the attitude of his fellow Muslims in Palestine. While strongly urging Jews not to associate their religion with political ambitions, he assured them that those Jews who "returned" to Palestine would find a warm welcome among the native Arabs.[138]

In the months following the Balfour Declaration, as French Zionist activity continued to grow, *L'Univers israélite* at once gave voice to the profound ambivalence of traditional French Jewry regarding the prospect of a Jewish home in Palestine, and recognized the historical significance of the moment, devoting increasing enthusiasm and attention to the Jewish presence in Palestine.[139] Consistent with its previous tone regarding Jews and Muslims, however, it painted a picture of positive Jewish-Muslim coexistence in Jerusalem and, stating that Muslims' "monotheistic faith makes them true children of Abraham," repeatedly underscored the need to respect the Muslim inhabitants and holy sites of

Palestine.[140] In a vivid illustration of the essential impact of World War I on French Jewish ideas about Muslims, in January 1918, as one writer gently advocated for a Jewish home in Palestine, in the same breath he lauded the tremendous sacrifice of Algeria's Muslims in the French war effort and alluded to the journal's already-stated support of citizenship for Algerian Muslim soldiers.[141] For the moment, then, transnational affiliations hardly undermined one's profession of French civic devotion; rather, they helped to shape yet another strand of identity and politics for a small but growing number of Jews, Muslims, and Christians in France. As the war drew to a close, both the meaning of Frenchness and the international order seemed open to countless new possibilities. Competing promises and movements over the same piece of land hardly registered as a source of Jewish-Muslim tension in the Hexagon.

World War I set a tone for Jewish-Muslim relations in France that would prevail for decades to come. These relations were from the outset triangular: the policies of the wartime state at once reinforced strict dichotomies of acceptance and exclusion in France and enabled many Jews and Muslims to negotiate more uncertain, multifaceted positions. The essential role of large numbers of colonized soldiers and workers that France was unprepared to make citizens in the foreseeable future, the reintroduction of religion as a source of active public identity, and the international political movements unleashed by the tectonic shifts in the Ottoman and Russian empires presented basic challenges to notions of singular French identity. In these ways, the war forced France to grapple with the implications of becoming a multiethnic empire and a multiconfessional republican nation-state. By the end of the war, seventy-five hundred Jews and between thirty-six and forty-five thousand North African Muslims had died for "mother France."[142] Throughout, both groups insisted, implicitly on the battlefield and at times explicitly through their patriotic rhetoric, that "Frenchness" might incorporate a greater range of differences than ever before.

By following and interrogating the narratives of wartime documents, we have seen that this foundational event catalyzed a wide range of Jewish-Muslim interactions. To be sure, the war not only challenged but also sharpened differences in Jews' and Muslims' respective legal status, relative power, and relationship to the French state and empire. Carrying experiences from North Africa and responding to new conditions in the metropole, many Jews and Muslims already confronted and sought to negotiate colonial, religious, and transnational elements of status and identity. Yet the meaning and import of these elements could be highly situational, as witnessed in the story of the comrades Habib and Rahmoun, philosophically discussing their religions while fighting next to each other in the trenches. Many Muslims and Jews interacted both according to the official poles of categories and in the spaces in between: as fellow soldiers, North Africans with common cultural sensibilities, monotheists of minority faiths with overlapping religious knowledge and heritage, or optimistic republicans. As would occur repeatedly in the twentieth century, the rhetoric of binaries ran up against a more fluid space: wherein Jews and Muslims laid claim to myriad ways of encountering each other and relating to France.

2

PUSHING THE BOUNDARIES OF MEDITERRANEAN FRANCE

World War I transformed French society, politics, and culture. At war's end, France lay physically and psychologically devastated. The country had lost much of a generation of able-bodied men and faced a crisis of demography and masculinity; the economy was decimated. The war brought not only massive destruction in its wake but also renewal and change. Charred French landscapes soon became sites of both commemoration and reconstruction. The shortfall in manpower, both demographic and economic, fueled a wave of interwar immigration that introduced an unprecedented variety of interethnic contact into France. The empire, whose subjects the war had engaged in such large numbers as soldiers and laborers, became more present than ever before in metropolitan life. In this context, France's Jewish and Muslim populations began to interact on a wider scale in a series of new settings.

For the first time in its history, France was becoming a nation of immigrants. This reflected a combination of factors: a growing pronatalist movement that favored immigration from select European societies in the face of France's long-standing low birth rates (a situation exacerbated by the overwhelming toll of war); the economic necessity of a productive labor force to rebuild the nation and support industrial expansion; and republican universal ideals about France as a nation of inclusion, integration, and successful assimilation.[1] After the United States instituted its quota system in 1924, France became the country with the highest rate of foreign population growth in the world.[2] The nearly 2.2 million foreigners recorded in the 1936 census made up 5.34 percent of the overall population, a number five times greater than their proportion had been in the mid-nineteenth century. This figure did not include the half-million naturalized French men and women who were 1.25 percent of the population, or the roughly 150,000 colonial migrants residing in the country.[3] By 1942, these groups together would account for 11 percent of mainland France's overall population.[4]

At the height of the interwar migration in the early to mid-1930s, over 100,000 Muslims and 150,000 newly arrived Jews (of an overall population of 260,000) together made up nearly 8 percent of the approximately 3.2 million total immigrants and colonial migrants living in France. After being "repatriated" immediately following World War I, Muslims from North Africa began to arrive in France in large numbers again, now as recruited workers. Most were men who came to France alone, for seasonal work in unskilled manual labor positions, sending back much of their salary to their families in North Africa and rotating home at least once every eighteen months. Many of France's newly arrived Jews sought to flee antisemitism or political instability; waves of refugees would swell the Jewish population to over 300,000 by the outbreak of World War II. Seventy-five percent, or roughly 130,000, of France's Jewish immigrants hailed from Eastern Europe, primarily Poland and Russia. Among the other fourth, some 25,000 came from the Balkans and the Levant and about 12,000 from either Germany or North Africa. Added to the existing presence of Jews from the southern Mediterranean, this brought the total Levantine or Maghrebian Jewish presence to 35,000, or 11 percent of Jews in France.[5]

Between the wars, France's Jews and Muslims encountered many common opportunities and challenges, but rarely on equal terms. By the mid- to late 1930s, as France faced economic depression with high unemployment, political ineffectiveness and instability, and a sense of cultural malaise, Jews confronted increasingly shrill antisemitism and xenophobia. Eventually this took the form of outwardly antisemitic political parties, demonstrations, and attacks, as well as government expulsions and detention centers for immigrants and refugees without permits, a large percentage of them Jews.[6] Nonetheless, Jewish immigrants generally benefited from at least one of three factors that did not apply to Muslims: the rights of foreign nationals secured through treaties, a sizable pro-refugee lobby, and France's relative openness to those fleeing persecution.[7]

The 1920s witnessed the establishment of several new institutions meant to recognize, attend to, and closely surveil the North African Muslim presence on the mainland. Muslims in Algeria and France were disappointed by the rather limited reforms of the 1919 Jonnart Law, which offered voting rights to a select group of Muslim men but only in local elections in Algeria and for specifically Muslim candidates. The Service des affaires indigènes nord-africaines (SAINA), created in Paris in 1923 (and established on a smaller scale in a number of other cities over the next several years), undertook substantial social assistance work to aid Muslims in meeting their basic needs. At the same time, under the supervision of the Paris Prefecture of Police, SAINA was tasked with intense monitoring of the North African Muslim population.[8] Another major institution that served to oversee and isolate allegedly dangerous Muslim bodies was the Grand Mosque of Paris. The mosque, completed in 1926, housed in the central 5th arrondissement, was built ostensibly to honor Muslims who died for France in World War I. In reality, it operated on many levels. It was a site for Muslim practice and a spectacle of imperial glory at the heart of Paris. Perhaps most important, it was the primary institution that expressed the paradoxes of "Islam français": the state claimed that the mosque would cultivate an Islam compatible with republican ideals of laïcité, while simultaneously designing the mosque architecturally around assumptions about the peculiarly and immutably physical nature of Muslim religious practice.[9]

The character and presence of SAINA and the Grand Mosque of Paris emblematized how shifts in France's population makeup, state policies, and culture during the interwar years were reshaping the Hexagon in myriad and far-reaching ways. Many of these changes were part of France's markedly increased orientation toward the wider Mediterranean, a shift linked to the heightened importance of the empire more broadly to metropolitan French politics and society during the interwar period. Alongside a plethora of advertisements, exhibits, ceremonies, and publications, growing numbers of colonial workers and students became both subjects of constant police surveillance and frequent agents of political change (Figure 2.1).[10] Yet other factors in the turn toward the Mediterranean included the increasing centrality of Algeria specifically to metropolitan politics; the substantial presence of immigrants from Italy and Spain, constituting roughly 45 percent of France's overall interwar migration; and the expanding importance of France as a Mediterranean empire, with mandates in Syria and Lebanon and a growing colonial rivalry with Italy.[11] Dramatic improvements in the speed of nautical transport and the advent of the airplane made the French Mediterranean a place that seemed considerably smaller and more interconnected than only a few years prior.

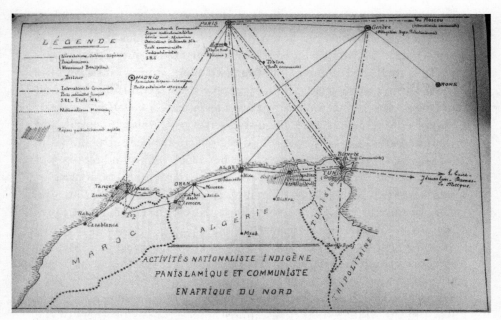

Figure 2.1. Map of trans-Mediterranean subversive political networks, from a French state report on North African political activity of 1935. (Archives départementales des Bouches-du-Rhône, 1 M 759.)

In the years after World War I, as metropolitan France became increasingly defined by its Mediterranean context, Jews and Muslims played a critical role in this transformation. Indeed, a focus on Jews and Muslims permits, even compels us to recenter the history of France and its empire between the wars, placing it as much in the northern portion of a burgeoning French Mediterranean as at the heart of Western Europe.[12] For, if World War I rendered metropolitan France a new site for the widespread passage and encounters of Jews and Muslims from across the Mediterranean, in the interwar period France became a major space of trans-Mediterranean migration, circulation, and cultural interaction on a far wider and deeper scale. More than ever before, the Hexagon constituted a meeting point of three continents and three monotheistic religions.[13] Now mainland France was being peopled by growing numbers of Christian, Jewish, and Muslim travelers, activists, and immigrants of subcultures all along the Great Sea, from not only southern Europe and North Africa but more distant places such as Egypt, Greece, and Asia Minor.

To understand these changes, we need to attend to three overlapping stories: about demography and everyday life, struggles to define the French nation and empire, and transnational subaltern political movements on mainland French soil. Together, these stories illustrate how France became characterized both by unprecedented ethnic diversity, and by what some scholars have called Mediterranean *connectivity*, a set of linkages—along commercial, linguistic, religious, culinary, musical, and other lines—that cross distinct micro-regions and subcultures along the sea.[14] At the same time, we can also see how such long-standing ties and networks were increasingly redefined by the hardening boundaries of modern politics. This occurred through the rise of the nation-state, the rivalry of empires, and the growing alternatives to the colonial order presented by a series of indigenous movements.[15]

In the first story, the dramatic growth of France's Jewish and Muslim populations led to the establishment of sociocultural spaces such as neighborhoods, cafés, and musical performances, where Muslims and Jews recreated and adapted aspects of the culture and coexistence they had known in the Maghreb, at times almost interacting as brothers of the same ethnicity. This took different forms, with Paris as the imperial capital and Marseille as the Mediterranean crossroads. By the mid- to late 1930s, the interaction of Jews and Muslims in both cities exemplified the French imperial nation-state's multiethnic and multiconfessional character in all its contradictions. Strasbourg, with virtually no Muslim population at this time, makes for an instructive contrast: the Mediterranean remained far more distant and optical than readily present in this borderland commercial center in the East.

In the second story, the two groups found themselves in the crosshairs of competing visions of French nationhood, wherein France's Mediterranean colonial possessions and subjects, particularly in Algeria, took on unprecedented importance. These visions played out in particular around a pair of debates: the struggle between fascism and antifascism and the growing question of Algeria's future. Often in articulations both about and by Jews and Muslims, the two issues became interrelated. The importance of these struggles crystallized following the 1934 riots in Constantine and during the emergence of the Popular Front.

These events in part shaped the third story, wherein a series of political movements with links across the wider Mediterranean established footholds in France. Ranging from anticolonial nationalism to Islamic reform to Zionism, some emerged in opposition to French colonial policies, others as part of a wider Jewish or Muslim transnational politics. Here, ongoing basic differences in French legal status and brewing conflicts across the Mediterranean frequently burdened many Jews and Muslims with markers or self-understandings of opposed ethnic or religious movements.

Because these three stories featured some of the same actors and unfolded concurrently, they enable us to see in what situations Jewish and Muslim ethnoreligious identity came to the fore and how the meaning of that identity varied according to context. In spaces of daily sociability, many Jews and Muslims formed harmonious, even close relationships with one another, but by the late 1930s, the political discussion around Muslim-Jewish relations became increasingly (if not entirely) tense and even hostile. This juxtaposition of overlapping everyday lives with frequently conflicting political attachments, of connectivity with boundary, meant that many of the same Jews and Muslims tended to assign different meanings to religion and ethnicity in different geographical spaces and social settings.

The Beginning of Shared Sociocultural Milieux

Many historians have focused on Jewish or Muslim geographic quarters of this period as spaces apart, defined by a distinct linguistic, cultural, religious, and often political character.[16] Yet the insularity of such quarters was rarely so absolute. A close examination of two neighborhoods—the "Jewish" Marais in Paris and the Porte d'Aix in Marseille, often labeled a "Muslim" quarter—illustrates how these spaces became sites of multilayered Jewish-Muslim interaction.[17] These relations, largely between Jews and Muslims from the Maghreb or Levant, reflected both common traditions from North Africa, the Balkans, and the Middle East and the specific spatial and social contexts of the metropolitan setting. In the process, Jews and Muslims turned these quarters from insular ethnic neighborhoods to outposts of North African culture within the new Mediterranean France.

Interwar Paris was undergoing rapid change demographically, culturally, and at the level of daily experience. If the nineteenth century saw the emergence of what historian Julia Clancy-Smith has dubbed a "central Mediterranean corridor" that crossed through France via Marseille, by the 1920s, the empire's increasingly cosmopolitan capital could be said to anchor a new extension, an elongated embayment by which mainland

France opened onto the Mediterranean—and vice versa.[18] Various Mediterranean subcultures were creating pockets of vital community, politics, and culture in countless Parisian spaces.[19] During the 1930 celebrations of the centenary of the Algerian conquest, one Jewish observer spotted groups of visiting Muslim notables in traditional attire entering the kosher restaurants of the 9th arrondissement, drawn by both the compatibility of Jewish ritual slaughter practices with Muslim rules of halal and the familiar menu.[20] Indeed, the daily experience of the city was changing: Parisians out walking in certain quarters might regularly pass by a restaurant with North African or Balkan cuisine and smell the wafting scent of couscous, merguez, baklava, or other traditional "Oriental" or "Arabic" foods; see Jews or Muslims dressed in "North African" garb going about their daily lives in the city; or hear previously unfamiliar Arabic musical modes and instruments emanating from cafés, restaurants, and concert halls.

Between 1905 and 1939, Paris's Jewish population grew from 60,000 to 200,000.[21] During this time, even as Jews in the capital were largely Ashkenazic, a significant North African and Levantine Jewish presence began to take root. In the 1930s, approximately 60 percent of Jews in Paris were Eastern European immigrants, 30 percent were native French, 7 to 8 percent Sephardim from North Africa or the Levant, and 2 to 3 percent recent German Jewish immigrants.[22] Meanwhile, as France's Muslim population increased during the 1920s and 1930s, it became more dispersed. While Paris housed 80,000 Muslims as of 1925, by 1932 that number had shrunk to 60,000. Nonetheless, the capital remained the principal destination for Muslim arrivals from North Africa.[23] Other immigrants from the Mediterranean were a sizable presence as well: between 1921 and 1926, Paris welcomed more than 101,000 Italians, 31,000 Spaniards, and 18,300 Turks or Armenians, meaning that those from the Mediterranean constituted nearly half of all immigrants in Paris at this time.[24]

The majority of Muslims and Jews in Paris concentrated heavily in particular neighborhoods, and the geographic overlap of the two groups was fairly limited.[25] Because most North African Muslims in Paris and its environs were employed in firms of heavy industry like automotive factories and metalworks located in the north and northwest suburbs, about two-thirds of them lived in communes like Aubervilliers, Saint-Denis, Nanterre, Boulogne-Billancourt, and Argenteuil, often inhabiting cramped quarters in ramshackle settings.[26] Within the city itself, police

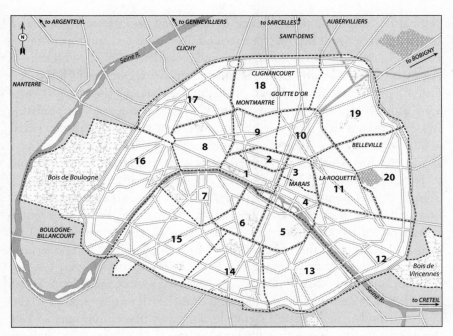

Map 2.1. City of Paris with surrounding areas. (Map by Isabelle Lewis; copyright © 2015 by Ethan B. Katz.)

reports focused on anticolonial militants suggest that the 5th arrondissement on the Left Bank, and the outer arrondissements—particularly the 15th and 13th in the south and the 19th in the northeast—were those most heavily populated by Muslims (Map 2.1). The same reports indicate that only small numbers settled in most of the central and middle- or upper-class parts of the city.[27] Among Jews, large numbers of East European immigrants, particularly artisans and workers, settled in Belleville, situated at the meeting point of the 11th, 19th, and 20th arrondissements in the northeast corner of Paris. Significant numbers settled as well in the working-class districts of Montmartre and Clignancourt north of the Seine. Jews from the former Ottoman Empire made up 4 to 5 percent of the overall population in La Roquette in the 11th arrondissement in eastern Paris. Paris's French-born Jews and some of its previous generation of immigrants who had become economically successful moved westward toward more affluent districts of the city.[28]

Although Jews and Muslims tended to live in distinct parts of Paris, certain regions of contact developed. The case of Paris's traditional Jewish neighborhood of the Marais illustrates how even in neighborhoods with substantial population imbalance between the two groups, Jews' and Muslims' lives could become intertwined. Paris's largest concentration of Eastern European Jewish immigrants and a smaller number of North African Jews resided in the Marais, located on the Right Bank in the 3rd and 4th arrondissements. Much of the quarter became the heart of Parisian Yiddish culture, nicknamed the Pletzl ("little place" in Yiddish). Lesser known is that its lower portion, the Saint-Gervais, housed a small group of Jews from Algeria, Morocco, and Tunisia and their cultural spaces.[29] A few Muslims also settled in the area, and larger numbers came to partake of what became its shared Maghrebian ambiance.[30]

In this Jewish space of the lower Marais, cafés, grocery stores, and homes became sites of shared Jewish-Muslim culture. Small in number and attracted to one another by all that they shared in common, Muslims and Jews from the territories of Morocco, Tunisia, and Algeria—whose histories and cultures were interwoven but distinct—were forging new kinds of trans–North African connections, spaces, and identities on French soil. When the Gharbis, an Algerian Jewish family, arrived in the capital from Marseille in 1927, they became part of a community of 189 Jews from North Africa living in the quarter.[31] Over three dozen Jews from the Levant joined them. At the heart of quarter, combined these Jews made up 1.6 percent of the total population of about 14,000. By 1936, nearly 250 North African Jews and more than 50 Levantine Jews lived in the neighborhood, and the number continued to grow.[32] Most adults worked as merchants, artisans, or commercial employees like hairdressers or waiters. As of 1926, 25 to 30 Muslims also lived in the quarter; within a decade, that number had more than tripled.[33] Mostly Algerian, these Muslims were almost entirely men ages twenty to fifty. Mainly manual laborers, a few worked in restaurants or as grocers, drivers, or artisans. A small number, like heating engineer Omar Merfed and accountant Hadj Bachir, practiced liberal professions. By the mid-1930s, many were unemployed.

Jews from the Maghreb soon formed a community with shared experiences, tastes, and sensibilities. Coffeehouses in particular became key social gathering points. The central hub of activity, located a stone's throw from the fashionable old Parisian neighborhood of île Saint-Louis in the city's heart, ran along the rue François Miron and the intersecting rue de Jouy (Map 2.2). Together these streets included eight North African Jewish-owned cafés. The 1936 census recorded about a dozen Muslims and nearly sixty North African or Levantine Jews living along the rue

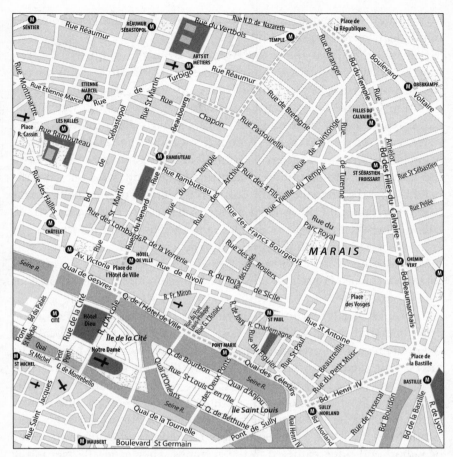

Map 2.2. Marais neighborhood, Paris. (Map by Isabelle Lewis; copyright © 2015 by Ethan B. Katz.)

François Miron. Beginning in 1937, René Moïse Gharbi opened a café-restaurant on the street, the Petit marseillais, where his mother, Esther Gharbi, became the chef. With four family-sized tables just inside the entrance, four more toward the back, and a large bar, plus the Gharbis's adjacent apartment, the space could hold a crowd. The café specialized in couscous, a staple across North Africa.[34] Years later, Félix Amanou, grandson of Esther Gharbi, explained that "the great majority of the clientele [were] former soldiers of [the Great] War who were either Jews or Muslims. . . . [They] were functionaries . . . and each trimester they awaited the payment of their pensions. They were [mostly] men who had been [brutally wounded, handicapped, or even disfigured] by the war—blind, deaf, '*gueules cassées.*' "[35]

Several other Jews and a few Muslims from the Maghreb also ran North African cafés along the same streets. These attracted Jews and Muslims into what became shared spaces for eating, drinking, and even common Jewish-Muslim musical traditions. Esther Gharbi's grandson Roger recalled: "We were on good terms. [The Muslim neighbors] came to our café, we went to theirs." A minute's walk from the Gharbis' establishment lay the Tunisian Jew Gaston Elbaz's café. In a room just above the café, one could often find a number of Jews and Muslims from the neighborhood gathered to drink coffee and, secretly, play games of cards (the latter being illegal in Paris at the time). Farther down the street, halfway between the Petit marseillais and the Saint-Paul Métro, lay the *épicerie* of Madame Boukhalter, a Jewish widow whose clientele was mostly Muslim. Ayache Suissa, another North African Jew of the quarter, toted two suitcases to sell his goods to Muslim immigrants in Paris's banlieues (outskirts).[36]

Louise Fhal, a Jew who arrived with her family from Constantine in 1937, met and married Maurice Jaïs, who ran a North African café on the rue François Miron with a sizable clientele of Jews and Muslims. The intersecting rue de Jouy had more Muslims than Jews, with two Muslim café managers, Méziane and Mustapha, being particularly friendly with several Jewish café owners.[37] Louise Jaïs (née Fhal) recounted how in the late 1930s, and until the German Occupation of Paris, her husband, Méziane, their Catholic neighbor Robert, and other men of the neighborhood often gathered in the evenings. They generally met in the Petit marseillais, where they would have an apéritif together and sit and talk into the night. Jaïs became friendly with Méziane's wife.

During the same period, on Saturday nights, the Petit marseillais was home to soirées of Arabic music, another critical element in the period's Mediterranean crossings. The Arabic music developing in the French Mediterranean at this time had several distinctive components. Its modes and melodies emerged from what has become known as the classical tradition of Arabo-Andalusian music. By the early twentieth century, however, it was marked increasingly by the fusion of that tradition with newer sounds like jazz, rumba, and flamenco, a pattern that intensified in the interwar years, especially in France. Arabic music had been characterized since at least the late nineteenth century by the presence of Jews among its leading figures, and by the frequent collaboration of Jews and Muslims as fellow performers and composers, teachers of one another, and partners in the business of recording and production. Reflecting its trans-Mediterranean history and character, this music was written in a wide range of languages, predominantly colloquial and classical Arabic but often with phrases and occasionally whole compositions in Judeo-Arabic, French, Hebrew, and Spanish. Finally, already in the 1930s, Arabic music in France repeatedly took up themes of exile, separation, and nostalgia; these would become all the more salient especially among Jews in the era following decolonization. Such themes had been present since the Iberian expulsions of the fifteenth century but had particular personal significance for many Muslims and Jews who relocated to France across the twentieth century.[38]

At the Petit marseillais, a typical Arabic musical performance consisted of three North African Jewish musicians, playing some combination of the tambourine, the *darbuka* (Arabic drum), the oud (Arabic lute), and violin, to melodies from the *maalouf,* the traditional Arabo-Andalusian song. Two Muslim dancers stood on a makeshift stage, and a crowd of as many as 100 Jews, Muslims, and Catholics sang and danced together from around 8:30 p.m. until as late as 5:00 a.m.[39]

Spaces of North African Culture and Family

In many respects, the shared sites of the lower Marais were hybrid spaces. For all of their North African character, spots like the Petit marseillais were also neighborhood cafés on a long-standing Parisian model. Since the nineteenth century, cafés in Paris had been spaces substantially shaped by the manual and skilled working class that made up most of their clientele. Like so many other Parisian workers, Jews and Muslims from the Maghreb recently arrived in the Saint-Gervais could escape their cramped apartments in part via the more open and neutral space of the café. They refashioned the latter into places of leisure and hospitality where they felt "at home."[40]

Indeed, Louise Jaïs describes the Muslims who participated in the social networks of the neighborhood as "very Frenchified." In addition to soldiers who had fought for France during World War I, Muslims like Méziane, who ran a café and whose wife lived in France, were unusually integrated. These Muslims contradicted widely disseminated images, echoed in the reports of Paris police, about the "abnormality" of the family, gender, and sexuality of North African Muslims. One French observer had written in 1930, "Among the differences which oppose our Western society to Muslim society . . . that which is primordial, is the family."[41] Traditional conceptions of family and faith within French nationhood saw the nuclear family as both metaphor and building block of the nation and its religious communities, the latter understood as confessional bodies confined to the private sphere. The vast majority of France's Muslims remained male seasonal laborers whose families stayed in North Africa. Yet among the Muslim men living in the lower Marais, over 7 percent lived with their wives or children, or both.[42] Roger Gharbi recalls the presence of Muslims at his neighborhood elementary school, on the rue Geoffrey L'Asnier, where children from the two groups played together.[43] As both physically impaired warriors of World War I and family men, a number of Muslims partook of the French neighborhood café's specificity as a space of working-class sociability, conviviality, and intimacy.

The quarter also became the site of domestic interactions. In some apartment buildings, Jews and Muslims lived on the same floor, crossing paths daily. In 1926, for instance, at 23 rue des Jardins Saint Paul, two blocks east of the rue François Miron, the forty-seven residents included at least eleven Jews and eight Muslims from the Maghreb or Levant. Romantic relationships, however occasional, also appeared. In 1936, Chaja Seghin, a thirty-six-year-old Jew from Poland, lived with her Algerian Muslim husband, Mohamed Kadri, three years her senior, on the rue des Ecouffes.[44]

While these Jewish-Muslim neighborhood (and even family) relations in certain respects typified those of French working-class neighborhoods, they also introduced aspects distinctive to Maghrebi culture into metropolitan spaces. The simultaneous self-sufficiency and porous boundaries of the North African Jewish spaces around Saint-Paul were akin to the character of Jewish minority areas in cities of the Muslim Mediterranean.[45] Not only in France but also in many cities of North Africa and the Middle East, spaces of coffee consumption had long been central to social life for the working class in particular.[46] In their largely male sociability, these Maghrebi cafés paralleled less the typical Paris working-class café (with its significant number of families) and more the coffeehouses of Algiers, Tunis, and Istanbul.[47] Moreover, many Muslims in the Maghreb had experienced a range of associations with both coffeehouses and the Jewish quarter. At times, each space could be understood as linked to the world of the mosque and traditional religious culture; at other times, these were places with an illicit reputation at once forbidden and alluring: sites of cards and dice, female dancing and sensuality, and alcohol consumption. In all these ways, certain aspects of the Saint-Gervais were quite familiar.[48] Perhaps the most crucial import of all was Arabic music, a constant through the many historic evolutions in the Arab coffeehouse. Music's presence extended here, as in North Africa, to family and religious festivities.[49]

Moreover, at this very moment, the Arab coffeehouse of North Africa was undergoing significant modernization. Only a generation prior, in the cafés of cities like Algiers, men had typically relaxed on an earthen floor and taken their coffee in cups prepared individually. By the 1920s and 1930s, however, the new presence of tables and chairs, an oven, and the bar counter, on a cement floor, had reshaped—along more European lines—the serving and consuming of coffee, and even the posture and attire of customers. In addition, a growing number of Muslims, particularly those young and well educated, were patronizing European cafés in Algeria. For a segment of both the Jewish and Muslim immigrant populations, all of these factors likely helped to render the cafés of Paris familiar places of culture and sociability.[50]

And yet the broader spatial context of Paris was significantly different from that of the southern Mediterranean: in the Maghreb, the Levant, and Anatolia, cafés had often formed the central component in a wider world of urban sociability. While many cities along the Mediterranean were becoming more modern and Western in their character under colonial and European influence, well into the twentieth century, spaces like the *hamam,* or public bathhouse, as well as neighborhood bread ovens, streets, outdoor markets, open courtyards between houses, and even multifamily homes frequently remained sites of interaction between Jews and Muslims, particularly for women. Many of these spaces were at once public and amenable to intimacy.[51] The relative absence of Muslim women on the French mainland at this time meant that common family responsibilities, proximate domestic interiors, or parallel religious or medical practices around water rarely created social glue between Jews and their Muslim acquaintances.

Moreover, such spaces as communal ovens, public bathhouses, and shared courtyards, while not unheard of, were much less typical to cities of mainland France. These types of common use spaces did not correspond to notions of modern, bourgeois domesticity, hygiene, privacy, and respectability that were exerting pressure on the urban fabric of metropole and colony. During this period French officials were reshaping colonial North African spaces like the *hara*, or Jewish quarter, in Tunis. In 1931, Tunis's municipal council decided to construct new apartments for the city's Jews where, they insisted, each unit would have its own kitchen. This accorded with French bourgeois norms that saw cooking as something done in private rather than using a communal oven. More broadly, many French officials and Jewish leaders thought it necessary to isolate Jews from the filth and immorality of the Tunisian Jewish quarter in order to reshape them to fit the model of the modern French family.[52] Those North African Jews and Muslims in the interwar Marais had migrated to a city already designed in a way that corresponded more closely to bourgeois norms. And at the same time, reformers and hygienists in the 1930s repeatedly expressed concerns about the Marais itself as a place that they claimed was overcrowded, ethnically insular, dirty, and dangerous, even proposing its demolition. The period's rising xenophobia, antisemitism, and anxiety over the "health of the nation" made such a space Other for more than a few Parisians; hostility to the Saint-Gervais focused on Eastern European Jews, but the entire neighborhood was affected.[53]

Spaces of Ethnicity and Empire

In these two contexts, one in which opportunities for urban sociability were more limited and circumscribed and the other in which the residents of the Saint-Gervais found themselves fairly isolated from the rest of the French population, the interactions and relationships around cafés became all the more important. For this first generation of Jewish and Muslim immigrants, cafés were French and North African spaces of identity formation, sociability, and intimacy. For certain Jews and Muslims, the closeness fostered by drinking and eating together combined with common customs and values from North Africa to offer the ingredients for a sense of interconfessional Maghrebi ethnicity.[54]

As they had in North Africa, Jews and Muslims in the Marais occasionally entered each other's ritual spaces or enjoyed the familiarity of similar religious practices. Cafés like the Petit marseillais served the traditional North African Jewish festival meal of the *berbouche,* an elaborate couscous dish, every Friday afternoon.[55] The evocative scents and tastes of this food drew a packed crowd of largely Jews but also Muslims.[56] Among North African Jews of the Marais, festive religious gatherings such as a brit milah circumcision ceremony, bar mitzvah, or wedding, remembers Félix Amanou, "nearly always" featured Jewish and Muslim musicians playing North African wedding music "in a totally familial atmosphere."[57] Yossef Fhal, Louise's father and a noted violinist and composer, regularly participated in such events.[58] These celebrations often included Muslim guests.[59] Jews occasionally visited Muslim religious spaces. Amanou recalled that he and Jewish friends would go to the Grand Mosque of Paris. There they found a warm welcome and would have a North African pastry, eat in the Muslim restaurant, or go to the Turkish bath.[60] Amanou explains that the Muslims at Jewish family celebrations tended to be "very Europeanized . . . former soldiers, or [functionaries] in the French administration, that is people who considered themselves French before anything else." Those Muslims at the Grand Mosque also appear to have typically been the more "Frenchified" among the immigrant population.

Repeated descriptions of these Muslims in such terms suggest that for many Muslims and Jews of the Saint-Gervais, aspirations to greater belonging in France, adaptation to French modes of working-class sociability, and cultural and religious ties to parts of North Africa together shaped their common outlook. That is, a sense of Algerian, Moroccan, Tunisian, or Maghrebi ethnic identity did not necessarily imply a rejection of France. France's empire was at its height and presumed secure. Therefore, the vast majority of its subjects sought to negotiate a dignified existence under French sovereignty, which often included the assertion of religious or cultural pride.[61]

Such was certainly the outlook of an important catalyst for Jewish-Muslim sociocultural relations in both France and Algeria at this time, Mahieddine Bachetarzi, a noted Algerian Muslim musician, one of the fathers of modern popular theater in Algeria, and a key figure in the development of Arabic music in the interwar French Mediterranean. Politically, Bachetarzi both supported Muslim integration into the republic and Algerian cultural revival. Among the musicians who participated occasionally in the musical soirées of the Marais were three notable Algerian Jews: Salim Hallali; his mother, Chelbiya Hallali; and Lili Labassi. The younger Hallali and Labassi were both part of El Moutribia, Bachetarzi's famous musical and theater troupe.[62] In 1934, the fourteen-year-old singer Hallali, of Berber origin, and gifted with a soaring voice, arrived in the metropole from Annaba, Algeria. Soon he became a sensation in Paris's Spanish nightclubs. In May 1937, at the Algerian booth of the international exposition in Paris, Hallali encountered Bachetarzi, whose troupe was performing there.[63]

Bachetarzi had long been involved in joint Jewish-Muslim musical ventures. He had received his first musical training as a Quran reader at a mosque in Constantine. Algerian Jewish musician Edmond Yafil, a key figure in the Andalusian musical revival in Algeria in the early twentieth century, would sneak into mosques to hear Muslim liturgical melodies; he first approached Bachetarzi in the late teens and took him under his wing. Within a few years, Bachetarzi became the leading musician and then, by 1923, the day-to-day manager of Yafil's orchestra, El Moutribia. At the time, the orchestra had mostly Jewish musicians and few Muslims—according to one count of Bachetarzi, seventy-eight young Jews and three Muslims joined the group between 1924 and 1930—and performed before largely Muslim audiences that always also included some Jews. In the early 1920s, the orchestra began to focus attention on not only music but also theater, adding skits and then plays to its repertoire. Bachetarzi's career soon took off, and he brought his troupe to the metropole for tours on a regular basis. In order to promote his tours, Bachetarzi would write to a few Muslim friends from Algeria living in Paris as migrant workers, who spread the news via word of mouth; after arriving in the metropole, musicians from the troupe would distribute posters and notices in Arab and Kabyle cafés. The result would invariably be large crowds at the performances.[64]

During the mid- to late 1930s, as Bachetarzi wrote and put on plays in Algeria and France, the plots and characters of many performances, like the makeup of his orchestra and theater troupe, defied conventional hierarchies or binary oppositions. Frequently plays like *Faqo, Les Beni-Oui-Oui,* and *Houb Enessa* deliberately inverted or blurred the positions of "Europeans" and "indigènes," Muslims and Jews, men and women, rich and poor, city and country folk, even as distinctions were never eliminated. Bachetarzi thus implied his own vision of a Mediterranean France where differences, while recognized, needed to be negotiated within a more equitable and tolerant coexistence. The troupe's leader saw his endeavor to establish an Algerian theatrical canon, with plays set mostly in Arabic, as in part an effort to cultivate the emergence of an Algerian Muslim public.[65] Yet for years he relied on a group of largely Jewish performers, who periodically came to the metropole, where they advertised in Muslim-owned cafés and performed in meeting halls before mostly Algerian Muslim workers.

While all of this implied that religious distinctions could give way to something akin to a common ethnicity in such artistic settings, the French state fostered other group boundaries. Sharp differences in Jewish and Muslim legal status were at times an unavoidable dividing factor. Bachetarzi would recall, for instance, how in 1931, following a law severely limiting the movement of Algerian Muslims within the metropole, administrative measures created fissures in the experiences of fellow musicians:

> See here the consequences in an association like "El-Moutribia," made up of a very amicable mix of Muslims and Jews. Joseph or Solomon or Samuel, being a French citizen, was traveling as he wished from Perpignan to Dunkirk and from Biarritz to Strasbourg, while his buddy near whom he was seated like a brother every night in the orchestra, calling himself Kaddour or Ahmed was benefiting from a special authorization of the Prefecture limiting his visit to the time necessary to our concerts and obligating him to return home immediately.

Nonetheless, relative amity prevailed; Bachetarzi describes the Jewish members of the group as "equally distressed" as the Muslims by these measures.[66]

It was in such a context that Hallali and Bachetarzi's fateful encounter occurred. Hallali went on to perform with the latter's company in cities across France and began a close collaboration with comic singer and songwriter Mohamed el-Kamal. Together, with pieces like "La Sevillana" and "Andalusia" that el-Kamal wrote for oud, maracas, castanets, and Hallali's voice, the two created a new musical genre, the flamenco in Arabic. Some of their songs became hit records in the Maghreb. By the late 1930s, they had a leading role in the growing Paris scene of "Oriental cabarets" that had spread far beyond the Marais. These cabarets had a French-Arab sound that combined traditional Arabo-Andalusian and more modern musical styles and featured Jewish and Muslim musicians from the Maghreb.[67] Such spaces included "El Djazaïr," opened by the Algerian composer Mohamed Iguerbouchène on the rue de la Huchette in the Latin Quarter. By its name, meaning Algiers in Arabic, this immigrant establishment self-identified—like many others of the time—with a famous faraway city. Hallali, for whom Iguerbouchène wrote numerous songs, became the club's featured act. Indeed, Jews and Muslims constantly imagined themselves and were imagined in a range of terms beyond Jewish, Muslim, and French: colonial, immigrant, Algerian, Oriental, Arab, natives of a particular Mediterranean locality, and more. Like the spaces in which they occurred, interreligious musical performances bridged North African and French tastes, combined Jewish and Muslim participants and mixed audiences, and creatively reworked long-standing traditions from Andalusia and the Maghreb.[68]

Marseille: Mediterranean Passageway

If interwar Paris was effectively the northernmost Mediterranean hub opening a new embayment onto the Great Sea, then nearly 650 kilometers to the south in France's leading port city lay the country's widely recognized Mediterranean crossroads. Due to its geographic position and importance as a port, in the nineteenth century with France's colonial expansion Marseille became the third key city on an axis of trade, migration, travel, and imperial imagination that ran from Paris to Algiers. Since at least the 1860s it had called itself "Gateway to the Orient."[69] The interwar years were a time of burgeoning interest in achieving a "Mediterranean" style of urbanism and architecture in cities like Algiers and Marseille; designers drew up various plans for buildings, roads, rail lines, and even dams that would bridge physical and cultural distances and render Marseille central to the empire and to world commerce.[70]

In human terms, Marseille's docks were already the site of constant movement by cargo ships, passenger vessels, and immigrants. Although Marseille's population was just over 600,000 in the early 1930s, approximately 782,000 travelers were recorded coming through the port in 1925 alone. Such an atmosphere led journalist Albert Londres to call the city "a monumental door, where hundreds of faces from the world over would pass, in a constant ebb and flow."[71] Many of them stayed and settled in Marseille. The city grew significantly in the years between the wars (from a population of 490,000 to 550,000 in 1911 to more than 600,000 by 1931), becoming a magnet for immigrants.[72] By the mid-1930s the city's long-standing Italian presence had grown to more than 100,000 and was joined by substantial numbers of Spanish, Armenians, Corsicans, Greeks, Levantines, North Africans, and black Africans. Foreigners at this point made up roughly 25 percent of the city's overall population.[73] Their presence, attires, and cuisines helped establish a reputation for cosmopolitanism that fed competing visions of its future. Some, like the Jamaican writer Claude McKay, saw its diversity as a source of inspiration; others leveled savage critiques, like Far Right thinker Charles Maurras, who wrote, "One must refrain from judging ancient Marseille by a corner of the modern city, the meeting place of North Africans, Negroes, and Jews."[74]

Jews and Muslims helped to define Marseille not only as an imagined but a lived space. Between the wars, the city became an important center of Jewish and Muslim life. The city's Jewish population grew from 3,500 to 8,500 between 1899 and 1923, reaching 12,000 to 15,000 in the late 1930s, when foreign-born Jews constituted a majority of the community. Unlike in Paris, 80 percent of Marseille's Jewish immigrants came not from Eastern or Central Europe but from the old lands of the Ottoman Empire: Turkey, Greece, and the Maghreb.[75] The city also became home to France's second largest Muslim population. Roughly 15,000 North African laborers, over 97 percent Algerian, lived in Marseille by 1929. By the end of the interwar period, this was closer to 20,000, and Jews and Muslims together made up more than 4 percent of the city's population.[76] Most Jews worked as unskilled laborers, commercial employees, merchants, or artisans. Mediterranean immigrant Jews, with the exception of those from Greece, tended to lack professional skills and economic means, forcing many children to work at an early age. Among Muslims, most were seasonal unskilled laborers or employees, but about one-fourth were out of work and one-fifth had taken up domestic residence in Marseille.[77]

In Marseille, no neighborhood became a Jewish cultural enclave on the order of the Marais or Belleville in Paris.[78] Nonetheless, most of Marseille's Jews were concentrated in a relatively small geographic area, with (by one calculation) 62 percent living within 1.5 kilometers of the Vieux Port (Old Port, so called because major commerce had moved northward to the Joliette docks in the mid-nineteenth century) (Map 2.3).[79] Most of Marseille's native-born French Jews inhabited the 6th arrondissement to the southeast of the Vieux Port, with the largest concentration in the bourgeois quartiers of the Palais de Justice and the Préfecture. In the same quarters many Sephardic Jewish immigrants from Greece and North Africa, particularly Algeria, were also housed.[80] Substantial numbers of Jews lived as well in the 2nd and 1st arrondissements to the north and east, respectively, of the Vieux Port. In the 2nd arrondissement, Turkish, Greek, and North African Jews resided in significant numbers, especially around the Hôtel de Ville, as did a majority of the city's Eastern European Jewish immigrants, concentrated around the Joliette and Grandes Carmes

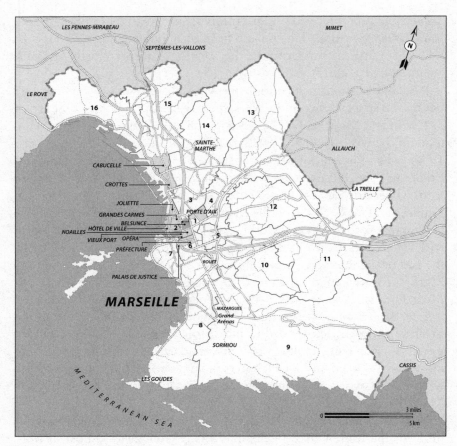

Map 2.3. City of Marseille with surrounding areas. (Map by Isabelle Lewis; copyright © 2015 by Ethan B. Katz.)

quartiers. Slightly east, the 1st arrondissement was home to many native-born French Jews, especially around Noailles, and to the vast majority of Turkish Jews, mostly around Opéra, an area also inhabited by Greek and North African Jews.[81]

By contrast, just as in Paris, given their income and their status generally as men in France on their own, Muslims in Marseille often lived in the cheapest housing under squalid conditions. Well to the north of the city center where most Jews resided, in the 15th arrondissement, Muslims often found very low-rent housing in the quartiers of Crottes, Cabucelle, and Rouet, not far from the refineries of Saint-Louis where many were employed. In the early 1920s, after the opening of the camp of Sainte-Marthe in the 15th, and the foyer musulman on boulevard

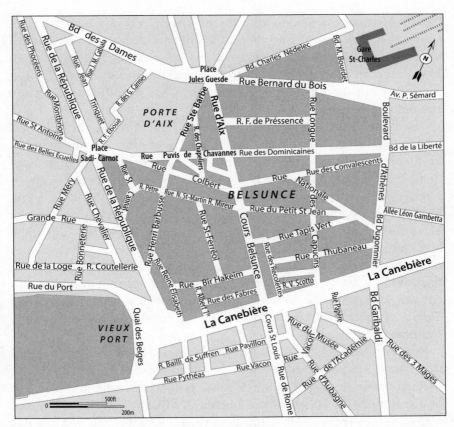

Map 2.4. Belsunce neighborhood, Marseille. (Map by Isabelle Lewis; copyright © 2015 by Ethan B. Katz.)

Burel in the city's eastern periphery, both also became widely used low-income housing for many Muslim workers.[82]

Unlike in Paris, however, the quarter of Marseille that buzzed with North African and Muslim culture, the Porte d'Aix neighborhood—where most Muslims came first on arrival in Marseille and returned many times, and where substantial numbers worked and lived—was near the heart of the city. This neighborhood was situated only a few hundred meters from the Canebière, Marseille's legendary central street, lined in the interwar years with numerous fashionable restaurants, hotels, and cafés. Beginning on the eve of World War I, the Porte d'Aix, centered on the tiny, narrow rue des Chapeliers, with the adjoining rues Saint-Barbe and Puvis de Chavannes, became home to numerous North African cafés, grocers, and lodging rooms, as well as a network of basic services for newly arrived Muslims (Map 2.4).

North Africans often socialized in the street, and one man later re-called that "we were living there, like all the Arabs; it was what we were used to." An observer remarked that "the classic Rue des Chape-liers . . . recalls the souks of North Africa"; another declared, "Ten minutes from the Canebière, North Africa has installed itself on the rue des Chapeliers."[83]

The Porte d'Aix was situated within the larger area of the Belsunce, which acted as the quarter for large numbers of often transitory immi-grants, including many southern Europeans, colonial migrants, large numbers of Jews from Eastern Europe, and smaller numbers of Jews from North Africa and the former Ottoman lands. Between the wars, a few hundred Jews settled in the Belsunce, with several families right at the heart of the Porte d'Aix neighborhood.[84] Many others set up shop in the area: on the neighborhood's central artery of the Cours de Belsunce as of 1936, at least a dozen Jews ran businesses, with several hailing from the Middle East or North Africa.[85] Many more Ottoman and North African Jews were not far away, having settled in nearby quarters like Opéra to the south, Hôtel de Ville to the west, and Noailles to the southeast.[86]

Relations between Jews and Muslims in and around the Belsunce and the Porte d'Aix paralleled and diverged from those in Paris. The shared Mediterranean ambiance of the Belsunce produced certain notable cases of cultural and social interactions between Muslims and Jews. On sev-eral occasions from the late 1920s to the mid-1930s, Mahieddine Ba-chetarzi brought his musical troupe to perform in Marseille near the end of the summer, often to large crowds and considerable acclaim. One of their chosen venues was the historic Alcazar performance hall on the Cours de Belsunce, where they gave a concert in August 1932. At a more intimate level, it was in Marseille that Ottoman Jewish immi-grant Alex Danon, an exporter of metallurgic goods born in Smyrna, Turkey, met French Muslim Yvonne Sidi. In May 1915, while many Jews and Muslims met on the French battlefront, the two wed. By the early 1920s, they had three children.[87] Yet on the whole in Marseille, we have less evidence for personal contact and more for commercial interactions.

Certain Jewish merchants did business almost daily with Muslims in the Belsunce.[88] These included Moïse Maurice Farhi, who had emigrated from Smyrna, Turkey, with his wife, Rachel. By the late 1930s, with their daughter, Jacqueline (b. 1926), the Farhis lived in a four-room apartment on the avenue du Maréchal Foch to the east in the 4th arrondissement. In 1921, the twenty-four-year-old Farhi opened an épicerie at 60 rue Sainte-Barbe, just adjacent to the place Jules Guesde and not far from the intersecting rue des Chapeliers. Farhi's store, named Products from Algeria, specialized in North African food, particularly couscous. Farhi was well placed to do business with numerous Muslim-run restaurants, cafés, and bars in the area, like the Sadji-Tahar establishment just down the street or that of Akli Rabhi, practically across the street where the place Jules Guesde met the rue des Chapeliers. It was only a few minutes farther to walk for the employees of the other Muslim-run food and drink establishments located on rue des Chapeliers—as of 1936, a dozen of them had registered with the local chamber of commerce. On occasions like Aïd el-Fitr, the end of the holy fast of Ramadan, these restaurants needed large amounts of certain specialty items like Arabic tea and coffee and couscous. By the late 1930s Farhi's grocery store was a popular destination, with a near monopoly locally on couscous in particular. These circumstances created an interreliant relationship between Farhi and many Muslims that had economic, religious, and cultural dimensions; the situation engendered loyalty from some Muslim clients and resentment from others.[89]

While Farhi's case was in certain respects unique, it reflected Marseille's distinctive atmosphere and geography more broadly. Interactions in the southern port occurred through the presence of Jews in "Muslim" spaces rather than vice versa. Jews and Muslims interacted, moreover, within a wider web of largely Mediterranean diversity in the city's immigrant quarter and other districts around the Vieux Port and city center. At the same time, Muslims here had created a robust social network for welcoming their coreligionists and weaving them into an existing community. Thus by comparison with Paris, Muslims in Marseille were simultaneously less isolated and more self-sufficient. As open, fluid locales of social life, like the cafés of the lower Marais, the culinary establishments and even the pavement of the streets in the Porte d'Aix seemed to mimic the shared spaces of many North African and Middle Eastern cities, but Muslims here predominated in most of those spaces. Furthermore, for many immigrants, Marseille, and specifically the Belsunce, were places of transit rather than destinations. Absent a situation of necessity, the development of personal relationships with members of other ethnoreligious groups thus became less likely.

Strasbourg: The Mediterranean as Distant Optic

The sociocultural relations discussed thus far partly reflected the particular origins, demographics, and urban location of Jews and Muslims in Paris and Marseille. Strasbourg in Alsace offers a telling counterpoint. The city's interactions between Jews and Muslims at this time were extremely limited. Strasbourg illustrates both the unevenness of France as a burgeoning space of trans-Mediterranean mobility and the way that in certain regions of France, the French Mediterranean was experienced voyeuristically as an entity distant from everyday life.

In 1918, when it returned from German to French sovereignty, Alsace remained a center of distinctive Jewish culture, shaped by centuries of local tradition, long-standing connections to France, and nearly fifty years in the German Kaiserreich. The area housed a majority of France's Jews until the 1860s and produced numerous leading Jewish thinkers. Because Alsace was part of Germany at the time of the 1905 law, it successfully resisted the imposition of *laïcité* following the war and retained state-sponsored religious institutions and salaries for priests, pastors, and rabbis. In Strasbourg, therefore, more than in Paris or Marseille, the consistory remained at the center of Jewish life. As of 1936, Strasbourg and its surrounding area housed over 10,000 Jews, more than one-third of all those in Alsace.[90] While this number included many Eastern European and German Jewish immigrants, Strasbourg, unlike Paris and Marseille, had no Mediterranean Jewish presence.[91]

Moreover, there were few, if any, Muslims in Strasbourg.[92] Thus Jewish-Muslim interactions in the Strasbourg region proved rare. Léon Nisand, born in Strasbourg in 1923 and raised in the German Ashkenazic world of Alsatian Jewry and the Hasidic milieu of his Polish grandparents, recalls that Jews of Strasbourg had little knowledge of the Muslim world. They only occasionally encountered the area's few North African itinerant merchants, who lived apart from the French population. Still, he describes them as "poor, brave people," exclaiming, "In general, the colonialist France did not respect them . . . but, we, the Jews, we knew that a man who is not from our homeland is an exile, and we respected them, we did not mock them."[93]

However, in the absence of many actual encounters, it was primarily within the broader colonial imagination that most Strasbourg residents came to experience France's growing orientation toward the Mediterranean. Strasbourg's 1924 colonial exposition, which drew a million visitors, was specifically designed to aid in Alsace's reintegration into "Greater France." Organizers sought both to educate Alsatians about the French empire from which they had been separated for forty-seven years and to market Alsace to the rest of France in terms of its value and patriotism for the empire.[94] Moreover, just over the border was the much-remarked specter of North African, black African, and Madagascan French troops serving in the Rhineland-occupying army. Such developments were creating, for the first time, a "colonial culture" in the region.[95]

Muslims were among those prominently on display. In 1926, as part of his tour of France for the opening of the Grand Mosque of Paris, the Moroccan sultan, Moulay Youssef, paid an official visit to Strasbourg. He brought with him a sizable entourage of Moroccan and French officials, and careful arrangements were made for a motorcade procession, official meals, ceremonies, and a reception, for which several prominent local Jews including Strasbourg's chief rabbi Isaïe Schwartz were invited guests.[96] Thus many Jews and other residents of Strasbourg experienced firsthand the colonial Mediterranean as not only a growing optic but also a site of occasional cultural exchange.

The Constantine Riots and Categories of Conflict

In the 1930s, as France faced economic depression, political crises both domestic and foreign, a sense of cultural malaise, and increasing xenophobia and antisemitism, Jews and Muslims repeatedly sought to renegotiate their political relationship to France and to each other. In the shadow of two issues, the fascist menace and the Algerian question, Jews and Muslims often found themselves in the crosshairs of competing visions of not just the Hexagon but the French Mediterranean. Jewish-Muslim interactions in political spaces (in contrast to neighborhoods) were largely between North African Muslims and Ashkenazic rather than Sephardic Jews.[97] At times, however, even common sociocultural spaces felt the effects of the period's political developments.

Few events illustrated better, or did more to shape, the impact from North Africa on Jewish and Muslim life in interwar France than the Constantine riots of August 3–6, 1934. In the mid-1930s, with 14,000 Jews among a total population of 106,000 (the rest 56,000 Muslims and 34,000 colons), Constantine had the largest proportion of Jews of any major Algerian city.[98] The riots began on the Friday night of August 3, when Jewish tailor and Zouave Elie Khalifa, arriving home drunk, insulted a group of Muslims whom he saw washing themselves in the nearby mosque. Khalifa later admitted that he cursed the Muslims, their nudity, and Islam; the Muslims claimed that he also urinated on them and the wall of the mosque. Large numbers of Muslims soon gathered outside Khalifa's home, located at the junction of the city's Jewish and Muslim quarters. Many attacked Jews and Jewish-owned businesses and fought with police. From the windows of homes, Jews hurled projectiles and fired shots. Before the police could quell the violence, six Jewish-owned shops were ransacked and fifteen people injured; among the injured was a Muslim man, wounded in the stomach, who died several days later.

The next day, local authorities and communal leaders sought to ease tensions, and calm appeared to return. Yet on Sunday morning, news of the cancellation of a large meeting planned by popular local Muslim leader Dr. Mohamed Salah Bendjelloul, and the brief rumor of Bendjelloul's murder by Jews, triggered further agitation. From inside their homes and out in the street, some Jews fired shots. Muslim crowds vandalized numerous Jewish-owned businesses; some threw goods into the street or even lit shops on fire. In at least two instances, Muslim attackers entered Jewish homes and murdered the families inside. French authorities proved to be extremely slow to respond. The following day, Muslims assaulted Jews or Jewish-owned property in several neighboring towns. In the end, twenty-four Jews and four Muslims lay dead, and scores had been injured.[99]

The Constantine riots became a defining moment for the relations of Jews and Muslims in Algeria and the metropole, both with each other and with France. For French officials, Algerian colonists, and many of France's most fervent nationalists, this event provoked new uncertainty about the physical and ethnic boundaries of the French nation. The French administration undertook a formal inquiry, arrested hundreds of Algerian Muslims, and instituted repressive measures. In the minds of many officials and colonists, the assault by native Algerian Muslims against Jews constituted a terrifying prequel to an impending direct attack on the French colonial state and the "European" settlers of Algeria.[100] Muslim and Jewish responses also centered on each group's relationship to France. From the press to meeting halls to synagogues, the riots were spotlighted in a series of emerging Mediterranean spaces of the metropole, where Algeria felt closer than ever before.

What nearly all responses to the riots shared was an almost total disregard for Jews' and Muslims' complex allegiances and frequently overlapping identities in Algeria. Instead Jewish versus Muslim quickly became the dominant narrative frame. By far the strongest Muslim reaction to the riots in the mainland appeared among the followers of the Étoile nord-africaine (ENA), the nascent Algerian nationalist party under the leadership of Messali Hadj that emerged first not in Algeria but among North African workers in the metropole. This was particularly the case in the French capital, quickly becoming the northernmost hub for a series of often trans-Mediterranean, radical political movements. Founded in 1926 under the aegis of the French Communist Party, the ENA had long since set out in its own direction. Nonetheless it remained not only nationalist but radically leftist and working class. For more than two months following the violence in Constantine, thousands of Muslims in Paris and its environs attended meetings and distributed pamphlets. After a period when the ENA's membership and finances had ebbed, the riots reenergized the party. Whereas most Muslim leaders in Algeria made solemn declarations that reiterated Muslims' attachment to France, the ENA used the riots to launch bold calls to resist French rule.[101]

ENA militants and other Muslim migrant workers also discussed the riots regularly in cafés across the Paris region. Many of Paris's Arab and Kabyle cafés constituted the spaces through which the lifeblood of the nascent Algerian nationalist movement flowed. This North African café culture took a different form from in the Marais, becoming the site of oppositional politics. Once again, however, the space was a hybrid: the ENA tapped a long-standing tradition of the café as a space for French working-class political activism, and echoed the growing presence of indigenous politics in many Arab cafés of Algeria.[102]

The first ENA meeting in Paris regarding the riots occurred on the evening of August 10 before nearly 700 North African Muslims. In a hall on the rue Cambronne in the 15th arrondissement, green-and-red nationalist flags flew, and banners hung above the stage that read: "Let us fight to deliver Abd el-Krim and Emir Khaled. Down with the *Code de l'indigénat*, long live liberty!"[103] The first speaker was ENA founder and central leader Messali Hadj, a World War I veteran and émigré from Tlemcen. He depicted "the Jews" as partners in the French conquest of 1830 and said that ever since acquiring citizenship with the Crémieux Decree of 1870 they had become the country's "true masters" and Muslims' most virulent enemies. Messali described the incidents in Constantine as a provocation meant as a diversion, and he called on Muslims of Algeria, Morocco, and Tunisia to join the ENA's battle for North African independence.[104] In a revealing manner, the prevailing discourse of Messali and others simply equated Jews with French imperialism. Algeria's Jews, implied the ENA, had no attachment to their Muslim neighbors or North African culture but had simply been grafted onto the French colonial project; Jews thus became subsumed within a larger indictment of France.

Between August 10 and October 1, at nine more meetings, speakers invoked the same message before engaged, often raucous crowds ranging from 100 to 1000; these crowds were drawn from the same ranks as the Kabyle manual laborers who had cheered for the Jewish musicians of Mahieddine Bachetarzi's orchestra. Both Jews and Muslims occupied multiple spheres; their identities formed through practices of common sociability were now becoming increasingly politicized. For example, one of these ENA meetings, with more than 500 spectators, began with chants of "Down with the Jews! Down with France!"[105] In these meetings and in its press and pamphlets, the ENA crafted a distinct narrative of Constantine: the French imperialists and their Jewish collaborators had provoked events; the Muslims had justly defended themselves. ENA voices repeatedly extolled the Muslims as victims, martyrs, or nationalist heroes who were receiving unfair treatment at the hands of the French justice system.[106] In this manner, their actions marked the opening salvo of a new phase in the battle for North African national liberation.

Religion also quickly came to the fore. In an August–September special issue of the ENA's organ *El Ouma*, Imache Amar declared: "May our union be sealed forever by the blood of the glorious fighters of Constantine, so that their sacrifice will be for us a signal of the common battle to break our executioners. . . . The Cross is too fragile to break the Crescent."[107] This final phrase framed the riots as a signal moment in the renewal of an epochal clash of civilizations across the Mediterranean, between Islam and Christendom, embodied by colonial France. Like the ENA newspaper's name *El Ouma*, which translates literally as "nation" but connotes sacred community, the regularly invoked metaphor of crescent versus cross was part of a growing emphasis on the part of the nationalists on the notion of an Arab (as distinct from Berber) Islamic civilization whose glory could effectively oppose French claims to European civilizational superiority over the "barbaric" indigènes.[108] Such a formulation in response to a Muslim-Jewish riot implied that Jews had betrayed their long-standing ties to their Muslim neighbors and become co-opted entirely by Christian European imperialism. At other meetings on Constantine, speakers read verses from the Quran and led chants of "Vive l'islam."[109] Rather than celebrating a sense of shared Abrahamic faith like many Jewish and Muslim comrades during World War I, the ENA was merging its nationalist and religious commitments, asserting a distinctly Islamic heritage for North Africa.[110]

It is difficult to measure precisely the broader impact of the riots among Muslims in France. However, within several weeks of the riots, the ENA's membership, finances, and print runs for its newspaper all increased dramatically. By October, political activity among Paris's Muslims had become noticeable enough that French police forcibly intervened on multiple occasions to prevent further ENA meetings related to Constantine.[111] Radjef Belkacem would later recall, "The events of Constantine, where hundreds of ours were massacred, took matters to a new level— declarations of Morinaud and others, pursuit against militants, abusive condemnations [in] the press from right to left; [this all] furnish[ed] new yeast for Algerian nationalism."[112] At the same time, the formation by other Muslim organizations in Paris of a Committee of Action and Solidarity on Behalf of the Muslim Victims of the Repression in Constantine appeared short-lived and unsuccessful.[113] By contrast with Paris, French officials in Marseille reported that despite its sizable Muslim population, the city seemed not to register even a ripple of political action after the riots.[114] Nonetheless, the ENA held large gatherings and drew significant monetary support in other major Muslim communities in Clermont-Ferrand, Lille, Lyon, and Saint-Etienne.[115]

The riots' impact was widespread enough that it marred the reception of Bachetarzi's troupe when they arrived in France in August for their annual tour. Bachetarzi's sponsors told him that under the circumstances, "It would be impossible for them to come to applaud the Jewish musicians." Ultimately, in a compromise, the organizers attended the first of three performances; on the other two nights, sparse crowds booed Jews Lili Labassi and Alfred Sassi. Subsequently the Kabylian leaders of the Muslim association that had brought El Moutribia to France showed their ongoing affection for the entire group by compensating them for the lost revenue with a much-needed donation of 10,000 francs. Yet tensions persisted. Bachetarzi responded to the generous donation by scheduling a special set of six or seven benefit concerts for the ENA the following year in which only Muslim performers would take part. Some Jewish and Muslim musicians in the group were even at odds: Muslim Rachid Ksentini and his one-time love interest, the Jewish singer Marie Soussan, were on the outs. Later Ksentini became embroiled in a feud where he accused Lili Labassi of trying to kill him.[116] The riots well illustrated the situational nature of Jewish and Muslim ethnicity. It appeared that at least for the moment, the violence had turned the Jewish performers from North African fellow musicians of the Jewish faith into Jews exclusively, at odds with Muslims, and absent from the nascent perception of an Algerian nation.

Jewish Narratives of Colonialism and Violence

France's Jewish community, for its part, devoted considerable attention to the riots. Jewish reactions to the riots included traditional demonstrations of Franco-Jewish religious solidarity, in the form of memorial services for the victims in various French synagogues and substantial fund drives through a number of communal organizations.[117] More publicly, even as France's Jewish leadership remained quiet, numerous Jewish associations and journals in mainland France responded immediately and forcefully, often drawing on the extended reports and petitions produced by their Algerian brothers.[118] Rather than in meeting halls, Jews largely spoke through the pages of their thriving communal press. Journals for all sorts of Jewish audiences—traditionalist, liberal, Zionist, youth, war veteran, and Eastern European—covered the riots. The mobilizations on the part of the ENA did not go altogether unnoticed by Jews. A writer for *Paix et droit,* the organ of the Alliance israélite universelle, described "meetings organized in Paris by the journal *El Ouma,* the most extreme designated organ of Islam, accustomed to the provocation to murder."[119] Yet this hyperbolic story proved rather exceptional, as most Jewish coverage focused on the actions of Muslims in Algeria. Whereas the ENA used the event as a rallying point for anticolonialism, Jews promoted solidarity with their Algerian coreligionists and insisted on the latter's full Frenchness.

Concentrating heavily on the events of Sunday, August 5, the most established Jewish organs, the liberal *Archives israélites* and the traditionalist *L'Univers israélite,* repeatedly termed the event a "massacre." For weeks, both organs filled their pages with poignant and horrifying details of murder and destruction by Muslim attackers against Jewish persons and property. A typical account read, "The streets [were] suddenly invaded by a swarming and uncontrollable multitude. These devastating waves unfurled without a pause, destroying without mercy, burning and killing."[120]

Henri Lellouche, a leader of the Jewish community in Constantine and a member of the city's municipal council, authored a detailed report on the riots that became the official account of Constantine's Jewish community and attempted to shape the forthcoming report from the French government.[121] Large portions of the report—which alleged, like most other stories on the riots, that the violence against the Jews of Constantine, rather than spontaneous, had been carefully planned—were reprinted in Jewish newspapers.[122] Lellouche's report framed its most forceful critique of Algeria's Muslims in terms of their relationship to France. Rather than an age-old tribal hatred of Jews, the riots reflected Muslims' strongly "antinational" sentiments; he termed as "illusory" any signs of their loyalty to France. Muslims could not tolerate that Jews, "formerly their slaves," now held superior status as French citizens, and moreover, they begrudged Jews' "profoundly French" loyalties.[123]

Throughout the Jewish accounts of the riots, the difference in status between the Algerian Jewish French citizens and Muslim colonial subjects held a central place. From the first press reports on the riots, authors almost never used the word *Muslim* or *Arab* but rather the colonial term *indigène*. This word, roughly translating to "native," designated the legal category of all noncitizen Muslims in Algeria. In the colonial context, it often had a pejorative connotation suggestive of savagery.[124] By contrast, reports referred to Jews as *israélites*, the title that most French Jews took for themselves in the nineteenth century in order to insist that their Jewishness represented a matter of confession rather than nationhood. Such terminology, while hardly new, implied through its constant reiteration that whereas Jews could move beyond their ethnicity and become French, Muslims remained bound to their Maghrebian past. Jewish accounts of the riots constantly searched for their "real" cause, by turns implicating the provocations of Muslim leaders, antisemitic propaganda of Germany or the French Right, Arab nationalist campaigns, and French officials' negligence or even acquiescence.[125] While such accusations reflected heartfelt suspicions, they also suggested that Muslims were easily manipulated and that without the French imposition of law and order, they might become violent. Moreover, by connecting the rioters' actions to the Nazis, antirepublican forces, or Arab nationalism, these accounts separated Muslims and their motivations from the French nation.

Thus in an opposite but analogous way to Muslims, Jews used the lens of Frenchness to frame their accounts of the riots. In their critiques of the French administration, many Jewish voices highlighted Algerian Jews' claim to full membership in the French national family. Jews in Algeria and France expressed deep disappointment at the inaction, or worse, of French authorities during the riots, frequently reminding readers of Algerian Jews' sacrifice in the Great War and their status as equal citizens.

The toughest critiques in this vein came from the International League Against Racism and Antisemitism (LICA), founded in 1928, which cut against the prevailing quietist grain of republican Judaism.[126] Through its confrontational stance against antisemitism and the impassioned speeches of its leader, Bernard Lecache, the organization appealed particularly to young French and immigrant Jews. By 1934, it was a growing force, with its membership reaching 30,000 in 1936.[127] LICA printed a special edition of its weekly newspaper, *Le Droit de Vivre,* that bore the headline, "Jewish blood has flowed in France!" and carried two opposing front-page images: one of Jews rushing off in August 1914 to "die for France" and the other of the wreckage in Constantine with the date August 1934, where the newspaper announced Jews had "died by the fault of the authorities" (Figure 2.2).[128] Just under the headline ran a story entitled "Nous accusons . . ." (We accuse), an evident attempt to connect the newspaper's outrage at the French government with that of the defenders of Alfred Dreyfus thirty-some years earlier, and specifically with the Dreyfusard Émile Zola's famous essay, "J'accuse!" On August 22, the LICA convened a meeting of 1,500 people in Paris, where participants called for an investigation and punishment of those authorities that had failed to act with proper diligence.[129] The LICA, then, saw the riots less in terms of Jewish-Muslim conflict and more through the lens of the league's larger struggle against fascism.

For groups like the LICA that advocated Jewish-Muslim dialogue, the riots were both inauspicious and a wakeup call. Six weeks earlier, in late June, Bernard Lecache had called on Muslims in France to resist joining the ranks of "the enemy," that is, the racist forces of the Far Right, and spoke of "extending fraternal hands" to "our Muslim comrades."[130] Following the riots, the LICA was not alone in its desire to build bridges with Muslims. Alongside graphic accounts of Muslim attacks, mainstream Jewish organs included articles praising certain Muslim leaders for their efforts to mend relations.[131] Such reports counteracted the negative representations of the Muslim attackers ubiquitous in the Jewish press.

Figure 2.2. The cover of the special issue of the LICA's organ *Le Droit de Vivre* published in response to the August 1934 riots of Constantine. (Courtesy of Le Droit de Vivre of the LICRA.)

On the whole, by identifying solely with their own ethnoreligious community, Jews and Muslims revealed both long-standing solidarities and tensions of the colonial Mediterranean and the power of French colonial law to define group categories. Press and government accounts of the riots repeatedly described three sets of actors: the "Muslims" or "indigènes," the "Jews" or "israélites," and the French military and colonists. These categories, encoded in the electoral laws and politics of the interwar period, carried connotations of belonging or exclusion, of proximity and distance from French "civilization."[132] The ethnoreligious terms in which the riots were instantly understood would become frozen in their narrative: soon, the events became a powerful touchstone for Jews and Muslims in Algeria and France.

Yet the suddenness with which these categories came to the fore, and the persistence of countervailing developments, illustrate as well the situational nature of both the prominence and meaning of Jewishness and Muslimness in the weeks and months following the violence in Constantine. Bounded ethnoreligious categories defined many of the spaces in which the riots' impact played out in mainland France. But in other spaces, different logics of identification and self-understanding prevailed, even for some touched directly by the riots. Among those Jews who came to the French capital in the wake of the riots (as many as 1,000 left Constantine for Paris or Tunis), several settled alongside other North African Jews in the Marais.[133] Louise Jaïs never forgot the terrifying experience of barely escaping the riots as a fourteen-year-old. Yet in the Marais, she became part of the North African Jewish cultural milieu frequented by many Muslims.[134]

Jews' and Muslims' Perilous Positions in Far Right Visions of France

In the special issue of *Le Droit de Vivre* devoted to the Constantine riots, one writer, pointing the finger at right-wing leagues like the Croix-de-feu (CF) and Solidarité française (SF), claimed that they "buy at 30 francs a day delinquent Arabs of [Paris] to beat up Jews and democrats."[135] These accusations were not without foundation. At the very moment when events in Algeria articulated and prompted competing boundaries of French nationhood that divided Jews and Muslims, so too did the emergence of an extreme Right that threatened the republic. In the face of economic downturn, a series of public scandals, and the successes of fascism in Germany and Italy, a whole array of extreme right political formations blossomed in France from 1933 to 1936. Despite ranging from militant peasant to neomonarchist in their outlook, these groups shared certain characteristics. All focused on veterans and the war experience; articulated an ardent, often xenophobic French nationalism; supported traditional social hierarchies; were fiercely anticommunist; and had ambitions to replace republican democracy with an authoritarian system. Most leagues had paramilitary dimensions and used symbols and gestures that drew on the imagery of German and Italian fascism. The Far Right and the perception of a fascist menace had an impact on Jewish-Muslim relations through several groups. These were France's two largest extreme right movements, the CF and, from 1936, onward, the Parti populaire français (PPF); a more ephemeral one, the SF, and several Algeria-based "Latinist" movements, most notably the Unions latines and the Amitiés latines.

As the right-wing leagues grew in stature, particularly after their massive, deadly altercation with police in the streets of Paris on the night of February 6, 1934, Jews and Muslims became both potential joiners and oppositional "Others," standing as important signifiers for the breadth and limits of the leagues' recruitment efforts and imagined national community. The CF and the SF sought to recreate the national unity of the *union sacrée;* the former even declared on occasion that whether one was Christian, Jewish, or Muslim did not matter so much as what one had done during World War I.[136] Yet eventually each movement turned to the politics of antisemitism. Likewise, even as they recruited Algerian Muslims, the CF and the SF defended the inequalities of colonial society. In time, the CF and its successor, the Parti social français (PSF), became the most successful of France's interwar right-wing movements, peaking at 700,000 to 1 million adherents in 1938.[137] The SF, led by former French officer Jean Renaud, had a brief burst of success in 1933 and 1934, but even at its peak, its membership appears never to have exceeded 10,000 despite its own claims of far higher numbers.[138]

It was in Algeria that the right-wing leagues, including the CF and PPF branches there, found their greatest success, mobilizing large portions of settler society, particularly in Oran and Constantine. Despite moments of tactical moderation, moreover, the Algeria-based parties were the most unrelenting and virulent in their exclusionary outlook and even frequent violence toward both Muslims and Jews. For groups like the Amitiés latines, both Jews and Muslims played a constitutive role as racially abhorrent "Others" within a vision of a "Latinist" Mediterranean that ran outward from Paris and saw Europe continuing to spread its civilizational superiority as the successor of ancient Rome.[139]

The CF's broader relationship with Jews followed a tortuous path. Founded in 1928 as a veterans' association, the CF had transformed within several years into a militant right-wing league with fascist tendencies.[140] A cadre of Jewish community leaders and mostly conservative wealthy Jews supported its ideals; the consistory even allowed the group to participate for several years in ceremonies at Parisian synagogues honoring Jewish veterans of the Great War.[141] Until the late 1930s, its leader, Colonel François de La Rocque repeatedly rejected antisemitism. Financial backer Ernest Mercier, leading activist Ferdinand Robbe, and more than a few members were Jewish.[142] Yet local provincial sections of the CF sought to stir up anti-Jewish sentiment. This was particularly the case in Algeria, where by 1935, CF activists entered Jewish neighborhoods to chant, "Long live La Rocque" and "Long live Hitler." In Algeria in particular, the league recruited Muslims with some success, and its leaders employed antisemitism as a strategy.[143] In Paris, according to a report of the same period, certain CF members attacked the Crémieux Decree in order to attract Algerian Muslims.[144] It was also in spring 1936 that La Rocque insinuated that certain Jews were provoking a wave of French antisemitism.[145] The league's increasingly vocal hostility toward Jews sparked conflict within the Jewish community. In June 1936, LICA and CF members came to blows following a synagogue ceremony in which the CF participated; the consistory leadership broke ties with the CF shortly after, and the league's reputation with Jews declined.[146]

Indeed, for much of the Far Right, it was increasingly clear that some measure of inclusion for Muslims was far more palatable than for Jews. Muslims, moreover, seemed like a useful tool for antisemitic aims: Jews were increasingly the primary racial Other of the hour. Put differently, colonial racism had long been basic to hierarchical visions of France, but antisemitism was a rising political program. Clarity on these issues came earlier for the SF than groups like the Croix-de-feu. Most SF members were Catholic, petty bourgeois native Frenchmen, but the SF also found a ready audience among certain Muslims, particularly in Paris.[147] While denying any affiliations with Nazi racial ideology, the SF denounced Eastern European Jewish immigrants, Jewish leftists, and alleged Jewish power.[148] Leading SF backer François Coty's newspaper L'Ami du peuple had once described Paris's North Africans as "hereditary-syphilitics" lacking hygiene. But by 1933, the league offered unemployed Algerians blue shirts, army boots, cigarette packs, and 50 to 300 francs a month in salary.[149] In summer 1934, the SF created a "North African brigade" designed for street fighting, with 50 to 100 members.[150] The North African presence in the SF even prompted some to mockingly term the organization "Sidilarité française."[151] For Muslims, however, entering such fascist militias could have far greater significance than the material benefits: away from their families, and unemployed, in the uniform and weapon of the SF, they found a measure of dignity, even a place to recover their threatened manhood.

The SF was not alone on the Right in its attempt to use antisemitism in pursuit of Muslim adherents, but it stood apart in mobilizing them so early for anti-Jewish violence.[152] During several of its street actions, North African SF members came to blows with Jews.[153] As the SF targeted Jewish neighborhoods like the Marais, the same spaces where certain Jews and Muslims had built a sense of North African community became vulnerable to divisive acts of violence at once nationalistic and ethnoreligious in character.

Amid rising tensions between the SF and the LICA, the night of September 25, 1935, witnessed the most significant known instance of Muslim-Jewish violence in interwar metropolitan France.[154] Shortly after 11:00 p.m., at least fifty SF shock troops, including many Muslims, by some accounts chanting, "Death to the Jews," proceeded to the Gamin de Paris, a café at the corner of the rue Vieille du Temple and the rue des Blancs Manteaux in the Marais.[155] The café had a largely Jewish clientele and was the regular meeting place of a LICA defense group. These Muslim SF troops seemingly hoped to cement through violence their allegiance to an ethnic vision of France that treated Jews as oppositional Other, thereby "proving" their own French bona-fides. Armed with sticks, billy clubs, and a few revolvers, the SF thugs tossed objects through an open door, ransacked the café, and fired shots into the air. As the dozen or so largely Jewish customers ran into the street, SF members came from the shadows to attack. Helped by LICA defense forces, the Jews held the SF at bay until French police arrived. The incident proved brief and contained. Nonetheless, it illustrated how the right-wing leagues were etching new battle lines of French nationhood that frequently divided Jews and Muslims, occasionally even in those spaces where they sought to forge coexistence.

Rallying to the Republic? Jewish-Muslim Unity and Dissonance in the Popular Front

During the same period, in the face of the challenges posed by the extreme right to democracy, national unity, and the republic, a left-wing alliance emerged that articulated a more inclusive vision of French nationhood and empire. This coalition, first called the Rassemblement populaire and then the Front populaire (Popular Front), found its roots in the period following the Nazis' attainment of power in Germany in 1933 and, more immediately, the antirepublican riots of February 6, 1934. The rise of fascism not only internationally but at home brought about a fairly sudden rapprochement between the French socialists (SFIO) and communists (PCF), who had been bitterly divided since their split in 1920. By July 1934, the PCF and SFIO signed a pact of common action against fascism, war, and France's conservative economic policies. In time, they would negotiate a united front with the Parti radical, the large center-left formation at the heart of most governing coalitions during the Third Republic; their alliance was displayed powerfully as the three groups marched with the trade unionists in an enormous demonstration in the streets of Paris on July 14, 1935.

Many Muslims and Jews were among the demonstrators that day.[156] Their respective concerns over workers' and immigrants' rights, the threat of fascism, and Algeria's future overlapped around shared ideals and drew them together in support of the Front populaire (FP). From the start, the FP became strongly identified with Jews. The Jewish socialist deputy Léon Blum led the coalition, and with its electoral triumph in May 1936, he became *président du conseil* (French premier). Though not religious, Blum had vocally supported Zionism, spoken proudly of his Judaism on the floor of parliament, and grown up in a traditional Jewish home.[157] The first government of the Front populaire had several other Jews in prominent roles: Jules Moch, a rabbi's grandson, as undersecretary of state; the socialist Marx Dormoy as minister of the interior; and suffragette leader Cécile Brunsvicg as secretary of state for national education. Jean Zay, minister of national education and fine arts, was "half-Jewish," born to an Alsatian Jewish father and Protestant mother. Large numbers of Jews also received lower-ranking administrative posts.[158]

Taking the tradition of the "state Jew" to its ultimate logic, Blum and his Jewish colleagues prepared to defend the republic in a moment of peril.[159] They would soon make policy decisions crucial to the lives of Jewish immigrants and Muslim colonial subjects. They would also confront virulent antisemitism (which at times became linked to anti-Muslim racism). Shortly after the Front populaire's victory, on the floor of the Chamber of Deputies, Xavier Vallat, future head of the Commissariat général aux questions juives during World War II, questioned Blum's qualifications to be premier, calling him "a subtle Talmudist" rather than one "deeply rooted in [French] soil."[160]

Among French Jews, this unprecedented situation provoked divergent reactions. These exposed deep communal divisions, particularly between the Jewish leadership and laity; the pre– and post–World War I generations; and native French Jews and those from Eastern Europe. Much of the French Jewish establishment treated Blum's candidacy with marked ambivalence or even downright hostility. Nonetheless, indications are that Parisian Jews, particularly in immigrant quarters, voted heavily for the Front populaire; crowds cheered loudly for Blum at Jewish rallies and numerous synagogues held prayers for the new premier's health and protection.[161] At a more organized level, left-wing Eastern European Jewish immigrants teamed with young French Jews to form the Mouvement populaire juif (MPJ), or Jewish Popular Front. It began in July 1934 as the United Front, a labor alliance of the Jewish communists, the Bund (Jewish workers' party), and the Socialist Zionists of the Left Poalei Tsiyon (Socialist Zionists), who joined forces to focus on preventing antiforeigner legislation and antiforeigner sentiment among French workers, promote Jewish commitment to the international proletarian cause, and oppose fascism in both France and the Jewish community. The LICA also played a leading role, advocating direct confrontation of fascism and antisemitism, and cooperation with like-minded non-Jewish leftists. While the MPJ, formed officially in October 1935, failed to gain the adherence of the Federation of Jewish Societies, the umbrella organization of Jewish immigrant associations, and saw the defection of the Bund, it garnered a wide spectrum of support that included the Jewish veterans' association and numerous smaller groups of Jewish artisans, merchants, socialists, and immigrants. By summer 1936, inspired by the success of the Front populaire, in Paris alone, about 12,000 Jewish workers had joined the labor movement.[162]

In an analogous fashion, a variety of Muslim political forces gravitated toward the Front populaire. Though in 1933 the ENA had called for outright independence and broken ties with its erstwhile patron the PCF, both the Messalists and the communists soon took a more pragmatic approach, each seeing the struggles against fascism and colonialism as linked. In 1934 PCF colonial representative André Ferrat reached an agreement with Messali on an alliance between communist organizations and the ENA: together they would work to end the Code de l'indigénat, or brutally discriminatory Native's Code in Algeria, and for eventual North African independence. By 1935, the nationalists joined the Rassemblement populaire. Rhetorically Messali focused less on independence and more on demanding the creation of an Algerian parliament.[163] Two other major Algeria-based Muslim political movements that were making inroads in the metropole also lent their support to the new government. Founded in 1931, under the leadership of Sheik Abdelhamid Ben-Badis, the Association des ulamas musulmans algériens (AUMA, often called the ulama) advocated Islamic reform—a "return" to the ways of the "pious ancestors." Politically, they sought greater cultural and religious recognition for Algerian Muslims.[164] Doctor Mohamed Salah Bendjelloul's Fédération des élus musulmans de Constantine (the élus) fought to make Algerian Muslims full French citizens who could maintain their "personal status" as Muslim. In January 1936, Ben-Badis proposed the formation of a unified Muslim party, the Congrès musulman (Muslim Congress) to sound out wider Muslim opinion regarding the Front populaire.

In such circumstances, many Jews and Muslims found common interests and even possibilities for rapprochement in the Front populaire around two causes in particular: antifascism and reform in Algeria. As they had on the battlefields of World War I, through their participation in the FP, these Jews and Muslims staked claims to their own belonging within an expansive vision of French nationhood. At the same time, while joint struggles on these issues were alluring, they occurred on terms that were never equal and through which ethnoreligious attachments remained at the fore, with tensions often more hidden than forgotten. The rapidly growing LICA and its president, Bernard Lecache, active in both the Mouvement populaire juif and the larger FP, continued their longtime advocacy of Jewish-Muslim alliance. In early 1936, Lecache undertook a speaking tour of North Africa to combat antisemitism and racism. Before a diverse audience in Constantine, he expressed sympathy for all victims of the riots of August 1934 and asked people of all faiths to join the cause of antiracism.[165] His tour of Morocco's large cities led to the creation of the Union marocaine des juifs et des musulmans, composed of Jewish intellectuals and certain Moroccan nationalists.[166] In mid-March, Lecache and Bendjelloul presided at a meeting in Paris of numerous LICA members and Muslims of various political persuasions. Despite a number of disagreements, all preached the need for unity and for reform for Algerian Muslims. In the pages of the Jewish weekly *Samedi,* the Algerian Jewish leader Elie Gozlan framed the meeting as exemplary of a fraternal spirit across North Africa and predicted a harmonious future.[167] In March 1936, several young Algerian Jewish leaders published an article in which they faulted the Crémieux Decree for not applying to Algerian Muslims, declaring, "If one wants to attach forever the [Muslim] population . . . to the Motherland, is there any better way than to make them French?"[168]

At times, however, Muslims expressed ambivalence about the coalition's Jewish elements. In September 1935, reform advocate Ferhat Abbas, leader of the assimilationist Young Algerians, penned an article in his newspaper, *L'Entente franco-musulmane,* where he sharply criticized the "Jewish bourgeoisie" for making the Muslim and Jewish proletariat suffer.[169] He focused his ire on Jews in positions of power, claiming that despite their involvement in numerous left-wing causes, "the problem

Figure 2.3. A caricature from the cover of *Le Droit de Vivre* of April 1936. (Courtesy of Le Droit de Vivre of the LICRA.)

of the Algerian proletariat alone remains foreign to them"; their "silence and forgetfulness" on this issue, he said, spoke volumes. An equally pointed expression of ambivalence followed an assassination attempt against Léon Blum in early February 1936. In the large FP demonstration on Blum's behalf, 250 Muslims marched, with several carrying the ENA flag. When explaining to police, however, why their participation was not greater, Muslims cited Blum's Jewishness: "M. Léon Blum being israélite, many declar[ed] that they did not want to show solidarity with a Jew."[170] Such sentiments suggested that even within the FP, many Muslims perceived Jews in terms of ethnoreligious difference and power inequality.

Many of the contradictions of the period are well captured in a bitingly satirical cartoon of early April 1936 found in the LICA's weekly newspaper *Le Droit de Vivre* and aimed at the CF (Figure 2.3). The cartoon featured the CF's leader, La Rocque, as a Janus-like figure, with one face turned toward several Muslims, the other to a group of Jews. To the

Muslims, he declared, "The Frenchman is not your oppressor. Your enemy is the Jew, who robs you and ruins you." To the Jewish audience, he exclaimed, "A wave of antisemitism would be disastrous for our country." Even with the cartoon's evident call to Jewish-Muslim solidarity that continued its long-standing campaigns, the set of images—which visibly contrasted Muslims, depicted as monolithically traditionalist, credulous, and fearful, with Jews as bourgeois, diverse, and frequently skeptical—echoed colonial stereotypes about Muslims.

Not long after this cartoon appeared, Muslim-Jewish violence exploded elsewhere in the Mediterranean, as what soon became known as the Great Arab Revolt began in Palestine. What started on April 19 with riots in Jaffa and a general strike quickly became a period of sustained violence. In France, these developments brought transnational Jewish and Muslim allegiances around Zionism and Arab nationalism to the fore, adding another layer of tension and complexity to Jewish-Muslim relations in the era of the Front populaire. In the interwar period, Zionism constituted a growing force in French Jewish life. While the majority of activists in Zionist organizations were Eastern European Jewish immigrants, native French Jewry also lent the movement crucial support: communal press outlets like the *Archives israélites* (and subsequently *Samedi*) and *L'Univers israélite* gave substantial coverage to Jewish life in Palestine; numerous visible French Jews, including Léon Blum, joined organizations like France-Palestine, founded in 1926.[171] Since the emergence of Muslim political activism in France in the late 1920s, small groups of Muslim workers had begun to express their support for the national rights of Palestinian Arabs in connection to larger causes like North African nationalism, anticolonialism, and Muslim revival. During the 1920s and early 1930s, these movements had little impact on Jewish-Muslim relations, save for a few isolated altercations and short-lived attempts at antiimperial solidarity.[172] With the Arab Revolt of 1936–1939, the question of Palestine took on more pressing importance for many Muslims and Jews across the French Mediterranean.

Yet the impact of the revolt on Jewish-Muslim relations in France was profoundly interconnected with the more central battles of the period: to defeat fascism and define the future of Algeria. Frequently Jews and Muslims articulated their positions on events in Palestine through the lens of one or both of these larger struggles. During the opening weeks of the rebellion, cover stories in *Samedi* detailed the attacks on Jews that they termed Arab aggression. In the same stories, however, the newspaper repeatedly expressed optimism about the possibility of Jewish-Arab rap-prochement, often placing primary blame for the Arab violence on German propaganda or the mistakes of British imperial rule of the mandate. The newspaper's writers used language that echoed idealistic portrayals of the French "civilizing mission" and of "Frenchification" in Algeria. Discussions of the Zionists and Arabs paralleled portrayals of colonists in Algeria as pioneers and native Algerians as both uncivilized and welcoming of the French presence. Occasionally Jews explicitly linked their outlook on the Palestinian context to the Algerian one. A *Samedi* cover editorial several days after the riots began declared, "Once more let us recall what a few men of good will are in the process of doing in North Africa. The 'hatreds of races' are still myths forged by the needs of an unjust cause."[173]

In these heady days of the Front populaire, even the ENA offered a rather measured response to the revolt. While the North African national-ists had hardly made Palestine a central issue, leaders like Messali often traveled in the same transnational Muslim and Arab political circles—like that of the influential Geneva-based Lebanese émigré Shakib Arslan—as the most passionate advocates for an Arab Palestine. But in late April, ENA leaders resisted the pressure of some members and postponed the possibility of a meeting regarding events in Palestine.[174]

Indeed, for the moment, solidarity prevailed. In early May, the elec-tion of Blum and his coalition brought almost unbridled optimism from all corners of France and its empire. Just after the government took of-fice, massive labor strikes occurred across France, with many Jewish and Muslim workers participating; these led to the Matignon Accords that brought landmark reforms such as the right to strike, major pay increases, the forty-hour workweek, and paid vacations.[175] Blum soon disbanded the right-wing leagues and enabled political refugees, many of them Jews from Eastern and Central Europe, to receive work permits.[176] By autumn, the new regime reestablished full freedom of movement for Algerian workers to the mainland, through its political prisoner amnesties freed Messali to return from his incarceration in Geneva, set minimum sala-ries for Algerian farmworkers, and budgeted 100 million francs specifi-cally for the needs of colonized populations.[177]

Many Muslim groups agitated for much larger changes in Algeria and Blum's government contemplated proposals for reform. In June 1936, the ulama, the élus, the Young Algerians, the Algerian Communist Party, and even ENA members came together in Algiers for the first meeting of the

Congrès musulman. Delegates drafted a charter of proposed reforms; in July, a delegation of Muslim leaders including Ben-Badis and Bendjelloul arrived in Paris to present the demands to the new government. Among others, Blum and Jules Moch received the group warmly and offered many promises. Tellingly, Blum even exclaimed to the group, "Me, as a French Jew, I am very happy to receive a French Muslim delegation."[178] These words signaled that Jewish-Muslim alliance within the FP was not incidental but self-conscious; they expressed support from one histori-cally marginalized group to another and a desire to overcome tensions between Jews and Muslims elsewhere in the Mediterranean.

Such tensions, kept at bay for the moment, were an increasing pres-ence in relations among some of the same Jews and Muslims joining forces in the Front populaire. On the evening of June 19 in Paris, the ENA, Jewish communists, and Bundists, along with leaders from the Parti radical and the PCF, took part in a meeting that drew a largely Muslim crowd of nearly 500. One ENA speaker expressed sadness at the Arab-Jewish conflict in Palestine in a manner that recalled the party's Marxist heritage: "Our duty is to reconcile them by making them understand that they are [both] victims of capitalism and British imperialism." A speaker from the anti-Zionist Bund said that Jews were not enemies of Arabs, blaming Zionism and British imperialism for the current situa-tion.[179] Other voices were more confrontational. Ferdinand Corcos, a Jewish leader of the League of the Rights of Man, acknowledged that Arabs had rights to citizenship in Palestine, but argued that Jews had an unassailable claim to the land. Messali called for Jewish-Arab unity but argued that the Jews in Palestine would be sacrificed eventually if they did not grasp "the sick work of Zionism." The statement adopted at the meeting's end papered over any divisions, however, declaring solidarity with all residents of Palestine and hatred for fascism, imperialism, and antisemitism.

The simultaneity of group boundaries and possibilities for entente that characterized this moment appeared not only in political but cultural spaces. Following the FP's election, responding to the support among Al-gerian Muslims for the new French premier, Bachetarzi dedicated a song to Léon Blum, whom he later described as, for Muslims at this time, "our great man." He concluded the work, entitled "The Voice of Algeria," and otherwise written entirely in Arabic, with a French phrase that exclaimed: "It is really thanks to Léon Blum that I have been able to speak."[180] Such a combination of linguistic, cultural, and political references was typical of Bachetarzi and emblematic of a moment where particularism and universalism coexisted uneasily in liberal visions of the imperial nation-state. When performed in France in autumn 1936, the song drew huge, enthusiastic crowds of Muslims in Paris. Bachetarzi recalled, "It was not without pleasure that our israélite comrades of 'El-Moutribia' heard the ecstatic roar that greeted the name of Léon Blum. They found here a revenge for the unfortunate incidents [following the riots of Constantine] two years prior."[181]

During the same period, the Front populaire government announced its long-awaited reform proposal for Algeria, to which Blum and Minister of State Maurice Viollette—reformist former governor-general of Algeria and the plan's primary architect—lent their names. The Blum-Viollette plan proposed citizenship for 21,000 to 25,000 Algerian Muslims, based on the attainment of a certain degree of military rank or higher education, without their having to surrender their status as Muslims. In this manner, a leading French Jew's name became attached to the government's controversial plan to enfranchise a limited number of Muslim colonial subjects. The measure also contained several other reforms to improve the social, economic, and cultural situation of Algerian Muslims. To the disappointment of many Muslims, the Blum-Viollette plan was decidedly modest in its proposals; nonetheless, it had potentially far-reaching implications for the status of Algerian Muslims. Thus, for a time, the plan galvanized the support of integrationist Muslim activists like Bendjelloul and Abbas. Setting aside previous objections to similar proposals, the ulama and the Algerian communists rallied in support. The Congrès musulman formally endorsed the plan.[182]

The Breakdown of Jewish-Muslim Political Unity

The Jewish-Muslim alliances of the early months of the Front populaire government and the presence of both universalist ideals and assertions of ethnoreligious particularism illustrated the possibilities of France as a Mediterranean imperial nation-state of a multiethnic and multiconfessional character. Yet the period also exposed the profound contradictions and conflicts within France and its empire. The Blum-Viollette plan provoked opposition from a variety of quarters—among Algerian nationalists, from some of the FP's own supporters in the republican mainstream, and, most vociferously, on the extreme Right. In the first instance, Messali spoke out immediately against the plan, famously declaring in early

August before 8,000 spectators in Algiers: "One does not sell his country! One does not assimilate his country!" This moment signaled the ENA's gradual isolation from the Front populaire but also its rise as a force not only on the mainland but in Algeria itself.[183] By January 1937, faced with the Algerian nationalists' increasing attacks on the FP and urged on by the PCF due to its rival interests, Blum's government dissolved the ENA.[184] Reconstituted soon as the Parti du peuple algerien (PPA), the group spoke out repeatedly against Blum-Viollette as far too timid and attacked the party's erstwhile FP allies, Muslims included, for what the nationalists deemed profound disappointments and betrayals.[185] Many members of the Parti radical, which controlled the French Senate, objected to Blum-Viollette because they saw the provision that permitted Muslims to keep their personal status as antirepublican. Within a disparate, fragile coalition held together by antifascism alone, such opposition was a major blow.

But it was the extreme Right, particularly in Algeria, that responded first to the Popular Front's election and then the Blum-Viollette plan with a furious and even violent countermobilization. The events of May and June 1936 appeared to realize the worst nightmares of colonial settler society. Their response was a surge of aggressive rhetoric, protest actions, and numerous physical attacks meant to rid Algeria of the threats posed by Jews, Muslims, socialists, and communists. In June, several parties in the right-wing stronghold of Oran formed the Rassemblement national d'action social (RNAS). Later that month in Oran, members of the CF—reconstituted as the Parti social français (PSF) after its ban by the FP, and one of the partners in the RNAS coalition—trashed the inside of a local bar as they chanted anticommunist slogans. They then proceeded to the Jewish quarter yelling, "Down with the Jews," "Blum to the gallows!" and, "Long live fascism!" Such incidents rapidly became commonplace in many parts of Algeria. By October, Constantine's federation of mayors threatened mass resignations if the FP tried to impose reform by decree. Fear of Jewish power, Muslim revolt, and leftist reform had become unified into a single movement of political obfuscation and violence.[186]

The Far Right's countermobilization at times took a more cynically strategic view toward Muslims and sought to recruit them, frequently through antisemitism. Both the PSF and Jacques Doriot's Parti populaire français (PPF), founded in June 1936, were particularly aggressive in this effort.[187] Doriot, a former communist opposed to French colonial policy and popular mayor and deputy of the heavily Muslim Parisian banlieue of Saint-Denis, had unique credibility with North Africans. This may explain the PPF's initial relative success; the party, which had at its height perhaps 60,000 members, attracted about 175 Muslim members in Marseille and 100 shock troops in Paris.[188] Despite its own ambivalence toward Jews, eventually the PPF decisively embraced antisemitism (particularly following the death of leading member and Jew David Abramski in February 1937). Both the PPF and PSF accelerated their Muslim recruitment following the government's dissolving of the ENA and the growing Muslim disappointment with the Popular Front as the Blum-Viollette plan stalled. Marseille, where local party head Simon Sabiani was counselor to the mayor and a deputy to the National Assembly, became a PPF stronghold. One July 1938 prefectoral report summarized the party's message to Marseille's Muslims: "France is in the hands of the israélites. That is [why] North Africans do not find work and are in misery, because the Jew, being your enemy, only looks to do you harm."[189] Nonetheless, perhaps because their agendas were fundamentally opposed to greater rights for Algerian Muslims, between them the PPF and PSF never appear to have had more than several hundred Muslim adherents in all of mainland France.[190]

If for the moment the politics of antisemitism bore little fruit among Muslims, by June 1937, when Blum resigned as premier (he would later return for another tenure) with many of the movement's highest hopes in tatters, the relative Jewish-Muslim unity of the Front populaire had substantially broken down. The Mouvement populaire juif gradually split at the seams: Bundists and dissident communists criticized the Jewish communists as too concerned with the French nation and the Jewish bourgeoisie, and not focused enough on the "Jewish masses." The PCF leadership, by contrast, attacked its Jewish subsection as "too Jewish" in its concerns, and the party's frequent attacks on Zionism alienated the Left Poalei Tsiyon from the MPJ.[191] When the Congrès musulman gathered again in Algiers in July 1937, even as it pledged adherence to the FP once more and committed itself to Blum-Viollette, it lacked its former energy, previewing a steady decline.[192]

As their own camps were increasingly divided over the Popular Front, Jews and Muslims were further challenged by an escalation of violence in Palestine. The Arab Revolt's second phase, lasting from autumn 1937 through spring 1939, witnessed dramatic growth in the number of rebels, the beginning of Jewish terrorism against Arabs, and markedly increased attacks and casualties that for a time upended British control of large parts of Palestine. For many French Jews, increasing antisemitism in Germany and Eastern Europe meant that rather than their earlier hopes for colonial reform, now it was fears of fascist influence in the Muslim world that inflected their perceptions of events. In numerous speeches in meetings and articles in the press, Zionists and other Jewish activists depicted the attacks on Jews in Palestine as part of a wider crisis of anti-Jewish persecution.[193] A September gathering of the Left Poalei Tsiyon featured a report on Jewish antifascist volunteers in Spain and a documentation of the growing influence of Nazi propaganda among Palestinian Arabs.[194] The Zionist press reported that in Algeria, Muslim-targeted propaganda from the Nazis and the French Far Right was increasing friction in the context of the revolt. This issue aroused anxiety for Jews' larger prospects in the Muslim world.[195]

The ENA/PPA also focused on Palestine in a newly assertive fashion. A December 1937 *El Ouma* article alluded to increased antisemitism in Europe, but declared that Jewish migration to Palestine was not the right way to address the problem. The writer denounced the Jews of Palestine as British imperial agents and used the language of Arab Muslim solidarity: "From the banks of the Ganges to the coasts of the Atlantic no Arab or Muslim can remain indifferent or insensitive to the sacrifices and sufferings of his brothers in Jerusalem or in Jaffa."[196] Such rhetoric, through its new engagement with the Palestinian question and relative indifference to the fate of European Jewry, signaled the sharp divergence of transnational solidarities among France's Jews and Muslims. From autumn 1938 through spring 1939, *El Ouma* articles repeatedly described Zionists as invaders set on driving Arabs from the land, and increasingly blurred the line between attacks on Zionists and Jews. One author declared that Arabs could not welcome "the invasion of their country by a den of insects ready to devour them."[197] By the eve of World War II, direct Muslim activism on behalf of Palestinian Arabs had emerged in mainland France. Muslim students organized to support pan-Arabism and Palestinian Arab nationalism.[198] In February 1939, a small group of Muslims in Paris founded the Comité nord-africain de solidarité et d'aide aux victimes arabes en Palestine.[199]

And yet the period from mid-1937 to 1939 is equally remarkable, in a way too often ignored by historians, for the persistence of two radically opposed visions of the French Mediterranean. Although Blum-Viollette never came to a vote in the French parliament and long after it appeared a dead letter to many in Paris, the proposal continued to arouse fierce passions in which the prospect of Jewish-Muslim entente remained central. Leading Jewish and Muslim individuals and organizations continued to advocate forcefully for one another's causes, often explicitly linking Jewish and Muslim rights. In March 1938, *L'Univers israélite,* in an uncharacteristically political gesture, featured a front-page interview with Alsatian deputy Pierre Bloch, of Jewish origin, where Bloch endorsed the Blum-Viollette bill, comparing it to the emancipations of French and Algerian Jewry.[200] In April 1939, Bernard Lecache demanded an antiracism law in the name of France's Jews, blacks, and Muslims. Referencing the ethnic slurs used against all three groups, Lecache concluded his plea: "It is a 'yid' ('youpin') who, in the name of the 'bicots' (short for 'Arabicots') [and] the 'dirty niggers' ('sales nègres'), respectively [calls on] you, Mr. Daladier."[201] In late March 1938, meanwhile, *L'Entente franco-musulman,* Abbas and Bendjelloul's reformist newspaper, bitterly condemned attempts to stir Muslim antisemitism, writing, "No one wants a second August Fifth 1934 in which, before the laughter [of these hateful opponents of France], Muslims and Jews again kill each other."[202] In July 1938, on the eve of the Constantine municipal elections, Abbas denounced the antisemitic politics of Emile Morinaud; calling for unity, he labeled efforts to unite French Catholics against Jews "as sacrilegious" as the campaign of Algeria's mayors against greater equality for Muslims.[203]

Ongoing efforts at Jewish-Muslim cooperation extended occasionally to the Palestinian issue. At the end of July 1938, the International Congress of the World Assembly against Racism and Antisemitism in Paris included a discussion of Palestine among several French Jewish and Muslim leaders. Zionist Marc Jarblum echoed Muslim delegate M. Chalidi's call for Jewish-Arab reconciliation. The congress issued a plea to end the violence in Palestine and decided to create an investigative commission with equal Jewish and Arab representation.[204]

Further indications of the hopes excited by the FP and Blum-Viollette can be found through a return to a regional comparative perspective. In Marseille, beginning in spring 1937, the Congrès musulman, with a message of both traditional Islamic learning and Franco-Algerian partnership, established a vibrant presence (its local membership peaked around five thousand), holding its first meeting in the Belsunce at the Cinéma Alcazar.[205] Well into 1938, local Congrès musulman leaders teamed with the LICA and, on at least one occasion, Marseille's chief rabbi and leading pastor, in antiracist initiatives.[206] The contrast with the radical politics of Paris, where the ENA remained the leading Muslim voice, can be explained by several factors: the relative geographical proximity of large numbers of Jews and Muslims in a wider immigrant environment broadly supportive of the Front populaire, the local strength of the PPF that made the cause of antifascism more immediately resonant, and the city's everyday reality as an imperial crossroads with cultural intermingling that rendered the Franco-Algerian vision of colonial liberals more plausible and appealing.

The wider Mediterranean context proves crucial for understanding how Jews and Muslims experienced France in the interwar years. In select neighborhoods of Paris, Marseille, and other cities, France's first generation of Jewish and Muslim immigrants from Algeria, Morocco, and Tunisia forged what would come to be seen as "North African" spaces. These settings were characterized by a range of everyday encounters, in which the meanings of culture and ethnicity remained fluid and contingent. At the same time, the statuses of Jews and Muslims and how the two groups perceived each other continued to be shaped profoundly by their relationship to the state. Jews remained far more integrated into the French polity than Muslims, and individual Jews came to hold significant power in policymaking that affected millions of Muslims. But both groups resided now in a republic where they could press claims for civic equality. Between 1934 and 1939, large numbers of Jews and Muslims did just that, seeking to navigate a place within the national and imperial boundary lines of competing political visions. Along the way, the darkening shadow of Palestine cast other divisions between many Jews and Muslims. While the period's shared sociocultural spaces largely endured, the solidarities expressed in everyday interaction became strained by the late 1930s by the increasingly accepted ethnoreligious terms of French and international politics. These terms had helped to set the stage for newly racial boundaries of French nationhood, and of Jewish-Muslim interaction, under Vichy and the German Occupation.

3

JEWS AS MUSLIMS AND MUSLIMS AS JEWS

One day in early August 1941, Louis Gayet, an inspector for the Commissariat général aux questions juives (CGQJ), paid a visit to Little Hungary, a restaurant on the rue de Surènes in Paris.[1] Gayet came to investigate a unique site of interwar Jewish-Muslim interaction. From its opening in 1934, Little Hungary developed a reputation as an exceptionally authentic locale of Hungarian culture and cuisine in Paris.[2] Sebastien Hassid, an Iranian Muslim born in 1886 in Salonika, who had emigrated to Hungary and then Paris, was the restaurant's founder and primary owner. In 1917 at the Iranian legation in Budapest, Hassid had married Ilonka Laufer, a Hungarian of Jewish origin ten years his junior.[3] By the mid-1920s, the couple had two children, Denise and Ego. Ilonka Laufer, now Ilonka Hassid, became a practicing Muslim.[4] When the Hassids came to Paris and opened their café in 1933, Blanche Luckas, Laufer's Jewish sister, joined them.[5] Blanche held a small amount of stock in the restaurant and acted as its manager. Eleven thousand Hungarian Jewish immigrants lived in Paris in the 1930s.[6] Given the restaurant's unusual profile, at least a few of them likely took a regular meal or drink at Little Hungary.

The spring and summer of 1940 saw, in rapid succession, German entry into France (May 10), the Occupation of Paris (June 14), the surrender of France (June 17), and the end of the Third Republic (July 10). France soon became divided, primarily into an occupied zone in the north, directly controlled by the Germans, and a "free zone" in the south, run by the new authoritarian Vichy government under Marshal Philippe Pétain.[7] As Germany sought to confiscate all Jewish-owned property in the occupied zone, Little Hungary claimed itself, despite Blanche Luckas's ongoing role, to be fully "Aryanized." On October 28, ten days after a

German ordinance that gave all Jewish property to "provisional administrators," Luckas ceased to be the legal manager of the restaurant.[8] In
April 1941, days before a new German law allowing provisional administrators to sell or close Jewish businesses, Luckas sold her remaining
stock in the restaurant.[9]

In August 1941, the German authorities and the CGQJ continued to
harbor doubts about the restaurant's Aryanization. On this day, Louis
Gayet had arrived to investigate the situation.[10] He met with Sebastien
Hassid, who could provide him no documentation. Gayet thus proceeded
to Paris's Chamber of Commerce, where he discovered that Blanche
Luckas had been the restaurant's manager until October 1940. Vichy's
racial laws stipulated that in order to be considered Aryan, an establishment had to be free of all Jewish influence no later than May 23, 1940.
Luckas had not sold out until well after that. The establishment could
therefore still be assigned to a provisional administrator—and in October
1941, the German authorities and the CGQJ did exactly that.

But those same parties soon questioned the decision. All of the restaurant's owners signed oaths attesting to their status as Aryans "totally
independent of any Jewish influence." The Iranian consulate supplied
letters attesting to the fact that Hassid, as well as his entire family, was
Muslim. By spring 1942 the Germans and the CGQJ narrowed their focus
to Ilonka Hassid, Sebastien's wife. They had two suspicions: first, that
she was Jewish; second, that through the Hassids' marriage contract,
Ilonka might jointly own all of her husband's possessions, including
the vast majority of shares in Little Hungary. Beginning in May 1942, the
authorities sent Sebastien Hassid numerous letters that sought to resolve
these concerns. In his initial reply, Hassid declared, "My wife is Aryan,"
and explained that under Iranian law, his property and his wife's were
separated.[11] When repeatedly asked for written evidence, Hassid appeared
to stall, taking weeks or even months to reply. In time, he produced limited documentation of their marriage and a letter from the Swiss embassy,
responsible for Iranian nationals in Paris, stating that Iranian records
indicated Ilonka Hassid was Muslim. Despite failing to obtain further information, the authorities concluded in February 1943 that Ilonka Hassid
was indeed a Muslim and that the Hassids' marriage contract made her
husband's property separate from her own. They thereby maintained that
the restaurant should be returned to the Hassids.[12]

While Sebastien and Ilonka Hassid and their children ultimately eluded
apprehension at the hands of Nazi and Vichy antisemitic policy, the in-

vestigation of Little Hungary had upended their livelihood and their identities.[13] Having lived comfortably as a multiethnic Muslim family in Paris for the previous six years, the Hassids unexpectedly saw frightening new questions of religion and race enter their professional and domestic spaces. Sebastien Hassid found himself in the unexpected role of not just a Muslim but an Aryan husband who sought to protect his wife and conceal her Jewish past. Under the Nazi occupation, Ilonka Hassid and other Muslims of Jewish descent[14] must have felt something akin to the memorable exclamation of the German Jew Peter Gay: "Suddenly, we had become Jews."[15] Moreover, Sebastien found that his sister-in-law had become a perilous liability. Indeed, for this Muslim in Paris, as for so many other ordinary people in France, the Occupation produced unenviable, torturous choices: either imperil oneself by lying to the administrators of a police state, or endanger one's wife by telling them the truth; either cut professional ties with close family members or risk losing one's business.

As the story of Sebastien Hassid and Ilonka and Blanche Laufer illustrates, from 1940 to 1945 the conditions of the Occupation, France's internal struggles, and the Shoah dramatically altered the terms of Jewish-Muslim interaction in France. Whereas political and sociocultural relations had often remained separated during the 1930s, the new identity politics produced by Nazi and Vichy policies pervaded all spheres of life. These policies, and the choices of individuals who responded to them, racialized the terms of Jewish-Muslim relations in an unprecedented manner. Turning the right-wing visions of the late interwar years into legal reality, tightly linked notions of religion and descent now defined one's eligibility for membership in the French nation. No longer just an undercurrent in Jewish-Muslim relations, race became overriding, acting as the principal, official lens for one's status in the eye of both Vichy and the German occupiers.

Beginning with the German anti-Jewish ordinance of late September 1940 and Vichy's Statut des juifs of early October, France's more than 300,000 Jews became "non-Aryans" and suffered dramatic persecution.[16] While many other marginal groups such as foreigners, Freemasons, "gypsies," and communists also faced growing exclusion under the Nazis and Vichy, the case of Muslims was far more complicated. Although nearly all of the 100,000 (mostly Algerian) Muslims in France still lacked citizenship, they now became defined by their racial status, superior to that of Jews and legally akin to "Aryan."[17]

The new categories of Jewish and Muslim identity subverted older power dynamics. Instead of Jews having the capacity to advocate, write, or implement policies directly affecting the lives of thousands of Muslims, they became largely powerless to defend even their own interests. Muslims, accustomed to being unequal colonial subjects, achieved new respect, both symbolic and material, from the French state. Two key factors accounted for this shift: Vichy's obsession with the North African empire, seen as France's remaining power base and bargaining chip to be maintained at all costs—particularly against both nationalist activity and Nazi propaganda—and the regime's broader antisecularist effort to bring state and religion back together. Under these circumstances, Vichy gave new public recognition to Muslims and attention to their ritual needs while also monitoring them with unprecedented intensity.[18] Muslims had to navigate as well the entreaties of the Nazi authorities, French collaborationist groups, and resisters, all of whom sought their support. The power imbalance that had informed distinctions in Jewish and Muslim religious and colonial status during the preceding twenty-five years was turned on its head.

With this context in mind, we can begin to offer a more detailed and nuanced story of Muslims and Jews during World War II than the one that has too often been told. The position of Muslims was in many respects quite similar to that of other ordinary people of France, especially others living on the margins, such as foreigners or the very poor. While it has been all too easy to rely on misleading oversimplifications about French behavior during the war, in reality we cannot accurately divide France into two camps of "good" resisters versus "bad" collaborators. Instead, we need to attend to the ambiguity that defined so many people's behavior.[19]

Muslims too cannot be reduced to either eager allies of the Nazis or sympathetic defenders of the Jews. Moreover, we need to understand Muslims' wartime behavior and sentiment in terms that go beyond simply assessing their level of antisemitism.[20] To be sure, we can hardly ignore the implications of many Muslim choices, even if their motivations were often more prudent than ideological. Still, like the rest of French society, particularly other marginal individuals, most Muslims made decisions informed by their sense of how best to improve their lives and that of their community. They assessed the most "good" or least "bad" path as it appeared in the precise historical moment. Examining Jews and Muslims side by side highlights how both groups navigated the period's challenges with remarkable creativity and imagination akin to that found among the wider French population. Yet such an analysis also illuminates how Muslims, along with their distinctive cultural practices, had an unusual combination of colonized vulnerability and newfound recognition—of what one scholar of the period terms "constraints" and "privileges"—that lent their approach to the war's challenges specific political, economic, and religious considerations.[21]

While a plurality of politically active Muslims showed support for Vichy or the Germans, or both, a close reading of their behavior reveals that their motivations were complex, and antisemitism was often not a leading factor. Like much of the wider French population, Muslims did display markedly increased hostility toward Jews, yet their status as colonial subjects seeking greater equality or autonomy and the resonance of Vichy and collaborationist antisecularism often acted as more central reasons to support Vichy or Germany. In certain quarters of Paris and Marseille, positive relations with Jews and a measure of contingency in status and identity persisted. Many Muslims joined the Resistance or fought in the Liberation armies, occasionally serving alongside or even helping to save Jews. Jewish and Muslim activism within the Resistance, in the context of the war's changing stakes, meant joint combat for freedom, but it also would lead to new tensions around increasingly assertive Zionist and anticolonial nationalist movements. Analyzed in terms of precise historical options, local and group particularities, and multicausality, Muslim choices begin to look very different.

Furthermore, certain Jewish choices vis-à-vis Muslims also defy conventional understandings of World War II, the Holocaust, and the two groups' relations during this period. Small numbers of North African and Levantine Jews in France moved in the opposite direction of Ilonka Hassid, suddenly seeking to take on a new racial and religious label: that of Muslims. They drew on centuries of coexistence and older Sephardi and Mizrahi histories of religious fluidity and adaptability and on overlapping elements of North African Muslim and Jewish culture, knowledge, and ritual. These Jews thereby drew closer than ever before to Islam, but purely as a survival strategy, treating religion as a cloak of protection. In this manner, as the setting of the Occupation placed Jews and Muslims in immutably opposed racial categories, it also opened possibilities for new ambiguities in the positions and relations of certain Muslims and Jews.

Moreover, this story illuminates how, like the many Ashkenazic Jews in France who hid as Catholics or undertook various forms of Resistance, these Jews from the Maghreb, the Middle East, and the Balkans used what cultural resources they could to maneuver and attempt to maintain a measure of agency.

Jewish "Muslims"

For Jews across France, the Occupation quickly became a struggle for survival. In the occupied zone, beginning in September 1940, the Nazis expropriated enormous quantities of Jewish property. In May and August 1941, with French police cooperation, they carried out the first large-scale arrests of Jews.[22] By June 1942, Jews of the occupied zone had to wear the yellow star. In the free zone, without any initial pressure from the Nazis, Vichy also wasted little time. In autumn 1940, the new regime stripped all Algerian Jews and many naturalized Jewish immigrants of their French citizenship. Over the next year, Vichy progressively barred or severely restricted the Jewish presence in most sectors of the French economy. Beginning in earnest with the infamous Vel d'Hiv roundup of July 16–17, 1942, in Paris, in which 9,000 French police participated, 76,000 Jews (about one-third of them French citizens and the rest foreigners) would be deported from France before the war's end.[23]

Muslims' racial position was far more favorable than that of Jews. In the 1930s, responding to pressures from the Arab world, Nazi racial experts and diplomats had created categories that reassured Muslims that they were not classified like Jews as racially inferior Semites, even as they were not considered exactly Aryans.[24] Vichy, meanwhile, took its own solicitous interest in France's Muslims from the start.[25] In September 1940, Marshal Pétain exclaimed, "I do not differentiate among the French; Catholics, Protestants and Muslims are all my children."[26] Such gestures persisted throughout the Vichy regime. Speaking to the inhabitants of Algeria in February 1942, Pétain declared, "To you all, French of Algeria, Christians who pursue here our civilizing work, Muslims who carry to us the magnificent example of a faith [kept] intact, I speak to you all of my affectionate concern."[27] Such statements, coupled with extensive Muslim-targeted propaganda around the figure of the marshal, made Pétain quite popular with North African Muslims in France.[28] Multiple state-produced newsreels that emphasized French suffering under Allied bombardments featured Si Kaddour Benghabrit or the Paris Mosque alongside Catholic clerics and churches. In these accounts, Jewish suffering received no mention. This represented a dramatic reversal from twenty-five years prior, when during World War I, the oft-discussed union sacrée had included Jews alongside Catholics and Protestants but typically ignored Muslims. Now, state symbolism implied that Muslims rather than Jews merited a place, however secondary, in the religious tapestry of wartime France.

Vichy's Muslim outreach also took more material forms. Even with wartime rationing and deficits, the regime found significant resources to support Islamic practices. For example, in 1943 in Marseille on Aïd el-Fitr, the holiday marking the end of Ramadan, the government furnished more than 1,300 pounds of couscous, 880 pounds of lamb, 440 pounds of sugar, and 44 pounds of green tea.[29] That same year, the regime promised to build a Muslim prayer hall in the town of Saint-Étienne, which it described as "a new manifestation of the Government's solicitude for the Metropole's North African" population. The Ministry of the Interior allotted more than 1.4 million francs for the project over the next two years.[30] One ministerial memo, explicitly linking such largesse with the regime's emphasis on empire, explained its aid efforts for Muslims and other colonial prisoners of war: "It is indeed important from a higher point of view that the Indigenous have a very clear feeling that even in their present misery the French Government keeps all of its benevolence toward them."[31] This wording reflects how Muslims' wartime status could carry its own pejorative racialization, often linked to older colonial histories.

Pétain's government did not treat Muslims in France as anything like full equals, and it expressed significant ambiguity about their precise racial status. The new regime declined to offer Muslims an easier path to full French citizenship; at times, policies grouped Muslims, other colonial subjects, and Jews together, such as prohibitions against "people of color" crossing the demarcation line from the northern occupied zone to the southern free zone.[32] A ministerial memo of February 1942 expressed fears about how North African laborers could "contaminate" the French through interacting with French workers.[33] At the same time, both Vichy and the Nazis, particularly within prisoner-of-war camps, placed North Africans at the top of a racial hierarchy of France's colonial subjects.[34] Moreover, many of the architects of Vichy's "National Revolution" situated themselves within a tradition of the French Far Right that had, since the late nineteenth century, seen Arabs as the "good Semites," a kind of positive foil for "the Jew."[35] On the whole, the very ambiguities of Vichy racial attitudes toward North African Muslims placed the latter somewhere in between full Aryans and racial "undesirables," with no doubt as to their superiority—racially and in many respects legally—to Jews.

As Jews realized they could no longer count on their place within the French nation-state, they looked elsewhere for protection, often seeking to conceal their Jewishness through false identities.[36] It is well known that during the war, many Ashkenazic Jews attempted to pass for or were hidden as Catholics or Protestants.[37] What is less well known is that a significant number of Jews from the Levant or North Africa tried to camouflage themselves as Muslims.[38] Both disguises mirrored the way that Vichy had legally subsumed much of religion within race. Calling oneself Muslim introduced a new level of commonality, both intimate and uncomfortable, into the religious and colonial components of Jewish-Muslim relations. Jews who took this route offered the ultimate statement of shared Judeo-Islamic heritage; at the same time, they appropriated Islam as their own, for their own purposes.

With the revocation of the Crémieux Decree on October 7, 1940, Algerian Jews lost their French citizenship. They became undesirables and legally of the same status as native Muslims; four days later, Vichy relegated them to a category beneath Muslims, barring Jews from the path of naturalization established for Algerian Muslims with the Jonnart Law of 1919. Most Algerian Jews living on the mainland also lost French citizenship. Jews of Morocco and Tunisia, who had never received French citizenship en masse, faced intensive new levels of surveillance and identification, severe professional quotas, and for many, imprisonment in labor camps. Thus, for the first time since they had been ruled as dhimmi under Islamic law in the precolonial era, all North African Jews were of inferior status to Muslims.[39] But whereas under the dhimmi, North African Jews faced restrictions on their clothing and could not feign equality with the ruling Muslim majority, under the conditions of the Occupation, some of them made a public claim to Islam.

In individual encounters with Nazi or Vichy agents, various Jews from North Africa, the Levant, and Central Asia improvised a range of Muslim disguises. When arrested by Vichy authorities in the street, for instance, Algerian-born musician Yoseff Fhal began speaking Arabic rapidly.[40] As she departed the Métro during a roundup, Lucette Bouchoucha, a Jewish girl of North African origin, followed her mother's instructions: she hid her yellow star and, when approached by an officer, gave a false, Arabicsounding name.[41] As he was inspected physically by a "race expert" at the Drancy concentration camp, the Iranian-Afghani Michel Mamon offered to read from the Quran, referred casually to performing the Muslim rite of ablution, and relied on his "Oriental" appearance and the physical similarity borne of the common rite of circumcision.[42]

Other Jews sought more official recognition that they were Muslim, and thereby of "Aryan"-like status. In Paris in autumn 1940, at the office of the Service des affaires indigènes nord-africaines (SAINA), numerous Jews from Algeria who had just lost their citizenship attempted to register as Muslims. Such a situation reflected how drastically the Occupation had already shifted the power dynamics of Muslim-Jewish relations. On the war's eve, because six of the inspectors of SAINA's Brigade nord africain (BNA)—the police force long charged with tracking North African Muslims—were Jewish, many Algerian Jews used this inside connection to attempt to get their metropolitan papers in order. Within a year, in German-occupied Paris, the BNA had turned most of its attention from the pursuit of Muslims to Jews. When Algerian Jews came covertly seeking Muslim identity cards, some SAINA personnel, whose ranks included a number of Muslims, worked to assist Jews; others directed suspect characters toward the more informed and often brutal Service des affaires juives.[43]

Rather than chance an encounter with a Vichy or Nazi agent, many Jews claimed in writing to be Muslim, attempting to acquire formal documentation of "Aryan" status.[44] Certain individuals went to elaborate, creative ends to fool the authorities. In Marseille, Emile Chaouat claimed that with Muslim Berber ancestry on his father's side and Catholic ancestors on his mother's side, he had registered as a Jew by mistake because he took "Semite" to include all indigènes.[45] Another Jew from Algeria, René Baccouche, living in the town of Saint-Clair le Levendau in the Var, alleged that his paternal grandparents were Turkish Muslims. At the time of the Crémieux Decree, he explained, his grandparents registered as Jews merely in order to acquire French citizenship.[46] Through his self-presentation as Muslim, Baccouche underscored the way Algerian Jews had long been positioned at the edge of French nationhood, fellow natives to the Muslims but legally French citizens. That is, in alleging that his grandparents had registered as Jews instead of Muslims in the wake of the Crémieux Decree, he acknowledged the deep inequalities that the decree had created. At the same time, only if Mediterranean Jews and Muslims had shared similar customs for centuries—and most crucial, if the French colonial authorities of 1870 had perceived them as highly similar—could his grandparents' guise, and therefore his story, be remotely plausible.[47] In order to explain himself, Chaouat too pointed toward cultural commonalities, both real and perceived. Yet by referring to both Algerian Jews and Muslims as indigènes, he treated a pejorative colonial term and legal category specifically designed for Muslims as applying also to Jews. Whereas Baccouche anchored his claim in a tale about confusion at the moment of Algerian Jewish emancipation, Chouat in a sense had to forget that this historic moment—and its decisive act of legal differentiation—had even occurred at all.

Under the Occupation, immediate daily needs could make events such as recognized Muslim holidays opportunities for temporary disguise. In Marseille, at the 1942 celebration of Aïd el-Fitr, many Jews attempted to take advantage of public distributions of couscous to Muslims. These Jews, often with typically Muslim last names like Bou Khoubza, Tayeb, and Kalifa, sought to fool distributors and obtain couscous for themselves. A number of Muslims in Marseille reported to the authorities that many Algerian Jews, hoping to camouflage their Jewishness, sought fake identity cards that said simply "North African indigène."[48]

Like the attempts of many Ashkenazic French Jews to pass themselves or their children off as Christian, the disguise of North African and Levantine Jews as Muslims constituted, first and foremost, a survival strategy.[49] Such strategies had multiple precedents. These included older Sephardi Jewish histories of Crypto-Jews and of rabbinic leniency regarding Jewish conversion to Islam in the face of danger. More recently, thousands of Jews living under imperial rule had sought to negotiate shifting boundaries and regimes of legal status.[50] Just as important, these Jews displayed a measure of ongoing agency under extreme circumstances and a comfort with Islam rooted in a long history of cohabitation and cultural commonalities.[51] Their particular disguise, however, also acknowledged that Muslims and Jews now stood on opposing sides of the new racial barriers erected in occupied France.

The Grand Mosque of Paris:
A Haven of Resistance and Rescue?

Few individuals better exemplify the shifting balance of Jewish-Muslim power and the complexity of Muslim choices in Vichy France than Si Kaddour Benghabrit, rector of the Grand Mosque of Paris and of the

Institut musulman.[52] Benghabrit was born in Algeria in 1868, and as a child, seemingly both attended a traditional madrasa and mastered French language and culture. Cosmopolitan and comfortable in the corridors of power from a young age, familiar with both Europe and the Islamic world, and noted by many observers for his savvy as an intermediary, Benghabrit worked first for the sultan of Morocco and then the French Ministry of Foreign Affairs. As the Grand Mosque's rector from its founding in 1926 until his death in 1954, he tirelessly defended the interests of his community and clung tightly to his own power.[53] Benghabrit proved capable of creating lasting relationships with diverse individuals and groups, including at least a few North African Jews. Among them were some of the performers in Mahieddine Bachetarzi's El-Moutribia, the Algerian orchestral and acting company of Jews and Muslims that frequently toured France in the 1920s and 1930s. He was also close to Maurice Mantout, the Jewish architect of the mosque.[54]

All of these components in Benghabrit's history, position, and personality informed his wartime conduct. Benghabrit's complicated position as an agent of resistance, collaboration, and accommodation serves as a paradigm for the conflicting loyalties, calculations, and ambiguities at the heart of many Muslims' choices in occupied France. Such complexities mimicked those found among France's broader population during the war.[55]

Over twenty-five years ago, a story began to circulate that during World War II Benghabrit used his position to help save Jews. An Algerian Jew named Albert Assouline became the leading advocate of this story. In September 1940, Assouline and a Muslim fellow soldier, having escaped from camps in Germany, found refuge in the mosque before crossing the demarcation line into the unoccupied zone. According to Assouline, during the war the mosque offered refuge mostly to British parachutists and Jewish children, and smaller numbers of Freemasons and resisters. Typically individuals spent a few nights in the mosque before they arranged to hide or move elsewhere. Benghabrit often provided false documents of Islamic ancestry for North African Jews. Assouline recounted how Si Mohamed Benzouaou, the first imam of the mosque, "took considerable risks in order to camouflage Jews by furnishing them with certificates saying that they were Muslim." Benzouaou even disguised as a Muslim one Rabbi Netter and led him from Metz to Narbonne. Ultimately, Assouline contended, based on his count of ration cards he found in the mosque after the war, that Benghabrit and other personnel of the mosque had helped to save no fewer than 1,732 individuals.[56] Assouline repeated his account with elaboration in Derri Berkani's 1991 film, *Une résistance oubliée*.[57] Yet it was only in the early twenty-first century, in the face of both the renewed violence of the Middle East conflict and France's Jewish-Muslim crisis, that the story began to receive unprecedented attention, featuring in a spate of popular renderings.[58]

Certain elements demonstrate that Benghabrit and others around the mosque did help to save Jews. Salim Hallali, the Jew from Algeria who teamed with Mohamed el-Kamal in the late 1930s to produce Arabic music that became immensely popular with both Jews and Muslims, often told his personal story. It is one that underscores both the possibilities and constraints for Jewish-Muslim cultural cooperation during this period. Hallali found himself abandoned by many erstwhile partners and friends: both Mohamed el-Kamal and Mohamed Igherbouchène agreed to collaborate with the Nazis at Radio-Berlin. Even Mahieddine Bachetarzi, desperate to maintain his troupe, severely compromised his values. He mounted an officially sponsored tour in Algeria to promote support for Vichy, composed an adoring hymn to Pétain in Arabic, and at least once made remarks from the stage before a performance in which he warned Muslims to be on their guard against Jews.[59]

Thus Hallali found himself alone and exposed in occupied Paris. Benghabrit loved Hallali's music and endeavored to protect him. The former provided the latter with false certificates as a Muslim, had the name of Hallali's grandfather inscribed on a tomb in the Muslim cemetery in Bobigny, and enabled Hallali to perform regularly at the mosque's café with well-known Muslim musicians such as Ali Sriti and Ibrahim Salah. Thus not only did Hallali's false identity blur Jewish-Muslim ethnic boundaries; Hallali made the mosque a rare space where elements of shared Judeo-Muslim culture persisted.[60] In addition, a few other testimonies have emerged from individuals whose family members received aid or offers of help from the mosque. Moreover, documentation exists regarding a resistance network around the Franco-Muslim hospital, also under Benghabrit's control.[61]

Other evidence suggests that the German occupiers discovered and sought to halt the rector's subversive activities. On September 24, 1940, the French Interior Ministry received a note explaining that the Germans suspected that employees of the mosque had been giving Jews fraudulent documents certifying them as Muslim. German officials, the note explained, had confronted the mosque's imam (likely meaning Benghabrit) in a threatening manner and told him that the practice had to stop.[62] In

Figure 3.1. Si Kaddour Benghabrit and German soldiers at the Grand Mosque of Paris. A: In a formal pose, outside the mosque. B: In a lighthearted moment, inside the mosque. (Memorial de la Shoah, Centre de Documentation Juive Contemporaine.)

late January 1941, for reasons that remain unclear, the German authorities briefly arrested Benghabrit but released him shortly after.[63]

Photographs and newsreels of Benghabrit with German soldiers from 1941, however, appear to show friendlier relations (Figure 3.1).[64] Yet these pictures and film clips were taken in a specific context: after Benghabrit, with Vichy's help, successfully lobbied the occupiers to reopen the Franco-Muslim hospital.[65] From autumn 1940 through summer 1941, German soldiers regularly visited the mosque.[66] The Germans attempted to turn the mosque into a center of pro-German propaganda, to manipulate Benghabrit for positive press in the Muslim world, and perhaps to watch him closely.[67] Benghabrit used these contacts to wrest concessions for his constituents and maintain cordial relations with the occupiers. With an eye toward public opinion in the Muslim world, the Germans made sure that the Parisian press photographed and filmed the hospital's reopening and their visit to the mosque. While initially Benghabrit thought it natural enough that pictures would appear in newspapers like *Le Petit Parisien,* whatever his attitude at the time toward German propaganda, he soon became dismayed by the German exploitation of these images.[68] In the months to come, the rector stringently fought against subsequent efforts to manipulate him for pro-German purposes.[69]

Thus there is significant evidence to suggest that Benghabrit was indeed a resister and, to a limited degree, a "righteous among the nations," the honor given by Yad Vashem, Israel's Holocaust Museum, to those recognized as non-Jews who risked themselves to help save Jews during the Holocaust.[70] Furthermore, the rector's youngest daughter has recently recounted how shortly after his death in 1954, she heard stories about him saving Jews.[71] The government's *Journal officiel* of July 26, 1947, documents that after the war, Benghabrit was honored with the prestigious Medal of the Resistance with the Rosette.[72]

But other evidence paints a far murkier picture. Most notable, Benghabrit had a warm relationship with the Commissariat générale aux questions juives (CGQJ). When individuals whom the commissariat regarded as Jewish claimed to be Muslim, officials often consulted Benghabrit. From autumn 1943 through summer 1944, in five known cases in which he was consulted, Benghabrit appears to have identified each individual in question not as Muslim but as Jewish.[73] Strikingly, these actions occurred during a period that saw the rapid growth of the French Resistance, the increasingly evident probability of German defeat, and more widespread knowledge of the fate that awaited captured Jews in France.[74]

When taken as a whole, the surviving documentation indicates that the rector made a series of choices that encompass resistance, collaboration, and accommodation. The Muslim leader's efforts to stop the Germans from using him or the mosque for propaganda, and more so his efforts to save several Jews, meet the definitions of symbolic resistance and the resistance of aid and protection, respectively.[75] Benghabrit's assistance to the CGQJ in identifying Jews falls within most historians' definition of collaboration: direct cooperation at the level of the state or political activism. Accommodation, by contrast, describes friendly everyday acts, ranging from reading a collaborationist newspaper to becoming friends with Germans.[76] Along these very lines, Benghabrit maintained cordial relations with the Nazis, Vichy, and many collaborationists throughout the war.

While Benghabrit's choices may appear contradictory, they constituted a careful balancing act that was in many ways emblematic of Jewish-Muslim relations under the Occupation. Even as he sought to help a certain number of Jews, his accommodations of the occupiers and Vichy reflected his efforts, as ever, to maintain his institution and its position outside politics. Illustrating the differences in the war's meaning for Jews and Muslims, he seems to have tried, with mixed results, to weigh the protection of his community and himself against the ethical imperatives of the moment. The mosque's efforts to enable certain North African Jews to pass as Muslims offered solidarity around shared cultural and religious customs and common minority status. Yet Benghabrit's reports to the CGQJ, like those of Muslims in Marseille in 1942 regarding Jews seeking Muslim identity cards, rebuked many Jews' efforts to use their familiarity with Islamic culture for protection. The Muslim leader's actions thus highlighted the lethal ethnic boundaries of the Occupation and the new Muslim-Jewish power imbalances these boundaries had created.

Muslim Collaboration and Accommodation

In contrast to the complex interactions of many of France's North African Jews and Muslims, often anchored in cultural similarities, wartime relations between Muslims and France's much larger Ashkenazic Jewish population generally occurred at a greater distance, through political status and action.[77] With Vichy displaced from Paris by the Nazis, the regime, deeply concerned about the constant Muslim-targeted German propaganda, set up three centers for police and secret service to monitor North Africans: Marseille, Châteauroux, and Clermond-Ferrand.[78] As the home of France's second-most-important Muslim population, as well as an already sizable administrative apparatus for North African affairs, Marseille became the de facto center of operations for surveillance of Muslims in the metropole. The prefecture of the Bouches-du-Rhône department, while concentrating its reports on the Marseille region, also offered regular, highly detailed information on Muslims in Paris and other parts of the occupied zone.

These reports, in tandem with similar records from the occupied zone, demonstrate how, particularly during the first two years of the war, large numbers of Muslims either collaborated with or accommodated the Nazi occupiers. Inevitably, it is difficult to draw the line between the two categories. But it will suffice to note that at least several hundred Muslims opted for collaboration, and thousands more made choices that constituted active accommodation with the enemy. For some Muslims, advocacy or sympathy for the German side expressed a desire to live under German rule. For others, it was part of a collaborationist, ardently French nationalistic platform that sought to racialize Frenchness along new boundaries similar to those articulated by the Far Right during the 1930s. Thus they supported the pro-German parties' platforms that included reforms giving Muslims greater equality and autonomy and excluding Jews altogether. In this sense antisemitism was merely one motivation for Muslim collaboration and accommodation. Aspirations to basic material, cultural, or political needs often proved more central.

Attention to what became an intense imperial struggle for Muslim hearts and minds complicates the well-known picture of the period's political battles. Conventional accounts pit Vichy and the Germans on one side, and a growing resistance movement on the other. Vichy and the occupiers, however, frequently competed fiercely for Muslim support.[79] Reflecting the regime's concerns, the authors of reports written at Vichy's behest carefully separated out Muslim expressions of support for Vichy, the Germans, the Italians, and Resistance movements, respectively. German efforts to woo Muslims, visible in Nazi officers' attempts to utilize the Grand Mosque of Paris as a propaganda tool, focused largely on antisemitism, critiques of French policy and military capacity, claims of resonance between Islam and National Socialism, and, after November 1942, demonic portrayals of Anglo-American imperialism and capitalism.[80] German soldiers in the metropole treated Muslims with marked benevolence, often impressing them with their Arabic or Kabyle language skills.[81] The occupiers also spread promises of impending self-determination in Algeria and Morocco, though never outright independence.[82]

Such German outreach achieved a certain resonance, particularly among anticolonial nationalists. Already beginning on the war's eve, several members of the nascent Algerian nationalist party (the Parti du peuple algérien, or PPA), along with student activists, formed the Comité d'action révolutionnaire nord-africain (CARNA). Disillusioned by the French Left in the wake of the failures of the Front populaire, the organization's founders sought aid from the Germans to take on the French. Former PPA activist and CARNA member Mahmoud Abdoun explained the group's at least initially opportunistic motivations: "[We] were united around . . . a common feeling that we were only able to acquire our independence by allying ourselves to a great power enemy of France, [that is] Germany. Our position had no connection with the political program [of] Nazism. . . . We had adopted in sum, the old adage that says that the enemy of the enemy is my friend." Abdoun, who as a young man in Algeria had worked alongside Jews in a shoemaker's shop, added: "We had never adhered to the anti-Jewish politics of Marshal Pétain and of Hitler and we carried on good relations with Algerian israélites."[83]

CARNA hoped that a strategic alliance with the Germans would furnish them with weapons. Thus in July 1939, members of the group traveled to Berlin, where they met German agents who promised to supply them with ample arms. But the promised arms never materialized. What did occur was that many of the anticolonial militants became (however ironically) committed supporters of Nazism and were made key figures in a Muslim propaganda organization created by the Nazis shortly after the latter occupied Paris. At the head of the Nazis' Algerian section, for instance, were two former PPA leaders, Radjef Belkacem and Mohamed Igherbouchène, who participated in such activities as pro-German radio propaganda and surveillance of Muslim milieux.[84]

These individuals worked with like-minded Muslims at the heart of an aggressive propaganda machine seeking Muslim support in France and the Maghreb.[85] Some took part in spy networks for the occupiers. In Paris, El Djazaïr, the Algerian café opened by Igherbouchène on the rue de la Huchette, where Salim Hallali had been a star in the late 1930s, now regularly had a large German clientele. Even as it maintained its Oriental flavor, early in the war its present owner Louaib Seghir operated as an information agent for the Germans. According to reports, he employed four other Muslims who recorded Muslim expressions of anti-German sentiment; through their repressive vigilance, in time they provoked fear and resentment among many Muslims still loyal to France.[86] In autumn 1941 in Paris, the Germans opened at least one "propaganda school" to train Muslims to spread pro-German sentiment in North Africa.[87] Germany also made its prisoner-of-war camps—camps that held tens of thousands of North African soldiers from the campaign of 1940—into sites of intensive propaganda. Imams and marabouts, or traditional Muslim religious leaders, were sent to the camps dressed in religious attire and instructed to place a pro-German spin on their message. A select number of Muslim prisoners were sent to the special camp of Luckenwalde just south of Berlin, where they listened to extensive German propaganda, enjoyed perks like morning coffee by their bedside, and in many cases concluded their stay with a tour of Berlin before being sent to France or North Africa to spread a pro-German message.[88]

Also supporting German victory but in a French nationalist framework, significant numbers of Muslims took an active role in many French collaborationist political parties. Many collaborationist groups launched aggressive campaigns for Muslim support.[89] The two largest collaborationist parties, the Parti populaire français (PPF), led by Jacques Doriot, and the Rassemblement national populaire (RNP) of Marcel Déat, took the lead. Both groups employed Muslim leaders and recruited specifically Muslim contingents.

During the Occupation, the PPF intensified its recruitment of Muslims that had already begun under the Popular Front. As Doriot's push for personal power at Vichy reached its apex in 1942, so too did his effort to gain Muslim support in France. Undertaking a massive publicity campaign, the party produced 100,000 leaflets and 2,700 posters advertising a gathering of March 29, 1942, at the "Magic City" meeting hall on the theme of "French Imperial Unity."[90] Three leading Muslim members of the PPF, Sheikh Mohamed Zouani, Mostefa Bendjamaa, and Si Ahmed Belghoul, traveled from Algeria for the occasion.[91]

The events of their visit illustrate how these Muslims, like many other activists among the broader French population, became collaborationists not for one single reason but due to a complex series of factors. The three Muslim leaders repeatedly underscored their enthusiasm for Vichy, the PPF and its leader, and collaboration with Germany. Yet they placed these familiar themes in distinctly religious and antisecular terms. When explaining their support for the PPF in a newspaper interview shortly

Figure 3.2. Sheikh Mohamed Zouani, Mostefa Bendjamaa, and Si Ahmed Belghoul, Muslim leaders of the PPF, meet with Cardinal Baudrillart at Paris's *Institut Catholique*, March 1942. (Memorial de la Shoah, CDJC.)

after their arrival, Zouani and Bendjamaa emphasized the party's virulent anticommunism and lamented the Soviet regime's destruction of mosques. Bendjamaa recounted an anecdote from his hadj to Mecca, where he met a Muslim from the Caucasus who described in moving detail the challenges and persecutions that Muslims in Soviet Russia faced.[92]

On March 22, Bendjamaa, Zouani, and Belghoul paid a visit to Paris's Institut catholique, where they met with the institute's eminent leader, Cardinal Alfred Baudrillart (Figure 3.2). Despite different backgrounds, the meeting's participants had convergent ideologies and interests. Like his guests, Baudrillart's wartime politics were motivated in major part by an avowed anticommunism, and the cardinal also saw his position in decidedly religious terms, declaring the German invasion of the Soviet Union a "crusade" that "pleases God."[93] In an enthusiastic account, occupied France's most widely read daily newspaper, *Le Petit Parisien*, spoke of the occasion in terms reminiscent of the union sacrée, celebrating this "new contact between great spiritual personalities" at a time when "all dissidence is attempting to break French unity."[94] The meeting's atmosphere became so amicable that by the end, Baudrillart exclaimed that there was no god but Allah, and the Muslim representatives extolled Jesus.[95]

One week later, at the March 29 rally, before an audience of 800, including 350 to 400 Muslims, Belghoul, Bendjemaa, and Zouani delivered impassioned speeches with similar themes, but with a new emphasis on antisemitism (Figure 3.3). Zouani spoke of his hopes for growing cooperation "between French of Catholic confession and French of the Quranic religion." He declared, "[Communism] fights God with relentlessness and destroys religions. It scoffs at our holy book, the foundation of our society and guide of our life in every domain." In his speech, Bendjamaa articulated an exclusionary religious politics. A few days prior, he had made statements about the teaching of the Prophet Muhammad to respect all "peoples of the book." Now, however, he explained that "God tells us in our Quran: 'the greatest enemy of Islam, it is the Jew,'" lamented that "Jews at any price, want to destroy Islam," and linked Judaism with communism as a "two-headed serpent" that Muslims had to fight.[96] While these words echoed certain premodern Islamic polemics against non-Muslims, Bendjamaa's formulation carried a more modern anti-Jewish focus that departed from much of Islamic history and textual tradition.[97]

The same day, Zouani's Sufi brotherhood, El amaria, held its religious services for the Prophet Muhammad's birthday, with an unusual twist. Zouani added a solemn ceremony where he made Jacques Doriot an honorary member of the brotherhood. Afterward, Doriot joined the other guests for a traditional North African meal (Figure 3.4).[98] This meeting and ceremony marked the culmination of what may be described as the sacralization of Muslim participation in the PPF. The emphasis on both mutual Muslim-Christian religious respect and hostility toward communism illustrated the complex, multifaceted motivations that had attracted many Muslims to the PPF. Yet these choices also revealed the danger for Muslims in associating religious expressions and sacred alliance with Nazi and Vichy racial thought. By invoking Islam and the Quran, Mostefa Bendjamaa attempted to give his antisemitism the stamp of religious authenticity. By inducting Doriot into El amaria in an event wrapped in ritual symbolism, Sheikh Zouani placed collaboration on a sacred plane. It is unclear, however, if such a message resonated widely among Muslims in France. Despite all the fanfare, the PPF's series of Muslim-targeted

Figure 3.3. The PPF meeting at the Magic City, March 1942. A: The speakers. B: The audience. (Memorial de la Shoah, CDJC.)

Figure 3.4. Jacques Doriot becomes an honorary member of Zouani's Sufi brotherhood *El amaria*. A: The ceremony. B: The meal. (Memorial de la Shoah, CDJC.)

events in spring 1942 drew only several hundred participants, and the party's Muslim following appears to have declined thereafter.[99]

The RNP carried out its own intensive recruitment of Muslims.[100] Its most lasting effort emerged within its labor syndicate, the Front social du travail (FST), which in April 1942 created a Muslim section called the Union des travailleurs nord-africains (UTNA).[101] In another instance of North African nationalists-turned-collaborationists, the leading members of the UTNA were all former PPA activists.[102] The organization's membership eventually reached 3,000, and with sections across France and a wide range of programs, it claimed to influence as many as 15 to 20 percent of North African workers.[103] The group's platform focused on improving Muslims' basic conditions, with demands including the liberation of Muslim political prisoners, family benefits for North African workers, bilingual education in North Africa, and complete equality between Muslim natives and French colonists. Only rarely did its publications or speakers attack Jews.[104] Indeed, the UTNA serves as a reminder that for many collaborationist Muslims, antisemitism was absent or marginal.

At the same time, it was also initially under the auspices of the RNP that emerged the most virulently antisemitic Muslim group in occupied France: the Comité nord-africain (CNA), headed by the ardent antisemite and Germanophile Mohamed El-Maadi.[105] During the war, El-Maadi merged themes of Islamic pride, resistance, and loyalty with notions of racial superiority that echoed both National Socialist and French colonial ideas. El-Maadi was born in 1902 in the village of Sfahli in the department of Constantine.[106] Described already by French security services in the late 1930s as expressing a "ferocious hatred [for] communists and Jews," he participated in extreme Right groups, including the Action française and Algérie française, of which he was founder and president.[107] He was arrested in November 1937 for his role in the Cagoule, a Far Right conspiracy to overthrow the republic.[108] Nonetheless, French educated and a French citizen, El-Maadi became a career military officer who was highly decorated for his service during the campaign of 1939–1940.[109] During the Occupation, El-Maadi worked frenetically for collaboration. He wrote dozens of collaborationist and antisemitic pamphlets, made pro-German radio broadcasts, recruited Muslims for pro-German parties and militias, worked closely with the Gestapo in Paris, and personally led military attacks against resisters.[110] In late October 1941, the CGQJ even assigned El-Maadi the official responsibility of considering all issues in the commissariat's orbit relating to North Africa.[111]

The CNA's platform, underscored in widely disseminated tracts, called for equality, bilingual education, and the abolition of the oppressive Code de l'indigénat for France's Muslims in a unified North African territory; social aid programs to improve Muslim agriculture and infrastructure; and collaboration with Germany in a new "European" France, from which Jews, Freemasons, and Trusts—"agents of war and famine"— would be banished.[112] The committee further demanded the expulsion of Jews from government positions and the expropriation of Jewish property. While El-Maadi's impassioned leadership initially attracted a following of several hundred, the CNA was struggling to stay afloat by early 1942. Its fortunes improved markedly, however, following the Allied landing in North Africa in November 1942.[113]

The committee responded to this event by printing 5,000 copies of a leaflet in the form of an open letter from El-Maadi to his fellow Muslims in France. In this letter, El-Maadi lamented the plight of North Africa's Muslims, victims of the Gaullists and the Anglo Americans who "received from their Jewish masters the mission of neutralizing [Muslims]."[114] "Our brothers," El-Maadi exclaimed, "know the most terrible of colonizations: that of the Judeo-Americans." He implored France's Muslims to join "in the 'Djihad' at the side of the heroic soldiers of the Axis." Yet this was not merely a stamp of Islamic approval on anticolonial sentiments: it was a wholesale endorsement of German racialist thinking. Tellingly, El-Maadi spoke of "our race," signaling his adoption of a more racialized version of Islam, akin to that of Vichy and the Nazis, for his own politics. He closed his letter by insisting, "Only the Strong and the Brave will be honored in the new world." Perhaps this was a jihadist message, a reference to Muslim martyrs receiving honors in the next life. It was also, however, a political message pointing to Muslims' place in the new Europe and North Africa that El-Maadi expected to emerge from a Nazi victory.

In 1943, after becoming an independent organization and changing its name to the Comité musulman de l'Afrique du Nord (CMAN), El-Maadi's group continued to articulate themes of racial division, religious war, and pro-German collaboration. It did so largely through the pages of its widely read journal, *Er Rachid (The Messenger)*.[115] Appearing biweekly and then weekly until the eve of the liberation of Paris, the journal expended a re- markably large share of its ink on an obsessive hatred of Jews.[116] The violent, bloodthirsty Jew had been "unchangeable" since ancient times.[117] The war was "inspired, wanted, and unleashed by the Jews."[118] American president Franklin Roosevelt sought "nothing less than to install in North Africa the omnipotent rule of the Jew."[119] Jews were, by turns, "international criminals," "the author of all ills of France," and "masters" who had "enslaved the world and us [Muslims]."[120] Altogether the newspaper depicted the war as a struggle between potentially monstrous Jewish masters controlling the Allied forces and proud Muslims, defended by the Germans and fighting for freedom.[121] For El-Maadi and his followers, the Jew became the racial and religious mortal enemy of the Muslim (Figure 3.5).

While it is difficult to determine how many Muslims supported El Maadi, he clearly had a sizable following by early 1943. According to Paris police, Er Rachid's print run eventually reached 25,000.[122] In January 1943, the newspaper claimed that the CMAN had "nearly 10,000 members"; Paris police placed the number at "several thousand" in November 1943.[123] While these figures seem inflated given the total number of Muslims in France, they suggest that more than a few Muslims participated in El-Maadi's committee and read its newsletter. Within Er Rachid's first month of existence, even amid wartime economic hardships, a subscription drive from the CMAN elicited eighty-eight individual Muslims or Muslim-owned businesses to give a total of 5,575 francs in donations.[124] At least a dozen of Paris's Muslim-owned businesses advertised, most of them regularly, in the journal.[125] In another indication of the organization's reach, despite being centered in Paris, one police report mentions members as far away as Brittany (in the northwest of France).[126]

Small numbers of Muslims took their support for the German cause to another level. In July 1941, the PPF, RNP, and other collaborationist parties in Paris formed the Anti-Bolshevik Legion (LVF). LVF members showed the highest level of commitment, preparing to fight on the Russian front, wearing the uniform of the Reich, and swearing a loyalty oath to the führer.[127] By the end of October 1941, at least 130 Muslims had volunteered for the LVF, a somewhat disproportionate figure considering that under 3,000 men total had volunteered at that time in all of France.[128] Ironically or perhaps alluringly for some Muslims, the LVF's self-image relied on notions of a racially binary, life-or-death struggle between Western civilization and the barbaric East. Jews were a central target of its rhetoric and desired combat. The primary motivations of most men who volunteered for the LVF were ideological affinity, personal opportunism, a

Figure 3.5. A cover of *Er Rachid* that depicts the Jew as a sleazy banker and a pig suddenly barred from Europe: "Goddam, I think they played a dirty trick on me." (Bibliothèque Nationale de France.)

thirst for adventure, and an ego-driven desire for military pride; Muslim motives were undoubtedly similar, but they also carried an anticolonial bent.[129] A May 1942 letter from thirty-six-year-old factory worker Makhlouf Aichoun to his brother is suggestive in this regard.[130] Aichoun exclaimed:

We are very happy . . . well nourished and well-fed . . . and also well-paid. . . .
The Muslims are loved by the Germans and their leader Adolf Hitler. . . .
Above all, don't listen to the Jewish and Gaullist propaganda. One who
is a Gaullist is a Communist and we say again death to the Jews and
communists. . . . We have lived nearly all imaginable injustices and physical
and moral sufferings and that is why we have decided *to win or to die*. . . .
I conclude by begging you to shout with me, *Heil Hitler Deutsche Reich
und Heil Afrika*.[131]

Ultimately, however, those who recruited Muslims for the LVF found limited interest. Even as some Muslims participated from summer 1942
into 1944, it appears that their numbers steadily dwindled.[132]

Yet as the war dragged on, violent collaboration by Muslims took other
forms. In early 1944, El-Maadi signed up 300 Arabs and Kabyles for the
North-African Brigade, which would fight in the Dordogne.[133] Most of
the brigade eventually became part of the Milice, which assassinated resisters and showed particular ruthlessness in its pursuit of Jews.[134] More
than sixty years later, for the Parisian Jew Louise Jaïs, originally from
Algeria, the sight of Muslims, like so many native Frenchmen, in the Milice
uniform, remained seared in her memory. She recalled categorically that
for all of her friendly encounters with Muslims in both the interwar and
postwar eras, "during the war, they were with the Germans."[135]

Outside of parties and militias, Muslims' paths of collaboration or accommodation could take myriad forms. Beginning in late 1941, 15,000
to 20,000 Muslim laborers contributed to the Nazi war machine by
working for the Todt Organization, an engineering group of the Third
Reich that carried out a number of large-scale military construction
projects in Germany. Paid as much as 400 francs an hour, many joined
for material reasons; others had idyllic impressions of Germany or its
leader.[136] In certain North African cafés, Gestapo members made up much
of the clientele or German soldiers entered to cheers of "Heil Hitler."[137]
In June 1941, a small group of Moroccans came to see the infamous Nazi
propaganda film, *The Jew Süss,* applauding excitedly at its conclusion.[138]
At least a few individual Muslims sought to take over confiscated Jewish
businesses.[139]

An examination of broader Muslim sentiment clarifies to what degree
the choices of individual Muslim collaborators and accommodators (as

well as resisters) reflected current Muslim attitudes toward Jews. Such a perspective also illuminates shifting patterns in Muslims' outlook and choices over the course of the war. Particularly during the first two years of the Occupation, an atmosphere of multilayered antisemitism prevailed among large numbers of Muslims in France. From March 1941 to December 1942, the Service of Algerian Affairs of Marseille produced at least forty reports that discussed Muslim expressions of explicitly antisemitic sentiments.[140] One report of December 1941 went so far as to maintain, undoubtedly in exaggeration (but revealingly no less), that "hardly a [Muslim] conversation in Marseille takes place without complaints expressed against the Jews."[141] Haj Amin al-Husseini, the grand mufti of Jerusalem who collaborated visibly with Hitler and actively supported his antisemitic policies, seemed to garner considerable respect among many of France's Muslims.[142]

In contemporary expressions of Muslim antisemitic sentiment, several key themes appear repeatedly. Many Muslims, whether aware or not of Vichy's anti-Jewish measures, described Jews as receiving favorable or sympathetic treatment from the French. Muslims often blamed Jewish exploitation for the tight wartime rations on basic supplies, echoing one of the most widespread French antisemitic ideas of the time and a major theme in German propaganda disseminated among North African prisoners of war.[143] More broadly, this outlook corresponded with the traditional antisemitic stereotype that Jews were secretly powerful, wealthy, and responsible for France's defeat. Finally, Muslim complaints frequently linked Jews to the British or the Bolsheviks, or both, as imperialist enemies of Islam. These attitudes were not isolated to one or two strands of the Muslim population but came from individuals of a broad range of backgrounds that included humble laborers and French-educated elites.[144]

The last recorded spike in Muslim antisemitism during the war, immediately following the Allied landing in North Africa in November 1942, illuminates the context in which such sentiments emerged. Along with deep concerns for their own economic well-being and the fate of their family and homeland, many Muslims in the metropole expressed fears that the Americans would "restore Jewish power" in Algeria, Morocco, and Tunisia.[145] This was long before the Allies made any legislative decisions about Jewish rights. Soon after the mid-November arrival of one Kabyle in Marseille, the city's Muslims took up popular slogans from Algeria such as, "The Americans are brutal" and "Roosevelt is a

Jew."[146] More than two years earlier, despite Vichy's designs, the repeal of the Crémieux Decree had provoked little enthusiasm among Algerian Muslims and no discernible reaction among their metropolitan coreligionists.[147] North African Muslims did not seek a shared state of oppression with native Jews, but rather one of recognition or full equality, or both, with French colonists. In the absence of tangible improvements in Muslim status, however, the possibility of restoring Jews to French citizenship seemed to symbolize their own persistent lack of equality.[148]

These ideas point to the three principal influences on contemporary Muslim antisemitism. The first was the propaganda of certain Muslim nationalist leaders and the French Far Right, starting in the mid- to late 1930s, regarding events in Algeria and Palestine. This propaganda sought to link Jews to French and British imperialism in the Muslim popular imagination. Second, reflecting the wider environment of Vichy political rhetoric and French public opinion, many of the most frequently stated Muslim prejudices corresponded strongly to those of the surrounding metropolitan French population. Finally, from the moment they seized power in 1933, the Nazis had attempted to prime the pump of Muslim anti-Jewish sentiment through aggressive propaganda in North Africa; such efforts had accelerated under the Occupation, taking on particular intensity among Muslim soldiers in POW camps.[149]

Despite its evident importance, however, it would be a mistake to see antisemitism as the primary motivating factor in the decision of most Muslims who chose to collaborate or accommodate. A close reading of Muslims' actions during the war indicates that many Muslims who expressed antisemitic sentiment did not necessarily actively collaborate; some of these individuals even expressed hostility toward the occupiers.[150] At least a few Muslims who did collaborate simultaneously had positive professional or personal ties to Jews.[151] Much of the propaganda from groups like the PPF and the RNP that specifically targeted Muslims barely mentioned Jews or ignored them altogether. Other considerations appeared more pressing. Given their already fragile economic standing, Muslims living under the hardship of occupation found themselves in a more precarious position than many native Frenchmen. Those who chose to work for the occupiers or join militias like the LVF received comparatively high salaries and often cited economic advantage as a leading motivation.[152] Ideologically, many Muslims had become embittered toward France for its colonial policies. The defeat of 1940 brought expressions of both a sense of revenge and the shock of seeing the illusion of French imperial invincibility shattered.[153] Many Muslims were thus receptive to the themes of Germany's anti-French propaganda and the notably friendly treatment of German soldiers—they hoped they might fare better under German than French rule.[154] For the many Muslims who still professed loyalty to France, the greater rights and autonomy offered in the colonial policy of the collaborationist parties may have carried considerable appeal. Moreover, given their ironically ultranationalist posture, these parties offered the opportunity to Muslims to prove their Frenchness once and for all. Such a set of competing considerations belies various scholars' insistence on either long-standing Muslim or European-imported antisemitism as a leading causal factor in the wartime actions of Muslims in the French orbit.[155]

Events in the summer of 1942 seemed to begin to turn Muslim opinion, like that of the wider French population, toward the Resistance.[156] On the holiday of 14 juillet, 100,000 people demonstrated against Vichy and the Nazis in the streets of Marseille, and collaborationists killed two protesters and wounded numerous others.[157] In the days that followed, many Muslims in the region appeared to adopt a more critical attitude toward Germany and Vichy and to question their stereotypes about communists and Jews.[158] While the June decree that all Jews of the occupied zone had to wear the yellow star, along with the first large-scale roundups of Jews in Paris in July, shocked many French people, these events elicited little evident sympathy among Muslims.[159] Yet the severity of these measures may have contributed to the growing resonance among Muslims of Resistance appeals to the cause of human rights. Having once placed their faith in Germany, significant numbers of Muslims appeared to reconsider in the summer and early autumn of 1942, fearing that they might lose their current liberties under German rule. Some even began to hope that France would "take revenge" on Germany. While a number of Muslims who had chosen the path of collaboration during the early days of the Occupation appeared too invested to shift their allegiances, others who had worked for the occupiers now switched sides or sought to boast anew their loyalty to France.[160]

As had been the case from the start of the Occupation, support for France did not necessarily mean identification with the Resistance, but it pointed increasingly in this direction. By autumn 1942, openly pro-German Muslim circles in Paris, once quite widespread, dwindled to a small, devoted core of largely paid collaborators.[161] Encouraged by anti-

German propaganda, many Muslim laborers requisitioned by the occupiers failed to show up for work or abandoned their jobs.[162] During this period, Muslims in Marseille grew more receptive to daily Jewish claims of brotherhood and the need to unite in the face of common oppression.[163] True, the Allied landing in November elicited short-term anger toward the Americans, British, French, and Jews, but for many, such sentiments soon gave way to an altered perspective on the war's stakes that linked the Resistance with the fate of France's colonial subjects. In September 1944, a group of formerly pro-German Muslim militants in the capital responded to the arrest of several Muslim collaborators by organizing a committee designed to cultivate relations with the provisional authorities of the Resistance.[164] But by autumn 1944, the war's stakes had also begun to bring acute frustration and fear among certain Muslims regarding the as-yet-unmet demands of equality for Muslims and the postwar governance of North Africa and the Middle East, including Palestine.

Friendlier Terms: Muslims and Jews Living and Fighting Side by Side

Even during the moments of the war that highlighted Jewish-Muslim distinctions most sharply and made collaboration most alluring for Muslims, stories of daily life show us how encounters between members of the two groups could take surprising turns of coexistence, compassion, and courage. To be sure, regular interaction did not necessarily equal warm relations. In Marseille, the Turkish-born Jew Maurice Farhi continued to operate his North African épicerie in the heart of the city's most Muslim neighborhood, even as relations with his Muslim clientele grew increasingly tense. More than ever before, a number of Muslim clients resented Farhi's near-monopoly and allegedly unfair business practices, making bitter complaints to Vichy authorities, some intended to expose him as a Jew. Yet because he was a French citizen working in a profession not forbidden to Jews, the government allowed him to continue to operate; until March 1944, he remained one of the city's main couscous suppliers for Muslim families and restaurants, playing a crucial role on occasions like Ramadan.[165] After summer 1942, commercial interactions often took on more positive ideological dimensions, as other Jewish merchants in Marseille sought to rally Muslims to the Resistance. With growing resonance, these Jews repeatedly told their Muslim customers:

"We are of the same race [or] country," "After us, they will hunt you down," and "We must unite in the face of those who oppress us."[166]

At a far more intimate level, echoing the story of Sebastien and Ilonka Hassid in Paris, a few cases of romantic Jewish-Muslim relations unfolded in Marseille. In spring 1941, a Kabyle Muslim man known as Amar Hamou, a member of the CGT with openly anti-Vichy sentiments, frequently was seen with a Jewish woman named Zakyia.[167] In late May of the same year, Allala Belhouane, a Muslim Tunisian nationalist leader imprisoned in Marseille received a letter from his Jewish lover, Miss Chérif Tunina, still in Tunis.[168] Lakmissi Matouk, an Algerian Muslim man, lived with a Turkish Jewish woman separated from her husband and was responsible for the care of her children.[169] These instances reveal that even as Nazi and Vichy racial policies sharpened ethnic differences between Jews and Muslims, individual lives often rejected those differences. Like the continuing commercial relations discussed above, such love stories also suggest the endurance in at least a few quarters of positive trans-Mediterranean ties. That each of these cases occurred in Marseille seems hardly a coincidence: France's Mediterranean port had long been a place of entry, passage, and intermingling for numerous Levantine and Maghrebi Jews and Muslims; during the Occupation, Jews there never experienced the brutal social isolation of wearing the yellow star, and the Germans did not occupy the city until November 1942.[170]

One Marseille story of Muslim-Jewish love gone bad, replete with contradictions, reminds us just how fluid and complex Jewish and Muslim loyalties and motivations could become during the Occupation. In the spring of 1944, "Marguerite X," an Alsatian Jew, moved in with the Muslim café owner Belkacem Bouzid as his mistress. According to Belkacem's account, one evening when he saw Marguerite kiss a sergeant from the colonial infantry in the restaurant's doorway, he grew angry and told her that he would not tolerate such behavior. In reply she mocked him, and he asked her to take her things from the apartment (just upstairs) and leave. Then, curiously, not only out of spite but seemingly as part of her larger Aryan facade, Marguerite, in heading up the stairs, turned to a German officer present and said of Belkacem, "He does propaganda for the English." In the ensuing tumult, a German soldier killed another resister and Belkacem fled through a window. When he returned later, he found that the Germans had ransacked his apartment and stolen his money. Soon after, Marguerite was arrested, and the Germans ordered Belkacem's restaurant closed.[171]

In this story, Marguerite positioned herself remarkably along colonialist and racial lines. She angered Belkacem by cavorting with a colonial soldier, the very symbol of repressive French rule, and in the colonial context, of "white" supremacy; by dismissing Belkacem's jealousy, she carried out a power play around these differences. Then, in denouncing Belkacem to the Germans as a resister, she sought to burnish further her Aryan credentials. Somehow, along the way, she obliterated her Jewish origins and forgot the real peril in which her own identity placed her.

Other Muslims reached out to Jews with less fraught results. In spring 1941, two Kabyles made a profit by helping Jews in the occupied zone to cross the demarcation line.[172] In June 1941, Belkacem Chably, a well-known athlete in Marseille, voiced hatred for the Axis and admiration for Jews. He condemned France's persecution of its Jews as "contrary to the cause of human liberty."[173] Roger Gharbi tells of how during a *rafle* (round-up) on the rue François Miron, Gharbi's aunt Marthe sought protection from the family's Muslim friend Mustapha Galy, who owned a café on the rue de Jouy in the Marais in Paris. For twenty-four hours, Mustapha hid Marthe in his café, and she evaded capture.[174]

Also in Paris, the infamous *grande rafle* of July 16–17, 1942, appears to have provided the context for one of the most remarkable surviving testaments of Muslim efforts toward resistance and rescue. Found in Paris, a handwritten note in Kabyle, presumably crafted and disseminated among the capital's Algerian laborers, exclaimed: "Yesterday evening, the Jews of Paris were arrested—the elderly, women, and children. In exile like us, workers like us, these are our brothers. Their children are like our children. If you encounter one of their children, you must give him asylum and protection until the time that the misfortune—or the sorrow—passes. Oh, man of my country, your heart is generous."[175] The wording of the last three sentences echoed Islam's traditional emphasis on hospitality and the historic welcome afforded by many Islamic rulers to Jews as a fellow "people of the book." At the same time, *workers* alluded to bonds of class, *exile* to those of exclusion from the French nation and distance from homeland. These words sounded a call to equality, freedom, and solidarity. Like many other pronouncements of the Resistance, this note connected itself to themes of republican universalism.

Indeed, the Resistance offered many Jews and Muslims an opportunity to assert their Frenchness in a manner that both recalled the republican model and rejected the moment's racial politics. For the mostly Ashkenazic Jewish resisters, this meant reclaiming their vision of the France of 1789. For Muslims, it conversely meant paving the way for their postwar acceptance as fully French. Indeed, just as Muslims could embrace collaboration and accommodation for a range of ideological or self-interested reasons, many Muslims who fought in the Resistance or the liberation armies hoped that their alignment with the Allied cause would further their own efforts toward greater freedom and autonomy. Regardless, thousands of Jews and Muslims ultimately fought together in the name of French liberty from fascist tyranny, with consequences that would reach far beyond the war itself.

Jewish resistance followed multiple paths. Some individuals, like Charles de Gaulle's key early lieutenant, René Cassin, took action within the broader Resistance as French citizens first, following the tradition of republican Judaism. Others focused on saving Jews: several Jewish groups organized the hiding of Jewish children in non-Jewish homes, as well as escape routes to Spain and Switzerland. Finally, some mirrored the regime's racial laws and wore their ethnicity not as a stigma but a badge of honor—they chose political and military resistance in specifically Jewish groups. In the occupied zone, under the aegis of the Communist Party, Jewish workers, eventually including many noncommunists, organized themselves in a section of the party's Main d'oeuvre immigré (MOI). Others created specifically Jewish groups within the party's guerrilla force, the Franc-tireurs et partisans (FTP). Eventually Jewish communists regrouped in the Union des juifs pour la résistance et l'entraide. French Zionists, who achieved new unity during the war, played a key role in Jewish resistance, as well as in communal efforts to meet the basic needs of French Jewry. In the southern zone, Zionists formed a "Jewish army" in 1941, drawing largely from the Jewish scouting movement, and focusing initially on immigration to Palestine. By 1944, the group became the Organisation juive de combat, and integrated into the larger Resistance.[176]

Muslims, like the broader French population, also undertook multiple forms of resistance. The personnel and locale of the Grand Mosque of Paris helped to save a small number of Jews. In other quarters, political resistance emerged quickly. Following de Gaulle's June 1940 call from London, Othman Garouia, a Tunisian immigrant, organized a Resistance group around Grenoble.[177] Larger numbers of Muslims affiliated with communist and anticolonial resistance movements. In summer 1941, not long after Hitler's invasion of the Soviet Union, communist resisters launched propaganda efforts in Muslim neighborhoods of Paris and Marseille.[178] Earlier, groups of Kabyle Algerian Muslim workers formed among the ethnic sections of the communist MOI and within the party's guerrilla resistance force, the FTP.[179] In 1941, Mohamed Lakhdar, a young Algerian metalworker, became a major activist in the communists' network in Paris. Until his arrest in January 1943, Lakhdar worked to spread resistance propaganda through conversations in cafés, wall and street graffiti, and the distribution of pamphlets.[180]

Some Muslim resistance took the form of refusal, even at personal risk, of German invitations to collaborate.[181] Perhaps most famous, nationalist leader Messali Hadj repeatedly refused invitations and pressures to collaborate with Vichy and the Nazis. As a result, in March 1941, he found himself condemned to sixteen years of forced labor, was banned from visiting France for twenty years, and had all of his property confiscated.[182] When he learned of CARNA's collaboration with the Nazis, he denounced its leaders and expelled them from the PPA.[183] Despite previously pejorative comments about the French citizenship of Algeria's Jews following the 1934 Constantine riots, Messali did not celebrate the revocation of the Crémieux Decree. This event, he exclaimed, "cannot be considered as progress for the Algerian people—lowering the rights of Jews did not increase the rights of Muslims."[184]

Many of the key Muslim figures who articulated forms of resistance were based in Algeria. Over time, a series of factors—the shifting meaning of the Allied war effort toward a struggle explicitly for freedom; more precisely, the August 1941 Atlantic Charter, issued by Churchill and Roosevelt and signed by France, which included in its pronouncements the right to self-determination of all peoples; and the centrality of the North African front after the Allied landing in November 1942—created an atmosphere in which Muslim political leaders found the Allied cause attractive.[185] By autumn 1941, the Algerian longtime reformist Ferhat Abbas grew frustrated by Vichy's nonresponsiveness to his entreaties and became inspired by the ideals of the Atlantic Charter. Abbas subsequently played a leading role in moving many Algerian Muslims to oppose Vichy and, particularly after November 1942, to demand formally the right to set their own path as a people.

While he declined to use the word *independence,* Abbas renounced his earlier work for assimilation and spoke for the first time of an "Algerian nation." In time, he authored a document, the so-called *manifeste,* that brought together the key ideas of most major Algerian Muslim political currents. Presented to Algerian governor-general Marcel Peyrouton and sent to Charles de Gaulle in spring 1943, the manifeste made several core demands: abolition of colonization, application of the principle of self-determination, liberation of all political prisoners, and establishment of an Algerian constitution that guaranteed basic rights, equality, education, the recognition of Arabic as Algeria's official language, and the separation of church and state. Thus the document at once had nationalistic overtones and articulated its platform largely with the principles of the republic. Such a fusion had immediate resonance: by 1944, as many as 500,000 Algerians formally supported the manifeste by joining Abbas's new party, the Amis du manifeste et de la liberté.[186]

It was in this atmosphere of reformist demands and democratic language from far-flung Algerian Muslim quarters that Charles de Gaulle arrived in Algiers in May 1943. He soon formed the Comité français de la libération nationale (CFLN), successfully uniting all the French Resistance movements, including the communists. The CFLN immediately created a commission of Muslim reforms. In December, de Gaulle announced the opening of French citizenship to tens of thousands more Muslims. In March 1944, against the bitter opposition of French colonists, he signed a law that made all civil and military positions accessible to Muslims, expanded their representation in municipal assemblies from one-third to two-fifths, and ended the detested Code de l'indigénat. These reforms fell far short of many Algerian Muslim political leaders' demands. Yet they evinced the potential of the war and Muslim actions to open once more spaces for Muslim claims to full French citizenship.

Well before the publication of the manifeste, Abbas and other key Algerian Muslim leaders began to resist selectively. They refused, for instance, to join fascism's policies of racial exclusion. In January 1941, the newspaper coedited by Abbas, *L'Entente franco-musulmane,* exclaimed: "Islam, spiritual and global power, is essentially good and humane, fraternal, tolerant, and democratic. It rejects proselytizing, hatred, and racial prejudices. It has always been welcoming to the weak and to the oppressed. It is what has contributed to its greatness." Coming a few months after the revocation of the Crémieux Decree, this statement seemed to refer clearly, if indirectly, to solidarity with Algeria's Jews; it corresponded to previous articles in the *Entente*'s pages preaching the practice of traditional Islamic tolerance for Jews.[187] Abbas later described how he saw in the revocation of the Crémieux Decree not promise but danger. It revealed that "the word of France, even guaranteed by law, meant nothing."[188] He eventually told Vichy officials, "Your racism runs in all directions. Today against the Jews and always against the Arabs."[189]

Even as they maintained friendly relations with the new order or declined to join the wider Resistance, other figures sent signals of their solidarity with Jews. One key example was Sheikh Tayeb el-Oqbi, a preacher and writer and prominent advocate for the *ulama,* or Islamic reformists, and a key partner with Jews and Christians in interconfessional dialogue in the 1930s. While el-Oqbi sought to stay in the good graces of Vichy, he resisted pressure to give Islamic sanction to the regime's antisemitic racial laws.[190] Shortly after the revocation of the Crémieux Decree, he declared: "We know . . . that the future of Algeria is in its definitive fusion with France. Catholics, Israélites, Muslims, we are all its sons, we all have to work for its greatness."[191] Such words directly challenged Vichy's version of a new union sacrée that included Muslims but not Jews. At a religious gathering in May 1942, El-Oqbi framed the issue as a basic tenet of his faith, exclaiming, "Islam respects all men without distinction of beliefs."[192] Such explicit referencing of Islam as a humane, tolerant religion, and implicit support for tolerance of Jews harkened back to long-standing Islamic traditions about Jews and Christians as peoples of the book, worthy of a certain respect, and about there being "no compulsion in matters of faith."[193]

While it is not clear how far the messages of Abbas, El-Oqbi, and others traveled from Algeria to mainland France, their invocations of Islam constituted a significant counterweight to those of El-Maadi, Bendjamaa, Zouani, and other Muslim collaborators.[194] Those employing religion to promote collaboration treated Islam's foundational tenets as a basis to demonize and persecute Jews. By contrast, leaders like Abbas and El-Oqbi saw Islamic tradition as the source for a struggle for tolerance and freedom. In another crucial contrast, these Muslim opponents of Vichy's anti-Jewish policies not only did not link Islam to racial thought but explicitly decoupled the two.

For many, the growing unity around the Allied cause and the growing Muslim sentiment that that cause could become a larger fight for freedom and universal brotherhood made the last year of the war a moment of almost limitless optimism about the postwar order. In the metropole in June 1944, a group calling itself the Future of North Africa published and widely disseminated an underground journal, *El Hayet (Life).*[195] In its editorial, after denouncing Hitler and Vichy, the newspaper implored its readers by invoking the presumed linkage between military service and persistent aspirations to citizenship and equality: "North African brothers, let us unite and act so that tomorrow, in liberated France, we can look the French people in the eye and say, 'You know now what oppression is, together we all have thrown it off. . . . You want a free France, strong and happy, and so do we, we want North Africa to be thrown off from tyranny, slavery, and oppression.'"[196] Further articles directed their rhetorical fire at Muslim collaborationists and reclaimed the mantle of Islam for the cause of liberty. "[A] *misérable,*" declared one writer, "named Mohamed el Maadi, sellout to the Germans, is trying to enroll some of our people . . . in a band of criminals [the Milice]."[197] Another writer offered an appeal that, in opposition to collaborationists, made Islam a source of common spirituality for antifascists: "Men who you have always known to be devoted to the North African cause are now [on our side]. They call you to holy war against the enemy of Islam, against the enemy of humanity, Hitler and the Nazi regime."[198]

Growing numbers of ordinary Muslims saw the battle against fascism as connected to their own struggle for equality in France. Eventually, side by side on the barricades with other Resistance groups (including a Jewish unit), many Muslim members of the Resistance participated in the battles of Paris in August 1944.[199] Sizable numbers of Muslim resisters shot down Germans, took German prisoners, and captured German vehicles.[200] On a larger scale, from the North African campaign of 1943 through the German surrender in 1945, between 200,000 and 250,000 North African Muslims served in the French armies on the Allied side.[201] Many of these fought their way across France during the Liberation, at times alongside Jewish soldiers and resisters. The battles in Alsace, and particularly around Strasbourg, in the winter of 1944–1945, provide a striking example. On November 23, 1944, as the French liberated Strasbourg, more than 200 of their soldiers fell, among them at least 6 Jews and 4 Muslims.[202] Many more Jewish and Muslim soldiers perished in the liberation of the surrounding region. Today their tombs in Strasbourg's military cemetery and the nearby Jewish cemetery of Cronenbourg testify to this joint Jewish-Muslim sacrifice. They act as a touchstone of a growing local historical consciousness regarding the ecumenical character of the Liberation armies (Figure 3.6).[203]

Admittedly, fighting together hardly guaranteed regular interaction. During the battles for the Vosges in autumn 1944, Jewish resister Léon

Figure 3.6. Tombs in Strasbourg's military cemetery of Jews, Muslims, and Christians who died together in the November 1944 liberation of the city. (Photo by the author; © 2015 by Ethan B. Katz.)

Nisand's French army unit teamed with Moroccan goumiers and Algerian tirailleurs. Yet Nisand's only memory of contact comes from a single moment of combat that occurred on the road from Belfort to Chaux. Hundreds of colonial soldiers, following an ill-fated attempt to take the German position above, suddenly raced back down the mountain in panic toward Nisand and his comrades.[204] On the other hand, when the Twenty-Second North African Marching Battalion liberated Dambach-la-Ville in lower Alsace in December 1944, soldiers discovered that the Germans had ransacked the town's synagogue. Jews, Muslims, and Corsican Catholics from this multiconfessional unit set about cleaning the site.[205]

These stories suggest that the Resistance had a paradoxical impact on Jewish-Muslim relations, and in particular on the importance of transnational loyalties. On the one hand, Jewish and Muslim resisters sought to prove their French national bona fides. They largely submerged communist, Zionist, and North African nationalist demands in the common struggle for French liberation and the republican vision. On the other hand, Jews and Muslims often fought in their own distinctive units within the larger resistance effort. Their proud participation, and the war's stakes, galvanized transnational movements within each community and increased their sometimes complementary, sometimes competing demands. Above all, the war spurred both groups' hopes for the postwar period—hopes that often centered on North Africa and the Middle East.

Palestine in Paris: A New Cause for Conflict?

As the triumph of the Resistance and the Allied cause became imminent by mid-1944, these particularist currents of Jewish and Muslim resistance did not disappear in a sea of unanimity. Rather, in many instances, they multiplied. During the war's last year, an upsurge appeared in French expressions of antisemitism; many French people, such as the provisional owners of confiscated Jewish businesses, articulated the fear that Jews would be too visible, too demanding, and use their position to seek unfair advantage.[206] Such an environment contributed to the increase in ethnic solidarity among many Jews, often in the form of Zionism. Léon Meiss, head of the Central Consistory, explained in April 1945 how even those who previously felt integrated under current circumstances "tighten the bonds that link them to Jewish communities abroad." Isaïe Schwartz, then chief rabbi of France, added that after feeling abandoned by the authorities, French Jews "no longer feel the same reservations about Zionism as formerly; henceforth they feel a true and effective sympathy for this movement."[207]

During the same period, a significant number of Muslims expressed their own growing dissatisfaction with France. Many North African Muslims who had enlisted in the cause of the Liberation after the Allied landing in November 1942 shared a collective memory of World War I's broken promises and were determined not to feel duped again. By autumn 1944, the disappointingly moderate nature of reforms in Algeria, along with the displacement of many tirailleurs by "white troops" in the Liberation armies, combined with heavy losses and fatigue to undermine tirailleur morale. Many Muslims concluded that their only option for improving their lot was to join the nationalist forces.[208] In April 1944, meanwhile, a group of collaborationist North African nationalists organized a meeting, with 350 attendees about the need to unify Muslims against Jewish immigration to Palestine, the "Jewish peril."[209] In the early autumn of 1944, the widely esteemed Haj Amin al-Husseini, in a broadcast over Radio-Berlin, captured Muslim attention by warning against the impending prospect of a Jewish occupation of Palestine.[210]

The growing strength of both Zionism and anticolonialism in France, a combination of aspirations and frustrations toward the French state among Jews and Muslims, and the ongoing effects of Muslim collaborationist propaganda and activity made for a potent combination. Such simmering undercurrents burst into the open on October 29, 1944, in the first large-scale altercation between Jews and Muslims in France over the Palestinian question. That afternoon in Paris, an estimated 1,400 to 2,000 people gathered for a meeting of the Organisation sioniste de France. While most attendees were Jewish, 200 to 300 of them were Muslim.[211] Before the gathering began, several Muslims gained permission to speak.[212] As the meeting started, French Zionist leader Marc Jarblum spoke first, lamenting the horrors of deportation and highlighting the heroism of Jewish resisters. He also saluted the presence of Muslims at the meeting and assured them of the Zionists' desire not to dominate but to work with the Arabs of Palestine.[213]

Soon after, a Muslim named Zadoca took to the podium and began speaking from a prepared text in the name of the Arab youth of Paris. After mentioning the diverse crowd of Arabs at the meeting, including "soldiers of the glorious Allied armies," he declared that all the Arabs present "salute with fervor the liberation of France and the return of . . . democratic liberties." He then pivoted: "These freedoms . . . enable us also, North African, Egyptian, Syrian, Iraqi, and Palestinian Arabs to make our voices heard and to say our piece on a matter that is for us a question of life and death: the Palestinian question."[214] Zadoca then made a distinction that seemed ever more important at the moment, stating that he and his fellow Arabs had never been "anti-Jewish" and their outlook "was not dictated by any racial or religious consideration," but they were "and will always be, anti-Zionist." The speaker emphasized that since Jews "left" Palestine 2,000 years ago, Arabs (who, he noted, did not drive them out but rather arrived after the Jews) had become deeply attached to the soil. Signaling that he sought more to lobby the French state than to persuade the audience, he compared the Arab attachment to Palestine to the French sentiment in relation to its own long-disputed territory, Alsace-Lorraine.

Then the real trouble began. Zadoca spoke next of how "bizarre" it was to see that the Jews, having just suffered deportation and forced dispossession, were preparing to become persecutors "determined to deport and dispossess on a grand scale an innocent and peaceful people." He also insisted that "Zionist atrocities in Palestine" should provoke the same universal reaction of horror as had those of the Nazis in Europe. At this point, widespread outcry erupted from the audience. Yet Zadoca continued. Ignoring Jarblum's instructions, first to tame his remarks and then to leave the stage promptly, he reminded the audience of the thousands of Arabs fighting for the Allies and declared, "The French Empire includes millions of Arabs who consider Palestine as the most beautiful and holy part of our Fatherland and are ready to defend it against any imperialist attempt no matter where it comes from."

A Zionist orator sought to respond to Zadoca but quickly found himself drowned out by the repeated Muslim chanting of "Palestine to the Arabs!" and "Palestine to the Muslims!"[215] As the atmosphere briefly calmed, French Zionist leader Joseph Fisher confronted the protesters: "For the first time since the Liberation, such a demonstration takes place. It is an outrage against the harmony that currently reigns in France. Certain leaders of ours are in Jerusalem, but yours, the Mufti, is in Berlin, which explains everything." Muslims continued to shout their slogans. Zionist speakers could not be heard, and Jews instead sang the Zionist anthem "Hatikvah."[216] French police had to disband the meeting.[217]

Recounting the events, France's Zionist organ *La Terre retrouvée* underscored the extreme personal difficulties that Jewish attendees faced; many still wondered about the fate of family and friends who had been deported or murdered in the Shoah. As a stark contrast, the writer contended that certain Muslim protesters were connected to the Comité musulman nord-africaine.[218] Implying further disparities between the two groups, the newspaper's coverage recounted the conciliatory efforts of the meeting's Zionist leaders, asserted that most Muslims present "did not even understand French," and classified the protesters as part of the same treacherous fifth column that had collaborated with the Germans and continued to sabotage French interests.[219] Likewise, internal Zionist correspondence referred to Zadoca as a "hooligan," and reported that certain protesters came from the ranks of antisemitic fascist groups.[220] Meanwhile, the day after the meeting, K. Hakkim, a representative of the Arab Youth of Paris, sent a copy of Zadoc's speech, which had also been printed as a flyer, to the minister of foreign affairs. Expressing his belief that France would "not remain indifferent to the unanimous aspirations of the Arab world," Hakkim asked the foreign minister to take seriously the fact that "our opposition to Zionism is not dictated by any racist or religious doctrine, but by our attachment to our country and to the integrity of our territories."[221]

The events of October 29, 1944, and their subsequent, competing renderings, reflected fundamental shifts over the preceding four years: the Occupation, France's internal struggles, and the Shoah dramatically reshaped Jewish-Muslim relations in France. The new racial order imposed by the Nazis and Vichy, along with the individual choices of many Muslims, largely obliterated the positive, shared components of Jews' and Muslims' colonial, religious, and transnational positions—largely, but not entirely. Cordial relations continued or were reinvented in a limited number of sociocultural spaces like neighborhoods, cafés, and grocery stores. The period's rigid racial categories, while generally narrowing possible terms of interaction and eliminating many fluidities, paradoxically also facilitated openings, whereby a select number of North African and Levantine Jews sought to pass as Muslims. Over time, the war's ideological stakes created opportunities for Jewish-Muslim solidarity in defense of the republican ideal.

Ultimately, however, as seen in the Zionist meeting of October 29, the war had such disparate meanings for many members of the two groups that it was as if Jews and Muslims had lived the period in parallel worlds. Shocked by France's betrayal, Jews had struggled daily to evade capture and deportation; as the war drew to a close, they had to reassess their politics and their relationship to France. The tensions of that reassessment were evident in the dissonance between the growing public confidence of French Zionism and the way that, in recounting the meeting, France's Zionists defined themselves insistently as loyal French citizens in contrast to their Muslim counterparts. Tying colonialist assumptions to an emerging Holocaust consciousness, Jewish statements during and after the meeting depicted a struggle between French Jews, as citizens, survivors and resisters, and unruly Muslim colonial subjects, branded here as Nazi collaborators.

As they contemplated their own future in France, Muslims also negotiated shifting relationships and loyalties. While some shared the antisemitic attitudes prevalent around them, Muslim political choices, including opposition to Zionism, emerged from a much wider set of factors. In emphasizing the service of Muslim soldiers, Zadoca's speech sought to establish common values and sacrifice with the rest of the French population. The speech and pamphlet's chosen themes, as well as the decision to send it immediately to the foreign ministry, indicated that the Muslim leaders appealed above all to France as an empire and Great Power. Yet the text also repeatedly framed the group as "Arabs" under French rule whose "fatherland" included Palestine but not necessarily Paris, and concluded by overtly threatening anti-imperial resistance.

Such were the contradictions of the war experience for many Muslims. Faced with the choice of competing political forces of collaboration, accommodation, and resistance, individual Muslims, more vulnerable than many others in France, made decisions with their civil, economic, and political rights in mind, as well as their sense of allegiance and ethics. With the veneer of security ripped off the French empire by the defeat of 1940, Muslims suddenly saw new political possibilities on the horizon. All the while, they wondered if political leaders' promises of the moment would prove more lasting than those of the previous war. In a mirror of Jewish assumptions, the rhetoric of October 29 signaled that for many Muslims in France, the war's propaganda had helped to cement a connection between Jewish power and Muslim colonial suffering in North Africa and Palestine.

Indeed, in a political move that highlighted the stark differences in the war's significance for the two groups, Zadoca made the claim—at a moment when the Nazi regime still continued its destruction of European Jewry and as he stood before numerous Holocaust survivors and their families—that Jews were preparing to transform themselves rapidly into perpetrators of their own genocidal campaign. The victims would become the victors, and Muslims would again suffer as a result.

Exemplifying further the divergent meanings of the period were the events of May 8, 1945. French citizens celebrated the Allied victory in the streets of Paris. Far away in the streets of Sétif, Algeria, French police responded to unrest with a repression that soon led to the massacre of thousands of Muslims. These events helped to guarantee that the contrasts of Jewish and Muslim experience during World War II would become conflicts in the postwar period. Those conflicts, at times violent, would concern not only the future of France, North Africa, and the Middle East; they also became struggles over how to remember and understand the events of World War II.

4

EXPANDING THE REPUBLIC
OR ENDING THE EMPIRE?

In September 1954, the fictional story "David and Ali" appeared in the Jewish communal organ of Alsace, the *Bulletin de nos communautés*. The tale recounted the friendship of a Jew, David, and a Muslim, Ali.[1] Descended from Polish grandparents and born in Paris, David had a twin brother, also named David. Their father, a World War I veteran, worked as a hatmaker, furrier, and tailor. Ali, from a traditional Muslim family, was also Parisian by birth. His father came to France as a tirailleur during the war and then settled in Paris. Each morning, young Ali brought peanuts and sunflower seeds to sell in the Marais, where he had Jewish clients.

At the start of World War II, serving in the same garrison in the East near the Maginot Line, the two Davids and Ali bonded as they discovered their common experiences in the streets of Paris and its Jewish quarter. When David's brother was killed, he grew closer to Ali. Here the author wrote that "Ali bec[ame] for the remaining David . . . another brother . . . having the same heart," and cited this as evidence that racial conflicts were in no way inevitable. After the fall of France, David and Ali went their separate ways. Eventually David became a Zionist resister and donned the yellow star with pride. Still, at his first chance, he joined the French troops landing on the coasts of Provence. Ali was interned in a camp in Spain, where he became friends with a Hungarian Jew, Sigismond. The two escaped and made their way through the Pyrenees to join France's African Army. They fought side by side until Sigismond was mortally wounded. As he lay near death, explained the author, "It was Ali, the Arab," who "closed the eyes of Sigismond, the Jew!" This moment evoked the episode from World War I when Rabbi Abraham Bloch had been struck with a mortal wound while placing a crucifix on a dying

155

Christian soldier and appeared to reflect the author's hopes for a new kind of "sacred union."[2] After the war, David migrated to Palestine. Years later, he encountered Ali in an emotional reunion. The two reminisced about childhood and the war. In the story's closing lines, the author used the characters and their names as a metaphor for the hope of Jewish-Arab and Judeo-Islamic rapprochement in Israel.

This story reflected both possibilities and challenges of the postwar moment. The two men's divergent backgrounds emblematized the large-scale Eastern European and colonial migrations between the wars; their common experiences among the artisans and workers of the Marais revealed how neighborhood Jewish-Muslim interactions often relied as much on status and class as on Mediterranean sensibilities. By carrying this story, Alsace's Jewish weekly demonstrated the growing post-1945 interest in Jewish-Muslim relations in the region. The bonds between David and Ali forged in the common experiences of antifascist Resistance and wartime persecution were a microcosm for the enduring legacies of the Occupation period in postwar French life.

Perhaps the most important changes underway were occurring in the wider Mediterranean. The author signaled the impact of the newly created Jewish state in Palestine. Aspirations for entente between Jews and Muslims everywhere took on new significance in light of the 1947–1948 War, Israel's embattled existence, and the Palestinian refugee crisis. David and Ali's paths of identity and relations suggested that opposed ethnoreligious allegiances linked to the Israeli-Arab conflict need not define Jewish-Muslim relations broadly. Yet could this hope transcend the gathering storm? Following the establishment of Israel, large numbers of the 750,000 Jews who then lived in the Middle East and North Africa had begun a process of mass migration to Israel or the West; within decades, their former communities would be largely empty. A crucial development in this upheaval was decolonization in French North Africa; by this time, the process was well underway in Morocco and Tunisia and approaching its violent crescendo in the French-Algerian War, which would begin on November 1, 1954.

The so-called events in Algeria from 1954 to 1962 would redefine the terms of Jewish-Muslim relations in France. To an unprecedented degree, the French-Algerian War tested whether the French republic constituted a bridge or barrier between Jews and Muslims. In Algeria and the metropole, most leading wartime actors believed there were only two choices available for Muslims and Jews. On one side stood a vision of France as a great empire, civilizing force, and bulwark of the Christian West that ruled by a combination of integration and coercion over millions of citizens and subjects of diverse backgrounds.[3] On the other side stood rejection of such a vision, in favor of anticolonialism and Algerian self-determination. The expositors of both outlooks contended that all interested parties had to choose one position or the other, with no viable options in between. Throughout the war, the French government, the advocates of Algérie française who eventually formed the Organisation de l'armée secrète (OAS), the Algerian Muslim rebels of the Front de libération nationale (FLN), and much of the Jewish communal leadership of France and Algeria embraced this Manichaean reading of political choices.

These dichotomies have too often overwhelmed historical narratives of the French-Algerian War and Jews and Muslims therein. Historians have typically assumed a sharply divided outcome—between France and Algeria, between Jews and Muslims, and between those supporting the republic and anticolonial nationalists, respectively—and projected it backward in a rigid manner. The options articulated throughout the war were certainly potent and influential, yet transforming them into dichotomous historical frameworks implies a set of fixed entities, ideologies, and actions when in reality the period witnessed constant shifts. Moreover, an emphasis on frozen divisions has typically obscured important, competing strands in the history of Jews, Muslims, and their relations as they unfolded during the war.[4] Such tautologies may relate to fairly rigid boundaries within most scholarship: works on Jews during the French-Algerian War rarely treat Muslims in depth and vice versa; developments in mainland France and Algeria generally are not studied together.[5]

By considering both Muslims and Jews at the elite and the grassroots level in France and Algeria, we can glimpse a remarkably multidirectional and uncertain lived experience for many ordinary people throughout much of the war. We can also begin to discern the complex interplay between such everyday complexity and the Manichaean logics of so many of the conflict's leading groups and actors. The war also looks different when we remind ourselves that its outcome was neither inevitable nor known at the time. Thus we concentrate here specifically on the period from the November 1954 uprising to autumn 1960, an era during which many questions regarding Algeria's future remained unresolved.

For the first six years of the conflict in Algeria, many developments on the ground could not be reduced to the black-and-white choices so prevalent in contemporary political rhetoric. Legally, the French state introduced possibilities for dual identities for Algerian Muslims, offering a new conception of the relationship between the republic and ethnicity.[6] Such openings and fluctuations occurred not only at the state level but also through the actions of grassroots activists. Muslims and Jews increasingly found ways to offer new, multifaceted visions of what it meant to be French. For Muslims, this took the form of an uprising that, intentionally or not, catalyzed a new hybrid category of French citizens—French Muslims of Algeria (FMAs)—and, for many, of a corresponding new assertiveness in their formal demands to the French state. With their own new assertiveness, numerous Jews challenged official assumptions of public secularism, often by foregrounding Jewishness or Judaism as fundamental to their political choices. The FLN itself debated possibilities for a multiethnic, multiconfessional Algerian republic.

Thus, between the war's outbreak in 1954 and autumn 1960, Jews and Muslims constantly renegotiated their triangular relationship with one another and the republic. Moreover, Jewish and Muslim choices were critical to a series of developments that linked France in new ways with the wider Mediterranean. The two groups drew not only on the language of rights and French universalism. They also revealed the impact of other factors on their allegiances and identities: ongoing sociocultural relations among diverse migrants from North Africa; competing memories of the Occupation and the history of colonial Algeria; and the founding of the state of Israel and the emergence of Nasserism, both of which altered the complexion of the wider Middle East. Fluid possibilities for identification and status, though, remained in constant tension with the either-or logic of official French republicanism, mainstream Algerian nationalism, and much of official Jewish communal rhetoric. This contradiction played out daily for Jews and Muslims in the myriad ways the two groups continued to interact: in disagreements and solidarities spelled out in organizational and political meetings and publications, in violent altercations, and in the ongoing coexistence of neighborhoods and cafés.

Postwar Evolutions in Jewish and Muslim Life

The nine years between the end of World War II and the outbreak of the Algerian revolution witnessed critical changes in French society, and for the country's Jewish and Muslim populations. In 1947, France's economy began a period of sustained growth that would last for almost thirty years; this economic boom occurred in the context of dramatic urbanization, the growth of mass consumerism, cultural renaissance, and de-colonization. In the postwar years, the country witnessed the beginnings of the waning of its imperial might with the stunning defeat at Dien Bien Phu in 1954 and the loss of French Indochina. France's North African protectorates, Morocco and Tunisia, both moved rapidly toward autonomy and then achieved independence in 1956. With the October 1946 Constitution of the Fourth Republic, the country finally granted most French women the vote and affirmed citizenship for all Algerian Muslims.

Algerian Muslims, however, remained on decidedly unequal footing. Unlike women in the metropole and France's other overseas territories, Muslim women in Algeria did not gain the right to vote. Algerian Muslim men continued to vote in a separate electoral college, which was the same size as that of the colonists, and therefore much smaller than the native Muslim proportion of the Algerian population. Algeria became part of a "French union," the new term for the country's colonial possessions that implied a more federalist system. In 1947, pressure from the Algerian colons succeeded in bringing about a new distinction between Algeria and metropole that gave a certain number of metropolitan-residing Muslims greater rights than their Algerian coreligionists. The former gained fully equal voting rights in the mainland. All Algerian Muslims had new freedom of circulation between their native territory and metropolitan France. Nonetheless, in three critical areas—access to public administration posts, ability to obtain social protection services from the government, and required forms of official identification—French Muslims from Algeria, increasingly called FMAs, faced ongoing inequalities. Furthermore, their new legal status, by challenging traditional colonial hierarchies, provoked frequent anti-Muslim violence by both French police on the mainland and colonists in Algeria.[7]

And yet due to Algerian Muslims' improved position and rights and France's growing postwar economic labor needs, Algerian migration to France soared.[8] From 1947 to 1953 the Algerian Muslim presence in the Hexagon increased by a net total of 185,000.[9] Kabyles no longer made up the decisive majority; increasing numbers of workers hailed from the departments of Oran and Constantine and from the Algerian south. Arab Muslims thus became a growing proportion of the Algerian presence in France.[10] The new population included an increasing number of Muslim families.[11] Immigration destinations also diversified. The sizable interwar Muslim presence in Paris, Marseille, and Lyon continued to grow. Elsewhere, booming industry in both the Lille-Roubaix-Tourcoing cluster in the far north and in the Moselle in the East brought substantial increases in Muslim population.[12]

During the same period Algerian nationalism gathered renewed strength. The movement's momentum resulted from the dashed hopes for more substantial post–World War II colonial status reform; the potent memory of the Sétif massacres of May 8, 1945; the changing face of the Middle East; and the growing presence of anticolonialism throughout much of Africa and Asia. In 1946, Messali Hadj's Algerian nationalist party changed its name to the Mouvement pour le triomphe des libertés démocratiques (MTLD). By the late 1940s, major fissures within the party led to a series of crises around various issues: the party's increasingly Arab-Islamic orientation versus a more multiethnic makeup, its relationship to Marxism, its leadership structure, and its radicalism and the possibility of armed resistance.[13] Nonetheless, by 1950 the MTLD had managed to co-opt much of the religious message of the ulama and had no real rival among France's Algerian immigrants.[14]

For French Jews, the experiences of the Occupation and the Shoah—and the founding of the state of Israel—had begun to shift the contours of outward identification. Between 1940 and 1945 one-fourth of France's prewar Jewish population had been deported.[15] Nonetheless, following the war, many of the country's remaining and newly arrived Jews (about 250,000 total in 1949) reiterated their devotion to the republic and its ideals. Yet a growing number also undertook their political engagements on increasingly Jewish terms. Within four years after the war's end most Jewish cultural, political, and social organizations joined forces to form the Fonds social juif unifié (FSJU), a united fundraising apparatus influenced by similar American Jewish models. In its emphasis on "attachment to Judaism in whatever form," the FSJU continued the interwar movement away from religion as the centerpiece of Jewish identification in France. At the same time, it reflected a new unity, born of the horrors of the Shoah, among competing interests within organized French Jewry.[16]

These developments linked with another shift begun in the interwar period and accelerated by the war: the broader acceptance of Zionism by much of the French Jewish establishment. World War II had necessitated greater self-reliance in the French Jewish community. French Zionism therefore achieved the organizational unity that had long eluded it and partnered with communal organizations to meet the basic needs of French Jews. Many Zionists took a leading role in the Jewish resistance and helped found the Conseil représentatif des israélites de France (CRIF) in 1944. By conceiving of itself as the representative political body of all French Jewish organizations, CRIF played a key role in altering the guiding principles of Franco-Judaism.[17] Moreover, in its opening charter, the organization included all of the Zionists' major demands regarding Palestine.[18] Even leading representatives of the two bastions of republican Judaism, the Central Consistory and the Alliance israélite universelle (AIU), backed the cause of a Jewish national home. This new support offered Zionism unprecedented legitimacy among French Jews.[19]

Such support broadened with the creation of the state of Israel. Shortly after the Jewish state's founding, an official of the American Joint Distribution Committee reported that concern with Israel was "the strongest single cohesive force" in the French Jewish community. By the early to mid-1950s the French Jewish press was saturated with coverage of life in Israel, its relations with its neighbors, and Franco-Israeli connections. Numerous Jewish charitable groups donated a substantial portion of their annual funds to Israel. Between 1948 and 1955, 25,000 French Jews took the more decisive step of emigrating to Israel.[20]

Jewish demographics in France were also undergoing changes. Soon after the Liberation, North African Jewish migration surged as many sought greater economic opportunity in France. From 1947 to 1949, in the context of the First Arab-Israeli War, Jewish departures increased substantially, particularly from Morocco, for Israel, France, and North America. Beginning in 1953, growing political instability across the Maghreb, fear about the Jewish future in Morocco and Tunisia, and Jewish economic decline led to dramatic spikes in migration.[21] From 1950 to 1959, 75,000 Jews from the Maghreb settled in France, constituting the majority of a total of 108,000 Jewish immigrants during this period.[22]

Despite the growth of France's Jewish and Muslim populations from "Arab lands" and the coincident events in Israel/Palestine, the Middle East conflict seldom directly affected relations between the two groups. French Jewish engagement during the 1947–1948 war rarely touched on the question of Muslims in France or its colonies. Particularly in Paris, Algerian nationalist propagandists gave significant attention to the war but largely within the rubric of anticolonial politics. Their approach, which elicited popular support for the Arab cause from certain quarters, had little to say about Jews outside Palestine. The nationalists accused France and Britain of breaking their promises to the Arabs after each of the world wars, inventing Zionism, and creating a false Jewish home-land in Palestine. MTLD statements claimed that the battle for Palestine was part of a larger struggle for the independence of the Arab world from Western domination and called on all North Africans to support the Arab side.[23]

In particular instances where the First Arab-Israeli War defined a space shared by Jews and Muslims, tensions arose. This occurred, for example, in the port of Marseille when Muslim dockworkers protested France's pro-Israel stance and the permitting of large numbers of Israel-bound per-sons and arms to pass through the port. Muslim dockworkers refused to load or threatened to sabotage suspicious vessels, and in at least one in-stance in late May 1948, they even briefly set fire to a French ship carrying Jews and Jewish supplies to Haifa. In early June, certain Muslims claimed that in a Marseille movie theater, a newsreel's depictions of the Arab-Israeli war had been heavily biased toward the Israeli side; according to the Muslims in attendance, the "foreign" Jews—who, they insisted, had little right to insult French Muslims—had cheered audibly for the Israelis.[24] Yet these episodes were rare. As had often been the case previ-ously, Jewish-Muslim relations in France became infused with the mean-ings and tensions of the Middle East only if a local setting was directly subject to the conflict. When this occurred, such a development was inex-tricably linked to each group's relationship to the French state. Jewish-Muslim interactions and mutual perceptions, that is, remained situational and triangular.

New Challenges, New Choices

More than the 1948 war, a conflict closer to home would define a new phase in relations between Jews and Muslims. From 1954 to 1962, the French-Algerian War would claim the lives of over 140,000 Algerian na-tionalist fighters and more than 27,000 French soldiers and would wreak untold havoc on the civilian populations of both the mainland and Algeria.[25] The French-Algerian war brought to the fore the shifting, mul-tifaceted public allegiances of Jews and Muslims in the postwar era. One can trace four stages in interactions between Jews and Muslims during the war. In the first stage, from November 1954 to summer 1956, Jews and Muslims hardly engaged one another politically over the Algerian question. Likewise, political divisions did not define the two groups' so-ciocultural interactions in metropolitan France. In summer and autumn

1956, however, Jewish-Muslim political relations moved to the fore. This initially took the form of heavy recruitment of Jews by the leading independence movement, the Front de libération nationale (FLN), occasioning responses of nationalist solidarity from certain Jewish individuals and groups. The same period witnessed numerous FLN attacks on Jews and Jewish-owned institutions. Over the next two years, a series of developments heightened the war's impact on the wider French and Algerian populations: military conscription became far more widespread, the political situation in both the metropole and Algeria deteriorated, revelations of widespread torture by the military scandalized the French public, and the Fourth Republic collapsed. Nonetheless, much of Algerian Jewry still sought to remain above the fray, emphasizing both attachments to France and fraternal relations with Muslims. In the third phase, from 1958 to 1960, as Charles de Gaulle "returned" and the Fifth Republic was established, an atmosphere of new possibility briefly prevailed. For a time, it appeared that de Gaulle might bring about what he termed a "peace of the brave," an arrangement through which Algeria could remain French but become autonomous. Definitions of French identity, for both Muslims and Jews, became even more malleable. Yet from late 1960 to 1962, FLN attacks on Jews increased, and independence became patently inevitable. In Algeria during this time, Jewish support for the OAS dramatically grew; in the metropole, the brutality of the OAS prompted many Jews and others to condemn the organization as reminiscent of the Nazis. The openings of the war's first six years gave way to a torturous moment of choice for Jews, for Muslims, and for the future of Algeria and France.

Jews and Muslims far from the Conflict

At the outbreak of the Algerian revolution on November 1, 1954, approximately 8 million Muslims, 135,000 Jews, and 1.1 million Christians lived in Algeria.[26] For the war's first twenty months, most Jews, and even many Muslims in Algeria and the metropole, commented little on what the French press and authorities dubbed "the events." The summer of 1955 witnessed two notable episodes of nationalist violence against Jews: an attack on the rabbi of Batna in July and the murder in August of a well-known Jewish family of Constantine.[27] Still, in December 1955, at a meeting of the executive council of the Comité juif algérien d'etudes sociales (CJAES), the leading representative body of Algerian Jewry, participants referred to the conflict quickly as "the present difficulties."[28]

Likewise, for the first few years of the war, Jews in the metropole, like much of the wider French population, often regarded the Algerian conflict with both geographical and psychological distance.[29]

Yet well before the outbreak of the revolt, metropolitan police, particularly in Paris, had homed in relentlessly on Algerian Muslims, often criminalizing them as a group.[30] The postwar acquisition of full citizenship by Algerian Muslims on the mainland created tremendous anxiety among police throughout the decolonization period. Though "protectees" without citizenship within the "French union" and thus technically foreigners, even the small minority of Muslims from Morocco and Tunisia now had a French identity card that gave them certain visitation rights. After 1950 they did not need a work contract to be authorized to cross to France. Parisian police sought repeatedly to reestablish stricter control using new instruments of order and hierarchy; proposals for Algerian Muslims ranged from required identity cards to mandatory migration authorizations. In essence, police wished to sharpen once more the suddenly fuzzier boundaries between colonizer and colonized.[31]

Only in this context can we appreciate many of the reports from this time produced by the Paris Prefecture of Police. In 1955, Paris remained the most important center of Jewish and Muslim life and interaction in France. The city and its suburbs absorbed a significant portion of the ongoing Jewish migration from North Africa and would reach an estimated Jewish population of 175,000 by 1957.[32] By 1958, meanwhile, about 126,000 of the approximately 350,000 North African Muslims in France lived in Paris and its surroundings, the majority in the banlieues, or outskirts.[33] One police report of 1955 claimed that the city's Muslims always gathered after work in cafés, "most particularly those . . . establishments which are directed or managed by coreligionists." Such behavior, insisted the authors, "contribute[s] to making the metropolitans consider them as beings apart, living on the margins of the ways and customs commonly accepted in the Paris region."[34] The narrative of these reports treats North African Muslims as inherently segregated—due to both their own clannishness and non-Muslims' aversion to living near them—and prone to bouts of violence and criminality. According to such logic, the possibility of assimilation and integration remained distant and only rarely attained.

Furthermore, these accounts repeatedly use phrases like "North Africans and their coreligionists" to portray "North African" as synonymous with "Muslim." The authors generally ignore the crucial Jewish presence in several "North African" neighborhoods. The few documents on "North Africans" in Paris that do mention Jews obscure more than they reveal. A 1952 report, for instance, speaks of the "hostility of Muslims toward israélites," but provides no evidence.[35] Too often historians have taken aspects of these reports at face value, in particular describing the life of Muslim immigrants of this period as extremely insular and ignoring their relations with Jews.[36]

Indeed, each of these narratives found in the archives—of Muslim isolation and violence, Jewish absence, and inevitable conflict—neglected key components of Muslim life and Jewish-Muslim relations in Paris. Such blind spots resulted in significant part from the desperate yet ill-equipped police effort to combat Muslims' new legal status by circumscribing their movements and contacts among the wider French population. In 1951, for example, the Ministry of the Interior, concerned about North African nationalism in Parisian cafés, requested from the prefect of police a report on all eating and drinking establishments in the area owned or operated "by Muslims native to North Africa."[37] When one examines the lists compiled and takes into account conventions for Jewish and Muslim names, oral histories, and other evidence, it becomes clear that many cafés described as "run by Muslims originally from North Africa" were in fact owned or operated by North African Jews. In addition, reports describe the customers at a number of Jewish-frequented cafés simply as "North African." Such documents show a colonial administration determined to impose fixed labels and exclusions on the fluidities of changing legal realities and everyday relations.[38]

Furthermore, these reports illuminate the growth of Jewish-Muslim sociocultural interactions. By the mid-1950s, the types of shared spaces of North African culture forged during the interwar period had reemerged in Paris on a wider scale. In 1952, according to the reports' admittedly inexact population estimates, the majority of Paris's 40,000 or so Muslims lived in the city's outer arrondissements, and therefore not in close proximity to Jews.[39] But among the more central arrondissements where Muslims resided (the 1st through 10th), the 4th was the second most popular, with 1,300 to 1,600 Muslim residents. More than 70 percent of them lived in the Saint-Gervais or the lower Marais. Often inhabiting cramped quarters in one of the areas' many "hôtels" (subsidized apartments), Jews and Muslims accounted for over 10 percent of the quarter's 22,000 residents.[40] The 4th had twenty-four "North African" cafés, restaurants and bars, nineteen of them located in the Saint-Gervais. Of the latter number, Jews owned or operated at least nine, Muslims no fewer than eight.[41]

In one of these cafés, the Chez Orsay on the rue François Miron, Maurice Jaïs had returned to work soon after the end of World War II. Not far away was his Muslim acquaintance Mustapha Galy, with his café on the rue de Jouy. Louise Jaïs recalls this period through nostalgic eyes but with telling detail: once again, "Arabs came to the café, to take an *apéritif* . . . there was Mustapha, there was Méziane, there was 'Robert l'Arabe' as we called him." She explains, "We [and these Arabs] visited each other often just the same [as before]." Jewish-Muslim relations in the Marais continued to touch on sacred aspects of each other's traditions. On several occasions, recounted Jaïs, "when [we knew or worked with] an Arab and he died . . . the Jews made the collection . . . for his interment in the Arab cemetery." Until his death in 1966, Maurice Jaïs's café's clientele remained in significant part Muslim.[42]

Under challenging circumstances, the Gharbi family resumed operation of the Petit marseillais. The father, René, had died in 1943. When his son Roger returned to Paris after the Liberation, he found the café "Aryanized" by Vichy, emptied of his family's property. Still, he reopened it quickly. By the early 1950s Roger gave management over to Maxim Hayotte, a Moroccan Jew. Under Hayotte the café retained much of its former character, including evenings of Judeo-Arabic music. Yet Roger and his cousin Félix Amanou recall that the ambiance of the prewar years could not be recreated.[43] Such memories likely reflect how the neighborhood's innocence saw itself shattered by the Shoah; many Jewish inhabitants never returned.

Even so, the cousins remember ongoing manifestations of Jewish-Muslim entente and even intimacy. Shortly after returning to Paris, Roger paid a call to Mustapha Galy.[44] Gharbi thanked him for protecting Gharbi's aunt during a roundup of Jews. "[Mustapha]," he recalls, "told me the story of how he had saved her, and otherwise, she would have been arrested." Around the time of the Liberation, Elie Tordjemann, another Algerian Jew, arrived to open a café at 19 rue François Miron. Tordjemann soon met a Muslim woman named Julia who, with her sister Louise, had long been friendly with the Gharbis. Elie and Julia fell in love, Julia converted to Judaism, and the two married in the quartier. They remained into the 1960s, when they emigrated to Israel (Figure 4.1).[45]

On an intersecting street, the rue du Pont Louis-Philippe, Félix Amanou's father, Maurice, opened a food market in 1947 that featured

Figure 4.1. Photograph of Julia Tordjemann (far left), Roger Gharbi (second from left), and other members of the extended Gharbi family seated in a café in the Marais, 1950s. (Courtesy of Roger Gharbi.)

"colonial" products like olive oil, tea, dates, and alcohol. For the next nineteen years the store would draw a largely North African Muslim clientele. Amanou's work kept him traveling, but he came to Paris each month. He always visited the restaurant of his best friend, Simon Sabba—son of Elie Sabba who had owned a café in the Marais in the 1930s—on the rue des Rosiers. This was a Franco-Oriental restaurant with a mixed clientele of Catholics, Jews, and Muslims. The medium-sized establishment, with about fifteen tables, served French and Tunisian dishes and included a bar. Occasionally the restaurant hosted Arabic music concerts; an orchestra of lute, mandolin, *kanoun* (North African sitar), and tambourine entertained guests late into the evening.[46]

In fact, in the years following World War II Jewish-Muslim musical collaboration grew within and beyond the Marais, with Paris at the heart of a buzzing set of trans-Mediterranean networks. During this period, the Librairie du Progrès, a Jewish-owned bookshop on the rue des Rosiers in the Marais, which had long sold Yiddish literature and music, became a major vendor of Arabic music and a regular stop for North African

Jewish musicians like Luc Cherki, Albert Rouimi (better known as "Blond-Blond"), Raymond Leyris ("Sheikh Raymond"), and the young starlet Line Monty. Not far away Salim Hallali lived for a time on the rue François Miron, and Samy El Maghribi, a Moroccan Jewish cantor and virtuoso of Andalusian music, had a record shop on the rue des Ecouffes. In the Faubourg-Montmartre in the 9th arrondissement, Roger Gharbi was one of many Jews running cafés frequented by Jews, Muslims, and Christians. Among these was the *Soleil d'Alger,* where a twenty-two-year-old Algerian Jewish prodigy, Lili Boniche, the "crooner of the Kasbah," arrived in 1946 or 1947 to become a star.[47] But it was in Paris's Latin Quarter around the rue de la Huchette that a host of Oriental cabarets, including "El Djazaïr" once more, and "Le Kasbah," "Tam-Tam," and "Nuits de Liban," created a dynamic Arabic music scene with Jewish-Muslim cooperation at its heart. It was a moment of overflowing creative interchange, as Algerian Muslim stars Ahmed Wahby, Slimane Azem, and Cheikh El Hasnaoui relocated to Paris, and collaborations included leading musicians from Egypt and Lebanon. When Salim Hallali moved to Casablanca to open his own cabaret, the Coq d'Or, where he performed with an orchestra of Jewish and Muslim musicians, it quickly became a legendary regional draw. Cherki, Monty, and Blond-Blond would leave the rue de la Huchette and cross the sea to perform there, and Arabic music greats Umm Kulthum and Mohamed Abdel Wahab came from Egypt just to watch. Listeners across France and the Maghreb could also hear many of these musicians on Radio Alger and Radio Tunis.[48]

If shared Jewish-Muslim musical spaces reached into many quarters of Paris, so too did daily coexistence. One area of increasing contact was Belleville, a working-class neighborhood situated along narrow, often dilapidated streets running mostly in the northwest corner of the 20th arrondissement and bleeding into the 11th to the east and the 19th to the north. A popular quarter for Eastern European Jews during the interwar period, Belleville by 1955 had begun to transform into a Tunisian and, to a lesser extent, Algerian quarter. In January 1956, a Jewish journalist was surprised to discover how, along the rue Louis Bonnet, the rue Julien-Lacroix, and the rue de la Présentation, foods like couscous, *makrouds* (Tunisian honey cakes), and *boukha* (Tunisian fig alcohol) increasingly mingled with the older presence of gefilte fish and other Ashkenazic Jewish standards. Several North African–style Jewish grocers and restaurants already appeared.[49] About 2,000 mostly working-class Muslim laborers from Algeria had also recently settled in the neighborhood. These Muslims lived along some common and many adjoining streets to those of Jews; many opened North African cafés and restaurants.[50]

From 1954 to 1956, sociocultural relations in these neighborhoods unfolded at a distance from the fierce contest for sovereignty over Algeria. At the same time, the lack of incident or political influence recorded by police in the "North African" establishments of these quarters suggested that most clients, whatever their ethnoreligious background, roughly accepted the status quo: they embraced Algeria and France becoming evermore contiguous spaces legally, culturally, and politically.[51] To be sure, there were differences that ran through the Jewish and Muslim streets and establishments of the Marais, Belleville, and other quarters, including those of ethnicity, religion, class, effective legal status, and gender. Yet in part because of commonly held political assumptions, these Jews and Muslims could largely, for the moment, select their own affiliations and categories of inclusion and exclusion. Ethnoreligious differences often became, as they had between the wars, more blurred than pronounced. Here, in the heart of the empire, a North African Jewish presence reinforced many Muslims' ability to maintain their attachments to the Maghreb. As we shall see, by the late 1950s the relatively blurry categories of coexistence within these spaces, like the political assumptions that underlined such fluidity, would be sorely tested.

The Beginnings of Engagement

The Algerian nationalists who began the revolt called themselves the Front de libération nationale (FLN), and claimed affiliation with the FLN's military arm, the Armée de libération nationale (ALN). FLN leaders accompanied the violent attacks of November 1, 1954, with a statement demanding "the restoration of the Algerian state, sovereign, democratic and social, within a framework provided by Islamic principles."[52] Previously unknown, the FLN was a splinter group of the MTLD, which stood 20,000 strong on the insurrection's eve. The FLN was formed largely of young activists who advocated violent revolt rather than the nationalists' traditional tactics of strikes, demonstrations, and the like. Following the government dissolution of the MTLD after the start of the revolt, Messali Hadj founded the Mouvement national algérien (MNA). Over the next two years, the FLN and MNA moved from possible entente to a brutal struggle for control of the war for independence. Though the infighting continued throughout the conflict, the FLN had gained the decisive upper hand by autumn 1956 in both Algeria and the MNA's stronghold, the metropole.[53]

The Algerian revolutionaries rejected decades of efforts by the French state and certain Muslims to foster a Franco-Muslim identity. Such efforts, however, only intensified in the years preceding the French departure from Algeria.[54] The dream of Algerian nationhood would in time gain the support of a majority of Muslims in Algeria and the mainland. Yet contrary to the selective national memories in Algeria and France, and the assumptions of much historiography, this did not occur without significant contestation.[55] Many Muslims sought to negotiate a complex relationship of optimistic allegiance to France.

At times, French officials endeavored to simplify the terms of this relationship. For example, state efforts continued to forge an "Islam français" at the Grand Mosque of Paris. Following the death of Si Kaddour Benghabrit in summer 1954, his nephew, Si Ahmed Benghabrit, became the mosque's provisional rector. During his brief tenure, a much freer political atmosphere reigned inside the mosque, with imams sometimes voicing support for North African nationalists in their messages at prayer services.[56] In May 1957 the government intervened to appoint Si Hamza Boubakeur, a liberal Algerian Muslim academic and strong supporter of Algérie française, as the new rector.[57] Even if Boubakeur's presence restored the mosque as a bulwark of Islam français, the French imposition of a new rector also seemed to provoke suspicion and even hostility among many of Paris's Muslims.[58]

Other state efforts to capture Muslim support proved more successful. Large numbers of Muslim Algerians offered loyalty to France—both symbolic and real—through military service. As of late 1960, some 120,000 served in the *harkis*, or Algerian Muslim self-defense and auxiliary forces, and another 60,000 in the regular French army. The harkis served several purposes. They enabled France to reduce its number of draftees, had knowledge of local conditions, and acted as an invaluable propaganda tool. The reasons for serving ranged from desire to avenge an FLN attack, to rivalries with another village or clan, to threats from French officials, to the modest if useful daily pay (750 francs).[59]

The government's recruitment of Muslim soldiers, like its stamping out of FLN propaganda at the mosque, suggested a binary understanding of the period's choices: assimilation versus rejection; imperial loyalty versus independence. Yet the terms of identity and interaction articulated by the French state, as well as by many Muslims, often reveal a messier reality of new options in both law and political discourse. Certain French politicians sought to respond to the insurrection by advocating more aggressively egalitarian policies for France's Muslim Algerian subjects. In doing so, they expressed an increasingly flexible framework for the place of Muslimness within French citizenship.[60] Disputing the notion that the uprising threw colonialism into question, French leaders argued that they needed merely to address an issue of discrimination within the French nation. They contended that most Algerian Muslims did not desire statehood; instead, they wanted equal economic, social, and political opportunity.

In this vein, beginning in February 1955, the newly appointed governor-general of Algeria, Jacques Soustelle, undertook a plan of "integrationism." This French policy gave new legal substance to a category of citizens first outlined in the reforms of 1944 to 1947: French Muslim citizens from Algeria (FMAs). The move represented a major departure from the legal strictures of republican orthodoxy: the reforms created a separate group of citizens, explicitly defined by its ethnic origins (and not, despite the word *Muslim,* its religious practices). In addition, against both the long-standing assumptions of citizenship policy in Algeria and the logics of French secularism more broadly, FMAs could both maintain their Muslim personal status and enjoy all the rights of full French citizens (officials envisioned such a situation as temporary). Finally, integrationism included new measures deemed "exceptional promotion," akin to the American affirmative action policies that would emerge a decade later. By mid-1956, officials in Algeria established quotas, from 10 to 70 percent, for the proportion of FMAs to be appointed to various public posts; in 1958 the new Fifth Republic government extended these rules to the metropole. Likewise, the 1958 constitution eliminated any legal separation between Algeria and the mainland; in the process it finally extended full French citizenship to all Muslims of Algeria while enabling them to maintain their Muslim "personal status." This series of reforms demonstrated France's commitment to making Algeria "French," as well as a willingness to think more creatively about the place of ethnicity and religion within French citizenship. These policies contrasted the binaries of conventional republicanism and contributed to an atmosphere of new openings for relationships among Jews, Muslims, and the French nation-state. During the same period French propaganda films like *Visages d'Algérie* and *One Thousand New Villages* portrayed Algeria and France as part of a common Mediterranean civilization.[61]

Simultaneously, however, the very act of seeking to integrate Muslims into the nation as members of a distinct ethnoreligious group rather than as individuals underscored once more the group label as a kind of asterisk to their Frenchness. French Muslims from Algeria, as their right to difference gained legal recognition, also became marked legally as ethnically different from the rest of the French polity. Despite the inclusive nature of the reforms around FMA status, they contained the seeds of future exclusions. Moreover, integrationism entailed the creation of an unprecedented number of institutions for the social assistance of Algerian Muslims in France; these institutions could—and soon would—operate not only as new instruments of republican assimilation but as apparatuses of republican surveillance and repression.[62]

Integrationism, moreover, unfolded alongside private statements by many French policymakers who remained starkly binary in their visions of France and its Muslims. In 1959 de Gaulle himself expressed to his young confidant, Alain Peyrefitte, tremendous fears about the implications of the policy. "Arabs are Arabs, Frenchmen are Frenchmen," stated the president, comparing the two groups to oil and water. Predicting rapid Muslim demographic growth, he went on to say: "If we pursue integration, if all the Arabs and Berbers of Algeria were considered French, how would we prevent them from coming to settle in the metropole. . . . My village would no longer be called Colombey-les-Deux-Eglises but Colombey-les-Deux-Mosqués."[63]

The FLN had its own very different fears of integration, a word that Ferhat Abbas declared in 1958, "means war."[64] Abbas and others understood that if the notion of France as an imperial republic that could integrate its Algerian Muslim colonial subjects became widely plausible to their compatriots, then the FLN's very raison d'être would be imperiled. At the same time, the Front had a complex relationship to republicanism. Its political platform, while vague, emphasized socioeconomic equality, Islamic heritage, destruction of the colonial system, and, above all, unanimity.[65] Often, however, the movement's spokesmen articulated these ideals in their own decidedly republican terms. Such an outlook found vivid expression in efforts to rally Jewish support. These efforts began in earnest at the Congress of Soummam in August 1956, when the FLN set out its platform, created a tighter organization, and attempted to unify all Algerian nationalists. The architect of the congress was Ramdane Abbane, a leading revolutionary with Western-influenced, secularist leanings, opposed to military authoritarianism and Islamism. Soummam constituted a temporary triumph for Abbane and other like-minded "interior" leaders over those operating outside Algeria, wedded to greater military power and often linked to pan-Arab and Islamist currents.[66] The Soummam platform proclaimed the revolution "the battle for the rebirth of an Algerian state under the form of a democratic and social republic and not a monarchic restoration or a revived theocracy."[67]

Not coincidentally, the same document made an effort to reassure Jews after the attacks of Constantine that the FLN was moderate and inclusive. The authors treated Jews as compatriots in waiting: "The Algerians of Jewish origin have not yet overcome their trouble of conscience, nor chosen [a side]. Let us hope that they will follow in large numbers the path of those who have responded to the call of the generous fatherland, given their friendship to the Revolution and already demanded proudly their Algerian nationalism." In a more explicitly critical vein, the statement contrasted the silence of the chief rabbi of Algeria to the Algerian archbishop's condemnation of colonialism, but nevertheless stated, "the vast majority of Algerians keep themselves from considering the Jewish community as having passed definitively into the enemy camp." The call of Soummam spoke fraternally but sternly, implying that Algerian Jews were bound by birth and justice to join the insurrection.[68]

This declaration constituted the opening salvo of an extended effort to recruit Jews. In October 1956 the FLN sent an open letter to Algerian Jewish communal leaders and the November 1956 and January 1957 issues of FLN publication *La Résistance algérienne* included long articles directed at Jews. These articles cited small groups of Jews who publicly supported the revolution. Repeatedly, the FLN underscored the longevity of Jews' attachment to Algeria. One article recalled a time when "Algeria was a refuge and land of liberty for all Jews fleeing the inhuman terrors of the Inquisition." Writers often mentioned the horrors Jews in Algeria faced during the Holocaust and used the phrase *colonial-fascists* to link past atrocities and present right-wing extremists.[69] This term tied French colonialism to Nazism and the independence struggle to the Resistance. The nationalists thus sought to place themselves on the right side of the defining event of recent French history, thereby connecting as well to the last great defense of the republic.

The FLN made distinct narratives of World War II and longer-term Algerian history central to its message toward Jews. One text highlighted how Muslims had rebuffed Vichy's appeals and showed solidarity with Jews. Reaching further back, the FLN argued that with the Crémieux

Decree of 1870 Jews had merely "artificially" joined the French nation. "We do not want to believe," declared the author, "that the Jews of Algeria tolerate living uprooted in a society that is not theirs, so their true fatherland reclaims them."[70] As the Jews assimilated French customs, exclaimed another FLN plea, "the israélite, speaking of the Muslims, would say 'the indigènes.' . . . This term has a pejorative meaning in the mouth of the occupier; coming from a compatriot, it is just completely odious."[71] Such appeals attempted to convince Jews that, contrary to their long-held perceptions, France was defined not by republican principles of equality and liberty but instead by racism, colonialism, and even fascism. The Jews remained, as they had been for centuries, part of the Algerian people; the French arrival had poisoned Jewish attitudes toward their Muslim fellow natives.

In such a manner, FLN rhetoric sought to separate the Jews of Algeria from one vision of their republican past and future and to bind them to another.[72] Despite the revolution's Islamic symbols and overtones, the FLN promised a democratic, egalitarian republic in which Jews would have "their place."[73] One appeal of November 1959 declared, "You are an integral part of the Algerian people. It is not a matter for you of choosing between France and Algeria but of becoming effective citizens of your true country."[74] The same document warned, however, "Those [Jews] who have [been] zealous servants of the colonialist regime and its army are irrevocably excluded from the national community."

The FLN's outreach to Jews followed multiple motives. Certain more secular and inclusive nationalist leaders, particularly Mohamed Lebjaoui and Mohamed Harbi, genuinely sought Jewish participation in the formation of the Algerian nation.[75] The former was coauthor of the Soummam Platform—wherein he insisted on a statement welcoming Jews to join the movement—and first head of the FLN's metropolitan branch, the Fédération de France; the latter was secretary-general for the Ministry of Foreign Affairs in the provisional government of 1961–1962 and a lead counselor to Algeria's first president, Ahmed Ben Bella.[76] Lebjaoui and other FLN leaders also saw outreach to Jews as a powerful way to demonstrate political maturity in the crucial arena of international diplomacy.[77] Some hoped the support of Algerian Jewry might influence supposedly key Jewish power brokers in various Western countries; at the very least, they believed that Jewish support would give the movement greater legitimacy.[78]

Reflecting further the FLN's complex attitude toward Jews, during the period from the Soummam Congress of August 1956 until de Gaulle's "return" in May 1958, the group's official warm words were accompanied by upward of some ninety attacks by Algerian nationalists against Jews or Jewish-owned institutions.[79] In September 1957, one source estimated that FLN violence had killed several hundred Algerian Jews and led 6,000 more to depart for the metropole. By that time many Algerian Jews suspected that certain FLN attacks specifically targeted Jews.[80]

For two years following de Gaulle's return, FLN violence against Jews lessened substantially.[81] Jewish departures from Algeria sharply declined, and some who had left even returned.[82] This coincided with a larger drop in attacks over the same period. The new optimism of May 1958 created a brief moment of calm. French Interior Ministry officials attributed the longer-term reduction in violence to military successes against key terrorists and to the FLN's triumph in its struggle with the MNA.[83] With specific regard to Jews, however, a secret FLN memo from early 1958 reveals other dynamics at work. The author expressed serious concern about recent attacks that had killed many Jews. The memo outlined a strategy to win Jewish support: convince Jews they were fellow victims of colonialism; make Jews feel secure within the nationalist movement and regarding their future in an independent Algeria; and control violence against Jews, particularly in urban centers.[84] Nonetheless, even the more stable period between May 1958 and late 1960 witnessed several jarring incidents of explicitly anti-Jewish terror, including grenade attacks on synagogues in the north-central towns of Boghari and Bou-Saâda. In the aftermath of both episodes, however, the local Muslim population expressed sympathy and even outrage.[85]

This disconnect between the FLN's charm offensive on the one hand, and anti-Jewish violence on the other hand, partly reflected intensifying internal struggles. Following the assassination of Ramdane Abbane by hardliners in December 1957, those who equated Algerianness with Arabness or Islam were gaining the upper hand over the ecumenical and democratic vision of those like Lebjaoui and Harbi. The former group included leading activists Ahmed Ben Bella and Larbi Ben M'Hidi. Ben M'Hidi had called Soummam's posture toward Jews too "fraternal" and "warm"; Ben Bella complained in a letter to the FLN central committee of "the importance that you seem to assign to the role of the Jewish minority."[86] In Paris, Algerian nationalist student leader Abdesselam Belaïd held a similar outlook, at one point telling an Algerian Jewish supporter, "You are Jewish, you can't defend Algeria as well as an Arab." He later explained his rationale by referring to Jews' higher position under French rule: "We're sorry, [the Jews] are not Algerian like the others; they benefit from different conditions."[87] Nonetheless, from 1958 to 1960, courting Jewish support remained an important part of the nationalists' diplomatic strategy, and the character of the future Algerian nation continued to be fiercely contested.

Jewish Organizations in the Face of "the Events"

In July 1957 Jacques Lazarus, head of the CJAES and the North African office of the World Jewish Congress, confided to a friend: "For the Jews [of Algeria] . . . now it is a matter of choosing, of *choosing between two worlds, between modes of life.* Algerian Judaism is too integrated into the Western world, to the detriment even of its own ancestral values, to take another path forward than that which it has followed for more than a century."[88] These words echoed the binary visions of both official French colonialism and the FLN. They revealed that Lazarus saw Jewish life as inseparable from the French presence, while hinting at many Algerian Jews' dilemma in the face of complex attachments. Throughout the war, Lazarus and the CJAES responded to FLN appeals by underscoring their constituents' place in the republic, but did so in terms that were distinctive to Algerian Jewry. In what became its guiding statement of principles, published in November 1956 partly as a response to the "call of Soummam," the CJAES called its character entirely "confessional" and contended that no single organization could speak for all Algerian Jews, who, like other French citizens, made up a diverse body of individuals.[89] The same declaration, published in the CJAES's monthly journal, *L'Information juive,* underscored Algerian Jewry's "profound recogn[ition] of France, to whom we owe so much." Yet the CJAES recalled the Jews' 2,000-year presence in Algeria and emphasized the cordiality of historical Jewish-Muslim relations and hopes of future coexistence. Evoking Jews' suffering due to racism and Judaism's tradition of "ma[king] justice and equality between men an absolute demand," the organization called its community "unshakably attached to these principles." Over the next four years, in the face of mounting pressures, the CJAES repeatedly reaffirmed this declaration.[90]

As the war continued, in the widely read pages of *L'Information juive,* public meetings, and private correspondence, leading members of the CJAES reiterated and expanded on this set of ideas.[91] As early as January 1957 Lazarus wrote confidentially to World Jewish Congress representative Maurice Perlzweig: "I remain persuaded that the future of the Jewish collectivity in North Africa is conditioned, in large part, on the maintenance of France in Algeria." Echoing many Jewish liberals, Lazarus wrote that the community needed to "fight for the justice and equality of rights of all, for access of all to more well-being."[92]

We can in part understand the contradiction here—between fealty to France and a commitment to justice for Muslims—through the Jewish community's particular narratives of the Algerian past, which it saw as portents for a more promising future.[93] These renderings of history differed markedly from those of the FLN. Jewish leaders celebrated the Crémieux Decree as a glorious turning point in their history.[94] They saw it not as a betrayal but as a defining step on a path to a freer French Algeria, along which they remained hopeful to the end, Algerian Muslims were also moving. Unlike the FLN, Lazarus and others did not perceive attachments to Muslims and to France in either-or terms. Rather, offering sympathetic statements like, "We understand the aspirations of the Muslim masses, today walled off in silence, to a better life, to complete equality," they lionized historical cases of Jewish support for reform in Algeria, such as the failed Blum-Viollette plan of the Front populaire era.[95] These Jews envisioned France moving Muslims ever closer to full equality, strengthening ties between the mainland and Algeria, and thereby creating a Mediterranean imperial republic.

Like the FLN, the CJAES regularly recalled Jews' long-standing ties with their Muslim neighbors and the latter's decency and solidarity under Vichy.[96] In contradistinction to the nationalists, for whom this history revealed the correct stance in the present, Jewish leaders refused to have their community members' choices and identities bound by any one consideration. Lazarus repeatedly defined the outlook of Algerian Jewry with the phrase, "We are French; we are republicans; we are liberals."[97] The CJAES insisted that regardless of the war's outcome, Jews had to retain their "self-determination," and thus their right to French citizenship.[98]

Tied to Algeria by competing allegiances and fortified with nearly limitless faith in the republic's capacity to mold citizens, few Jews imagined leaving until late 1960.[99] The community continued unabated with a series of renewal projects that had begun in the postwar years. These included, among other things, the construction of a new rabbinical seminary from 1956 to 1959. Such initiatives often consumed greater attention than the political situation.[100] In a similar vein, Algerian Jewry offered highly measured responses to attacks on Jews or Jewish-owned property. Of the more than 100 such attacks catalogued personally by Lazarus from summer 1956 to autumn 1960, fewer than ten became news stories in L'information juive. Where they did appear, they took little space and were placed well inside the issue.[101] The CJAES endeavored to make sure that the worst episodes of violence, which sometimes elicited Jewish reprisals, did not escalate tensions. In summer 1957, for instance, the council mourned the "horrible terrorist attacks that, once more, test particularly the cities of Algiers and Constantine," but cautioned Jews: "Neither sadness, nor indignation and anger, as justified as they are, can in fact excuse [cases where] unbridled passions lead to indefensible acts, whose victims are also innocent."[102]

The events surrounding General de Gaulle taking the reins of power in May 1958 and his visit to Algeria soon after witnessed demonstrations in which Christians, Muslims, and Jews repeatedly mingled spontaneously; these developments prompted widespread renewed optimism about Algeria's future. In June 1958 L'Information juive spoke glowingly of the general as historically "the restorer of the Republic and the ideal that it incarnates, and who, in the worst moments of the Nazi persecution, had affirmed his will to reestablish, after the victory, at once equality of rights and that of duties of all citizens in the French territory."[103] Algerian Jewry thereby linked its own aspirations for Algeria to the memory of the Resistance. In 1962, in his brief retrospective of the war's key moments for Algerian Jews, communal leader Henri Chemouilli wrote nostalgically of May 1958: "Fraternisation mixes Christians, Muslims and Jews on the Forum [in Algiers]. Agreement is made around General de Gaulle; peace seems imminent; *the Muslims are full citizens, the major injustice of colonialism is abolished, time will do the rest*."[104] Even in the face of mounting difficulties, Algerian Jewry continued to see its own "Frenchification" as a model for that of Muslims, part of an ever-more-equal France blossoming along the northern and southern shores of the Mediterranean.

During the same period between 1956 and 1960, it became clear that events beyond the metropole and Algeria were having a substantial impact on Jewish and Muslim outlooks. As Maud Mandel has argued, Algerian Jews considered their fate within what French policymakers, international Jewish organizations, and Jews in the Maghreb were coming to see as a larger North African Jewish story of decolonization.[105] In this context, Algerian Jews watched both Morocco and Tunisia for hints of what to expect in the event of an independent Algeria. There, the battles for independence, while far less bloody, had nonetheless reshaped Jewish life. Although Moroccan and Tunisian nationalists had focused most of their attacks, both verbal and physical, on France, they also occasionally had targeted Jews. Unlike in Algeria, most Moroccan and Tunisian Jews did not have French citizenship. While about 70 percent of Tunisian Jews became citizens of their new country, a significant number held French citizenship due to the 1923 Morinaud Law. Long-standing Italian influence in Tunisia also meant that many Jews were of Italian nationality. In Morocco, where most Jews had long been considered nationally Moroccan by the French (due to a provision of the Madrid Convention of 1880), a majority soon became recognized by the new sovereign state as citizens.[106]

In both Tunisia and Morocco, the emergence of the Israeli-Arab conflict became the leading source of Jewish-Muslim tensions. Each country carefully negotiated a complicated relationship to the rest of the Arab world, facing internal political battles between more moderate or Western-friendly and pan-Arabist or Islamist factions. This context raised questions such as how Jewish migration from these countries to Israel might contribute to manpower that could be used against the Arab world or if dual loyalties would make Jews a potential fifth column in the event of war with Israel.

Within a short time of both countries' independence in 1956, substantial numbers of Moroccan and Tunisian Jews had immigrated to Israel; smaller numbers went to France. At the same time, Tunisian and Moroccan leaders invited Jews to become part of the new nation. Tunisia's first president, Habib Bourguiba, and Morocco's king, Mohamed V, undertook gestures of respect for Jews, including appointing a Jew to a cabinet ministry. Yet particularly in Morocco, efforts toward Muslim-Jewish entente proved short-lived. Egyptian president Gamel Abdel Nasser's growing influence, Morocco's membership in the Arab League after mid-1958, and the regime's staunch opposition to Zionism and ban on immigration to Israel all fostered tensions. Even in Tunisia, which took a friendlier attitude toward Israel, obstacles to Jewish emigration emerged by 1959. As examples for Jewish prospects in North Africa, then, the two countries sent decidedly mixed signals. International Jewish observers, colonial officials, and Algerian Jews regularly received and disseminated news, rhetoric, and images of both promise and foreboding about the wider destiny of North African Jewry.[107]

The conflict also could hardly escape the shadow of two Israeli-Arab wars: the one that had established the state in 1947–1949 and the Suez campaign of 1956. The former, despite its muted impact on Jewish-Muslim relations in France, meant that interactions between Jews and Muslims everywhere occurred against the background of an ongoing state of belligerence between Jewish and Arab nation-states. The Arab-Israeli conflict at times became a parallel frame for binary conceptions of Algeria: many advocates of both French Algeria and independence mapped the Arab and Israeli causes onto those of anticolonialism and French civilization, respectively. For French policymakers, the decision to attack Egypt in the Suez War was tightly linked to their increasing sense of the Algerian conflict as, in the words of Governor-General Robert Lacoste, a contest of "civilization against anarchy," and more specifically their fears about the imminent spread of pan-Islamism.[108] These connections resonated as well in an unexpected place: among many activists of the traditionally antisemitic French extreme Right. Following the Suez War, Israel's military performance provoked admiration from the editor of the Far Right newspaper *Rivarol*. Jean-Louis Tixier-Vignancour, a former member of Charles Maurras's Action française and ardent Pétainist, referred enthusiastically to Israel in parliament. This marked the beginning of an important shift, whereby portions of the extreme Right came to see Jews increasingly as possible allies with shared values and interests and to focus more of their racism on Muslims. A significant factor in these developments was Israel's military success against its Arab neighbors and the events of the French-Algerian War.[109]

For many Jews and Muslims, the Suez War—by coinciding with the Algerian conflict's escalation—highlighted issues of competing loyalties and transnational identities. Yet articulated linkages between the Middle Eastern and Algerian conflicts took myriad forms. Among Muslims, certain FLN leaders, particularly the moderate Ferhat Abbas, sought to gain Israeli support for votes on Algeria in the United Nations. In a September 1957 statement to the Jewish Telegraph Agency, Abbas promised that Jews in an independent Algeria would have full rights, including emigration to Israel. Pushing further, he exclaimed, "There is no paradox between the Franco-Israeli friendship and the eventual support of Israel [for] the Algerian cause. This support is the only way of bridging the gap that separates Israel from the rest of the Afro-Asiatic nations."[110] In fact, Israel's close relationship with France—its primary weapons supplier, ally in the Suez War, and key supporter in the international community—rendered such a move by the young Jewish state unthinkable.

Perspectives like that of Abbas remind us that during much of the war, Israel had a complicated relationship to the Algerian nationalists and the broader emerging "global south." With Israel having recently emerged from British imperial control, many Israelis saw themselves as taking part in an anticolonial struggle. Those holding such an outlook ranged from mainstream Labor Zionists with their deep commitment to socialism, to the militant Israeli right that had championed guerilla warfare against the British. An instructive story comes from the Egyptian Jewish writer Jacqueline Shohet Kahanoff, who reports that Ahmed Ben Bella was housed off and on by her parents in Cairo during much of the war's first two years and became very close with the family. At the time, he shared with Kahanoff's mother his copy of the Israeli right-wing leader Menachem Begin's book *The Revolt.* Kahanoff's mother claimed that Ben Bella called Begin's writings his "Bible," explained intricacies of Israeli society, and extolled the young Jewish state as a "civilization of the avant-garde." Whatever his later statements about Jews and Israel, at the time Ben Bella claimed that following the war, when Algeria would be freed of the necessity of an alliance with Nasser, the new state could look to Israel as a model in confronting many challenges.[111]

Another favorable FLN perspective on Israel came from the Marxist Abd al-Razik Abd al-Qadir—the Syrian-born great-grandson of the nineteenth-century Algerian Abd al-Qadir, seen as the first Algerian nationalist hero—who had joined the FLN at the start of the uprising. Prior to the revolution, he lived in Israel, where he had originally come to volunteer (unsuccessfully) to fight in the 1948 War, worked on a kibbutz, and married a Jewish Marxist. The FLN had made Abd al-Razik its ambassador to Switzerland and West Germany.[112] In his 1961 book, *The Jewish-Arab Conflict,* he vocally rejected typical equations, from either pan-Arabists or militants of Algérie française, of the Algerian struggle and the one between Israel and its Arab neighbors. Rather, he saw an affinity between the founding liberation struggles of the young Jewish state and the nascent Algerian one. Abd al-Razik, whose book garnered praise in the left-wing French Jewish press, perceived within the Algerian revolution the ingredients for a genuinely popular, social democracy in the Arab world, which he regarded as the sine qua non for the Jewish-Arab reconciliation that he sought.[113]

Many Algerian nationalists took a far dimmer view of any connections between Algeria and Israel.[114] The most violent manifestation of anti-Israel sentiments from the nationalists occurred in 1958 when the FLN kidnapped and murdered Jacob Hassan and Raphaël Ben Guera, a pair of Israeli emissaries to Algeria. In this morose affair, FLN militants took the men captive in February, held them until April, and then murdered them. The FLN continued to promise their good health and imminent release until the discovery of their bodies in September, provoking outrage in the Jewish community.[115] Still, until spring 1962, the FLN internally debated future relations with Israel, and FLN and Israeli representatives made occasional overtures through back channels and secret meetings.[116]

Even more than for Muslims, the issue of Israel proved significant and problematic for Jews in Algeria and France. In its defining statement of November 1956, the CJAES declared, "The events which are unfolding currently in the Middle East should not alter the sentiments which exist here between israélites and Muslims." Even as it sought, however, to keep the Israeli-Arab conflict at a distance, the CJAES asserted Algerian Jews' attachment to Israel; Lazarus and others insisted on guarantees regarding visitation and migration rights to Israel for the Jews of a future Algerian state.[117] French Zionist groups across the political spectrum framed their position on the war in terms of Israel's interests. By 1957, former Algerian governor-general Jacques Soustelle, now a hard-line advocate for Algérie française, drew significant Zionist support for his campaign to strengthen the Franco-Israeli alliance. Like a growing segment of the Far Right, he depicted Israel's conflict with the Arabs as coterminous with the fight to keep Algeria French.[118] Algerian-born Jewish intellectual Jean Daniel, increasingly sympathetic to the Algerian nationalist cause, fiercely contested such formulations.[119] In spring 1958, when the left-wing Zionist Cercle Bernard Lazare critiqued Soustelle and called for a negotiated peace, the organization connected its position to Israel's need for peace and stability.[120]

Certain Israelis found themselves implicated directly in the war's events. In May 1956, the Misgeret, an Israeli-organized underground Jewish self-defense force, played a leading role in violent altercations in Constantine that resulted in as many as 230 Muslim deaths.[121] During the later stages of the war, accusations circulated linking Israel to the forces fighting for Algérie française.[122] Several Israelis established an Israeli Committee for a Free Algeria, hoping their presence would improve Arab-Israeli relations.[123] Israel's influence and occasional presence in the conflict thus simultaneously raised the issue of dual loyalties and became a screen onto which various actors projected their positions regarding Algeria's future.

Wider Mediterranean contexts had less impact on the outlook of metropolitan Jewish community leaders and institutions. Their positions on the war reflected the more conventional binaries of imperial republicanism: between loyalty to French Algeria and opposition to colonialism and between publicly French and privately Jewish selves. Much of the French Jewish leadership and press treated the conflict with relative silence until 1958, and often as late as autumn 1960. In September 1956, in an annual message to French Jews that touched on many issues, CRIF president Vidal Modiano conspicuously avoided the subject of Algeria.[124] Moreover, the CRIF discussed Algeria on only six occasions in its general assembly and bureau meetings during the four-year span between the Soummam Congress and de Gaulle's first mention of the future "Algerian republic" in November 1960.[125] Twice, the CRIF even expressed vehement disapproval of member associations that took a position on the war without prior approval from the larger council.[126] The consistory's official organ, the *Journal des communautés,* and many of the body's spokesmen appeared determined to avoid giving attention to the conflict.[127] The relative silence of the CRIF and the consistory around attacks on Jews in Algeria maintained Franco-Judaism's loyalty to republican colonial ideology. Such a posture suggested that "the events" in Algeria were indeed limited in scope and would not fundamentally alter the relationship of this land or its people to France. Moreover, their scant attention accorded with assimilationist assumptions of republican Judaism, implying that these victims of attacks were French of Algeria who happened, secondarily, to be Jewish.

The traditional outlook of Franco-Judaism could be heard as well on the rare occasions when community leaders openly discussed Algeria. In his widely disseminated September 1956 Rosh Hashanah message, France's chief rabbi Jacob Kaplan saluted "our dear soldiers" in Algeria, prayed for peace, and invoked demonstrations of Jewish-Christian-Muslim unity.[128] Two years later, Meyer Jaïs, chief rabbi of Paris and himself Algerian born, spoke in his Rosh Hashanah message in more urgent terms, reflecting the war's shifting tenor and impact: "A blind terrorism continues to rage ... on this beautiful land of Africa where France, after having introduced order, hygiene, prosperity, and doing everything for the intellectual progress of the least favored element, was preparing to lead it [toward] political emancipation, [the] ultimate objective of its civilizing mission."[129] These two metropolitan Jewish leaders responded to the war by underscoring, in more unequivocal terms than their Algerian-based counterparts, loyalty to the French war effort; like Algerian Jewish leaders, they spoke proudly of the liberating, ecumenical character of France's presence on the opposite side of the Mediterranean.

Kaplan's mention of soldiers in Algeria reflected the sizable Jewish presence in the French forces.[130] As in previous wars, the Jewish community offered support for soldiers' religious needs. In 1957, during Passover, Rabbi David Feuerwerker, Jewish chaplain of the French Navy, worked to secure exceptional leave time and made matzo available for Jews in the Navy.[131] For Purim in March 1960, the Jewish chaplaincy of the Army Corps of Algiers sent 700 traditional Purim baskets to Jews in its unit.[132] Perhaps reflecting wider public ambivalence about the French war effort, the Jewish press gave far less attention to Jewish soldiers than it had during World War I or II. Still, certain communal organs paid homage to a number of decorated and deceased Jewish soldiers.[133] Jews' service, of course, brought them into regular violent confrontation with Muslims.[134]

The war's battle lines, physical or otherwise, framed many Jewish leaders' perspective on Jewish-Muslim relations. French and Algerian Jewish leaders recognized neither the daily Jewish-Muslim coexistence in many French neighborhoods nor the commonalities between many Jews and Muslims arriving in France from North Africa. Instead, they typically sought to sharply distinguish Jews from Muslims. A striking example appeared in an article by Algerian Jewish leader Émile Touati in the March 1956 issue of the *Revue du FSJU*. While acknowledging that Algerian Muslims sometimes migrated to France for the same reasons as Jews, Touati drew a series of contrasts between the two groups' arrivals in the French mainland.[135] The Jewish immigration was "Francophone," while most Muslims spoke little or no French. In contrast to Muslims, Algerian Jews were not so different from French citizens of the metropole. French Jewish organizations stood prepared to assist Jewish newcomers, whereas "nothing comparable" existed among metropolitan Muslims. Most Algerian Jews resided in cities; the majority of Muslims were from rural areas, mainly the mountainous region of Kabylia. Further, he noted, Jews generally brought large families, a desire to stay in France, middle-class status, and at least some economic resources to build their own enterprise. Muslims usually arrived as single men, for transient reasons, from agricultural settings and were qualified to work only as unskilled laborers.

In the face of both colonial antisemitism and skepticism from some French Jews about Algerian Jews' level of integration, Touati sent a clear message: Jews from the Maghreb, especially Algeria, had already attained middle-class French standards of language, education, labor, and gender and family relations. They would adapt quickly and offer vital cultural, economic, and demographic resources. Muslims lacked these attributes, and their migration might provoke legitimate concerns, but there was nothing to fear from Jews. Such a depiction, echoing long-standing French state and Jewish discourses, contrasted Algerian Jews as increasingly French and modern, with Muslims as frozen in precolonial modes of life.[136]

Individualized Jewish and Muslim Responses

As the war escalated from 1956, individual Jews increasingly chose paths of activism, with some mimicking and others eliding the fixed boundaries of statist, nationalist, and communal conceptions. From early in the war, numerous Jews followed the conventional form of Franco-Jewish activism. At all levels and across the political spectrum, they took positions on the war as French citizens rather than as Jews. Several Jews from highly assimilated backgrounds played critical roles in shaping public opinion toward the war. In 1958, Henri Alleg, a thirty-six-year-old Jewish communist living in Algeria, and Pierre Vidal-Naquet, a young professor of Greek history in France, each published a seminal exposé of French torture in Algeria.[137] Two years later, Vidal-Naquet and other Jewish intellectuals, including filmmaker Claude Lanzmann, philosopher Edgar Morin, and mathematician Laurent Schwartz, were among those who signed the influential Manifesto of the 121 in September 1960, a widely disseminated document defending the right of French people to refuse to serve in Algeria and to aid the nationalists and calling the revolution "the cause of all free men."[138]

At the grassroots level, the Franco-Jewish tradition was the default option for many lesser-known Jews as well. A number of young Jews from

Algeria studying in Paris became pro-FLN activists. Many of these students lived with Muslims in the dormitories on the rue Férou and ate at the cafeteria of the Association of Muslim Students from North Africa on the boulevard Saint-Michel. Never really feeling fully French, these Algerian Jews were drawn to their Muslim compatriots by shared language and music from their common homeland and saw themselves as part of the future Algerian nation; typically, alongside a handful of Muslims and more numerous "Europeans," they were members of the Algerian language section of the French Communist Party.[139] Henri Curiel, a militant Jewish communist from Egypt, became one of the leading "suitcase carriers," the nickname given to the members of the Jeanson network, a group of mostly French militants who lent considerable aid to the FLN. On the side of French Algeria, in summer 1956, a Strasbourg rabbi offered active support to the newly formed Union for the Salvation and Renewal of French Algeria.[140]

In Algeria, a handful of Jews, often migrating from the Communist Party, joined or assisted the FLN. Until his arrest in October 1956, communist medical student Daniel Timsit worked with the FLN to build explosives used in terror attacks; his brothers also joined.[141] Jean Bensimon began the war as a French soldier, but in 1957 he became moved by the culture and consciousness of the natives of Kabylia where he served. For a time, he pursued the dream of an ecumenical Algeria by supporting the FLN.[142] Such cases were rare but not singular. In her research, Jessica Hammerman has found numerous letters from the FLN to Jewish activists who chose to enlist in the national liberation struggle, ensuring them their place in the future Algeria.[143] In 1959, Frantz Fanon claimed that in many Algerian cities, Jewish tradesmen were supplying the ALN with military clothes, blankets, and other necessities; it was well known, he said, "that since 1954 several Jewish tradesmen have been arrested for aiding and abetting the Algerian Revolution."[144] In the late stages of the war, as we shall see in the next chapter, many more Jews of Algeria would support the OAS as it fought to keep Algeria French; some would bring these efforts with them to the metropole. With their individual choices, many of these Jews revealed their struggles to weave together multiple strands of identity and positionality among those laid out by Jacques Lazarus: republican, liberal, Jewish, Algerian, and French.

Few Jews, however, were so explicit or lucid about the complexity of their attachments as an influential young writer from Tunisia, Albert Memmi. Memmi's semiautobiographical 1953 novel, *The Pillar of Salt*, portrays a young Tunisian Jew, Alexandre Mordechai Benillouche, whose three names reflect his position caught between Jewish, North African, and French culture, drawn at various times to ideologies of colonial progress, anticolonial Tunisian nationalism, and Zionism. Eventually he leaves these seemingly insoluble conflicts behind and moves to Argentina to start a new life. Four years later, Memmi published *The Colonizer and the Colonized*, his devastating indictment of the structure of colonialism that became an instant classic for many anticolonial activists in Algeria and elsewhere; in it, he wrote explicitly of the impact of his Jewishness on his perspectives and how he saw Jews across the French Maghreb as situated between colonizer and colonized, at once both and neither.[145] In a follow-up article, "The Colonized Jew," Memmi argued that North African Jews faced three choices that reflected the three parts of their being: if they aspired to continued Westernization, they should migrate to France; they could instead "return" to their Jewishness and thus choose immigration to Israel; or if they felt most bound to the Maghreb, they could decide to be full members of their new nation-states, and only secondarily Jews, and therefore remain.[146] Memmi's work embodies the contradictions of so many Jewish and Muslim lives of this period: even as he openly engages the in-between positionalities and multiple attachments for North African Jews, he ultimately suggests that they cannot occupy multiple identities successfully and must choose one.

Within a few years, Memmi seemed to decide in favor of publicly emphasizing one's Jewishness. In December 1961, he penned an article in *L'Information juive* in which he critiqued the lack of "Jewish politics" in France: "Numerous Jews try to act, even do act politically, but almost never *as Jews*."[147] In particular, he derided the attempts of some to fight antisemitism "as Frenchmen" rather than openly recognize the particular danger for Jews. While Memmi's critique, set forth in several forums, reflected a dimension of historical and contemporary reality, fundamentally it missed the mark.[148] Perhaps due to his own experiences of struggling with multiple pulls on his identity, the author failed to realize that many Jews coming of age under decolonization sought to express simultaneously two or three parts of their being.

When Memmi wrote, many Jews had already begun to step out of the traditional model of republican Judaism to articulate their stance on the war in distinctly Jewish terms. Small groups of Algerian Jews responded to the FLN's calls by affirming their support for independence and echoing the nationalists' historical arguments for Jewish support. In 1957, a

"Group of Algerian Jews" published a notice that depicted the French conferral of citizenship in 1870 as a way to make the Jews of Algeria abandon their authentic heritage. "Can we," they asked, "repudiate our names, which were generally Arab names? Ought we to refuse to understand our parents, who are attached to Algerian customs, traditions and music?" Further underscoring its own form of ethnic nationalism, this group insisted that "in the common struggle, Muslims and Jews discover themselves to be racial brothers, and . . . they experience a profound and definite attachment to the Algerian homeland."[149]

In the metropole, several left-wing Jewish political organizations advocated visibly for peace or independence in Algeria and for Jewish-Muslim entente.[150] One of the most striking examples was the French Jewish Student Union (UEJF).[151] In 1955, the UEJF took a position against sending French troops to North Africa.[152] The group had a significant following, boasting over 1,500 members and ten sections across France. Beginning in 1957, the UEJF focused conferences and issues of its journal, *Kadimah,* around themes like Jewish students in the face of decolonization and Christians and Jews confronting Islam.[153] The same year, at the urging of Mohamed Lebjaoui and Mohammed Harbi, Claude Sixou and other Algerian Jews living in Paris formed the Committee of Algerian Israélites for Negotiation in Algeria. In an early statement, the committee explained that its members were moved by the sentiments of the "Call of Soummam," and that an affirmation of Jewish support would "dissipate any misunderstandings and extirpate the germs of hatred engendered by French colonialism."[154] While short-lived, the group offered a specifically Jewish affirmation of belonging in the Algerian nation, and lodged a further protest against the official binaries of the war and in favor of an inclusive Algeria.[155]

By 1958, in the face of growing political instability and evidence of renewed anti-Arab and anti-Jewish racism, small numbers of Jews in the Strasbourg region began to challenge the community's official position of pro-French "neutrality."[156] Through Alsace's Jewish newspaper, *Le Bulletin de nos communautés,* closely tied to the Consistory of the Bas-Rhin, the Jewish leadership took a conservative position that implicitly supported French actions, depicted the FLN as antisemitic, and commented little on growing signs of intolerance toward Muslims and Jews in the metropole.[157] In time a chorus of voices objected, calling for a more activist Jewish stance and in many cases directly urging sympathy for the insurgents.

In April 1958 writer Louis Bloch published a short story in *Le Bulletin* in which the protagonist, Simon, awakes to find that the nightmare he just dreamed is real. Racism, antisemitism, the pursuit of communists, and torture—all reminiscent of World War II—have begun again amid "total" indifference. "Some think," in reaction to Simon, "that one should not exaggerate: we only torture in Algeria; others say that the Arabs and the communists do worse; still others that the Jews should not mix themselves in politics." Simon replies in exasperation: "But do you understand nothing? . . . It is not a matter of politics, nor of [Arabs], nor of communism. . . . It is a matter of a fascist upsurge. If one can torture with impunity the reds and the Moors under the simple pretext of their political convictions or their race, tomorrow it will be us." Met by "the shrugging of shoulders," Simon searches for "a new Cardinal Salièges," referring to the archbishop of Toulouse who courageously denounced Nazi persecution of Jews.[158]

Five months later, in a biting attack sent to the same newsletter, Jewish student leader Freddy Raphaël said that the journal's recent support for de Gaulle and the new constitution had "eluded the principal problem, that of the Jewish attitude before a bloody war, where the infernal cycle of terror, of torture and of injustice crushes thousands of human lives." Raphaël contended that Jews needed "to affirm our Jewish self in all our relations with the world as well as in the political domain." While the editor largely dismissed this as "juvenile indignation," the writer's words clearly reflected wider sentiments.[159] The willingness of Strasbourg's Jewish community to discuss these issues so openly through its communal press was a distinctive aspect of the city as a site of Jewish engagement during the war. In a territory with no legal separation of church and state, Jews seemed to link their Frenchness and Jewishness in public speech more easily than elsewhere. Moreover, Alsatian Jewry maintained a strong intellectual tradition that lent itself to open communal debates about current questions.

Jews, then, took a wide array of positions on the war and often asserted their French civic duty as Jews. In a parallel development—too often obscured by the eventual triumph of the FLN and the nationalists' wartime and postindependence insistence on absolute unity—French Muslims responded to the war and the question of Algeria's future in myriad ways. A cache of Muslim letters from this period, written to the commissariat of police in Marseille, reveals how in and around France's port to the Mediterranean, numerous Muslims sought to push through the openings provided by their new legal equality. In September 1957 forty-seven-year-old Mohamed Iddir, a badly wounded Muslim military veteran who had fought for France, appealed to the prefect for help in building his fledgling local Association of French Muslim Veterans.[160] Five members of the Hakkoum family, when learning in February 1959 that their relatives' homes had been attacked by the FLN in Algiers and that four family members were serving in the French military, appealed to the prefect of police for permission to return to Algeria to join the French army.[161] In August, Habib Lakidar, a French Muslim from Tunisia living in Marseille, reported an incident in which his pregnant wife was physically attacked and called a "dirty Arab" by another woman. In his letter to the prefect, Lakidar spoke of his love for France and his appreciation for all that de Gaulle and the local government were doing "so that confidence will reign, so that peace will prevail," something he claimed that most of the "peoples of Africa and of metropolitan France desire ardently"; he also saluted how "each day, the Common Brothers die for this ideal." He lamented how people "without scruples" could undermine the efforts and sacrifices of these statesmen and soldiers at such a time.[162]

By appealing to France, even in the face of discrimination, FLN harassment, or French police brutality, these Muslims evinced a persistent faith in France's ongoing capacity for integration. Like young Jews who took a public stand on the war specifically as Jewish activists, these Muslims sought to actualize a new form of French citizenship. In a key difference, Islam's more burdened position prevented them from foregrounding their Muslimness. Nonetheless, as proud Muslims or North Africans, they followed in the footsteps of those who had spoken of France as their fatherland while serving in the trenches of World War I or who had demonstrated on July 14 with other supporters of the Front populaire while advocating reform in Algeria.

In a manner that echoed Albert Memmi's writings about Jews, the young Muslim Algerian writer and activist Yacine Kateb more explicitly articulated Algeria's multiple identities and complex challenges. A nationalist from an educated Berber family of Constantine, Kateb attained literary fame with the novel Nedjma in 1956. The title character descends from a tribe native to Algeria for centuries; each of her four lovers tells his own story in a splintered narrative.[163] Set in 1945, the work twice recounts the massacres at Sétif, a formative experience in the author's life. Nedjma herself is the product of an act of brutality, the rape of a French

Jewish woman by four Algerian men. Depicted in an epic, mythical fashion, Nedjma symbolizes the Algerian nation-in-waiting; the protagonist never speaks herself, suggesting that the Algerians still must master their destiny. The circumstances of her conception and the prevalence of violence throughout the story imply inevitable brutality in the birth of Algeria. Nedjma's mother appears to stand in not only for the France that must be violated to achieve independence but also for the Jews. She represents their predicament: so often caught in the crosshairs of colonial and anticolonial violence, at once integral to the Algerian people and bound to the French.[164]

The view of Jews only hinted at in *Nedjma* emerged more overtly in Kateb's political activism. In November 1956 he spoke at a meeting in Paris devoted to the question of "Jews as seen by others." In the wake of the recent Suez War, Kateb brought a message of coexistence that made Jews central to the history of the Algerian nation. "In North Africa," he declared, "the thousand-year-old Jewish communities have always lived in peace." More pointedly, he noted the historic and ongoing importance of Jews to Algerian culture: "*La Kahena,* national Berber heroine, was Jewish; the Jews have kept intact the music of the Algerian artisans." Even in discussing the Middle East conflict, he remained respectful: "At the current moment . . . Algeria has certain real links with the Arab countries but it recognizes the legitimacy of the State of Israel; it has the right to exist but not to impose itself by force or to do the bidding of the great colonialist powers; the public opinion of the two sides should act for a peace based on reciprocal concession." The next summer, Kateb issued a "message to the Jews of Israel and the world." While advocating for a Palestinian state, he spoke of the necessity of "assuring the place of Israel in the new community of peoples of the free East" and emphasized how common Jewish-Muslim suffering should be a source of unity.[165]

Jews and Muslims in the War for City Spaces

As the Algerian crisis became a fixture of metropolitan daily life, many Jews and Muslims found that the competing political loyalties at the heart of the conflict—Algerian nationalism versus French colonialism—became crucial categories for mutual perception and daily interaction. French state actors, Algerian nationalists, and Jewish communal leaders all approached shared spaces of Jewish and Muslim life through increasingly narrow, opposed, politically determined definitions of Jewishness and

Muslimness. While these binary conceptions did not overtake altogether other terms of Jewish-Muslim interaction, they did sharpen boundaries and identity markers within many neighborhood relationships, redefining possibilities for intercultural exchange and occasionally provoking violence. In their own distinctive ways, Paris, Marseille, and Strasbourg each witnessed the effects of these changes.

By 1958, the Jewish demographic shifts underway in France had considerably altered Paris—and the Marais quarter specifically. According to one estimate, 40,000 North African Jews lived in Paris, with the majority of them concentrated in and around the Marais.[166] By 1958, every Friday night, no fewer than eight North African Jewish prayer gatherings took place in the neighborhood, and each drew at least 450 participants. The thousands of North African Jews in the increasingly crowded Marais regularly encountered sizable numbers of Muslims. A 1959 estimate approximated that 1,280 French Muslims from Algeria (FMAs) lived in the 4th arrondissement; 550 of these resided in the Saint-Gervais, with most situated along the longtime Maghrebian hub of the rue François Miron and the intersecting rue de Jouy.[167] Even as the war intensified in the metropole, several North African Jews of the quarter recall it having little or no impact on their relations with Muslims. Félix Amanou stresses the fact that "the Algerian War was a conflict [that] was not anti-Jewish; it was anti-French." Similarly, Louise Jaïs declares that in the Marais, "all was still very good, with Mustapha, with the Arabs who frequented the café." Sylvain Strock, who had run a hotel nearby on the rue Ferdinand Duval since the late 1930s, continued to receive Muslims there.[168]

Patricia Jaïs, the youngest daughter of Louise and Maurice, was born the year of the outbreak of the war. Though the family moved to the rue Jacob in the 6th arrondissement when she was only a few months old, she still spent considerable time as a child in the Marais due to her father's café there. She remembers her earliest years in the neighborhood fondly, as a time of fluidity between categories of "Jew" and "Arab."[169] In her memory, its character was not exactly "Jewish" but more "Oriental." Many of the Jews living on streets like the rue François Miron, the rue des Ecouffes, and the rue des Rosiers "had Arab culture," she says: "Old people in their sun chairs, women with their foulard [Arab veil]. . . . For me, when I was very young, [the quarter's] . . . sensations, odors, sounds . . . were completely Arab." Sometimes, Patricia "even mixed up the Jewish religion and the Arab religion." As a young child, she explains,

"When my sister [Claude], was dressed up [as Queen Esther] for the holiday of Purim, she was photographed in front of Mustapha's café. I no longer knew if this was a thing that had to do with Jewish religion or with Arab culture! For me, all these colorful costumes, these things . . . that was more Arab than Jewish." Such experiences connected to the sensibilities transmitted to Patricia by her mother, who shared memories of her youth in Algeria. Louise recounted not only terribly violent episodes like the 1934 riots of Constantine, but stories about "making perfume with roses that were crushed on the terrace . . . the taste of [Algerian] cakes, dates, olive oil . . . the [particular angle of the] light, all of that."

Notwithstanding the nostalgia apparent in Patricia's recollections, they suggest that in these years, many of the quarter's cafés remained spaces characterized by Jewish-Muslim social relations and blurred ethnic boundaries. While much of Maurice Jaïs's clientele was Algerian Jews, it continued to include many Muslims. Customers often came to pass the afternoon in the café, where Jews and Muslims interacted amiably, if not entirely as equals. "There were already," says Patricia, "perhaps slightly hierarchical relations of class, where Jews already felt a bit better than Arabs." Yet ultimately, she claims: "These people loved each other, they shared the same culture." Mustapha Galy, who still ran his café on the rue de Jouy, remained a nearby Muslim friend. "I suppose," she says, "that my father would go into his café to play cards. . . . They had the same interests: cards, racing, boxing . . . the children, the quarter, beef, couscous."

As much as shared North African culture or immigrant status, masculinity remained a key basis for many such friendly Jewish-Muslim relations in the Marais of the 1950s. Patricia's father made it clear that his café was not a place for his daughters. She characterizes the cafés as a men's world, where they played cards and dice, smoked, and spoke about matters they preferred not discuss in mixed company. The one exception occurred on Fridays, which Patricia spent in the café with her mother. As she had for years, on Friday, Louise made the traditional North African Jewish festival meal of the *berbouche,* and a huge crowd of largely North African Jews but also Muslims came to partake.

Such an atmosphere unfolded amid major wartime intrusions on urban space. Beginning in 1956, the metropolitan branch of the FLN (the Fédération française du front de libération nationale, or FFFLN) and MNA waged a brutal struggle for control of Muslim emigrant communities that would result eventually in roughly 4,000 deaths and up to 9,000 injuries.[170] Within this larger battle for turf, the two groups competed fiercely for control of Paris's cafés and restaurants with significant Muslim clientele. Activists used posters, personal recruitment and pressure, the purchase of establishments, and even death threats and violent attacks.[171] By 1958, as the FLN brought its larger guerrilla campaign to the Hexagon with a wave of attacks, it monitored intently its activists and supporters. It offered social services to replace those of the French state, minimized outside contact, and enforced Muslim religious practices, partly aiming to inculcate the ideology of the new nation it sought to build. With the growth of the war in the metropole, police surveillance of "North African" cafés also intensified.[172]

In many instances, these struggles did not intrude directly on spaces of regular Jewish-Muslim contact. In reports of November 1956 and April 1957, of fifty-seven total Parisian North African food and drink establishments recorded by police as sites of Algerian nationalist activity, none were owned by Jews or in a neighborhood where Jews and Muslims often interacted in cafés.[173] This pattern suggests that those Muslims interacting amicably with Jews in neighborhoods like the Marais and Belleville remained the most "Frenchified," and continued optimistically to support French Algeria. But Jewish-Muslim relations did not restrict themselves to these quarters. In the 18th arrondissement, for instance, in and around the Goutte d'or quarter that became the FLN's Paris headquarters, at least three Algerian Jews operated cafés.[174]

Moreover, musical spaces and relationships were increasingly circumscribed by the war's intensifying violence. In Algeria, the Jewish-Muslim orchestra "El Gusto," a group of virtuosos in the populist Algerian song tradition of the *chaabi*, was torn apart by the pressures of the conflict.[175] Muslim performers in Paris like Zerrouki Allaoua and Ahmed Wahby who had played for years alongside Jewish musicians like Lili Labassi, Blond-Blond, and José de Suza increasingly turned their music to the cause of Algerian independence; they composed songs that resonated with themes of the nationalist struggle.[176] Oriental cabarets like El Djazaïr became sites of surveillance by both police and the FLN, who tried, for example, to control contacts between Muslim belly dancers and French patrons. One belly dancer at El Djazaïr, a seventeen-year-old named Shéhérazade, recalled later that if she drank with a Frenchman at an evening performance, she would be summoned the next day by FLN militants.[177]

Likewise, on occasion, the war encroached violently on long-standing Jewish-Muslim neighborhood interactions. In April 1958, police agents investigating an altercation between two Muslims in the street burst into a popular Jewish-owned café on the rue François Miron. Shouting "Death to the Jews," "Hitler didn't exterminate you enough!" and other slogans, the police struck and wounded fourteen Jews seated in the café. They then took them to the nearby police station for "identity verification" and kept them for three hours, hitting and insulting them further. By the end, the victims had sustained significant injuries, with one reportedly losing a liter of blood.[178]

Numerous Jewish organizations responded immediately; their accounts revealed the sharp dissonance between competing understandings of France as an imperial republic. In the Alsatian *Bulletin,* Jewish community leader Roger Berg noted that Jews and Muslims both lived in the Marais and recounted that "a patrol of police was the other day in search of Muslims when it penetrated in the Café, 'La Potiniere.' The owner himself declared that the customers found there did not belong to the religion of Mohamed. They were israélites, French in virtue of the Crémieux Decree and therefore not belonging to the milieux against which the public powers have deployed a vigilant activity for too many months."[179] Berg's words sharply distinguished Jews from Muslims: the two groups' lives in the Marais were adjacent but did not intersect; the Jews were above all loyal French citizens, but the Muslims were religious in essence and a menace to public order. Berg's depiction echoed the assumptions of state reports about Muslim social segregation and violence and the fears, common to French officials and many French and international Jewish organizations, of inevitable Jewish-Muslim conflict in response to events in Israel/Palestine.[180]

The Jewish Left responded rather differently. A writer in the Jewish communist weekly *La Presse nouvelle* expressed shock that antisemitism could return after World War II and treated the incidents as a sign of the larger "fascist menace" confronting France and an effort to camouflage the true source of France's current problems: the war in Algeria. Such incidents, he said, "sap the national unity and flou[t] republican principles." In response to this and other incidents, the UEJF printed a tract, "Antisemitism Becomes Public Again," that referenced the Holocaust and called for direct action, insisting that "silen[ce] would be complicity."[181] Unlike the more official communal press, these accounts regarded the attack on the rue François Miron as reflecting a wider plague of racism that reminded one of the Shoah and imperiled France. Threats to Jews, Muslims, and their coexistence were also threats to a multiethnic republic.

Such a perspective remained largely absent from the reaction to a subsequent altercation in summer 1960 that again punctured Jewish-Muslim interactions in the Marais. On July 17 two members of the Force de police auxiliaire (FPA), a unit of Muslims formed in 1959 by the French government to combat Algerian nationalists in the capital, entered another café on the rue François-Miron. Revolvers in hand, they hurled antisemitic insults and attacked customers at random, wounding one before fleeing the scene. This was the first of two attacks on Jews in Parisian cafés by FPAs in a matter of weeks. The pair of incidents suggested significant hostility toward Jews among these Muslim police officers, with two likely sources. Certain FPAs may have resented that many Jews from the Maghreb found greater acceptance in the metropole than even those Muslims serving on the French side in the war. Second, at a time of intensifying racism, these FPAs perhaps believed that attacks on Jews would show them to be "super-French."

In recounting the July 17 incident months later, the consistory's organ recalled the 1958 altercation and echoed Roger Berg's narrative of the earlier incident. The newspaper noted that according to witnesses, on entering the café, the FPAs had yelled insults in Arabic to the effect of "Dirty Jews!" The story described the attackers as "2 Muslim police, confined to the capital."[182] Such an account set the FPAs apart from other French people linguistically even as it mentioned the presumably Jewish "witnesses," who could have reported what the officers said only by virtue of their own knowledge of Arabic. The emphasis on the religion of the two policemen distinguished them from regular French police; calling the former "confined" suggested that Muslim police in Paris—and Muslims serving on the French side broadly—were a forced anomaly, by contrast with the resident Jews whom these men assaulted. Furthermore, the image of these essentially Muslim bodies that had to be tightly controlled lest they become violent echoed long-standing French notions about the immutability and corporeality of Islam, as well as specific contemporary anxieties in French media and policy regarding Algerian gender and sexuality.[183] It remained the case that masculinity had multiple meanings for Jewish-Muslim relations.

These two incidents in the Marais illustrated how the war had introduced new political categories into the lexicon of Jewish-Muslim mutual perceptions and interactions in Paris. In each instance, the tension within a café came not from a local disagreement but an external source. These altercations, which reflected in part the very proximity of Jewish and Muslim lives in the Marais, became only more volatile through their framing within certain organs of the Jewish press. Like the actions of the FPAs, such narrative frames implied a desire to map binary conceptions of politics onto daily social relations.

Other French cities too saw the war reshape the local context of Jewish-Muslim relations. In Marseille, the Muslim and Jewish populations grew throughout the Algerian War. The former jumped from 12,500 in 1953 to 21,000 in January 1958, remaining largely Algerian with a small Moroccan and Tunisian presence.[184] Through the arrival of Egyptian, Moroccan, Tunisian, and finally Algerian Jews, the city's Jewish population jumped as well, to 12,000 by 1957 and 30,000 to 35,000 by 1961.[185] While Jewish and Muslim newcomers faced common challenges, they encountered sharply contrasting receptions.

In the immigrant quarter of the Belsunce, from early in the war, the area around the rue des Chapeliers where Muslims had long congregated became critical to local FLN organizing, fundraising, and propaganda; this provoked periodic police raids. Already a suspect neighborhood, the Belsunce became increasingly isolated. More broadly, the war's atmosphere separated many Algerian Muslims from others living in Marseille.[186] Whereas earlier, a number of Jews from Mediterranean subcultures had lived and worked in the Belsunce, the fairly established nature of both many Marseillais Jews and the city's Jewish communal institutions appears to have limited any Jewish presence in the quarter at this time.[187]

Newly arrived Jews, even those classified as refugees, tended to encounter greater communal and state support mechanisms than French Muslim citizens and to live, tellingly, among *rapatriés* (repatriates). For the mostly stateless 10,000 Egyptian Jews who came to France after 1956, for instance, the French government budgeted at least 34 million francs over thirty-one months to support the work of Jewish relief agencies.[188] A number of these Jews settled in areas not physically far from the Belsunce but quite socially segregated. By 1961, 120 Jewish refugee families from Egypt and North Africa lived in the Félix Pyat-Parc Bellevue development, eight apartment buildings constructed specifically for settler colonists emigrating from North Africa, who began to arrive in 1957.[189]

The contrasts in Jews' and Muslims' capacities to integrate into the cityscape fostered tensions. In 1960 Abed Guendouz, a factory worker from Algeria, wrote to Marseille's mayor in exasperation. He and his wife and children had sought adequate housing from the local authorities for four years. Mentioning his citizenship, Guendouz wrote that he had "chosen France" and "married a European in order to penetrate further the French Family." But none of this seemed to offer him any advantage. Guendouz focused his greatest anger on the failure of the republic to live up to its promise. "I can cite to you," he exclaimed, "numerous cases of demands [of housing] deposited by French Muslims since 1950 and even before, and which are still pending, while the families of how many *israélites* and other French people departed from Egypt and elsewhere barely since 1957 are already lodged." Guendouz decried this practice as "not only revolting by its injustice, but above all by its separatism and all the hatreds that it arouses."[190] Guendouz's critique took its framework from republican principles. Yet to his frustration, circumstances dictated that he depict his situation as that of a French *Muslim* seeking integration along the lines enjoyed by *Jews,* among others.

In Strasbourg, smaller numbers of Jews and especially Muslims meant fewer opportunities for direct interaction. In autumn 1957, alongside a rebuilding postwar community of 10,500 Jews, the city housed a growing population of 1,500 to 1,600 mostly Algerian Muslim laborers. Like in Paris and Marseille, in Strasbourg, Muslim places of lodging, work, and socializing were subject to both intense pressure from Algerian nationalists and close surveillance by local police.[191] These political circumstances, and the prevalence of subsidized low-income housing among most Muslims, created social isolation that left few opportunities for the majority of Muslims and Jews to interact. Still, the first significant number of Muslims in the city's history resituated the meaning of Jewish-Muslim relations.

First, the Muslim presence raised the profile of the war. As we have already seen, by 1958, the Alsatian Jewish press became the site of fierce arguments about the proper Jewish position toward Muslims; such disagreements would become more acute in the final stages of the war. Beyond heightening conversation about Algeria's Muslims and the nationalists' cause among local Jews, Strasbourg's shifting demographics also created occasional opportunities for more personal interrelations. In autumn 1959, the city's university enrolled ninety-four students from North Africa; most were Muslims, and several were Jews.[192] Yet that year, it was with Evelyne Rueff, a twenty-year-old Ashkenazic Jew and medical student from Colmar, that Habib Hihi, a Moroccan medical student of Muslim descent, fell in love. The two met one morning standing in line next to each other at the start of class. Before long, their romance grew serious and they became engaged. Writing from Morocco, Hihi's father responded to the news with a letter full of anti-Jewish stereotypes. Rueff's father was friendlier, specifically not wanting to insist that Hihi convert to Judaism; unable to find a rabbi who would agree to marry them, the two wed in a civil ceremony. The couple's respective upbringings—in which Rueff learned she was Jewish only at the age of six due to her parents' fears during the Occupation, and Hihi's childhood home included rather faint connections to Islamic tradition—may have cultivated a shared ecumenical outlook. Indeed, rather than let prejudice or current tensions decide their allegiance, Hihi and Rueff went briefly to Algeria in summer 1962 in a neutral role to help fill a shortage of medical personnel.[193]

Through a remarkable range of ever-evolving mobilities and encounters, transnational connections, and often brutal divisions, Jews and Muslims during the French-Algerian War laid bare more than ever the possibilities and paradoxes of France as a both a space of trans-Mediterranean mobility and a Mediterranean empire. This occurred at the level of politics, demography, culture, and collective memory. By the late 1950s, the French-Algerian conflict was waged simultaneously in both Algeria and the mainland, with persons, arms, and ideas constantly crossing borders. New equality for Algerian Muslims under French law shrank the legal distance between the mainland and Algeria, even as it also triggered new types of anti-Muslim discrimination. Jews and Muslims from North Africa arrived, settled, and interacted in France in ever-growing numbers. The Arab-Israeli conflict and the wider story of decolonization in North Africa each had a major impact, from demographics to ideology, on French politics and culture. At the war's conclusion, nearly all Algerian Jews and *pieds-noirs* (the term, literally "black feet," by which the colonial settlers would soon become widely known), and large numbers of Muslims, came to France. For those who saw the French-Algerian conflict upend their lives, the experience would remain formative in shaping their future perceptions and interactions.

Habib Hihi and Evelyne Rueff's marriage constituted a telling sign of the fluid ethnoreligious boundaries and integrative capacities that crested in France during the height of the Algerian conflict. Yet by the time the two young doctors arrived in Algeria to offer medical aid, they came as foreigners to a newly independent land. Even as these newlyweds from diverse backgrounds sought to maintain their humanitarian, universal ideals, they saw that the war's final stage had rendered the binary visions of the French-Algerian relationship all too real.

5

A TIME OF CHOOSING

After nearly six years of violent struggle, autumn 1960 marked a turning point in the French-Algerian War. Earlier that summer, briefly promising negotiations for a cease-fire and Algerian self-determination had collapsed. On September 5, 1960, the French government opened trial against the "suitcase carriers" of the Jeanson network. The following day, the so-called Manifesto of the 121, calling itself a "declaration on the right of insubordination in the Algerian War," was published in the French press. In November 1960, French president Charles de Gaulle referred for the first time to "an Algerian republic, which will exist one day." These events galvanized large segments of mainland French opinion in anticipation of a negotiated peace and an independent Algeria. In Algeria, de Gaulle's declaration prompted a new militancy among supporters of Algérie française—largely European colonists and numerous current and former members of the French military. In February 1961, these activists coalesced around the newly formed, militant Organisation de l'armée secrète (OAS), which would wage a formidable, if last-ditch, war of propaganda and terror designed to keep Algeria French at any cost.

During the period from autumn 1960 to the end of hostilities and the independence of Algeria in the summer of 1962, as violence escalated first in Algeria and then the metropole, and negotiations unfolded between the government and the Front de libération nationale (FLN), Jews and Muslims faced narrowing political choices. During the preceding six years, many Jews and Muslims had found ways to articulate multiple or fluid versions of belonging and nationhood in both the French republic and the prospective Algerian one. Now, however, the French and Algerian nations, and Jews and Muslims of the Francophone world, stood at a hinge point of their history: the war's closing phase and its immediate aftermath witnessed shifts in the meaning of nationhood and ethnicity in France, with far-reaching consequences.

Most scholarship on the French-Algerian War and on Jewish and Muslim migrations to France has treated 1962 simply as a rupture point with a clear before and after. Yet the key changes had already begun to occur over the final year and a half of the war; they then continued into the post-decolonization period, making the early to mid-1960s a defining period of transformation. Understanding these changes requires us to examine two distinct but interconnected sets of developments. First, as the war neared its conclusion, Jews and Muslims increasingly framed their political positions in a binary manner that either embraced or rejected notions of French Algeria, and many did so in terms that foregrounded religion or ethnicity. At the same time, in numerous cases, configurations of identity and relations remained open-ended and multifaceted. In the second development, the migrations of the late colonial period brought larger numbers of North African Jews and Muslims than ever before into close proximity on metropolitan French soil. In Marseille, Paris, Strasbourg, and elsewhere, Jewish and Muslim emigrants forged ties in new "North African" neighborhoods, cafés, corner stores, even an athletic association. Yet the process of decolonization—through its traumatic end points and the changes it produced in French citizenship policy—also entailed significant changes in the terms on which Jews and Muslims related to each other and to France. At the everyday level, even as Jews and Muslims found ways to interact amicably in a number of contexts, they had to negotiate new rules that would govern their encounters as they faced a wider environment of increasing racialization.

Recent studies have illuminated how, as it became clearer that the French would leave Algeria, the state etched new, more rigid, ethnically defined boundary lines around national belonging.[1] In key respects, these boundaries constricted the possible meanings of Frenchness and of Jewish and Muslim ethnoreligious identifications. Yet an emphasis on legal categories and national political discourse alone obscures other parts of a multilayered story. Put differently, if the Latinist colonial dream of Mediterraneanism died with the polarization and then official break between France and Algeria, the same events brought to mainland France an unprecedented number of people, material objects, and cultural practices from various subcultures across the Mediterranean.

The Future Algeria: A Space for Muslim-Jewish Brotherhood?

Over the last year and a half of the French-Algerian War, Jews and Muslims in Algeria increasingly perceived and depicted themselves on opposing sides of two competing national visions. By now, most Muslims in both Algeria and France supported Algerian independence. Jews, however, sharply split between Algeria and the metropole: the majority of the former tied their fate to that of France, with many supporting or even joining the OAS; increasing numbers of the latter showed solidarity with the Algerian nationalists. And yet while for many, particularly in Algeria, Muslim and Jewish identity became linked automatically with the causes of Algerian nationalism and French Algeria, respectively, others rejected or evaded these alignments and their oppositions.

In December 1960, the FLN declared, "By inviting the israélite community not to take part in the battle of national liberation, the authorities of this community . . . have affirmed themselves as accomplices of the colonialist crimes perpetrated everyday [in] our country."[2] The nationalists had expressed increasing frustration with the indecisiveness of the Algerian Jewish community during the preceding four years, and they would offer more temperate, even conciliatory rhetoric again in the future. But these inflammatory statements signaled a turning point. In significant part due to its own internal struggles that had gradually tilted away from secular nationalism toward notions of Algeria as an Islamic nation linked to the wider Arab world, the FLN was hardening its position with regard to the Jews. Increasingly, the nationalists' new outlook took the form of violent action. Particularly jarring was the December 12, 1960, attack on the Great Synagogue of Algiers. A group of Muslims pillaged the synagogue, smashing the furniture and desecrating and trampling on the Torah scrolls. The attackers planted an FLN flag and left inscriptions such as "Death to the Jews" and, tellingly, "Long Live the Algerian Republic." The FLN disavowed the attack; in the event's aftermath, many Muslims in the surrounding quarter offered their Jewish neighbors protection.[3] Yet for many, the religiously tinged anti-Jewish violence of December 1960 created a sense of profound insecurity about Jewish prospects in an independent Algeria.[4]

During the next fifteen months, over 130 attacks against Jews or Jewish establishments occurred in Algeria, with the vast majority perpetrated by the FLN or its supporters.[5] Among the most symbolically significant of these was the assassination in June 1961 of the beloved Jewish Algerian musician Raymond Leyris, a *chaabi* maestro affectionately nicknamed by Muslims "Sheikh Raymond."[6] Only weeks before, a self-styled Group of Jewish Algerian Patriots had published an optimistic article in which they wrote, "The Constantinian singer and musician Raymond, is he not dear in the eyes of the Muslims? They love him because he contributed to conserving and enriching the Algerian folklore that the colonialists wanted to destroy."[7] Leyris was, according to at least one report of the time, a known supporter of the FLN. He embodied the liminal identity of Algerian Jews, situated between the native Muslims with whom they continued to share customs and sensibilities and the liberating presence of French civilization, culture, and citizenship.[8] For many, the Algerian nationalists' decision to murder him signaled that Jews would have no place in the future Algerian republic.

Nonetheless, the FLN and its supporters continued to court Jews. On both sides of the Mediterranean, conversations continued between Jews and Muslims over the Algerian future. FLN tracts printed in 1961 and 1962 spoke of the Jews as "authentic children of Algeria" and exclaimed that the Muslims of Algeria, having endured racism themselves, would not wish to inflict it on the country's Jews in the future. Internal directives from 1961 urged FLN activists to communicate a message of inclusion that would lead Europeans and Jews to remain.[9] Moreover, several nationalist pamphlets targeting Jews equated the OAS with fascism and the Holocaust.[10] In the metropole in spring 1961, a certain number of nationalist Muslims studying in Paris used similar arguments in an effort to persuade Jewish fellow students of the justice of their cause. As the Jewish leftist Jacques Greilsammer explained in a public debate about Jewish positions on the war:

> For a large part of the Jewish youth, up until the Algerian problem, they had the feeling of being on the good side of the fence, on the side of those who had defeated Nazism, but there was the war in Algeria, and when we encountered students from black Africa and Algerian students, when they spoke to us of the tortures and the concentration camps, of villages razed and all the rest, we perceived that we were able, us as well, to be on the bad side of the fence, that we had to choose right away, because if not . . . [then] the face that we [as Jews] could present to others was no longer the face of liberty or of great principles but the face of the butcher, of the torturer, and that [could happen] very simply and very easily.[11]

During the same period, *Kadimah,* the newsletter of the French Jewish Student Union (UEJF), published selected portions of a long letter to the editors from Mohamed Ben Bachir, a Muslim student and nationalist. Bachir objected to a recent *Kadimah* article that had voiced anxieties about the fate of Jews in an independent Algeria; he termed such concern "without foundation." More specifically, even as he spoke critically of Israel, Bachir called it "inopportune" and "premature" to worry about the future relationship of Algeria with Israel or Cairo. Instead, the author wished to focus on how, regardless of religion, all who opposed colonialism were comrades in the Algerian revolution. He echoed previous claims of the FLN that the Crémieux Decree had sought to divide Jews from Muslims; colonialism alone, he insisted, created discord between the two populations. Reflecting the multiple strands within both the nationalist movement and Muslim-Jewish relations, Bachir made his claims not only in nationalistic or historical but also religious terms. In an invocation of Islamic traditions of respect for the other monotheistic religions, he insisted, "Universal morality, from Moses to Jesus and Mohamed, calls believers to be on the side of the weak and the oppressed, without other considerations." As he concluded his article, he contrasted the stakes of the present moment with the economic disagreements of Jews and Muslims in ninth-century Medina, declaring, "In 1960, Algerian Jews and Muslims have greater and nobler things to do than argue over the spice market."[12]

Read carefully, Bachir's words did not simply call for Jewish support for Algerian nationalism; implicitly, they went much further than that. Bachir sent the not unimportant message that he was a young Algerian nationalist who bothered to read the newsletter of his Jewish peers and sought to respond to their specifically Jewish concerns. His reference to traditional Muslim respect for the central figures of biblical Judaism and Christianity, and to coexistence between Jews and Muslims in the very cradle of Islamic civilization, suggested that Jewish and Muslim destinies were ultimately inseparable. Only forces of Western imperialism could divide Jews and Muslims; the two groups might have disagreements, but ultimately they shared fundamental values and common roots.

Yet by spring 1961, these disagreements had opened a growing chasm that even those Jews most sympathetic to the Algerian uprising found difficult to bridge. Numerous UEJF-organized gatherings and other meetings of Jews and Muslims had done little to achieve greater mutual understanding. Following one such meeting, the Tunisian Jewish writer Albert Memmi, though he remained committed to dialogue, wrote, "Must I acknowledge that reticence was almost equal on both sides? That the non-Jews and the non-Arabs who were with us were full of goodwill but skeptical. In brief, we failed; we must acknowledge it because nobody expected it." Even when *Kadimah* published Bachir's letter, it preceded it with a disclaimer that explained the editors had excised potentially provocative passages, described his conclusions as fundamentally flawed, and printed multiple rebuttals.[13]

Disillusionment was mutual. As the Islamist, pan-Arab portions of the FLN leadership gained the upper hand, Muslim voices like that of Bachir were becoming rather lonely. The question of Israel played a significant part in increasing hostility toward Jews. In 1960, the Algerian-born Jew Jean Daniel, prominent journalist and FLN sympathizer, asked two leading nationalist representatives privately about whether the "religious fanatics" in the FLN would allow non-Muslims to live in an independent Algeria. The two leaders explained frankly that the severity and duration of French colonialism meant "the pendulum" would swing the other way with a brutal vengeance that would leave no place for non-Muslims. They said that they understood the powerful allure of such an outlook and would not try to change it.[14] Numerous French newspapers reported that when the independent Algerian government gathered in Tunis in early 1961, it promised that in a free Algeria, it would revoke the Crémieux Decree and bar Algerian Jews from emigrating to Israel.[15] In essence, Jews would be asked to negate their multifaceted attachments and choose their Algerienness alone over any connection to France or to Jewish peoplehood. In spring 1962, representatives of the American Jewish Joint Distribution Committee (commonly called the Joint) reported growing numbers of FLN kidnappings and executions of Jews. During an April visit in Cairo with Gamal Abdel Nasser, Ahmed Ben Bella—recently liberated from prison by the Evian Accords and now vice president of the Algerian provisional government—gave a widely reported news interview that offered no sign of his previous admiration for Israel. Ben Bella attacked Zionism by linking it to the OAS, said the Algerian revolution would only be complete upon the "liberation of Palestine," and promised to send 100,000 Algerians to fight for the cause.[16]

Algerian Jewry and the OAS as the Last, Best Hope

During the same period when the FLN appeared to turn more decisively against the Jews of Algeria, developments in Morocco and Tunisia made conditions more precarious for Jews there as well. In July 1961, Tunisian president Habib Bourguiba demanded that de Gaulle evacuate the French naval bases at Bizerte, which constituted some of the country's last vestiges of French colonialism. What began as a blockade designed to force the French to leave devolved quickly into a bloody conflict in which many Tunisians died; the French ultimately overran the town of Bizerte, and Tunisia had to accept a humiliating military defeat. On the basis of unsubstantiated rumors, many Tunisians believed that their Jewish compatriots had fought on the French side. Jews quickly became targets of hostility and even antisemitic violence. Months earlier, in Morocco, Nasser had visited the Casablanca Conference on January 3, 1961, with a delegation that included FLN members. A week later, the *Pisces,* a boat with forty-three Jewish passengers secretly bound from Morocco for Israel, sank and all the passengers drowned. These incidents linked Muslim-Jewish relations in Morocco more tightly to hostility between Israel and its Arab neighbors, provoking antisemitic attacks and the arrests of numerous Jews. In the aftermath of the *Pisces* sinking, a Zionist pamphlet criticizing Moroccan mistreatment of Jews only further fueled antisemitism. In this context, 1961 saw many Jewish immigrants leave both countries for France or Israel; for Algerian Jews, such developments heightened the sense of insecurity.[17]

In this atmosphere, at both individual and institutional levels, Algerian Jewry came to view its future as linked inextricably to France. Most hoped that France would somehow remain in Algeria, and they insisted that regardless of the war's outcome, they had to retain their French citizenship. Consequently, increasing numbers of Algerian Jews supported the OAS.[18] Shocked by what they viewed as de Gaulle's profound betrayal in moving toward Algerian self-determination, the OAS considered a French departure unthinkable and waged its own war to stop it. Until and even after Algerian independence became official in July 1962, the group used terror, intimidation, and propaganda to mobilize against the FLN, the French army, and any French citizen who wished to flee Algeria.

It may appear counterintuitive that the OAS would have garnered widespread Jewish support in Algeria. In addition to its violent tactics and ultranationalist rhetoric, many OAS members had formerly supported Vichy during World War II and Far Right movements in the 1950s. In a manner that connected to the longtime rhetoric of Latinist Mediterraneanism, the fiercest partisans of Algérie française spoke of their struggle as key to the larger defense of the "Christian West."[19] In both Algeria and the mainland, the group's propaganda savagely attacked "the trusts," "the bankers," and "the Masons," as well as the Rothschilds and other prominent Jews.[20] Militants murdered a number of Algerian Jewish individuals. For all these reasons, the OAS provoked repeated charges of fascism and antisemitism.[21] Yet its leaders adamantly denied any such tendencies. In fact, the group anchored many of its harshest critiques of de Gaulle in calls for republican legality. The OAS repeatedly assailed instruments by which the government, in its efforts to leave Algeria, appeared to subvert the new constitution of the Fifth Republic.[22] The organization also touted Muslim support, connecting repeatedly to France's thirteen-decade-old effort to "Frenchify" Algeria (one that de Gaulle's government hastened to forget). The OAS even sought to position itself within the tradition of the Revolution of 1789 and the French Resistance.[23] In turn, it compared de Gaulle and his policies to Nazism.

A tract from early 1962 described the martyrdom of a young Jewish boy in Algeria who died when a French soldier shot at a group of high school students hanging "patriotic posters." The author exclaimed: "No, the scene did not take place in the Warsaw Ghetto in 1942, but in Bône, in the European quarter, 19 January 1962. . . . The man in uniform is not an SS, but an officer of the Military Court of Bône." This story served to justify the broader assertion that "to fight the OAS today is to prepare the genocide and the pogroms of tomorrow."[24] Like all other political forces at the time, the OAS superimposed the memory of World War II over present events. The specific emphasis here on a young Jewish boy and the Shoah also aimed to rally Jewish support. Indeed, here was, among other things, a striking signal of the shifting attitudes toward Jews among parts of the Far Right in the context of the Algerian struggle.

Jews in Algeria reacted in a variety of ways to the OAS. Much of the Algerian Jewish leadership appeared uncomfortable with the organization's tactics, if not necessarily its goals. A May 1961 editorial in *L'Information juive,* the monthly organ of Algerian Jews, lambasted the French press for its insinuations of connections between Zionist groups and the OAS.[25] Longtime CJAES secretary-general Jacques Lazarus was never contacted personally by the OAS, but said later that he long lived in dread of the prospect. "Because," explained Lazarus, "I was *hostile* to the action of the OAS, I was finding it *inadmissible* when they killed Muslims in the street, which [people] testified and which I saw [myself]."[26]

Yet amid the escalating FLN violence and growing signs of French departure, many Algerian Jews grew increasingly receptive to OAS appeals. As it became ever clearer that Algeria would become independent, many Jews feared, in the words of French Jewish observer Arnold Mandel, that "the revenge of the former subject populace would be directed against them, not only as Europeans but also as Jews and as friends of Israel." Thus, according to Mandel, "the majority of Algerian Jews slipped bit by bit into the camp of the ultras and even, in the last period before the signing of the Evian agreement, into that of the [OAS]."[27] Autumn 1961, when the OAS reached its zenith as a popular movement, appears to have been the turning point.[28] In Oran, where a wait-and-see attitude had long prevailed among most of the 35,000 Jews, the move was particularly striking.[29] On Rosh Hashanah in September 1961, Jewish-Muslim tension exploded in the city's Jewish quarter. The FLN murder of Jew Henri Choukroun provoked Jewish and then Muslim reprisals. Participants exchanged chants of "Algérie française" and "Algérie musulmane," revealing the degree to which binary, exclusionary outlooks regarding the future of both the French Republic and the imminent Algerian one were taking hold.[30] In early 1962, one resident of Oran's Jewish quarter confided to a friend in Paris: "We live in total insecurity. . . . We risk our lives at each moment, and it is a climate of Terror."[31] According to numerous accounts, by this point the city's Jews had chosen, widely and often actively, to support the OAS.[32]

Still, claims to multifaceted rather than monolithic forms of French citizenship played a role in many Jews' engagement on the side of Algérie française. As OAS attacks intensified in late 1961, in Oran, a unit dubbed the "Commandos Israélites" led the way, carrying out numerous assassinations of French officials and Muslims.[33] In February 1962, the group participated in an attack in the Muslim quarter of the Planteurs that left forty dead and one hundred wounded. One Jewish member described the Commandos' purpose as "the self-defense of the Israélite quarter of Oran, in order to prevent the Arabs from penetrating there."[34] Given this stated mission, the unit's activity implied that these Algerian Jews saw any advocate for either Algerian independence or French departure as a threat to their community's security. Algerian Jewish leader and OAS supporter Henri Chemouilli defended his position with different politics but similar references to security and invoked, as so many other actors of the period did, the terms of the World War II: "The OAS, as I knew it, was made of veterans, often *résistants,* always former Gaullists. All men of the left as well! We were not looking for a posthumous revenge for Pétain, we were not contemplating overthrowing the regime. We just simply did not want to die."[35]

As a member of the CJAES, Chemouilli was unusual in his activism for Algérie française. But in their own way, most Algerian Jewish leaders demonstrated during the late stages of the war that they viewed Algerian Jewry's future as tied irrevocably to France. Along with others, Jacques Lazarus worked relentlessly to emphasize the community's Frenchness. In February 1960, Socialist Party leader and former prime minister Guy Mollet penned an article in *Démocratie 60* that alarmed Algerian Jewry. He relayed a recent conversation with President de Gaulle in which the general had referred to "the rights of the Arab, Chaouia, Mozabite, Jewish, and French communities" that he foresaw in a future federal Algerian state. The separation of "Jewish" from "French" stunned Jewish leaders. Lazarus and many of his colleagues contacted Mollet and de Gaulle directly to express their concerns and underscored the longevity and intensity of Algerian Jews' attachment to French citizenship.[36] When negotiations took place the following year over the future of Algeria and its inhabitants, the Jewish community leaned heavily on key allies and participants Bernard Tricot and Louis Joxe to protect Jews' status.[37] The pressure ultimately succeeded. French official language about groups in Algeria ceased to treat "israélites" as a separate category, mentioning them only as part of the broader set of "Europeans." At the very same moment, however, officials tightened the meaning of the latter category to exclude Muslims loyal to France. In underscoring the assimilability of Jews, this followed classical French republican conceptions; in rejecting that of Muslims, particularly those already legally French, it violated them. This signaled the narrowing window of Frenchness emerging in the war's closing months.[38]

The FLN's own outlook ultimately reinforced the same developments. The nationalists had long prioritized strict national unity above all else, thus framing as unthinkable the prospect that a Muslim of Algeria would choose France over his newly independent homeland. Furthermore, after long insisting that the Jews must be considered indigenous Algerians rather than French, the FLN, for pragmatic reasons, elected not to make a major issue of this in the final negotiations at Evian.[39]

As France and Algeria neared the mutual breaking point, so too did numerous personal relationships between Jews and Muslims in Algeria. In many small towns like Tiaret and Relizane in the Oran region, Muslims warned their Jewish friends and neighbors that they should flee before independence, as they feared that Jews would be the victims of an OAS-targeted spree of violent retribution once the FLN took power.[40] Another development that served to underscore the new distinction between the assimilability of Jews and the ethnic otherness of Muslims occurred with regard to the Jews of the Mzab region of the Algerian Sahara. In the Sahara, Jews had never gained the French citizenship bestowed on the rest of the population by the Crémieux Decree; consequently, the area's Jews and Muslims had continued to live as fellow natives, with close daily relations that remained undisturbed by the war—until July 1961, that is, when the French government elected to grant all Mzabi Jews French citizenship. This move transformed overnight the climate for Jewish-Muslim relations in communities across the region. A newspaper report from the village of Comomb-Béchar, for instance, detailed how Jews (few of whom imagined leaving Algeria) were thrilled by their new status, seeing it as "a ticket of protection" against possible times of persecution; Muslims, for their part, saw their Jewish neighbors' acceptance of French citizenship as nothing less than an act of treason. All speech between Muslims and Jews, the author claimed, suddenly became aggressive and threatening, leading quickly to violence in which French soldiers had to intervene. Before long, Jews began to depart the region en masse.[41] Here, at least for many, the association of Jews with French Algeria and Muslims with anticolonial nationalism had indeed become quite absolute.[42]

Years later, Jews from Dar-Refayil, a large house in Sétif shared by Jewish and Muslim families for decades, offered conflicting memories of the period. They portrayed the domestic sphere of the home, long a shared space, as one that remained relatively insulated from the war, recalling in particular Jewish and Muslim children playing together in the courtyard of the house. At the same time, they noted how Jews separated themselves from Muslims in new ways in this period due to Muslim aspirations that the Jews did not share. Jews became more selective about the Muslims with whom they interacted, trusting only those they already knew. For Muslims, the Jewish decision to depart was seen as "a kind of support of the oppressive colonial power." And yet Muslims saw these Jews' position as ambiguous, still different from that of "real Europeans"; when the Jews of Dar-Refayil left for France, Muslim families looked on with tears in their eyes.[43]

Yet Algerian Jews did not entirely move in sync with the increasing rigidity of French legal categories. Leaders like Lazarus continued to insist at times on an amalgam of identities for the Algerian Jewish population, implicitly pushing for more fluid understandings of Frenchness. In February 1961, Lazarus proclaimed: "Algerians, French, liberals, the Jews of this country are also and want to remain Jews." Jewish leaders even discussed the possibility of dual French and Algerian citizenship.[44]

Beginning in late 1961, however, Algerian Jews would opt decisively for France with their feet. By late summer 1962, 130,000 of Algeria's approximately 140,000 Jews had left for the French mainland.[45] These Jews had been largely impervious to efforts by the Jewish Agency to recruit them for *Aliyah,* or migration to Israel (a path chosen by only about 10,000).[46] Algerian Jews' departure en masse for France reflected their long-standing French citizenship and attachments to French culture, as well as their growing sense that their security depended on continued French rule in Algeria; it coincided with the larger "repatriation" of the so-called European colonists. For these reasons, along with their equivalent legal status, some historians have argued that these Jews undertook, in essence, a *French* migration rather than a Jewish one, and became themselves *pieds-noirs,* the frequently used term for the French colonists in Algeria.[47] Yet such a perspective overlooks a larger picture. As we have seen, the questions that animated Algerian Jews as they decided whether to migrate were constantly centered on their position as Jews: What would the war mean specifically for the Jewish community and Jewish individuals in Algeria? What would it mean for their capacity to migrate to Israel or visit family there? As Jews native to Algeria and its language and customs for centuries, how could they abandon this land and culture they loved? Moreover, while community leaders insisted that Algerian Jewry was made up of a diverse body of individuals, they elected to represent Jews as a collective; in insisting to the French government that they were French, they did so specifically as Jews and cited all that France had done for Jews specifically throughout its history in Algeria, and vice versa. Even as they departed, these Jews sought to maintain a measure of Algerian-Jewish ethnic identity, organizing as a distinctive community on their arrival in France.[48]

Metropolitan Jewry and the OAS as Return of Fascism

In October 1960, Jeanine Cahen, one of the "suitcase carriers," after being told at the conclusion of her trial that the FLN was antisemitic, responded defiantly: "It is *because* I am Jewish that I helped the FLN; one must know that those who cry, 'Algérie Française' are the same who write 'Death to the Jews.'"[49] Few other moments captured better the way that numerous ordinary French Jews in the metropole were publicly engaging the question of Algeria on their own multifaceted terms, often distinct from those of either their coreligionists in Algeria or conventional Franco-Judaism. Many of the most outspoken of these Jews had come of age during or following World War II. Such ethnic and generational contrasts reflected divergences of historical experience and previewed conflicts of the years to come.

By late 1960, the long-simmering tensions over Algeria within Strasbourg's Jewish community burst into the open. In a December 1960 cover story in *Le Bulletin de nos communautés*, leading community activist Lucien Lazare sharply criticized the heads of organized French Jewry. Lazare's outlook reflected both a religious perspective born of his traditional Jewish education and a personal history of engagement in the Jewish Resistance during World War II. Acknowledging that the Jewish community indeed should not speak politically and admitting that not only the French but also the FLN had committed atrocities, Lazare called nonetheless for what he deemed spiritual engagement. Citing passages from both the Torah and the Talmud regarding collective responsibility for bloodshed, Lazare declared: "When the innocent die of assassination, it is thus the entire society that is guilty, but above all its leaders and its guides." He argued, therefore, that "pleading for justice, when Muslims are persecuted, is an absolute demand of the Jewish spiritual tradition. . . . Heads of our community, make yourselves the mouthpiece of the cry of the Jewish conscience."[50] Soon after, two other cover editorials took opposing positions. In the first, Joseph Weill, president of the Bas-Rhin Consistory, wrote in response to several recent brutal anti-Jewish attacks by nationalists in Algeria. Weill's response demonstrated that by this point, a flood of negative, often demonic images of Arabs in the Jewish press during the 1950s, coupled with the departure of growing numbers of Jews from North Africa, had created deep anti-Arab hostility among many Ashkenazic French Jews. Weill lamented the latest acts as the result of systemic antisemitism, which he linked to Arab attitudes toward Israel, the dissemination in Arabic of "The Protocols of the Elders of Zion" (a notorious antisemitic forgery claiming to document a Jewish plan for world domination), and consultation by Arab leaders with Nazi war criminals.[51] In February another editorial argued that as a community, Jews could not take a stance, labeling as "naive" those who critiqued French rabbis on this score.[52]

In January 1961 Lionel Cohn, a Jewish student activist, and, like Lazare, from a traditional religious background, wrote in *Kadimah* that Jews found themselves torn in the conflict. They felt compelled by Jewish tradition's support for a people's right to independence and opposition to inhumane methods like torture. But in accordance with another traditional value, that of Jewish solidarity, they also cared deeply for the welfare of Algerian Jews, including their rights regarding visiting and communicating with Israel.[53] In the spring of 1961, these competing concerns framed a debate in a special issue of *Kadimah* and then were expressed by one speaker after another in a lengthy conference session on "engagement and nonengagement." These developments reflected the ongoing emergence of a new generation of Jews speaking publicly about the war not simply as French citizens but as Jews.[54]

In its ultimate support for Algerian self-determination, the UEJF, like many metropolitan Jews, responded to the issue differently from most Jewish activists in Algeria. Widespread attacks and discrimination against Muslims provoked a growing engagement on their behalf by French Jewish leaders and groups. On the night of October 17, 1961, in response to an FFLN protest against a curfew for Algerian Muslims in Paris, Parisian police unleashed a wave of repression in which they killed 30 to 200 Algerian Muslims and rounded up 12,000 more. In February 1962, a communist-led anti-OAS demonstration near the Charonne Métro station was brutally suppressed by French police, leading to the deaths of eight protesters. By early 1962, the OAS increasingly brought its ultranationalist propaganda and terror campaign to the metropole.

Leading Jewish figures and groups responded to this climate with denunciations that compared current events to those of Nazism and the Shoah. René Sirat, the Paris Consistory's youth rabbi, declared that the murder and roundups of Algerian Muslims "touches me personally." Indeed, Sirat had, like so many other Algerian Jewish schoolchildren, not only lost his citizenship during World War II but also endured humiliating wartime experiences of antisemitism at his lycée.[55] Now, he exclaimed: "I only am able to be reminded of twenty years ago, when every Jew was able to be led into the high places of civilization that are Vel d'Hiv and Drancy. We must do something so that that does not begin again." Sirat, like Lazare, took a position that he deemed more religious than political, also citing the Talmud to invoke the halakhic (Jewish legal) obligation to stand up against the shedding of blood.[56] On a broader scale, Jewish leftist groups like the UEJF and the Union des juifs pour la résistance et l'entraide (UJRE) organized meetings and coalitions to mobilize Jews against the "danger of French Nazism.[57] Thus, in definitively Jewish terms, many individuals and groups reframed the stakes of the Algerian conflict and the cause of rights for Algerian Muslims as a continuation of those of World War II, that is, as a defense of republican values against fascism.

Despite this trend in Paris and many national organizations, Jewish politics and its relationship to metropolitan violence in the late stages of the war took diverse forms. Due to their locations on the German border and the Mediterranean, respectively, both Strasbourg and Marseille witnessed greater human traffic throughout the war than most other cities. This made them particular targets of not only the FLN but also of OAS efforts to spread to the metropole. In the meantime, along with its geographical accessibility, each city's established Jewish community made it more attractive for those Jewish so-called rapatriés already arriving in late 1961 and early 1962. These coinciding developments led Jewish OAS activists to both cities. In late 1961, Messaoud Chouraqui, a thirty-seven-year-old Jew from Algiers who went by the nickname "Gaston the Jew," orchestrated OAS explosives attacks in Marseille.[58] In June 1962, at least nine North African Jews appeared to be among 149 rapatriés coming to Marseille listed as "dangerous" for activism on behalf of French Algeria.[59] In May 1962 in Strasbourg, two recently arrived Algerian rapatriés with Jewish names, Gabriel Sebbah and Georges Sarraf, drew suspicion from local police of attempting to foment OAS activity.[60]

These new arrivals underscored the contrast between many Algerian Jews and those of the metropole in their attitudes toward the OAS. For Algerian Jewry, the group emerged at a moment of tremendous vulnerability. As the community came to equate French departure with the liquidation of the Jewish presence in Algeria, the OAS, as the last bastion of pro-French Algeria resistance, became alluring. The group seemed all that stood between Algerian Jewry and an untenable life in an independent Arab state. For metropolitan Jews, on the other hand, many of whom had experienced the Shoah more directly than in Algeria, the arrival of the OAS in the Hexagon appeared to threaten the stability of French democracy and its basic values. On the heels of postwar movements like the Far Right Poujadists, the OAS, along with instances of police brutality like the "October massacre" and Charonne, constituted only the latest and most lethal manifestation of rising racism and antisemitism in France.[61] For one group of Jews, then, the OAS offered a last hope of security; for the other, it imperiled a basic sense of security.

As the war drew to a close, consternation among many metropolitan Jews even prompted engagement by the Jewish communal leadership. Among the French rabbinate, this mostly took the form of efforts to promote peace and condemn racism.[62] Pushing further, the CRIF, beginning in December 1961, debated a possible resolution condemning the OAS. In the end, however, in significant part due to its fears for the security of Algerian Jews, the committee settled on a statement that simply spoke of dedication to French tradition, recalled past persecution of Jews, and condemned all violence.[63] This decision not only exhibited the competing stakes of the war for many Algerian and metropolitan French Jews, respectively; it highlighted as well the ongoing tension between traditional republican Judaism and the emergent, more actively Jewish politics.

The New France Defines the New Arrivals

While the Algerian War and decolonization did much to shift the relationships of Muslims and Jews to the French state, North African nationalisms, and one another, these events were equally transformative at the level of demographics. Somewhat paradoxically, the Algerian War had witnessed the largest Algerian Muslim migration yet to metropolitan France. By 1958, roughly 350,000 Algerian Muslims lived in France.[64] The nationalist "myth of the return" had long claimed that all Algerians would return to their native land following independence, but this hardly proved true in the event. A certain number of Algerian workers continued to flock to France for the employment opportunities of its humming economy; almost by definition, those coming in the wake of the Evian Accords tended to be the least political, with little investment in the new state. Indeed, during the same period, many militant Algerian nationalists long active in France returned to Algeria to continue their work on behalf of the independent nation. In time, however, a significant number of them, disillusioned with their national dream as reality, came back to France. For many, the aspirations and unity of the Revolution proved unsustainable in the context of a repressive regime, all the more so after the military coup d'état of 1965 that replaced Ahmed Ben Bella's socialist one-party state with a military dictatorship under Houari Boumediene.[65]

In the early 1960s, as the Algerian migration slowed, the proportion of Moroccan and Tunisian Muslims among the French Muslim population began to grow. In 1962 approximately 350,000 Algerians, 33,000 Moroccans, and 27,000 Tunisians lived in France. At that time, Algerians constituted 85 percent of France's North African Muslim population; by 1970 their relative presence had dropped to around 70 percent. The country's population of Muslim noncitizens, by then over 800,000, counted approximately 608,000 Algerians, but also 143,000 Moroccans and 89,000 Tunisians. While the strong majority were male manual laborers, the proportion of women and children had increased substantially since World War II. In addition, those who arrived in France from Algeria in 1962 had included 40,000 harkis and their families; by 1968, 138,000 "repatriated" French Muslim citizens of Algerian origin lived in France.[66]

For the majority of Muslims, the precise form of the French departure from Algeria rapidly redefined their relationship to France. In a basic sense, Algerian, Moroccan, and Tunisian independence gave most Muslims in France formal ties to newly established sovereign states. As citizens of these countries, the majority of Muslims in France became what they had never been previously: foreign nationals like the country's many immigrants from places such as Italy, Portugal, and Yugoslavia.[67] Though this granted them diplomatic representation and legal recourse, it also meant that they no longer occupied the uncertain position of French colonial subjects or, in the case of Algeria, equal French citizens since 1958. Indeed, the shift was far more pronounced in the case of Muslims from Algeria than those from Morocco or Tunisia. This reflected the longevity and size of the French presence in Algeria, the official status of much of the territory as part of France proper, and the enormous effort that had accelerated during the Algerian War to "make French" the land and its native inhabitants.

The segregation of most Muslims from the French body politic, already suggested by the exclusion of Muslims from the category of "European" in the course of the negotiations leading to the Evian Accords, would become encoded into law by late 1962.[68] Such a stark change in status was hardly inevitable. A telegram from French National Defense headquarters in March 1962 declared that following independence, Muslim French

citizens of Algeria would "have the same possibilities as 'French of origin' to settle in the metropole with French citizenship" and all the legal
benefits of "French repatriates." The telegram also stated that such a
possibility certainly "would remain available to French Muslims" who
chose to return to the metropole "at any moment after self-determination,"
wherein they could "reclaim French nationality under French law." A
message from the minister of the armies had guaranteed that "French
Muslims serving in the armed forces and as auxiliaries" would have "their
legitimate interests as soldiers and citizens" protected.[69]

In late spring 1962, however, as the government witnessed the massive exodus underway from Algeria, it began to adopt different policies.
A secret memo of late May from President de Gaulle's office stated that
those assisting Muslims in Algeria had to "cease all initiatives linked to
the repatriation of harkis." The same month, the French secretary of state
for repatriates created a new set of categories, dividing French of Algeria
into "repatriates of European origin" and "repatriates of Muslim origin." This marked a crucial shift, for it moved the question of citizenship from the realm of territory, where it had long resided in republican
law, into that of ethnicity or race, a fixed category antithetical to the assimilationist republican model. This revealed the paradox of the recognition contained within the new category of citizens, French Muslims of
Algeria (FMAs), established during the French-Algerian conflict; these
measures maintained the category's identification of a specific ethnic
group but now did so for the purposes of legal exclusion. By late July, de
Gaulle would completely ignore the legal categories that had existed up
to and through the Evian Accords and declare: "The term 'repatriates'
obviously does not apply to the Muslims. In their case, we are dealing
only with refugees."[70] This statement came on the heels of an ordinance
that allowed "European" French from Algeria to retain automatically
their French nationality even if they became Algerian, but explained that
"Muslims" from Algeria now officially had to apply for French citizenship, with approval entirely in the hands of a French official on a case-
by-case basis. Thus, the French effectively revived a requirement that must
have reminded many Muslims of the one they or their parents had lived
under until the last decades of colonial rule.

These developments enabled the French to ignore willfully the needs
of numerous harkis, who now sought to flee to France. Estimates of Muslims loyal to the French side during the war that were killed by the FLN
or in other reprisals by the end of 1962 range from 10,000 to 100,000.[71]

For the tens of thousands of harki families who came to France, most were citizens either under civil status or local law, and their status therefore was converted by default to Algerian citizenship, forcing them to undergo the often humiliating process of a recorded declaration or "reintegration" measures.[72]

The state thus chose to forget that Algeria and its natives had ever been "French," or, more precisely, that France's republican mission had failed to *make them fully French*. This decision had far-reaching implications. De Gaulle's government was breaking with not only its own recent promises but also republican law, the assimilatory traditions of French republican nationalism, and the aggressive integrationist policies of the previous seven years. In place of the official flexibility within French citizenship opened up for Muslims during the Algerian War, the binary vision of much of the war's rhetoric, between French Algeria and an independent Algeria, had in a sense become real. Algerian independence, implied French policy, had to mean mutual rejection on a massive scale. For Algerian Jews, previously in an ambiguous position between Algerian natives and European society, this meant that in successfully choosing France at the war's end, they had "become" Europeans.

Decolonization would reshape French Jewry. From about 350,000 in the late 1950s, France's Jewish population grew to approximately 535,000 by the end of the 1960s. Between 1949 and 1969, some 250,000 Jews arrived from North Africa. Most left Morocco, Tunisia, or Algeria preceding or following independence.[73] As with France's Muslim population, such shifts represented more than demographic changes. By comparison with French Ashkenazic Jews, the newcomers tended to be less affluent and from more lower and lower-middle-class professions, religiously more observant, and accustomed to greater demonstrations of Jewish identity in public; they also had higher birthrates.[74] These differences, along with their distinctly North African sensibilities in cuisine, attire, and liturgy, meant that the new arrivals threw the long-standing assumptions of republican Judaism into question. Once a small minority of the metropolitan French Jewish population, Jews from the Maghreb and their descendants were soon to assume a position of demographic and cultural prevalence. A series of factors would make their differences, from the rest of the Jewish and the broader French population, particularly significant in this moment. Thus their relations with Muslims—in a manner that echoed the colonial period—became defined in large part around their simultaneous proximity to "European" and "Arab" cultures and identities.

The French state's decisions in the months preceding and following the cessation of hostilities in Algeria had created sharply contrasting legal situations for many Muslim and Jewish immigrants from the Maghreb. Unlike most Muslims, the 130,000 Algerian Jewish emigrants had passed definitively into the same legal category as the more than 1 million newly arrived pieds-noirs. By 1962, through inclusion in the group described as "Europeans" and, parenthetically, "essentially French by origin," Jews disappeared as a separate ethnic category in ministerial reports on the migration. In 1962, approximately 79,000 Jews took advantage of a recent law that offered loans, housing assistance, employment and educational aid, and other social benefits to all rapatriés.[75] Furthermore, most newly arrived Tunisian and Moroccan Jews, unlike their Muslim counterparts, had strong familiarity with French culture. Many had attended French or Alliance israélite universelle (AIU) schools, and on the eve of decolonization, 90 percent of Tunisian and 60 percent of Moroccan Jewry read and wrote French compared to 13 percent of these countries' Muslims. The vast majority of Moroccan and Tunisian Jews who came to France were among those who were more "Frenchified." While Jewish immigrants without French citizenship were initially classified as refugees, they anticipated (correctly) that they would acquire citizenship within a short time.[76]

As North African Jewish immigrants negotiated their way in the larger French Jewish community, challenges, but also further advantages, awaited them.[77] To be sure, a good deal of paternalism and a certain degree of fear—of demographic, and thereby cultural, eclipse—characterized the attitude of many Ashkenazic French Jewish leaders to the newcomers. Consequently, those like the Bas-Rhin chief rabbi J. Cohen argued forcefully in favor of molding the newcomers to fit the ethos of republican Judaism.[78] Yet on the whole, French Jewish leaders—in part influenced by the experience of the Holocaust and the way its losses had created new communal solidarities and priorities of Jewish renewal—were determined to avoid the mistakes of the 1930s; during the earlier period, much of the native French Jewish community became divided from Eastern European immigrants around issues of assimilation.[79] This time, they sought a warmer and subtler approach to integration. In the months preceding Algerian independence, French Jewish leaders pleaded and planned for a major mobilization of communal resources to meet the religious needs of the newcomers. By spring and summer 1962, as the trickle became a flood, the French Jewish press filled with stories about the challenge of "repatriating" huge numbers of Algerian Jews. Chief rabbi Jacob Kaplan implored "all the israélites of our country" to take up a portion of what he termed "the heavy responsibilities incumbent upon us." Kaplan asked that French Jews help their coreligionists to find lodging and work, as well as prayer and study spaces, urging the building of new facilities where necessary.[80]

Beginning in 1961, numerous Jewish associations in France—most importantly the social welfare organization CBIP (Comité de bienfaisance israélite de Paris, which became the Comité d'action sociale israélite de Paris, or CASIP, in 1964), the united communal fundraising operation of the Fonds social des juifs unifié (FSJU), and the Joint—worked tirelessly to meet the enormous challenges posed not only by the increasing numbers of Algerian Jews, but also, for instance, by the rapid migration of 3,500 Jews from Tunisia after the Bizerte incidents of July 1961.[81] In April 1962 the FSJU held a special assembly in which it outlined a plan: Jewish social workers would be ready to welcome North Africans everywhere from Paris to the provinces; a large housing fund would help to lodge families with the greatest needs.[82] In September, working with the European Jewish Community and the French government, the FSJU set up an emergency fund designated specifically for the rapatriés. Between 1962 and 1965 it spent 26.2 million new francs from this fund, and 16 million, or more than half of its annual budget, to help the newly arrived Jews from North Africa find their footing in France.[83]

It bears mentioning briefly the stark contrast between this combination of Jewish community organization, solidarity, and resources and the welcome that awaited the period's newly arrived Muslims. Without anything like a similar Muslim communal or associational apparatus, Muslim immigrants in France had to seek assistance almost exclusively from public agencies. These offices faced the same strains that beset all government efforts to aid newcomers from North Africa at this time. Compounding matters further, of course, was the shift that had occurred in most of these Muslims' status. Two documents from the French Service for Muslim Affairs encapsulate well the dramatic consequences of de Gaulle's policies: in 1958 a report from the service had spoken of France's Muslims as "320,000 legally French citizens"; by 1963 it defined most of the same group as "480,000 foreigners."[84] Even for the harkis, who would regain their French citizenship fairly quickly, conditions were often dreadful, as they were generally placed in French camps, foresting villages, or specially built social assistance urban housing units. In each instance, many would remain for years in substandard living conditions, stuck on the fringes of society.[85]

Beyond material necessities, leaders in the Jewish community sought to ensure the spiritual well-being of their new arrivals. They feared that failing to do so might result in widespread loss of Jewish observance. Many saw the mass migration, if greeted properly, as an unprecedented opportunity to reinvigorate the French Jewish community. In July 1962 consistorial leader and rabbi Simon Schwarzfuchs wrote that nothing less than "the union and the unity of our communities" depended on the understanding of French Jews toward their North African coreligionists.[86] Overall, the French state and Jewish community proved remarkably successful at integrating most Jewish immigrants. Within a few years, large numbers of adult newcomers achieved the same professional status they had known in North Africa; youth and children attained high education levels.[87] New Jewish communities emerged across France and old ones revived. The Joint, the FSJU, and other bodies managed to account for the particular religious and cultural needs of North African Jews and to facilitate measures toward adaptation and integration. Despite tensions with the Ashkenazic host community, Sephardic Jews found an accepted place in France's Jewish fabric, and increasingly occupied leadership positions.[88] Once more, with respect to educational levels and economic opportunity, the contrast with Muslims becomes striking. Only 3 percent of Jewish immigrants from the Maghreb had less than a grade school education; in three-quarters of Muslim households, neither parent had completed primary school. After starting as artisans, shopkeepers, or industrial workers, Jews, like other "European" postcolonial arrivals from the Maghreb, moved quickly into more middle-class professions, frequently becoming skilled workers, civil servants, managers, lawyers, and doctors. The vast majority of Muslims, by contrast, for decades had jobs in factories, mines, construction, and other blue-collar, often unskilled sectors.[89]

Nevertheless, North African Jews' integration, while relatively smooth, did not occur overnight. Many of the new arrivals sought to maintain elements of North African culture but were being challenged to remake themselves in a more "European" image. One effort to safeguard long-standing traditions from the Maghreb occurred through the formation of a series of Algerian, Tunisian, Moroccan, and locale-specific Jewish associations. In the words of the largest such group—the Association des juifs originaires d'Algérie (AJOA), founded in December 1962 by Jacques Lazarus and other luminaries of the Algerian Jewish community—these associations strove to work with leaders of the consistory and the AIU for the "fusion" of their constituents "within metropolitan Jewry," but also to maintain each group's distinct "personality" and traditions.[90] On a smaller scale, individuals and communities from Algeria carefully brought Torah scrolls and other ritual objects to France.[91] All of these efforts did not merely transport touchstones of memory and elements of continuity from North Africa; they played a vital role in the immigrants' integration process and, in time, helped transform the character of French Jewry.[92]

In this context, the lack of outreach toward Muslim representatives, groups, or individuals on the part of the newcomers becomes telling. Many leading figures in groups like the AJOA had concerned themselves with interactions with Muslims until the moment of departure from the Maghreb. Now, though, with the occasional exception of a crisis moment, they gave the subject virtually no attention.[93] More broadly, a 1966–1967 survey of over 600 North African Jews in France found that few if any respondents had chosen Muslims as their friends since arriving in France.[94] This undoubtedly reflected daily challenges of arrival and adaptation. Yet in the context of efforts to maintain traditions often drawn from surrounding Muslim culture, it represented a notable absence. Two other factors help to account for the lack of engagement. First, Algerian Jews in particular attempted to forget the often traumatic experience of suddenly fleeing the society that had housed their families and culture for generations. Second, in the newly racialized national environment, these Jews were no longer seen as among the most assimilable citizens and subjects of a great empire with a far-reaching "civilizing mission"; instead, they were immigrants, deeply and visibly tied to their North African religious and cultural heritage in a way that reminded their hosts of France's recent loss of colonial glory. These attachments could now render North African Jews different, foreign, and, for many, more specifically "Arab." Therefore, many Jewish immigrants, in their quest for integration, had little desire to associate with a group considered inherently less French.

Indeed, due to the prevailing atmosphere, even among many Jews, these newcomers from the Maghreb regularly found themselves depicted as North African "others" and lumped with Muslims. As Jewish immigration intensified in the late 1950s, the director of the FSJU in Marseille exclaimed, prior to his removal in 1959, that he did not wish to care for "Arabs," that is, North African Jews.[95] In his November 1960 article that argued for forceful integration into the Franco-Jewish tradition, chief rabbi Cohen spoke of the "clear superiority" of Ashkenazic Judaism, describing its Sephardic counterpart as currently "of an incredible religious poverty" and "penetrated by a fundamentally Arab orientalism."[96] In the years following decolonization, open conflict in a number of local communities emerged between the native French and North African Jews. Certain neighborhoods witnessed confrontations over which liturgical tradition would prevail in a given prayer space. Many from the Maghreb saw their French hosts as too secularized; more than a few of the latter spoke about the former as too "Arab," even sometimes designating them as "Schwarz," a Yiddish racial term meaning "black," or as "savages," taking up a longtime colonialist stereotype about North Africans.[97] Not long after her arrival, one Algerian Jewish woman discovered she had a French Jewish neighbor but realized that the woman's husband had warned her: "Watch out, it seems that they are Algerians. . . . Be careful, close the door and don't open it, because Algerians, they play with knives."[98]

Daily Interactions on Changing Terms: Marseille, Strasbourg, and Paris

Like political interactions between many ordinary Jews and Muslims at the end of the Algerian War, postcolonial neighborhood relationships among the two groups were, on the one hand, significantly shaped by the period's narrowing options for citizenship and belonging and, on the other hand, produced by individuals capable of navigating spaces found between and along the boundaries. Even as France had defined the meaning of Frenchness in a more rigidly white, secular, "European" manner, numerous Jews and Muslims retained the multifaceted attachments that had become increasingly public during the Algerian War. Consequently, as Jews and Muslims from North Africa settled across France, the careful revival of Mediterranean cultural meeting points competed with the delineation of Jewish and Muslim boundary lines and divisions between public and private expression. Different levels of education, income, and adherence to tradition between and within the Jewish and Muslim populations proved crucial as well. The degree and type of in-

teraction, then, between North African Jews and Muslims in postcolonial France was, as it had long been, situational, dependent on factors of
geography, politics, demography, culture, class, and individual initiative.
Yet such components were now aligning in new ways, producing new
rules of the game through which many of the periods' Jews and Muslims
would define and stabilize their increasingly ubiquitous daily encounters.

Most Jews, Muslims, and Christians who arrived from North Africa in
the mass migrations entered the metropole via Marseille. In summer 1962,
the city's docks, lodging capacity, and social welfare institutions became
overwhelmed; in June alone, a net total of over 300,000 newcomers
arrived.[99] Alongside larger numbers of pieds-noirs and Jews, this figure
included approximately 26,000 harkis.[100] Thus it was in Marseille in
1962, at the prefecture of the department of the Bouches-du-Rhône, that
the shifting meaning of the republic for Jews and Muslims from Algeria
took the form of hardened ethnic categories. Every week, on large foldout
forms, officials of the Service d'accueil des rapatriés (Service for Welcome
of the Repatriated) diligently recorded the numbers of new arrivals. The
categories were simply "Europeans" and "Muslims." Tellingly, only on
the European side did the form have spaces designated to record the fact
and details of "persons welcomed by the service," the implication being
that no Muslims would qualify for its assistance.[101] Nothing distinguished
the Algerian Jews from other "Europeans." Occasionally, accompanying
statistical reports on the migration from the Ministry of Rapatriés mentioned "israélites," but as a footnote. Their information came from a
study by the FSJU, not the French administration, and appeared alongside such anodyne observations as the professional, gender, or age breakdown of the rapatriés.[102] The state's attempt to eliminate the ambiguity
that had long marked both Jews' and Muslims' existence in Algeria began
to apply, then, the moment they entered the metropole's great Mediterranean port city.

Such absolute distinctions, however, did not characterize the tenor of
many of the interactions that occurred between Jews and Muslims within
the space of Marseille, particularly in the period immediately following
their arrival. From the late 1950s to the early 1970s, for many Jews and
Muslims the city acted as a crucial transitional entry point to France.
After the summer of 1962, 80 percent of the newcomers from Algeria
would leave to settle elsewhere in the Hexagon.[103] Yet large numbers of

Moroccan and Tunisian Jews, as well as Muslim seasonal laborers from the former French protectorates and Algeria, continued to arrive in Marseille. Others sought to return to their now independent North African homelands. Thus in places like the Belsunce immigrant quarter a sense of constant motion and persistent Mediterranean border crossings prevailed. More than ever before, to quote a longtime Belsunce resident, "There [was] always someone preparing to leave for Algeria or who [just] return[ed] from it."[104] Such a situation often facilitated contact, however ephemeral, between Jews and Muslims. The Grand arénas transit camp, with its temporary housing units, had acted in the late 1940s and early 1950s as a holdover point for thousands of Jews en route to Israel, also housing smaller numbers of North African Muslims transits. Now it again became a site of interaction. Alongside the largely Algerian Muslim population, as of February 1961, up to one-fourth of the camp's 1,000 inhabitants were Egyptian and North African Jewish refugees.[105]

In many cases, Jewish-Muslim relations unfolded on a longer-term basis. About 100,000 "European" rapatriés from Algeria remained in Marseille after the summer of 1962.[106] From 1959 to 1969 the city's Jewish community more than quadrupled, reaching 50,000 to 65,000 by the end of the decade.[107] Marseille's Muslim population also grew markedly during this period. Whereas slightly under 25,000 Muslims resided in the entire department of the Bouches-du-Rhône in spring 1958, by 1975, almost 44,000 lived in Marseille alone. The population had diversified as well. Algerians, once almost the sole Muslim presence, had grown to 35,000, but about 6,300 Tunisians and 2,700 Moroccans now joined them.[108]

Many Muslim newcomers settled in the Belsunce (more than 2,000 lived there as of 1968), but they made up only part of the quarter's increasingly Arab image and character.[109] Large numbers of Maghrebian Jews took part in the quarter's commercial life, as the Belsunce became an international crossroads for not only persons but also products moving to and from North Africa.[110] In the early 1970s an ethnographic examination of the narrow rue des Chapeliers, still a key artery at the heart of the Belsunce, revealed the presence there of thirty-two North African Muslim–owned businesses and twenty-seven Jewish shopkeepers of mostly North African origin (as well as a few businesses owned by "Europeans," Armenians, and Greeks). In a typical situation, described the authors, "a fabric boutique, with a Jewish owner, finds itself between a Tunisian restaurant and a food business with very old Marseillais roots."[111] Just minutes away, North African Jewish shop owners, especially jewelers, made up a major presence along the rue d'Aix. In many of these Jewish-owned businesses, Muslims constituted most of the clientele. On the intersecting rue Sainte-Barbe, Muslims owned several bazaars.[112] On weekends, Jews often did business with Muslims in these markets. Until halal shops became widespread in Marseille in the mid- to late 1960s, many newly arrived Muslims went to kosher butcheries here and elsewhere in the city to buy their meat.[113] Language remained another key linkage: one Muslim recalled that all women of the quarter, regardless of religion, spoke Arabic.[114] The strong ties of the Jews of the Belsunce to North African culture, and their modest economic level, reflects the fact that in Marseille and elsewhere, traditional Jews of lower educational and income levels were often those most likely to maintain close proximity and connections to Muslims.

Alongside the continuity from the Maghreb of shared cultural elements, territorial boundaries that mimicked class disparities and newly racialized understandings of Frenchness also emerged. Particularly for those from Algeria, within the resettlement experience, the two groups became "Europeans" and "Muslims." While few Algerian-born Jews joined the numerous pied-noir associations formed in Marseille, the two groups now had a shared legal status as privileged Europeans counterposed to Muslims. Moreover, many Jews held similar socioeconomic positions to the pieds-noirs and had shared the latter's staunch support for French Algeria and harrowing exodus experience.[115] Forging a crucial new dimension of pied-noir identity, the tremendous challenges of arrival and settlement in Marseille in summer 1962 reinforced these ties and helped to overcome older ethnic boundaries.[116] These commonalities and solidarities persisted in social geography patterns. A number of Jews and other "European" rapatriés from North Africa in Marseille initially lived in certain housing projects with Muslims, but greater segregation soon emerged. In part, as the former groups' economic circumstances improved, they tended to move elsewhere. Local housing policies proved crucial as well. As the city constructed the *habitation de loyer modérée* (HLM), or new public housing units intended for relocating immigrants from the projects, it reserved 30 percent of their apartments over five years for "European" rapatriés. Yet many Muslims remained stuck in what was meant to be only temporary outlying areas, sometimes for decades. Urban renewal projects that pushed Muslims out of dilapidated inner-city areas exacerbated geographic division along lines of socioeconomic and legal status.[117] By 1968, this evolution meant that Algerian Muslims lived largely in the often bleak settings of the outer industrial arrondissements, particularly the 14th, 15th, and 16th along the city's northern periphery, often referred to as *bidonvilles* (slums); most rapatriés, including Jews, populated the more affluent, middle-class, and commercial districts in the center and south and around the port.[118]

At odds with the period's growing Jewish-Muslim distance, one Muslim from Algeria who had lived initially in the Grand arénas (closed down in 1966) later recalled: "We didn't know much about the Maghreb. . . . And we learned about our country through these people who were North African before they were Jews."[119] Such a statement illustrates the splits of experience that emerged across space and time in postcolonial Marseille. Located a boat ride of less than 500 miles from the North African coastline, home for decades to a wide mix of European and North African Mediterranean immigrants and long a transit point for persons and goods circulating between colony and metropole, Marseille, more than any other mainland French city, became contiguous with many aspects— both convivial and divisive—of the colonial settings of the Maghreb. Particularly in the uncertain initial years of settlement, in transient immigrant quarters with a distinctly North African flavor, like the Grand arénas and especially the Belsunce, many Jewish and Muslim residents and visitors remained intertwined through ties of language and culture. In these spaces, ethnicity and religion did not always align; boundaries were porous. Yet across Marseille, the distinctions of status that had marked much of colonial Algeria's history, and the decisions of the French state in the closing months of the war, slowly crystallized in the settlement patterns of Jews, Muslims, and former colonists. In this manner, the postcolonial influx of Jews and Muslims both maintained the connectivity of France's Mediterranean crossroads and rendered the city plan more divided along ethnic and religious boundary lines.

As many Jewish and Muslim immigrants passed from Marseille to other parts of France, another consequence of decolonization became the unprecedented diffusion of both Jewish and Muslim communities throughout the country. This development facilitated new centers of interaction; among them was Strasbourg.[120] From the late 1950s to the mid-1960s, Strasbourg's North African Muslim population roughly doubled. By spring 1965 more than 5,000 North Africans lived in the department of the Bas-Rhin: over 4,000 Algerians, about 700 Moroccans, and almost 600 Tunisians. While 70 percent were male laborers, about 500 worked as shop owners or service employees. In addition, reflecting the growing presence of Muslim families, the group included 487 women and 828 children. Of these Muslim workers and families, 75 percent lived in Strasbourg. Other signs pointed to the increasing permanence of many Muslims in the area. By spring 1967, 737, or 22 percent of the nearly 3,300 Algerian Muslims living in Strasbourg, were French citizens.[121]

During the same period, Strasbourg's Jewish population also markedly increased and diversified. Its size reached 14,000 by 1963, with 3,500 having recently immigrated from North Africa.[122] Like the Muslim newcomers, many of these Jews settled in outlying areas of the city like Schiltigheim and Bishheim to the north, Cronenbourg and Hautepierre to the west, and La Meinau in the south; at least initially they frequently lived in the same HLMs (Map 5.1).[123] The growing North African Jewish presence included a few Moroccan Jewish university students there since the late 1950s; a number of Jewish families from Morocco who came in the early 1960s; hundreds of Algerian Jewish children brought for safety near the end of the war by a local initiative, Aide aux jeunes israélites repliés d'Algérie; and several hundred Jews from the Mzab in the Algerian Sahara who arrived in 1962. Relatively few Algerian Jews came to Strasbourg overall. Yet the Mzabites, who had a highly unified, distinctive Jewish culture and set of religious practices, were rarely highly educated or wealthy, often still spoke Judeo-Arabic rather than French, and unlike all other Algerian Jews, had received French citizenship only in 1961, found the city appealing for its significant resources for traditional Jewish life.[124] The predominantly Ashkenazic community undertook major efforts to integrate the new arrivals, providing social services, a Sephardic-designated prayer space, a kosher restaurant for Jewish students, and religious study and recreational activities for children.[125] Gradually this border city, long seen as on the outskirts of Central Europe, was experiencing the Mediterranean not simply through colonial voyeurism or political debate but as immediate demographic and cultural reality.

The city's small but vibrant North African Jewish and Muslim populations, their particular origins, personal histories, and memories, and the unusual place of religion in Alsace all helped to shape a distinctive setting for Jewish-Muslim interactions. Simon Dahan, a Moroccan Jew who arrived in 1964 at the age of seven, insists, "Jews and Muslims lived in

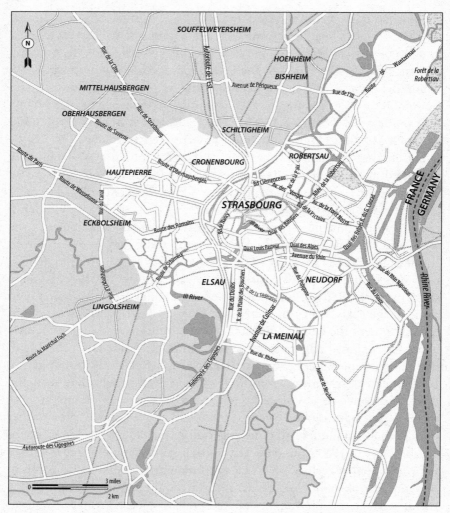

Map 5.1. Strasbourg with surrounding area. (Map by Isabelle Lewis; copyright © 2015 by Ethan B. Katz.)

Morocco and Algeria always in great harmony."[126] Dahan speaks, for instance, with great affection of a Muslim woman in Morocco born around the same time as he was to a family very close to his, whom he still visits when he returns to Morocco on vacation. "One of [the family's] children," he explains, "is my sister, because she sucked milk from my mother's breast. . . . Her mother had no milk, so my mother breastfed her, therefore, she's my sister." Here Dahan has adapted the language of a practice widespread among Muslims in certain parts of North Africa known as milk kinship, spoken of in Arabic as *rida'* (a nursing bond), that creates so-called milk siblings. Traditionally such a relationship has great social significance, often creating tight bonds between mothers and children from families of different social status or ethnicity. In the words of one anthropologist of Morocco, according to popular belief, "love is fostered only between siblings who drank from the same breast" and so-called milk kin are expected to "comfort you, encourage you and be your intermediary."[127] Here we see an example of a Jewish-Muslim relationship that gained new meaning as one or both groups crossed to the French mainland. Whereas in many Moroccan communities, milk kinship could mediate hierarchical differences of status between families, Dahan later spoke of his closeness with this woman in order to minimize a new set of political divisions, between Jews and Muslims in postcolonial France.

For Dahan, the connection between the two experiences is more seamless: "For us with this sensibility [from North Africa]," Muslim-Jewish cordiality in Strasbourg "is just a logical continuation of our *'histoire ami.'*" Indeed, Jewish-Muslim interactions in Strasbourg in this era appeared largely to elide the difficult history of colonialism and decolonization and to connect rather to memories (however idealized) of harmonious coexistence.[128] The more traditional nature of the Moroccan and Mzabite Algerian Jewish communities, the critical way in which each remained connected to surrounding Islamic culture and populations until the time of their departure, the common language of Arabic that many of them still shared, and the gap many found between their own outlook and that of their Alsatian Ashkenazic hosts all made Muslims in Strasbourg important intermediaries in many of these Jews' process of transitioning to French culture.[129]

From age seven to twenty-nine, Simon Dahan lived in the cité of Cronenbourg, a working-class area northwest of the city center. Cronenbourg soon became home to not only large numbers of North African laborers but also one of the first sizable North African Jewish communities in Strasbourg. In 1962 a small prayer space opened in the neighborhood; within a few years, under the leadership of Rabbi Raphael Perez, himself from North Africa, a synagogue was constructed in Cronenbourg.[130] Many of the area's North African Jews lived on the rue du Champ de Manoeuvre and along the intersecting route de Mittelhausbergen and rue Curie and the parallel rue de Loess, where significant numbers of Muslims from Morocco and Algeria also settled. Simon Dahan recalls how he and his Jewish and Muslim neighbors spoke Arabic and shared common sensibilities and traditions. He remembers the continuation of a custom that had occurred in parts of North Africa, whereby on Jewish holidays "when we gave out cakes, we gave cakes to our Arab neighbors." Dahan also explains that in his quarter in France, neighbors sustained the long-standing Muslim-Jewish ritual of the Mimouna. He recounts, "In Morocco, there is a tradition . . . that the last day of *Pesach* [Passover], the Arabs bring the Jews milk and butter, always something white—in order to wish the Jews 'good luck, good continuity.'" He notes that here, tradition overrode *halakhah* (strict Jewish law): "But, normally, according to the halakhah, it's not so authorized, because it's still *chametz* [food with leavening] and it's still Pesach. But this was the tradition! From 2 PM, the Arabs would bring Jews milk and butter. . . . In Cronenbourg, we [still] knew this tradition. Arabs brought Jews things like that . . . maybe not every year, but [often]."[131] In North Africa, the Mimouna had at times carried implications of hierarchy and temporary role reversal, wherein Jews, receiving gifts and services from Muslims and sometimes even dressing as Muslims, could briefly overcome their subservient status as dhimmis.[132] Here again, however, in Dahan's rendering, for these Jews and Muslims from Morocco transplanted to the very different social and cultural context of France, the ritual became simply a signifier of deep, enduring ties of tradition and kinship.

Within Cronenbourg, another milieu of interaction emerged. Founded in 1963, the Association sportive menora, popularly called "A. S. Menora," originally the idea of André Neher and other leading figures in the local Jewish community, sought to provide recreational opportunities for the children of newly arrived Jews from North Africa. The club started in a very humble setting. Near what is today Cronenbourg's "tramway terrain," the team had a locale with no locker room and a large basin of cold water for the shower. While it participated in the broader Alsatian athletic leagues, the A. S. Menora's teams received support from the Jewish community and used a blue-and-white letterhead with a menorah, made it a rule never to play matches on the Jewish Sabbath, and eventually had a kosher clubhouse. The association's overwhelmingly North African Jewish participants, however, also gave it a distinctly Maghrebian flavor. This quickly attracted many Christian and Muslim new arrivals from the Maghreb. The association developed an unusual ecumenicism, coming to take pride in the fact that it drew individuals

Figure 5.1. The Association Sportive Menora, ca. 1965. A: The insignia. B: The players. (Courtesy of A. S. Menora.)

from numerous ethnic backgrounds. Dahan, now president of the A. S. Menora, recounts that "in this club prevailed an outlook that had been brought from Morocco and Algeria. Thus non-Jews quickly integrated into the club, because they rediscovered exactly the same ambiance as there [in North Africa]" (Figure 5.1).[133]

In particular, the soccer teams at the A. S. Menora became sites of Jewish-Muslim interaction and frequent camaraderie. "This club," explains Dahan, "has always welcomed young Arab players."[134] Maxime Elkaim, an Algerian Jew, longtime soccer coach, and one of the founding members of A. S. Menora, remembered thirty years later: "We had to build teams of young men and seniors, with boys from a whole spectrum. . . . I had to be tough with everyone as a way of creating a climate of camaraderie, of sporting fraternity, and above all, the spirit of a club."[135] Like Dahan, other early participants at A. S. Menora saw the group as continuing their experiences in North Africa. Robert Garcia, a Catholic rapatrié from Algeria, recalls playing in his local soccer league in Algeria and that teams of Jews, Catholics, and Muslims competed fiercely but on good terms. By the mid-1960s, Garcia was coaching soccer teams at A. S. Menora that included Jewish, Christian, and a few Muslim players.[136]

The club's ambiance overlapped with other spaces. The brother of Maxime Elkaim also ran a restaurant, Le Penalty, centrally located along the Ill River on the quai des Bateliers. There, players and coaches regularly gathered in what Dahan calls the second "anchor point for all these families arriving at A. S. Menora, Jewish and non-Jewish." Serving drinks like the anisette, a Mediterranean liqueur, the bar also had a distinctly North African flavor.[137] Many of Dahan's best friends were Muslim players at the club who shared in family celebrations at his house. In particular, they came for Shabbat, as his "mother would make the same foods [these Muslims] had known in Morocco." An Algerian Muslim friend of Dahan who played and coached at the A. S. Menora regularly called to wish Dahan and his family a Happy Passover or a Shabbat Shalom.

Not far from Cronenbourg, the Bagouchas, an Algerian Jewish family, opened the city's first "Oriental" grocery store, with products from North Africa. "All the Muslims," remembers Dahan, "went to this épicerie, because they found there someone who spoke Arabic, who dressed like them, who served the great sacks of spices to which they were accustomed in North Africa." For many years before Strasbourg had halal shops, religious Muslims purchased their meat at kosher butcheries.[138] At North African Jewish celebrations of holidays like Purim and life cycle events like bar mitzvahs and weddings, Muslim musicians from the Maghreb often participated in the Arabic music that continued to constitute an important part of the ambiance.[139]

At this time, in Schiltigheim, a town to the immediate north of Cronen-bourg, Zoubida Tribak, a Muslim girl from Morocco who arrived in Strasbourg in 1967 at the age of eight, had begun to discover common-alities with certain North African Jewish neighbors. Tribak came from a traditional Muslim family of modest means. Her parents had, in her words, "a spirit of openness" and "big ideas" that brought them to France in order to give their children a French education and greater opportuni-ties. In school Tribak met a classmate named Annie Attia: "She said to me, 'Me I'm from Algeria.' Her name was Annie. I said, 'you're from Algeria your name can't be Annie.' She said, 'but no, me I'm Jewish.' . . . And I was happy and I returned home and I said, 'Mama, there's a girl who comes from Algeria. It's great,' and so forth. And Mama said, 'Ah, really, what's the story?' I said 'the Jewish mother, she also wears the *foulard*.' "

The Attia family, which had come from Tlemcen, Algeria, following the end of the war, was active in the sizable North African immigrant Jewish community that had formed by this time in Schiltigheim.[140] It turned out the family lived in the same apartment building as the Tribaks; the Attias were on the seventh floor and the Tribaks resided three floors below. Tribak's mother at the time knew not a word of French, and in Annie's mother she found someone with whom to speak Arabic, some-thing that was, Tribak explains, "very important for us." Annie's mother, lonely after the death of her husband in an auto accident, found a nearby companion. The two women would sit and talk for hours and exchanged cakes on Jewish and Muslim religious occasions. Madame Attia, like Tribak's family, was religiously observant, refusing to eat anything when she visited the Tribaks' apartment and asking someone to push the elevator button on the Jewish Sabbath. Young Zoubida was learning about Judaism and what she found to be striking similarities with Islam: similar holiday traditions, circumcisions, and wedding rituals in-cluding the ceremony of the *henna*.[141] Tribak's mother often consulted her friend's knowledge of the Jewish lunar calendar, similar to that used by Muslims, to find the correct date for upcoming Muslim holidays. In a new setting, these two families discovered each other as fellow North Africans.

Despite the unequal positions of Jews and Muslims in France at this time, these two families illustrate once more how difficult life experiences and a basic vulnerability as immigrants could be as critical as cultural commonality in fostering ties. Tribak tells the story of one day being asked by Annie's mother, who had fallen in the snow, to go and get her "papers" for her. Zoubida rushed to the Attias' apartment, grabbed the necessary materials, went to the local administrative office, got Madame Attia's identification and other documentation for her, and brought them to her. Madame Attia then insisted that Zoubida take a box of chocolates as a token of gratitude. In response, Zoubida explains, "I said: 'May God bless you with a long life.' She began to cry and say, 'I don't want [that]. I've already lived enough. It's enough for us. I suffer because my husband is no longer here.'"[142]

Jewish-Muslim relations in Strasbourg both echoed and diverged from those in Marseille. Once more, traditional lifestyles and modest means were common to most participants. To an even greater degree than in Belsunce, Muslims displayed comfort with Jewish spaces and culture, having little trouble playing for a "Jewish" soccer team or sharing in Jewish rituals or religious knowledge. For years, Muslims in Strasbourg could buy North African food or ritually permissible meat only from a Jew. For their part, Jews turned to their Muslim neighbors to share in North African traditions that took on new meanings; they welcomed them as well into their athletic activities. Such open displays of religious attachment occurred more easily in Strasbourg, where no official separation existed between church and state. The city's Jewish community has long remained one of France's most traditional. Here, integration never required compartmentalizing religious observance or cultural particularity. The move toward greater Jewish and Muslim visibility in postcolonial France, often a source of tension elsewhere, thus echoed the city's religious environment rather than violating it. Such capacity for public religiosity may have given Jews and Muslims greater security in their own identity, making spatial boundaries at once usefully implicit and semipermeable. Moreover, due to the small size of each population, North African Jews and Muslims in Strasbourg needed one another to perpetuate the customs and ambiance they had known in the Maghreb.

Despite Jews' and Muslims' dispersal across France, Paris remained their leading destination. Between 1962 and 1968, close to 30 percent of North African Jewish immigrants settled in the region, swelling the area's Jewish population to 313,000 by 1966 (the city itself had about 250,000 Jews). By 1968, the area was also home to 200,000 Algerian, and several thousand Moroccan and Tunisian, Muslims.[143] Paris's geography of Jewish-Muslim relations at once expanded and shifted. While Jews continued to arrive in large numbers in the Jewish quarter of the Marais, the quarter became a less frequent site of Jewish-Muslim interaction than previously by the mid-1960s. Following Algerian independence, many Muslims who had frequented the cafés of earlier Algerian Jewish immigrants like Roger Gharbi and Maurice Jaïs, for instance, returned to Algeria.[144]

Decolonization and mass migration brought continuities and ruptures in Paris's key Jewish-Muslim meeting points. The rue de la Huchette remained the site of Oriental Cabarets, with Salim Hallali and Line Monty now the leading stars there. On the rue du Faubourg-Montmartre, with its many Jewish-owned cafés, other leading Jewish musicians from the Maghreb like Lili Labassi, Maurice El Medioni, Blond-Blond, and Luc Cherki turned a restaurant called "Le Poussin Bleu" into a new hub for Arabic music. In both settings, these musicians wrote and performed songs that frequently evoked the moment's deep sense of loss, and more specifically sentiments of exile *(el ghorba)*, separation *(el faraq)*, and nostalgia *(el wahash)* shared by many Jews and Muslims. Particularly between 1962 and Labassi's death in 1969, Jewish musicians performed in these spaces, often alongside Muslims, though now before mostly Jewish recent arrivals from North Africa.[145]

Neighborhood relations were evolving as well. The trend of increasing Muslim settlement in areas of Paris's outer arrondissements and banlieues continued; the same neighborhoods often attracted newly arrived Jews from the Maghreb. Belleville, located in the northeast of Paris, was one such neighborhood. Tunisian Jews and Algerian Muslims started to arrive in Belleville in the 1950s, and it soon became a site of daily contact on a far larger scale than the Marais had ever been. Tunisian Jews were drawn to the quarter by several factors. It had a long-standing, established Jewish presence that by the 1950s included several Tunisian families. With only 17 percent of Tunisian Jews being French citizens at the time of independence, most newcomers were ineligible for state benefits and therefore relied heavily on geographical concentration and communal networks to meet basic needs. Tunisian Jewry was, on average, the poorest of the Maghrebi Jewish populations, and this marginal quarter could better accommodate many immigrants' economic limitations.[146] The "Kabyle hôtels" of the quarter had drawn many Algerian Muslims in the early 1950s.[147] In time, their presence, as well as that of

Tunisian (Jewish) compatriots, the quarter's Maghrebi culture, and its economic affordability, would bring larger numbers.

Jewish social service workers envisioned Belleville, with its cramped quarters and poor living conditions, as a transitional space. Indeed, having gained the necessary financial security, a significant number of Jews moved from the neighborhood into more affluent, integrated portions of Paris. For many, the quarter remained a center of Tunisian Jewish culture but no longer a place of residence. Large numbers of Jews who lived elsewhere in the region visited Belleville to enjoy its Jewish-owned food establishments and atmosphere.[148] Yet for thousands of Jews, it became a place of longer-term abode: the site of an effort to reestablish traditional Tunisian Jewish neighborhood life on metropolitan soil.[149] Thus, in the course of the 1950s and 1960s numerous tailors, plumbers, and painters, followed soon by butchers, grocers, hairdressers, and the like, arrived from the Hara, or Jewish quarter, in the capital city of Tunis.[150] By 1968 Belleville's Jewish population swelled to 15,000. As of 1970, 82 percent of the quarter's Jews were of Tunisian origin, with 90 percent of this group from Tunis.[151] They were largely employed in artisanal and working-class jobs.[152] Most Muslims were male Algerian laborers who worked for modest wages in large companies like the automaker Renault.[153]

The heart of the quarter's North African Jewish community lived in a circle that ran along the rues Ramponeau, Dénoyez, Tourtille, and de la Présentation (Map 5.2). Here, as of 1970, Jews made up between 15 and 27 percent of the inhabitants on each street. The rue Julien-Lacroix to the north, the rues de Palikao and Vilin to the east, the rue de l'Orillon and Moulin-Joly to the south, and the rue de Belleville to the west formed the boundary of this area. Significant numbers of Jews (between 7 and 10 percent of the population) lived along outlying streets to the west like the rue Jules Verne and to the North like the rue Piat. Throughout these streets, Tunisian Jewish grocers sold olives and Mediterranean seasonings; patisseries baked desserts like baklava and manicotti; and in North African cafés, customers played the Mediterranean card game *scopa* while listening to Arabic chants or music. These Jews most often spoke to one another, in private and public, in Judeo-Arabic rather than French.[154]

Tunisian Jews' sizable numbers in Belleville enabled them to recreate an insular world of North African Jewish culture. Yet they also drew from the Muslims who surrounded them. The daily itineraries of Jews and Muslims intersected constantly. The rue Ramponeau included not only

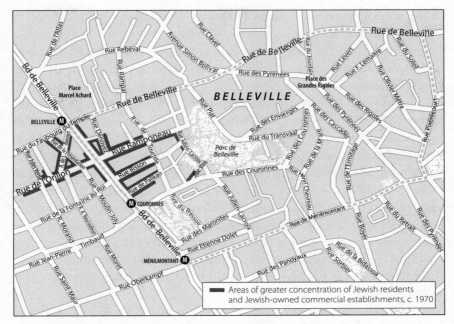

Map 5.2. Belleville neighborhood, Paris. (Map by Isabelle Lewis; copyright © 2015 by Ethan B. Katz.)

nineteen Jewish-owned food establishments but also seven Muslim-owned cafés and a Muslim grocer.[155] On the intersecting boulevard de Belleville, the Arab travel agency El Djazaïr sat right next to Chez Frido, a Jewish grocer specializing in condiments. Farther down, Jewish bars served boukha, the Tunisian fig alcohol, just across from Arab cafés where Muslims played cards.[156] Aspects of this world offered striking continuities with long traditions from Tunisia and other parts of North Africa. When one European reporting on Tunisia in the late nineteenth century emphasized the universal importance of café culture, and, more specifically, that "Tunisians love to chat and play cards," he could have been writing about Belleville in the mid-1960s.[157] Equally enduring was the Muslim popularity of boukha; in Tunis and elsewhere in the Maghreb, because of the Islamic prohibition on alcohol, Jews had often been the suppliers to Muslims of this and other alcoholic beverages.[158] Once again, the dynamics in Belleville were in significant part ethnically specific: among North African Jewish emigrants, those from Tunisia were much more likely than either their Moroccan or Algerian counterparts to maintain both literacy in Arabic and traditional religious customs, particularly in the second generation. Each of these elements kept them connected to many of their Muslim neighbors.[159]

Jews' and Muslims' mutual familiarity, common customs and language, and physical proximity gave way to social, economic, cultural, and even religious relations. In many North African cafés, Jews and Muslims played cards and listened to Arabic music together.[160] Mediterranean grocery stores regularly featured mixed Jewish and Muslim clienteles. Many Jews and Muslims lived in the same apartment building.[161] A number of Tunisian Muslims who found their way to Belleville took jobs in the quarter working for Jewish-owned food establishments.[162] North African Jews in Belleville often had greater resources than their Muslim counterparts and reached out to them. As an organizer for Logique, a Jewish voluntary association helping underprivileged children in Belleville, Patricia Jaïs remembers working with both Jewish and Muslim families in need. She recalls as well a Jewish friend whose father kept his neighborhood North African café open after hours each night to allow Muslims who came with no money to eat for free.[163]

Community boundaries were at once porous and fixed. With fifteen kosher and twelve halal butcheries in the short stretch between the Ménilmontant and Belleville Metro stops, Jews and Muslims generally purchased ritually slaughtered meat that accorded precisely with their own, rather than each other's comparable, traditions.[164] Reviving customs popular in North Africa, Jews and Muslims also exchanged foods around the Muslim holiday of Ramadan. During the fast month itself, Jewish grocers often offered fruits, vegetables, and fresh herbs that Muslims used to prepare their evening meals. On Aïd el-Fitr, the feast that concludes the holiday, Muslims would bring pastries and grilled mutton to their Jewish neighbors. As in North Africa, these exchanges highlighted a sense of community. By their festive, occasional nature, though, they under-scored the way that many Jewish and Muslim neighbors, while speaking in the street and remaining amicable, stayed at arm's length.[165] The mixing of Jews and Muslims was accepted here, but it occurred in a precise, con-trolled context and thus relied on understood boundaries.

In the postcolonial environment of the 1960s such respectful dis-tance, often articulated through ethnic symbols, became a centerpiece of Jewish-Muslim coexistence in Belleville and elsewhere.[166] Not surpris-ingly, given Paris's longtime position as a center of immigrant and trans-national politics, signs of identification in Belleville increasingly mixed the ethnoreligious and the political. Jewish- and Muslim-owned shops used insignia like a *maguen David,* a crescent and star, Hebrew or Arabic lettering, or pro-Zionist or Palestinian graffiti, to mark territory.[167] Communal social welfare and religious institutions, as well as individuals wearing attire like Orthodox Jewish black hats or Muslim foulards, served similar purposes. By indicating places with predominantly Jewish or Muslim clientele or residents, these displays of religious or transnational affiliation all made a subtle but unmistakable claim on a portion of a tight, shared urban space. In this manner they were at once more circumscribed and expressive than the unabashedly interreligious Jewish-Muslim relations emerging in Strasbourg or the sense of shared North Africanness in the markets and shops of Marseille's Belsunce. In all three instances, outward uses of extranational signs of affiliation threatened to violate the notion of "neutral" public space at the heart of republican *laïcité* and French nationalism, particularly as asserted along more racial lines since the close of the French-Algerian War.[168] A delicate balance was required.

Across France, many individuals were seeking to negotiate new rules for interethnic coexistence in the increasingly dichotomous postcolonial environment, where ethnicity was proving less fluid than under the empire. In order to live together peacefully, Jews and Muslims found that they had to offer, albeit carefully and semiprivately, outward indications and emblems that marked their ethnoreligious affiliation. In addition, they needed to structure their interactions around mutually agreed-on permissible and prohibited types of contact. The latter was key for three reasons: it respected suddenly stricter French notions of neutral public space, it enabled the two groups to protect one another's boundaries and group identities, and it reduced the likelihood of confrontations around disparate religious or political allegiances. These tied into an additional rule: the boundaries and dynamics characterizing their encounters and their place in the wider French public sphere had to remain stable.[169] By the mid-1960s, however, events within and far beyond France threatened to upend such stability and its accompanying social harmony. When Jews or Muslims who coexisted daily perceived a breach of the rules by members of the other group, the results could quickly become explosive.

6

HIGHER FENCES, BETTER NEIGHBORS?

In the late afternoon on June 12, 1968, two immigrants to France from Tunisia—one Jewish and the other Muslim—were playing cards in the café Kairouan, at the corner of the rue de l'Orillon and the rue de Louis-Bonnet in the Belleville quartier of Paris. This benign encounter soon turned ugly. Accounts vary, but it appears that the Muslim lost the game and then refused to pay the winnings. Soon the two exchanged blows, and a group of Jews broke the café windows. Rioters fought in the street, and before police restored order around midnight, Muslim demonstrators attacked at least half a dozen Jewish-owned establishments.

The following day, rioting resumed around midday as large groups of Jews and Muslims threw bottles, rocks, and other projectiles at one another. They also exchanged blows, with some reports speaking of Muslims taking razors from Jewish barbershops and knives from kosher butcheries. Then many more cafés and stores were attacked. At the synagogue on the rue Julien-Lacroix, because of the holiday of Shavuot, many Jews had gathered in prayer. Muslim attackers broke the synagogue's windows, defaced the door, and launched Molotov cocktails toward the building. A Jewish "self-defense force" set up barricades at the synagogue. Wild rumors circulated, keeping many participants in a frenzy. By midafternoon, police finally dispersed the agitators. In the early evening, Belleville rabbi Emmanuel Chouchena, originally from Algeria, and Tunisian ambassador Mohamed Masmoudi walked about the quartier together and called for calm. Crowds of Jews and Muslims mingled around them amicably as order returned. Yet twelve people had been injured and forty to fifty Jewish- or Muslim-owned stores attacked or set on fire.[1]

The 1968 riots stunned many Jews and Muslims of Belleville. Until this time, the neighborhood had seemed largely impervious to tensions elsewhere. In close quarters, sizable numbers of Jews and Muslims respected one another's communal boundary lines at the same time that their daily lives intermingled. Certain members of the two groups felt a shared identity as *maghrébins* (North Africans). The outbreak of violence appeared as a lethal threat to the coexistence of the quarter.

Occurring almost exactly one year after the outbreak of the 1967 Six Day War in the Middle East, for many, the Belleville riots of 1968 seemed to show that the Israeli-Arab conflict had now arrived on French shores. Even playing cards in a coffee shop—an activity characteristic of amicable Jewish-Muslim relations in Tunis, Paris, and beyond for over a century—could be overtaken by political strife. The reality was more complex. To be sure, over a period of decades the impact in France of the Zionist-Arab conflict had grown, particularly since the founding of the state of Israel and in light of the substantial role the conflict played in both the ideological frameworks and human migrations of decolonization. But contrary to the common assumption of scholars that the 1967 war in itself reconfigured Jewish-Muslim relations across the Mediterranean, the war's impact in France can be appreciated only by considering it in combination with several other factors. As shown in the previous chapter, decolonization transformed Jewish and Muslim demography, culture, and relations with the French state. By the mid-1960s, major political changes were also afoot as a series of postcolonial entities spanning the Mediterranean emerged. On the one hand, alongside North African Jewish cultural associations like the Association des juifs originaires d'Algérie (AJOA) and a new generation's Jewish politics, newly independent Algeria, Morocco, and Tunisia established a consular presence in major French cities; a spate of organizations from these countries sought to extend or even anchor their political and social movements among Muslim migrant workers and students. On the other hand, as we have seen, large numbers of Jews and Muslims were forming Maghrebian spaces within neighborhoods like Belleville, where commonalities of food, language, attire, and other cultural sensibilities created ties beyond the control of governments, political parties, and workers' associations. These spaces at once transcended territorial boundaries and appropriated territory in the French cityscape for the newcomers' distinctive cultures.[2]

But despite ongoing cultural interaction, politicization was the defining development in Jewish-Muslim encounters of the late 1960s. Political groups with agendas rooted in the Middle East and North Africa and milieus of shared Maghrebi culture operated in productive tension, forging a new model for daily interactions between Jewish and Muslim neighbors. According to the rules that governed such settings, high and clearly delineated fences marked the borders of Jews' and Muslims' semi-private ethnoreligious spheres. Jewish-Muslim harmony in more public spaces depended directly on respecting these community boundaries and confining visible displays of ethnoreligious identity to the spaces within them.

These Mediterranean crossings, deeply contested, were in dialectic with the period's more racialized notions of Frenchness. The opposition between "Europeans" and "Muslims" (frequently called "Arabs" regardless of their ethnicity) that had taken new legal form with the French departure from Algeria would render Jewish, and even more so Muslim, difference all the more pronounced by the late 1960s. During and following the 1967 war French state policies, frequent political rhetoric (especially on the Right) and occasional violence would create a new sense of vulnerability among many Muslims and Jews. This sense of insecurity coincided with new transnational activism on behalf of both sides in the Israeli-Palestinian conflict. Alongside the increasingly visible support for Israel among France's Jews brought on by the war itself, the period of May '68 and its aftermath saw the rise of a radical leftist politics that included a growing pro-Palestinian movement.

In this context, many Jews and Muslims would mutually perceive their group identities as less situational than they had once been and now tied by definition to political movements and entities potentially at odds with one another or with wider French politics and culture. These attachments, while often out of sight, could come to the fore at a moment's notice. Ultimately, for both populations, a constellation of international, national, and group-specific developments was producing a new ethnoreligious identity politics. This politics saturated with political significance even those who did not wish to be politicized.[3] Such politicization in all of its dimensions can be appreciated only with sufficient attention to the changing dynamics of Jewish-Muslim spaces of daily interaction. Thus the riots of 1968 and 1970 in Belleville offer an illuminating lens through which to trace the convergence of many developments.

The 1967 War: The Arab-Israeli Conflict Comes to the Fore

In the late spring and early summer of 1967, the escalating tensions in the Middle East echoed among Jews and Muslims in France. The June 1967 war elicited countless public manifestations of Jewish and Muslim allegiance to Zionism and Palestinian nationalism. Although Jews and Muslims often sought to frame such affiliation as coterminous with their citizenship or presence in France, their ethnoreligious visibility still cut against the grain of the republican "abstract individual" and more specifically violated current prevailing notions of Frenchness—as largely white, European, and publicly secular. Following the war, journalists, state actors, and a number of Jews and Muslims increasingly articulated a direct link between events in the Middle East and Jewish-Muslim relations in France. However exaggerated, such an understanding gained growing acceptance and had far-reaching consequences.

In the days and weeks preceding the outbreak of war on June 5, 1967, French Jews expressed grave concerns for the fate of Israel. Various sectors of the Jewish community displayed solidarity with the Jewish state in an unprecedentedly public and assertive fashion. While this echoed some displays of distinctly Jewish politics seen during the Algerian War, it marked a notable shift for communal institutions, as the leadership of French Jewry broke from its long-standing quietist posture on hot-button political matters. In late May, representatives of diverse Jewish organizations formed the Coordinating Committee. The group sought to rally French public opinion and officials behind Israel, solicited financial donations from French Jews for Israel, and tried to coordinate all demonstrations of Jewish public support.[4] While the group's leaders did not agree altogether on the nature of its activism, the new embrace of a communal Jewish politics was palpable, and for some, quite explicit. Coordinating Committee vice president Claude Kelman declared: "Without ambiguities or equivocations; we are acting as Jews, our reactions are Jewish reactions." After a period of passivity, he said, French Jewry "has emerged from its lethargy."[5]

The new posture endured beyond this moment. In the first days of June, the organs of both the Consistory and Fonds social juif unifié (FSJU) published special issues. Their headlines conveyed an apocalyptic atmosphere in which, in light of threats from Arab leaders, many feared that war could bring a second Shoah.[6] "The Jewish community of France supports Israel in danger," somberly declared the *Journal des communautés.*

More optimistic, *L'Arche,* the FSJU's review, exclaimed in huge letters, "Israel Will Live!" This ancient Jewish rallying cry evoked the moment's aspiration but also its underlying anxieties.[7] Large pro-Israel demonstrations, which included many non-Jews, occurred across France. Thirty thousand rallied in front of the Israeli embassy in Paris; 2,500 Jews marched silently in Strasbourg; 6,000 did the same in Marseille, and thousands marched in several other cities as well.[8] In Jewish schools, teachers struggled to keep students from constantly tuning into their radios for the latest news; children made cakes and sold them at recess to raise money for solidarity funds.[9]

A few Jewish groups attempted to defuse potential Jewish-Muslim tensions in France. Their words, however, often revealed how decolonization and the Middle East conflict increasingly challenged Jewish-Muslim coexistence. The AJOA, for instance, made the unusual choice to speak about Jewish-Muslim relations. It issued a statement that reminded readers that "100,000 israélites of Algeria [were forced] to leave a land where they had lived for many centuries. They left here their tombs and property of considerable value. . . . Nevertheless, they have never spread either hatred or resentment toward Arabs." The same declaration went on to condemn the Palestinian refugees, by contrast, for having spent twenty years not looking for "constructive peaceful solutions" but instead engaging only in "vengeful provocation." In offering "absolute solidarity with Israel," the AJOA evoked recent histories of Jewish-Muslim tension, as it termed Israel the "land of exile for hundreds of thousands of persecuted . . . from the Nazi camps and exiles of Iraq, Egypt, Yemen, and Syria."[10] While the AJOA sought to express a peaceful orientation, it repeatedly evoked episodes of conflict in a manner that underscored Jewish victimhood and Muslim transgression. Moreover, it suddenly defined the groups' encounter almost entirely as one forged in the conflicts of decolonization and the struggle for Israel/Palestine.

More broadly, the presence of Jews from North Africa, who had not grown up with the same type of expectations about public displays of loyalty to Jewish nationhood or religion, proved vital to the shift underway. Ady Steg, president of the Conseil représentatif des israélites de France (CRIF), later explained that at the moment the war broke out, "The Jews of North Africa uninhibited us [the Ashkenazim]. They pushed us to scream, to cry, to sing, to invade the streets. They had no complex. And France observed with curiosity the extraverted Judaism."[11]

Confidence in such public support for Israel benefited as well from the unflinching solidarity of most major national political leaders and parties—including on the Left, with the exception of the French Communist Party (PCF)—and of many left-wing intellectuals like Jean-Paul Sartre and Simone de Beauvoir. In an unlikely alliance, their position was echoed by many pieds-noirs on the Right. Three national associations of rapatriés or former colonists from North Africa took part in pro-Israel demonstrations. Whereas the quasi-unanimity of the mainstream Left in favor of Israel confounded many Muslims and supporters of the Palestinians, who recalled a number of the same figures' advocacy for Algerian independence, displays of pied-noir support appeared once more to map the struggle over Algeria onto the one over Israel/Palestine. Drivers in traffic even began beeping their horns again in the way that first became fashionable to the syllables of *Al-gé-rie fran-çaise* (French Algeria), now applying it instead to *Is-ra-ël vain-cra* (Israel will win).[12]

Soon, as Israel's military successes rapidly remade the borders of the Middle East, French Jewry offered an unprecedented outpouring of visible support for the Jewish state. The *Journal des communautés* spoke for many when it described a "radical reversal," moving from "the attempt of genocide that was, still just a few days ago, announced publicly over the Arab radio airwaves," to the Israeli conquests of East Jerusalem, the West Bank, the Golan Heights, the Gaza Strip, and the Sinai Peninsula.[13] Indeed, to perceive how Israel moved from the margins to the center in communal life in just a few weeks, one need look no further than the French Jewish press. The Alsatian Jewish weekly, *Bulletin de nos communautés,* which had seldom featured any cover images related to Israel, ran nothing else from June 2 to October 18, 1967, portraying everything from pilgrims at the Western Wall to the Dead Sea Scrolls to holidays in Jerusalem.[14] For weeks after the war, numerous Jewish organs featured firsthand accounts and photographs from the war. Community leaders, rabbis, and commentators assessed the event's political and religious significance.[15] Substantial coverage focused on how Israel might finally make peace.[16]

Jewish communities across France launched numerous initiatives to support Israel. Not long after the war, leaders in Strasbourg reported having collected 1 million francs, and those in Marseille half a million, for solidarity funds. These were part of a massive nationwide fundraising haul: in the few weeks following Israel's victory, some 60,000 contributors across France gave more than 50 million francs to support Israel, a far greater sum than any previously gathered among French Jewry on behalf of the Jewish state.[17] Attention to Israel permeated all aspects of communal life. In daily prayers, some congregations added readings regarding individuals' responsibility toward Israel; other communities held parades.[18] Delegations of French Jews, from leaders to ordinary community members, undertook organized trips to Israel.[19]

Unsurprisingly, then, Jewish coverage and initiatives around the 1967 war gave primary attention to Israel and Jewish solidarity. Particularly after the war began, few Jews focused on the potential repercussions for Jews' relations with their Muslim neighbors in France. Some, however, were concerned by the public alliance of Algerian rapatrié and other Far Right groups with the Zionist cause, particularly in an atmosphere of rising anti-Arab racism connected to the war's events.[20] The French Jewish Student Union (UEJF), consistent with the concerns it had expressed for both Jewish solidarity and fundamental human rights during the Algerian conflict, printed tracts that said, "Long live Israel, not anti-Arab racism!"[21] A Jewish Coordinating Committee statement of early July reflected the combination of emerging considerations. There, Jewish leaders called on Jews and non-Jews in France to do three things: support and publicize Israel's will to peace, promote Israeli-Arab negotiation, and "fight energetically any racist spirit whatever it is, in any forms, wherever it shows itself."[22]

One notes the absence, here and elsewhere, of great appeals for migration to Israel. Even amid the fervor of 1967, few French Jews took this step. Immigration did increase substantially over the preceding years, but, nonetheless, between 1965 and 1971, a mere 6,852 Jews left France for Israel.[23] In part, this reflected the ongoing tradition of a Jewish community that saw French Jews' primary devotion to their native country as integrally connected to their concern for international Jewry. Such an outlook, however, had begun to change perceptibly. The publicly transnational nature of the French Jewish response to the 1967 war—and its departure from the more reserved history of French Zionism—were inescapable. Such a shift reflected numerous factors: Zionism's new credibility following World War II and Israel's birth, the memory of the Shoah and its precise relationship to current events, the relative unity of postwar Jewish associational life, and the more multifaceted nature of Jewish identity in the public sphere for both the North African newcomers

and the new generation that had begun to speak up during decolonization as Jews.

The same period witnessed the start of important shifts in the relationship
of France's Muslims to Israel/Palestine. By mid- to late May 1967, through
the pages of *El Moudjahid,* the widely disseminated state newspaper
of Algeria, large numbers of Muslim workers in France could read constantly about the Middle East conflict. In late May, the Boumediene
government, which would ultimately participate on the Arab side, used
its organ to beat the drum for war. Headlines, photographs, and cartoons
glorified the Algerian leadership and the Arab cause and demonized the
Jewish state while portending its imminent demise. The newspaper repeated
belligerent slogans such as Nasser's, "The war of liberation is inevitable."[24]
In the early days of June, the journal relayed Algerian leaders' declarations
such as, "The Palestinian cause is yours," which sought to personalize
the conflict.[25]

Within France itself, the largest organization of Algerian workers—the
Amicale des algériens en France (ADAF), renamed in 1965 the Amicale
des algériens en Europe (ADAE)—sounded the call for pro-Palestinian
solidarity. Founded as the successor to the French Federation of the Front
de libération nationale (FFFLN), its credibility suffered when most of the
French Federation's leaders, loyal to the Algerian provisional government,
ended up on the losing side in the civil war that followed independence
in 1962.[26] The FLN, quickly the only legal party in Algeria, took over
the ADAF and sought to make it the recognized representative of Algerians in France. The ADAF and then the Amicale des algériens en Europe
(ADAE) acted as a patriotic association, organized Algerian workers,
women, and students, and provided them social and cultural services. It
spread its message through the distribution of *El Moudjahid,* as well its
own journal, *L'Algérien en Europe.*[27] Hardly uncontested on the terrain
of Algerian politics in France, the ADAE experienced competition, particularly after the 1965 coup d'état, from several opposition groups that
sought to make inroads among France's Algerian workers and students.
By the late 1960s, the ADAE, in the face of rival organizations, its founding
circumstances, and its tainted ties to a series of embattled Algerian regimes, struggled to gain traction in France.[28] While the Algerian government claimed that the association had 100,000 members, French officials

estimated the ADAE's adherents at not more than 15,000.[29] In an atmosphere of relative political apathy, the Algerian opposition parties attracted far smaller followings.[30]

Within this context, the 1967 war emerged in part as an opportunity for mobilization. When war appeared imminent, the ADAE, which had previously avoided direct political engagements, suddenly moved from relative silence to saturation on the issue of Palestine. On June 1, *L'Algérien en Europe,* in step with the Algerian government, tied the Arab cause to anti-imperialism and evoked the Vietnam War to dismiss American condemnations of Egypt's closing of the Gulf of Aqaba.[31] The day the war began, the Amicale's council convened a special meeting, from which it issued a statement supporting the Algerian government, defending the Palestinian cause, and attacking Israel.[32] Between June 7 and 18, 1967, fourteen ADAE gatherings took place in the Paris region, seeking to rally Muslims to action.[33]

Before the war such intense propaganda prompted little grassroots action on the part of Muslims in France.[34] Yet after Israel's attack on June 5 large numbers of Algerian Muslims quickly became engaged.[35] Thousands of Muslims, including as many as 9,000 Algerians, reported to Algerian and various Arab consulates in France to volunteer for the Arab cause. Hundreds turned out for the ADAE's meetings around Paris.[36] The Inter-Arab Student Committee formed, grouping thirteen "Arab" student groups in Paris. Soon the committee wrote a letter to President de Gaulle urging condemnation of the Israeli attack; it subsequently issued a statement bitterly complaining, "the American and British imperialisms have just proven their collusion with Zionism against the Arab people."[37] In several other French cities, including Strasbourg, Algerian student associations issued statements that supported their homeland's government and denounced the "imperialist aggressions against the Arab fatherland."[38] In the context of the longer history of ethnic diversity within France's Muslim population, the repeated use of the term *Arab* here and elsewhere, as synonymous with all Muslims throughout the Mediterranean, becomes striking. Such an equation reflects several factors: long-term shifts in the demographics of North African Muslim migration; the ideology of those who won the struggle for power in independent Algeria; and the growing importance of Middle East politics in France, including Nasserism and calls for Arab unity.

Following the war, the Algerian government and the ADAE continued to call on Algerians everywhere to take up arms, donate blood, and organize on behalf of their Palestinian brothers and sisters.[39] The June 15 issue of *L'Algérien en Europe* included maps to show Israel "encircling" the Arab world, rather than vice versa, and a chronology of "20 years of repeated Zionist and imperialist aggressions" that began with the establishment of Israel in May 1948.[40] Two weeks later, it proudly described Algerian Muslims in France as directly at war with Israel: "In the face of the Zionist aggression, the Algerian immigration rediscovered its taste for battle." Indeed, numerous Algerian Muslims in France, at least momentarily, expressed shock at the crushing military defeat of the Arab countries.[41]

The ADAE synthesized the sentiments and experiences of pain that it had observed among Muslims in France into the declaration of a single fictive worker: "For me, this week of 5 to 10 June, I am not ready to forget it. To tell you what I have experienced . . . is impossible. I did not sleep; I had no desire to eat. There was something burning inside me." Just as important, many stories in both *El Moudjahid* and *L'Algérien en Europe* complained of pro-Israel bias in France, and even of a "sudden rise of racial violence against Algerians [which] risks extending into all of France." The largest student union in France, the UNEF, which by July would condemn Israel for military aggression and come out in favor of Palestinian statehood, issued a statement in early June that exclaimed: "The demonstrations of support for Israel are providing the pretext for racist acts of violence. . . . Everywhere . . . incidents are tending to multiply."[42] Several scholars have argued that this wave of racism was the greatest France had witnessed in decades and that in the popular imagination "the Arab was substituted for the Jew as incarnation of evil."[43]

Indeed, the war's opposing sides appear to have become intertwined with the racialized divisions forged by the events of 1961–1962, bringing to the surface larger undercurrents of anti–North African prejudice among wide swaths of the French population. For many Muslims, this wave of racism provoked an acute sense of vulnerability. As we shall see, for large numbers of both Muslims and Jews, the months following the war became a period of fear and isolation, with important long-term consequences for their relations.

The Amicale sought, at the same moment, to bitterly condemn Zionism and Zionists while reaching out to certain Jews. As the organization did so, it linked its own struggles to the fault lines that had emerged in the closing period of the French-Algerian War. In the June 30 issue of *L'Algérien en Europe,* a headline read, "Not all Jews are Zionists." This implied, of course, that those who were remained decided enemies. According to the historical definition of Zionism—as support for a sovereign Jewish state in a portion of historic Palestine—few Jews in France by 1967 were non-Zionists. Yet among the anti-Zionist Left, a number of Jews figured prominently. Such were the authors of the column, a "Liaison Committee of Jewish Students," which stated flatly that Israel had no right to exist and defined the country's recent action as a "war of aggression and conquest." Condemning uncritical Jewish support for Israel in France, the students concluded by arguing: "the battle against antisemitism has become the pretext for anti-Arab racism and for '*Algérie française*' vengeance and the ideological timidity of the right."[44] The committee thereby linked Zionism with the Organisation de l'armée secrète (OAS). This association reignited an accusation made during the Algerian conflict—one that would appear elsewhere in anti-Israel Muslim and left-wing propaganda in France during and after the 1967 war.

As they blamed Zionists in significant part for anti-Arab sentiments and attacks in France, the ADAE and the Algerian government projected this narrative of spillover onto older binaries. They made the nationalist memory of the French-Algerian War a steady undercurrent in their propaganda and sought as well to separate themselves from their enemies around French traditions of public secularism and antiracism. The Amicale's statement of June 5 against Israel and in support of Algeria insistently denied any link to racism or antisemitism.[45] Later, the Amicale complained that in the course of the war, "there was an attempt to expand the action taking place in the Middle East. They had wanted, by acts planned and carried out, to provoke a reaction in order to prove that what was occurring on Palestinian soil was nothing more, nothing less than a war between Arabs and Jews, between those of the Muslim and Jewish faiths."[46] FLN accounts linked "Zionist adventurers" and former OAS elements, accused them of racist attacks, and then labeled these actions as outside French tradition. Both the pages of *El Moudjahid* and the UNEF blamed "Zionists" and "[OAS] ultras" for one incident in particular, an arson attack in a North African slum in Nice and the subsequent murder of two Algerians.[47] One report exclaimed, "We know . . . that the French people have always disapproved of the actions of these adventurers that are still in the defense of lost causes."[48]

For these and other groups tied to Algeria, responses to the 1967 war often showed that past and present struggles for Algeria's future remained paramount and that the Palestinian cause had more instrumental than vital significance. In Strasbourg, despite aggressive efforts, the local ADAE struggled to rally much support for the Palestinian cause among what remained a relatively small local Muslim population. Nonetheless, organizers at a pro-Palestinian meeting in late June refused entry to ten harkis who came to participate.[49] In addition, according to one French report on Muslim attitudes, while most harkis took a similar view to their Algerian coreligionists on the recent war, they hoped that recent events in the Middle East might lead to the fall of Boumediene, which could open the door for them to return to their native country.[50]

Some activists saw in the war's outcome an opportunity for more vocal opposition. In September, the Organisation clandestine de la révolution algérienne (OCRA), formed the previous year by Benbellist opponents of the Boumedienne regime, including Mohamed Lebjaoui, broke with a short-lived policy of supporting the Algerian government during the war. Lebjaoui, who as an FLN militant had advocated a more moderate, secularist version of Algerian nationalism with a place for Jews, authored a scathing editorial in the group's organ, *Révolution algérienne*. Here he expressed approval for the "positive resolutions" of the recent Khartoum conference and encouraged all means of resistance by the Arab populations in the territories conquered by Israel.[51] Yet he also accused the current Algerian government of using the war as an excuse for the "looting of the Algerian budget" and an "avalanche of new taxes," as well as of taking a demagogically stubborn position on the Palestinian question, destroying Arab unity (this presumably referred to Boumediene's open opposition to Egypt's decision to sign a cease-fire at the war's end).[52] Here we can detect not only the deep political divisions of postindependence Algeria, but also the vestiges of alternative paths envisioned by many nationalists before 1962.

Even the fervency of the ADAE's efforts to arouse passion regarding recent events in Palestine made limited headway among most Muslims in France. Likewise, the war's immediate impact on direct Jewish-Muslim relations varied considerably from one locale to another. The events of 1968 would confirm that Paris remained a center of national political activism as well as international leftist and anti-imperial politics. These larger contexts would in time reshape day-to-day Jewish-Muslim reactions in the city. During and immediately following the war, however, in Belleville, Muslims continued to sit in Arab cafés beneath posters of Nasser that seemed to compete with the images of Israeli war hero Moshe Dayan that hung in many Jewish businesses. While such signposts continued to help claim territory for Jews and Muslims, they did not generate any recorded altercations, even amid the actual fighting.[53]

In Strasbourg, where interactions were more limited but ethnoreligious identities more publicly oriented, two spheres of interaction revealed the war's limited effects. At the A. S. Menora athletic club, the war provoked no discernible tension among the mostly Jewish footballers and the small number of Muslim players.[54] The University of Strasbourg, where Habib Hihi and Evelyne Rueff had met, was now home to one of the largest North African Muslim student populations in France.[55] Like many other French universities, it was becoming a key site of Jewish-Muslim interaction. In the days preceding the outbreak of hostilities, a pamphlet from Arab students in the Comité anti-colonialiste attacked Zionism and claimed it was destroying Judaism, even as the author took pains to distinguish the two. The local UEJF chapter responded with a leaflet that denounced the anti-Zionist tract as "base propaganda." An item appearing soon after in *Bulletin de nos communautés* quoted and condemned a far shriller Muslim student pamphlet published in Brussels. By saying that the prior leaflet's "nuance was rapidly forgotten," the story lumped all Muslim students together, implying that the two publications constituted a sequential escalation from anti-Zionism to antisemitism. But actual altercations did not appear to occur during or following the war.[56]

Marseille, with its geographical proximity to the Mediterranean, felt the weight of the conflict most acutely, in a manner that reflected both the emerging rules for Jewish-Muslim coexistence and the city's own particularities of postcolonial social geography. In the days preceding the war, large demonstrations on behalf of Israel brought thousands of Jews into the streets. These rallies also made visible the significant non-Jewish support in the city for the Jewish state, particularly on the part of socialist mayor Gaston Defferre, a longtime pro-Israel enthusiast who at the start of June became president of the newly formed Committee of Support for Israel.[57] On the war's second day, police reported "numerous commentaries within the Algerian community that hold Israel responsible for the conflict and immediately declare solidarity with the Arab countries." By the end of the war's first day, the Algerian consulate in Marseille, with the collaboration of the local Amicale, had recruited 150 Algerian volunteers to fight on the Arab side. The Algerian and Tunisian consulates continued these efforts in the coming days as Muslim agents recruited coreligionists in the housing projects on the city outskirts; the Israeli consulate of Marseille opened its own registration for Jews to enlist on the Israeli side.[58]

Many Muslims in Marseille, particularly as they witnessed large-scale demonstrations of solidarity with Israel, became both uncomfortable about the wider political environment and nervous about the possibility of interreligious confrontation. Here Defferre's ardent support for Israel seems to have helped catalyze among Muslims a locally specific sense of the anti-Arab bias and isolation being experienced across France. Meanwhile, Muslim fears of altercation repeatedly centered on potential provocations by Jewish youth. As calm prevailed, one state report attributed the lack of Jewish-Muslim violence to the physical distance between most heavily Jewish and Muslim neighborhoods.[59] Shortly after the war, a representative at the local Algerian consulate urged Muslims to boycott Jewish-owned stores where they normally shopped. One French official noted that such a boycott "could have unfortunate consequences for certain small shopkeepers installed in the Muslim quarters."[60] Presumably the author of this report spoke in part of the Belsunce. Nevertheless, it does not appear that such fears or schemes materialized: just as no reported confrontations by young Jews with Muslims occurred, Muslim customers did not discernibly let the war push their business away from Jewish-owned shops. For the time being, the rules of coexistence held.

Long-Term Effects of 1967

Thus it was hardly apparent that a major change had occurred in the terms of Jewish-Muslim relations in France in the immediate aftermath of the Six Day War. Over the next eleven months, however, the potency of events in the Middle East as a catalyst for tension grew. President de Gaulle's press conference of November 27, 1967, in which he outlined the beginnings of a major shift in foreign policy, away from support for Israel and toward closer ties with the Arab world, marked a key event in this process. Since the early nineteenth century French Jewish leaders had articulated and taught their children the similarity between the values of the French Revolution and the Hebrew Bible, often equating their Judaism and their patriotic devotion to France.[61] The close relationship between France and Israel that developed in the early years of the Jewish state must have appeared to many French Jews as simply the logical extension of such shared values. After the 1956 Suez War France alone had stood with Israel when the rest of the Security Council condemned the nation; until the 1967 war, France had been Israel's primary weapons supplier, and many Jews felt particular affection for de Gaulle as leader of the Resistance.

On the eve of the Six Day War de Gaulle had troubled many Jews by imposing an arms embargo on all parties. But at his press conference, when the president made official his new posture toward Israel and described Jews as "an elite people, sure of itself and domineering," he left many French Jews dumbfounded, with a deep sense of betrayal. Two days later, when 4,000 Jews gathered at the Mutualité in Paris to commemorate Israel's birth, groups approved motions that criticized de Gaulle's rendition of Jewish history as erroneous, called on him to reverse recent French policy changes toward Israel, and contrasted recent events with de Gaulle's own former heroism and defense of Jewish rights during World War II. Some in the crowd even chanted derisively, "Charles Pétain." Stunned, the French Jewish press devoted extensive critique and commentary to the president's choice of words.[62]

Invoking the Vichy chief of state to attack de Gaulle was hardly an arbitrary choice. Joan B. Wolf has argued persuasively that the sequence of events—from fears of a second Holocaust on the war's eve, to the sense soon after the euphoria of victory that the French state had abandoned Israel and severed its close relationship with Jews—awakened a new kind of activist Holocaust consciousness. The connection between the memory of World War II and solidarity with Israel catalyzed Jewish demands for public recognition as a distinct ethnoreligious community with a history of suffering.[63]

In part, this new Jewish politics emerged from a Jewish sense of vulnerability spurred by the war's events. Perhaps the most articulate expression of this connection came from a seemingly unlikely source: prominent conservative social theorist Raymond Aron. Aron, a longtime friend and public supporter of de Gaulle, was a nonobservant Jew who had called himself more Catholic than Jewish. He had previously written that French Jewish support for Israel would understandably provoke concerns about dual loyalties. But for Aron, the war's events and the president's press conference proved transformative. By way of "some half a dozen words, loaded with resonance," Aron exclaimed, de Gaulle "rehabilitated" what had long remained a "latent antisemitism." Aron admitted that on the whole, he felt "less removed from an antisemitic French person than from a southern Moroccan Jew who speaks only Arabic and who has scarcely emerged from what appears to me to be the Middle Ages." But the philosopher declared that, nonetheless, "the day when a sovereign power declares that Jews around the world constitute 'a people sure of themselves and domineering,' I do not have any choice." He had to speak out, he explained, and as a Jew. Furthermore, suddenly Aron realized: "I also know, more clearly than yesterday, that even the possibility of the destruction of the state of Israel . . . strikes me in the depths of my soul."[64] In this manner, France's ongoing foreign policy shift away from full-throated support for Israel and the president's critical comments about the Jewish people made the months following the Six Day War a period of rupture for French Jewry. Jews, like Muslims, experienced a sense of acute uncertainty about their security and their relationship with the French state and wider society.

Contrary to Aron's fears, a wave of antisemitism was not forthcoming. In part this reflected the fact that the traditional base for antisemitic politics in France, the Far Right, now rarely demonized Israel or Jews. In fact, due to the defining power of the French-Algerian War for the world-view of many of their adherents, extreme Right parties and publications were deeply anti-Gaullist and aligned with pied-noir nostalgia; both of these factors put them squarely in Israel's camp in the French political dynamics of 1967.[65] More broadly, opinion surveys of the French population reveal that Jews in fact enjoyed a far less stigmatized position than Muslims at this time, a dichotomy that seemed both to reflect and map onto views of the Arab-Israeli conflict before, during, and immediately following the Six Day War. In 1966 one survey had shown that 62 percent of French people thought that too many "North Africans" (that is, Muslims) lived in France, while only 13 percent said the same about Jews. In an October 1967 survey 65 percent of respondents said they had racist attitudes toward Arabs, and 23 percent said they were racist toward Jews.[66] Three separate polls from early June to September all showed overwhelming majorities of the French who supported Israel versus tiny numbers favoring the Arabs, suggesting possible links in the popular imagination between the Middle East conflict and the Jews and Muslims residing in France.

Following de Gaulle's press conference 37 percent refused to comment on the president's position; 30 percent even supported it. By January 1970, support for Israel had declined precipitously from a high of 68 percent in September 1967 to 33 percent, even as Arab support remained quite low at 6 percent. Another survey from the same year would show that the percentage of the French population calling themselves racist against Jews had risen to 34 percent.[67] Thus even as broader French attitudes toward Muslims and the Arab world remained far harsher than against Jews, it was not without reason that French Jews experienced the president's infamous statement as a turning point of new vulnerability.

For the Algerian government, the shift in French policy constituted a welcome surprise and an opportunity for Franco-Arab reconciliation: officials praised de Gaulle and pushed for closer diplomatic and economic ties with France.[68] Algeria also continued to seek a larger role in Middle East politics. In January 1968 the FLN helped organize a conference of Islamic political organizations from across Europe with most of the leading groups coming from France. The FLN hoped to use the conference to build a coordinated position among these groups in support of the Arabs in the Middle East conflict.[69] In March, among young Algerian Muslims living in the northern French coastal town of Le Havre, popular rumors circulated about the imminent selection of particularly fit Algerians for special camps in Algeria. Once there, sources claimed, the young recruits would undergo intensive training that would prepare them to fight as shock troops for Egypt in the event of another war with Israel.[70] In May 1968, as many Jewish organizations planned celebrations marking the war's one-year anniversary, Algeria and its representatives in France called for an international day of Arab mourning.[71] Continuing their growing engagement with the Middle East conflict, Muslim university students in Paris affiliated with the Palestinian nationalist group Fatah, the leading party within the growing Palestine Liberation Organization (PLO), planned a meeting to commemorate what they termed "the Imperial-Zionist aggression of 5 June 1967."[72]

These developments coincided with another dimension of growing transnational Jewish and Muslim allegiances in France: anti-Jewish violence in North Africa and subsequent Jewish migration. In Tunis, on the first day of the 1967 war, Muslims violently attacked Jews, synagogues, and Jewish-owned shops as they chanted slogans like, "Into the Sea with the Jews."[73] In Morocco, while government protection succeeded in ensuring relative calm, many Jews still faced visible hostility from Muslims.[74] Between the start of the war and April 1968 at least 15,000 Jews from these two countries, 60 percent of them from Tunisia, came to France.[75] A number of Tunisian and Moroccan Jews would long recall this moment as one of violence or fear.[76] Through numerous letters to family and friends in France and the stories immigrants shared on arrival, many of them brought these memories to a wider audience.[77] Large numbers of Tunisian arrivals in particular came to Paris, with a high percentage

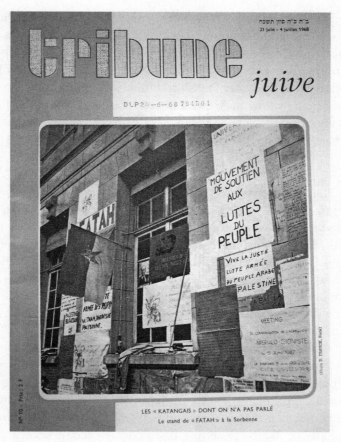

Figure 6.1. The pro-Palestinian movement of May 1968 on the cover of *La Tribune juive*. The caption reads: "The 'Katangais' that no one talks about—the 'Fatah' stand at the Sorbonne." (Courtesy of La Tribune juive.)

following their compatriots to Belleville, as the quarter's Jewish population grew to 15,000.[78] It hardly seems coincidental that the quarter in which a Jewish-Muslim riot broke out one year later housed largely Tunisian Jews and Algerian, and to a lesser extent Tunisian, Muslims.

The riot's immediate context, however, also drew from internal upheavals in France. As a wave of student and worker strikes all but shut down parts of the country in the events of what was soon deemed "May '68," many Jews and Muslims in Belleville found themselves financially strapped, restless, and bored. The large-scale protests and confrontations of the moment in places like the Latin Quarter had created an allure around the heroic street action of young people.[79] Meanwhile, during the student sit-ins at the Sorbonne supporters of the Palestinian cause and, soon after, Zionist socialists, had set up their own posters and tables, producing numerous tense conversations.[80] These confrontations had not gone unnoticed in the wider Jewish community. *Tribune juive,* the recently renamed organ of Jews in Alsace-Lorraine, ran a photograph of the pro-Palestinian kiosk at the Sorbonne with a pejorative caption that dubbed its activists "the Katangais that no one talks about" (Figure 6.1).[81]

The Belleville Riots: Parenthesis or Turning Point?

Several interrelated factors converged, then, in the 1968 riots in Belleville: the experience of decolonization, the fragile proximity of many Jews and Muslims in shared spaces, the 1967 war, and its implications for various transnational allegiances in France, and the immediate context of May '68.[82] Despite these multifaceted causalities, the riots were framed in much simpler terms. The French press tended to trace the violence directly to the one-year mark of the Six Day War; in fact, a number of journalists immediately dubbed the riots "the six hour war."[83] Some observers later commented that Jews and Muslims in the quarter became increasingly wary with the approach of the war's anniversary.[84] Press reports, official statements, and individual reactions among Jews and Muslims typically fashioned rather one-sided versions of this narrative. Many members of each community blamed the other for allowing the Middle East conflict to penetrate daily coexistence in France and then underscored their own close relationship to France and its values of public secularism.

In the same manner, each side accused the other of violating the new rules for interethnic coexistence. Yet in the process, they often unwittingly reinforced precisely what they blamed their neighbors for doing: the imposition of divisive political meanings onto previously fluid personal identities, neighborhood interactions, and urban spaces. Several Jewish residents of Belleville, for instance, insisted that the card game represented a mere pretext. They said they had never experienced friction with their Muslim neighbors before, but in recent days, the latter had avoided them or acted disagreeably. "We understood," said one, "it was about the approaching anniversary."[85] The president of the synagogue on the rue Julien-Lacroix declared: "A game of cards cannot explain the importance and the gravity of what took place. It is the anniversary of the beginning of the 'Six Day War,' and that's not simply a coincidence."[86]

One Tunisian Jew claimed that "the Arabs prepared to avenge their defeat of last year. . . . They told me that there would have to be something on June 11. In any case, they leaped at the opportunity of the fight of the 'Kairouan' in order to attack us."[87]

Muslims often expressed analogous reactions. One Muslim man exclaimed: "The Jews [can't] have [a] modest victory. Israel won the war, it's true; but why, while we live here together, must they remind us at every opportunity, at each instance, that we are the defeated? While we, like them, did not participate in the Six Day War."[88] A number of North African Muslim leaders, troubled by the implications for the entire community, suggested that coreligionists who had acted as antagonists in the riots in the Latin Quarter or the Belleville incidents should be deported from France. Many Muslims from North Africa articulated their concerns about recent developments by turning to the Service d'assistance technique aux migrants to share their fears and seek advice.[89]

Widespread reports spoke of a tract distributed in Arabic that called for a "holy war" in Paris on the upcoming anniversary of the Six Day War. In a declaration issued on behalf of all the Muslim and Arab student associations in France, the Inter-Arab Student Committee (CEIA) denied claims that it was the source of these tracts and condemned the riots. In the same statement, however, the CEIA called the incidents "racist" and blamed them on "well-known provocateurs."[90] Other Muslim groups helped to clarify such coded language. The day after the riots, the ADAE published a pamphlet that exclaimed: "It appears that the Zionist organization has profited from a minor incident opposing a Tunisian national to an israélite in order to launch itself against the Algerian community, attacking pedestrians and burning their establishments."[91] Once again, the ADAE's interpretation of Zionist aggression in the wider Mediterranean became imposed onto its depiction of Jewish actors in France.

Many of these statements contained a striking tension. First, they acknowledged the prevalence of everyday Jewish-Muslim contact in Belleville, signaling the groups' commonalities as neighboring immigrants in France. But then, in the same breath, each side sought to link foreign nationals within the other community to a transnational politics that ran counter to French public secularism and the mutually understood boundaries for signs of ethnoreligious allegiance in this shared neighborhood. One of the more tortured examples of this came from a writer in *El Moudjahid*. "It is known," he declared, that "Muslims and Jews in Paris visit each other regularly. It is well known that one third of the Jewish emigrants are Tunisian and have kept their original nationality. Because of this [these Jews] feel much closer to Israel than to the France that welcomed them. 'They belong,' [it is said], 'to the Israeli movements, they remain affiliated to the ex-Irgun.' "[92] According to this account, for Jews, Tunisian nationality and friendly relations with Muslims became the catalysts not for coexistence but rather for ties to an Israeli paramilitary organization and a lack of devotion to France.

Another set of responses from leading Jewish and Muslim figures sought to minimize the importance of the Middle East conflict for interactions in France. They too, however, hinted at a new kind of politicization of neighbors and spaces and a breakdown of the laws of coexistence. As the riots created a stir among Muslims and Jews across France, Algerian officials grew concerned about the potential deterioration of the warming Franco-Algerian relationship.[93] The Algerian minister of foreign affairs instructed his ambassador to work for a quick solution to prevent a "war of religion."[94] Tunisian ambassador Masmoudi, credited for helping to quell the violence, said he was ready to serve "all of my compatriots, of the Muslim or israélite confession" (Figure 6.2). Calling the rioters "a group of imbeciles," he said that as "guests" in France, Tunisians of all confessions had an obligation not to cause trouble "by our useless fights."[95]

That these reactions came from foreign representatives of a country with many Muslim immigrants was highly significant. The source revealed how the presence on French soil of new North African transnational entities in the postcolonial era had multiple dimensions of separation and potential conviviality. In the first instance, the positions of the Algerian foreign minister and Ambassador Masmoudi signaled the dramatic change that had occurred for many of France's former Muslim and, to a lesser extent, Jewish subjects with decolonization. These North Africans living in France were no longer French subjects aspiring to equal citizenship; they were foreign nationals more clearly delineated from the French people. At the same time, the choices these leaders made showed that such clear markers of ethnic difference need not automatically lead to greater conflict. Algerian and Tunisian officials articulated the need for a group of Muslims based outside France to maintain friendly relations with their host country. The Tunisian ambassador, furthermore, highlighted the interreligious nature of his country's migration and transnational community, implicitly insisting that *Tunisian* was not simply coterminous with *Muslim*.

Figure 6.2. Rabbi Emmanuel Chouchena and Tunisian ambassador Mohamed Masmoudi walk through Belleville to restore calm following the riots of June 1968. (Courtesy of La Tribune juive.)

French chief rabbi Jacob Kaplan's actions prove equally revealing of the narrowing landscape but ongoing possibilities for Jewish and Muslim allegiances in postcolonial France. Following the riots, Kaplan carefully addressed a plea for calm to "the israélite and Muslim populations of the Belleville quarter," thereby categorizing the groups by their religious identities but seeking to subordinate these to their common neighborhood. He went on to exclaim: "We rejoice in noting that the tension between the two communities has noticeably diminished. A confrontation between israélites and Muslims would be indeed dramatic for [both communities]."[96] With these words, Kaplan seemed to acknowledge that the Middle East conflict might easily reignite intercommunal tensions without warning.

Indeed, many Muslims and Jews appeared ready to embrace the largely mythical view of the Belleville riots as the signal of new Jewish-Muslim tensions that extended directly from those in Israel/Palestine. This occurred in spite of the riots' complex causes and their exceptionality within Belleville, a space of daily Jewish-Muslim interaction, as well as the quick return to calm that followed them. In the minds of many, these riots made real the previously theoretical prospect of spillover from the Middle East conflict into France and showed how Zionist and Palestinian activism could saturate the outlooks and mutual perceptions of Jews and Muslims. A few weeks later, *L'Arche* tellingly made the mistake of referring to the events as occurring on June 5, the anniversary of the outbreak of the Six Day War, rather than their actual dates of June 2–3.[97] Within days of the riots tracts appeared in Grenoble in Arabic attacking the Jewish community; these preceded a sizable local meeting of North African and Middle Eastern Muslims.[98] In the department of the Var in the south, Muslims, upset about the riots, blamed Jews. Rumors spread that the Algerian embassy might create Muslim "commandos," or "moudjahidine" to combat "the aggression of Zionist Jews in France."[99]

In the same period, Marseille showed itself once more to be a site where the combination of spheres of interaction, socioeconomic divisions, and local politics could produce Jewish-Muslim tension. Jewish leaders feared that "Arabs" might demonstrate on June 5 and asked for police protection for the city's consistory.[100] Marseille's ADAE chapter held a meeting attended by 100 Muslims, where it offered its account of the riots and founded a "committee of intervention," ready to act in case the events in Belleville provoked local trouble.[101] In the end, however, even as such developments highlighted further Jewish-Muslim differences and saw communal leaders seek literally to police group boundaries, calm appeared to prevail once more in France's Mediterranean port.

Radicalizing and Racializing Jewish and Muslim Space, 1968–1970

One of the major short-term catalysts of the Belleville riots—the events of May '68—proved to have lasting ramifications for the importance of the Israeli-Arab conflict among Jews and Muslims in France. To be sure, the larger contexts of decolonization, ethnic politics, the Six Day War, and shifting French policies and opinions regarding the Middle East were crucial. Yet the rise of a group of radical, anticolonial, internationalist, and student political movements, coming of age in May '68, gave pro-Palestinian activism its organizational roots in France and the question of Palestine a growing place in French public consciousness.[102] By the late 1960s Marxists, Maoists, Trotskyites, and other far leftists saw in France's immigrant workers both a new cause and potential army of activists. While the 1967 war mobilized a certain number of these leftists in favor of the Palestinians, particularly on French university campuses, it was developments the following year that unleashed new political alliances. A substantial minority of France's immigrant workers, including many from North Africa, took part in the explosion of strikes and protests in May.[103] Earlier that spring heated battles between the Israeli military and Fatah around the Jordanian town of Karameh had attracted worldwide attention from the Left, including important declarations of pro-Palestinian support from Vietnamese and Chinese activists, who were highly influential among French radicals. In the context of May '68, many French leftists, taken with Maoist connections between violence and revolution, saw Palestinian resistance as symbolic of their larger struggles and started to forge connections with Muslim workers.[104]

During the months after the June 1968 Belleville riots pro-Palestinian militants began to make their own inroads in France. Beginning in January 1969, Muhammad Abou Mayer and then Mahmoud Hamchari, the latter of whom had worked closely with Yasir Arafat, came to Paris to build support for the Palestinian cause. In the coming months, they laid the groundwork for the movement. They founded a newspaper in French, *Fedayin;* partnered with several revolutionary organizations—many of whose leading figures continued to be leftist Jews—with whom they created Committees of Palestine Action (commonly referred to as Palestine Committees) at a number of universities; and established a legally recognized presence that could lobby the French government on behalf of Palestinian nationalism. In August 1969 they led two leaders of the Maoist Gauche prolétarienne, Alain Geismar and Léo Lévy, both Jewish, on a tour of the Palestinian refugee camp of Karameh in Jordan.[105]

Indeed, even in an environment where Jews and Muslims found themselves increasingly divided along political lines, a small group of Jews like the Maoists Léo and (her husband) Benny Lévy and Geismar, the Marxist Maxime Rodinson (an important scholar of Islam), and a number of others were among the most influential figures in the early pro-Palestinian movements. At the time of the outbreak of the Six Day War several of these Jewish leftists had reached out to Muslim students to declare their solidarity with the Arab cause, even forming the Committee of Anti-Zionist Jewish Students. They often framed their critiques or opposition to Zionism as coterminous with a larger defense of oppressed peoples born in significant part of a universalistic view of the Holocaust and its lessons.[106] At times such an outlook entailed a very self-conscious assertion of the Jewishness of an individual's politics.[107] Rabbi Emmanuel Lévyne, for example, whose father had died at Auschwitz, wrote a book entitled *Judaism against Zionism.* The worker Patrick Rabiaz who joined a pro-Palestinian hunger strike explained his actions by drawing an analogy between the persecution of members of his family in concentration camps of the Nazis and the current suffering of Palestinians under Zionism.

Since the vast majority of such figures were Ashkenazic Jews, their position—and its contrast with that of most Jews from North Africa at this time—is highly revealing.[108] Many of the "68ers" more broadly came of age during the French-Algerian War, particularly around events such as the brutal police repression against Algerians on October 17, 1961, which at the time provoked comparisons with the Shoah.[109] Likewise, many Jews of the anti-Zionist Left of this generation had developed their political consciousness through an experience of decolonization and a collective memory of World War II that, as we saw in chapter 5, differed markedly from that of their North African coreligionists. Geismar was stopped by French police numerous times during the Algerian War due to his dark skin, followed by apologies like, "Pardon us, we thought you were Algerian." He called this racism "intolerable" and reminiscent of that faced by "Jews who were arrested fifteen years before." For the eighteen-year-old Geismar, the experience proved formative.[110]

Many young Muslims in the pro-Palestinian movement in France favored the presence of Jews in their ranks. Saïd Bouziri, a twenty-year-old student from Tunisia who had come to France the year before the Six Day War and would become a major figure in the working-class struggles of Muslims in the 1970s, was moved by the stunning defeat of the Arabs to take up the Palestinian cause. From a traditionally observant family but himself an atheist, Bouziri nonetheless had a very strong sense of Muslim cultural identity. At the time of the war, he began to take part in discussions about the history of the Palestinians and the Middle East conflict with his fellow university students in Lyon; before long, Bouziri and other Muslim students reached out to young Jews on the Left. Years later, Bouziri explained that because their vision was one of coexistence, "It was very important for us to be in contact with Jews in France." "We had," he says, "the will to familiarize ourselves with the Palestinian question but also to not completely demonize the Jews. . . . We [wanted] anti-Zionism not to equal antisemitism."[111]

During the same period that Fatah was spreading into France, the ADAE, not to be outdone, sought to create a network of support for the Palestinian nationalist cause in Europe. The leading figure in this effort was M'hammed Yazid, longtime international spokesman for the FLN. Yazid had played a key role in the nationalists' successful lobbying at the United Nations during the French-Algerian War; now he was head of the Algerian Committee of Afro-Asiatic Solidarity. By the autumn of 1969

Yazid was making regular trips to France to meet with Algerian diplomats and activists on behalf of the Palestinian cause. Subsequently the ADAE would team with Fatah in a variety of efforts including fundraising and distributing literature.[112]

Mayer, Hamchari, Yazid, and others found their loudest echo in a growing pro-Palestinian movement of Muslim university students. Even before the 1967 war student militants played a leading role in advocating for the Palestinians in France and thereby fueling tensions with Jews. One year prior to the war's outbreak the Association des étudiants musulmans nord-africains en France (AEMNA) and the Union générale des étudiants palestiniens (UGEP) had drawn a crowd of 100 to the first rally for the Palestinian cause that had occurred in France since the establishment of the state of Israel.[113] Within the larger student and pro-Palestinian activism of 1968, these efforts gained momentum. Among France's 6,500 North African Muslim students, for instance, several groups organized in the wake of the Belleville riots around opposition to Zionism and imperialism and support for Palestine.[114] Continuing in the same vein, by late 1969, the AEMNA distributed bulletins that denounced France and the sitting governments in the Maghreb and described Israel as the "veritable Nazi regime."[115] Even the Union des étudiants marocains (UNEM), previously hesitant on the issue of Palestine, now debated how best to oppose the regime in Morocco and support the Arab cause in the Middle East.[116]

Just as few Jews from France elected to show the ultimate commitment to Zionism through emigration to Israel, Muslim support for the Palestinian cause in France, while seemingly widespread at the level of sentiment, rarely took more tangible forms. The ADAE, for instance, continued to solicit donations of money, clothing, medicine, and blood from Muslims in France, but with little evident impact.[117] In 1969, working in tandem with Yazid and Dr. Adel Aher, head of the Arab League's Paris office, the ADAE also stepped up its efforts to convince Muslims to fight for the Arab armies. The recruiters' successive target audiences—North African laborers, the unemployed, and now even former Algerian harkis—remained fairly reticent.[118] On the one hand, this suggested Algerian Muslims in France were most ready to engage politically with causes directly linked to their native or host country, not those in the Middle East. On the other hand, many did not equate solidarity with the Palestinian cause with a willingness to give of their possessions or their being on its behalf. Moreover, in a wider environment of intense police surveillance where too much activism could put their legal standing in France at risk, fears of becoming too visible politically likely also limited outward displays of pro-Palestinian sentiment.

Yet together, Fatah, the early Palestine committees, and the ADAE were already finding increasing success in framing Jewish-Muslim relations in France as an extension of the Zionist-Arab struggle on the Mediterranean's southern shore. In December 1968, immediately following a shooting that left two dead and three wounded inside a North African café in the Paris suburb of Aubervilliers, the leadership of the ADAE blamed the incident on "Jews." Soon after, the group contended that further attacks were the work of a Zionist organization run by Jewish extremists in France. In September 1969 some armed attacks in Muslim-owned cafés, including one in Belleville, left several wounded. In this and subsequent cases the ADAE expressed certainty that the perpetrators were racists, former OAS members, and those working on behalf of Zionists.[119] At the popular level many Algerian Muslims living in Paris accepted such allegations as fact.[120] Numerous Muslims long criticized Si Hamza Boubakeur, who remained rector of the Grand Mosque of Paris, for his participation in the Fraternité d'Abraham dialogue group with Christians and Jews and his larger positive relationships with representatives of the French Jewish community.[121] At times, despite the organization's repeated insistence to the contrary, ADAE distinctions between Jews and Zionists became invisible. In January 1970, when L'Algérien en Europe alleged that Zionists held influence throughout the French press, it did so simply by listing Jews in high-level positions with various publications, without regard for their politics.[122]

In such a climate, even those with greater optimism about Jewish-Muslim relations seemed to accept that Middle Eastern encroachment had now become an ever-present danger. Jacques Lazarus responded to the 1968 Belleville riots with a letter to a Muslim leader insisting that the Middle East conflict should remain afar and not hinder coexistence in France.[123] In 1971, a Jewish doctor in Belleville exclaimed that "relations with the Arab milieu are excellent when they are not poisoned by the Israeli problem."[124] Rosette Senoussi, an Algerian Jew who had lived for years in Dar-Refayil—the house in Sétif shared by Jewish and Muslim families until the last stages of the French-Algerian War—maintained close relations with certain Muslims in Marseille. Yet she made a careful distinction between "different kinds of Arabs." "When we say 'the Arabs,'" she explained, "I feel hatred, but those are Middle Eastern Arabs. I am not talking about the Arabs who live here [in France]. . . . They work, they

earn their living, they have children and families like us, *à la française*. . . .
But the problem in Israel is still not solved. So since I've known the
Israeli problem, I am anti-Arab, but not against the Arabs of France."[125]
For Senoussi and many others, the specific geographical spaces and political contexts in which Jews and Muslims encountered each other determined the possible parameters of their relations. Yet the Middle East
conflict was becoming present in all manner of interactions.

Even daily encounters sometimes gave way to violent altercations, like
the fight between Jewish and Muslim customers that broke out inside a
café on the rue Faubourg de Temple in Paris's 11th arrondissement in
January 1969.[126] Among youth and students, small groups of both
Muslim and Jewish activists occasionally instigated violent incidents quite
deliberately. The militant Zionist youth movement Betar, for instance,
had become increasingly visible in France since 1967 and showed a
willingness to resort to physical attacks. The Front des étudiants juifs
(FEJ), a Far Right breakaway from the UEJF formed after the 1968 Belleville riots in protest of the latter's moderation, was also quite aggressive,
aiming to put Jewish students on guard against growing antisemitism,
particularly from Arab students. By early 1970 both groups had taken
part in protests that resulted in physical clashes with Muslim students at
the newly opened branch of the Sorbonne in the banlieue of Censier.[127]
Such occurrences reflected two distinct but interrelated developments:
first, ethnoreligious affiliations and labels were shaping the active choices
of a growing number Jews and Muslims in daily life, sometimes in the
heat of the moment; and second, Jewish-Muslim conflict linked to the
Middle East was becoming the most pervasive narrative frame for explaining any case of tension between individuals of Jewish and Muslim
background.

In June 1970 a second set of Jewish-Muslim riots in Belleville crystallized many developments of the preceding three years. On the evening of
June 15, 1970, between the rue Ramponneau and the rue des Couronnes
and in the neighboring streets of the 11th arrondissement, groups of Jews
and Muslims came to blows. Within a few hours of the initial incident,
the antagonists had smashed an estimated twenty-eight mostly Jewish
storefronts with iron bars, thrown bottles at one another, injured numerous persons, and set one car on fire. M. Belaiche, a sixty-year-old
Algerian Jew, died of a heart attack. Order returned only around 1:00

a.m. As had occurred two years prior, Jews and Muslims disputed the origins of the riots. Many Jews claimed that Muslims planned them to coincide with the anniversary of the Six Day War; some Muslims blamed a disputed game of cards; others cited an attack on a Muslim by Jews. Journalists also noted how the combination of an ongoing transportation strike and extremely hot temperatures had kept large numbers of Jews and Muslims indoors and on edge all day. Regardless of the origins of the incidents, organized elements within each community quickly took hold of them, exchanging chants of, "Vive Israël," and "Vive la Palestine" or "Fatah will win" and "Israel will win." Within several days of the riots, police charged seven Muslims; a judge later sentenced them to brief prison terms and fines.[128]

Jewish groups' statements on the 1970 riots took a variety of approaches. The CRIF condemned the violence and called on leaders of each community and the authorities to calm emotions and restore order. Yet its statement also noted that Jews had suffered the overwhelming majority of damages and that most of the antagonists had been Muslims carrying illegal weapons.[129] The FEJ took a far more aggressive tack by issuing a tract, "Stop the Arab Pogromists," that spoke of the group's readiness to defend "the Jewish community of France." It asserted that "this attack coincided with the coming to Paris of Fatah's henchmen who recruit mercenaries against Israel and against the Jews of France." Going further, the FEJ blamed the events on "the antisemitic coalition directed by the 'Palestinian progressives' and their left-wing and Nazi allies."[130] From the opposite end of the political spectrum, the next day, the Mouvement contre le racisme, l'antisémitisme et pour la paix (MRAP), affiliated with the PCF and in which many Jewish leftists had sought to facilitate dialogue with Muslims, issued its own statement that insisted, "We must prevent an exterior conflict from setting two communities against each other."[131]

Regardless of their diffuse sources, these responses developed themes that overlapped in important ways. The MRAP accepted the narrative of the Middle East conflict as the source of Jewish-Muslim violence in Belleville. So too did the FEJ, but it blamed Muslims and their allies exclusively, contrasting a violent image of Palestinian nationalists with an integrated one of a religious community in the conventional mode of laïcité. The CRIF also demonized the Muslim participants, albeit in a different way, using stern words that echoed wider stereotypes about

North African criminality. The FEJ and the CRIF implicitly positioned Jews firmly within the republican nation while questioning the place of Muslims. This framework responded to the larger atmosphere of the moment, wherein North Africans had become increasingly racialized as "Arab" and un-French and Jews sought to harmonize their more public ethnoreligious politics with their ongoing attachment to the republic.

Public reactions from Muslim organizations were more muted. The ADAE placed the blame on "Jewish residents" and "Zionist provocateurs," blurring once more any distinction between the two groups.[132] The AEMNA and several other Muslim student groups planned a meeting to follow up the incidents, clearly seeing them as a potential political problem for their pro-Palestinian, anti-Zionist campaigns. In a pamphlet, these groups exclaimed: "The Arab student organizations consider the recent events in Belleville as only working to serve the interests of Zionist propaganda and anti-Arab and antisemitic racism."[133] Reflecting the radical politics of the emerging international leftist immigrant labor movements, the Maoist pro-Palestinian newsletter *Lutte palestinienne* called the riots a "fascist escalation," blaming Betar militants. It described the incidents as part of a provocation meant to hide "the real problem," that of the merciless exploitation of immigrant workers, mostly Arabs, and their rising political consciousness. The newsletter called on all workers, foreign and French, to unite against their common enemies of racism, capitalism, and imperialism.[134] In this way, even as these Muslim organizations connected the riots to the Middle East conflict, they spoke in universalist terms that echoed both internationalist and, to an extent, republican themes. Moreover, they connected directly the plight of workers living in France to the suffering of Palestinians across the Mediterranean, previewing a central theme of organized politics among France's Muslim workers in the years ahead.

Events like the riots in Belleville became important not simply because of their meaning for Jews and Muslims, but in the triangular context of each group's relationship to France. These riots at once strengthened Jewish and Muslim consciousness around certain group oppositions and, in a dialectical manner, hardened narratives of Jewish and Muslim difference among many French nationalists, media outlets, and local authorities. If, however, they often "darkened" racially both Jews and

Muslims, they rarely did so equally. Muslims were increasingly seen more than Jews as France's defining Other, counterposed to exclusionary definitions of Frenchness. According to one left-wing account of the 1968 riots, French police intervened quickly with overwhelming force and in a way that fomented tensions: police warned Jews that "Arabs" were about to attack their shops, encouraged Jews to wear armbands to distinguish themselves from their Muslim neighbors, and proceeded to an "immense roundup" of the Muslim workers in the area.[135] L'Aurore, a conservative daily that had long taken up the perspective of the pieds-noirs (including racialized images of Algerians), used the 1968 incidents to suggest that Jews, but even more so "Arabs," could not resist bloody confrontation.[136] On its June 4 cover, beneath the words "Arabs and Is-raélites Have Continued to Do Battle," it featured an enormous photograph in which mostly dark-skinned individuals generally appeared to hurl projectiles, scheme, or, most clearly in the lower-right corner, flee in panic. The few persons present with evidently pale faces walked calmly and sought to avoid the chaos (Figure 6.3).

Other elements focused particular attention on an image of Muslims as violent Arab men. Further down, the story's subheads included a single item in bold: "20 Muslims Arrested." Inside, under a large headline that read, "'The Arabs Wanted to Avenge the Victory of Israel over Egypt,'" the newspaper printed a map that depicted Belleville as a site of North African violence on every corner (Figure 6.4). Alongside markers for sites of altercation, the artist included a church, perhaps suggesting that the French Catholic nation was suddenly threatened by the growing North African Jewish, but especially Muslim, presence.[137] While we should be careful not to overread such representations, given L'Aurore's tendencies and the context of this period of social upheaval, these headlines and illustrations appear to fit a larger contemporary pattern of exclusion. The Paris Prefecture of Police reported: "During this troubled period, it was possible to measure the weariness, not to say xenophobia of the 'petits Français' [lower middle or working-class French] living in the quarters with a strong density of Muslims or israélites from North Africa."[138]

Two years later, L'Aurore's headline described the recurrence of violence as "racial fights in Belleville." Other newspapers took different yet complementary tacks. The center-right France-Soir's story on the June 1970 riots described Belleville as a "little Parisian Medina." Such words connected the area to long-standing, largely mythical European images of the immutable Islamic city, divided into the medina, the popular quarter

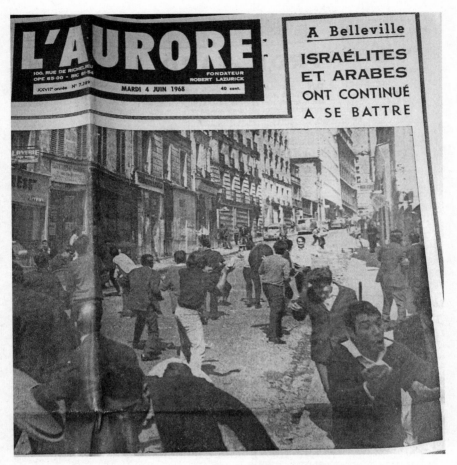

Figure 6.3. The cover of *L'Aurore,* June 4, 1968. (Courtesy of Le Figaro.)

inhabited by mostly Muslim lower classes; the kasbah, where the Muslim upper classes (and later Europeans) lived; and the mellah or hara, similar in this understanding to the European Jewish ghetto.[139] By the early 1970s, the specter of the "medina" was in wider circulation as a synonym for a rundown (Muslim) urban neighborhood.[140] By treating this quarter of Jewish-Muslim coexistence with this term, *France-Soir*'s report suggested an equation between the otherness of the two groups. Like the images of two years prior in *L'Aurore,* the story also represented Belleville not as transitional space, as it was for many Jewish immigrants in particular who spent a few years there before relocating to more integrated

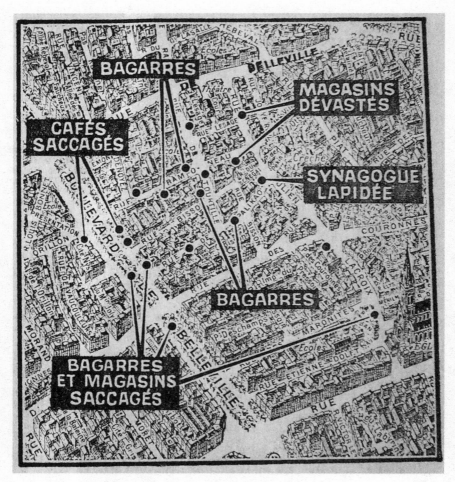

Figure 6.4. *L'Aurore*'s map of the 1968 Belleville riots. (Courtesy of Le Figaro.)

areas of Paris, or as a neighborhood inhabited by immigrants with multiple identities, as many of the quarter's residents sought to define it, but rather as a space of Otherness, foreign to France and its values.

Such stigmatization of Belleville as a North African space did not occur in isolation. First, it took place in the midst of a wave of construction in the Paris region that included 300,000 low-income housing units that were meant to be temporary but quickly became long-term sites of economic and racial exclusion for countless Muslims from North Africa.[141] Second, this type of rhetoric had wider echoes, not least of all among the residents of Belleville themselves: when sociologist Claude Tapia interviewed almost 200 school-aged Jewish children in Belleville in 1970 the majority described their neighborhood in negative terms, with the sentiment of "what upsets me most is what others think of the quarter. They say to us [even other Jewish kids] that [it] is a poor, dirty, crowded quarter."[142] Thus racial rhetoric around the riots could only underscore a wider sense of physical isolation.

The left-wing *Nouvel observateur* reinforced this message in its coverage, calling Belleville "at once the medina and the ghetto of Paris." The same author spoke of an "Arab colony" and emphasized legal separation: "Rare are those [Arabs] who demand French citizenship. It is the Ambassador of Algeria to France who represents authority for them." By contrast, he claimed, "50% of the Jews have become French or await with impatience the naturalization that will make them full citizens."[143] In this manner, while separating both Jews and Muslims in Belleville from the French body politic, many representations did so on relative terms. Despite the parallel challenges Jews and Muslims faced in the racialized environment of the years following decolonization, Jews far more often than Muslims found themselves inside the boundaries of accepted belonging.

Belleville's otherness, and particularly that of its Muslims, also appeared in police and municipal officials' assessments of the riots. A January 1970 Paris police report cited the violence as the first example of interethnic altercations in Paris since 1968, claiming "the events of the Middle East have contributed to oppose Muslims and israélites and we have thus witnessed dangers and even confrontations."[144] In addition to implying that transnational allegiances could explain every Jewish or Muslim move, the account spoke separately of the "European population," thereby placing Jews and Muslims (as well as black Africans) in ethnic categories outside of European Frenchness. Ever at war, Jews and Muslims threatened republican order by bringing their violence to the French capital.

Broader attention to ethnic difference characterized official reports on both Jews and Muslims during this period. In the mid- to late 1960s, numerous ministerial memos on numbers of immigrants repeatedly counted Algerians and sometimes all North Africans separately from other foreigners in France. These reports often termed their subject the "Algerian problem."[145] In the same period, Paris police compiled an extensive contemporary dossier on the "Jewish community in the Paris region." Even as this wording treated Jews as part of a confessional group with a natural place inside the French nation, the report itself contained 320 "individual notices" on various Jewish activists, a few of whom were at least as prominent outside the Jewish community as they were within it.[146] Such an endeavor, difficult to imagine for Protestants or Catholics or those of Italian or Spanish origin, implied that the state attached special significance to a public figure's Jewishness, and especially to his or her affiliation with any part of the Jewish community. Thus reactions to Belleville formed part of a larger picture. French journalists, police, politicians, and administrators implied that the ongoing possibilities of republican integration coexisted uneasily with contemporary efforts to mark certain people by ethnicity, particularly Muslims and Jews.

Three years after the second Belleville riots, in late June 1973, a ten-minute news program about the neighborhood aired on French television.[147] To the rhythms, instruments, harmonies, and lyrics of Arabic music, the opening shots rotate between residents of the neighborhood and scenes of the Mediterranean Sea crashing against the shore, with an Arab woman singing and swaying on the beach. As the camera moves out from her, viewers realize this footage comes from a television program being watched in a restaurant of the quarter. At the start, the narrator intones, "Rue de Belleville still serves as a place of refuge and welcome. Jews who took refuge from North Africa, Muslim laborers— they live together without, all the same, mixing." For the last word, the narrator uses the French term *se confondre,* also meaning "to become confused." Such a phrase revealed the narrator's binary understanding of Jews and Muslims even in shared spaces. These initial sites, sounds, and words conveyed a message that Jews and Muslims from North Africa gave the quarter a rather exotic, foreign aesthetic but at the same time, the two groups neither regularly interacted nor became fused in the eyes of the wider population.

Subsequently the journalist Claude-Jean Philippe proceeds to interview several individuals: two native Frenchmen, two Muslim electricians from Algeria, and a Monsieur Beriti, an active member of the Jewish community, asking them about life in Belleville. The two *français de souche* (inhabitants long native to France) communicate profound discomfort at France's postcolonial condition. Asked directly, the first says that indeed the presence of Jews, Arabs, and Africans has disrupted the neighborhood, as he no longer hears French spoken all the time and the Jewish and Muslim immigrants act as if, in his words, "they think they [are occupiers] in a conquered country." The second interviewee gestures with scorn toward the boulevard de Belleville as a place where there are "israélites . . . Arabs . . . Muslims," explaining that "it's not good" and "completely changing," and he does not go there.

From there, the Muslims and Jews interviewed offer counternarratives that begin to break the frame of Belleville as a space of foreign invasion and interethnic violence, utterly apart. The two Muslim workers say that their life in the neighborhood is all right, though they acknowledge instances of racism. Monsieur Beriti from the Jewish community contends that the quarter does not deserve the bad reputation it has. He highlights the communal, economic, and small gastronomic and cultural elements that fulfill the needs of many Jews from Tunisia when they arrive here, noting that many move on soon to other neighborhoods. Contrary to certain assertions, he says that he and many other Jews in Belleville enter Muslim cafés and vice versa, and if they do not, it is an issue of habit, not discrimination; he notes that Jews and Muslims would "enjoy an apéritif together in Tunisia," and asks why they should not do so in France. Speaking specifically of the riots of 1968, Beriti links them to the larger events and atmosphere of May; one of the Algerian workers says he does not recall the origins but notes that he has many good friends who are Jewish. In its final seconds, seeking a hopeful ending, the camera returns to an interview with one of the native Frenchmen who, when asked if people will find a way to coexist, says, "Yes why not?" with a smile, but then notes that this is "not the old Belleville."

This television broadcast revealed several key elements of Jewish-Muslim relations in France by the early 1970s. Decolonization had brought substantial numbers of Jews and Muslims together on French soil. This led to the proliferation of shared spaces of Mediterranean culture—like those of Arabic music—often rooted in common experiences in North Africa. Yet such proximity also produced tensions, often around conflicting transnational allegiances. This was particularly the case in a broader French environment where changing demography and loss of empire helped to fuel widespread discrimination, to some extent against Jews but particularly against Muslims arriving from North Africa. Unspoken altogether in this telecast but implicitly present at moments was the Middle East conflict and the afterlives on French soil—real and perceived—of the 1967 Six Day War. In part because of other issues, the Israeli-Palestinian conflict had become more present in France than prior to the 1967 war, and played a new role in the public lives of growing numbers of Jews and Muslims. The question, hinted at in this television program, was if such diverse and often opposing interethnic allegiances led inevitably to greater conflict. For the rest of the twentieth century, France and its Jews and Muslims would wrestle repeatedly with that conundrum.

7

JEWS AS JEWS AND MUSLIMS AS MUSLIMS

"The first thing I have to tell you is that we lived on the seventh-floor walk-up, so you can take my word for it that Madame Rosa, with all the pounds she had to lug around with her, had more than her share of daily life with all its sorrows and cares. She said so too, whenever she wasn't complaining about something else, because to make matters worse she was Jewish."[1] Thus begins the Muslim narrator Momo (short for Mohamed) at the start of Romain Gary's 1975 prize-winning novel, *La vie devant soi (The Life before Us)*. The novel, which sold 1.2 million copies and was soon adapted into a successful film starring Simone Signoret, takes place in Belleville and is peopled by a varied and eccentric cast of characters reflective of the neighborhood's diversity: Eastern European Jews, Algerians, Senegalese, and native French; doctors, shopkeepers, dying old wise men, prostitutes, pimps, transvestites, and drug dealers all coexist, often amicably.[2] The story centers on the close relationship between Madame Rosa, a Polish-born Jewish Holocaust survivor in ill health, and her ten-year old Muslim tenant, Momo, the abandoned son of a prostitute. Madame Rosa is forever haunted by her experience in the Holocaust, Momo constantly searching for his father and his identity. Throughout the novel, amid the diversity of Belleville, the young narrator's perceptions highlight the tension between people's universal commonalities and strict classifications according to ethnicity, religion, or class. When Momo's father shows up to take him from Madame Rosa, she convinces the man that Momo and his fellow tenant, Moses, a Jewish boy, were accidentally swapped at an early age. She explains: "It's only an identical mistake. Identity can make mistakes, you know, it's not foolproof. A three-year-old child has very little identity, you know, even when circumcised. I got the circumcisions mixed up and brought up your

279

little Mohammed as a good little Jew, you needn't worry." Enraged, Momo's father rails, "I want my son back . . . in good Arab condition and not in bad Jewish condition." Madame Rosa replies: "Arab and Jew are all the same to us here."[3] In this dramatic scene, the author at once acknowledges the rigid power of ethnic and religious differences and then collapses all distinctions between Jews and Muslims, poking fun at the very tribalistic ethnic determinism often articulated by Momo himself.

On many levels, the book constantly reconfigures categories of Jew and Muslim. Gary, born to a Russian Jewish mother in Poland, often claimed that his father, never known with certainty, had been of Tatar-Mongol (Muslim) descent.[4] The book was published under the pseudonym Émile Ajar, an elaborate invention of Gary in the early 1970s: Ajar was allegedly a thirty-four-year-old Algerian Muslim medical student in Paris who had fled to Brazil after carrying out a failed abortion operation that killed his young French patient. Many critics at the time, unaware of the true author, described the work as an "authentically Arab" novel.[5] Linguistically, Madame Rosa, having spent time in North Africa, speaks "Arabic as well as you or me"; frequently she and Momo also speak Yiddish together.[6] Even the divisions of the Middle East conflict become fluid. Momo saves Madame Rosa from endless hospitalizations by taking her to die in peace in her "Jewish hiding place" in the basement, after telling everyone that he has arranged for her to go to Israel. Stunned at the latter possibility, her Jewish friend Dr. Katz tells Momo, "It's the first time an Arab has ever sent a Jew to Israel."[7] With Madame Rosa dead, Momo finds his way to a bourgeois French family that warmly accepts him, despite his impressions earlier in the novel that its children and he "just weren't from the same block."[8]

The Life before Us captures many of the possibilities, tensions, and complexities of French republicanism and Jewish-Muslim relations at a particular historical moment, one shaped by decolonization, the growing impact of the Israeli-Palestinian conflict, and the efforts of many Jews, Muslims, and other ethnic and religious minorities to articulate a public right to difference. Despite its persistent attention to group-based identity, suffering, and memory, the book appears optimistic ultimately that France can negotiate the challenge of republican universalism and public difference that pressed itself anew in the 1970s, and therein preserve peaceful coexistence between its Jews and Muslims. In short, the novel suggests that even widely recognized ethnoreligious difference need not define one's every loyalty or relationship.

It is tempting to see Romain Gary's novel as simply the figment of a fertile literary imagination, a lonely call for humanity at a time of ethnic strife or a nostalgic snapshot of more halcyon days.[9] Likewise, when recounting the history of Jewish-Muslim relations in France, one can all too easily dismiss the impact of the 1970s. As the story goes, on the heels of hardening boundaries, growing anti-Arab sentiment, and public Israeli activism after the 1967 war, the early part of the decade witnessed further movement in the direction of Jewish-Muslim tension; the remarkable escalation of racial violence against North African Muslims and the growing profile of the Palestinian question in France reinforced such an outlook. According to this account, the elements for Jewish-Muslim polarization were in place by the early to mid-1970s. These elements did little to shift until a brief moment of optimism in the context of the election of François Mitterrand and the rise of pluriculturalism and antiracist activism in the 1980s.[10]

Such a perspective omits critical pieces of the story. In fact, just as the enormous popular and critical success of *The Life before Us* suggests a deeper resonance with contemporaneous developments in France, a closer examination of the 1970s illuminates it as an era both important and paradoxical. The period was characterized by competing currents within greater Jewish and Muslim claims on French public space that constituted a kind of multiculturalism *avant la lettre:* in crucial respects, the decade previewed and even catalyzed the events of the 1980s. To be sure, the public difference of—and differences between—Jews and Muslims became more pronounced. But as the tensions of Romain Gary's novel exemplify, the 1970s oscillated between signs of ethnoreligious conflict and possibilities for Muslim-Jewish coexistence based on mutually respected differences. The 1970s also witnessed, in this connection, the reemergence of immigration as a national political issue and the quiet mutation of the Far Right. Both developments previewed more dramatic struggles a decade later. Within this context, the multiculturalism of the Mitterrand years may be understood as a critical testing ground for ideas that had gathered momentum over an extended period. The 1980s saw the boundaries of acceptable public difference first expand and then contract, shifting yet again the respective positions of Jews and Muslims vis-à-vis each other and the French nation-state.

The possibilities and tensions of Jewish and Muslim life in late-twentieth-century France are particularly apparent in three overlapping areas: the ongoing presence of the Israeli-Palestinian conflict for Jewish-Muslim public identities, the increasingly entangled public memories of the Holocaust and colonialism, and the rise of new forms of mass politics through which Jews and Muslims made claims at once particularistic and universalistic on the French state. These factors continued to affect Paris, Marseille, and Strasbourg in distinctive, locally determined ways. Such an understanding casts the violent Jewish-Muslim conflict of the early twenty-first century in a new light as merely one of many possible paths along which recent history moved, in some respects more of a departure from the preceding decades than a linear progression.

Postcolonial Muslim Politics

The 1970s tested the possibilities of the postcolonial republic as a place where markers of difference were, on the whole, less ambiguous and often more stigmatized than during the colonial era and where larger numbers of Jews and Muslims, as well as other postcolonial and Mediterranean immigrants, had come to reside in France. By the mid-1970s, visible attachments to Muslim and Jewish identities in public, increasingly tied to the Israeli and Palestinian causes, respectively, proliferated. During the same period, Holocaust memory, already politicized in new ways following the Six Day War, became a topic, historical reference point, and metaphor in public conversation.

In the early 1970s a series of developments transformed the situation of Muslim migrant laborers in France. A number of factors—including Algeria's increasing economic independence from France (highlighted by its nationalization of French gas and oil corporations), France's economic slowdown, growing anti-Muslim discrimination, and French fears about Muslim radical politics—led to a halt in Muslim migration. In 1972, with the so-called Marcellin-Fontanet decrees, France suddenly required workers to obtain a job contract and an employer-approved housing certificate before they were eligible to receive the coveted *carte de séjour* (residency card). This meant that North African Muslim workers could no longer regularize their status after arrival; a new category, that of the "illegal immigrant," was born. Meanwhile, a series of deadly anti-Muslim incidents occurred in the early 1970s. These culminated in August 1973: following the murder in Marseille of French bus driver Désiré-Emile Gerlache by Salah Bougrine, a mentally disturbed Algerian man, a wave of revenge attacks erupted against North Africans, killing ten people within a week. This provided the impetus for the Algerian government to ban all immigration in September 1973; in July 1974, in the face of economic recession, France instituted its own ban. Fearful about their ability to return if they left, Muslim workers tended to remain in France and urged their family members to join them. Many laborers' spouses and children came as tourists and stayed, their presence being difficult to track or prevent. In 1975 France legalized this changing reality by exempting family reunion immigrants from its ban on immigration. Muslim demography in France was undergoing dramatic change.[11]

France's economic downturn began to bring the issue of immigration to the forefront of national debate for the first time in forty years. At the same moment a new political force emerged on the extreme Right, the Front national (FN) party, founded in 1972. Though the FN would not gain traction with French voters until the 1980s, its rhetoric revealed the shifting politics of nationalism and difference with regard to Jews and Muslims. The patterns of racialization seen in some of the press coverage of the Belleville riots of 1968 and 1970 now found more pronounced expression on the Far Right. The FN's founder was Jean-Marie Le Pen, a former National Assembly member and activist on behalf of Algérie française during the French-Algerian War. The party sought to cultivate a more mainstream image than its predecessors, but Le Pen nonetheless took increasingly harsh anti-immigrant positions. As early as a September 1973 press conference, Le Pen referred to Algerian immigrant laborers as "some fifty divisions of infantry," a fifth column waiting to be mobilized. By the 1978 FN party congress, Le Pen spoke about "the defense of the West," and claimed immigration constituted a danger for "the safety and health of our compatriots . . . even the existence of our people."[12] This outlook resumed a shift that had begun during the Algerian War and continued in the 1960s, wherein the Far Right concentrated more on protecting Western civilization against "Arabs" or "North Africans," and less on antisemitism. This was the case in spite of enduring prejudice against Jews on the part of many FN party activists and rank and file, including a number of former collaborators and Vichy sympathizers. Muslims, simply put, were now far more racialized in ultranationalist rhetoric than Jews.[13]

During the same period, politics among France's Muslims was entering a new era. The years following the 1967 war and May '68 witnessed the founding of the Palestine Committees and then the Mouvement des travailleurs arabes (Movement of Arab Laborers, MTA), the first major movements to focus principally on both Muslim workers' rights in France and the Palestinian question abroad. Like earlier generations of Muslim activists, those of the 1970s combined the terms of contemporary French politics with their own distinctive positioning and cultural currents. In contrast to many of their forebears, they gave less attention to Islamic symbols, identifications, or practices and forged a largely areligious politics around shared Arabness and class consciousness. They used language that emphasized their legal rights and economic power as laborers, linking these to larger notions of French citizenship and to various strands of class politics and Marxist internationalism on the French Left. At the same time, activists placed such issues in the terms of pan-Arab solidarity, the model of the Palestinian *fedai* (freedom fighter), and the particular vulnerabilities of Muslim migrant workers in France. These workers repeatedly came up against deeply rooted postcolonial racism and severe legal restrictions on their status and activity; nonetheless, they combined the above elements to forge a compelling set of claims that pushed the state toward greater accommodation, in the process opening unanticipated possibilities within the French polity.

North African Muslims did not do this alone. Critical to the atmosphere of the period and the successes of various campaigns was the enduring alliance that had emerged in May '68 between many North African and other immigrant workers, generally also from former French colonial possessions or other parts of the Mediterranean. Frequently such groups worked to oppose the oppressive policies of their native country's government. Political developments in Mediterranean Europe, moreover, especially Portugal—with its Carnation Revolution of April 1974 and large number of immigrant workers in France—both drew influences from the spirit of France's so-called '68 years and helped to catalyze greater immigrant activism in France.[14] Many immigrant coalitions sought to build a more equal France and transcend ethnic differences, previewing the terms of the so-called pluriculturalism that became critical to the antiracist campaigns of the 1980s.[15]

The transnational, multicultural setting of these wider immigrant politics proved ripe for the emergence of France's home-grown pro-Palestinian movement, in which radical leftists teamed with North

African Muslim workers and students. The spring of 1969 witnessed the publication of the first pro-Palestinian newsletter in France, *Lutte palestinienne,* produced by a group of Maoist Muslim students, and following the Marxist-Leninist line of the Democratic Popular Front for the Liberation of Palestine (DPFLP), a recent splinter group from Georges Habache's Popular Front for the Liberation of Palestine (PFLP).[16] *Lutte palestinienne* focused on not only the Palestinian struggle or anticolonial freedom fighters but also the everyday concerns of North African laborers. The newsletter soon published articles in both French and Arabic and covered topics like the squalid conditions and regular expulsions in the housing projects where many of these workers lived.[17] It also promoted the ideas and activities of the recently formed Palestine committees. The committees, active in a number of French cities and other parts of Europe by early 1969, were established by a combination of North African and Levantine workers and students, Fatah representatives in France, and Maoists like those of the Gauche prolétarienne, led by among others the Jewish leftists Alain Geismar and Benny Lévy.[18]

The events of Black September in autumn 1970—when an uprising by the Palestinian militants against King Hussein of Jordan led to the murder of thousands of Palestinians, the leveling of refugee camps, and the eventual expulsion of the PLO from Jordan—spurred a new level of intensity in the pro-Palestinian movement. Shortly after these events, groups calling themselves Committees for the Support of the Palestinian Revolution (CSRP) began to form throughout France. These new Palestine Committees followed much of the platform of those formed in February the previous year. Here the committees had called popular resistance the sole means for the Palestinian people to reclaim their historic rights; expressed support for the goal of the Palestine liberation movement to destroy the State of Israel; and insisted that the committees "battle[d] against Zionism and anti-Jewish racism," both of which were "at the origin of the creation of the State of Israel." Finally, the committees termed the Palestinian cause an "integral part of the world Revolution" and said the movement could help to create "an anti-imperialist consciousness in Europe and in France."[19]

The new Palestine Committees made more significant inroads than their predecessors among North African workers. Seeking to politicize urban space in a manner reminiscent of the Algerian nationalists, these movements endeavored to penetrate neighborhoods, high schools, and dormitories where high concentrations of North Africans resided.[20] In Nanterre in November 1970, six hundred North African workers and one hundred French and other immigrant workers gathered for a Palestine Committee meeting. In another city, activists managed to raise 2,000 francs, which, however modest, represented a sizable body of contributions given the salaries of most Muslim workers. Despite brutal police repression in the form of constant surveillance, frequent arrests, and even deportations, the Palestine Committees continued their work unabated in the months to come.[21]

The committees created a powerful link in the minds of many workers between the claims of Palestinian Arabs to their homeland and those of North African workers to equal rights in France.[22] The movement's newsletter *Fedai: Newsletter for the Support of the Palestinian Revolution,* widely distributed to workers inside shops and at factory exits, called for the mobilization of North African, other immigrant, and French workers together on behalf of the Palestinian cause and against anti-Arab and anti-immigrant discrimination in France. As suggested by the journal's name and its masthead, featuring a pair of Kalishnikov rifles, the organ valorized the Palestinian *fedai,* or freedom fighter, as a model for armed resistance (Figure 7.1).[23] The newsletter paired frequent images and stories of the fedayeen with calls for working class solidarity in France. The dissemination of ideas, language, and images in a manner that resonated locally gave the Middle East conflict a greater presence in Muslim political action and consciousness in France. In the fedayeen, Muslim working-class activists found at once a model of resistance and a source of pride. In the words of MTA activist Hamza Bouziri: "When united and organized to support Palestine, the Arab workers constitute a force that racists cannot break. In the [Palestine Committees], we have regained our dignity and the right to speak out that had been taken away from us. We stopped being 'wogs,' slaves, we became fighters, fedayeen."[24]

Yet what ultimately differentiated the Palestine committees from most Muslim organizations in France at this time was their substantial focus on the specific needs of North African migrant laborers rather than on political struggles within their home countries. The committees benefited from a growing disenchantment on the part of many with the repressive policies of the governments on the other side of the Mediterranean, the declining allure of return, and a correspondent lack of interest in movements like the Amicales and opposition groups that sought to enlist Muslims in France for their own political purposes in North Africa. Constructing an entire militant life of conversations, debates, and meals cen-

Figure 7.1. Cover cartoon from *Fedai* issue of April 8, 1971: "All united in support of the Palestinian Revolution Until Victory!" Note the combination of Palestinian guerilla and immigrant worker imagery. (Collection Bibliothèque de documentation contemporaine.)

tered around the Muslim student associations, especially the Association des étudiants musulmans nord-africains (AEMNA) on the boulevard Saint-Michel, the committees became incubators for a new generation of Muslim political activists.[25]

By 1972, the Palestine Committees' focus had begun to shift decisively away from Palestine as other issues took greater priority. In protest against the dilapidated state of public housing, leading sometimes to tragic incidents like a deadly fire in Aubervilliers in 1970, a movement had arisen for better lodging for immigrant laborers. Increasingly restricted access to residency cards and growing threats of expulsion produced an organized effort to regularize the legal status of workers made vulnerable by a lack of proper documentation. More than anything else, the racially motivated murder of Djellali Ben Ali, a fifteen-year-old Algerian boy, in October 1971 in the indigent Parisian immigrant neighborhood of the Goutte d'or, set off a firestorm of activism, mobilizing local protesters numbering in the thousands and attracting the support of leading left-wing intellectuals like François Mauriac, Jean-Paul Sartre, and Michel Foucault. For pro-Palestinian activists like the young Tunisian Saïd Bouziri, such events, along with growing complaints from Muslim workers about too much focus on Palestine, highlighted the greater urgency of immigrant laborers' basic needs.[26]

Under these circumstances, in the summer of 1972, the Palestine committees gave way to the Movement for Arab Workers (MTA). The MTA constituted the first postcolonial organization for the rights of North African laborers in France. The organization drew Muslims from throughout France, with the Paris and Marseille regions among those with the largest movements; within Ile-de-France, activists were particularly concentrated in many of the long-standing strongholds of Muslim political activism such as Paris's outer arrondissements and banlieues like Nanterre, Gennevilliers, and Clichy. An early MTA statement summarized the group's aims in revealing terms: "It is a movement of struggle for dignity, against racism, to support the Palestinian revolution and the Arab people struggling against Zionism and the Arab reactionaries . . . for decent living conditions and for the defense of our rights, against material and moral misery. Through these struggles, an Arab national consciousness (which is also a working-class consciousness) developed."[27]

The same period witnessed rising political tensions between the Jewish and Muslim populations in France. In 1972, a wave of violent attacks occurred against both Jews and Muslims, with members of each community accusing the other of having perpetrated the assaults. These included explosions at a Palestinian bookstore and the apartment of Fatah envoy Mahmoud Hamchari; threatening letters sent to several leading North African and Middle Eastern representatives; and fourteen attacks from September to year's end on Jews or Jewish institutions, including one against Marseille's central synagogue. Even pro-Palestinian Jewish leftists encountered occasional hostility. Benny Lévy was stunned when he heard new Arab recruits to the movement make antisemitic statements, but he did not want to cause a fracas that might hurt the movement's larger interests. The Amicale's *Algérien en Europe,* once more equating French Jews and Zionists, criticized Zionists in France for fueling "anti-Arab hysteria" in the aftermath of the Palestinian terrorist attack against Israelis at the 1972 Olympics in Munich.[28] Reflecting this wider environment, a number of Muslim rhetorical attacks on the leadership of Si

Hamza Boubakeur at the Grand Mosque of Paris, continued to center on his ties to Jews: he was criticized, among other things, for allegedly having been "breastfed by a Jew" as an infant and being an active member of the International League against Racism and Antisemitism (LICA).[29]

Yet the Palestine committees followed a different path. For all their emphasis on the heroism of the fedayeen and the need to liberate Palestine and for all the links they drew between the Palestinian cause and Muslim struggles in France, the committees said almost nothing publicly about Jews per se. They attacked King Hussein with as much vitriol as they did Zionism and did not spare other reactionary Arab leaders or American imperialism.[30] They repeatedly declared themselves antiracist. To be sure, according to numerous stories in *Fedai,* every Israeli, whether a government official, military officer, or shopkeeper, was among the "Zionist enemy" and worthy of violent attack.[31] But Zionism remained largely an abstraction; the focus was on the act of resistance and Arab unity rather than on vilifying Jews qua Jews. Critiques of Zionism never extended to the Jewish community or Jews in France, and thus did not seek to draw Muslims and Jews in France into a struggle that mimicked the Israeli-Arab conflict.

Rather, the MTA fused declarations of Arab cultural pride and transnational unity with a distinctly French language of antiracism, class struggle, and civic rights.[32] This pattern would continue through a series of bold political actions well into the mid-1970s. In October 1972, the Tunisian activist Saïd Bouziri undertook a hunger strike to protest an expulsion order for him and his wife. The hunger strike, one of the few tactics of political action legally available to foreigners at that time, garnered an immediate outpouring of solidarity from Tunisian and French supporters and convinced the authorities to offer a fifteen-day authorization for the Bouziris's stay in France that could be renewed (a bimonthly process to which they would remain subject for years). Bouziri's successful action became a model for many immigrants of effective protest in the face of dire circumstances and legal constraints. In response to the Marcellin-Fontanet decrees that went into effect in fall 1972, hunger strikes emerged across France, with most participants Tunisians, along with Moroccans, Portuguese, and French supporters. One pamphlet, addressing its reader as "brother Arab worker," reminded workers that they did "the most dangerous and difficult work for the lowest wages" and called on them to "wake up and claim your rights," reminding them that "all Arabs will be with you." Such language encapsulated how cultural unity and collective labor struggle could together be tapped to combat legal vulnerability and actualize rights current and future. In the end, every hunger striker saw his legal status normalized, as well as that of 35,000 other workers; the Marcellin-Fantanet decrees were softened, if not eliminated. This marked the birth of the first *sans-papiers* movement, a phrase coined during the strikes to speak of immigrants of irregular status threatened with expulsion organizing their own nonviolent resistance.[33]

Large-scale Muslim political mobilizations grew with time, and continued to center on a combination of universalist and particularist claims. Protests against squalid living conditions, and in solidarity with the ongoing plight of the sans-papiers, transformed into major strikes. Muslim workers insisted on greater respect and representation within France's largest labor union, the General Labor Confederation (CGT), renewing a longtime demand of immigrant and colonial laborers: equal work for equal pay. They also responded in no uncertain terms to racist crimes like the lethal bombing of the Algerian consulate in Marseille in December 1973, which brought 20,000 North Africans to strike and follow the funeral procession through the streets.[34] In part, Saïd Bouziri explained, this activism was about asserting as never before a permanent place in France for these erstwhile rotational laborers: "People began to consider themselves—today you would say as citizens, in any case at the time, to consider themselves as being from here . . . and that they shouldn't put up with things . . . whereas before there was a total inhibition."[35] In the 1974 presidential campaign a Tunisian activist under the pseudonym of Djellali Kamal decided to run, though he had neither the right to be a candidate nor to vote. Kamal explained that his running had a very serious purpose: "My candidacy is not a joke, it is not a publicity stunt, it is the cry of millions of men reduced to serfdom in the middle of the twentieth century." Kamal framed his campaign around a call for legal equality with French workers.[36] In this manner, then, Bouziri, Kamal, and many of their fellow Muslim immigrants were at once performing French citizenship and seeking to expand its meaning and possibilities (Figure 7.2).

In another sign of this strategy and the growing support for North African worker rights, the movement successfully reached out to numerous Catholic clergy. In autumn 1972 churches like the Saint-Bernard in

Figure 7.2. Photograph of leading North African immigrant-rights activists Saïd Bouziri (left) and Driss El-Yazami (right) and a man only identified as "Jamal" (middle), at the site of *Génériques*, a Paris-based association and archive for the history of immigration that they helped to create, 1994. (Collection Génériques © Beatrice Lagarde.)

Paris began to shelter hunger strikers in their annexes; one of the church's priests, the abbé Gallimardet, became a particularly important supporter of the sans-papiers movement. That Christmas, a group of four priests refused to celebrate midnight mass, a show of solidarity that garnered considerable attention. By spring 1973 most bishops and archbishops had publicly given their support to the sans-papiers movement.[37] A number of clergy, such as Père Loubier of Notre Dame de la Croix de Ménilmonant in Belleville, also played key roles in helping Muslim workers to find prayer spaces.[38] In a country where the church remained central to many people's daily life or understanding of French culture, these shows of solidarity had not only practical but symbolic implications.

The efforts of the MTA and its allies to build a movement at once North African and French yielded tangible benefits. By the mid- to late 1970s, they had placed a series of issues specific to immigrant workers on the national agenda. With hindsight, we can see how their achievements, even in the face of enormous structural obstacles, laid the groundwork for many of the key reforms in immigrant and foreigner rights of the early 1980s. In 1974, the state created a new post at the Ministry of Labor, a secretary of state for foreign workers, and drafted a new policy for immigrant workers, largely designed to provide the same freedoms enjoyed by French workers. This entailed not only freedom of movement but also a right to maintain one's linguistic, religious, and cultural identity.[39] The National Office for the Cultural Promotion of Immigrants was created in 1975; by the next year, a ministerial memo laid out a religious sites program with support for both the creation of new sites and the material needs of existing mosques and prayer rooms.[40] At the level of electoral politics, in 1972, the Socialist Party came out in favor of key immigrant demands for better housing, education, and job training; a moratorium on expulsions and the creation of greater judicial oversight; and the vote for foreigners in local elections. By 1976 the party supported full freedom of association for foreigners. During the 1981 presidential elections the rights of immigrants gained a place in campaign discussions.[41] Thus what has often been painted as the watershed emergence of multicultural immigrant inclusion following the 1981 victory of François Mitterrand constituted more continuity than rupture and was as much a product of subaltern actors as elite ones.[42]

Even venues for Muslim religious and cultural life proliferated during this time, in spite of both the major French stigma that persisted against Islam and the secularism of the "Arab" worker movements. In fact, a number of Muslim working-class associations and unions petitioned the state or employers asking for spaces that they could use for prayer; these were among the demands made when Muslim workers carried out strikes in factories and SONACOTRA workers' hostels.[43] From 1970 to 1980, the number of Muslim places of worship in France, mostly set in small, informal spaces, grew from 33 to 274; during the same period, the number of Islamic associations mushroomed from 7 to 192.[44]

In the same atmosphere, as Jews witnessed the persistence and virulence of anti-Arab racism in France, many Jewish organizations grew more openly sympathetic, anticipating the Jewish-Muslim alliances around antiracism that would emerge in the 1980s. The CRIF's shift was perhaps the most striking. In 1973, amid the torrent of racist attacks against Muslims, the group had issued a fairly banal statement about the biblical principles of loving your neighbor and loving the stranger. By 1979 following the murder of two African workers, which came on the heels of several fires in synagogues and desecrations of Jewish cemeteries, the organization spoke out forcefully, declaring itself "in solidarity with all immigrant workers no matter their origin."[45] Such an outlook suggested both greater concern with the impact of racism on Jews and the impact of the political movements of the preceding decade on organized Jewry's perceptions of the place of postcolonial immigrants in France.

The late arrival of most Jews to the cause of immigrant workers contrasted earlier periods such as the Popular Front or the French-Algerian War, when Jewish individuals and even organizations had often played a critical role in supporting Muslim rights. One reason for the shift was the significant decline in the working-class, largely Ashkenazic Jewish Left in France by the 1970s; previously, this group had often made common cause with certain Muslim activists. But equally crucial was the question of Israel/Palestine. In petitions distributed in 1974 that garnered nearly eight hundred signatures, for instance, the MTA spoke not only of workers' rights and antiracism but its support for "the Palestinians chased from their land" and demanded the "pursuit and arrest of the Zionist criminals in France."[46] The Palestinian struggle thus remained a key source of inspiration for the new postcolonial Maghrebi activism. At the very same moment, Zionism had emerged as increasingly fundamental to French Jewish identity.

During the 1970s both the solidarity of antiracism and the opposing loyalties of the Palestinian-Israeli conflict informed day-to-day relationships between many Muslims and Jews. These relationships bore the mark of the period's fundamental tensions: between frequent Jewish-Muslim public engagement around mutually hostile transnational causes; a set of multicultural popular movements for immigrant rights and public difference; and ongoing daily coexistence. Here once more, national and international events were perceived in the context of individuals' local experiences; by the same token, local claims to belonging took on new meanings when shone in the national limelight.

The Parisian neighborhood of Belleville again proves instructive. By this time, it was one among many poorer immigrant quarters in the capital with a distinctive ethnic character and an emerging transnational, radical politics. Belleville, still home to many North African Jews and Muslims, became a hub for the Palestine committees and then the MTA. Militants of the Arab working-class movements repeatedly made the neighborhood's streets, apartments, and Métro stations sites of protest on behalf of greater labor and civil rights, frequently leading to altercations with French police.[47] Groups disseminated leaflets not only in Belleville's "Arab" cafés but also sometimes in those owned by Jews and in common neutral spaces like street markets.[48] In an interview years later, Saïd Bouziri remembered how he and his fellow activists regularly stood in the streets of the neighborhood, disseminating pamphlets and newsletters to passersby, including Jews. When a Jew would keep walking and say "Long live Israel," the activists would try to stop him or her and engage a discussion, asking: "Okay but what about the Palestinians?" Such encounters, admitted Bouziri, only occasionally won Jewish converts to the Palestinian cause, but the discussions were almost always respectful.[49] Furthermore, these movements' politicization of urban space—even if it included regular references to the Palestinian cause—did not center on the Middle East conflict but, rather, the daily needs of North African workers.

Indeed, Jews and Muslims in Belleville continued to interact on an array of both locally and internationally shaped terms, signaling that the Israeli-Arab conflict was neither the sole nor necessarily the most important lens through which most individuals perceived one another.[50] When Claude Tapia published his sociology of Belleville in 1974, he found that many Tunisian and Algerian Muslims of the neighborhood were regular customers at Jewish butcher shops, restaurants, and bakeries. Respectful distance prevailed in public spaces: along the central avenue of the boulevard de Belleville, Jews largely stuck to the northern sidewalks and Muslims to the southern and eastern ones, with a mutually understood kind of no-man's-land in between.[51] Muslims often sought and obtained guidance and social assistance from leading, more bourgeois figures in the quarter's Jewish community. At the time of Tapia's study, eighty Muslims had been recruited for salaried positions in Jewish-owned businesses, most commonly restaurants or corner grocery stores.[52] Many Jewish and Muslim children attended school together; a few even became close friends. Such circumstances, along with the fact that the vast majority of the quarter's Jews were either lower middle class or poor, likely produced substantial sympathy among Jews for the basic demands of their Muslim activist neighbors who took to the streets. A twelve-year-old Jewish schoolgirl named Joëlle told Tapia: "People are right to strike for better lodging. I saw that on television. One can see that this quarter is not like others. People are shocked when they come [here] from another quarter."[53] Indeed, by the early to mid-1970s, the neighborhood was declining economically, noticeably overcrowded and physically dilapidated.

Particularly in the context of Belleville's increasingly dire material state, the quarter's interethnic coexistence was repeatedly tested, if never altogether upended, by the resonance of national and international political developments. In the racially charged atmosphere of the early 1970s many Jews expressed embarrassment at the stigma attached to Belleville. A number of Jewish residents, including many schoolchildren, spoke frequently in interviews of tensions between Jews and Arabs or regular street altercations between members of different groups. These were among the reasons cited for many Jews moving to more middle-class and spacious neighborhoods in Paris. Moreover, in the thirty months that followed the Six Day War 501 Jews left Belleville for Israel; many more told Tapia they planned to follow suit.[54] Even in a neighborhood where a common cultural background in North Africa and mutual economic interests shaped Jewish-Muslim coexistence, other factors were often taking precedent for a new generation raised in France: the politicization of Jewish-Muslim places and people along the lines of the Israeli-Arab conflict and the divisions of postcolonial French society and politics.

Jews and Muslims Take to the Streets

Among France's Jewish population, the Six Day War and its aftermath became a watershed in terms of the unabashed articulation of claims to public space on behalf of Israel, in dialectic with another shift in the form of a newly perceived divide between many leading French Jews and their government. Marseille, whose mayor remained the ardently pro-Israel Gaston Defferre, continued to be a particular stronghold for visible pro-Israel activism. The city remained a magnet for Jewish and Muslim immigrants, and through its sizable Jewish (80,000) and Muslim presence (30,000) and its proximity to the Middle East, became a hub of both pro-Zionist and pro-Palestinian activism. In the context of international tensions, the differences in economic opportunity, housing quarter, and legal status between many of Marseille's Jews and Muslims often burst forth in the terms of a fairly one-sided Zionist-Arab proxy struggle for supremacy in the local public sphere.

Authorities in Marseille worried in the years following the Six Day War that the conflict might once more spill onto routes of transportation that ran through the city to and from Israel and North Africa. In 1970, French police repeatedly spoke of rumors or intelligence about planned attacks by Palestinian groups or North Africans against Israeli planes and ships stopping in Marseille.[55] While concerns about attacks on transport appeared to dissipate in time, they informed an atmosphere in which Marseille's location as a Mediterranean transit point now made it volatile, as the Middle East conflict seemed unusually close at hand. Activists from Jewish and pro-Palestinian organizations engaged in what amounted to a local propaganda war. In May 1972, young Jews were caught distributing tracts showing a Jew under a guillotine and demanding "the liberation of the Jews [who are] hostage to the antisemitic Arab governments."[56] In January 1973, a Palestine Committee helped organize protests of the upcoming visit of Israeli prime minister Golda Meier, distributing leaflets dubbing her "assassin" and accusing her of organizing terrorist attacks in Europe, fomenting intra-Jewish racial discrimination, and oppressing and bombarding Palestinians.[57]

Tensions crested around the October 1973 Israeli-Arab War, but with limited impact in terms of actual altercations. During the war, the Jewish community undertook a major public fundraising campaign through the "French United Jewish Appeal." Supporters of Israel now faced a much more divided French public than six years prior and a government far removed from its former position as one of Israel's staunchest allies. On October 8, two days after the war's outbreak, in a demonstration organized by the Jewish community and led by Gaston Defferre, thousands took to La Canebière, the central avenue of the city, to show solidarity with Israel. They waved Israeli flags and carried banners: "Israel will win" and "Let's fight for a just and lasting peace." Demonstrators sang the Israeli national anthem and uttered prayers on behalf of the Jewish state. Police reported that the rally produced no visible reaction in either North African neighborhoods or the vicinity of the Algerian consulate of Marseille.[58] During the days that followed, in a smaller demonstration and a series of tracts, Jewish groups called on France to cease all arms sales to the Arab world.[59]

On October 13, two hundred to three hundred demonstrators participated in a pro-Palestinian rally. One MTA activist bitterly complained, "We don't have the right to [demonstrate] on the Canebière."[60] In this manner, local politics in Marseille, as they had in 1967, rendered the heart of the city more pro-Israeli than pro-Palestinian, mimicking the city's postcolonial social geography that saw the majority of Jews and pieds-noirs residing in more central quarters and most Muslims at the periphery. The respective demonstrations also illustrated how at least in Marseille with its favorable local government, Jews—despite an often pro-Arab French foreign policy, increasingly ambivalent attitudes toward the

Middle East conflict among the French public, and long-standing conventions of Jewish political quietism in France—could now make a transnational, ethnoreligious claim to public space that remained far less viable for Muslims.

At the same time, despite the opposing ethnic solidarities and struggles over certain pieces of the urban fabric, the dynamics in the immigrant quarter of the Belsunce, long home to many Jewish and Muslim immigrants from North Africa, seemed little changed. One report recounted how the Jewish jewelers of the rue d'Aix and the merchants of the Arab souk on the neighboring rue Sainte-Barbe went about their business with "no perceptible change in their attitude [save] for a few transistor radios stuck to their ears and connected to Radio-Alger [for news of the war]." Still, following both the pro-Israeli and pro-Palestinian demonstrations, Marseille police set up barriers to keep Jews and Muslims in the neighborhood from coming into contact. Jewish leaders urged all community members, particularly youth, to avoid any conflict with local Arabs.[61]

One year later, in response to the French decision to recognize the PLO, Marseille was the site of further Jewish and Muslim political competition. The coordinating committee of the Associations juives de Marseille described the French as capitulating before Middle East oil in a manner that "recalls the tragic self-abnegation before Nazi Germany" and argued that the current policy "if pursued, would put in danger the courageous State of Israel."[62] Here, the committee's words at once drew historical parallels, lessons, and continuities. This was hardly isolated rhetoric. In a climate where World War II and its memory were gaining new resonance in France far beyond the Jewish community, communal leaders invoked the Holocaust with increasing frequency in connection to their support for Israel.[63] Indeed, several weeks later the Marseille committee for the CRIF, in denouncing France's action, "reaffirmed" the wartime words of one French Resistance hero: "This assault of two million men against a handful of Jews is not a just fight."[64] Making clear that Jews' ability to assert particularity remained highly contested, French president Giscard d'Estaing responded to such condemnations by declaring, "If the French of Israelite origin put the interests of Israel before those of their own country, this is bound to create difficulties."[65]

Here the persistent question of the era—whether public affirmation of difference would lead necessarily to conflict or marginalization—had been posed by the president of the republic. Many Jews insisted that their loyalty to Israel in no way threatened their "deep attachment to the *mère patrie*" of France.[66] Within a short time public assertions of Jewish specificity would become institutionalized. In 1976, at the first of what would become an annual event, roughly 100,000 Jews took part in the Twelve Hours for Israel festival that included films, music concerts, and intellectual and spiritual panels with leading Jewish figures.[67] The next year, the CRIF revised its charter, claiming a communal "responsibility" to "contribute its views that stem from its Jewish identity to the national debate." Moreover, the charter declared that the French Jewish community considered Israel as "the privileged expression of Jewish existence."[68] Thus, far removed from its insistent reserve during the French-Algerian War some fifteen years earlier, the CRIF affirmed the need for Jews to speak publicly *as Jews* and framed Israel as coterminous with French Jewish identity.

In November 1974 in Marseille, hundreds of Jews and Muslims took to the streets of the city on the same day in response to France's recognition of the PLO, demonstrating on behalf of their respective allegiances. Once again, a significant police presence helped to ensure that no conflict ensued.[69] Nonetheless, during the same period, Jewish leaders in Marseille expressed apprehensions that France's strident support for the PLO was shifting local dynamics, leading to a breakdown in the relationships between Jewish employers and their Muslim employees.[70] Whether through an activist standoff in its urban core or day-to-day business interactions, it appeared that few of Marseille's Jewish and Muslim residents attempted or had the ability to escape altogether the latest saturation of their neighborhoods and beings with political significance.

In significant part, moments like this illustrated that France's foreign policy shift of 1967 regarding the Arab-Israeli conflict, coupled with the growing acceptance of a more permanent Muslim presence in France, had created a newly competitive political dynamic. France's position on the Middle East conflict was now seen as hanging in the balance. From opposing sides, many Jews and Muslims began openly using public statements and political mobilization in an effort to lobby the government.[71]

And yet the new attention to distinctly different Jewish and Arab populations did not predetermine conflict. Some of the same Jews and Muslims of Marseille who held opposing foreign policy positions came together around questions of equal rights in a manner that previewed more visible multicultural alliances to come. Local Jewish leader Prosper Elkouby, of North African origin and often at the forefront of pro-Israel activism in the region, condemned anti-Arab racism in France in the strongest possible terms. "We must always remain vigilant," he declared, "when we see anti-Arab campaigns develop; we condemn them. . . . Anti-Arab racism can very well transform itself into anti-Jewish racism."[72]

Jewish and Muslim Holocaust Talk

The period's marked increase in what Joan Wolf terms "Holocaust talk" also played a rather ambivalent role in Jewish-Muslim relations.[73] Jews and Muslims repeatedly found themselves appropriating the Holocaust in ways that we might deem, in Michael Rothberg's formulation, both "competitive" and "multidirectional." The former type of memory is one seen by advocates, critics, and observers alike as "a zero-sum game over scarce resources." Rothberg contends that the latter, by contrast, is understood as "subject to ongoing negotiation, cross-referencing, and borrowing; as productive and not privative."[74] In a striking instance of multidirectional memory, on September 2, 1970, the MTA and the Committee to Defend the Lives and Rights of Immigrant Workers, the major organizer of hunger strikes for the sans-papiers, held a ceremony at the Monument to the Deportation. This stark, stone memorial on the Seine in Paris honors the 200,000 men and women deported from France to concentration camps during World War II. Before a silent audience that included several human rights advocates, the widow of the PLO's recently assassinated Paris representative, and two survivors of concentration camps, a speaker recalled for the audience that "fascism and racism made 6 million victims" and then read the names of seven of those killed in the recent wave of racist murders in Marseille that followed the killing of Désiré-Emile Gerlache.[75] Thus the site of Holocaust mourning par excellence in France became a space for highlighting contemporary racist violence, and in a manner that paid full recognition to the horrors of World War II.

By the end of the decade, competitive memory was also playing a major role. The February-to-March 1979 screening of the American mini-series *Holocaust* on French television became occasion for fierce debates around the relationship of Holocaust memory to the state of Israel. On February 27, 1979, a pair of sharply opposed Jewish and Muslim reactions appeared in the pages of *Le Monde*. Prominent Moroccan writer Tahar Ben Jelloun wrote a letter to the editor in which he spoke of first learning about the Holocaust when he saw the film *Night and Fog* in high school but then learning soon after of the Zionist massacre of Palestinian Arabs at Deir Yassin during the 1947–1948 war. Not far from this letter appeared an article by Zionist activist Paul Giniewski about how Israel's victories constituted a triumph wherein victims of the Holocaust became "less atrociously, less uselessly, and less truly dead."[76] For Ben Jelloun, the Holocaust constituted the tragic antecedent of Israel's own crimes, for Giniewski the Jewish state's ongoing raison d'être.

The next year, the bombing attack at the synagogue on rue Copernic in Paris, in which four people were killed and more than forty injured, provoked a more complex dynamic. Jewish vulnerability and criticism of the French state burst into the open in an unprecedented manner, with frequent reference to the Holocaust. At a rally at the synagogue the morning after the attack, one man screamed at a police officer, "Six million Jews in 1940, this isn't enough for you? It is your uniform that sent our fathers and mothers to the crematory ovens."[77] Yet far from merely a moment for the assertion of Jewish particularity, the aftermath of Copernic became an occasion for a politically and ethnically diverse antiracist coalition; some saw the bombing as above all a racist attack on "France itself." In a demonstration against the attack in Paris soon after, a remarkably wide array of groups participated, including not only Jewish organizations but antiracist and human rights activists, feminists, the Association of Muslim Students, and several Palestinian organizations. While all of the protesters marched together and Jews and non-Jews carried banners that read, "Never again!" each group had as well its own placards and advocated for its particular organization. The occasion became one for some Muslims to denounce racism against Jews in a reverse of the more typical pattern. One editorial in an Algerian newspaper contended that violence by Europeans against North Africans was linked to bombs in synagogues, declaring that "resolute adversaries of all forms of racist persecution and religious intolerance, we can only join this general condemnation without equivocation and express our solidarity with the victims of this racist attack."[78] By 1980, unlike most ethnic minorities in France, Jews had established a successful claim to speak qua Jews in the public sphere. But a whole host of other groups, including Muslim workers and students and pro-Palestinian activists, were finding their public voices as well.

New Cooperation, New Challenges

The 1980s would test whether the tensions established in grassroots Muslim and Jewish activism and relations of the previous decade, between increasingly opposed transnational identifications in the public sphere and frequently shared spaces and political interests, could be resolved or even sustained. In 1981, François Mitterrand became France's first left-wing head of government since the Front populaire. During the campaign, he had invoked a "right to difference" and discussed human rights and immigrants' rights.[79] Soon his government offered amnesty to 131,000 irregular immigrants, simplified naturalization and family reunion processes, and forbade the deportation of any French-born foreigner. Moreover, a new law permitted foreigners to form associations without permission from the Interior Ministry, and some of these associations became eligible for public subsidies.[80] These measures enabled the rich associational life that had emerged over the preceding decade to move from the edges of legality and politics toward the center; discussions of diversity and difference that had begun in the 1970s became more public and widespread. Visions of a republic more accommodating to public difference appeared to actualize.

One of the first and most visible manifestations of this shifting environment was the so-called *Beur* movement. The Beurs were a new generation of Muslim citizens: French-born children of North African immigrants, particularly Algerians, who articulated a set of hybrid public identities that embraced Frenchness while maintaining strong cultural connections to the Maghreb. The Beurs, partly influenced by the ongoing activism of many former MTA militants, continued the focus of the previous movement on immigrant rights, equality, antiracism, and the establishment of a North African cultural and civic presence in the French public sphere.

But the Beurs also marked important departures from the movements of the 1970s. Having grown up entirely in France and living mostly in the banlieues rather than traditional immigrant neighborhoods like Belleville or the Goutte d'or, the Beurs were largely divorced from direct contact with the North African society of their parents; instead, they were shaped by both the growing unemployment and desolation of the banlieues and many currents of mainstream French and European culture. In a sign of their self-conscious generational separation, their very name Beur was *verlan*—a language game common to the banlieues wherein speakers change a French word by inverting its syllables—for Arab, the term used so often to label these Muslims' parents. Following the 1981 reforms, Beur activists founded hundreds of new associations dedicated to causes ranging from urban development to North African art or music. The movement reached its peak in autumn 1983 when, in response to a wave of racial violence, hundreds of thousands of Beurs participated in the March for Equality and against Racism that began in Marseille and ended in Paris two months later, where President Mitterrand greeted the 100,000 marchers in the place de la République.[81]

From early on, the underlying tensions of the Arab-Israeli conflict plagued many Beurs' relations with Jews in national politics. Many Jews, despite their long-standing affinity for left-of-center politics and antiracism, were not terribly sympathetic to the movement. Jews would long remember how at rallies during the 1982 Lebanese War, Beurs showed their support for the Palestinian cause by wearing kaffiyehs and chanting "Death to the Jews." Later, in a statement that became a headline in the socialist daily *Libération,* a Beur named Samya described the hundreds of victims of racist crimes of France in terms that stung many Jews: "We are in the process of living a quiet Sabra and Shatilla."[82] (This comment referred to the notorious event of September 1982 in which Lebanese Christian Phalangists carried out large massacres in Palestinian refugee camps while the Israeli military stood by.) Once more, for many French Muslims, the Palestinian cause had become a source of public identification and a metaphor for their own suffering. Yet chants of "death to the Jews" or "Jewish assassins" (as also occurred) were a major shift from the virulent but strictly focused anti-Zionism of the Palestine committees and the MTA; attacking "Jews," particularly in a climate of increasing Holocaust consciousness, implied broader accusations against all Jews, presumably including those in France.[83] Here was a sign that the Muslim and Jewish activists of a new generation took for granted the two groups' opposed attachments in the Israeli-Arab conflict. Moreover, despite their frequently common North African origins, most had little sense of any shared Maghrebi culture. There were, as it were, no Jewish Beurs.

Indeed, the impetus for a new Jewish-Muslim entente would be much more political than cultural. The same new left-wing politics that animated the Beur movement—antiracism rooted in asserting both a right to cultural difference and pride as equal French citizens (rather than in internationalism and class struggle)—soon helped to shape an emerging Muslim-Jewish alliance that crystallized with the founding of SOS Racisme in 1984. In part, this was a response to repeated spikes in racist violence against both Muslims and Jews, along with the electoral break-through on the far right of Jean-Marie Le Pen's FN.

Beginning in 1983 the FN achieved a stunning string of double-digit vote percentages in local, national, and European elections. While the FN's rise centered on the changing politics of the immigration issue, it deeply concerned both Muslims and Jews. In the 1970s FN rhetoric on immigration had been only a few steps removed from the fairly restric-tive policies of right-wing governments. Yet with the relative openness of the Mitterrand government toward immigrant worker rights, the FN suddenly found itself sharply opposed to state policy in a manner useful for political purposes. Moreover, the large number of North Africans among France's immigrant population (roughly 40 percent), as well as their increased visibility everywhere from cultural associations to sites of worship to radio programs, meant that the FN's racialized rhetoric about threats to Western civilization suddenly resonated with many more French voters.[84]

Meanwhile, the FN and others on the Far Right repeatedly joined the heated discussions of the memory of the Holocaust and World War II, frequently revealing deep attachment on the part of many to a positive view of Vichy and collaboration. After the FN's chief strategist, François Duprat, was murdered in mysterious circumstances in 1978, the obituary in the FN newspaper *Le National* insinuated that he had been killed by a Jewish plot, claimed that his revisionist writings on the Holocaust had cost him his life, and praised the way he had taken on "all of those ta-boos inherited from the Second World War."[85] In 1982 the editors of the longtime extreme-right weekly *Le Rivarol* spoke with pride of the maga-zine as "a meeting place for those who were 'Pétainists but not collabo-rators,' those who were 'collaborators but not Pétainists,' and those who were neither but who were a little slow to understand that the Allies had killed 'the wrong pig.'"[86] If Jews were less of a present target for the Far Right than Muslims, Jewish memory of World War II—a critical aspect in contemporary assertions of public Jewishness—was an ever-present problem.

In this context, SOS Racisme found itself in the crosshairs of debates about the meaning of the French nation. Indeed, the group was promoted as part of a Socialist effort to facilitate the creation of associations that could provide backing and outreach for the party. SOS Racisme sought to be an umbrella for the antiracist movement, therefore including Beur activists but within a more diverse coalition. Whereas the Beur movement exemplified the period's frequently particularist politics, emphasizing the interests of a particular ethnic group, SOS Racisme took a pluricultural approach that saw diverse groups working together to create a more welcoming and equal society, enriched by difference. This inherent tension between particularism and pluriculturalism—already visible in the political struggles of the 1970s—would plague the antiracist coalition's efforts and prove central to the movement's challenges and possibilities for Jewish-Muslim relations.[87]

From early on, the partnership of significant numbers of young Muslim and Jewish activists became crucial to both the substance and optics of SOS Racisme. Along with founder and leading activist Julien Dray, an Algerian Jew, Eric Ghébali, president of the French Jewish Student Union (UEJF), became the new group's secretary-general. Under Ghébali's leadership, the UEJF revitalized after a period of relative inactivity and became a key ally of the new antiracism. At the same time, like the Beur movement, the UEJF maintained its own more particularistic program, including an ardent commitment to Zionism and the state of Israel. Dray and Ghébali worked alongside several Muslims who took on leading roles in SOS Racisme. Soon noted Jewish intellectuals Marek Halter and Bernard Henry-Lévy became visible supporters. The group often partnered with Beur activists around common goals and initiatives.[88]

SOS Racisme rapidly gathered steam. The group spread its message through the sale of yellow badges in the shape of a hand that sported the slogan, "Touche pas à mon pôte!"("Don't touch my friend!"). By March 1985, 300,000 people had purchased badges; by year's end the number would be 1.5 million.[89] The alliance between SOS Racisme and the UEJF gained traction as well. Following three racist attacks in late March, demonstrators could be heard to chant: "Arabs in Menton, Jews in Paris, they are killing our friends [pôtes]." A number of Jewish and Muslim leaders and news commentators saw this as a moment when Jews and Muslims knew that racism against the one affected the other and barriers between the two groups were beginning to come down. In early May, when American president Ronald Reagan paid a controversial visit to Bitburg cemetery in Germany and placed a wreath on the graves of German soldiers, forty-nine of whom had been SS troops, several leading Muslim figures protested in a written statement. The signatories, who argued that all victims of racism needed to work together, included several former MTA activists and writers such as Leïla Sebbar and Tajar Ben Jelloun.[90]

Ben Jelloun's presence is particularly striking, for he was several years and seemingly a political universe removed from his confrontational stance in response to the television miniseries *Holocaust.* Now, rather than competitive memory, in the face of what Muslims and Jews increasingly saw as a shared threat, the Moroccan writer embraced an opportunity to show the Holocaust's multidirectional potential within antiracist politics. Not long after, Ben Jelloun and the Jewish writer Marek Halter were interviewed together for a weekend story in *Libération,* both speaking about the activism of Jews and Arabs together in SOS Racisme. When asked about the decision of many Muslim intellectuals to sign the protest against Reagan's visit to Bitburg, Ben Jelloun explained that for him and many other Arabs, a crucial turning point toward greater sympathy with Jews was the protest of large numbers of Israelis against their military's conduct in Lebanon during the 1982 War. Both he and Halter agreed that rather than placing the Israeli-Palestinian conflict "in parentheses" as some antiracist activists advocated, Jews and Muslims had to have solidarity around a message of compassion for all victims of the conflict.[91]

Even at this moment of tremendous optimism for Jewish-Muslim entente, then, tensions over the Middle East conflict were not entirely obscured. At a meeting several weeks earlier, called to address the question of how Jews and Arabs could work together within the movement, Marc Bitton, a Jewish participant and member of both UEJF and SOS Racisme, exclaimed: "You must understand that when an Israeli is killed, it is like our own blood flows." Driss Yazami, a veteran of the struggles of the 1970s and now part of the team at the immigrant rights magazine *Sans frontières* (which helped to link the two generations of activists), spoke in reply: "I accept that you are Zionists. So long as that does not prevent you from working together with us to build a real antiracist movement."[92]

Yet the conflict between particularistic concerns of groups like the Beurs and the UEJF and the effort of SOS Racisme to build a pluriculturalist movement never truly dissipated, and over time, greater friction emerged. From a range of vantage points, an increasing number of Muslims and Jews publicly emphasized differences, rather than similarities, between the two groups. On the one hand, Muslims like *Sans frontières* founder Mejid Daboussi Ammar were not necessarily ready to set aside the particularist demands that had fueled the Beur movement. In a December 1985 joint interview with Julien Dray in *Libération,* Ammar pushed back on Dray's enthusiasm for pluriculturalism: "[Intermingling] is a luxury that I cannot permit myself. Before saying let's move toward mixture, the pluricultural, we must establish as well a certain equality between communities." Jews, on the other hand, frequently shared the fears of André Wormser, head of a center for research on antisemitism, who protested that associations with "Arab" activists could "make it seem as if Jews are foreigners to the French nation."[93] If for Muslims Jews constituted a minority community that had already achieved the acceptance to which they still aspired, for Jews proximity to Muslims risked isolation that they hoped they had overcome.[94]

Over time, a series of external developments posed growing challenges to Jewish-Muslim entente within the antiracist movement. For many Jewish and Muslim activists, their respective ethnoreligious loyalties overtook the group's larger claims of pluriculturalism. Tensions in this regard were exacerbated when the First Intifada in Israel/Palestine that began in late 1987 and the Gulf War of 1991 brought the Middle East conflict to the fore. But other domestic challenges separated Jews from Muslims. The FN's persistent successes had made it a perceived threat to the mainstream right-wing parties. After the latter won the 1986 legislative elections and Mitterrand had to name a prime minister from the Gaullist center-right party the Rassemblement pour la République (RPR), the new government thus responded with a series of anti-immigrant proposals that sought to co-opt central tenets of Le Pen's platform. New laws granted police greater powers of surveillance, identity verification, and detention and limited more severely immigration from countries outside of the European Economic Community. The government pursued a major, if ultimately unsuccessful effort to pass a more restrictive nationality code. In 1988 Interior Minister Charles Pasqua even insisted that the mainstream right-wing parties shared not only the FN's program but "the same preoccupations, the same values."[95] In the meantime, rather than responding with a robust defense of a right to ethnic difference, the Socialists had sought to channel the Beurs in a more integrationist direction. This effort robbed the movement of much of its grassroots authenticity and bite.[96] With a political consensus emerging that treated Muslim public difference as the symptom of a new immigration "problem," fears again became widespread among Jews that association with Muslims could link them to foreignness.[97] By the late 1980s the Jewish-Muslim alliances of SOS Racisme that had once seemed so promising had reached a breaking point.

It was in this context in October 1989 that the first "headscarf affair" erupted. The affair would reveal the sharp yet uneven strictures on ethnoreligious particularity that had emerged from the failed effort of the preceding years to establish a right to difference. The controversy began when the expulsion of three Muslim girls from a middle school in the town of Creil became a national debate over *laïcité*. The affair took place against the backdrop of wider developments that included public disagreement about the meaning of the republic surrounding the bicentennial of the French Revolution, the ongoing First Intifada in Israel/ Palestine, and a fatwa issued in February 1989 against Salman Rushdie by the Ayatollah Khomeini of Iran in response to the former's publication of *The Satanic Verses*. The first headscarf affair marked the beginning of a series of disputes that would recur during the next twenty years over female Muslim religious attire in schools and, more broadly, in public. French ethnic nationalists had found a new way to frame Muslims as outside French norms of gender, family, and sexuality. Despite many Jews' own "conspicuous religious attire," throughout these debates, Judaism was never scrutinized in a manner analogous to Islam.

Public Jewish responses to the affair were varied. Chief Rabbi Joseph Sitruk showed solidarity with the three girls, arguing that both the veil and the kippa should be permitted in schools. Others strongly objected to this position. Several secular Jewish public intellectuals like philosopher Alain Finkielkraut took a hard line that betrayed fears that the republic might deviate from a singular vision of total assimilation as the way that one "becomes French."[98] A stronger disagreement with Sitruk came from those like one letter writer to *Tribune juive* who differentiated sharply between Judaism and Islam. The writer insisted that banning the kippa from French public schools "would be an intolerable attack on human rights," whereas by contrast "Islam is waging a systematic offensive against our tolerant, Judeo-Christian society" and thus the wearing of the veil was unacceptable.[99]

Despite the way that Jewish-Muslim relations during this period were both nationalized and internationalized, as we have seen, we should not lose sight of the specificity of the local. In the unfolding of Jewish-Muslim interaction in the postcolonial era, many cities followed their own rhythms. So too with Strasbourg, a city that in this era became increasingly emblematic of the idea of a unified Europe with fluid national borders.

More so than in Paris and Marseille, where in certain neighborhoods Jews and Muslims had interacted for decades, in Strasbourg the two populations were still discovering each other in the 1970s. In this period, the growth of Jewish-Muslim contact in university and athletic settings, as well as the region's first moves toward interreligious dialogue, made for a range of relations. Alsace's long history of competing nationalist and regionalist Far Right groups was reawakening. Indeed, the region would quickly become a stronghold of Le Pen's party following its breakthrough in the early 1980s. At the same time, a changing urban landscape of numerous European institutions, accompanied by growing numbers of what the locals dubbed "Eurocrats," cultivated an emerging notion of Strasbourg as the most "European" of French cities and a symbol of Franco-German reconciliation.[100] In this simultaneously provincial and international context, certain Muslims and Jews from North Africa continued to find strength in one another's cultural commonalities and their mutual predicament as relatively isolated minorities. But the frictions of their frequently opposing transnational allegiances were never far beneath the surface.

Following the decision of many Muslim workers to remain in France and the arrival of many children after the 1975 family reunification laws, the late 1970s and early 1980s witnessed a significant increase in the number of Muslim university students throughout France. In Strasbourg, Moroccan Muslim students were a particularly large and visible group. Two future leaders in the local Muslim community arrived to study at the University of Strasbourg between 1979 and 1981—Mohamed Latahy and Fouad Daoui—both from traditional Muslim households in the region of Meknès and both having grown up around Jews in relations that they remember as quite amicable. Each recalls that nonetheless, despite his background, the Palestinian-Israeli conflict was a basic obstacle in his relations with Jewish students, as it powerfully shaped the two groups' mutual perceptions.[101]

Zoubida Tribak had a rather different experience that may have partly grown out of her childhood in Schiltigheim, where she had grown close to her Algerian Jewish neighbors. As the daughter of immigrants, she felt stigmatized at the university by many Moroccan Muslims who had grown up in Morocco and came to France only to study. She found her place socially largely among her Moroccan Jewish fellow students. They, she explained, reminded her of the Maghreb and were, like her, searching for contacts. Soon she and these Jewish students were studying together, eating together in the cafeteria, and even celebrating each other's holidays together. Yet the Middle East conflict lurked, especially at moments like the Lebanese War. It was a taboo subject, not spoken about because it was occurring elsewhere, and these students wanted to avoid importing the conflict; they thus resisted imposing, as it were, international meaning on locally defined relationships.[102] Only a few years earlier Tribak's father had been instrumental in founding, in autumn 1977, the second mosque in the Strasbourg region, in the northern suburb of Bischeim. Ahmed Tribak, the imam of the mosque, elected to invite the leading local rabbi, priest, and pastor to participate in the mosque's opening ceremony, seeking already, says his daughter, to find a way to live together in France.[103]

By the time Mostafa Elqoch, a traditional Muslim from Morocco, arrived in Strasbourg in 1985 and found his way quickly to the A. S. Menora, he discovered a football (soccer) club that had long had its own distinct dynamic of ecumenicism.[104] There, he explains, "one did not foreground religion," and the welcome was so warm that the club became his family; he would remain active until he moved away from Strasbourg seven years later. When he experienced financial difficulties, the coaches and leadership of A. S. Menora helped him to find work. In time, Elqoch became close to Simon Dahan and Denis Elkaim, Moroccan Jews long involved in the club. Elqoch spent many Shabbat meals in the Dahans' home and attended a number of Jewish family celebrations like weddings and bar mitzvahs, where he frequently delighted in the Arabic music.

During his years on the club, Elqoch estimates that there were about ten Muslim players a year at the club out of several dozen total. Audiences at the team's matches included both Jews and Muslims. During the 1987–1988 season, by one estimate, the club featured players of twenty nationalities.[105] Elqoch explains that in this environment of athletic camaraderie, "there were no longer . . . 'Jewish-Muslim' relations. We didn't see that. The relations they [were] based on many things." During periods of violence in the Middle East, Elqoch recalled that there was disagreement, but then the conversation would quickly move to another subject, "because there was another relationship, above that. It's like with your brother . . . there was so much around us that brought us back [together]." At the A. S. Menora, identities were perceived to be multilayered and fungible. Jews and Muslims saw each other above all as fellow athletes who enjoyed each other's company and often shared links to North African culture. The context of international conflict was not absent, but here it inflected their harmonious relations with a more self-consciously multicultural meaning.

At the same time, Middle East politics could color other daily interactions with darker hues, even for someone like Elqoch who did not wish to be politicized. Le Penalty, the pizzeria run by the Elkaim family, where for years many players often gathered after games, had become by this time less a place of conviviality and more one of conflict. Living nearby, Elqoch frequently went there for a meal or a late-night coffee. But over time, he found that his conversations with one of the Elkaim brothers turned increasingly hostile: "We had very instructive conversations that transformed themselves into hatred on his part. He helped me discover that there are Jews who are . . . ready to die, even to send [their] child to kill, in order not to give even a centimeter to the Palestinians." Yet as these few examples show, while Strasbourg surely felt the impact of national and international developments, as elsewhere, individual Jews and Muslims in specific local settings made choices about how to respond, and about where to draw group boundaries for themselves and each other.

Hopes and Uncertainties in the 1990s

The events of the late 1980s suggested that pluriculturalism was in eclipse and ethnic politics had taken a more decisively particularistic turn. Nonetheless, interreligious solidarity like that of Rabbi Sitruk during the first headscarf affair revealed a truth that had repeatedly been in evidence since the hardening of boundaries in the late 1960s: public displays of particularism were not in themselves necessarily harbingers of Jewish-Muslim conflict. The question of if and how Jews, Muslims, and other ethnic and religious minorities could coexist within the republic continued to play out with uncertainty through the turn of the century. Although the 1991 Gulf War engendered intercommunal tensions and fears of violence between Jews and Muslims around opposing transnational allegiances, calm ultimately prevailed.[106] For the politics of memory, the 1990s produced watershed moments of recognition for France's Jews and, to a lesser extent, Muslims of Algerian descent. In 1995, President Jacques Chirac offered a long-awaited and warmly received official apology for the role of the French state in the persecution of Jews during World War II. A series of books, documentaries, and public controversies also began the first open conversations in France about French atrocities during the Algerian War. Leading French officials took pains to insist that the archives for both World War II and the Algerian War, long tightly sealed, should be opened fully to researchers. Less clear, however, was whether these two memories could share space in the public sphere. The 1998 trial of former French official Maurice Papon for war crimes under Vichy provoked a series of controversies around Papon's far more direct participation in the events of October 17, 1961. Although the ensuing discussion pointed up a sense of historical continuity between the Holocaust and the atrocities of the Algerian War, it also frequently became the site for articulating competitive memories of Jewish and Muslim suffering.[107]

Nevertheless, the seemingly imminent prospect of Middle East peace appeared to encourage other developments on the order of amicable relations and mutual recognition. As France's Muslim population continued to grow and Islamic religious life became more publicly visible, an increasing number of initiatives for interreligious cooperation emerged. Local dialogue initiatives sprang up among Jewish, Muslim, Christian, and other ethnic and religious leaders in cities like Marseille and Strasbourg. One participant, Alsatian chief rabbi René Guthman, spoke with pride of participating in the groundbreaking ceremony for a large mosque being built in Strasbourg; he repeatedly summarized the context succinctly: "We are looking for a way to live together [vivre ensemble]."[108] Popular culture reflected this aspiration as well, as a growing number of novels, memoirs, films, and even comic books depicting Jewish-Muslim relations in other times and places, some real, others fictional, began to appear. In at least one instance, Belleville was once more the setting, this time for a comic rather than macabre tale. A cartoon series by Farid Boudjellal, which became popular with Belleville's Jewish and Muslim residents alike, recounts the relationship between a religious Jewish father and traditional Muslim father in the neighborhood, whose children are dating one another in defiance of their fathers' adamant opposition. In spite of themselves, the two men bond as fellow minorities in France while poking fun at their own and each other's traditions. The relationship between this unlikely pair seems to communicate the same idea as that of Romain Gary's protagonists some twenty years before: ethnic difference between Jews and Muslims need not be an obstacle to mutual understanding and even friendship; in a multiethnic republic, universal dimensions of the human experience can redefine the meaning of group distinctions.[109]

Yet during the preceding three decades, what it meant to be Jewish and Muslim in public had substantially hardened around particularistic ethnoreligious categories. Jews, Muslims, and the French state and society had struggled periodically with the implications of the public expression of such identifications. Jewish and Muslim claims to an ethnoreligious politics were sometimes competing, at other moments mutually compatible. Opposing visions of the Israeli-Palestinian conflict came to define increasingly the public political expression of large numbers of Jews and Muslims. While public disagreement about this struggle was far from a guarantee of mutual hostility, outbreaks of violence in the Middle East repeatedly troubled the mutual perceptions, and at times the relations, of Jews and Muslims in France. Moreover, as evidenced by the FN's ongoing success—not only at the ballot box but in shifting the broader conversation about immigration onto harsher and more racialized grounds—and the first headscarf affair and the debates that succeeded it in the 1990s, the visible public expression of ethnicity and religion remained contested, though much more sharply for Muslims than for Jews.[110] All the same, increasing interreligious dialogues and landscapes, recognition of histories of both Jewish and Muslim suffering, and popular representations and discussions of a multiethnic France all suggested that the visible presence of Jews as Jews and Muslims as Muslims could follow a path other than that of ineluctable conflict. As we know, events in the new century would quickly undermine such optimistic indications.

CONCLUSION

Jews and Muslims Always and Forever?

On Wednesday, January 6, 2015, the brothers Saïd and Chérif Kouachi entered the offices of the French satirical magazine *Charlie Hebdo* with AK-47 assault rifles. They shot many of the publication's journalists and staff, claiming retaliation for the magazine's caricatures of Islam and, in particular, the Prophet Muhammad. During their assault, the Kouachi brothers, who had ties to al-Qaeda in the Arabian Peninsula, murdered twelve people and wounded eleven more. As they left the building, they cried out, "Allahu Akbar," and declared triumph. Two days later, on Friday morning, French authorities tracked the brothers to a printing shop in the town of Dammartin-en-Goële about twenty miles northeast of Paris. That afternoon, and in coordination with the brothers, their friend Amedy Coulibaly, who claimed allegiance to the Islamic State (ISIS), orchestrated a second act of terror meant to distract the authorities. Coulibaly took hostage the customers and staff of Hyper Cacher, a kosher supermarket in the Paris suburb of Porte de Vincennes. Coulibaly eventually murdered four people; fifteen other hostages would survive. The violence finally concluded when police units stormed both buildings, killing all of the assailants.[1]

These incidents instantly transfixed France and the rest of the world. Commentators in the Hexagon and far beyond declared the events "France's 9/11." Days later, more than 1 million people, most of them French but among them many world leaders, marched across Paris in defense of free speech and republicanism, and against hatred and violence. Marchers held signs reading "I am Charlie," often "I am Jewish," and occasionally, "I am Muslim." French prime minister Manuel Valls declared in front of the Hyper Cacher the day after the murders there, "France without Jews is not France," and shortly after gave a speech in the

313

National Assembly in which he said, "I don't want any Jews in our country to be afraid and I don't want any Muslims to be ashamed."[2] Israeli prime minister Benjamin Netanyahu, meanwhile, invited France's Jews to come to Israel, calling it "your home." Following another lethal antisemitic attack in Europe by Islamists, this time on a synagogue in Copenhagen, and a group of cemetery desecrations in eastern France, Netanyahu said that he expected the wave of antisemitic incidents would continue and that Israel was preparing for the absorption of a "mass immigration of Jews from Europe." French officials strongly objected to these comments, insisting that Jews should remain in France.[3] Meanwhile, national leaders considered a range of reform, surveillance, and education projects designed to address not only the spread of militant Islamic ideologies but the underlying social conditions that help make it possible.

Thus Jews and Muslims in France found themselves once more in the national and international spotlight. And perhaps more than ever before, the image was one of violent, unmitigated conflict. Muslims had attacked an emblem of French free expression and within two days linked this attack to violence against Jews. Such a connection was hardly altogether new, but the unprecedented ferocity and shock value of these events did provoke a newly acute sense of crisis for France and many of its Jews and Muslims. The attacks threatened to overwhelm the ethnic and religious diversity of French society, which officials like Valls were now attempting to defend. For all the challenges French multiculturalism has faced, by the early twenty-first century a visibly ethnic supermarket like Hyper Cacher was standard fare, and a Mali Muslim named Lassana Bathily, working inside the supermarket, saved several Jews during the siege by hiding them in a walk-in freezer. As this book has partly sought to show, this multiethnic fabric has deep roots in a long and little-known history, one that risks being further overwhelmed by the sharp divisions and black-and-white logic of contemporary events.

The Common Vocabulary of Conflict and Coexistence

The shooting in Hyper Cacher was among the most shocking and deadly manifestations of a shift that has occurred since 2000: whatever the uncertainties of Jewish-Muslim relations in France at the dawn of the twenty-first century, the period since has taken a decidedly conflictual turn. From the outbreak of the Second Intifada in Israel/Palestine in autumn 2000 through 2012, France witnessed an average of nearly six hundred recorded antisemitic incidents each year.[4] A disproportionate number of the known perpetrators in these incidents were Muslims of North African (and to a lesser extent sub-Saharan African) descent.[5] Since 2012, the crisis has become more violent, with lethal attacks on a Jewish school in Toulouse in March 2012 by a French Muslim and against the Jewish museum in Brussels in May 2014 by another French Muslim, as well as anti-Jewish riots in which many Muslims participated in various parts of France during the Gaza war of summer 2014.

If we take seriously not only the horrific actions of the perpetrators of each deadly attack but also their targets and many of their words, then we must understand their assaults in part as the outcome of a series of foundational beliefs. Each attacker defined himself above all as a certain kind of Muslim, linked as a religious freedom fighter with fellow Muslims in radical organizations like al-Qaeda and ISIS, and in places like Afghanistan, Yemen, Syria, and Israel/Palestine. As he took them hostage, for instance, Amedy Coulibaly told the Jews in Hyper Cacher that they were not innocent: they were, he said, financing the killing of women and children and therefore culpable, and he linked this charge to his Islamic faith with a cry of "Allahu Akbar."[6] Indeed, it would appear that the attackers have frequently amalgamated the French state, the West, Zionists, and by extension of the latter, Jews as enemy targets worthy of murder. Some have been shaped by clerics who encourage such attacks as a strategy to provoke a wider civilizational struggle between Islam and the West.[7]

In the early twenty-first century, even as Jews were by far the most frequent targets of racism in France, Muslims were next, with more than 2,700 anti-North African, anti-Arab, or anti-Muslim incidents recorded from 2000 through 2011. In a small but noticeable number of these cases, Jews from militant Zionist groups like Betar or the Jewish Defense League have attacked Muslim targets.[8] On December 2, 2001, for instance, as a pro-Zionist rally dispersed, several militant Zionist activists chased North Africans to the Métro lines and into the Paris Métro tunnels, even provoking an interruption of service on the Number 1 line.[9] In 2004 there were six separate attacks on Muslims by Jewish activists, resulting in injuries to six Muslims.[10] While waiting to enter a pro-Palestinian film showing in Paris in April 2009, two Muslims were assaulted by several Jewish Defense League militants who yelled "dirty Arab" and "death to the Arabs, long live Israel."[11] The JDL helped to provoke several altercations with pro-Palestinian demonstrators during the strife of the summer of 2014.[12] Even as Jewish-authored anti-Muslim incidents have remained isolated, they mirror the logic of Muslim antisemitism in revealing ways. Relationships between Jews and Muslims have become reduced once more to a proxy struggle in an international conflict. For the attackers, their Zionism and Jewishness merge into a single and dominant identity; in addition, they treat their victims' Muslimness as equivalent to support for the Arab side in the Middle East conflict and therefore deserving of violent attack.

It has been a basic contention of this book that the outlooks shaping episodes of Muslim-Jewish hostility have been in no way self-evident, eternal, or the inevitable products of history. To be sure, the Muslim individuals and small groups who have carried out lethal attacks against Jews in recent years have enunciated views common to a new extremism among certain young Muslim activists in contemporary France. Yet these murderers' narrow ethnic labels, and the actions they saw as their logical outcome, were the product of a confluence of specific circumstances. These attackers articulated one strain of various competing understandings of what it means to be Muslim and Jewish in France.

Well before the statements of the French prime minister that followed the Charlie Hebdo and Hyper Cacher attacks, France's Jewish-Muslim crisis had prompted a number of Jewish and Muslim leaders to promote other kinds of relationships. In 2004, the Moroccan-born rabbi Michel Serfaty worked with other Jewish and Muslim community figures to create the Amitié judéo-musulmane de France (Muslim-Jewish Friendship of France, AJ-MF). The group aimed to effect greater understanding, knowledge, and respect between France's Jews and Muslims, through joint cultural, sporting, and travel events. The organization's very name, and its purposes, implied that using an interfaith framework to define relations between Jews and Muslims did not necessitate conflict. The AJ-MF's work suggested that while the terms of interaction might be predetermined, their meaning was not. Depending on circumstances, the same categories that some treated as inherently oppositional could facilitate coexistence.[13]

In spring 2006, the group undertook its first "Friendship Tour of Île-de-France." The plan called for a bus of Jewish and Muslim leaders to visit numerous Jewish and Muslim communities of the Paris banlieues. These troubled neighborhoods have frequently had high rates of poverty, crime, and unemployment and, in many instances, widespread hostility toward Jews on the part of Muslims from North Africa and sub-Saharan

Africa. The tour took place in the aftermath of a series of particularly violent events in the banlieues, including the kidnapping, torture, and murder of twenty-three-year-old Moroccan-born Jew Ilan Halimi in the town of Bagneux by a group calling itself the Gang of Barbarians, consisting largely of young men from Muslim Arab or black African descent. In these circumstances, as it visited the banlieues, including—controversially—Bagneux itself, Serfaty explains that the organizers sought to convey a distinct message to young Muslims: "We came in order to meet them, not to track them, but to listen to them."[14]

Throughout this tour of Île-de-France and subsequent tours across the rest of France, the AJ-MF encountered mixed reactions within the Jewish and Muslim communities. These ranged from warm welcomes in one another's religious spaces, to expressions of hatred from individuals, from logistical cooperation to obstruction on the part of community leaders. In one episode in Toulouse that epitomized the ambivalence of many Jews and Muslims encountered on the tours, Serfaty spoke for half an hour with a religious Muslim man. The man began the conversation quite skeptical, but said by the end that the rabbi had convinced him of the importance of Jewish-Muslim friendship. But when Serfaty reached for a "Jewish-Muslim friendship" T-shirt to hand to him, the man said, "No, I cannot take that from *your hands*." And so Serfaty gave it to his Muslim colleague to his right, from whose hands the man gladly accepted the T-shirt.[15]

At first glance, these efforts to engage in productive dialogue in Toulouse in 2006 seem diametrically opposed to events like the terrifying attack by Mohamed Merah at a Jewish school in the same city six years later. On closer examination, however, these contrasting developments share a larger set of assumptions about the nature of Jewish and Muslim identification, community, and interaction in France. That is, just as Merah, Amedy Coulibaly, and the Kouachi brothers appeared to understand their attacks as part of a life-or-death struggle between Muslims and the French military, Western powers, and Zionists on the other side, the work of the AJ-MF relies on its own reductive, binary logic. The association's very name implies that relationships between individuals considered in some manner "Jewish" and others considered in some manner "Muslim" must be understood as "Jewish-Muslim" relationships, facilitated by leaders of the respective communities, often in specifically religious communal spaces. Further, it suggests a need for an active effort toward friendlier interactions and understanding between these groups because both ethnoreligious identities and conflict have become so defining of their relationship. A conversation like the one that Michel Serfaty had with the Muslim man in Toulouse who refused to take the T-shirt from his hands speaks volumes. Serfaty struggled, with some success, to convince the man specifically of the merits of *Jewish-Muslim dialogue*. He approached him not as a fellow Frenchman but *as a Jew speaking to a Muslim*, with all the implied complicated attachments. It was on these terms that the man, despite his greater openness at the end of the conversation, could not take the T-shirt from Serfaty's hands: he saw him above all as *a Jew*.

This story thus, in one sense, validates the assumptions of the AJ-MF about the overriding nature of Jewish and Muslim ethnicity and how these categories have taken on a social life of their own. In another sense, however, it reminds us of how much of the depth and breadth of human experience, identification, and interaction can become concealed once "Jew" and "Muslim" overrun all other possible ways of understanding the relations and mutual perceptions of those who identify in any manner as Jewish and Muslim.

The Contingencies of History

As this book has sought to show, hostility cannot be considered the norm in the long history of Jewish-Muslim encounters in France. Nor have Jewish-Muslim relations in France necessarily mimicked the divisions of national and international conflicts. There have been three main strands to this argument. First, contrary to popular conceptions, for roughly a century, Jews and Muslims in France have interacted not solely or even primarily as members of their respective religious or ethnic groups but according to a myriad of other categories. Second, the meaning of Jewish or Muslim ethnoreligious identities in France has been highly situational, and only at specific historical moments, most often in the postcolonial period, became perceived as definitional. Third, from their very inception, Jewish-Muslim relations in France have not been solely about Jews' and Muslims' relations to each other. Rather, they have constituted what I call a triangular affair, with France as the third party. That is, the French state and empire, and notions of what it means to be French, have always been crucial to Jewish-Muslim relations in France.

Thus, the dramatic escalation of Jewish-Muslim tension in France in the early twenty-first century has reflected several factors that converged at a precise moment in history. The process and legacy of decolonization, particularly from Algeria, at once challenged the long-standing assumptions of the French civilizing mission and served to racialize definitions of Frenchness and otherness. In addition, since 1967, the Middle East conflict, and more specifically its intensification and internationalization, has led to the greater politicization of Jewish and Muslim spaces and bodies in France. For many Muslims and Jews, this politicization connected to a sense of vulnerability in relation to the French state and society and to increased transnational and religious assertiveness in public spaces. Another factor was a newly militant French secularism that began to emerge in the late 1980s; an allegedly universal idea of religious neutrality became linked to efforts to exclude minority religious expressions, especially Muslim ones, from the French public sphere. International events—namely, September 11, 2001, and its aftermath; and Europeanization and its attendant discourses of an "Islamic invasion" of a "secular" or "Christian" continent—have created a climate of fear that has strengthened considerably this development.[16] Moreover, gaping inequalities between Jews and Muslims in education, employment, and income levels, existent for decades, have persisted and even grown.[17]

Not least important has been the endurance of the Far Right Front national (FN) party as a factor in national politics, culminating in the advance of Jean-Marie Le Pen to the runoff in the 2002 presidential election. The FN has managed to make immigration a pressing issue in the minds of millions of French voters, with Muslims the central target of a racist nationalist rhetoric that now reaches far beyond the extreme Right. Most recently, under the new leadership of Jean-Marie Le Pen's daughter Marine Le Pen, the FN—in a manner echoed more broadly—has framed its attacks on Islam as a defense not of an older ethnonationalism but of the republic itself.[18] Such an outlook has made efforts to integrate Muslims even more difficult.

These factors have helped to produce a new dynamic, especially among Jews and Muslims who grew up in the 1980s, 1990s, and early 2000s. Through their encounters with French and communal institutions, large numbers of youth and young adults in the two populations took on sharply divergent self-understandings and cultural identifications. In both instances, many came to identify first as "Jewish" and "Muslim," in part as a response to a sense of being stuck in between other entities to which they could never ultimately relate, like the North African heritage of their parents and an elusive sense of belonging in France.[19] The strong claims of Jewish and Muslim activists to a place in the public sphere along eth-noreligious, often transnational lines, which burgeoned in the 1970s, have grown; now, however, they seem less often framed within the France-centered hopes of equal rights or multiculturalism that had character-ized earlier periods.

These larger factors have played themselves out among Muslims and Jews in a variety of ways. Given the basic challenges attached to Muslim immigrants' settlement in France and the persistent discrimination they and their children have faced in French society, they have continued to struggle to integrate successfully.[20] Many have perceived Jews, despite their frequently common North African origins and the very real chal-lenges also posed to Jewish immigrants, as having a series of unfair ad-vantages. Moreover, many Muslims attribute Jews' relative success to favorable treatment of Jews by the French, Jews selling out their North African or "Semitic" heritage, Jews' unique access to key decision makers in French society, and international Jewish power (often supported by the United States).[21] According to this view, Jews are unusually wealthy, powerful, integrated insiders in French society. Some of these percep-tions correspond, of course, to traditional antisemitic stereotypes, still espoused actively by portions of both the extreme Right and Left in France and at times embraced more passively by other elements of the French population. In addition, increasingly since 1967, and especially since the late 1990s, many Muslims in France have seen the suffering of the Palestinian people not simply as a case of fellow Arabs suffering, but as a powerful metaphor for their own struggles in France. Correspond-ingly, they regard French Jews' increasingly visible support for Israel, like these Jews' greater "Frenchness," as a sign of Jewish identification with the imperialist oppressors of innocent Muslim victims. In a way that was not the case for earlier generations, for many Muslims in France today, Jews have become Zionist colonialists or their close allies.

It is in part in the face of a wave of antisemitism and anti-Muslim racism that many French Jews—the majority of whom migrated or were born to parents who migrated from North Africa—have defended their Frenchness by seeking to differentiate themselves from "Arabness." To the degree that some, particularly of the youngest generation, express affinity for "Tunisian" or "Moroccan" or "Oriental" culture, they tend to insist that this culture is Jewish.[22] We hear echoes of this discourse in a range of places, from the distinctive fashion in Jewish youth culture in Paris to the repeated insistence of certain Jewish intellectuals that Jews are not immigrants and that the Jewish-Muslim comparison is invalid. At the same time, since 2000, as their frustrations have grown with French state policies and responses to antisemitism, many Jews have anchored their universe of belonging more in Israel than in France, ironically making it even harder to be accepted as French.[23]

The environment at the A. S. Menora sports club in Strasbourg during the early to mid-2000s illustrates both the unprecedented extent of this politicization and its less than total scope. In April 2002, at the height of the Second Intifada, three Muslim soccer players suddenly refused to play. They objected to the active support of the Conseil représentatif des israélites de France (CRIF) for Israeli policy. "The CRIF calls for demonstrating against antisemitism," one of the players explained, "which is normal, and [it calls] for supporting Sharon, which is not [normal]." This was a shocking turn of events at a place that had long prided itself on basing relations between its Jewish and Muslim players in sports, fellowship, and culture rather than the vicissitudes of Middle East politics. And yet, while the incident gained national press attention, it changed almost nothing of the larger culture at the club. Muslim former players of A. S. Menora came to express their sadness at the actions of these two players and their own ongoing fidelity to the association. All other Muslim players remained and continued to play. In 2005, A. S. Menora president Simon Dahan estimated that roughly a third of the two hundred players at the club were Muslim (with another third Christian and the remaining third Jewish).[24]

Broader studies of Muslim and Jewish opinion suggest that in the months preceding the attacks on Charlie Hebdo and Hyper Cacher, Muslim anti-Jewish hostility and Jewish fear of Muslims were already on the rise.[25] In November 2014, a survey from the French polling firm Fondapol showed that more than half of Muslims in France believed Jews had too much power in the media (61 percent), the economy (67 percent), and politics (51 percent). Fifty-seven percent agreed that Zionism is "an international organization that seeks to influence the world and society to the benefit of Jews."[26] Among French Jews, a study of May 2014 by the Sephardic organization Siona found that nearly 75 percent were considering migration to Israel, 57.5 percent agreed that "Jews have no future in France," and 93 percent said the French state could not effectively combat "Islamic exclusionist and pro-Palestinian propaganda."[27] Yet it is unclear how central anti-Jewish hostility is for Muslims, or fear of Muslims is for Jews. In the same study of November 2014, more than

90 percent of Muslims surveyed indicated no objection to having a Jewish neighbor; a higher number said they either don't think anything in particular (85 percent) or are even pleased (8 percent) when they learn someone they know is Jewish; and 63 percent said they rarely or never hear Jews spoken about among their family and friends (only 6 percent said it is a frequent topic). Likewise, despite their pessimism, of the Jews who stated in May 2014 that they are considering leaving France for Israel, only 30 percent cited antisemitism as the main reason; less than half of that number had personally experienced antisemitism in the past two years.[28]

Mediterranean Mobilities, Constraints, and Fantasies

This book has explored how Jews and Muslims substantially shaped and exhibited the possibilities and contradictions of France in the twentieth century as a space of trans-Mediterranean encounter—in terms of politics, religion, demography, and culture. This occurred through a range of constantly shifting Jewish and Muslim mobilities, networks, and interactions. These were characterized both by long-standing connectivity along linguistic, culinary, musical, and other lines, and by hardening boundaries wrought by the territorial and political ambitions of nation-states, empires, and ideologies. By the early twenty-first century, it appeared that the bitter struggles of modern Mediterranean history had landed on French shores in the form of violent Jewish-Muslim conflict. Mediterranean divisions melded with the exclusionary components of Far Right ideology and republican public sameness; the combination created calcified notions of Jewish and Muslim belonging among large swaths of both groups as well as the wider French population, making conflict often appear inevitable.

In a more long-term perspective, we can find the catalysts of hardened, conflictual notions of "Jewish" and "Muslim" within the encounters that shaped the modern French Mediterranean. These include French colonialism's penchant for dividing those under French sovereignty into citizens and others; Mediterraneanism as an Algerian colonial ideology that took particular interest in ideas about both Jews and Muslims as different and threatening; the manner in which North African anticolonial nationalisms mimicked the logic of colonialism by opposing Frenchness to anything authentically indigenous, and in time fused ethnicity and religion to the exclusion of most non-Muslims; and the claims made on Jews and Muslims by transnational movements such as Zionism, Arab nationalism, and Islamism. Recently French narratives of stark division between North and South—which depict a unidirectional population movement from the Mediterranean's southern shore that at once seeks and imperils the fruits of superior French civilization—have reinforced many of these ways of thinking.[29] All of these factors unwittingly pursued a common project: the gradual destruction, first in theory and then in practice, of the capacity of most Muslims and Jews to identify in a manner that did not fit precisely into an official, circumscribed, exclusionary category backed by state sponsorship, violent disciplinary power, or both.

And yet despite, or indeed in response to, the conflicts of the early twenty-first century, a spate of popular representations have emerged that seek to recover a Mediterranean of diverse peoples and encounters, where ethnoreligious categories and identities surely exist but do not exhaust all forms of self-understanding or identification. Here the French Mediterranean becomes once more the crucible not only of division and violence but of possibility and coexistence. For instance, in Eric Emmanuel-Schmitt's best-selling play and novella turned major motion picture *Monsieur Ibrahim and the Flowers of the Koran,* Monsieur Ibrahim, a Turkish Muslim who owns a corner market in a poor Parisian neighborhood, becomes a father figure to "Momo."[30] Unlike in Romain Gary's *The Life before Us,* this time Momo is a Jewish boy named Moses. Karin Albou's 2005 film, *Little Jerusalem,* set in the Parisian banlieue of Sarcelles, home to large Jewish and Muslim populations, centers on an impossible Jewish-Muslim love. The protagonist is the rebellious teenage girl Laura of an Orthodox Jewish family from Tunisia; she meets Djamel, a Muslim coworker from Algeria. The latter's vulnerability as a sans-papiers (undocumented immigrant) and the two characters' enduring attachments to community ultimately doom their relationship.[31]

Albou's follow-up feature, *The Wedding Song* (2008), moves back in time and crosses the Mediterranean to depict a fictional relationship in World War II Tunisia.[32] Childhood friends Nour (Muslim) and Myriam (Jewish) struggle to maintain their relationship in the face of Nazi racial laws and their differing paths in family and marriage. The 2007 film *Two Women,* set in France during the second Lebanese War, portrays an Algerian-born elderly Jew named Esther, and her caretaker, Halima, a pious Algerian Muslim.[33] Even as they disagree about the contemporary violence in the Middle East, they bond over shared musical and culinary tastes; Esther's money eventually allows Halima and her husband to make the holy Muslim hajj (pilgrimage) to Mecca. A flood of memoirs, particularly by Algerian Jews, have also appeared in recent years. Like the fictional renderings, these works frequently depict at once a harmonious story of coexistence and the constrained interactions and tensions for Jews and Muslims under the French colonial order.[34] In addition, since the early 2000s, after a period of relative dormancy, many Jewish and Muslim performers and listeners with North African roots have been reviving the two groups' shared heritage of Arabic music, rediscovering sounds that elicit nostalgia for Jewish-Muslim cultural interchanges and common traditions.[35]

Thus in the very period when Jews and Muslims in France became defined more by their ethnoreligious and transnational identities, works that reached wide audiences portrayed group boundaries as not entirely rigid. According to popular culture, Jews and Muslims, especially in light of their common Mediterranean pasts, could interact on a wider range of terms, even as they remained Jews and Muslims with potentially opposing loyalties.

A similar depiction appeared, often set on the Mediterranean's southern shore, among the three dozen or so Jews and Muslims I interviewed in spring and summer 2006. Numerous individuals from a range of backgrounds seemed to be seeking, in telling me their personal story, to piece together a logic by which Jewish-Muslim relations in France had reached a crisis point. As part of this effort, they often spoke with what anthropologist Michael Herzfeld calls "structural nostalgia," that is, a "collective representation of an Edenic order—a time before time—in which the balanced perfection of social relations has not yet suffered the decay that affects everything human."[36] That is, they described with frequent nostalgia a setting where they claimed that, in the words of one interviewee, "We did not feel that there were 'Muslims' and 'Jews.' It was the same culture."[37]

Various interviewees formulated in a number of ways this previous era during which "Jews" and "Muslims" as categories did not define the two groups' relations or blurred with one another. Strasbourg Muslim community leader Fouad Daoui, for example, who grew up in Morocco, recounted for me how his grandmother would successfully arbitrate spousal disputes of neighboring Jewish couples and how on Fridays, Jews and Muslims ate couscous together. Similarly, Moroccan Jewish doctor and president of A. S. Menora Simon Dahan insisted, "Jews and Muslims lived in Morocco and Algeria always in great harmony."[38] Such accounts implicitly argue that, contrary to the current terms and frameworks of interaction, in a previous time, identities and allegiances outside of being Jewish or Muslim formed the basis of relations between the two groups.

In other instances, categories were not obliterated or denied but rather blurred, such as when Zoubida Tribak described how she moved to France as a child and befriended an Algerian Jewish schoolmate and her family, discovering Muslim-Jewish commonalities of religion, custom, clothing, food, and language.[39] The Jewish artist Patricia Jais who grew up in the Marais to Algerian Jewish parents spoke of her confusion at times between what was Jewish and what was Arab, declaring, "For me, Arabs, they're the people who resemble us a great deal." Reflecting with a poignancy that reveals further her contemporary preoccupations, she exclaims, "I am very lost in this story, very, very lost. . . . I am neither Jewish nor Arab, or [perhaps] both."[40]

These renderings suggest, intentionally or not, that categories of "Jew" and "Muslim" have only recently become leading public signifiers for large portions of the two populations in France. Yet articulations of this narrative often contain internal contradictions. Fouad Daoui noted how, as he grew up in Morocco, he heard his father and others describe someone they considered tricky or clever as "Jewish"; Daoui hastened to explain that the phrase had no pejorative connotation. As she spoke to me, Zoubida Tribak repeatedly referred to Jewish friends of past and present with declarations such as, "They are Jews, but they are very good."

In crafting a coherent account that moves from an allegedly harmonious past into the fractured present, these oral histories have typically highlighted key moments or causes of rupture in Jewish-Muslim relations. The most frequently cited fault line is the Israeli-Palestinian conflict. Mohamed Latahy, another Muslim leader in Strasbourg originally from Morocco, said that Jews and Muslims have no religious disagreement but instead "a political problem [that] concerns, primarily, Israelis and Palestinians." Latahy pinpointed the founding of the state of Israel as a chronological break point, exclaiming, "In Morocco, you must understand that the comportment of Muslims toward Jews before '48 had nothing to do with the relations after '48."[41] Others cited different dates, focusing in particular on the Six Day War. Patricia Jais, who grew up hearing about Algeria from her parents and seeing them interact with their Muslim friends in the Marais, pointed to 1967 as a moment when common culture began to break down: "[The North African Jews of my parents' circle] began to reject the Judeo-Arabic music when there were the terrible remarks with Nasser—when he made his statements about throwing Jews into the sea and all that Jews stopped listening to Arabic singers." Gilles Taieb, a Jew from Tunisia, similarly recalled that after the antisemitic riots in Tunis in June 1967 that forced his family to flee to France, the Tunisian Jews whom he knew refused for many years to listen to the Arabic music they had previously loved.[42] Even if the individual cited no specific moment of rupture, he or she often seemed haunted by the Middle East. Fouad Daoui claimed that the Israeli-Palestinian conflict is a problem that all Muslims "will share . . . because there's an injustice at the start. . . . [And as long as that injustice remains uncorrected], this will remain in the feeling of every Muslim."

Yet the Israeli-Palestinian conflict is hardly the sole source of rupture in these narratives. The other major point of focus is the end of colonialism and the massive migration of Jews and Muslims from North Africa to France. More often, it is Jews who articulate this perspective. Patricia Jaïs offers another poignant set of formulations when she speaks of the deep nostalgia for North Africa among her parents' generation, the experience they conveyed of having been "kicked out of a paradise." In discussing how the conflicts of decolonization and the Middle East ripped asunder the bonds of culture between Jews and Muslims, she turns again to family, but this time as a metaphor. "It's like," she claims, "the parents who divorce and then the children think that all will be okay between brother and sister, but then it's over, something happens."

Thus we see how, when given the opportunity to tell their personal stories of Jewish-Muslim relations, individuals have crafted narratives that at once depict an idyllic past and try to explain a painful present. Many people struggle within their testimony to fashion a coherent narrative that overcomes the contradictions of their history. Most of these narratives, even as they reveal sources of division and difference, claim that Jews and Muslims in the Francophone world once got along seamlessly enough that "there were no Jews and Muslims" or they interacted in "a familial atmosphere" with "exactly the same" customs. The same narratives suggest that at some point, based on the Israeli-Palestinian conflict, decolonization, or both, all went horribly wrong.

These personal renderings both echo and challenge the history of Jewish-Muslim relations in France. Like many other accounts throughout this book, they give narrative voice to individual Jews and Muslims; in the process, they offer pieces of a history that cuts against the hegemonic national and archival grain of fixed notions about the two groups and their relations. Moreover, we should take seriously many interviewees' insistence that "Jews" and "Muslims" only emerged recently as defining categories and boundaries. This pattern reveals at a new level—that of the *mentalités* of countless individuals—the way that Jewish-Muslim relations in postcolonial France, and more so in the twenty-first century, became saturated by political divisions.

These interviewees' words suggest that Jews and Muslims not only can trace but also resist the striking evolution recounted in these pages. Thousands of people interacted as fellow immigrants, shopkeepers and clients, monotheists of their respective religions, musicians and artists with shared North African sensibilities, friends, and even lovers. Now, according to much of French society and to their own rendering, they have become, above all, Jews and Muslims. And yet, with their stories, these individuals seek to reclaim a more malleable coexistence not defined by fixed categories. They have not lost the capacity, then, to reimagine a complex history of Muslim-Jewish kinship, even brotherhood. In thinking their way out of the present, they remind us that the future, too, may yield an unexpected narrative.

NOTES

Abbreviations

ACCM   Archives de la Chambre de Commerce de Marseille, Marseille

ACICF   Archives du Consistoire Israélite Centrale de France, Paris

ADBdR   Archives Départementales des Bouches-du-Rhône, Marseille

ADBR   Archives Départementales du Bas-Rhin, Strasbourg

AG   Archives de l'Association Génériques, Paris

AIU   Archives de l'Alliance Israélite Universelle, Paris

AJDC   Archives of the American Joint Distribution Committee, Jerusalem

AMAE   Archives du Ministère des Affaires Etrangères, Paris and LaCourneuve

AMM   Archives Municipales de Marseille, Marseille

AN   Archives Nationales, Paris

APP   Archives de la Préfecture de Police, Paris

AVCUS   Archives de la Ville et de la Communauté Urbaine de Strasbourg, Strasbourg

AVP   Archives de la Ville de Paris, Paris

CAC   Centre des Archives Contemporaines, Fontainebleau

CADN   Centre des Archives Diplomatiques de Nantes, Nantes

CAOM   Centre des Archives d'Outre-mer, Aix-en-Provence

CDJC   Centre de Documentation Juive Contemporaine, Paris

CZA   Central Zionist Archives, Jerusalem

ICJ   Institute for Contemporary Jewry (Avraham Harman Institute), Jerusalem

IPFL Inventaire Provisoire du fonds Levant

M V-M M Vichy-Maroc

Introduction

1. Archives départementales des Bouches-du-Rhône (ADBdR) (Marseille), 137 W 463, Préfecture des Bouches-du-Rhône (PBR), Cabinet du préfet, Service des affaires musulmanes, "Liste de français en provenance d'Algérie reçus au service des affaires musulmanes," 1961–1962. In my observations about this document, I have drawn substantially from both the careful analysis of Sarah Sussman, "Changing Lands, Changing Identities: The Migration of Algerian Jewry to France, 1954–1967" (PhD diss., Stanford University, 2003), 172–73, and conversations with Sussman about this document and its context in the archives. The document simply records Benisti saying that "threats" were his reason for leaving; we do not know either the source or the nature of such threats.

2. The approximately 130,000 Algerian Jews who came to France between 1961 and 1963 were about 13 percent of the roughly 1 million overall "Europeans" who arrived from Algeria at this time.

3. Adding to the challenges, while the *rapatrié* law providing aid to all "Europeans" coming from France's colonies or former colonies was passed in December 1961, the law did not apply to those coming from Algeria until April 1962.

4. See, for example, Elizabeth Friedman, *Colonialism & After: An Algerian Jewish Community* (Boston: Bergin & Garvey, 1988), chaps. 4–5.

5. See Todd Shepard, *The Invention of Decolonization: The Algerian War and the Remaking of France* (Ithaca, NY: Cornell University Press, 2006), esp. chap. 9.

6. This formulation in part echoes Ann Laura Stoler, *Along the Archival Grain: Epistemic Anxieties and Colonial Common Sense* (Princeton, NJ: Princeton University Press, 2009).

7. These questions are partly inspired by parallel and related ones of Talal Asad, *Formations of the Secular: Christianity, Islam, Modernity* (Stanford, CA: Stanford University Press, 2003), 15.

8. Gary Wilder, *The French Imperial Nation-State: Negritude and Colonial Humanism between the Two World Wars* (Chicago: University of Chicago Press, 2005).

9. Because French law has long forbidden questions about ethnicity or religion in its censuses, such statistics are notoriously problematic and only offer best estimates.

10. See esp. Maud S. Mandel, *Muslims and Jews in France: History of a Conflict* (Princeton, NJ: Princeton University Press, 2014). Like this book, Man-

del's excellent study seeks to move beyond a narrative of inevitable conflict, accounts for local specificity, and weighs carefully the impact of events in the Middle East within a distinctly French story. Where my book differs substantially is in three areas: my significant attention to the crucial developments between 1914 and 1945 (Mandel's book begins in 1948); my effort to treat developments in France and North Africa not as separate but within a larger Mediterranean story; and most important, my emphasis on the messiness of lived experiences and relationships at the ground level and on their ongoing ability to resist and even disrupt larger narratives of Muslim-Jewish conflict.

11. Ibid. is the major exception. An important anthropological treatment of the Jewish side is Kimberly Arkin, *Rhinestones, Religion and the Republic: Fashioning Jewishness in France* (Stanford, CA: Stanford University Press, 2013). Arkin focuses significant attention on growing hostility toward Muslims among young Jews in contemporary France, and gives historical perspective. The book does not, however, treat substantially the views or experiences of Muslims themselves. For a pioneering sociological comparison, see Rémy Leveau and Dominique Schnapper, *Religion et politique: juifs et musulmans maghrébins en France* (Paris: Association française de science politique, Centre d'études et de recherches internationals, [1987]). Two insightful treatments with a presentist focus are Esther Benbassa, *La république face à ses minorités: les juifs hier, les musulmans aujourd'hui* (Paris: Mille et une nuits/Fayard, 2004) and Shmuel Trigano, *La démission de la république: juifs et musulmans en France* (Paris: Presses universitaires de France, 2003). Naomi Davidson, *Only Muslim: Embodying Islam in Twentieth-Century France* (Ithaca, NY: Cornell University Press, 2012), and Shepard, *Invention*, while focused on Muslims, give significant attention to similarities and differences with Jews.

12. For major exceptions to this, see esp. Maud S. Mandel, *In the Aftermath of Genocide: Armenians and Jews in Twentieth-Century France* (Durham, NC: Duke University Press, 2003); and for religious minorities, Patrick Cabanel, *Juifs et protestants en France: les affinités electives XVIe–XXIe siècle* (Paris: Fayard, 2000). More recently, comparison has appeared in immigration history; see esp. Mary Dewhurst Lewis, *Boundaries of the Republic: Migrant Rights and the Limits of Universalism in France, 1918–1940* (Stanford, CA: Stanford University Press, 2007), and Clifford Rosenberg, *Policing Paris: The Origins of Modern Immigration Control between the Wars* (Ithaca, NY: Cornell University Press, 2006).

13. The literature produced by the new attention to empire in French history is becoming vast. Among the works that have influenced me, see esp. Frederick Cooper and Ann Stoler, *Tensions of Empire: Colonial Cultures in a Bourgeois World* (Berkeley: University of California Press, 1997); Emmanuel Blanchard, *La police parisienne et les algériens (1944–1962)* (Paris: Nouveau monde, 2011); Laurent Dubois, *A Colony of Citizens: Revolution and Slave Emancipation in the French Caribbean, 1787–1804* (Chapel Hill: University of North Carolina Press,

2004); Rosenberg, *Policing Paris;* Emmanuelle Saada, *Les enfants de la colonie: les métis de l'empire français entre sujétion et citoyenneté* (Paris: Presses universitaires de France, 2007); Shepard, *Invention;* Wilder, *The French Imperial.*

14. For the older model, particularly influential were Arthur Hertzberg, *The French Enlightenment and the Jews: The Origins of Modern Anti-Semitism* (New York: Columbia University Press, 1968); Michael Marrus, *The Politics of Assimilation: A Study of the French Jewish Community at the Time of the Dreyfus Affair* (Oxford: Clarendon Press, 1971). For the newer scholarship showing a more multifaceted French Jewish modernity, see esp. Jay Berkovitz, *The Shaping of Jewish Identity in Nineteenth-Century France* (Detroit: Wayne State University Press, 1989); Berkovitz, *Rites and Passages: The Beginnings of Jewish Culture in Modern France* (Philadelphia: University of Pennsylvania Press, 2004); Paula Hyman, *The Emancipation of the Jews of Alsace: Acculturation and Tradition in the Nineteenth Century* (New Haven, CT: Yale University Press, 1991); Lisa Moses Leff, *Sacred Bonds of Solidarity: The Rise of Jewish Internationalism in Nineteenth-Century France* (Stanford, CA: Stanford University Press, 2006); Ronald Schechter, *Obstinate Hebrews: Representations of Jews in France, 1715–1815* (Berkeley: University of California Press, 2003).

15. Much of this literature has focused on French Algeria. See esp. Valérie Assan, *Les consistoires israélites d'Algérie au XIXᵉ siècle: "L'alliance de la civilisation et de la religion"* (Paris: Armand Colin, 2012); Joshua Schreier, *Arabs of the Jewish Faith: The Civilizing Mission in Colonial Algeria* (New Brunswick, NJ: Rutgers University Press, 2010); Sarah Abrevaya Stein, *Saharan Jews and the Fate of French Algeria* (Chicago: University of Chicago Press, 2014); Benjamin Stora, *Les trois exils: Juifs d'Algérie* (Paris: Stock, 2006); Colette Zytnicki, *Les juifs du Maghreb: Naissance d'une historiographie coloniale* (Paris: Presse Universitaire Paris-Sorbonne, 2011). Regarding the wider field of Jews in colonial history, see Sarah Abrevaya Stein, "Jews and European Imperialism," in Mitchell Hart and Tony Michels, eds., *The Cambridge History of Judaism: The Modern World* (Cambridge: Cambridge University Press, forthcoming); Ethan B. Katz, Lisa Moses Leff, and Maud S. Mandel, "Engaging Jewish History and Colonial History," in Katz, Leff, and Mandel, eds., *Colonialism and the Jews* (Bloomington: Indiana University Press, forthcoming).

16. Here I am inspired by the formulation of Cooper and Stoler, "Between Metropole and Colony," in Cooper and Stoler, eds., *Tensions of Empire,* 1–55, here 1.

17. The latter have been the subject of greater research in anthropology and sociology. See, for instance, Doris Bensimon-Donath, *L'intégration des juifs nord-africains en France* (Paris: La Haye, Mouton, 1971); Claude Tapia, *Les juifs sépharades en France (1965–1985): Études psychosociologiques et historiques* (Paris: L'Harmattan, 1986). Mandel, *Muslims and Jews,* is a recent exception in the historical literature that addresses substantially North African Jews in France.

18. For two useful examples of the numerous comparative books on Muslims in Europe from a more contemporary than historical perspective: Aziz Al-Azmeh and Effie Fokas, eds., *Islam in Europe: Diversity, Identity, and Influence* (Cambridge: Cambridge University Press, 2007); Shireen Hunter, ed., *Islam, Europe's Second Religion: The New Social, Cultural, and Political Landscape* (Westport, CT: Praeger, 2002).

19. For early work, see esp. Gilles Kepel, *Les banlieues de l'Islam: naissance d'une religion en France* (Paris: Seuil, 1991); Neil MacMaster, *Colonial Migrants and Racism: Algerians in France, 1900–1962* (New York: St. Martin's Press, 1997); Benjamin Stora, *Ils venaient d'Algérie: l'immigration algérienne en France (1912–1992)* (Paris: Fayard, 1992). More recent studies include notably Davidson, *Only Muslim*; Blanchard, *La police parisienne*; and Paul Silverstein, *Algeria in France: Transpolitics, Race, and Nation* (Bloomington: Indiana University Press, 2004), which gives greater attention than most others to the interior lives and multidirectional activism of Muslims.

20. I have been influenced by the so-called archival turn, esp. Stoler, *Along the Archival Grain*; Natalie Zemon Davis, *Fiction in the Archives: Pardon Tales and Their Tellers in Sixteenth-Century France* (Stanford, CA: Stanford University Press, 1987).

21. On this point, Cooper and Stoler, "Between Metropole," 8.

22. On the value of oral histories for both incorporating the voices of ordinary people and penetrating spaces of interior life, see Paul Thompson, "History and the Community," in David K. Dunaway and Willa K. Baum, eds., *Oral History: An Interdisciplinary Anthology* (Nashville, TN: American Association for State and Local History in cooperation with the Oral History Association, 1984), 37–50. While oral histories offer important voices from the margins often obscured by state sources, the historian must be careful not to assign them redemptive value simply because they speak for a persecuted minority. Regarding the latter issue, see Annette Wieviorka, *The Era of the Witness*, trans. Jared Stark (Ithaca, NY: Cornell University Press, 2006).

23. For a valuable discussion of related issues in oral histories of women, see Kathryn Anderson and Dana C. Jack, "Learning to Listen: Interview Techniques and Analyses," in Robert Perks and Alistair Thomson, eds., *The Oral History Reader* (London: Routledge, 1998), 157–71.

24. Regarding basic challenges to oral history and possible ways of addressing them, I have drawn on esp. Donald A. Ritchie, *Doing Oral History: A Practical Guide*, 2nd ed. (Oxford: Oxford University Press), and several essays in Dunaway and Baum, eds., *Oral History*.

25. While some advocate pointed questions that push on discrepancies throughout the interview as a way to test accuracy, I favored a more open-ended format because my interviews were concerned less with precise information such as names, dates, or the order of events, and more with following those who argue

the interviewer should "allow people to speak on their own terms." See Hugo Slim and Paul Thompson, with Olivia Bennett and Nigel Cross, "Ways of Listening," in Perks and Thomson, eds., *The Oral History Reader,* 114–25, here 115. Regarding the revealing nature of anecdotes within oral histories as a genre of narrative, see T. G. Ashplant, "Anecdote as Narrative Resource in Working-Class Life Stories: Parody, Dramatization and Sequence," in Mary Chamberlain and Paul Thompson, eds., *Narrative and Genre* (New York: Routledge, 1998), 99–113.

26. For an important review and critique of this opposition, see Mark Cohen, "Myth and Countermyth," in his *Under Crescent and Cross: The Jews in the Middle Ages* (Princeton, NJ: Princeton University Press, 1994).

27. Here I have been influenced by a growing corpus of works that move beyond conventional dichotomies. See esp. Orit Bashkin, *New Babylonians: A History of Jews in Modern Iraq* (Stanford, CA: Stanford University Press, 2012); Emily Gottreich, *The Mellah of Marrakesh: Jewish and Muslim Space in Morocco's Red City* (Bloomington: Indiana University Press, 2006); Jonathan Gribetz, *Defining Neighbors: Religion, Race, and the Early Zionist-Arab Encounter* (Princeton, NJ: Princeton University Press, 2014); Mark Mazower, *Salonica, City of Ghosts: Christians, Muslims, and Jews, 1430–1950* (New York: Knopf, 2004).

28. For this broader insight, I have been influenced by Jacob Katz, *Exclusiveness and Tolerance: Jewish-Gentile Relations in Medieval and Modern Times* (New York: Oxford University Press, 1961; reprint, New York: Schocken, 1962); Lawrence Rosen, *Bargaining for Reality: The Construction of Social Relations in a Muslim Community* (Chicago: University of Chicago Press, 1984).

29. I use this term as pioneered in Frederik Barth, *Ethnic Groups and Boundaries* (Boston: Little, Brown, 1969), and used to great effect by Till van Rahden in his *Jews and Other Germans: Civil Society, Religious Diversity, and Urban Politics in Breslau, 1860–1925,* trans. Marcus Brainard (Madison: University of Wisconsin Press, 2008). This book employs the terms *ethnicity* and *ethnic* as defined by John Hutchinson and Anthony D. Smith: an ethnic group is "a named human population with myths of common ancestry, shared historical memories, one or more elements of common culture [normally these include religion, customs, or language], a link with a homeland and a sense of solidarity among at least some of its members." "Introduction" to Hutchinson and Smith, eds., *Ethnicity* (Oxford: Oxford University Press, 1996), 6–7.

30. Van Rahden, *Jews and Other Germans;* Barth, *Ethnic Groups.*

31. Van Rahden, *Jews and Other Germans,* 9.

32. Each of these elements is explored in greater detail in Chapter 2.

33. For an important exception that emphasizes the contingency of the rights and status of immigrants in interwar France, see Lewis, *Boundaries.*

34. Similar observations appear in Miriam Feldblum, "Reconsidering the 'Republican' Model," in Wayne A. Cornelius, Philip L. Martin, and James F. Hol-

lifield, eds., *Controlling Immigration: A Global Perspective* (Stanford, CA: Stanford University Press, 1994); Lewis, *Boundaries,* 13–14.

35. Saada, *Les enfants* elaborates a similar critique.

36. On pragmatic versus assimilationist versions of French nationhood and the republic, see Véronique Dimier, "For a Republic 'Diverse and Indivisible'? France's Experience from the Colonial Past," *Contemporary European History* 13, no. 1 (2004): 45–66, and "French Secularism in Debate: Old Wine in New Bottles," *French Politics, Culture and Society* 26, no. 1 (Spring 2008): 92–110. For the examples given here, see, respectively, Jean-François Chanet, *L'école ré-publicaine et les petites patries* (Paris: Aubier, 1996); Saada, *Les enfants;* Wilder, *The French Imperial.* Regarding the broader history of French citizenship in terms of law, institutions, and ideology, see esp. Rogers Brubaker, *Citizenship and Nationhood in France and Germany* (Cambridge, MA: Harvard University Press, 1992); Gérard Noiriel, *The French Melting Pot: Immigration, Citizenship, and National Identity,* ed. Charles Tilly, trans. Geoffroy de Laforcade (Minneapolis: University of Minnesota Press, 1996); Patrick Weil, *How to Be French: Nationality in the Making since 1789,* trans. Catherine Porter (Durham, NC: Duke University Press, 2008).

37. With this formulation, I do not seek to separate republic from empire, but rather to emphasize both their simultaneity and the varying degrees to which the two were implicated in one another. Others pushing in parallel directions that emphasize uneven forms of governance and legal status under French sovereignty include Wilder, *The French Imperial;* Lewis, *Boundaries;* and Elizabeth Foster, *Faith in Empire: Religion, Politics, and Colonial Rule in French Senegal, 1880–1940* (Stanford, CA: Stanford University Press, 2013).

38. Here I draw on Joan Scott, *Only Paradoxes to Offer: French Feminists and the Rights of Man* (Cambridge, MA: Harvard University Press, 1996), and *The Politics of the Veil* (Princeton, NJ: Princeton University Press, 2007), 127–29; Dimier, "For a Republic 'Diverse and Indivisible'?" and "French Secularism in Debate."

39. In part, I draw here on Arkin, *Rhinestones,* 27–33.

40. This point is persuasively argued in Jessica Marglin, "In the Courts of the Nations; Jews, Muslims, and Legal Pluralism in Nineteenth-Century Morocco" (PhD diss., Princeton University, 2013).

41. Recent years have witnessed a renewed interest in the importance of Catholicism in modern France. For the Third Republic, see esp. Ruth Harris, *Lourdes: Body and Spirit in the Secular Age* (London: Allen Lane, 1999), and Caroline Ford, *Creating the Nation in Provincial France: Religion and Political Identity in Brittany* (Princeton, NJ: Princeton University Press, 1993); with particular regard to relations with Jews, see Vicki Caron, "Catholic Political Mobilization and Antisemitic Violence in Fin de Siècle France: The Case of the Union Nationale," *Journal of Modern History* 81, no. 2 (2009): 294–346.

42. Cited in Gregory Mann, *Native Sons: West African Veterans and France in the Twentieth Century* (Durham, NC: Duke University Press, 2006), 168. The image evoked here becomes all the more striking in light of the long-standing idea of the impossibility of trying to "wash a Moor white," evoked by soap advertisers throughout much of Europe since the late nineteenth century.

43. See Chapter 6.

44. Albert Memmi, *The Colonizer and the Colonized,* trans. Howard Greenfield, intro. Jean-Paul Sartre (Boston: Beacon Press, 1965), xiii–xiv.

45. There is a considerable literature on the importance of the family to conceptions of French nationhood. Two important books that have informed my own understanding are Lynn Hunt, *The Family Romance of the French Revolution* (Berkeley: University of California Press, 1992) and Mary Louise Roberts, *Civilization without Sexes: Reconstructing Gender in Postwar France, 1917–1927* (Chicago: University of Chicago Press, 1994).

46. As shown in Amelia Lyons, *The Civilizing Mission in the Metropole: Algerian Families and the French Welfare State during Decolonization* (Stanford, CA: Stanford University Press, 2013), Muslim workers who brought families to France long received little attention from the state, perpetuating an image of Muslims' presence as temporary.

47. On this issue, see Davidson, *Only Muslim.*

48. Here I follow ibid.

1. Jewish, Muslim, and Possibly French

1. Habib, "Action humaine et Providence divine: Tradition arabe," *L'Univers israélite (UI),* 6 April 1917. *Habib* is the name in the article's byline; given the piece's tenor and the meaning of the Arabic word *habib* (love), it is likely a pen name. I give only one name when there are no other names in the cited document. Throughout this book, all translations from French are my own unless otherwise indicated.

2. According to a footnote in the newspaper, the story comes not from the Quran but rather from authoritative commentators of Islam, as related by a member of the court of the sultan of Morocco.

3. Since Habib narrated this story in French, one imagines that the initial *h* was silent, thus rendering the pronunciation "attabib," Arabic for "the doctor."

4. *UI,* founded in 1844, was close to the French consistory and addressed a more traditional audience of practicing Jews, particularly those of Ashkenazic background. At the same time, it allied itself with the consistory's support of "Franco-Judaism," the combination of fervent French patriotism in public and more privatized religious or cultural attachments to Judaism.

5. The names and physical proximity of the soldiers suggest that they were in the same unit, and thus both were likely Algerian. For North African Jewish

names, I rely on Maurice Eisenbeth, *Les juifs de l'afrique du nord: démographie et onomastique* (Algiers: Imprimerie du Lycée, 1936), and Sarah Sussman, "Changing Lands, Changing Identities: The Migration of Algerian Jewry to France, 1954–1967" (PhD diss., Stanford University, 2003), 426–29.

6. See Eugen Weber, *Peasants into Frenchmen: The Modernization of Rural France, 1870–1914* (London: Chatto & Windus, 1977).

7. I am grateful to Annette Aronowicz for bringing this possibility to my attention.

8. This partly reflects demographics: on the war's eve, there were at most fifteen thousand Muslims on the French mainland. Pascal le Pautremat, *La politique musulmane de la France au XXe siècle: de l'hexagone aux terres d'islam. Espoirs, réussites, échecs* (Paris: Maisonneuve & Larose, 2003), 279.

9. See Richard S. Fogarty, *Race and War in France: Colonial Subjects in the French Army, 1914–1918* (Baltimore: Johns Hopkins University Press, 2008). On the army's role in nation building during the Third Republic, see Weber, *Peasants into Frenchmen*. For a study of the link between military service and claims to rights in the colonial context, see Gregory Mann, *Native Sons: West African Veterans and France in the Twentieth Century* (Durham, NC: Duke University Press, 2006).

10. For shorthand purposes, I often refer to Algerian Muslims as "subjects." But from the time that they became French in nationality with the 1865 *senatus-consulte,* they had some limited rights—eligibility for civil service jobs and the right to appear as a plaintiff or a witness in a French court—that separated them from other colonial subjects.

11. My attention to religion as a major factor corresponds to the broader assertion of Stéphane Audoin-Rouzeau and Annette Becker. See especially their *14–18, retrouver la guerre* (Paris: Gallimard, 2000), and Becker's *War and Faith: The Religious Imagination in France, 1914–1940* (Oxford: Berg, 1998).

12. On this contradiction, see Todd Shepard, *The Invention of Decolonization: The Algerian War and the Remaking of France* (Ithaca, NY: Cornell University Press, 2006), chap. 1.

13. Here I have drawn especially on Ann Laura Stoler, *Along the Archival Grain: Epistemic Anxieties and Colonial Common Sense* (Princeton, NJ: Princeton University Press, 2009).

14. For overall figures of colonial workers and soldiers during the war, see Tyler Stovall, "The Color Line behind the Lines: Racial Violence in France during the Great War," *American Historical Review* 103, no. 3 (1998): 741–42, 766. Among soldiers, 173,000 were Algerian, 50,000 Tunisian, and 37,000 Moroccan. Le Pautremat, *La politique*, 146, 173. An estimated 125,000 Algerians, 38,000 Tunisians, and 9,000 Moroccans fought specifically in Europe. Marina Bertheir, Albane Brunel, Véronique Goloubinaff, Constance Lemans, Lucie Moriceau, Emmanuel Thomassin, and Damien Vitry, "Images des maghrébins dans les collections historiques de l'ECPAD," *Migrance* 38, no. 2 (2011): 10.

Among the 132,321 laborers, 78,056 were Algerians, 35,506 were Moroccans, and 18,249 were Tunisians. Benjamin Stora, *Ils venaient d'Algérie: L'immigration algérienne en France (1912–1992)* (Paris: Fayard, 1992), 14. These figures for laborers are total, rather than the number in France at any one time. In October 1918, for instance, 64,871 North African laborers were employed in the metropole. B. Nogaro and Lucien Weil, *La main-d'oeuvre étrangère et coloniale pendant la guerre* (Paris: Presses Universitaires de France; New Haven, CT: Yale University Press, 1926), 26. Some 200,000 West Africans also fought in the war. Figure from Mann, *Native Sons,* 17. The numbers of Muslims among West African troops are difficult to determine. Even as parts of West Africa had been majority-Muslim for centuries and the war fell during a period when Islam was expanding its presence in the region (1880–1940), African animism still remained widely practiced. See Cécile Laborde, *La Confrérie Iayenne et les Lébou du Sénégal: Islam et culture traditionnelle en Afrique* (Bordeaux: Université Montesquieu-Bordeaux IV, 1995). Due to this lack of clarity, as well as the much smaller numbers of West Africans who resided in France during most of the period covered in this study, I concentrate heavily on North African Muslims. Unless otherwise indicated, when I refer to Muslims, I mean those from Algeria, Tunisia, or Morocco and their descendants.

15. Stovall, "The Color Line," treats such differentiation as almost immediate on arrival in France. Clifford Rosenberg, *Policing Paris: The Origins of Modern Immigration Control between the Wars* (Ithaca, NY: Cornell University Press, 2006), 116–19, 125, argues that the racial status of colonial immigrants was initially ambiguous and became ingrained only between the wars.

16. Of Jewish soldiers, sixteen thousand were native-born French Jews, eighty-five hundred Jewish immigrants, over thirteen thousand Algerian Jews, and several hundred Tunisian and Moroccan Jews, mostly in the Foreign Legion. For the numbers of native-born and Algerian Jews, see Philippe E. Landau, *Les juifs de france et la grande guerre: un patriotisme républicain, 1914–1941* (Paris: Editions CNRS, 2000), 26, 33. For the numbers of Jewish immigrants, see Esther Benbassa, *The Jews of France: A History from Antiquity to the Present,* trans. M. B. DeBevoise (Princeton: Princeton University Press, 1999), 137. In order to determine the number living in the metropole, I have subtracted out those native and immigrant Jews in the French armies from the commonly given population estimate of 110,000 for the eve of the war.

17. Because France had not yet completed its conquest of the Algerian south in 1870, the law did not give citizenship to the several thousand Jews living in the Mzab region of the Algerian Sahara.

18. There was considerable variation along lines of locale, educational background, and class. On the ways that Jews often publicly adopted a European identity but maintained Algerian traditions in interior spaces, see Elizabeth Friedman, *Colonialism & After: An Algerian Jewish Community* (South Hadley, MA: Bergin & Garvey, 1988).

19. See Derek J. Penslar, *Jews in the Military: A History* (Princeton, NJ: Princeton University Press, 2013), chap. 2.

20. For Jewish motivations during the war and the impact of the Dreyfus affair, see Landau, *Les juifs.*

21. Quoted and translated in Sylvain Halff, "The Participation of the Jews of France in the Great War," *American Jewish Yearbook* 21 (1919–1920): 78–79. I have made modifications for American spelling.

22. Initially foreign-born Jews volunteered for the Foreign Legion. After a wave of antisemitism that helped lead to a mutiny of legionnaires in summer 1915 and the subsequent disbanding of part of the legion, foreign Jews born in another allied country had the option of joining the regular French army or returning to their native country. Landau, *Les juifs,* 44–47; Halff, "The Participation," 81–82, and, for the case of Ottoman Jews, 86–89.

23. The *Archives israélites (AI),* founded in 1840, was the leading voice of acculturated republican Judaism. It addressed an educated audience, but not one particularly steeped in Jewish learning. Both *AI* and *UI* shied away from political controversy. For these journals' treatment of Jewish patriotic sacrifice, see, for instance, Hippolyte Prague, "Notre devoir envers la France," *AI,* 18 February 1915, and "Quelques traits 'd'union sacrée,'" *UI,* 13 April 1917.

24. On the antisemitic wave of 1915, see Rosenberg, *Policing Paris,* 45–46; on antisemitic publications, see Landau, *Les juifs,* 67–77.

25. See Gilbert Meynier, *L'Algérie révelée, la guerre de 1914–1918 et le premier quart du siècle* (Geneva: Librairie Droz, 1981), 88–104.

26. A number of Algerian Muslims volunteered, particularly early in the war; conscription was also instituted by 1915, and it intensified as the war lengthened. For the varying recruitment and conscription policies and procedures across the Maghreb, see Fogarty, *Race,* chap. 1; Le Pautremat, *La politique,* 144–47.

27. Quotation from Richard Fogarty, "Between Subjects and Citizens: Algerians, Islam and French National Identity during the Great War," in Paul Spickard, ed., *Race and Nation: Ethnic Systems in the Modern World* (New York: Routledge, 2005), 177.

28. On World War I citizenship debates, see ibid. Retaining their "personal status" meant that Muslims remained governed by Islamic courts in a limited domain that included questions of marriage, divorce, paternity, and inheritance. Such a situation had existed since the *senatus-consulte* of 1865 that gave Muslims of Algeria the right to apply for French citizenship, but only if they agreed to voluntarily give up their personal status.

29. Le Pautremat, *La politique,* 147–49, 157. One particularly significant piece of enemy propaganda was the booklet of an Algerian deserter, Boukabouya Rabah, under German and Ottoman patronage: Lieutenant El Hadj Abdallah [pseudonym of Boukabouya], *L'islam dans l'armée française (Guerre de 1914–1915)* (Constantinople, 1915; 2nd ed., Lausanne, 1917), briefly discussed below. On Boukabouya's publication and its impact, see Fogarty, *Race,* 183–89.

30. Le Pautremat, *La politique,* 151–58; Meynier, *L'Algérie révélée,* 415–18.

31. See Meynier, *L'Algérie révélée,* 415–59; Belkacem Recham, "Les musulmans dans l'armée française, 1830–1945: Mercenaires ou citoyens?" *Migrance* 38, no. 2 (2011): 28–29; Le Pautremat, *La politique,* 158–61. On the welcome of Muslims in the metropole, see Stovall, "The Color Line," 766–77; Meynier, *L'Algérie révélée,* 436–68; Mann, *Native Sons,* 164–65.

32. Admittedly, given the wartime ban on Algerian Muslim-owned press and the few French-educated Muslims, Muslim-authored or -oriented presses were likely to favor assimilationist positions. Neil MacMaster, *Colonial Migrants and Racism: Algerians in France, 1900–62* (New York: St. Martin's Press, 1997), 51, uses the term *indigénophile* for native French who supported greater Muslim rights in Algeria without opposing colonialism. In 1902 and 1903, Barrucand and Isabelle Eberhardt began to publish *El Akhbar* in French and Arabic, making it the first such newspaper in Algeria. Many Muslims contributed, and it appeared in Algeria and the metropole. On Barrucand, see Céline Keller, "Victor Barrucand, dilettante de la pensée," *Histoires littéraires* 8 (2001): 38–47; Christine Drouot and Olivier Vergniot, "Victor Barrucand, un indésirable à Alger," *Revue de l'Occident musulman et de la Méditerranée* 37 (1984): 31–36. *L'Islam,* run by Sadek Denden, a Muslim former functionary, was the mouthpiece of the Young Algerians movement, made up of Muslims from notable families or who had gained notice through the French schools, military, or administration. Allied with French liberal reformers, the movement demanded equality for Algerian Muslims. Due to a wartime shortage of resources, *L'Islam* published only during the opening months of combat, then reemerged as *L'Ikdam* in 1919.

33. Sadek Denden, "Aux musulmans algériens!" *L'Islam,* August 4, 1914. Similar themes were sounded by some Muslims as they went into battle. See, for instance, Fogarty, *Race,* 193.

34. On this issue in broader Jewish military history, see Derek Jonathan Penslar, "An Unlikely Internationalism: Jews at War in Modern Western Europe," *Journal of Modern Jewish Studies* 7, no. 3 (2008): 309–23.

35. Centre des archives d'outre-mer (CAOM) (Aix-en-Provence), 81 F 834, correspondence of the Interior Ministry, July–August 1915. The source mentions only Muslims, but the regiment also included Jews.

36. For Muslims, CAOM, 81 F 834, correspondence of the Direction of Municipal Affairs, April 1915; for Jews, see Halff, "Participation of the Jews," 93; Serge Barcellini, "Les monuments en homage aux combatants de la 'Grande France' (armee d'Afrique et armée coloniale)," in Claude Carlier and Guy Pedroncini, eds., *Les troupes coloniales dans la grande guerre* (Paris: Economica, 1997), 123. Barcellini notes that the vaguer language of instructions for Jews reflected the fact that the French were not in a propaganda war for their loyalty.

37. Twenty-one were army corps chaplains, eight were in heavily Jewish divisions, and five were at fortified locations. Halff, "Participation of the Jews," 90.

38. In spring 1915, for instance, Paris's chief rabbi, Jean Dreyfus, successfully solicited contributions from the community for Passover *matzah* for soldiers. "La paque de nos soldats," *AI*, 25 March 1915; "Le Péssah de nos soldats," *UI*, 23 April 1915.

39. Halff, "Participation of the Jews," 93–94. The quoted phrasing here comes from 93n23 (Halff was himself a Jewish veteran).

40. On the first point, see Naomi Davidson, *Only Muslim: Embodying Islam in Twentieth-Century France* (Ithaca, NY: Cornell University Press, 2012). Davidson sees the notion of Muslim practices as "embodied" as the leading factor in the state's greater wartime support for Islamic practices than Jewish ones. See ibid., 66–68.

41. For Muslim clerics and Quran distribution, see Meynier, *L'Algérie révélée*, 438–40, 455; Fogarty, *Race*, 187–89. For Muslim food, see Le Pautremat, *La politique*, 148, 153–54; Meynier, *L'Algérie révélée*, 455–56; Recham, "Les musulmans," 34.

42. See Richard S. Fogarty, "L'identité en question: l'islam, la captivité, et les soldats nord-africains pendant la Grande Guerre," *Migrance* 38, no. 2 (2011): 37–52.

43. On the debates about Islam's compatibility with Frenchness, see Fogarty, *Race*, 178–83, 230–69. Depont's quotation is cited on page 180.

44. Regarding the Foreign Legion, Muslim tirailleurs initially fought only in divisions of North Africans, but by 1918, twelve French infantry divisions included tirailleurs. The legion had long been part of the African Army, and so it often fought alongside the tirailleurs. Anthony Clayton, *France, Soldiers and Africa* (London: Brassey's Defence Publishers, 1988), 223–43. For a vivid example of Jewish-Muslim interaction in the legion, see Emile Cahen, "Les ouvrages blancs," *AI*, 17 June 1915.

45. The metropolitan-based component of La Coloniale, inaccurately but tellingly nicknamed Coloniale blanche, included infantry and artillery forces of metropolitan (and a few Algerian) French citizens, and colonial French citizens from the pre-Revolutionary colonies. These units fought alongside the *tirailleurs sénégalais,* the name given to 192,000 of France's 200,000 West African soldiers during the war, who included many Muslims (see note 14). Tiny numbers of Algerian Jews served in the tirailleurs sénégalais, with more in the colonial infantry, artillery, and medical units. The Algerian Jewish honor book, *Le Livre d'or du jüdaisme algérien* (Algiers: Comité algérien d'études sociales, 1919), includes five Jews in the Senegalese units and another twenty-three total from La Coloniale; ten Jews in the "African battalions" are cited in "Les juifs aux bataillons d'Afrique," *AI*, 24 January 1918. On La Coloniale's origins and development, see Clayton, *France, Soldiers,* chap. 10; Mann, *Native Sons.* Regarding West African soldiers in World War I, see esp. Marc Michel, *L'appel à l'Afrique: Contributions et reactions à l'effort de guerre en A.O.F., 1914–1919* (Paris: Publications de la Sorbonne, 1982).

46. France needed troops to monitor its African possessions and, at times, to put down insurrections. Many regiments moved between theaters. See Clayton, *France, Soldiers*, 94–106.

47. I have drawn this claim in part from Meynier, *L'Algérie révélée*, 441.

48. See ibid., 440–54, 456–58; Jean-Charles Jauffret, "La Grande Guerre et l'Afrique Française du Nord," in Carlier and Pedroncini, eds., *Les Troupes Coloniales*, 97–112.

49. Fogarty, *Race*, 78–80; Clayton, *France, Soldiers*, 96–97, 249. In each of these cases, the number of regiments expanded over the course of the war.

50. On Jews in the Zouaves, see Meynier, *L'Algérie révélée*, 85. Figures are from Le Pautremat, *La politique*, 144.

51. Conscription was never instituted in Morocco during the war, and Tunisian Jews served mostly in the Foreign Legion (see the discussion below for more detail on the latter). Yet the *Livre d'or* shows that a few Jews from both Morocco and Tunisia served in the tirailleurs.

52. Meynier, *L'Algérie révélée*, 395, 418; Clayton, *France, Soldiers*, 206. In 1917, Clayton notes, an additional "3ᵉ Mixte du Levant" regiment formed (249). In early 1918, the Zouave battalions were removed from all but one of these regiments (206).

53. These were the Thirty-Seventh, Thirty-Eighth, Forty-Fifth and "Moroccan" divisions (so called simply because they were stationed in Morocco at the outbreak of the war). See Clayton, *France, Soldiers*, 94–96; Meynier, *L'Algérie révélée*, 418; Halff, "Participation of the Jews," 73.

54. Each regiment of the Chasseurs included a Muslim contingent, and these units often fought alongside the Spahis; as of the mid-1940s, about 33 percent of artillery personnel were Muslims. Clayton, *France, Soldiers*, 216–20, 287–88.

55. *Livre d'or*. Since according to the 1905 law of separation, French government documents by law generally do not indicate the religious background of individuals, the *Livre d'or* is the rare type of source that identifies clearly Jews across various military units. Thus it becomes valuable, among other things, as the source for a statistical sample.

56. *Livre d'or*. Thirty-nine are listed simply as "tirailleurs," five as "Algerian tirailleurs," two "Moroccan tirailleurs," one "Kabyle worker," thirty-three in mixed Zouave-tirailleur units, five Spahis, and five interpreters. Fifty-four Jews come from artillery units that included Muslims, and thirty-one from the Chasseurs d'afrique. I have counted Jews as part of artillery units that included Muslims only if their unit name in the *Livre d'or* corresponds to known units or types of units in the African Army. The numbers of Chasseurs include Jews who may have served in the Spahis. In many cases, the soldier's unit is not indicated. A recent new edition with a names index has helped, but repeated names and missing biographical information make it impossible to determine an exact

total. *Le livre d'or du judaïsme algérien (1914–1918)* (Paris: Cercle de Généalogie Juive, 1919; with the collaboration of Georges Teboul and Jean-Pierre Bernard, 2000). While the reference to a Jewish "Kabyle worker" is surprising, other sources indicate that there were a few Jews among the North African laborers in France. See Nogaro and Weil, *La main-d'œuvre*, 26.

57. *Livre d'or.* Clayton, *France, Soldiers*, 248.

58. Divisional festivals typically included sporting competitions and performances of popular North African songs and dances; they culminated with a review of the troops during which Zouaves, French tirailleurs, and North African tirailleurs all sang together about the achievements of their division. See Meynier, *L'Algérie révélée*, 441–46. On Jews and Arabic coffee, "Nos illustrations," *UI*, 14 April 1916; for North African Jewish prayers, see, for example, Paul Hagauner, "Lettre d'un Aumônier," *AI*, 23 September 1915, and 26 October 1916. On Muslim religious practices, see Meynier, *L'Algérie révélée*, 455–56; on Muslims and coffee, see Le Pautremat, *La politique*, 148, 153; on Arabic spoken among Jewish soldiers, see, for example, Un aumônier israélite, "Le séder sur le front," *UI*, 9 April 1915.

59. Because tirailleurs from Senegal had the longest history, this name was given to describe all native infantrymen from France's colonies in sub-Saharan Africa.

60. Clayton, *France, Soldiers*, 93–105. For racial distinctions, see Fogarty, *Race*, chaps. 2–3. For mixed units, see 67–72.

61. *Livre d'or;* Clayton, *France, Soldiers*, 287–88.

62. Indochinese and Madagascans were the exception. See Fogarty, *Race*, 64–66.

63. On tasks of French and native soldiers, see Clayton, *France, Soldiers*, 287, and on North Africans as light-skinned, 244.

64. Quotation from Fogarty, "Between Subjects," 183.

65. A professional class of Jewish officers had emerged in the French military by the late nineteenth century; a number of Jews even took up posts in the colonies. See Penslar, *Jews in the Military,* chap. 3. During the war, some Jews were commanding officers in units that included Muslims, such as Captain Emile-Philippe Moog of the Fifth Regiment of Spahis, cited in the pamphlet *Les Juifs et la guerre, première partie* ([Paris], [1915–1916]), in Freidus Collection, Klau Library, Hebrew Union College, Cincinnati, 58. On this issue for Jewish Algerian soldiers during the war, Landau, *Les Juifs*, 34; for Muslims, Meynier, *L'Algérie révélée*, 416–17; Le Pautremat, *La politique*, 167–74.

66. *Livre d'or.*

67. Sometimes, for a particular mission, a two- or three-battalion regiment would first form a "tirailleur de marche" regiment, which was a single battalion regiment composed of trained field personnel. Clayton, *France, Soldiers,* 16.

68. Examples from *Livre d'or*, 19, 76, 165.

69. Excerpted in Centre des archives diplomatiques de Nantes (CADN), 1TU/125/11, extracts of letters from tirailleurs, n.d., circa November 1914.

70. "Un service patriotique à Alger," *AI*, 23 March 1916. Further citations of the speech from this source.

71. See Fogarty, *Race*, 12.

72. Fridman appears here to be quoting from Isaiah 63:8, which translates as: "For He [God] said: 'Surely they are My people, children that will not deal falsely'; so He was their Saviour." *Midrash* is the term used for Jewish commentaries, glosses, and explanatory stories in relation to the Bible.

73. The AIU aspired, largely through the establishment of hundreds of schools, to bring the model of civilized, successful French Jewry to coreligionists across North Africa, the Middle East, and Central Asia. See esp. Michael Graetz, *The Jews in Nineteenth Century France: From the French Revolution to the Alliance Israélite Universelle,* trans. Jane Marie Todd (Stanford, CA: Stanford University Press, 1996); Aron Rodrigue, *French Jews, Turkish Jews: The Alliance Israélite Universelle and the Politics of Jewish Schooling in Turkey, 1860–1925* (Bloomington: Indiana University Press, 1990).

74. Archives de l'Alliance Israélite Universelle (AIU) (Paris), Algeria, IIC-2, correspondence of 5 February and 10 March 1915. For broader issues of discrimination, see Landau, *Les juifs,* 70–71.

75. AIU, Algeria, IIC-3, unsigned letter from M. Guéron, 11 May 1915.

76. Abdallah [pseudonym of Boukabouya], *L'islam dans l'armée française,* 4, 14, 17.

77. CADN, 1TU/125/11, extracts of letters from tirailleurs, n.d., circa November 1914.

78. CADN, 1TU/125/10, memo from the Minister of the War to the Resident-General, 21 October 1916; Direction des affaires politiques et commerciales, memo from the Resident-General, "Incorporation des sujets tunisiens israélites," 16 November 1916. The quotations come from the second document.

79. For a balanced account of Tunisian Jewry during World War I that, while not discussing Alapetite's memo, offers a useful contrast to his claims, see Philippe E. Landau, "Les juifs de Tunisie et la grande guerre," *Archives juives* 32, no. 1 (1999): 40–52.

80. CADN, 1TU/125/13, Direction des Services Judiciaires, report of 21 December 1916.

81. Regarding both Jewish patriotism and anti-Jewish violence in Tunisia during the war, see Landau, "Les Juifs de Tunisie," 44–48.

82. Numerous documents in CADN, 1TU/125/31. Space does not permit greater detail here on this tumultuous period, but I hope to write a careful analysis of it in a future research project.

83. On the considerations for who the Europeans appointed as interpreters in the nineteenth century, Raymond Mopoho, "Statut de l'interprète dans

l'administration coloniale en Afrique francophone," *Meta* 46, no. 3 (2001): 615–26. For general remarks on Jews as frequent interpreters, H. Prague, "Revue de l'Année Israélite," *Annuaire des Archives israélites*, 1929–30; Meynier, *L'Algérie révélée*, 85. For greater detail (in the form of lists of names that can often be identified as Jewish), Jules Baruch, *Historique des corps des officiers interprètes de l'Armée d'Afrique* (Constantine: D. Braham, 1901). A few, like Baruch himself, served as interpreter-officers. *Livre d'or*, 22. On the role of interpreters during the war, see Meynier, *L'Algérie révélée*, 416, 438–39, 455; Fogarty, *Race*, 141–49.

84. CADN, 1TU/125/9, Direction des Services Militaires, 4ᵉ bureau, Afrique du Nord, report on "la visite du 4ᵉ Régiment de marche de tirailleurs (Tunisiens)," 22 March 1918.

85. CADN, 1TU/125/22, 8ème Région térritoriale, Etat-Major, surveillance report from military interpreter, 9 February 1915.

86. Ibid.

87. See Fogarty, *Race*, 191–201.

88. There were also a few Muslim interpreters. On sexual encounters and the colonial, see esp. Ann Laura Stoler, *Carnal Knowledge and Imperial Power: Race and the Intimate in Colonial Rule* (Berkeley: University of California Press, 2002). Regarding this issue during the war, see Stovall, "The Color Line"; Fogarty, *Race*, chap. 6.

89. Meynier, *L'Algérie révélée*, 273–74; see also 433. West Africans had substantially higher mortality rates and were even more often used as "cannon fodder." See Fogarty, *Race*, 86–87.

90. The rights of Muslims regarding vacation time improved significantly over the war. Meynier, *L'Algérie révélée*, 420–25.

91. This account, originally from the newspaper *La Sarthe*, then appeared in "Honneur à un Zouave israélite," *AI*, 22 April 1915, and elsewhere. It should not be altogether surprising that Leguay was able to address the Muslim soldiers in Arabic. He had spent considerable time in several North African posts in the late nineteenth century, when significant numbers of French officers were still becoming "Arabized" through special language training (this was less the case by the time of World War I). Moreover, for such ceremonies, even non-Arabic speakers might have a transliteration written out for them ahead of time by an interpreter. A sketch of Leguay's career appears at http://military-photos.com /leguay.htm. Regarding French Arabists and colonial Algeria, see Alain Messaoudi, *Les arabisants et la France coloniale: Savants, conseillers, médiateurs (1780–1930)* (Lyon: ENS Éditions, 2015). My thanks to Messaoudi for helping me think through this question.

92. While many Algerian Jews still spoke Judeo-Arabic, most, unlike many Muslims, also spoke French.

93. On the Kabyle myth, see Patricia Lorcin, *Imperial Identities: Stereotyping, Prejudice, and Race in Colonial Algeria* (New York: Saint Martin's Press,

1995). On perceptions of Kabyles and Arabs specifically as soldiers, see Fogarty, *Race,* 31.

94. AIU, Algeria, IIC3, unsigned letter to M. Guéron, May 1915. The story appeared in the *AI,* the *UI,* and, soon after the war, in Halff, "Participation of the Jews," 74, and the *Livre d'or,* 29–30.

95. See Joshua Schreier, *Arabs of the Jewish Faith: The Civilizing Mission in Colonial Algeria* (New Brunswick, NJ: Rutgers University Press, 2010), esp. chaps. 3 and 5.

96. "Israélites algériens et tirailleurs indigènes," *UI,* 22 September 1916.

97. For broader racial perceptions of colonial soldiers, see Fogarty, *Race.* On exoticized depictions of North Africans, Meynier, *L'Algérie révélée,* 436–40; Mann, *Native Sons,* 164. For racial anxieties about colonial subjects, Stovall, "The Color Line," 747–48, 761–62.

98. For such a mention of Jewish *tirailleurs,* see, for example, "La paque de nos soldats," *AI,* 25 March 1915.

99. "A la gloire des Zouaves israélites," *AI,* 28 October 1915.

100. Penslar, *Jews and the Military,* 69–70.

101. Regarding Protestant efforts to highlight participation in the *union sacrée,* see Laurent Gambarotto, *Foi et patrie: La prédication du protestantisme français pendant la Première Guerre mondiale* (Geneva: Labor et Fides, 1996), 2:358. My thanks to Emily Machen for recommending this source.

102. Maurice Barrès, *Les diverses familles spirituelles de la France* (Paris, 1917). *L'écho de Paris* had a sizable circulation: 430,000. Landau, *Les juifs,* 55.

103. On nineteenth-century Jewish anti-Catholicism, see esp. Ari Joskowicz, *The Modernity of Others: Jewish Anti-Catholicism in Germany and France* (Stanford, CA: Stanford University Press, 2014); Lisa Moses Leff, *Sacred Bonds of Solidarity: The Rise of Jewish Internationalism in Nineteenth-Century France* (Stanford, CA: Stanford University Press, 2006).

104. "Hier et aujourd'hui," *AI,* 25 May 1916.

105. Barrucand, "Familles spirituelles," *El Akhbar (EA),* 1 June 1917. For more on Barrucand and *EA,* see note 32.

106. Letter from Maurice Barrès, printed as part of story, "Dans la fraternité des armes," *EA,* 1 July 1917.

107. On Barrucand's previous history in the Dreyfus affair and his mission to Algeria, see Drouot and Vergniot, "Victor Barrucand," 31–32.

108. Grand-Rabbin Homel Meiss, "La paix" (1919), in his *Religion et patrie* (Paris: Librarie Durlacher, 1922), 341.

109. See Meiss, "Schabouot" (1915) and "Rosch-Haschana, le devoir" (1916), in his *Religion et patrie.*

110. For a typical example, Prague, "Et l'union sacrée," *AI,* 1 July 1915. For a rare exception in the press, Cahen, "Illusion Boche!" *AI,* 10 June 1915.

111. In terms of Protestant numbers: of five hundred pastors, evangelists, and missionaries who served in the war, forty-two died. A survey of memorial walls in fourteen Protestant churches totals over fifteen hundred soldiers. Yet it is unclear how many total Protestants fought and died in the war. Gambarotto, *Foi et patrie*, 2:358.

112. Nogaro and Weil, *La main-d'oeuvre*, 26.

113. On the SOTC, Stovall, "The Color Line," 744–46. On Algerian workers' interactions with French natives, Meynier, *L'Algérie révelée*, 459–84.

114. Driss Maghraoui, "The 'Grand Guerre Sainte': Moroccan Colonial Troops and Workers in the First World War," *Journal of North African Studies* 9, no. 1 (2004): 1–21; Augustin Bernard, *L'Afrique du nord pendant la guerre* (Paris: Presses universitaires de France; New Haven: Yale University Press, 1926), 13.

115. Maghraoui, "The 'Grand Guerre Sainte,'" 18. As of 1916, Moroccan workers generally made a minimum of 2 francs versus a minimum of 4.50 francs for French workers. Bernard, *L'Afrique du nord*, 18.

116. For Muslim neighborhood patterns and visits to kosher butchers, Meynier, *L'Algérie révelée*, 475–77. For Jewish neighborhoods, I have drawn from Michel Roblin, *Les juifs de Paris: Démographie—économie—culture* (Paris: Éditions A. et J. Picard, 1952), 82–85; Richard Ayoun and Bernard Cohen, *Les juifs d'Algérie: 2000 ans d'histoire* (Paris: Jean-Claude Lattès, 1982), 231–33; Annie Benveniste, *Le Bosphore à la Roquette: La communauté judéo-espagnole à Paris (1914–1940)* (Paris: L'Harmattan, 1989); Florence Berceot, "Renouvellement socio-démographique des juifs de Marseille 1901–1937," *Provence historique* 175 (1994): 39–57. For Muslim awareness of Jewish slaughter practices in North Africa and Muslim travelers visiting kosher butchers in nineteenth- and early twentieth-century Europe, see Stacy E. Holden, "Muslim and Jewish Interactions in Moroccan Meat Markets, 1873–1912," in Emily Benichou Gottreich and Daniel J. Schroeter, eds., *Jewish Culture and Society in North Africa* (Bloomington: Indiana University Press, 2012), esp. 160–63. Where there are differences between Jewish and Muslim ritual slaughter practices, the halacha (Jewish law) is generally stricter than the sharia (Islamic law). The one exception is that many interpretations of sharia require a blessing be said over each animal before killing it, whereas halacha allows for the slaughtering of a series of animals consecutively following a single blessing, so long as there is no significant pause between the killings.

117. "La fête du Ramadan," *Le journal*, 28 July 1916, in Archives de la préfecture de police (APP) (Paris), BA 2171, dossier on Ammou Missoum Chekroum, 1916–1917. Aïd el-Fitr ends the month-long holy fast of Ramadan.

118. APP, BA 2171, dossier on Chekroum. All subsequent information on this event comes from this dossier.

119. Quotation from APP, BA 2171, dossier on Chekroum, letter of 13 July 1917.

120. See Davidson, *Only Muslim,* 76–81.

121. Regarding the lack of Muslim response to wartime state-sponsored religious events and locales, see Meynier, *L'Algérie révélée,* 455. It is unclear whether Chekroum sought to mislead Muslims or was mistaken about the holiday's date.

122. The figure of seven hundred to eight hundred appears in two reports, but another speaks of only fifteen people.

123. APP, BA 2171, report of the Service des Renseignements Généraux (RG Report), 2 August 1916.

124. *Zaouïa,* the term for traditional Muslim (often Sufi) brotherhoods, literally refers to their physical space, typically a central complex featuring a prayer space, school, and living quarters.

125. On surveillance and Muslim gatherings during the war, Le Pautremat, *La politique,* 151–58; Meynier, *L'Algérie révélée,* 415–18.

126. See Pierre Birnbaum, *The Jews of the Republic: A Political History of State Jews in France from Gambetta to Vichy,* trans. Jane Marie Todd (Stanford, CA: Stanford University Press, 1996). For Reinach, I have drawn on ibid., 7–19; Wendy Ellen Perry, "Remembering Dreyfus: The Ligue des Droits de l'Homme and the Making of the Modern French Human Rights Movement" (PhD diss., University of North Carolina, 1998), 821–27; Steve Marquardt, "Joseph Reinach (1856–1921): A Political Biography" (PhD diss., University of Minnesota, 1978).

127. "De l'islam dans la guerre mondiale," *Le figaro,* 27 May 1917.

128. "Nouveaux motifs," *EA,* 16 June 1917.

129. "Une lettre de M. Joseph Reinach," *EA,* 1 July 1917.

130. For a much fuller discussion of the role and outlook of Reinach and other leading state Jews in the imperial context, see Ethan B. Katz, "Crémieux's Children: Joseph Reinach, Léon Blum, and René Cassin as Jews of French Empire," in Ethan Katz, Maud S. Mandel, and Lisa Moses Leff, eds., *Colonialism and the Jews* (Bloomington: Indiana University Press, forthcoming).

131. For the league's work in Algeria in the prewar years, see Meynier, *L'Algérie révélée,* 181. On the league's history, Perry, "Remembering Dreyfus"; William Irvine, *Between Justice and Politics: The Ligue des Droits de l'Homme, 1898–1945* (Stanford, CA: Stanford University Press, 2007). For overall figures and Jewish figures, respectively, ibid., 1, 9.

132. Meynier, *L'Algérie révélée,* 553.

133. Quote from both Zadoc-Kahn and *UI*'s response in P.R., "Un acte de justice," *UI,* 14 December 1917. During the affair, Edmond had played a role by showing his father that the document attributed to Dreyfus was a forgery. Jean-Philippe Chaumont and Monique Lévy, eds., *Dictionnaire biographique des rab-*

bins et autres ministres du culte israélite, France et Algérie, du Grand Sanhédrin (1807) à la loi de séparation (1905) (Paris: Berg International Éditeurs, 2007), 397.

134. "Un acte de justice," *UI*, 28 December 1917. See also P.R., "Un acte de justice," *EA*, 28 February 1918; "Pour les indigenes d'algérie," *UI*, 4 January 1918.

135. The Balfour Declaration, published in November 1917, stated that the British government officially supported the establishment of a Jewish homeland in Palestine, while promising not to infringe on the rights of the Arab natives.

136. Regarding Arab-Jewish relations around the question of Palestine on the eve of World War I, including in Paris, see Neville Mandel, *The Arabs and Zionism Before World War I* (Berkeley: University of California Press, 1976).

137. APP, BA 1811, Service des renseignements généraux (R-G), lengthy report of 30 July 1915, "Au sujet de sous-lieutenant Husson, du docteur Zalta, et du mouvement qu'ils ont provoqué dans les milieux syriens, libanais et sionistes." The report refers to Christians and Muslims. The ranks of the committee include those with clearly Levantine or North African Jewish names.

138. APP, BA 1811, report of 27 November 1916.

139. On Zionist activity during the war, see Paula Hyman, *From Dreyfus to Vichy: The Remaking of French Jewry, 1906–1939* (New York: Columbia University Press, 1979), 156–59. On coverage in *UI*, see, for example, letters from Lazare Dichter and Roger Lévy, *UI*, 18 January 1918; AP, "Les juifs français et le sionisme," *UI*, 12 July 1918.

140. See AP, "La route de Jerusalem," *UI*, 30 November 1917; AP, "Les réunions du dimanche 23: Conférence Victor Bérard," *UI*, 4 January 1918; AP, "Le temple et la mosqueé," *UI*, 15 February 1918 (quotation in text taken from here); Charles Wagner, "Jérusalem: centre de ralliement religieux du monde," speech reprinted in *UI*, 3 May 1918.

141. AP, "Les réunions," *UI*.

142. Landau, *Les juifs*, 35, 47, 176 cites 2,800 Algerian Jews, 1,600 foreign Jews, and therefore 3,100 native French Jews. Figures for North African Muslims vary considerably. Recham, "Les musulmans," 28. The second figure comes from combining a higher-end estimate of 35,900 Algerians and Tunisians with 9,000 Moroccans. Le Pautremat, *La politique*, 173.

2. Pushing the Boundaries of Mediterranean France

1. Elisa Camiscioli, "Reproducing the French Race: Immigration, Reproduction, and National Identity in France, 1900–1939" (PhD diss., University of Chicago, 2000).

2. Gérard Noiriel, *The French Melting Pot: Immigration, Citizenship and National Identity*, trans. Geoffroy de Laforcade (Minneapolis: University of Minnesota Press, 1996), 5.

3. Figures and proportions for foreigners and naturalized in Alain Girard and Jean Stoetzel, *Français et immigrés* (Paris: Presses universitaires de France, 1953), 17. Immigration figures, particularly for colonial migrants during this era, are inevitably approximations with estimates varying widely. The figure of 150,000 is arrived at by combining: nearly 119,000 Algerian Muslims in France (as of 1936); 10,000 to 15,000 West Africans and Madagascans (as of 1926); 4,000 to 5,000 Vietnamese (as of 1931), 10,000 Moroccans (1937), and a few hundred Tunisian and other Middle Eastern Muslim migrants (1932). For Algerian figures, Neil MacMaster, *Colonial Migrants and Racism: Algerians in France, 1900–1962* (New York: St. Martin's Press, 1997), 223; for West Africans and Madagascans, Philippe Dewitte, *Les mouvements nègres en France, 1919–1939* (Paris: L'Harmattan, 1985); on Vietnamese, Scott McConnell, *Leftward Journey: The Education of Vietnamese Students in France, 1919–1939* (New Brunswick, NJ: Transaction, 1989), 127n14, 157. For Moroccans, Archives de la prefecture de police (APP) (Paris), BA 2171, meeting of Haut comité méditerranéen (HCM), 28 October 1937. For other North African or Middle Eastern Muslims, Le Pautremat, *La politique musulmane de la France au XXe siècle: De l'hexagone aux terres d'Islam. Espoirs, réussites, échecs* (Paris: Maisonneuve & Larose, 2003), 302–3.

4. Camiscioli, "Reproducing," 13.

5. Girard and Stoetzel indicate that France's population of foreigners and naturalized peaked at almost 3.1 million in 1931. They give no indication of including colonial migrants. Therefore, I have added the above-cited figures for various groups of colonial migrants. For Jews, I have subtracted the pre–World War I population of 110,000 from the 1933 figure of 260,000 to arrive at roughly 150,000 immigrants by this time. For 1933 Jewish figures, Vicki Caron, *Uneasy Asylum: France and the Jewish Refugee Crisis, 1933–1942* (Stanford, CA: Stanford University Press, 1999), 41, 97; Jacques Adler, *The Jews of Paris and the Final Solution: Communal Response and Internal Conflicts, 1940–1944* (Oxford: Oxford University Press, 1987), 5. For pre–World War I Jewish numbers, Paula Hyman, *From Dreyfus to Vichy: The Remaking of French Jewry, 1906–1939* (New York: Columbia University Press, 1979), 16, 65, 68; Esther Benbassa, *The Jews of France: A History from Antiquity to the Present,* trans. M. B. DeBevoise (Princeton: Princeton University Press, 1999), 148–49.

6. Regarding rights and restrictions for Jews and other refugees in France at this time, see Caron, *Uneasy Asylum.*

7. For these and other key contrasts between colonial and most other immigrants in the interwar years, Clifford Rosenberg, *Policing Paris: The Origins of Modern Immigration Control between the Wars* (Ithaca, NY: Cornell University Press, 2006); Mary Lewis, *Boundaries of the Republic: Migrant Rights and the Limits of Universalism in France, 1918–1940* (Stanford, CA: Stanford University Press, 2007).

8. On SAINA's creation and evolution, Rosenberg, *Policing Paris.*

9. Here I follow Davidson, *Only Muslim: Embodying Islam in Twentieth-Century France* (Ithaca, NY: Cornell University Press, 2012), esp. 47–61.

10. On the importance of the colonial to metropolitan politics and society between the wars, see esp. Pascal Blanchard and Sandrine Lemaire, eds., *Culture impériale: Les colonies au coeur de la république, 1931–1961* (Paris: Éditions autrement, 2004); Jennifer Boittin, *Colonial Metropolis: The Urban Grounds of Anti-Imperialism and Feminism in Interwar Paris* (Lincoln: University of Nebraska Press, 2010); Elizabeth Ezra, *The Colonial Unconscious: Race and Culture in Interwar France* (Ithaca, NY: Cornell University Press, 2000); Rosenberg, *Policing Paris;* Martin Thomas, *The French Empire between the Wars: Imperialism, Politics, and Society* (Manchester: Manchester University Press, 2005); Gary Wilder, *The French Imperial Nation-State: Negritude and Colonial Humanism between the Two World Wars* (Chicago: University of Chicago Press, 2005).

11. For immigration figures, Girard and Stoetzel, *Français et immigrés,* 18.

12. In its claims about Mediterraneaness, this chapter builds on recent work showing how various migrations and relationships across the Mediterranean have long been important to France and French nationhood. See esp. Ian Coller, *Arab France: Islam and the Making of Modern Europe, 1798–1831* (Berkeley: University of California Press, 2011); Julia Clancy-Smith, *Mediterraneans: North Africa and Europe in the Age of Migration, c. 1800–1900* (Berkeley: University of California Press, 2010); and Gillian Weiss, *Corsairs and Captives: France and Slavery in the Early Modern Mediterranean* (Stanford, CA: Stanford University Press, 2011).

13. I draw this point in part from David Abulafia's definition of the distinctive historical aspects of the Mediterranean in his "Introduction: What Is the Mediterranean?" in Abulafia, ed., *The Mediterranean in History* (London: Thames & Hudson, 2003), 23, 26.

14. Peregrine Horden and Nicholas Purcell, *The Corrupting Sea: A Study of Mediterranean History* (Oxford: Wiley-Blackwell, 2000) have sought to utilize "connectivity" and diversity across microregions as a new framework for Mediterranean history, but have focused on the pre-modern period and largely on questions of physical environment. In attempting to apply this to the modern era and the kinds of linkages described here, I am influenced by Jessica M. Marglin, "Mediterranean Modernity through Jewish Eyes: The Transimperial Life of Abraham Ankawa," *Jewish Social Studies* n.s. 20, no. 2 (Winter 2014): 34–68.

15. On this set of countervailing forces as characteristic of the modern Mediterranean, see Marglin, "Mediterranean Modernity through Jewish Eyes."

16. See, for example, Hyman, *From Dreyfus;* MacMaster, *Colonial Migrants.*

17. Here in part I draw on the parallel work of Emily Gottreich, *The Mellah of Marrakesh: Jewish and Muslim Space in Morocco's Red City* (Bloomington: Indiana University Press, 2007).

18. See Clancy-Smith, *Mediterraneans,* 11.

19. Here I am significantly inspired by the framework of analysis for black Africans in Paris in this period employed in Boittin, *Colonial Metropolis.*

20. H. Boucri, "Les musulmans et la 'chehita,'" *UI,* 25 July 1930.

21. Hyman, *From Dreyfus,* 30; Adler, *The Jews,* 5.

22. See David H. Weinberg, *A Community on Trial: The Jews of Paris in the 1930s* (Chicago: University of Chicago Press, 1977), 4–5, 9n16; Michel Roblin, *Les juifs de Paris: Démographie—économie—culture* (Paris: Éditions A. et J. Picard, 1952), 72–73; Benbassa, *Jews of France,* 148–49.

23. Statistics from MacMaster, *Colonial Migrants,* 223; APP, DA 768, Official municipal bulletin of 14 December 1932.

24. Rosenberg, *Policing Paris,* 31.

25. Admittedly the question requires further study; throughout the book, I focus on neighborhoods with significant overlap that left records of everyday relations.

26. MacMaster, *Colonial Migrants,* 89–90.

27. See Benjamin Stora, *Ils venaient d'Algérie: L'immigration algérienne en France, 1912–1992* (Paris: Fayard, 1992), 446.

28. Benbassa, *Jews of France,* 148–49.

29. The focus and approach here draw on Laloum, "Des juifs d'Afrique du Nord au Pletzl? Une présence méconnue et des épreuves oubliées (1920–1945)," *Archives juives* 38, no. 2 (2005): 47–83.

30. Interview with Roger Gharbi, 6 June 2006.

31. For the Gharbis's arrival date, interview with Roger Gharbi. Figure here compiled from Archives de la ville de Paris (AVP), 2 Mi LN 1926/7, 4e, recensements de population: Saint-Gervais (jusqu'au 88 quai de l'Hotel de Ville); 2 Mi LN 1926/8, 4^e: Saint-Gervais. I examined the following streets: rues des Archives, de l'Ave Maria, d'Aubriot, des Ecouffes, Barres, Eginhard, Ferdinand Duval, du Figurier, de Fourcy, François Miron, Geoffrey l'Asnier, des Jardins Saint Paul, de Jouy, des Rosiers, Saint Antoine, and Saint Paul; Impasses d'Argenson, Guénine, and Putigneux, and the Quai and Fort de l'Hôtel de Ville. Because the French do not include religion in the census, I have relied on name, birthplace, and profession. Figures include children of marriages with only one North African or Levantine parent (the other being typically European). I have separated North African and Levantine Jews because those from Palestine appear to have included many Ashkenazim, and there is little evidence that they participated in the North African Jewish milieu.

32. Numbers of Jews and Muslims for 1936 from AVP, 2 Mi LN 1936/5, 4e: Saint-Gervais, de la place Baudoyer au 7 rue de Sévigné; 2 Mi LN 1936/7,

4e: Saint-Gervais, du 87 rue Saint-Antoine au 26 rue des Rosiers. For later arrivals, Laloum, "Des juifs," 50–53. Laloum finds 168 Jews from the Maghreb on the 1941 lists of Jews registered by Vichy. Knowing the overall number of Jews registered in Paris by Vichy was roughly half of the prewar population, it seems reasonable to estimate the 1939 population at around 300.

33. My estimate for 1936 is ninety-two Muslims.

34. Interview with Roger Gharbi; Laloum, "Des juifs," 52, 55.

35. Interview with Félix Amanou, 11 June 2006.

36. Laloum, "Des juifs," 52–55, and "Sociabilité et convivialité juive nord-africaine dans les cafés du Marais," *Cahiers du judaïsme* 26 (2009): 52–61; Archives nationales (AN), Series AJ38, 3186, dossier 10728, dossier d'aryanisation du restaurant de Sabba, Elie; 3188, dossier 14094, dossier d'entreprise de Moise Draïe, 1941–1943; interviews with Roger Gharbi; with Félix Amanou, 11 July 2006; and with Louise Jaïs (née Fhal), 5 June 2006; AN, AJ38, 3190, dossier 16 423 (section VIII NR), dossier d'aryanisation établi au nom de Vve Boukhalter, 1941–1943, 1949.

37. Interview with Louise Jaïs; interview with Félix Amanou, 11 June 2006.

38. I refer to this as Arabic music because it was, in each instance, variations on the older tradition of Arabo-Andalusian music. Arabo-Andalusian music was in fact a wide-ranging supergenre that included many styles and various fusions, and was only transformed—in both discourse and practice—into a "classical tradition" by the dialectics of colonialism. While the important presence of Jews in the Arabic music discussed here has led some to call it "Judeo-Arabic music," this term did not come into existence until the 1960s and was contested by some of its Jewish practitioners. Speaking of it as North African music is too narrow, since influences and collaborations included songs and artists from the wider Arab Middle East. I have drawn here on Hisham D. Aidi, *Rebel Music: Race, Empire and the New Muslim Youth Culture* (New York: Pantheon Books, 2014), chap. 11; Jérémy Guedj, "La musique judéo-arabe, patrimoine d'exil," in Driss El Yazami, Yvan Gastaut, and Naïma Yahi, eds., *Générations: Un siècle d'histoire culturelle des Maghrébins en France* (Paris: Gallimard in cooperation with Génériques and the Cité nationale de l'histoire de l'immigration, 2009), 148–55; Mehenna Mahfoufi, "La chanson kabyle en immigration: une retrospective," *Hommes et Migrations* 1179 (September 1994): 32–39; Hadj Miliani, "Présence des musiques arabes en France: immigrations, diasporas et musiques du monde," *Migrance* 32 (2008): 91–99.

39. Interview with Félix Amanou, 11 June 2006; interview with Roger Gharbi; interview with Louise Jaïs; Laloum, "Sociabilité et convivialité," 54.

40. Regarding Paris cafés, I have drawn on W. Scott Haine, *The World of the Paris Café: Sociability among the French Working Class, 1789–1914* (Baltimore: Johns Hopkins University Press, 1996).

41. Cited in Joan Scott, *The Politics of the Veil* (Princeton, NJ: Princeton University Press, 2007), 59–60.

42. Archives de la Ville de Paris (AVP), 2 Mi LN, 1936/5, 4e: Saint-Gervais, de la place Baudoyer au 7 rue de Sévigné; 2 Mi LN 1936/7, 4e: Saint-Gervais, du 87 rue Saint-Antoine au 26 rue des Rosiers.

43. Interview with Roger Gharbi.

44. Compiled from AVP, 2 Mi LN 1926/7, 4e; 2 Mi LN 1926/8, 4e; 2 Mi LN 1936/7, 4e.

45. On this issue, see Susan Gilson Miller and Mauro Bertagnin, eds., *The Architecture and Memory of the Minority Quarter in the Muslim Mediterranean City* (Cambridge, MA: Harvard University Press, 2010).

46. See Selma Akyazici Özkoçak, "Coffeehouses: Rethinking the Public and Private in Early Modern Istanbul," *Journal of Urban History* 33, no. 6 (2007): 965–86; Omar Carlier, "Le café maure. Sociabilité masculine et effervescence citoyenne (Algerie XVIIe-XXe siècles)," *Annales. Économies, Sociétés, Civilisations* 45, no. 4 (1990): 975–1003; Clancy-Smith, *Mediterraneans*, 38, 134, 138–39.

47. Carlier, "Le café maure," 976, 981; Özkoçak, "Coffeehouses"; Clancy-Smith, *Mediterraneans*, 38, 134, 138–39; Elizabeth Friedman, *Colonialism & After: An Algerian Jewish Community* (Boston: Bergin & Garvey, 1988), chap. 4.

48. See esp. Carlier, "Le café maure," 976, 981, 983, 985; Clancy-Smith, *Mediterraneans*, 138–39, 146; Gottreich, *The Mellah of Marrakesh*, chap. 3; Miller and Bertagnin, *The Architecture*.

49. See Carlier, "Le café maure," 985, 991–93; on gender in Paris cafés, see Haine, *The World*, chap. 7.

50. See Carlier, "Le café maure," 988, 991.

51. See Clancy-Smith, *Mediterraneans*, 37–38, 103, 292, 295; Friedman, *Colonialism*, chap. 4.

52. Richard Parks, "The Jewish Quarters of Interwar Paris and Tunis: Destruction, Creation, and French Urban Design," *Jewish Social Studies* n.s. 17, no. 1 (2010): 67–87.

53. See ibid., esp. 69–74.

54. Here I draw on the ideas on ethnicity formation of Manning Nash, *The Cauldron of Ethnicity in the Modern World* (Chicago: University of Chicago Press, 1989), esp. 11.

55. On the Berbouche, see Joëlle Allouche-Benayoun and Doris Bensimon, *Les juifs d'Algerie: Mémoires et identités plurielles* (Paris: Éditions Stavit, 1998), 206–7, 415–16.

56. See Laloum, "Des juifs," 55; interview with Roger Gharbi.

57. Interview with Félix Amanou, 11 July 2006.

58. Laloum, "Des juifs," 56–57.

59. Louise Fhal corroborates this, saying that it was only Muslims "whom we knew."

60. Interview with Félix Amanou, 11 July 2006.

61. On this last point, see James McDougall, *History and the Culture of Nationalism in Algeria* (Cambridge: Cambridge University Press, 2006), chap. 2.

62. Laloum, "Des juifs," 55–56.

63. Aidi, *Rebel Music,* 262–63.

64. On Salim Hallali, Nidam Abdi, "La chanson maghrébine orpheline," *Libération,* 13 July 2005. On Bachetarzi's early acquaintance with Yafil, see Mahieddine Bachetarzi, *Mémoires, 1919–1939* (Algiers: Editions Nationales Algériennes, 1968), 22–26. On Hallali, ibid., 357–58; 387–88; on Jews in his orchestra, 155, 276–77; on spreading news of tours in France, 131–32. On Bachetarzi and Yafil, I have drawn insight from Joshua Cole, "'A chacun son public': Politique et culture dans Algérie des années 1930," *Sociétés et représentations* 38 (2014): 21–51; Jonathan Glasser, "Edmond Yafil and Andalusi Musical Revival in Early 20th-Century Algeria," *International Journal of Middle East Studies* 44 (2012): 671–92.

65. See Cole, "'A chacun."

66. Bachetarzi, *Mémoires,* 134.

67. Aidi, *Rebel Music,* 263; Hélène Hazéra, "La douce nostalgie des chants judéo-arabes," *Alger Info,* 10 May 1996.

68. On mixed audiences, see Bachetarzi, *Mémoires,* 276.

69. Sheila Crane, *Mediterranean Crossroads: Marseille and Modern Architecture* (Minneapolis: University of Minnesota Press, 2011), 68–69.

70. Ibid., chap. 2; Sherry McKay, "Mediterraneanism: The Politics of Architectural Production in Algiers during the 1930s," *City and Society* 12, no. 1 (2000): 79–102.

71. Figure and quotation in Crane, *Mediterranean Crossroads,* 71.

72. Figures of 490,000 and over 600,000 from ibid., 27. Figures vary; for 1911, 550,000 comes from Émile Temime, "Marseille XXe: de la dominante italienne à la diversité maghrébine," *Revue européenne de migrations internationales* 11, no. 1 (1995): 9–19.

73. Temime, "Marseille," 10–11.

74. See Crane, *Mediterranean Crossroads,* 29–30, 88–90; quotation from 89–90.

75. For more exact figures, Florence Berceot, "Renouvellement sociodémographique des juifs de Marseille 1901–1937," *Provence historique* 175 (1994): 39–40, 44.

76. First figure in Michel Renard, "Aperçu sur l'histoire de l'islam à Marseille, 1813–1962: Pratiques réligieuses et encadrements des nord-africains," *Revue française d'histoire d'outre-mer* 90, no. 340–41 (2003): 279–80. For the late 1930s, estimates vary. Archives départementales des Bouches-du-Rhône (ADBdR) (Marseille), 1 M 759, Service des affaires indigènes nord-africaines

de Marseille (SAINAM), report of 21 July 1936; 76 W 205, Service des Affaires Algériennes (SAA), report of 13 October 1941; Renard, "Aperçu," 280.

77. For Jews, Berceot, "Renouvellement," 49–50, 52. For Muslims, Renard, "Aperçu."

78. Donna Ryan, *The Holocaust and the Jews of Marseille: The Enforcement of Anti-Semitic Policies in Vichy France* (Urbana: University of Illinois Press, 1996), 9–10.

79. Ibid., 16.

80. Ibid., 16–18; Berceot, "Renouvellement," 48.

81. Berceot, "Renouvellement," 48–49.

82. Renard, "Aperçu," 277–80.

83. Émile Temime, *Marseille transit: les passagers de Belsunce* (Paris: Éditions autrement, 1995), 36–37.

84. Compiled from ADBdR, 76 W 168, individual fiches, 1941.

85. Entry for the Cours de Belsunce in *Indicateur marseillais, 1936: Guide de l'administration et du commerce, annuaire des Bouches-du-Rhône* (Marseille: Société anonyme de l'indicateur marseillais, 1936), in Archives de la chambre de commerce (ACC) (Marseille).

86. Berceot, "Renouvellement," 47–49.

87. ADBdR, 76 W 168. Individual fiches of Alex, Jacqueline, Jean, and Philippe Danon, 1941.

88. ADBdR, 76 W 205. SAA, report on "Les musulmans et l'agression de Madagascar," 24 September 1942 refers to the "daily transactions" of Jewish merchants with Muslims.

89. I have drawn on entries for the rues des Chapeliers, Puvis de Chavannes, and Sainte-Barbes in the *Indicateur marseillais, 1936,* in ACC; and various records of Farhi in ADBdR, 76 W 163, FARKHI dossier, documents dated 18 May to 3 August 1943; 76 W 205, Direction générale de la sureté nationale (DGSN), Commissariat Special Marseille (CSM), memo of 17 April 1941; 76 W 206, PBdR, SAA, report on the supply of couscous and grain to Muslims, 27 May 1943; 149 W 137, Service des affaires musulmanes nord-africaines (SAMNA) and other departmental bodies, reports of April–August 1945 and September 1946.

90. Overall, the region had 28,989 Jews. See Institute for Contemporary Jewry (ICJ) (Jerusalem), Demography section, FRO 4201, *Aspects particuliers des populations Alsacienne et Mosellane—Langues—Personnes Déplacées—Religions* (1956), 235–36, 242–43; Archives du consistoire israélite du Bas-Rhin (ACIBR), CIBR 185, population figures for Jews in the Bas-Rhin and the Haute-Rhin, undated document.

91. By 1937, two thousand Jewish immigrant families lived in Strasbourg. Hyman, *From Dreyfus,* 70.

92. This is confirmed by the near total absence of Muslims in the records from this period of press surveillance, associations, and immigration at the Archives départementales du Bas-Rhin (ADBR) (Strasbourg).

93. Interview with Léon and Laurette Nisand, 20 May 2006.

94. See Alison Carrol, "Greater France in the Provinces: The Strasbourg Colonial Exhibition of 1924," in Philip Whalen and Patrick Young, eds., *Place and Locality in Modern France* (New York: Bloomsbury Academic, 2014). On the empire as "Greater France" at this time, see Wilder, *French Imperial,* esp. chap. 2.

95. Pascal Blanchard, Nicolas Bancel, Ahmed Boubeker, and Éric Deroo, eds., *Frontière d'empire, du nord à l'est: Soldats coloniaux et immigrations des Suds* (Paris: Découverte, 2008), 14.

96. ADBR, 286 D 190, dossier on visit of S. M. Sultan Moulay Youssef, July 1926.

97. When I use the term Sephardic here and elsewhere to include North African Jews, it reflects my broad conception of Sephardic Jewry as a category that includes Jews of both Iberian and Mizrahi background.

98. These figures come from the 1936 census. Cited in Benjamin Stora, *Histoire de l'Algérie coloniale (1830–1954)* (Paris: Éditions la decouverte, 2004 [1991]), 58.

99. Secondary literature on the riots remains limited. For the most balanced account, see Charles-Robert Ageron, "Une émeute anti-juive à Constantine (August 1934)," *Revue de l'Occident Musulman et de la Méditerranée* 13–14 (1973): 23–40. Joshua Cole, "Antisémitisme et situation coloniale pendant l'entre-deux-guerres en Algérie: Les émeutes antijuives de Constantine," *Vingtième siècle* 108, no. 4 (2012): 2–23, analyzes the riots' meaning and offers several ideas that have influenced my own. Robert Attal, *Les émeutes de Constantine: 5 août 1934* (Paris: Romillat, 2002), is at once memoir, history, and sourcebook of the riots (Attal's father and mother were both murdered).

100. For example, see Attal, *Les émeutes,* chap. 7. On this point, I have drawn in part from Cole, "Antisémitisme."

101. In the first instance, see in particular the declaration of Muslim leaders in Constantine made to the governor-general of Algeria immediately following the riots, cited in Attal, *Les émeutes,* 170–71.

102. On the first point, see Haine, *The World;* on the second, Carlier, "Le café maure," 994–96.

103. APP, BA 2170, Service des affaires indigènes nord-africaines (SAINA), report of 11 August 1934; BA 2172, SAINA, "Note sur l'activité de l'Etoile Nord-africaine depuis sa création jusqu'au 15 novembre 1934," 91–92. Abd el-Krim (1882/3–1962) was the Berber leader of the Rif revolt in Morocco in 1925–1926; Emir Khaled (1875–1936) was the grandson of the anticolonial Algerian hero

Abd al-Qadir, and was himself an important figure in the early development of Algerian nationalism.

104. Ibid.

105. For the gathering of 19 August, one report estimated eighteen hundred people, while two others placed attendance at seven hundred to eight hundred. APP, BA 2170, SAINA, reports of 20 and 21 August and 10 September 1934 (quotation from latter); SAINA, "Note sur l'activité," 94.

106. APP, BA 2172, SAINA, "Note sur l'activité," 91–115, 148.

107. From *El Ouma,* September–October 1934, quoted in APP, BA 2171, SAINA, "Au sujet de la dissolution et de la reconstitution de l'étoile nord-africaine," 6 September 1935.

108. An insightful brief definition of *ouma* appears in Marshall G. S. Hodgson, "Cultural Patterning in Islamdom and the Occident," in his *Rethinking World History: Essays on Europe, Islam, and World History,* ed. Edmund Burke III (Cambridge: Cambridge University Press, 1993), 136.

109. APP, BA 2170, SAINA, reports of 10 August–1 October 1934; SAINA, "Note sur l'activité," 91–115.

110. On religion and civilization within the ENA outlook and rhetoric, Rabah Aissaoui, *Immigration and National Identity: North African Political Movements in Colonial and Postcolonial France* (London: I. B. Tauris, 2009), chap. 3, esp. 77–93.

111. APP, BA 2172, SAINA, "Note sur l'activité," 108–13.

112. Belkacem's memoir in Mahfoud Kaddache and Mohamed Guenaneche, eds., *L'étoile nord-africaine, 1926–1937: Documents et témoignages pour servir à l'étude du nationalisme algérien* (Algiers: Office des Publications Universitaires, 1994).

113. APP, BA 2171, SAINA, reports of 21–22 August and 15 December 1934.

114. ADBdR, 1 M 801, correspondence of Interior Ministry with local officials of Marseille, 21 August–18 September 1934.

115. APP, BA 2172, SAINA, "Note sur l'activité," 97–100; BA 2170, SAINA, correspondence of 20 October 1934.

116. Bachetarzi, *Mémoires,* 200–205, 219.

117. For memorial services, see, for example, "Paris: A la mémoire des victimes de Constantine," *L'Univers israélite (UI),* 17 August 1934. Archives de l'Alliance Israélite Universelle (AIU) (Paris), IC-5, letter from M. Angel in Constantine, 26 October 1934, discusses one of the many fundraising campaigns.

118. Four formal reports on the riots appeared, three by leaders in the Algerian Jewish community. "Le rapport officiel du consistoire israélite," *Chalom,* September 1934; AIU, IIC-1, "Rapport de M. Eisenbeth sur le rôle de M. Morinaud dans les événements de Constantine," 21 November 1934; Fonds Jacques Lazarus (FJL), dossier II, "Conférence juive mondiale: Pogrom de Constantine 3–5 août 1934," 20–23 August 1934; Algeria, IC1, report of Confino to AIU, 15 August 1934; report from A. Sultan, 9 August 1934.

119. Alfred Berl, "L'enquête ministérielle en Algérie," *Paix et droit,* March 1935.

120. Luciania, "Un effrayant récit du pogrom," *UI,* 17 August 1934.

121. See Cole, "Antisémitisme," 9.

122. See, for example, "Les massacres de Constantine," *Archives israélites (AI),* 30 August 1934.

123. "Le rapport officiel."

124. On the term *indigène*, see Laure Blévis, "Les avatars de la citoyenneté en Algérie coloniale ou les paradoxes d'une catégorisation," *Droit et société* 48 (2001): 557–80, esp. 571–79.

125. For an example of the first, see "Le rapport officiel"; for the second, see "La situation en Afrique du Nord," *La Terre retrouvée (TR),* 25 November 1934; for the third, see quotation of Lellouche interview in Ageron, "Une émeute anti-juive," 31; for examples of the last, see "Le rapport officiel."

126. The league changed its name to the International League Against Racism and Antisemitism in 1932 but maintained the same acronym until 1979, when it became the LICRA. On the interwar history of the LICA, see Emmanuel Debono, *Aux origines de l'antiracisme: La Ligue internationale contre l'antisémitisme (LICA), 1927–1940,* preface by Serge Berstein (Paris: CNRS Éditions, 2012).

127. Weinberg, *A Community,* 27; statistics from Benbassa, *Jews of France,* 162.

128. "Le sang juif a coulé en France!" *Le Droit de Vivre,* special edition, August 1934.

129. "Après les massacres de Constantine," *Le Populaire,* 23 August 1934, found in AIU, Algeria, IIC-6.

130. "Un appel fraternal de la L.I.C.A. à nos camarades musulmans," *Le Droit de Vivre,* 22 June 1934.

131. "Un échange de lettres entre le président de l'Association cultuelle musulmane d'Oran et le président du Consistoire israélite de cette ville," *UI,* 24 August 1934 (also published in *AI* of 30 August 1934).

132. Cole, "Antisémitisme."

133. For precise figures of Jews leaving after the riots, Claude Sitbon, "Août 1934: Le pogrom de Constantine," *La Vie sépharade,* August 1984, in AIU, FJL, "Chemise Algérie."

134. Interview with Louise Jaïs, 20 June 2006.

135. J. Hadjadj, "Les anciens combattants de la L.I.C.A. exigent," *Le Droit de Vivre,* special edition, August 1934. Pierre Emmanuel, "Constantine-rouge: Kichinev II," in the same issue, mentioned the CF and SF.

136. See "Les 'croix de feu,'" *UI,* 27 December 1935.

137. See Sean Kennedy, *Reconciling France against Democracy: The Croix de Feu and the Parti Social Français, 1927–1945* (Montreal: McGill–Queen's University Press, 2007), 37, 51–52.

138. Robert Soucy, *French Fascism: The Second Wave, 1933–1939* (New Haven, CT: Yale University Press, 1995), 61.

139. On movements in Algeria, Samuel Kalman, *French Colonial Fascism: The Extreme Right in Algeria, 1919–1939* (New York: Palgrave Macmillan, 2013).

140. The historiographic debate over the fascist nature of the Croix-de-feu is long-standing and beyond the bounds of this study. A good discussion is William Irvine, "Fascism in France and the Strange Case of the Croix-de-Feu," *Journal of Modern History* 63, no. 2 (1991): 271–95; Introduction to Kennedy, *Reconciling,* treats the more recent literature.

141. See, for instance, "Les 'croix de feu' et l'antisémitisme," *UI,* 17 April 1936.

142. Soucy, *French Fascism,* 152–53. We lack anything like precise membership counts for Jews in the CF.

143. See Kennedy, *Reconciling France,* 70, 90; "Les ligues paramilitaires," *Le Droit de Vivre,* 28 March 1936.

144. Cited in Soucy, *French Fascism,* 155.

145. "Et les croix de feu?" *Samedi: Hebdomadaire illustré de la vie juive,* 27 March 1936. This journal was founded in 1936 through the merger of *Les Archives israélites* and *Le Journal juif.*

146. See Kennedy, *Reconciling France,* 62.

147. Soucy, *French Fascism,* 61.

148. Ibid., 74–80.

149. Ibid., 65.

150. APP, BA 1960, reports of 16 May and 17 July 1934; Soucy, *French Fascism,* 65.

151. Henri Chemouilli, *Une diaspora méconnue: Les juifs d'Algérie* (Paris, 1976), 165; Rosenberg, *Policing Paris,* 194; "Cent cinquante apaches de la solidarité française attaquent une dizaine de members de la L.I.C.A.," *Le Populaire,* 27 September 1935, found in APP, BA 1960. *Sidi* is Arabic for "sir"; by the mid-1930s, it was a pejorative name for North Africans in France.

152. Beyond the CF, various reports indicated that the Jeunesses patriotes, Action française, and the Francistes also recruited Muslims in France. See, for example, APP, BA 2170, "Groupements politiques musulmans," 2 February 1937.

153. Soucy, *French Fascism,* 66, 80, 329–30.

154. I have drawn my account below from APP, BA 1960, files of 25–30 September 1935; Georges Stern, "Pogrome avorté dans le 4ᵉ," *Le Droit de Vivre,* October 1935; G. S., "Les incidents de la rue vieille-du-temple," *UI,* 4 October 1935; "Correspondence," *UI,* 11 October 1935. Numerical ranges reflect discrepancies in various reports. For rising LICA-SF tensions, see Bernard Lecache, "La L.I.C.A. parle directement aux électeurs et dénonce, dans Paris, la honte du racisme," *Le Droit de Vivre,* May 1935.

155. While many reports cite "large numbers" of North Africans, none gives a numerical estimate.

156. APP, BA 2171, "Liste des rapports transmis le 13 september 1935 à M. le Directeur de la Police Judiciaire"; report of 30 January 1936; Mahfoud Kaddache, *L'Algérie des Algériens, de la Préhistoire à 1954* (Éd. Paris-Méditerranée, 2003), 727; Léon Rudin, "Rapport morale du C.C.," *Le Droit de Vivre,* November 1935.

157. See Pierre Birnbaum, *Léon Blum: A Portrait* (New Haven, CT: Yale University Press, 2015).

158. Caron, *Uneasy Asylum,* 270–71.

159. See Pierre Birnbaum, *The Jews of the Republic: A Political History of State Jews in France from Gambetta to Vichy,* trans. Jane Marie Todd (Stanford, CA: Stanford University Press, 1996); Chapter 1, this volume.

160. "La chambre des députés," *UI,* 12 June 1936.

161. Hyman, *From Dreyfus,* and Weinberg, *A Community,* both detail these divisions. On Jewish support for Blum, see the latter, 106, 115.

162. APP, BA 2273, report of a schism in the MPJ, 28 October 1936; Hyman, *From Dreyfus,*107, 210–15; Weinberg, *A Community,* 91, 120–26.

163. See Benjamin Stora, *Nationalistes algériens et révolutionnaires français au temps du front populaire* (Paris: L'Harmattan, 1987).

164. On the Association des ulamas musulmans algériens, see McDougall, *History and the Culture.*

165. Germaine Corrot, "Une tournée triomphale," *Le Droit de Vivre,* 1 February 1936.

166. The alliance proved short-lived. Michel Abitbol, *The Jews of North Africa during the Second World War*, trans. Catherine Tahanyi Zentelis (Detroit: Wayne State University Press, 1989), 39–40.

167. Elie Gozlan, "Alger: Entente entre juifs et arabes," *Samedi,* 27 March 1936.

168. Cited in Benjamin Stora, *Les trois exils: juifs d'Algérie* (Paris: Stock, 2006), 63.

169. Ferhat Abbas, "Juifs et musulmans d'Algérie," *L'Entente franco-musulmane (EFM),* 12 September 1935.

170. APP, BA 2171, report of 26 February 1936.

171. Here I draw on Nadia Malinovich, *French and Jewish: Culture and the Politics of Identity in Early-Twentieth Century France* (Oxford: Littman Library of Jewish Civilization, 2008). For an older view that saw Zionism in this period as having little impact in France beyond small immigrant circles, see esp. Michel Abitbol, *Les deux terres promises: Les juifs de France et le sionisme* (Paris: Olivier Orban, 1989); Catherine Nicault, *La France et le sionisme, 1897–1948: Une rencontre manquée?* (Paris: Calmann-Lévy, 1992).

172. For greater detail, see Ethan Katz, "Tracing the Shadow of Palestine: The Zionist-Arab Conflict and Jewish-Muslim Relations in France, 1914–1945," in Nathalie Debrauwere-Miller, ed., *The Israeli-Palestinian Conflict in the Francophone World* (New York: Routledge, 2010), 25–40, esp. 27–30.

173. "Les résultats d'une politique," *Samedi,* 25 April 1936.

174. APP, BA 2170, reports of 12 February, 2 May 1936; BA 2171, reports of 4 March 1935, and 30 April 1936; the ENA's organ, *El Ouma,* does not survive from this period, admittedly limiting our perspective. For Arslan's impact on Muslims in Europe, see Martin Kramer, "Swiss Exile: The European Muslim Congress, 1935," in Kramer, *Islam Assembled: The Advent of the Muslim Congresses* (New York: Columbia University Press, 1986). Aissaoui, *Immigration* takes a different perspective, insisting on the importance of Palestine for the ENA from an early date.

175. The extent of Jewish and Muslim participation remains unclear. Hints for Jews can be found in Weinberg, *A Community,* 129; for Muslims, APP, BA 2171, report of 20 June 1936.

176. On the second point, see Weinberg, *A Community,* 131.

177. Charles-Robert Ageron, *"L'Algérie algérienne" de Napoléon III à de Gaulle* (Paris: Sindbad, 1980), 162; Thomas, *The French Empire,* 299.

178. APP, BA 2171, report of 22 July 1936; Stora, *Ils venaient,* 71. Quotation in Mahmoud Abdoun, *Témoignage d'un militant du mouvement nationaliste* (Algiers: Éditions Dahleb, 1990), 21.

179. APP, BA 2171, reports of 18 and 23 June 1936; BA 2172, report of 2 July 1936; HA 26, "Meeting organisé par la 'Ligue Anti-Impérialiste,'" 20 June 1936; RD, "Un meeting antisioniste à Paris," *UI,* 26 June 1936. Quotations from HA 26.

180. Posted by Michel Renard at http://islamenfrance.canalblog.com/archives/2006/08/31/2598343.html.

181. Bachetarzi, *Mémoires,* 277–78.

182. See Ageron, *"L'Algérie algérienne,"* 132–34, 139.

183. Stora, *Nationalistes,* 40.

184. APP, BA 2171, "Conseil de Cabinet," 25 January 1937.

185. See, for example, "Ce que fut pour nous l'expérience du front populaire," *El Ouma (EO),* 1 April 1938.

186. Ageron, *"L'Algérie algérienne,"* 134–35, 138, 161. I have drawn my material on Oran, as well as the interpretation offered here of the movement's violence, from Samuel Kalman, "Le combat par tous les moyens: Colonial Violence and the Extreme Right in 1930s Oran," *French Historical Studies* 34, no. 1 (Winter 2011): 125–53, quotation from 146.

187. By this time, the SF had declined considerably.

188. Figures from Irvine, "Fascism," 272; ADBdR, 1 M 759, SAINAM report of 21 July 1936; and Soucy, *French Fascism,* 220, respectively.

189. ADBdR, 1 M 759, lengthy report on the SAINAM, 17 June 1938.

190. I base this estimate on the sources cited in the preceding two notes.

191. See Weinberg, *A Community,* 125–37; Hyman, *From Dreyfus,* 107, 213–16.

192. Kaddache, *L'Algérie des Algériens,* 737–79.

193. "Tous dans la bataille pour la Palestine, tous pour la Palestine, seule terre de salut!" *TR,* 1 September 1938.

194. APP, BA 1811, "Meeting organisée par le 'Poalei Zion,' " 10 September 1938.

195. For example, El Habib, "Les relations judéo-musulmanes en Algérie," *TR,* 1 November 1938.

196. A. Yahiaoui, "La Palestine martyre," *EO,* December 1937.

197. Abdel-Moumen, "En Palestine: Les méfaits du sionisme," *EO,* 27 August 1938.

198. APP, BA 2172, reports of 10 May 1937 and 14 January and 14 February 1938.

199. "Comité de solidarité et d'aide aux victimes arabes en Palestine," *EFM,* 23 February 1939.

200. Raymond Raoul-Lambert, "Le problème Algérien: Déclarations de M. Pierre-Bloch, député de l'Aisne, vice-president de la commission d'enquête en Algérie," *UI,* 4 March 1938.

201. "Bernard Lecache, Président de la L.I.C.A. réclame une loi contre le racism," *EFM,* 13 April 1939.

202. M. M. Benslimane, "Au service de la Haine!!" *EFM,* 24 March 1938.

203. Ferhat Abbas, "Soyons sérieux! Soyons humains! Soyons unis!" *EFM,* 14 July 1938. Morinaud, the former mayor, was trying to reclaim his seat.

204. J.B., "Le 2ᵉ Congrès international du rassemblement mondial contre le racisme et l'antisémitisme," *UI,* 29 July 1938; M. El Azziz Kessous, "Lettre de Paris," *EFM,* 28 July 1938.

205. ADBdR, 1 M 801, series of documents on Congrès musulman of Marseille, May 1937–May 1938; Renard, "Aperçu," 281–83.

206. ADBdR, 8 Fi, "Pour la liberté de conscience contre le racisme," LICA poster, 1938; "Français! Les anciens combattants et mutiles de la L.I.C.A. s'addressent à vous," LICA poster, date uncertain.

3. Jews as Muslims and Muslims as Jews

1. The Commissariat (CGQJ) was created in spring 1941 in an effort by Vichy to take back French control of anti-Jewish policy in the occupied zone. In the course of the war, the CGQJ implemented both Vichy and German policies. "Little Hungary" is not a translation but the restaurant's actual name. The name may have been taken from a popular restaurant by the same name in New York,

founded decades earlier, that became a hub for Hungarian immigrants. All information and documentation here comes from Archives nationales (AN) (Paris), AJ38, 3190, dossier 16 709, "Little Hungary," 1941–1943. I have cited more specific documents for information that might only be gleaned from a single part of the dossier.

2. AN, AJ38, "Little Hungary" dossier (hereafter LHd), letter from Hungarian Royal General Consul of Paris to German authorities, 11 October 1941.

3. AN, AJ38, LHd, translated document (from Persian to French) from the Iranian consulate in Paris, translated 2 July 1942.

4. The Iranian authorities considered Laufer a Muslim.

5. There is no indication in the dossier of Luckas's level of Jewish practice or identification. But no one attempted to conceal her Jewish origins either.

6. David Weinberg, *A Community on Trial: The Jews of Paris in the 1930s* (Chicago: University of Chicago Press, 1977), 4.

7. There were further divisions. In the far north, Germany attached a region to Belgium; in the northeast, the Germans created two "reserved zones," ostensibly for German settlement; farther east, they annexed the long-disputed Alsace-Lorraine region. In the southeast, the Italians occupied a small zone that became larger in November 1942, before they retreated from France in September 1943.

8. AN, AJ38, LHd, report from Louis Gayet for CGQJ, 14 August 1941.

9. It is not clear if these actions responded to or anticipated the corresponding German measures.

10. Documents show that the visit occurred between 8 August and 14 August 1941, but the exact date is unclear.

11. AN, AJ38, LHd, letter from Sebastien Hassid to Robert Lafon, 19 May 1942.

12. AN, AJ38, LHd, letter from German military authority in France, 26 February 1942.

13. The dossier of Dénise Hassid suggests that the investigation convinced the authorities the family was Aryan. AJ38, 176, Hassid, Dénise, 2 August 1944.

14. Laufer's case does not appear to be entirely isolated. The limited evidence, for example, in the cases of Selim Asail, Lydie Barouche, and Nelly Hadjage suggests analogous experiences. AN, AJ38, 154, dossier of Asail, Selim; AN, AJ38, 155, dossier of Barouche, Lydie; AN, AJ38, 171, dossier of Hadjage, Nelly.

15. Peter Gay, *My German Question: Growing Up in Nazi Berlin* (New Haven, CT: Yale University Press, 1998), 47. Admittedly the context of Gay's experience was different: that of an assimilated Jewish family in Germany in 1933.

16. For Vichy and German definitions of a Jew under their respective racial laws, see Michael Marrus and Robert Paxton, *Vichy France and the Jews,* reprint ed. (Stanford, CA: Stanford University Press, 1995), esp. 12–13, 91–105.

17. Naomi Davidson, *Only Muslim: Embodying Islam in Twentieth-Century France* (Ithaca, NY: Cornell University Press, 2012), has a somewhat different outlook, contending that the French state racialized Muslim bodies and practices as Other and unassimilable already in World War I and the interwar period and all the more so during World War II. For the first population figure, Renée Poznanski, *Jews in France during World War II*, trans. Nathan Bracher (Hanover, NH: University Press of New England, 1997), 1; for the second, Neil MacMaster, *Colonial Migrants and Racism: Algerians in France, 1900–1962* (New York: St. Martin's Press, 1997), 223.

18. On Vichy's treatment of Muslim religious needs, see Davidson, *Only Muslim,* chap. 4. On the importance of empire for Vichy, see, among others, Eric T. Jennings, *Vichy in the Tropics: Pétain's National Revolution in Madagascar, Guadeloupe, and Indochina, 1940–1944* (Stanford, CA: Stanford University Press, 2001); Pascal Blanchard and Gilles Boëtsch, "La France de Pétain et l'Afrique: Images et propagandes coloniales," *Canadian Journal of African Studies/Revue canadienne des études africaines* 28, no. 1 (1994): 1–31; and Pascal Blanchard and Ruth Ginio, "Révolution impériale: Le mythe colonial de Vichy," in Blanchard and Sandrine Lemaire, eds., *Culture impériale: Les colonies au coeur de la république, 1931–1961* (Paris: Éditions autrement, 2004).

19. A recent wave of scholarship on France during the war has opened these more nuanced perspectives. Here and in the paragraph that follows I rely in particular on Philippe Burrin, *France under the Germans: Collaboration and Compromise,* trans. J. Lloyd (New York: The New Press, 1996); Robert Gildea, *Marianne in Chains: In Search of the German Occupation* (London: Macmillan, 2002); John Sweets, *Choices in Vichy France: The French under the Nazi Occupation* (New York: Oxford University Press, 1986); Richard Vinen, *The Unfree French: Life under the Occupation* (New Haven, CT: Yale University Press, 2006).

20. For Muslims as almost exclusively eager collaborators (in work focused more on the Arab Middle East), see Edwin Black, *The Farhud: Roots of the Arab-Nazi Alliance in the Holocaust* (Washington, DC: Dialog Press, 2010); Jeffrey Herf, *Nazi Propaganda for the Arab World* (New Haven, CT: Yale University Press, 2009). For accounts that treat Muslims as rarely complicit, see Gilbert Achcar, *The Arabs and the Holocaust: The Arab-Israeli War of Narratives,* trans. G. M. Goshgarian (New York: Holt, 2009); or that highlight and embellish resistance, Robert Assaraf, *Mohammed V et les juifs du Maroc: l'époque de Vichy* (Paris: Plon, 1997). Robert Satloff, *Among the Righteous: Lost Stories from the Holocaust's Long Reach into Arab Lands* (New York: Public Affairs Press, 2006), treats both Muslim collaborators and those who helped Jews, but emphasizes the former and sometimes exaggerates the heroic deeds of the latter. Michel Abitbol, *The Jews of North Africa during the Second World War*, trans.

Catherine Tahanyi Zentelis (Detroit: Wayne State University Press, 1989) offers a more balanced account, but focuses little on Muslims themselves.

21. This is one of Vinen's formulations.

22. Robert Paxton, *Vichy France: Old Guard and New Order, 1940–1944* (New York: Knopf, 1972; reprint with a new introduction by the author, New York: Columbia University Press, 1982), 181.

23. French police figure from Marrus and Paxton, *Vichy France*, 250–52; for figures and breakdown of deportations, Paxton, *Vichy France*, 183.

24. See Herf, *Nazi Propaganda*, 17–24.

25. Regarding the place of North Africa at the top of Vichy's imperial priorities, see Martin Thomas, "The Vichy Government and French Colonial Prisoners of War, 1940–1944," *French Historical Studies* 25, no. 4 (2002): 657–92.

26. Cited in Yves-Claude Aouate, "Les Algériens musulmans et les mesures antijuives du gouvernement de Vichy (1940–1942)," *Pardes* 16 (1992): 189.

27. Philippe Pétain, *Discours au français, 17 juin 1940–20 août 1944*, ed. Jean-Claude Barabs, with preface by Antoine Prost (Paris: Albin Michel, 1989), 231.

28. See Raffael Scheck, "Nazi Propaganda toward French Muslim Prisoners of War," *Holocaust and Genocide Studies* 26, no. 3 (2012): 447–77.

29. Archives départementales des Bouches-du-Rhône (ADBdR) (Marseille), 76 W 209, Ministère de l'intérieur (MdI), memo on "Célébration par les musulmans nord-africans de la fête de l'Aïd el Seghir," 14 September 1943.

30. Quotation and figure in Davidson, *Only Muslim*, 110.

31. Cited in Scheck, "Nazi Propaganda," 462.

32. See Blanchard and Boëtsch, "La France de Pétain," 27.

33. Archives du ministère des affaires étrangères (AMAE) (La Courneuve), Série guerre 1939–1945 (SG39–45), M Vichy-Maroc (M V-M), 20, memo from the Vice-Président du Conseil "sur les indigènes nord-africains séjournant en France," 22 February 1942.

34. See Thomas, "The Vichy Government."

35. Blanchard and Boëtsch, "La France de Pétain," 20.

36. For an overview of Vichy's role in anti-Jewish measures in wartime France, see Paxton, *Vichy France*, 173–85.

37. Regarding hidden Jewish children in Catholic homes, see Maurice Rajsfus, *N'oublie pas le petit Jésus! L'église catholique et les enfants juifs (1940–1945)* (Paris: Manya, 1994). For a more comprehensive assessment of Christian efforts to save and protect Jews, see Limore Yagil, *Chrétiens et juifs sous Vichy (1940–1944): Sauvetage et désobéissance civile* (Paris: Cerf, 2005).

38. For a fuller discussion of this history, see Ethan B. Katz, "Secular French Nationhood and Its Discontents: Jews as Muslims and Religion as Race in Occupied France," in Ari Joskowicz and Ethan B. Katz, eds., *Secularism in Ques-*

tion: Jews and Judaism in Modern Times (Philadelphia: University of Pennsylvania Press, 2015).

39. Beginning in the Middle Ages, as dhimmis, or a non-Muslim "people of the book," Jews living under Islamic law gained special protections and relative autonomy in their own affairs. In exchange, they had to pay certain taxes and faced restrictions in many aspects of daily life such as clothing, profession, and neighborhood of residence. In terms of Jews' changed status under colonialism, we should be careful not to generalize. The Jews of Morocco remained in dhimmi status during the colonial period, and in certain respects they were worse off legally than they had been prior to the establishment of the protectorate. Nonetheless, the Vichy period resulted in new legal and social barriers for Jews in Moroccan society. See Daniel Schroeter, "Vichy in Morocco: The Residency, Mohammed V, and His Indigenous Jewish Subjects," in Ethan B. Katz, Lisa Moses Leff, and Maud S. Mandel, eds., *Colonialism and the Jews* (Bloomington: Indiana University Press, forthcoming). On laws lowering Algerian Jews' status in both colony and metropole, see Henri Msellati, *Les juifs d'Algérie sous le régime de Vichy* (Paris: L'Harmattan, 1999), 67–71, 88; regarding Jewish treatment across North Africa, Abitbol, *The Jews,* esp. chap. 5.

40. Jean Laloum, "Des juifs d'Afrique du Nord au Pletzl? Une presence méconnue et des épreuves oubliées (1920–1945)," *Archives juives* 38, no. 2 (2005): 69; interview with Louise Jaïs, 20 June 2006.

41. Laloum, "Des juifs," 69.

42. Jacques Darville and Simon Wichené, *Drancy la juive ou la deuxième inquisition* (Cachan: A. Breger Frères, 1945), 104, 108–9. See also Gitta Amipaz-Silber, *Sephardi Jews in Occupied France* (Jerusalem: Rubin Mass, 1995), 284.

43. Emmanuel Blanchard, *La police parisienne et les algériens (1944–1962)* (Paris: Nouveau Monde, 2011), 62–65.

44. A limited examination of personal dossiers in the records of the CGQJ shows at least fourteen Jews who sought to benefit from their North African or Levantine heritage in this manner. See AN, AJ38. See 152, 154, and 156, dossiers of Amsellem, Salomon, Yacouta née Ben Rhamin, Ben Chemouan and Ben Aroch, Messaoudah; 155, dossier of Baccouche, René; 156, dossiers of Ben B'Diko, Messaoud and Benhamou, Emile; 170, dossier of Gourdji, Clément Rahmi, Gourdji, Huyemine, and Aster, Yourouchelmi; 176, dossier of Kriel, Joseph; 187, dossier of Saffar, Jules; 154, dossier of Azoulay, J. The latter two dossiers are cited in Laloum, "Des juifs," 70, 74–75, 82n82, 83n102. See also CDJC, CXV_164a, letter regarding status of Roland née Marzouk, Germaine.

45. ADBdR, 76 W 162, Affaire Chaouat, letters of November–December 1942.

46. AN, AJ38. 156, dossier of René Baccouche. While it is impossible to know if Baccouche was lying, his French name, his residence in the Var, and his lack of documentation for his story strain credibility.

47. Many Moroccan Jews and some Muslims did cross briefly into Algeria in the decades following the French conquest of 1830, and particularly after 1865, to obtain certifications of French nationality. See Jessica M. Marglin, "The Two Lives of Mas'ud Amoyal: Pseudo-Algerians in Morocco, 1830–1912," *International Journal of Middle East Studies* 44 (2012): 651–70.

48. ADBdR, 76 W 161, Préfecture des Bouches-du-Rhône (PBdR), Service des Affaires Algériennes (SAA), note of 9 November 1942. Such activity may have continued the following year. See "Ce qui furent à la fête," *Er Rachid (ER)*, 5 October 1943.

49. While we lack anything like precise numbers, certain documents suggest that the practice may have been quite widespread. For instance, AN, F1a, 5012, "Note sur les prévisions budgetaires pour 1944, fonctionnement du service des affaires musulmanes nord-africaines" requests additional funding to study the requests of Algerian Jews in the metropole seeking to retain French citizenship.

50. On Crypto-Jews and flexibility in Jewish law regarding conversion to Islam, see Lewis, *The Jews of Islam* (Princeton, NJ: Princeton University Press, 1984), 82–84, and Mark R. Cohen, *Under Crescent and Cross: The Jews in the Middle Ages* (Princeton, NJ: Princeton University Press, 1994), chap. 10, esp. 175–76, 183. Regarding fungible imperial regimes and statuses for Jews, Sarah Abravenal Stein, "Protected Persons? The Baghdadi Jewish Diaspora, the British State, and the Persistence of Empire," *American Historical Review* 116, no. 1 (2011): 80–108; and Marglin, "The Two Lives."

51. Both Poznanski, *Jews in France,* and, even more so, Daniel Lee, *Pétain's Jewish Children: French Jewish Youth and the Vichy Regime* (Oxford: Oxford University Press, 2014), show how Jews more broadly retained limited agency under the Occupation.

52. The job of rector, without foundation in Islam, is an invention of the French state, derived from the Catholic Church.

53. Remarkably little biographical information exists on Benghabrit. My account draws on Jalila Sbai, "Trajectoire d'un home et d'une idée: Si Kaddour Ben Ghabrit et l'islam de France, 1892–1926," *Hespéris-Tamuda* 39, fasc. 1 (2001): 45–58; Michel Renard, "Si Kaddour ben Ghabrit: biographie," http://islamenfrance .canalblog.com/archives/2007/02/10/4057434.html; and in particular for his education, Driss El Yazami, "Kaddour Ben Ghabrit (1873–1954)," in Magellan, *Génériques: histoire et mémoire de l'immigration,* http://www.generiques.org/db /biographie/?do=findall&row=130.

54. On Bachetarzi's troupe's relationship with Benghabrit, see Mahieddine Bachetarzi, *Mémoires: 1919–1939* (Algiers: Éditions nationales algériennes, 1968), 53–54, 88, 110. Regarding Mantout's relationship with Benghabrit, I have drawn from a letter in the private collection of Martine Bernheim. Mantout's Jewishness is confirmed by his wartime dossier: Bibliothèque Nationale du

Royaume du Maroc, Rabat, D614, in the United States Holocaust Memorial Museum, Record Group 81.001M.0004. My thanks to Daniel Schroeter for generously sharing this file with me.

55. For more on the mosque's wartime conduct and the debates around its memory, see Ethan Katz, "Did the Paris Mosque Save Jews? A Mystery and Its Memory," *Jewish Quarterly Review* 102, no. 2 (2012): 256–87.

56. Albert Assouline, "Une vocation ignorée de la mosquée de Paris," in *Almanach du combattant* (Paris: Comité National du Souvenir de Verdun, 1983); Assouline, "La paix sur lui," *Vae victis: Bulletin officiel d'information de l'amicale libre du 22eme B.M.N.A.*, no. 27 (October 1984).

57. *Une résistance oubliée: La mosquée de Paris,* DVD, directed by Derri Berkani (documentary made for *Racines de France 3,* 1991).

58. See Katz, "Did the Paris Mosque."

59. On Bachetarzi's wartime conduct, see Joshua Cole, "'A chacun son public': Politique et culture dans Algérie des années 1930," *Sociétés et représentations* 38 (2014): 21–51.

60. See Nidam Abdi, "La chanson maghrébine orpheline," *Libération,* 13 July 2005; *Une résistance oubliée.*

61. See Katz, "Did the Paris," 274–76.

62. AMAE, SG39–45, M V-M, 20, Mosquée de Paris. Note to the minister dated 24 September 1940. My thanks for Derri Berkani and Martine Bernheim for bringing these documents to my attention. It is unclear with whom the Germans spoke. Logically, it would have been Benghabrit as head of the mosque, and the Germans could have mistakenly described him as its imam, but multiple documents attest to Benghabrit's departure from Paris between June and October 1940, so it is possible they spoke with someone else. For documentation of his absence, see Mohamed Aïssaoui, *L'étoile jaune et le croissant* (Paris: Gallimard, 2012), 132, 136.

63. AMAE, SG39–45, M V-M, 20, Mosquée de Paris, telegrams of arrival of 31 January 1941. Benghabrit later denied his arrest to a Vichy officer. ADBdR, 76 W 205, prefect de Constantine, Centre d'information et d'études, report on Si Kaddour Ben Ghabrit and his relations with the German authorities, 23 April 1941.

64. For photographs, Centre de documentation juive contemporaine (CDJC), MXC_D4_70–73; newsreel found at http://www.ina.fr/video/AFE8 5000387/hopital-franco-musulman-a-bobigny.fr.html.

65. AMAE, SG39–45, M V-M, 20, Mosquée de Paris, note for Colonel Otzen, 22 January 1941; memo to German ambassador in Paris, 22 February 1941; and letter from Ambassador of France to General Doyen, 10 March 1941.

66. ADBdR, 76 W 204, MdI, report labeled top secret on propaganda among Algerian indigènes, 12 February 1941; ADBdR, 76 W 205, PBdR, SAA, report on Muslims in Paris, 5 July 1941.

67. Ibid.; ADBdR, 76 W 206, PBdR, SAA, report on a conversation of Muslims coming from North Africa, 28 March 1941.

68. AMAE, SG39–45, M V-M, 20, Mosquée de Paris, note from Benghabrit to Monsieur Amédée Outrey, conseiller d'ambassade, 29 October 1941. From the CDJC sources, we know that the images appeared in *Le Petit Parisien*.

69. AMAE, SG39–45, M V-M, 20, Mosquée de Paris, notes regarding imams for Muslim prisoners, 12 and 19 June 1941.

70. Benghabrit has received no such honor.

71. Aïssaoui, *L'étoile jaune*, 41.

72. *Journal officiel de la république française*, 26 July 1947, 7253. My thanks to Benjamin Stora for showing me this document. The rosette was a superior level of the Medal of the Resistance.

73. Four are from AN, AJ38, files 152, 154, and 156, dossiers of Amsellem, Salomon, Yacouta née Ben Rhamin, Ben Chemouan, and Ben Aroch, Messaoudah; 155, dossier of Baccouche, René; 170, dossier of Gourdji, Clément Rahmi, Gourdji, Huyemine, and Aster, Yourouchelmi; 176, dossier of Kriel, Joseph. The fifth is from CDJC, CXV_164a, CGQJ, Statut des personnes, letters dated 17 June, 12 July 1944. These documents do not reproduce Benghabrit's responses, but on each occasion, officials at the CGQJ indicate that he has insisted the individual in question was not Muslim.

74. For knowledge regarding the "Final Solution" in France, see Marrus and Paxton, *Vichy France*, 346–56.

75. Here I rely on Werner Rings, *Life with the Enemy: Collaboration and Resistance in Hitler's Europe, 1939–1945*, trans. J. M. Brownjohn (London: Weidenfeld and Nicolsan, 1982), esp. part 3.

76. On accommodation, see Burrin, *France under the Germans*.

77. Exceptionally rich surveillance reports provide a picture of the choices of thousands of Muslims in occupied France. While we must read such reports with great care, their authors increasingly told superiors what they did not wish to hear; such candidness offers the historian reassurance as to the information's veracity. Regarding wartime surveillance sources, see Marrus and Paxton, *Vichy France*, 181.

78. Scheck, "Nazi Propaganda," 450.

79. Blanchard and Boëtsch, "La France de Pétain," begin to suggest this, but they underestimate the intensity of Vichy Muslim-targeted propaganda. See esp. 21–28.

80. Charles-Robert Ageron, "Contribution à l'étude de la propaganda allemande au Maghreb pendant la deuxième guerre mondiale," *Revue d'histoire maghrébine*, nos. 7–8 (January 1977): 16–32.

81. ADBdR, 76 W 204, MdI, report labeled top secret on propaganda among Algerian indigènes, 12 February 1941; ADBdR, 76 W 206, PBdR, SAA, reports of 18 March, 22 April 1941.

82. ADBdR, 76 W 204, report of 18 April 1941; ADBdR, 76 W 206, PBdR, SAA, reports of 18 March, 28 March, and 12 and 19 November 1941. On propaganda themes, see Ageron, "Contribution."

83. Mahmoud Abdoun, *Temoignage d'un militant du mouvement nationaliste* (Algiers: Dahlab, 1990), 46.

84. ADBdR, 76 W 206, PBdR, SAA, reports of 17 April, 26 September 1941; Benjamin Stora, *Ils venaient d'Algérie: L'immigration algérienne en France (1912–1992)* (Paris: Fayard, 1992), 84–88; Pascal le Pautremat, *La politique musulmane de la France au XXᵉ siècle: De l'hexagone aux terres d'Islam. Espoirs, réussites, échecs* (Paris: Maisonneuve & Larose, 2003), 375–76.

85. Numerous reports attest to this. See, for example, ADBdR, 76 W 204, MdI, report on propaganda among Algerian indigènes, 12 February 1941.

86. On Seghir and his collaboration, ADBdR, 76 W 205, PBdR, SAA, reports of 23 April, 10 and 20 May 1941. Rachid Ksentini became the cabaret's new star. Hadj Miliani, "Présence des musiques arabes en France: immigrations, diasporas et musiques du monde," *Migrance* 32 (2008): 94. Despite cinematic depiction of Hallali continuing to perform in El Djazaïr during the war in the guise of a Muslim, I have yet to find evidence for this. See *Les Hommes Libres,* DVD, directed by Ismaël Ferroukhi (Pyramide, 2011).

87. ADBdR, 76 W 206, PBdR, SAA, reports of 24 September, 19 November 1941. The second report refers to an existing school in the Paris suburb of Argenteuil; the first reports one will open soon in Paris.

88. Scheck, "Nazi Propaganda." Estimates indicate that these camps, at their peak size in 1940–1941, held sixty thousand to ninety thousand Muslims. Le Pautremat, *La politique,* 378–79.

89. Smaller parties including the Ligue française, the Parti français national-collectiviste, and Le feu, as well as the large but more culturally focused Groupe collaboration, also sought to make inroads among Muslims.

90. Paris Police Archives (PPA), BA 1948, report entitled "Parti populaire français, delégation nationale à la propagande, rapport d'activité pour la période du 1ᵉʳ janvier au 31 mars 1942"; figures from APP, BA 1949, report of 23 March 1942.

91. Zouani headed the El amaria Sufi brotherhood; Bendjamaa was a former municipal councilor in Guelma and secretary-general of the Fédération des élus musulmans d'Algérie, and Belghoul, a founding militant of the Algerian nationalist movement during the interwar years and an old friend of the Emir Khaled, called himself the leader of the descendants of Algerian nationalist hero Abd al-Qadir (of whom Khaled was the grandson). Ageron, "Contribution," 25; Jacques Cantier, *L'Algérie sous le régime de Vichy* (Paris: Odile Jacob, 2002), 114, 262. Official reports express skepticism about these claims of Bendjamaa and Belghoul.

92. Interview by Y. Sicard in *Le Cri du peuple*, 25 March 1942, reprinted in ADBdR, 76 W 205. In particular between 1927 and 1931, the Soviets closed

numerous mosques, madrasas, and Islamic courts; arrested, exiled, or killed thousands of imams; confiscated property of the *waqf,* or communal Islamic trust; and undertook the *hujum,* a major campaign to unveil Islamic women. This lends credibility to such reports. See Shoshana Keller, *To Moscow, Not Mecca: The Soviet Campaign against Islam in Central Asia, 1917–1941* (Westport, CT: Praeger, 2001).

93. ADBdR, 76 W 205, PBdR, SAA, report of 27 March 1942. On Baudrillart's evolving attitudes and motivations, see Paul Christophe, "Le cardinal Baudrillart et ses choix pendant la seconde guerre mondiale," *Revue d'histoire de l'église de France* 78 (1992): 57–75 (quotations from 68).

94. "Le cardinal Baudrillart a reçu plusieurs personnalités musulmanes," *Le Petit Parisien,* 23 March 1942.

95. ADBdR, 76 W 205, secret report of wire-tapped phone conversation, 24 March 1942.

96. ADBdR, 76 W 205, "Le P.P.F. a réuni hier à Magic City des milliers de musulmans et de français," *Le Cri du peuple,* 30 March 1942, reprinted but mistakenly dated as from 1941. The Quranic passage referred to is unclear. One possibility is chapter 5, Sura 82: "You will find the Jews and idolaters most excessive in hatred of those who believe." *Al Qu'rān: A Contemporary Translation by Ahmed Ali* (Princeton, NJ: Princeton University Press, 2001), 108.

97. Certain of these polemics used similar language to that applied here to Jews. See, for instance, a thirteenth-century fatwa translated in Bernard Lewis, ed. and trans., *Islam: From the Prophet Muhammad to the Capture of Constantinople,* vol. 2 (New York: Oxford University Press, 1987), 228–29 (no. 83). On the comparatively restrained nature of medieval Muslim anti-Jewish polemics and the way they more often were against "nonbelievers" or dhimmis broadly, see Cohen, *Under Crescent,* chaps. 4, 9.

98. ADBdR, 76 W 205, "A l'occasion de l'anniversaire du prophète, le chef de la confrérie El Amaria remet à Jacques Doriot un dipleme [*sic*] d'honneur dans une 'Zaouia' de la région parisienne," *Le Cri du peuple,* 30 March 1942, reprinted as a report.

99. A burst of PPF propaganda toward North Africans after the November 1942 Allied landing seems to have elicited little response. In the extensive police dossiers on the PPF from the Occupation, Muslims make few appearances thereafter.

100. APP, BA 1914, MdI, reports of 17–18 April 1941.

101. ADBdR, 76 W 204, report on the publication "Le travailleur nord-africain," 8 September 1943.

102. APP, BA 1954, report of 1 July 1942.

103. Number from ADBdR, 76 W 204, report on the publication "Le travailleur nord-africain," 8 September 1943. Estimate from APP, BA 1954, "Note sur le front social du travail," attached to notice dated 18 December 1943.

104. ADBdR, 76 W 205, FST tract attached to PBdR, SAA report dated 6 May 1942; APP, BA 1954, tracts attached to report of 6 May 1942. Jews seldom appear in the extensive compiled files of UTNA in APP, BA 1954 and BA 1955. For an exception at a large UTNA event, see APP, BA 1954, report of 11 October 1943.

105. APP, BA 1954, report of 26 April 1941.

106. APP, BA 1954, report of 2 July 1941 on the Comité nord-africaine.

107. CAOM, 16 H 115, documents of French security services concerning El-Maadi, October 1937 to January 1938. Quotation from report of 28 October 1937.

108. Ibid.; APP, BA 2335, Préfecture de Police, report of 21 June 1943 on *Er Rachid*. Existing in 1936–1937, the Comité secret d'action révolutionnaire (CSAR), known as the Cagoule, stockpiled weapons, assassinated leftists, and planned a coup against the Front populaire. On the wartime return of many Cagoulards, see Bertram Gordon, *Collaborationism in France during the Second World War* (Ithaca, NY: Cornell University Press, 1980), 56–62.

109. APP, BA 2335, report of 14 August 1944 on *Er Rachid;* BA 2171, undated handwritten reports attached to report of 7 August 1942 on the Comité d'entraide des musulmans nord-africains.

110. For one highly detailed account, APP, BA 2335, report of 26 July 1945.

111. AN, AJ38, 176, Direction du statut des personnes, dossiers individuels, 1941–1944—KO à LANZ, dossier of Lakhdar, 29 October 1941.

112. APP, BA 1954, report of 2 July 1941 on CNA; CNA, quotations from undated tracts attached to report of 4 May 1941; report of 8 November 1943 on the CNA; report with attached tract of 4 February 1942.

113. For the group's early growth numbers, see APP, BA 1954, report of 17 June 1941. Yet very few notices of activities of the group appear for 1942, and Mohamed El-Maadi, "Bilan," *ER,* January 1943, indicates that the committee almost folded in mid-1942 due to financial trouble.

114. APP, BA 1914, report of 1 December 1942; tract of Comité musulman de l'afrique du nord, dated 19 November 1942. All subsequent quotations here are from the tract.

115. APP, BA 1954, report of 14 January 1943. It is not clear when the CNA left the Mouvement social révolutionnaire (MSR) of Eugène Deloncle, with which it had affiliated after the MSR split from the RNP in October 1941. The above-cited report of December 1942 still referred to it as affiliated.

116. The journal was biweekly during 1943 and then weekly in its new series through 9 August 1944.

117. "Le juif immuable," *ER,* 20 June 1943.

118. Chérif Aït Atmann, "Quand Israël se défend: saucisson de bataille," *ER,* 26 January 1944.

119. Jean-François Durand, "Le problème musulman-juif," *ER,* 20 March 1943.

120. These come from, respectively, Ulf Uweson, "Couleur du temps présent: Bolchevisme . . . et Socialisme"; El-Maadi, "Flâneries provençales," *ER,* 1 March 1943; Abd-el Hak, "Mots d'ordre," *ER,* January 1943.

121. For instance, see Aït Atmann, "Au delà de la voûte," *ER,* 14 June 1944.

122. This figure comes from APP, BA 2335, report on *Er Rachid* of 14 August 1944. In a small notice in its issue of 21 June 1944, the newspaper itself reports thirty thousand weekly readers.

123. For the first number, see "Le chef Mohamed El Maadi," *ER,* January 1943; for the second, APP, BA 1954, report of 8 November 1943.

124. "Pour que le comité musulman de l'afrique du nord vive, prospère et remporte la victoire," *ER,* January 1943.

125. Compiled from a close examination of advertisements throughout all issues of *Er Rachid.*

126. APP, BA 1954, report of 4 October 1943.

127. Burrin, *France under the Germans,* 433. For an overview of the LVF, J. G. Shields, "Charlemagne's Crusaders: French Collaboration in Arms, 1941–1945," *French Cultural Studies* 18, no. 1 (2007): 83–105.

128. Muslim numbers compiled from ADBdR, 76 W 205, reports on recruitment of Muslims to the legion, 22 September, 10 November, and 21 November; ADBdR, 76 W 206, report on Muslims in the legion, 29 September 1941. Overall numbers from Shields, "Charlemagne's Crusaders," 88. Numbers of volunteers were significantly greater than those permitted to join, as rigorous examinations meant numerous rejections.

129. On motivations for joining, see Gordon, *Collaborationism,* 253–60.

130. Aichoun is described as a member of the Légion tricolore, the name given to the LVF during Vichy's short-lived effort to wrest control of the legion from the Paris collaborationist parties. See Gordon, *Collaborationism,* 252–53.

131. ADBdR, 76 W 206, seized correspondence from Aichoun, Makhlouf, written 5 May 1942, reported 23 June 1942; individual notice of Aichoun, Makhlouf, 27 July 1942. Emphasis in document.

132. For evidence of their declining if continuous presence, see CAOM, 5 I 87, Ministère de la guerre, report of 24 September 1944; APP, BA 1793, assorted documents of October 1943–May 1944.

133. Stora, *Ils venaient,* 87; Satloff, *Among,* 86–87; Le Pautremat, *La politique,* 377–78; CAOM, 5 I 87, ministère de la guerre, report of 24 September 1944.

134. On the latter point, see Burrin, *France under the Germans,* 451; Marrus and Paxton, *Vichy France,* 335.

135. Interview with Louise Jaïs, 20 June 2006.

136. Le Pautremat, *La politique,* 387.

137. ADBdR, 76 W 204, MdI, report on propaganda among Algerian indigènes, 12 February 1941; APP, HA 25, report of 14 September 1944.

138. ADBdR, 76 W 206, report entitled, "Antisémitisme et germanophillie des indigènes," 12 June 1941. This reaction contrasted the wider French population's response. See Marrus and Paxton, *Vichy France,* 212.

139. AMAE, SG39–45, M V-M, 20, "Note sur les indigènes nord-africains séjournant en France," 22 February 1942.

140. These numbers are conservative, exempting many other files that suggest antisemitic sentiment. They reflect an exhaustive review of the dossiers in ADBdR, 76 W 204–206, and CAOM, 5 I 87.

141. ADBdR, 76 W 205, report on attitudes of Muslims in Marseille, 13 December 1941.

142. Reports repeatedly note Muslim attention to al-Husseini's activities. ADBdR, 76 W 206, PBdR, SAA, reports of 22 January and 29 May 1942.

143. On wider French opinion, see Marrus and Paxton, *Vichy France,* 183–84; regarding camps of North Africans, Scheck, "Nazi Propaganda," 451–52.

144. These observations reflect a composite view of the documents cited here. The diversity of Muslims holding such opinions is directly articulated in ADBdR, 76 W 205, PBdR, SAA, report on "attitude of North African indigènes," 10 November 1942.

145. On the first two points of discontent, see ADBdR, 76 W 205, PBdR, SAA, report on "attitude of North African indigènes," 10 November 1942; report on "attitude of North Africans and Annamites," 17 November 1942; report on the attitude of Muslims in light of current events, 17 November 1942; CAOM, 5 I 87, PBdR, SAA, report of 21 September 1942. On fears of Jewish power, APP, HA 7, préfecture de police (PP), service des affaires nord-africaines (SANA), report of 16 November 1942; ADBdR, 76 W 205, PBdR, SAA, report on "attitude of North African indigènes," 10 November 1942. My quotation comes from the first of the last two reports.

146. ADBdR, 76 W 205, PBdR, SAA, report on Tunisian Muslim sentiment, 19 November 1942; report on the Algerian indigènes and Americans, 21 November 1942.

147. It is virtually never mentioned in the reports cited here. On Muslim reaction in Algeria to the revocation of the decree, see Benjamin Stora, *Les trois exils: juifs d'Algérie* (France: Éditions Stock, 2006), 104–7.

148. CAOM, 8 CAB 19, file on Jewish-Muslim relations, "Le discours du Général Giraud," 16 March 1943.

149. See Charles-Robert Ageron, "Les populations du Maghreb face à la propagande allemande," *Revue d'histoire de la deuxième guerre mondiale,* no. 114 (April 1979): 1–39.

150. For example, see ADBdR, 76 W 205, report of 2 July 1941.

151. See, for instance, ADBdR, 76 W 206, PBdR, SAA, reports of 23, 26 September 1941.

152. ADBdR, 76 W 206, PBdR, SAA, "Note sur les nord africains de Paris," 26 September 1942.

153. ADBdR, 76 W 206, PBdR, SAA, report of 29 August 1941; ADBdR, 76 W 205, report of 17 February 1942.

154. Many Muslims considered themselves French culturally but politically inclined toward Germany. See CAOM, 5 I 87, PBdR, SAA, "Aperçu sur le peuplement algérien de Paris," report of 26 August 1942.

155. See esp. Abitbol, *The Jews;* Satloff, *Among;* Black, *The Farhud;* Herf, *Nazi Propaganda.*

156. On this point, see H. R. Kedward, *Resistance in Vichy France: A Study of Ideas and Motivation in the Southern Zone, 1940–1942* (New York: Oxford University Press, 1978), 221–28. For a contrasting view that sees this moment as less decisive, Pierre Laborie, *L'opinion française sous Vichy* (Paris: Seuil, 1990).

157. Olivier Ihl, *La fête républicaine,* preface by Mona Ozouf (France: Gallimard, 1996).

158. ADBdR, 76 W 206, SAA, PBdR, "Anti-Collaborationist Propaganda in Marseille," 21 July 1942.

159. Above I have cited seemingly exceptional cases of Muslim solidarity with Jews in the face of roundups. For their more discernible impact on wider opinion, see Marrus and Paxton, *Vichy France,* chap. 6.

160. ADBdR, 76 W 205, PBdR, SAA, reports of 17 July and 24, 31 August (multiple) 1942.

161. ADBdR, 76 W 206, PBdR, SAA, "Note sur les Nord Africains de Paris," 26 September 1942.

162. ADBdR, 76 W 205, PBdR, SAA, reports of 4, 7 August 1942.

163. ADBdR, 76 W 205, reports of 24 September, 14 October 1942. See more detail above.

164. APP, HA 25, report of 14 September 1944.

165. ADBdR, 76 W 163, FARKHI dossier, documents of 18 May to 3 August 1943; 76 W 205, Direction générale de la sureté nationale (DGSN), Commissariat special Marseille (CSM), memo of 17 April 1941; 76 W 206, PBdR, SAA, report on couscous for Ramadan, 4 December 1942; report on the supply of couscous and grain to Muslims, 27 May 1943. In early March 1944, for reasons that are not entirely clear, French authorities directed Muslims to use other couscous suppliers; later that month, Farhi and his wife were arrested and deported. ADBdR, 149 W 37, MdI, service des affaires musulmanes nord africaines, report regarding "convocation par telephone a/s plainte FARHI," 3 September 1945.

166. ADBdR, 76 W 205, reports of 24 September, 14 October 1942.

167. ADBdR, 76 W 204, PBdR, SAA, report of 19 April 1941.

168. ADBdR, 76 W 205, PBdR, SAA, report on correspondence of imprisoned members of the Neo-Destour, dated 7 June 1941.

169. ADBdR, 76 W 205, renseignements généraux (R-G), report of 21 June 1942.

170. Vichy kept the Germans from imposing the star in the unoccupied zone, fearing a bitter outcry from the French population.

171. "Marguerite X" is the name given in the report. ADBdR, 76 W 204, "affaire Bouzid Belkacem," dated 22 April 1944; Bureau des affaires musulmanes nord-africaines, memo about sanctions against Bouzid, 29 April 1944.

172. ADBdR, 76 W 205, PBdR, SAA, reports of 5, 9 April 1941.

173. ADBdR, 76 W 205, PBdR, SAA, report of 9 June 1941.

174. Interview with Roger Gharbi, 6 June 2006. For Mustapha's full name, APP, HA 15, "Restaurants nord-africains, région parisienne," 1951.

175. Document found in November 2004. My thanks to Derri Berkani for sharing a photograph of the document and his translation from Kabyle to French.

176. Here I use the categories of Renée Poznanski, "Reflections on Jewish Resistance and Jewish Resistants in France," *Jewish Social Studies* n.s. 2, no. 1 (Autumn 1995): 124–58, which offers a useful assessment of the literature and debates on Jewish resistance in France.

177. *Les oubliés de l'histoire, les étrangers dans la résistance et la libération,* DVD, directed by Daniel Kupferstein (1992).

178. For Paris, ADBdR, 76 W 206, PBdR, SAA, report of 29 August 1941; for Marseille, ADBdR, 76 W 205, PBdR, SAA, report of 27 September 1941.

179. Archives du musée de la résistance nationale (MRN) (Champigny-sur-Marne), fonds thématique, carton 112, "'Les immigrés en France," undated document. My thanks to Linda Amiri for sharing this with me.

180. APP, BS2, 41, Mohamed Lakhdar, January 1943. My thanks to Linda Amiri for directing me to this file.

181. For examples, see ADBdR, 76 W 206, PBdR, SAA, report on "activité diverse des allemands à Paris," 19 July 1941; and ADBdR, 76 W 205, PBdR, SAA, report of 1 May 1942.

182. On Messali's refusal, accounts vary slightly. I follow Jacques Simon, *L'immigration Algérienne en France, des origines à l'indépendence* (Paris: Paris-Méditerranée, 2000), 91. For other examples of refusal, see, for instance, ADBdR, 76 W 206, PBdR, SAA, report on "activité diverse des allemands à Paris," 19 July 1941.

183. Stora, *Ils venaient,* 85.

184. Quoted in Satloff, *Among,* 106 (translated by Satloff).

185. See Le Pautremat, *La politique,* 373. For an example of direct Muslim arguments based on the charter, see APP, HA 29, "Activité du parti du peuple algérien," undated report, 85–86.

186. Abbas was effectively replacing Bendjelloul as the leading Muslim political voice from the reformist wing. On wartime Muslim politics in Algeria, Annie Rey-Goldzeiguer, *Aux origins de la guerre d'Algérie, 1940–1945: de mers-el-kébir aux massacres du Nord-Constantionis* (Paris: Éditions la découverte, 2002), esp. 185, 189–90.

187. Aouate, "Les algériens," 196–97.

188. Quoted in Rey-Goldzeiguer, *Aux origins,* 90. Jeremy Lane, "Ferhat Abbas, Vichy's National Revolution, and the Memory of the Royaume arabe," *L'esprit créateur* 47, no. 1 (2007): 19–31, has a revisionist perspective, contending that Abbas may have initially seen the decree's revocation as a promising sign for the reform proposal he submitted to Pétain.

189. Quoted in Satloff, *Among,* 106 (trans. Satloff).

190. Sadek Sellam, "Le Cheikh el Oqbi au cercle du progress," *NAQD* 11 (1998): 84–90, http://assala-dz.net/old/index.php?option=com_content&view= article&id=1062:le-cheikh-el-oqbi-au-cercle-du-progres-sadek-sellam&catid =29:2012–03–04–19–18–26&Itemid=36; Aouate, "Les algériens," 196–98.

191. Quoted in Cantier, *L'Algérie sous le régime de Vichy,* 333.

192. Aouate, "Les algériens," esp. 196–97.

193. Sura 2, verse 256, *Al Qu'rān,* 45.

194. Traces of each figure's influence in the mainland appear in the archives, but further research is needed for a precise assessment.

195. The negative attention given to *El Hayet* in *Er Rachid* seems to confirm its wide circulation. See Mohamed El-Maadi, "Dedié à 'El hayet,'" *ER,* 28 June 1944.

196. "La guerre atteint de plus en plus son paroxysme," *El Hayet,* June 1944.

197. "La Milice de Darnand," *El Hayet,* June 1944.

198. "Nous avons retrouvé le chemin de la liberté," *El Hayet,* June 1944.

199. *Les oubliés de l'histoire.*

200. Rabah Adjoud, "Les nord-africains aux côtés du peuple français: les faits d'armes des Musulmans dans les combats de la capitale," *Liberté* (Algiers), 19 October 1944. Quoted by Michel Renard on his website: http://islamenfrance .canalblog.com/archives/2007/02/16/4072472.html.

201. Estimates vary. See Belkacem Recham, "Les musulmans algériens dans l'armée française (1919–1945)" (PhD diss., University of Strasbourg, 1995), 249.

202. I based my numbers here on Jewish cemetery records and traditionally Muslim names. Archives de la ville et de la communauté urbaine de Strasbourg (AVCUS), 456 W 11, list of soldiers buried in the Jewish cemetery of Cronen-bourg, Strasbourg; 456 W 12, lists of soldiers fallen and entombed in Strasbourg, 23 November 1944; Dossier Documentaire, militaires tombés à la libération de Strasbourg, 1944–1945.

203. Such consciousness appears in the form of an elaborate monument at the military cemetery and various projects around the memory of colonial soldiers in the liberation of Strasbourg.

204. Interview with Léon and Laurette Nisand, 20 May 2006.

205. Albert Assouline, "Le racisme et non seulement l'antisémitisme durant la France libre," *Vae victis: Bulletin officiel d'information de l'amicale libre du 22ᵉ B.M.N.A.* 26 (August 1982): 27–31.

206. Renée Poznanski, "French Apprehensions, Jewish Expectations: From a Social Imaginary to a Political Practice," in David Bankier, ed., *The Jews Are Coming Back: The Return of the Jews to Their Countries of Origin after WWII* (New York: Berghahn Books; Jerusalem: Yad Vashem, 2005), 44–52.

207. Both statements were made before a Ministry of Foreign Affairs special committee on Jewish Affairs. Cited in ibid., 55–56.

208. Emmanuel Blanchard, *La police,* 70; Belkacem Recham, "Les musulmans dans l'armée française, 1830–1945: Mercenaires ou citoyens?" *Migrance* 38, no. 2 (2011): 32–33.

209. Centre des archives diplomatiques de Nantes (CADN), 1 TU/1/V/1583, memo regarding "Meeting musulman contre l'immigration juive en Palestine," 14 April 1944; APP, HA 29, "Activité du parti du peuple algérien," undated report [1945].

210. CAOM, 5 I 73, "Relations entre israélites et musulmans à Oran," 3 October 1944.

211. Lower figures in APP, BA 1811, report of 29 October 1944; for the higher, Central Zionist Archives (CZA) (Jerusalem)/S25/1985, letter to Central Office of Karen Kayemet L'Yisrael (KKL), 11 November 1944 [Hebrew].

212. Rachel, "Le meeting du 29 octobre à la mutualité," *La Terre retrouvée (TR),* 1 December 1944.

213. Ibid.

214. The text of Zadoca's speech is reproduced in full in AMAE, Inventaire provisoire du fonds Levant (IPFL) 1944–1965, 373, L. 72, K. Hakki to Ministry of Foreign Affairs, 30 October 1944. I have relied on this text for each citation of Zadoca. Many thanks to Maud Mandel for sharing with me her transcription of this document.

215. APP, BA 1811, report of 29 October 1944; Rachel, "Le meeting."

216. Rachel, "Le meeting."

217. APP, BA 1811, report of 29 October 1944; CZA/KKL5/13146, letter from Fisher to Central Office of KKL, 30 October 1944.

218. Rachel, "Le meeting."

219. Ibid.; TG, "Toujours la même main," *TR,* 1 December 1944.

220. CZA/S25/1985, letter to Central Office of KKL.

221. AMAE, IPFL 1944–65, L. 72, K. Hakki to Ministry of Foreign Affairs, 30 October 1944.

4. Expanding the Republic or Ending the Empire?

1. Léo Labousquière, "David et Ali: Conte Judéo-Arabe," *Bulletin de nos communautés (BNC)*, 10, 24 September 1954.

2. See the discussion in Chapter 1.

3. On the increasing prevalence of such visions among French policy-makers during the war, see Matthew Connelly, *A Diplomatic Revolution: Algeria's Fight for Independence and the Origins of the Post–Cold War Era* (New York: Oxford University Press, 2002).

4. Certain recent scholarship offers greater nuance and wider context that also bridges mainland France and Algeria. See esp. Maud Mandel, *Muslims and Jews in France: History of a Conflict* (Princeton, NJ: Princeton University Press, 2014), chaps. 2–3; and Naomi Davidson, *Only Muslim: Embodying Islam in Twentieth-Century France* (Ithaca, NY: Cornell University Press, 2012), chap. 5.

5. Scholars have largely ignored the choices of mainland French Jews during the conflict. For notable exceptions, see Philippe Boukara, "La gauche juive en France et la guerre d'Algérie," *Archives juives* 29, no. 1 (1996): 72–81; Mandel, *Muslims and Jews*, chaps. 2–3. Previous research has shown well the challenges of the war for Algeria's Jews. See esp. Sarah Sussman, "Changing Lands, Changing Identities: The Migration of Algerian Jewry to France, 1954–1967" (PhD diss., Stanford University, 2003); Richard Ayoun, "Les juifs d'Algérie pendant la guerre d'indépendance (1954–1962)," *Archives juives* 29, no. 1 (1996): 15–29; David Cohen, "Le comité juif algérien d'études sociales dans le débat idéologique pendant la guerre d'Algérie (1954–1961)" *Archives juives* 29, no. 1 (1996): 30–50; Benjamin Stora, *Les trois exils: juifs d'Algérie* (Paris: Stock, 2006), part 3; Todd Shepard, *The Invention of Decolonization: The Algerian War and the Remaking of France* (Ithaca, NY: Cornell University Press, 2006), chap. 6; Michael Laskier, *North African Jewry in the Twentieth Century* (New York: New York University Press, 1994), chap. 10. Cohen, "Le comité juif," Sussman, "Changing Lands," and Shepard, *Invention*, emphasize how Jews elicited disproportionate attention from the FLN, the French government, and the OAS and sought to accommodate each of these forces.

6. See in particular Todd Shepard, "Thinking between Metropole and Colony: The French Republic, 'Exceptional Promotion,' and the 'Integration' of Algerians, 1955–1962," in Martin Thomas, ed., *The French Colonial Mind*, vol. 1 (Lincoln, NE: University of Nebraska Press, 2011); Shepard, *Invention*.

7. Already in 1944, France offered full French citizenship to a list of about 65,000 Muslim men in Algeria without their having to surrender their "local" status as Muslims. In May 1946, it made all Algerian males citizens with local status, reaffirmed in the October Constitution. Equal rights for Muslims living in the metropole applied only while they resided in mainland France. Regarding the persistent inequalities for French Muslims from Algeria in the mainland, see

Alexis Spire, "Semblables et pourtants différents. La citoyenneté paradoxale des 'Français musulmans d'Algérie' en metropole," *Genèses* 53 (2003): 48–68. Regarding the responses of French police and colonists to Algerian Muslims' attainment of full citizenship, Emmanuel Blanchard, "Encadrer des 'citoyens diminués': La police des algériens en région parisienne (1944–1962)" (PhD diss., University of Bourgogne, 2008), 68–69.

8. See Archives de la prefecture de police (APP) (Paris), HA 7, "Le problème nord-africaine," 22 November 1951.

9. This represented 746,000 arrivals versus 561,000 departures. Benjamin Stora, *Ils venaient d'Algérie: l'immigration algérienne en France, 1912–1992* (France: Fayard, 1992), 94.

10. Ibid., 94–95. We lack numerical data for this demographic shift.

11. In August 1953, the interior ministry estimated five thousand Muslim families and eleven thousand children residing in the metropole. Stora, *Ils venaient*, 94; APP, HA 7, "Le problème nord-africaine," 22 November 1951. On Muslim families in the Algerian migration, Amelia Lyons, *The Civilizing Mission in the Metropole: Algerian Families and the French Welfare State during Decolonization* (Stanford, CA: Stanford University Press, 2013).

12. Stora, *Ils venaient*, 95.

13. Here I follow Blanchard, "Encadrer des 'citoyens diminués,'" 103.

14. See ibid., 104–6.

15. Only about 2,500, or 3 percent of these, survived. Michael R. Marrus and Robert Paxton, *Vichy France and the Jews* (New York: Basic Books, 1981; reprint Stanford, CA: Stanford University Press, 1995), 343 (page references from reprint edition).

16. This discussion draws heavily on Maud S. Mandel, *In the Aftermath of Genocide: Armenians and Jews in Twentieth-Century France* (Durham, NC: Duke University Press, 2003), 167–76; for quotation from FSJU leader, 172.

17. Esther Benbassa, *The Jews of France: A History from Antiquity to the Present*, trans. M. B. DeBevoise (Princeton, NJ: Princeton University Press, 1999), 180.

18. At this time, these were revocation of the British White Paper of 1939, open Jewish immigration, and a solution to the political conflict that respected Jewish rights to national self-determination.

19. In my discussion of the war's significance for Zionism and the creation of CRIF, I have drawn largely on Mandel, *In the Aftermath*, esp. 135–48. Quotation cited in ibid., 139.

20. Examples and emigration figure from ibid., 137, 147.

21. Doris Bensimon-Donath, *L'integration des juifs Nord-Africains en France* (Paris: Mouton, 1971), 30.

22. Colette Zytnicki, "Du rapatrié au séfarade. L'intégration des juifs d'Afrique du Nord dans la société française: essai de bilan," *Archives Juives* 38, no. 2 (2005): 86. Others have given smaller figures for this period: Jacques

Taïeb, "Immigrés d'Afrique du Nord: Combien? Quand? Pourquoi?" in Zytnicki, ed., *Terre d'exil, terre d'asile: Migrations juives en France aux XIXe et XXe siècles* (Villefranche-de-Roudergue: Éclat, 2010), 50–51.

23. See esp APP, HA 7, "Situation des musulmans dans le département de la Seine," 1–15 August 1948.

24. On the first specific incident, Centre des archives diplomatiques de Nantes (CADN), 1TU/V/2793, Bureau du Maghreb Arabe, translated bulletin, "Le navire français 'La Providence' débarque mille deux cents juifs à Haïfa," 29 May 1948; for the second, Archives du ministère des affaires étrangères (AMAE) (La Courneuve), 148 W 85, folder on Jews and Arabs, Service départemental des renseignements généraux, Mle, "La guerre en Palestine—Projection de films jugés provocateurs par les arabes de Marseille," 10 June 1948. My thanks to Maud Mandel for generously sharing her notes on the second file with me. For more on these developments and their larger context, from which I have drawn in my interpretation, see Mandel, *Muslims and Jews,* chap. 1.

25. There are disputes about the casualty figures, with the Algerian state claiming much higher tolls for the Algerian rebels. For my figures and a good synopsis, see Davidson, *Only Muslim,* 139.

26. For figures, "Plusieurs centaines de juifs ont été tués en Algérie depuis le début des événements," *Journal des communautés (JDC),* 13 September 1957; Sussman, "Changing Lands," 93. Regarding the degree to which the FLN may properly be termed a "revolutionary movement," see Gilbert Meynier, *Histoire intérieure du FLN, 1954–1962* (Paris: Fayard, 2002), 157–68.

27. Ayoun, "Les juifs d'Algérie," 24.

28. Archives de l'Alliance Israélite Universelle (AIU) (Paris), Fonds Jacques Lazarus (FJL), Dossier XVI, report on meeting of the Conseil du CJAES, 8 December 1955.

29. A February 1958 survey found the war ranked sixth among French people's preoccupations. Benjamin Stora, *Histoire de la guerre d'Algérie (1954–1962)* (Paris: Éditions la découverte, 2002), 66.

30. For the interwar period, Clifford Rosenberg, *Policing Paris: The Origins of Modern Immigration Control between the Wars* (Ithaca, NY: Cornell University Press, 2006); for the postwar period, see Blanchard, "Encadrer des 'citoyens diminués.'"

31. Blanchard, "Encadrer des 'citoyens diminués,'" 98.

32. American Joint Distribution Committee (AJDC) (Jerusalem), Geneva II, Box 384, folder 12, France, Budget Department, population statistics for France, 15 February 1963.

33. APP, HA 7, Recensement de la population musulmane, 17 March 1958.

34. APP, HA 8, préfecture de police (PP), Direction de la police judiciaire (DPJ), "Etude de la population nord-africaine à Paris et dans le département de la Seine," 1955. For figures, 1–3; 11; for quotations, 14.

35. APP, HA 7, "La population nord-africaine de Paris et du département de la Seine," 1952.

36. See, for example, Stora, *Ils venaient,* chaps. 6 and 8, esp. 95–96, 149; and Neil MacMaster, *Colonial Migrants and Racism: Algerians in France, 1900–62* (New York: St. Martin's Press, 1997), chaps. 10–11, esp. 183–88, 190–95.

37. Reasons for this included a lack of agents for a large caseload, a pittance of Arabic speakers, and poor knowledge of Algerian nationalist networks. Blanchard, "Encadrer des 'citoyens diminués,' " 105–7.

38. In part I have drawn this idea from ibid., 98–100.

39. These population estimates were based on ration cards and employment statistics. Davidson, *Only Muslim,* 129.

40. APP, HA 7, "La population nord-africaine de Paris et du département de la Seine," 1952, 3–5. While we lack precise figures for Jews in the quarter at this moment, we know that they remained larger than those of Muslims, themselves about 5 percent.

41. APP, HA 15, PP, Police municipale (PM), IVe arrondissement, "Liste des hôtels, restaurants, débits de boissons tenus par nord-africains," 27 April 1951; "Restaurants nord-africains, région parisienne," 1951. As of 1954, it appears that nearly all of Paris's "North African" establishments of three years previously continued to operate. APP, HA 15, PP, Direction générale de la police municipale, report of 15 December 1954.

42. Interview with Louise Jaïs (née Fhal), 5 June 2006.

43. APP, HA 15, PP, PM, IVe arrondissement, "Liste des hôtels"; interview with Roger Gharbi, 6 June 2006; interview with Félix Amanou, 11 July 2006.

44. Full name found in APP, HA 15, "Restaurants nord-africains, région parisienne," 1951.

45. APP, HA 15, PP, PM, IVe arrondissement, "Liste des hôtels"; interview with Roger Gharbi. Gharbi referred to Tordjemann as Alexandre, but *Elie* is the name in the archives.

46. Interviews with Félix Amanou, 11 June, 11 July 2006; interview with Roger Gharbi.

47. For details on the Faubourg Montmartre and the Soleil d'Alger, I have drawn from APP, HA 15, Préfecture de Police, Police Municipale, 2e Division, 9e Arrondissement, "Liste des Hotels, Restaurants, Debits de Boissons tenus par les Nord-Africains," response to circular of 17 April 1951; interview with Roger Gharbi; "Lili Boniche, chanteur," *Le Monde,* 22 March 2008.

48. This paragraph draws much of its depiction from Hisham D. Aidi, *Rebel Music: Race, Empire and the New Muslim Youth Culture* (New York: Pantheon Books, 2014), esp. 259–60, 263, 279–80, 319–20.

49. Raphael Valensi, "Le temple de la rue Julien-Lacroix est devenu un creuset," *Terre retrouvée (TR),* 15 January 1956.

50. APP, HA 8, PP, "Etude de la population," 42–43; street-by-street map of "places of habitation" of FMAs in the Seine, 1958; HA 15, list of North African food establishments in the 20th arrondissement, 26 April 1951; "Etat des débits de boissons acquis par des nord-africains à des métropolitains, depuis 1er janvier 1957"; Patrick Simon and Claude Tapia, *Le Belleville des juifs tunisiens* (Paris: Éditions autrement, 1998), 62. For the further development of Belleville, see chaps. 5 and 6.

51. At this time, police noted "no particular incident" between Jews and Muslims in the Marais or Belleville. APP, HA 8, PP, "Étude de la population," 23. Moreover, in reports of both 1951 and 1957 on individual cafés, none noted for political activism were located in either quarter.

52. Quoted in Shepard, *Invention*, 43.

53. On the FLN-MNA struggle, see Stora, *Histoire de la guerre*, chap. 4; on the background of the FLN's activists, 10–13, 42–43.

54. See Shepard, "Thinking" and *Invention*, 45–54.

55. On national memory in both France and Algeria, see esp. Stora, *La gangrène et l'oubli: la mémoire de la guerre d'Algérie* (Paris: Découverte, 1991).

56. On the unique dynamics of this brief period, see Davidson, *Only Muslim*, esp. 142–49.

57. For French concern regarding nationalist activity at the mosque, see, for example, Centre des archives outre-mer (CAOM) (Aix-en-Provence), 81 F 833, report, "Cérémonie à la mosquée de Paris à l'occasion de l'Aïd-Es-Seghier," 23 May 1955. On Boubakeur's appointment and his wartime loyalty, see Centre des archives contemporaines (CAC) (Fontainebleau), 0019770346, art. 11, service des affaires musulmanes, memo on Institut musulman de la mosquée de Paris, 1 March 1963.

58. On the first point, see the lack of political concerns in reports such as CAOM, 81 F 833, report on Aïd-es-Seghir at the mosque, 20 April 1958. On the second point, CAOM, 81 F 832, "Institut musulman de la mosquée de Paris, projet de budget, propositions de dépenses et de recettes pour l'exercise 1961."

59. The term *harkis* originally designated Algerian Muslims in government-armed self-defense units but became the common term for any Muslim French citizens who supported the French. Estimates for total numbers vary considerably. The figures and explanation above come from William B. Cohen, "The Harkis: History and Memory," in Patricia M. E. Lorcin, ed., *Algeria and France, 1800–2000: Identity, Memory, Nostalgia* (Syracuse, NY: Syracuse University Press, 2006), 164–65.

60. Here I draw on Shepard, *Invention*, 45–54, and "Thinking."

61. See Connelly, *A Diplomatic Revolution*, 216–18.

62. Here I am influenced by the discussion in Joshua Cole, "Remembering the Battle of Paris: 17 October 1961 in French and Algerian Memory," *French Politics, Culture and Society* 21, no. 3 (2003): 21–50, esp. 36–40.

63. Quoted in Connelly, *A Diplomatic Revolution*, 179.

64. Quoted in ibid., 181.

65. On the FLN's platform, see Meynier, *Histoire intérieure*, 157–68; Stora, *Histoire de la guerre*, 42–44.

66. On Soummam, see Meynier, *Histoire intérieure*, 191–200.

67. *El Moudjahid*, special issue of 1 November 1956, found in APP, HA 26.

68. Quotations from ibid.; context from Mandel, *Muslims and Jews*, 50.

69. "Lettre du C.C.E. aux Israélites d'Algérie," 1 October 1956, reprinted in Fédération de France du front de libération nationale algérien, ed., *A l'adresse du peuple français—FLN documents*, no. 5: "Les juifs d'Algérie dans le combat pour l'independence" (Paris, December 1959).

70. "Les juifs du Maroc et la révolution," *Résistance algérienne*, 10 January 1957, excerpted in Fédération de France.

71. "Quelques points," *Résistance algérienne*, Edition B, 1 November 1956.

72. In part I draw here on Cohen, "Le comité juif algérien."

73. See, for instance, the introductory section to Fédération de France, ed.

74. "Appel de la fédération de France du FLN," 25 November 1959, quoted in Fédération de France, ed.

75. On Lebjaoui and Jews, see Meynier, *Histoire intérieure*, 256; Mohamed Lebjaoui, *Vérités sur la révolution algérienne* (Paris: Gallimard, 1970), 114–23.

76. See Lebjaoui, *Vérités*, 114–17; Mohamed Harbi, *Une vie debout. Mémoires politiques*, vol. 1: *1945–1962* (Paris, La Découverte et Syros, 2001).

77. Lebjaoui, *Vérités*, 117. On the international nature of the revolution, see Connelly, *A Diplomatic Revolution*.

78. Sussman, "Changing Lands," 115–17, 127–28.

79. The FLN authored most of these attacks. I compiled totals from press clippings kept by Lazarus of every incident known to him in which Jews were targeted from 1956 to the war's end, in AIU, FJL, dossier I, and I supplemented these with other cases mentioned in secondary sources.

80. Figure from "Plusieurs centaines"; for shifting Jewish perceptions regarding FLN attacks, Jessica Hammerman, "The Heart of the Diaspora: Algerian Jews during the War for Independence, 1954–1962" (PhD diss., City University of New York, 2013), 194–95.

81. Based again on compilations from AIU, FJL, dossier I, and secondary sources.

82. Mandel, *Muslims and Jews*, 47.

83. Hammerman, "The Heart," 194.

84. Hammerman discovered this document and details its contents in ibid., 211–12.

85. AIU, FJL, dossier 1, various files on Boghari attack, 1 October 1958; letter from Abraham Sellem to Lazarus, 16 October 1959; Sussman, 106–7; Stora, *Les trois*, 148.

86. Cited in Pierre-Jean Le Foll-Luciani, "Des étudiants juifs algériens dans le mouvement national algérien à Paris (1948–1962)," in Frédéric Abécassis, Karima Dirèche, and Rita Aouad, eds., *La bienvenue et l'adieu: migrants juifs et musulmans au Maghreb (XVᵉ-XXᵉ siècle)*, vol. 3 (Casablanca: Centre Jacques-Berque, 2012).

87. Quoted in Le Foll-Luciani, "Des étudants."

88. AIU, FJL, dossier III, letter from Lazarus to M. Rabi, 26 July 1957. Emphasis mine.

89. "Une déclaration du comité juif d'études sociales," *Information juive (IJ)*, November 1956.

90. In the first case, see, for example, Archives du consistoire israélite centrale de France (ACICF) (Paris), Fonds Jacques Lazarus (FJL), "Rapport aux assises du judaïsme algérien," Algiers, 13–14 March 1958. Individual cartons are not numbered.

91. As of late 1961, a low point due to disintegrating conditions, *IJ* reported a print run of 6,500. "Nous continuons," *IJ*, December 1961.

92. AIU, FJL, dossier III, letter from Lazarus to Maurice Perlzweig, 14 January 1957.

93. On Algerian Jewish collective memory, see Ethan Katz, "Between Emancipation and Persecution: Algerian Jewish Memory in the *Longue durée* (1930–1970)," *Journal of North African Studies* 17, no. 5 (2012): 793–820.

94. See, for example, statement of Lazarus, cited in ACICF, FJL, "Rapports aux assises."

95. See, for example, ibid.

96. See, for example, Lazarus, "Tels que," *IJ*, April 1961 and many of the cited files from ACICF, FJL.

97. Jacques Lazarus, "Fidelité à soi-même," *IJ*, June 1958.

98. See, for example, ACICF, FJL, Jacques Lazarus, "Mémoire," 1961.

99. At this time, one estimate placed Algeria's Jewish population at about 128,000, nearly equal to the war's eve. CAC, 0019920172, article 8, liasse 3, list of Algerian Jews by locality, beginning of 1961. Mandel, *Muslims and Jews*, chap. 2, argues differently, seeing the Jewish movement toward departure beginning at an earlier stage.

100. On the above points, see Sussman, "Changing Lands," 91, 102–6.

101. Lazarus claims that *IJ* published a story each time it knew of an attack. Interview with Jacques Lazarus, 15 June 2006. Yet in examining all issues of the period, I counted only seven stories about specific attacks.

102. "Une motion du comité juif algérien d'études sociales," *IJ*, May–June 1957. Hammerman, "The Heart," 202, interprets this statement differently.

103. Untitled editorial; see also Jacques Lazarus, "Fidelité à soi-même," both in *IJ*, June 1958.

104. Henri Chemouilli, "Sept ans," *Évidence* 94 (1962), found in AIU, FJL, dossier IV. Emphasis mine. By the late stages of the war, Chemouilli would align

himself with the fiercest supporters of Algérie française as they engaged in a bitter, searing struggle with de Gaulle. Thus his words should in part be understood as a political protest about what might have been.

105. See Mandel, *Muslims and Jews*, chap. 2. On North African Jewry in the era of decolonization, see Laskier, *North African*.

106. Figure for Tunisia from Benbassa, *Jews of France*, 186. On Moroccan Jews' complex identity and legal status under the protectorate, see Daniel J. Schroeter and Joseph Chetrit, "Emancipation and Its Discontents: Jews at the Formative Period of Colonial Rule in Morocco," *Jewish Social Studies* n.s. 13, no. 1 (2006): 170–206.

107. A primary source for such information was *Information juive*. See, for example, the issue of June 1956.

108. Regarding the interconnectedness of the Suez War with Algeria, see Connelly, *A Diplomatic Revolution*, chap. 4. Quotation from ibid., 109.

109. See Richard C. Vinen, "The End of an Ideology? Right-Wing Antisemitism in France, 1944–1970," *Historical Journal* 37, no. 2 (1994): 365–88, here 376–77.

110. "'Droit égaux en Algérie,'" *Nouvel observateur*, 13 September 1957, found in AIU, FJL, dossier II; see also Abbas's interview in Cairo, quoted at length in ACICF, FJL, "rapport aux assises."

111. Jacqueline Shohet Kahanoff, "Rebel, My Brother," in Kahanoff, *Mongrels or Marvels: The Levantine Writings of Jacqueline Shohet Kahanoff*, eds. Deborah Starr and Sasson Somekh (Oxford: Oxford University Press, 2011), 177–92, here 185. I am grateful to Deborah Starr for alerting me to this text. Regarding Ben Bella's later criticisms of Israel, see Chapter 5.

112. On Abd al-Qadir, see Michael M. Laskier, "Israel and Algeria amid French Colonialism and the Arab-Israeli Conflict, 1954–1978," *Israel Studies* 6, no. 2 (1998): 8–9.

113. A. Razak Abdel-Kader, *Le Conflit judéo-arabe* (Paris: François Maspero, 1961), esp. 373–86. (The publisher used the French spelling of the author's name.) The work received an enthusiastic review and was briefly excerpted in the *Cahiers Bernard Lazare (CBL)* of October 1961.

114. For example, see "Tract distribué en Algérie," *Voix du peuple algérien*, undated, circa September 1956.

115. "Un crime gratuit, un crime unjustifiable: l'assassinat de Jacob Hassan et de Raphaël ben Guera délégués de l'agence juive en Algérie," *IJ*, August–September 1958; "A la mémoire de Jacob Hassan et Raphaël ben Guera: Action de solidarité en faveur de leurs sept orphelins," *IJ*, October 1958.

116. See Laskier, "Israel and Algeria"; Stora, *Les trois*, 154–55.

117. See, for example, Lazarus, "Tels que"; André Narboni, "1948–1961," *IJ*, April 1961.

118. See, for example, Jacques Soustelle, "La tradition de la France," and "Pour l'alliance France-Israël," both in *TR*, 1 March 1957.

119. Jean Daniel, "Israël, la France et l'Algérie," *L'Arche*, October 1957.

120. "Le cercle Bernard Lazare pour la négociation et pour la paix" and Henry Bulawko, "Les contradictions de M. Soustelle," both in *CBL*, March–April 1958.

121. Estimates vary widely. See Meynier, *Histoire intérieure*, 255; Laskier, *North African*, 319–22; Stora, *Les trois*, 152–53.

122. See, for instance, "Une campagne criminelle," *IJ*, January 1961; Jean Maquet, "A Oran comme à Alger un passant invisible: la peur," *Paris Match*, 20 January 1962, 27.

123. CAC, 0019920172, article 8, liasse 3, Ministère de l'Intérieur, memo of 12 February 1961, "Création d'un comité israélien pour l'Algérie libre."

124. "Message du docteur Modiano, président du C.R.I.F.," *JDC*, 28 September 1956.

125. Centre de documentation juive contemporaine (CDJC), MDI 14–18, Procès-verbaux of CRIF general assembly meetings, 1956–1960; MDI 37–39, Réunions du bureau of CRIF, 1958–1960.

126. CDJC, MDI 14, meeting of 23 December 1955; MDI 18, meeting of July 1960.

127. A telling exception, in September 1957, was a report, buried several pages into the *Journal*, that several hundred Jews had died in attacks in Algeria since the start of the conflict. "Plusieurs centaines."

128. "Message de Roch-Hachana du grand rabbin de France," *JDC*, 31 August 1956. Kaplan also worked behind the scenes on France's behalf, helping to secure continuing positive coverage of the French position in the *New York Times* during the United Nations debates over Algeria. Connelly, *A Diplomatic Revolution*, 127.

129. "Roch Hachana 5719," *JDC*, 12 September 1958. It was broadcast on the national radio program "Ecoute Israël" and reprinted in full or in excerpts throughout most of the Jewish press.

130. The population's size and France's conscription suggest at least a few thousand Jews served.

131. "Les fêtes de paques dans la marine française," *BNC*, 5 April 1957.

132. "Pourim de nos soldats," *IJ*, March 1960.

133. See in particular the *Journal des communautés* and the *Bulletin de nos communautés*.

134. In the first instance, "Distinctions," under "Dans nos communautés," *BNC*, 23 August 1957.

135. Émile Touati, "Analyse de l'immigration nord-africaine," *Revue du FSJU*, March 1956.

136. See Katz, "Between Emancipation."

137. Henri Alleg, *La question* (Paris: Éditions de Minuit, 1958); Pierre Vidal-Naquet, *L'affaire Audin* (Paris: Éditions de Minuit, 1958).

138. "Le droit à l'insoumission," *Vérité-Liberté,* 6 September 1960.

139. Le Foll-Luciani, "Des étudiants."

140. Archives départementales du Bas-Rhin (ADBR) (Strasbourg), 544 D 171, Minister of the Interior, Renseignements-généraux (R-G) report of 26 June 1956.

141. See Jean Laloum, "Portrait d'un juif du FLN," *Archives juives* 29, no. 1 (1996): 65–71. Regarding Timsit's brothers, Sussman, "Changing Lands," 130–31.

142. Jean Bensimon, "Etre juif en Algérie: Une illusion perdue?" *Kadimah: Journal de l'union des étudiants juifs de France,* December 1962.

143. On this point and Jews in the FLN more broadly, see Hammerman, "The Heart," chap. 4.

144. Frantz Fanon, *A Dying Colonialism,* trans. Haakon Chevalier, with an introduction by Adolfo Gilly (New York: Grove Press, 1965), 154. Fanon (1925–1961), a psychiatrist and philosopher who became an immensely influential anticolonial thinker and activist, was originally from Martinique but moved to Algeria and joined the FLN. As a historical observer, he is admittedly not altogether reliable. He maintains, for instance, that 75 percent of Algerian Jews—a grossly exaggerated number—were "highly Arabized" so that for this group "there is no problem: they are Algerians" (155). I have cited him here because the specificity of his claim makes it appear credible.

145. Albert Memmi, *The Pillar of Salt,* trans. Edouard Roditi (Boston: Beacon Press, 1955), and *The Colonizer and the Colonized,* trans. Howard Greenfeld (New York: Orion Press, 1965).

146. Memmi, "Portrait du juif colonisé," *L'Arche,* June–July 1957.

147. Albert Memmi, "Le juif et la politique," *IJ,* December 1961. Emphasis mine.

148. See, for example, "Albert Memmi: Nous et la politique," *CBL,* June 1961.

149. "Un groupe de juifs algériens," in *Al Istiqlal,* 2 February 1957 and *Résistance algérienne,* Edition B, 28 February 1957. Quoted in *Fédération de France,* ed.

150. On the Jewish Left during the war, see Boukara, "La gauche juive."

151. Curt Niedermaier, "Union d'étudiants . . . en France," *Communauté,* December 1959–January 1960, 29.

152. CDJC, MDI 14, meeting of 23 December 1955.

153. Niedermaier, "Union d'étudiants," 26–28.

154. Quoted in APP, HA 25, dossier on Comité des algériens israélites pour la négociation en Algérie, 1958.

155. See Le Foll-Luciani, "Des étudiants."

156. For one striking instance of anti-Jewish propaganda at this time, see a pamphlet distributed in Paris the day of the 28 September 1958 referendum. CDJC, MDI-16, meeting of 20 October 1958.

157. Most of these patterns are discussed below. On the FLN as "antisemitic," see small, untitled notice from Algiers of *BNC,* 5 October 1956.

158. Louis Bloch, "De choses et d'autres," *BNC,* 4 April 1958.

159. Freddy Raphaël, "La tentation de faire de bien," *BNC,* 26 September 1958.

160. ADBdR, 138 W 74, dossier of Iddir, Mohamed and the Association des anciens combattants français musulmans, documents dated August 1957–July 1960.

161. ADBdR, 138 W 74, note of February 16, 1959.

162. ADBdR, 138 W 74, dossiers of Lakidar, Habib, documents of August 1959; Association des anciens combattants français musulmans, 1957–1960.

163. Yacine Kateb, *Nedjma* (Paris: Éditions du Seuil, 1956).

164. Here I follow Charles Bonn, "Le jeu avec l'histoire dans *Nedjma,*" in Jacques Girault and Bernard Lecherbonnier, eds., *Kateb Yacine: un intellectuel dans la révolution algérienne* (Paris: l'Harmattan, 2002), 35–46, and *Kateb Yacine, Nedjma* (Paris: Presses universitaires de France, 1990); Richard Keller, *Colonial Madness: Psychiatry in French North Africa* (Chicago: University of Chicago Press, 2007), 175.

165. Kateb Yacine, "'Message aux juifs d'Israël et du monde,'" *CBL,* June 1957. The history of the Kahena is rather more complex than Kateb made it sound, as she has been appropriated by various groups and not always defined as Jewish. See Abdelmajid Hannoum, *Colonial Histories, Post-Colonial Memories: The Legend of the Kahina, a North African Heroine* (Portsmouth, NH: Heinemann, 2001).

166. Figure from "Un temple du rite nord-africain à Paris," *JDC,* 23 May 1958. Geographical concentration noted in ibid. and Roger Berg, "Lettre de Paris," *BNC,* 18 November 1960. As a percentage of the Jewish population of the 3rd, 4th, 9th, 10th, and 11th arrondissements, Algerian Jewish immigrants jumped from 2 percent in the interwar period to 33.2 percent between 1940 and 1959. Richard Ayoun and Bernard Cohen, *Les juifs d'Algérie: Deux mille ans d'histoire* (Paris: Jean-Claude Lattès, 1982), appendix III.

167. APP, HA 8, Dénombrement des français musulmans algériens de la Seine, 1959; map of "places of habitation" of FMAs in the Seine, 1958. Figures for North African Jews in the Marais are hard to estimate, but based on those given in "Un temple du rite" appear to be at least in the low thousands.

168. Interviews with Félix Amanou, Roger Gharbi, and Louise Jaïs; APP, HA 15, PP, PM, IVe arrondissement, "Liste des hôtels"; Archives de la ville de Paris (AVP), 2 Mi LN 1936 / 7, 4ᵉ: Saint-Gervais, du 87 rue Saint-Antoine au 26 rue des Rosiers.

169. All material throughout this section comes from interview with Patricia Jaïs, 20 June 2006.

170. See Stora, *Ils venaient,* 206–7.

171. See numerous dossiers in APP, HA 15; HA 25; maps in HA 29.

172. See MacMaster, *Colonial migrants,* 192–99; Davidson, *Only Muslim,* 149–50.

173. Compiled from APP, HA 27, Reports on nationalist-affiliated establishments, 10 November 1956, 20 April 1957, in conjunction with other records cited above from HA 15.

174. APP, HA 15, "Liste des hôtels, restaurants, débits de boissons tenus par les nord-africains," 27 April 1951; Etat des débits de boissons acquis par des nord-africains." On the Goutte d'or, see Jean-Claude Toubon and Khelifa Messamah, *Centralité immigrée: Le quartier de la goutte d'or,* vol. 1 (Paris: l'Harmattan, 1990), esp. 209–12.

175. This story—as well as the group's reunification fifty years later—is told in the documentary *El Gusto,* directed by Safinez Bousbia (2012).

176. See Mehenna Mahfoufi, *Chants kabyles de la guerre d'indépendance, Algérie 1954–1962* (Paris: Éditions Séguier, 2002), esp. 95–98, 105.

177. Aidi, *Rebel Music,* 289–90.

178. "Des juifs maltraités par des agents de police dans le 4ᵉ arrondissement," *BNC,* 18 April 1958.

179. Roger Berg, "Lettre de Paris," *BNC,* 18 April 1958. Berg later became editor of the Central Consistory's organ.

180. On the latter point, see Mandel, *Muslims and Jews,* chaps. 1–2. I use the phrase Israel/Palestine here as elsewhere to refer to the territories over which Israelis, Palestinians, and neighboring Arab states have struggled since 1948. These include today's Israel, the West Bank, and the Gaza Strip.

181. Cited in "'L'antisémitisme redevient public,'" under "Coin des jeunes," *BNC,* 2 May 1958.

182. "Après les incidents de la rue François-Miron," *JDC,* 28 October 1960. On the second incident, "Des supplétifs algériens molestent des Juifs," *BNC,* 5 August 1960.

183. See esp. Neil MacMaster, *Burning the Veil: The Algerian War and the "Emancipation" of Algerian Women, 1954–1962* (Manchester: Manchester University Press, 2010); Davidson, *Only Muslim,* chap. 5; Shepard, *The Invention,* chap. 7.

184. Archives nationales (AN) (Paris), F1a, 5035, Ministère de l'intérieur (MdI), Direction des services de l'Algérie et des départements d'Outre-Mer, circulaire no. 310, 24 August 1953; MdI, Cabinet du ministre, Affaires sociales musulmanes en métropole, circulaire no. 65, 10 February 1958.

185. AJDC, Geneva II, Box 384, folder 12, France, Budget Department, population statistics for France; Box 382b, 7, France, Report on Visit to Marseille, 14–19 February 1961. On Jewish migration to Marseille at this time, Jean-Jacques Jordi, *De l'exode a l'exil: rapatriés et pieds-noirs en France, L'Exemple marseillais, 1954–1992* (Paris: Éditions l'Harmattan, 1993), 213.

186. Émile Temime, *Marseille transit: les passagers de Belsunce* (Paris: Éditions autrement, 1995), 70–71, 75.

187. There is no mention of Jews for this time in either ibid. or archival references.

188. Archives du CASIP-COJASOR (Paris), Fonds du comité juif d'action sociale et de reconstruction (COJASOR), COJASOR. R. Egy. A, COJASOR financial report on funds for relodging of refugees from Egypt, June 1957–December 1959.

189. On the Félix Pyat, see Abdelmalek Sayad, Jean-Jacques Jordi, and Émile Temime, *Migrance: Histoire des migrations à Marseille,* vol. 4 (Aix-en-Provence: Edisud, 1991), 150; on Jews there, AJDC, Box 382b, 7, France, Report on Visit to Marseille, 14–19 February 1961.

190. ADBdR, 138 W 73, dossier of Guendouz, Abed, documents of February 1960.

191. Jewish figure from AJDC, Geneva II, Box 384, folder 12, France, Budget Department, population statistics for France; for Muslim figure and account, ADBR, 544 D 171, series of dossiers.

192. ADBR, 544 D 183, MdI, DGSN, "Recensement de ressortissants d'Algérie, du Maroc et de Tunisie," 21 December 1959.

193. Interview with Habib Hihi and Evelyne Rueff-Hihi, 3 May 2006.

5. A Time of Choosing

1. See esp. Todd Shepard, *The Invention of Decolonization: The Algerian War and the Remaking of France* (Ithaca, NY: Cornell University Press, 2006).

2. "L'antisémitisme, cheval de bataille du colonialisme," *El Moudjahid,* 21 December 1960, quoted in Lazarus, "Tels que nous sommes," *Information juive (IJ),* January 1961.

3. "Le saccage de la grande synagogue d'Alger," *IJ,* December 1960; Benjamin Stora, *Les trois exils: juifs d'Algérie* (Paris: Stock, 2006), 155–56; Archives de l'Alliance Israélite Universelle (AIU) (Paris), Fonds Jacques Lazarus (FJL), Dossier II, photographs from the attack, December 1960. David Cohen, "Le comité juif algérien d'études sociales dans le débat idéologique pendant la guerre d'Algérie (1954–1961)," *Archives juives* 29, no. 1 (1996): 37–39 attributes the attack to the OAS, but with little evidence.

4. Sarah Sussman, "Changing Lands, Changing Identities: The Migration of Algerian Jewry to France, 1954–1967" (PhD diss., Stanford University, 2003), 107–9.

5. Compiled from AIU, FJL, Dossier I; and other attacks noted in several secondary sources: Sussman, "Changing Lands"; Richard Ayoun, "Les juifs d'Algérie pendant la guerre d'indépendance (1954–1962)," *Archives juives* 29, no. 1 (1996): 15–29; Cohen, "Le comité juif"; and Michael Laskier, *North*

African Jewry in the Twentieth Century (New York: New York University Press, 1994), chap. 10.

6. See "Attentats," *IJ*, June 1961; Ayoun, "Les juifs d'Algérie," 26–27.

7. From *Droit et liberté*, May 1961, cited in "Attentats," *IJ*, June 1961.

8. The claim here about Leyris's politics appears in Arnold Mandel, "Algeria," country-by-country reports, *American Jewish Yearbook (AJYB)*, 1963, 407. Leyris's personal politics, however, remain disputed and somewhat shrouded in mystery.

9. See Gilbert Meynier, *Histoire intérieure du FLN, 1954–1962* (Paris: Fayard, 2002), 255, 257.

10. See, for example, "Un tract F.L.N. adressé aux juifs," *Le Bulletin de nos communautés (BNC)*, 4 May 1962.

11. Central Zionist Archives (CZA) (Jerusalem)/C10/3303, transcript of debate on "engagement et non engagement," Colloque de la jeunesse juive en France, March 1961.

12. Mohamed Ben Bachir, "Un étudiant nous répond," *Kadimah*, April–May 1961.

13. Here I have drawn on the fuller discussion of Maud Mandel, *Muslims and Jews in France: History of a Conflict* (Princeton, NJ: Princeton University Press, 2014), 63–65, 192n36. Quotation from ibid., 64. For disclaimer and rebuttals, see "Un étudiant musulman nous répond," and "Réponse à la lettre de M. B. Bachir Ben Mohamed au sujet de 'Reflexions d'un étudiant juif religieux sur le problem algérien,'" in *Kadimah*, April–May 1961.

14. Jean Daniel, *Cet étranger qui me ressemble* (Paris: Grasset, 2004), cited in Stora, *Les trois*, 160–61.

15. Jessica Hammerman, "The Heart of the Diaspora: Algerian Jews during the War for Independence, 1954–1962" (PhD diss., City University of New York, 2013), 217–18.

16. H. B., "Ben Bella Chez Nasser," *Cahiers Bernard Lazare (CBL)*, April 1962; "La quinzaine dans le monde juif," *BNC*, 4 May 1962. Further research is needed to account for the dramatic shift on Ben Bella's part. His earlier private statements lauding Begin and Israel (see Chapter 4) suggest that perhaps the attitude he evinced near the war's end was more pragmatic than heartfelt. On the other hand, the Suez War, the hesitation of most Algerian Jews to join the FLN, and the rumors linking the OAS with Israel all could have turned him against Israel.

17. See Laskier, *North African*, 202–5, 299–301; Jacques Taïeb, "Immigrés d'Afrique du Nord: Combien? Quand? Pourquoi?" in Colette Zytnicki, ed., *Terre d'exil, terre d'asile: Migrations juives en France aux XIXe et XXe siècles* (Villefranche-de-Roudergue: Éclat, 2010), 151–53. These incidents received ample coverage in the pages of *Information juive*.

18. Shepard, *Invention*, chap. 6; Stora, *Les trois*, pt. 3; and Sussman, "Changing Lands," 113–15, 132–38.

19. Cited in Matthew Connelly, *A Diplomatic Revolution: Algeria's Fight for Independence and the Origins of the Post-Cold War Era* (Oxford: Oxford University Press, 2002), 221.

20. OAS, "Vive la France," found with report dated 4 December 1961, in Archives départementales du Bas-Rhin (ADBR) (Strasbourg), 589 D 241.

21. Quotations from multiple OAS tracts of late 1961. For examples of OAS attacks on Jews, see Ayoun, "Les juifs d'Algérie," 27. For depictions of the OAS as antisemitic, see, for example, ADBR, 589 D 241, Prefecture of the Bas-Rhin (PBR), report on pamphlet distributed by Association fédérative générale des étudiants de Strasbourg, 2 March 1962.

22. These included popular referenda to decide the future of an integral part of France; long-term use of "special powers" by the president; and the creation of exceptional tribunals. See Shepard, *Invention,* 89–99.

23. Ibid. On Muslim support, see, for example, "La courageuse intervention de M. Djebbour," *Appel de la France: demeurer français sur une terre française (le journal de l'O.A.S.),* no. 8, c. December 1961, found in ADBR, 589 D 243.

24. OAS, "Mon cher ami," stamped 3 February 1962, found in 589 D 243.

25. "La presse abusive," *IJ,* May 1961.

26. Interview with Jacques Lazarus, 6 April 2006.

27. Arnold Mandel, "Algeria," 404–5.

28. On the first point, Benjamin Stora, *Histoire de la guerre d'Algérie (1954–1962)* (Paris: Éditions la découverte, 2002), 61.

29. For this figure, Centre des Archives Contemporaines (CAC) (Fontainebleau), 0019920172, article 8, liasse 3, list of Algerian Jews by locality, beginning of 1961. Regarding Oran as a site of particular Jewish participation in the OAS, see, among others, Mandel, "Algeria," 405.

30. "Oran: Les graves incidents de Roch Hachana," *IJ,* August–September 1961.

31. CASIP-COJASOR Archives (Paris), Le Toit Familial, II, 1, Letter of LB to NS, 4 January 1962.

32. Maquet, "A Oran comme à Alger un passant invisible: La peur," *Paris-Match,* 20 January 1962, 26–31; "Pas de soutien israélien à l'O.A.S.," *BNC,* 19 January 1962; "Une conférence de W. Rabi: les juifs du Maghreb à l'heure de l'indépendance," *CBL,* April 1962; "Le quartier juif d'Oran en état de siége," *BNC,* 18 May 1962.

33. R. Goulatier, "Les juifs et l'O.A.S. en Oranie," in Centre nationale de la recherche scientifique, *Les relations entre juifs et musulmans en afrique du nord, XIXe-XXe siècles* (Paris: Éditions du CNRS, 1980), 188–96.

34. Ibid., 194.

35. Henri Chemouilli, *Une Diaspora méconnue: Les Juifs d'Algérie* (Paris: [n.p.], 1976), 300.

36. AIU, FJL, Dossier II, series of letters to Guy Mollet and Charles de Gaulle, February–March 1960.

37. Tricot was a diplomat on de Gaulle's staff; Joxe was Algerian foreign affairs minister.

38. Here I have drawn my account from Shepard, *Invention*, 170–73.

39. On this latter point, see Mandel, "Algeria," 405.

40. Ibid., 408.

41. R. A., "C'était à Colomb-Béchar: Comment on passe dans l'autre camp. La nationalité française accordée aux juifs apatrides a ruiné leur entente avec les arabes," *L'évènement du jeudi,* 5–11 March 1962, cited in Maud Mandel, "Migration and Ethnicity during the Decolonization of North Africa," unpublished paper. Many thanks to the author for sharing this work.

42. On the closing months of French Algeria for Jews of the Mzab in the context of their longer history, Sarah Abrevaya Stein, *Saharan Jews and the Fate of French Algeria* (Chicago: University of Chicago Press, 2014). See also Rebecca Wall, "The Jews of the Desert: Colonialism, Zionism, and the Jews of the Algerian M'zab" (Phd diss., University of Michigan, 2014).

43. Joëlle Bahloul, *The Architecture of Memory: A Jewish-Muslim Household in Colonial Algeria, 1937–1962,* trans. Catherine du Peloux Ménagé (Cambridge: Cambridge University Press, 1996), 81–82, 84–85. Quotation from 85.

44. For the quotation, Lazarus, "Tels que"; on second point, Archives du consistoire israélite centrale de France (ACICF) (Paris), Fonds Jacques Lazarus (FJL), Lazarus, "Mémoire"; Émile Touati, "Aspects Politiques de la Situation du Judaisme Algérien," 1960.

45. Stora, *Les trois,* 170.

46. See Shepard, *Invention,* chap. 6.

47. See esp. ibid.; Hammerman, "The Heart," chap. 6; Naomi Davidson, *Only Muslim: Embodying Islam in Twentieth-Century France* (Ithaca, NY: Cornell University Press, 2012), chap. 5.

48. Mandel, *Muslims and Jews* makes certain parallel arguments about Jewish migration. See chap. 2, esp. 44–45, 57–58.

49. Emphasis is mine. Quotation in Lionel Cohn, "Reflexions d'un étudiant juif religieux sur le problème algérien," *Kadimah,* December 1960–January 1961.

50. Lucien Lazare, "Nos mains n'ont pas versé ce sang," *BNC,* 2 December 1960.

51. Joseph Weill, "Un certain esprit," *BNC,* 30 December 1960.

52. Cedre, "Du politique et de la politique," *BNC,* 10 February 1961.

53. Cohn, "Reflexions d'un étudiant juif."

54. See issue of *Kadimah,* April–May 1961; CZA/C10/3303, transcript of debate on "engagement et non engagement."

55. See René-Samuel Sirat, *La joie austere: entretiens réalisés par Emmanuel Hirsch* (Paris: Les Éditions du Cerf, 1990), 11–12.

56. "Le judaisme contre la violence," *Journal des communautés (JDC)*, 24 November 1961.

57. For example, "Grand succès de la réunion d'information du C.J.A.A.," *CBL*, April 1962. Quotation from Philippe Boukara, "La gauche juive en France et la guerre d'Algérie," *Archives juives* 29, no. 1 (1996): 80.

58. Archives départementales des Bouches-du-Rhône (ADBdR) (Marseille), 137 W 434. Ministère de l'Intérieur (MdI), R-G report on attacks by the OAS, 6 December 1961.

59. ADBdR, 137 W 436, MdI, R-G report on the arrival of "elements considered dangerous," 22 June 1962.

60. ADBR, 589 D 243, extended dossiers on Sebbah, Gabriel, and "Sarraf-Rodier" conspiracy, 1962.

61. Stora, *Les trois,* 157–59, makes some similar points.

62. For example, "Pour la paix fraternelle en Algérie," *JDC,* 13 April 1962.

63. CDJC, MDI-19 and MDI-20, reports for meetings of 8 December 1961 and 18 and 25 January 1962.

64. APP, HA 7, Recensement de la population musulmane, 17 March 1958.

65. Abdellali Hajjat, "Les comités Palestine (1970–1972): aux origines du soutien à la cause palestinienne en France," *Revue d'études palestiniennes* 98 (2006): 76–77.

66. On 1962 figures and overall percentages, Rémy Leveau and Dominique Schnapper, *Religion et politique: juifs et musulmans maghrébins en France* ([Paris]: Association française de science politique, Centre d'études et de recherches internationales, [1987]), 12.2–12.3. On foreign Muslims as of 1970, Archives de la chambre de commerce de Marseille (ACCM), ML 42731, 03, "Population étrangère en France au 1er janvier 1970"; for harki figures, Pierre Baillet, "Notes et études documentaires: les rapatriés d'Algérie en France," *La documentation française* 4275–4276, March 1976, 51, found in AIU, FJL, Dossier II. While Leveau and Schnapper cite the figure of 70 percent for Algerians in 1970, the precise figures, which come from the second source, indicate something closer to 75 percent. Yet these numbers do not include any naturalized French Moroccan or Tunisian immigrants, which may help to explain the differential.

67. On differences between foreign immigrants and North African colonial migrants previously, see Clifford Rosenberg, *Policing Paris: The Origins of Modern Immigration Control between the Wars* (Ithaca, NY: Cornell University Press, 2006).

68. Shepard, *Invention,* esp. chap. 9.

69. All cited in ibid., 229–30, 236.

70. Citation and assessment from ibid., 230–31.

71. Ibid., 232–33.

72. Baillet, "Notes et études," 52.

73. Large numbers of immigrants went elsewhere, primarily Israel and North America. According to one estimate, about 355,000 went to Israel, with 270,000 of these from Morocco, about 25,000 from Algeria, and roughly 60,000 from Tunisia. Canada received 10,000 to 12,000 immigrants mostly from Morocco, and less than 10,000, largely from Morocco's former Spanish zone, went to Spain. Taïeb, "Immigrés d'Afrique du Nord," 149.

74. Figures and observations from Colette Zytnicki, "Du rapatrié au séfarade: l'intégration des juifs d'Afrique du Nord dans la société française: essai de bilan," *Archives juives* 38, no. 2 (2005): 85–88.

75. ADBdR, 137 W 464, Ministère des rapatriés, Direction de l'accueil et du logement, reports of 1962–1963, esp. 3 and 15 January 1963. Statistic from latter report. The December 1961 law for aid to rapatriés originally did not include those arriving from Algeria; this was changed and applied retroactively in April 1962. For a good discussion of the law's benefits, see Davidson, *Only Muslim,* 140.

76. Zytnicki, "Du rapatrié," 89. For figures, Michel Abitbol, "La cinquième république et l'accueil des juifs d'Afrique du Nord," in Jean-Jacques Becker and Annette Wieviorka, eds., *Les juifs de France: de la révolution française à nos jours* (France: Liana Levi, 1998), 289.

77. On the Algerian case, Sussman, "Changing Lands," chaps. 5–6.

78. See, for example, "Sépharad ou Ashkenaz?" *Le Bulletin de nos communautés (BNC),* 4 November 1960.

79. See, for instance, the remarks of one community leader cited in Colette Zytnicki, "Introduction," in Zytnicki, ed., *Terre d'exil, terre d'asile,* 14. On the importance of the Holocaust, see Sussman, "Changing Lands," 325.

80. Jacob Kaplan, "Pour nos coreligionnaires rapatriés d'Algérie," *JDC,* 11 May 1962, and "Appel aux juifs de France en faveur des rapatriés," *JDC,* 27 July 1962.

81. Figure from Zytnicki, "Du rapatrié," 93.

82. Ibid., 92–93.

83. Figures from Sussman, "Changing Lands," 273–74.

84. Statistics and comparison from Shepard, *Invention,* 234.

85. See Baillet, "Notes et études."

86. Zytnicki, "Du rapatrié," 88–92; for quotation, Simon Schwarzfuchs, "Aspects culturels et éducatifs du problème des réfugiés et rapatriés," *JDC,* 27 July 1962.

87. Abitbol, "La cinquième république," esp. 310–19.

88. See, on the first point, Zytnicki, "Du rapatrié," 86–88; on the second, for example, AJDC, Geneva II, Box 382b, folder 7, France, undated report, "Marseille, 1961: Jewish Boom Town."

89. Mandel, *Muslims and Jews,* 72; Richard Alba and Roxane Silberman, "Decolonization Immigrations and the Social Origins of the Second Generation: The Case of North Africans in France," *International Migration Review* 36, no. 4 (2002): 1169–93.

90. See ACICF, FJL, unnumbered AJOA dossiers, AJOA statements of 23 January, 9 September 1963; report on meeting among representatives of the AJOA, Consistory, and AIU of 6 March 1963; Abitbol, "La cinquième république," 315. First quotation from ACICF, FJL, AJOA dossiers, meeting of AJOA correspondents and representatives of the Jewish communities of the Parisian banlieues, 20 December 1964.

91. See Sussman, "Changing Lands," 13–15.

92. Ibid., chap. 5.

93. Correspondence and meeting minutes of the AJOA and its Moroccan counterpart through the mid-1970s contain only a handful of references to Muslims. ACICF, FJL, unnumbered AJOA dossiers; AIU, Fonds Benazeraf, boxes 1–3.

94. Doris Bensimon-Donath, *L'intégration des juifs nord-africains en France* (Paris: Mouton, 1971), 3, 176–78. Admittedly, it does not appear that the options given in the survey for friends within France included Muslims, but few even claimed that their friends in North Africa had been Muslim.

95. Archives of the American Jewish Joint Distribution Committee (AJDC) (Jerusalem), Geneva II, Box 382b, folder 7, France, "Report on Visit to Marseille," 14–19, 1961.

96. "Sépharad ou Ashkenaz?" *BNC,* 4 November 1960.

97. Jean Liberman, "Belleville juif d'aujourd'hui: les 'achkenazes' ont cédé la place," *La Presse Nouvelle Hebdomadaire,* 21 May 1971; Patrick Simon and Claude Tapia, *Le Belleville des juifs tunisiens* (Paris: Éditions autrement, 1998), 81–85.

98. Quoted in Sussman, "Changing Lands," 390–91.

99. ADBdR, 137 W 463, Ministère des Repatriés (MR), Direction de l'accueil et du logement (DAL), "Note hebdomadaire d'information sur les rapatriements d'Afrique du Nord et spécialement d'Algérie," 5 February 1963. For the impact on Marseille, Jean-Jacques Jordi, "L'été 62 à Marseille: tensions et incompréhensions," in Jordi and Émile Temime, eds., *Marseille et le choc des décolonisations: Les rapatriements, 1954–1964* (Aix-en-Provence: Edisud, 1996). On the state's lack of preparedness, Guy Pervillé, "Les conditions de départ: l'Algérie," in Jordi and Temime, *Marseille,* 54–65.

100. Statistic from Jordi, "L'été," 68.

101. ADBdR, 137 W 463–465, Préfecture des Bouches-du-Rhône (PBR), Service d'accueil des rapatriés, statistique hebdomadaire, weekly reports of 1962–1964.

102. See ADBdR, 137 W 464, MR, DAL, reports of 1962–1963, esp. 3 and 15 January 1963.

103. Jordi, "L'été," 73.

104. Émile Temime, *Marseille transit: les passagers de Belsunce* (Paris: Éditions autrement, 1995), 42–43.

105. On Jews, AJDC, Geneva II, Box 382b, France, "Report on visit"; on Muslims, Émile Temime and Nathalie Deguigné, *Le camp du Grand Arénas: Marseille, 1944–1966* (Paris: Éditions autrement, 2001). Regarding Jewish-Muslim interaction in the camp, see Mandel, *Muslims and Jews*, chaps. 1, 3.

106. Jordi, "L'été."

107. First number from Zytnicki, "Du rapatrié," 87; second from Bensimon-Donath, *L'intégration des juifs*, 55.

108. For the first figure, Archives nationales (AN) (Paris), F1a, 5025, MdI, Cabinet du Ministre, Affaires sociales musulmanes en métropole, Circulaire no. 65, 10 February 1958. For the second, Abdelmalek Sayad, Jean-Jacques Jordi, and Émile Temime, *Migrance: Histoire des migrations à Marseille* (Aix-en-Provence: Edisud, 1991), 121.

109. For figure, Sayad, Jordi, and Temime, *Migrance*, 120.

110. On the last point, see Temime, *Marseille transit*, esp. 86–109.

111. Jean André Carreno, Alain Hayot, and Francis Lesme, *Le quartier de la Porte d'Aix à Marseille: Ethnologie d'un centre urbain* (Aix-en-Provence, 1974), cited in ibid., 95–96.

112. AN, F1a, 5025, Direction générale des affaires politiques et de l'administration du territoire (DGAPAT), Service de Liaison et de Promotion des Migrants (SLPM), "Etat d'esprit dans les milieux musulmans à la suite des évènements du Moyen-Orient," 16 June 1967; Guy Porte, "En marge du conflit: A Marseille, juifs et arabes ont su éviter les pièges de racisme," *Le Monde,* 25 July 1973, found in Centre de documentation juive contemporaine (CDJC) (Paris), MDI-159.

113. On the last points, interview with Salah Bariki and Moulay Ghoul, 10 July 2006.

114. Mandel, *Muslims and Jews,* 71.

115. On the first point, Jean-Jacques Jordi, *De l'Exode à l'Exil: Rapatriés et Pieds-Noirs en France, L'Exemple marseillais, 1954–1992* (Paris: Éditions l'Harmattan, 1993), 216–17.

116. Here I draw on the arguments of Jordi, "L'été," 72–73; Sussman, "Changing Lands," 144–46, 172–74.

117. For much more on this process, see Mandel, *Muslims and Jews,* chap. 3, esp. 74, 76–77.

118. See ibid., 77; Sayad, Jordi, and Temime, *Migrance,* 105, 109, 120; AN, F1a, 5025, DGAPAT, SLPM, "Répercussions des évènements du Moyen-Orient sur la population algérienne et la communauté israélite de Marseille," 12 June 1967.

119. Quoted in Mandel, *Muslims and Jews,* 71.

120. For more specifics on Jewish mobility, see Bensimon-Donath, *L'intégration des juifs,* 55; Zytnicki, "Du rapatrié," 86–88. On Algerian Muslims, see Benjamin Stora, *Ils venaient d'Algérie: l'immigration algérienne en France, 1912–1992* (France: Fayard, 1992), 401.

121. Statistics compiled in ADBR, 709 D 133, MdI, Direction générale de la sureté nationale (DGSN), statistics on Muslims in Bas-Rhin, 1964–1971.

122. For the number of Jews, AJDC, Geneva II, Box 384, folder 12, France, AJDC budget department, population statistics report for France, 15 February 1963.

123. For useful discussions of social geography and life in the HLMs in Strasbourg, see John Western, *Cosmopolitan Europe: A Strasbourg Self-Portrait* (Burlington, VT: Ashgate, 2012), esp. chaps. 3, 7.

124. Max Warschawski, "1962"; Freddy Raphaël, "1962: la découverte d'un monde juif nouveau"; Charles Kleinkenecht, "L'exode des Juifs du M'Zab"; Vidal Serfaty, "La préhistoire de la communauté séfarade de Strasbourg"; Esther and David Abenhaim, "Directeur à l'AJIRA"; Albert Hazan, "Mémoire quand tu nous tiens," firsthand contemporary and memoir accounts found at URL (as of 26 April 2009): http://judaisme.sdv.fr/histoire/villes/strasbrg/sefarade/index.htm; Sussman, "Changing Lands," 304. For an in-depth examination of the Mzabite Jews and the challenges of integration they faced, Freddy Raphaël, "Les juifs du M'Zab dans l'est de la France: Problématique et premières étapes d'une recherché," in Centre nationale de la recherche scientifique, *Les relations entre juifs et musulmans,* 197–224.

125. AJDC, Geneva II, Box 384, folder 21, General Office, report on trip to Strasbourg, 29 May 1964.

126. All citations from interview with Simon Dahan, 17 May 2006.

127. Remco Ensel, *Saints and Servants in Southern Morocco* (Boston: Brill, 1999), 112–23. Quotation from 121. My thanks to Jessica Marglin for helping me better understand this issue.

128. Rabbi David Abergel, for example, who arrived from Morocco in 1965 and was the longtime rabbi in the Strasbourg suburb of Meinau, spoke of his congregants' frequent nostalgia for Morocco. Interview with Abergel, 7 May 2006.

129. For Moroccan Jews, I have drawn on interviews. On Mzabite Jews in Strasbourg, see Raphaël, "Les juifs du M'Zab." The subject of these Jews' local relations with Muslims demands greater investigation.

130. Warschawski, "1962."

131. Interview with Simon Dahan.

132. See Harvey Goldberg, "The Mimuna and the Minority Status of Moroccan Jews," *Ethnology* 17 (1978): 75–87.

133. Cited in undated press clipping, "Intégration et tolérance par le sport," *Actualité juive,* from A. S. Menora private collection (ASMPC), courtesy of Simon Dahan.

134. "Intégration et tolérance" and "Le sport et 'la connaissance de l'autre,'" *Derniéres nouvelles d'Alsace,* 23 June 2005, ASMPC.

135. *A. S. Menora 30ème Anniversaire, 1963–1993,* 25, ASMPC.

136. Interview with Robert Garcia, 1 May 2006

137. Interview with Dahan.

138. Ibid.; interview with Rabbi David Abergel, 7 May 2006.

139. Interview with Rabbi David Abergel; interview with Isaac Ben-David, 30 April 2006.

140. Regarding a larger North African Jewish community in Schiltigheim, CZA/S5/12533, letter of 19 May 1967 from M. Aron to M. Getz.

141. The *henna* is a ceremony to purify the bride that takes place in the days preceding her wedding. Her family and close friends surround her and place henna, a plant-based dye, on her head, hands, or feet. On the henna among Algerian Jews, see Joëlle Allouche-Benayoun and Doris Bensimon, *Les Juifs d'Algérie: Mémoires et identités plurielles* (Paris: Éditions Stavit, 1998), 163–66.

142. Interview with Zoubida Tribak, 4 May 2006.

143. CAC, 19850087, article 33, "La population algérienne en France," 8 February 1968. We lack precise figures for the latter two groups.

144. Interviews with Roger Gharbi, 6 June 2006, and Louis Jaïs, 5 June 2006.

145. Hisham D. Aidi, *Rebel Music: Race, Empire and the New Muslim Youth Culture* (New York: Pantheon Books, 2014), 284–86; Mehenna Mahfoufi, *Chants kabyles de la guerre d'indépendence, Algérie 1954–1962* (Paris: Éditions Séguier, 2002), 30; Jérémy Guedj, "La musique judéo-arabe: Un symbole de l'exil des juifs d'Afrique du Nord en France," *Ecarts d'identité* 114 (2009): 35–43.

146. Patrick Simon "Le Belleville des juifs: Yiddish et tunes en quartier populaire," *Passages* 80 (November–December 1996): 58.

147. Simon and Tapia, *Le Belleville,* 62.

148. See ibid., 102–4, 125, 149.

149. See ibid., 46–47.

150. Simon, "Le Belleville," 58.

151. For overall population figure, Gilbert Cohen-Tanugi and Raphael Valensi, "Belleville après la guerre des six heures," *L'Arche,* special issue of June-July 1968; for proportional figures, Simon and Tapia, *Le Belleville,* 89.

152. Claude Tapia, *Les juifs sépharades en France (1965–1985): études psychologiques et historiques* (Paris: L'Harmattan, 1986), 221.

153. Jean-Louis Bonnot, "La guerre de six heures," *Nouvel observateur,* 22 June 1970, found in CZA/C10/3947.

154. Tapia, *Les juifs sépharades,* 220–21; Simon and Tapia, *Le Belleville,* 90–91; see also ibid., 126, 146–47.

155. Ibid., 161, map on 110.

156. Drawn closely from Cohen-Tanugi and Valensi, "Belleville," 46.

157. Cited in Julia Clancy-Smith, *Mediterraneans: North Africa and Europe in an Age of Migration, c. 1800–1900* (Berkeley: University of California Press, 2011), 138–39.

158. Ibid., 146.

159. Bensimon-Donath, *L'intégration des juifs*, 23nn17–18, 200.

160. Ibid., 56.

161. Bonnot, "La guerre de six heures."

162. Drawn closely from Simon and Tapia, *Le Belleville*, 161.

163. Interview with Patricia Jaïs, 20 June 2006.

164. Simon and Tapia, *Le Belleville*, 113.

165. On the latter point, ibid., 100–101; Bonnot, "La guerre."

166. I have drawn here on Simon and Tapia, *Le Belleville*, esp. 108, 159–61; and Simon, "Les représentations des relations interethniques dans un quartier cosmopolite," *Recherches sociologiques* 28, no. 2 (1997): 5–37.

167. See for example, Bonnot, "La guerre."

168. I have drawn here from Simon and Tapia, *Le Belleville*, 165.

169. I am influenced here by Fredrik Barth, *Ethnic Groups and Boundaries* (Boston: Little, Brown, 1969).

6. Higher Fences, Better Neighbors?

1. My account is based on several sources: "Troubles à Belleville," *Le Journal des communautés (JDC)*, 14 June 1968; "Après les incidents de Belleville," *JDC*, 28 June 1968; "Les affrontements de Belleville: à qui profite le chauvinisme," *La Presse nouvelle hebdomadaire (PNH)*, 14–20 June 1968; Patrick Simon and Claude Tapia, *Le Belleville des juifs tunisiens* (Paris: Éditions autrement, 1998), 168–73; J.-M. Lermon, Gilles Patri, and Jean Nouailhac, "Les émeutes de Belleville," *L'Aurore*, 4 June 1968; J.-P. Norbert, "Belleville: ambassadeur de Tunisie et rabbin côte à côte," *La France soir*, 5 June 1968. Last two articles found in Archives de la préfecture de police (APP) (Paris), DB 626.

2. Here I draw on Paul Silverstein's notion of transpolitics in his *Algeria in France: Transpolitics, Race, and Nation* (Bloomington: Indiana University Press, 2004), esp. 5–6.

3. I owe this precise formulation to the work of Alma Heckman.

4. See the special issue of *JDC*, 2 June 1967.

5. Cited in Joan B. Wolf, *Harnessing the Holocaust: The Politics of Memory in France* (Stanford, CA: Stanford University Press, 2004), 36.

6. See, for instance, posters that read "Nasser=Hitler," Archives départementales des Bouches-du-Rhône (ADBdR) (Marseille), 137 W 363, Ministère de l'Intérieur (MdI), Direction générale de la sureté nationale (DGSN), with report dated 28 June 1967.

7. Ibid.; *L'Arche*, special issue of June 1967.

8. First number from Roger Berg, "Dans la Galouth: solidarité avec Israël," *Bulletin de nos communautés (BNC)*, 16 June 1967; second and third from "La France avec Israël," *JDC*, 9 June 1967.

9. Berg, "Dans la Galouth."

10. ADBdR, 137 W 363, MdI, renseignements généraux (R-G) report on the Israeli-Arab conflict, 8 June 1967.

11. Quoted in Michel Winock, *La France et les juifs* (Paris: Seuil, 2004), 323.

12. Yves Gastaut, "La guerre des six jours et la question du racisme en France," *Cahiers de la Méditerranée* 71 (2005), http://cdlm.revues.org/930?lang =en; Abdellali Hajjat, "Aux origines du soutien a la cause palestinienne en France," *Europe solidaire sans frontières,* 1 February 2006, http://www.europe -solidaire.org/spip.php?article3675, 8–9 (page numbers here and thereafter are for the online edition).

13. "La guerre israélo-arabe: premiéres consequences de la victoire," *JDC,* 23 June 1967.

14. See *BNC,* 2 June–18 October 1967.

15. See, for example, ibid.; René Weil, "Le chofar au mur des lamentations," *BNC,* 16 June 1967.

16. "La paix pour demain?" *L'Arche,* August–September 1967; in the latter case, for example, *Cahiers Bernard Lazare (CBL),* issues of October and November 1967.

17. This constituted a 50 percent increase in the number of individual contributors over any previous donations for Israel. Maud Mandel, *Muslims and Jews in France: History of a Conflict* (Princeton, NJ: Princeton University Press, 2014), 84. For specific Marseille and Strasbourg figures, "L'action hors de Paris," *JDC,* 23 June 1967.

18. "L'action."

19. See, for example, "Le Rabbin Kaplan en Israël," *JDC,* 23 June 1967; Central Zionist Archives (Jerusalem)/S5/12533/Eastern France (Strasbourg), 1967.

20. Gastaut, "La guerre," 5–6 (page numbers are for online edition).

21. Quoted in ibid., 6.

22. "Une déclaration du Comité de coordination," *JDC,* 14 July 1967.

23. Mandel, *Muslims and Jews,* 85.

24. "L'Algérie prête à faire face à l'aggression sioniste," *El Moudjahid (EM),* 27 May 1967; "La guerre de libération est inéluctable proclame le président NASSER devant trois cents journalistes," *EM,* 28–29 May 1967.

25. "Le FLN au peuple algérien: la cause palestinienne est la tienne," *EM,* 3 June 1967.

26. My thanks to Joshua Cole for alerting me to this issue. See Benjamin Stora, *Histoire de l'Algérie depuis indépendence,* vol. 1: *1962–1988,* 4th ed. (Paris: La Découverte, 2004), 11–18.

27. Centre des archives contemporaines (CAC) (Fontainebleau), 0019850087, 033, Direction centrale des renseignements généraux (DCRG), "Les problèmes posées par la colonie algérienne aux gouvernements algérien et français," 7 October 1969.

28. On the ADAE after the 1965 coup, Archives départementales du Bas-Rhin (ADBR) (Strasbourg), 709 D 133, MdI, DGSN, report of November 1966.

29. For the first claim, CAC, 0019850087, 031, Ministère des armes, memo on political attitudes of Algerians in France, 24 August 1968; for the second, CAC, 0019850087, 033, DCRG, "Les problèmes posées." The latter indicates that only generous support from the Algerian state (6 million francs in 1968) kept it afloat. The number of members may have been even lower; a report cited by Mandel, *Muslims and Jews,* 88, estimates only 4,000.

30. On oppositional parties, CAC, 0019850087, 033, "Les mouvements d'opposition algérienne en France," 24 October 1969; on frequent political apathy, CAC, 0019850087, 033, "Les problèmes posées."

31. Editorial, "La loi du plus fort"; "Proche-Orient: Au delà de l'état d'alerte," both in *L'Algérien en Europe (AE),* 1 June 1967.

32. "Les émigrés Algériens se tiennent prêts," *EM,* 6 June 1967.

33. "Devant l'aggression sioniste, l'émigration algérienne a retrouvé le sens du combat," *AE,* 30 June 1967.

34. See, for example, ADBdR, 137 W 363, MdI, R-G report on Algerians and the Middle East situation, 3 June 1967. For an exception, see "Journée internationale de Palestine à Paris," *EM,* 20 May 1967.

35. ADBdR, 137 W 363, MdI, R-G report on Algerians and Middle East tension, 6 June 1967.

36. "Les émigrés"; "Des milliers de volontaires pour le front en France," *EM,* 7 June 1967. Figure from the latter.

37. "Lettre du comité étudiant interabe au général de Gaulle," *EM,* 6 June 1967; "Les étudiants arabes en France dénoncent la collusion de l'impérialisme anglo-américain avec les sionistes," *EM,* 8 June 1967; "Création d'un comité interarabe des étudiants à Paris," *EM,* 9 June 1967.

38. "Messages de soutien," *EM,* 7 June 1967.

39. See, for instance, "Solidarité internationale," *EM,* 11–12 June 1967.

40. See *AE,* 15 June 1967.

41. See, for example, Archives nationales (AN) (Paris), F1a, 5025, Direction générale des affaires politiques et de l'administration du territoire (DGAPAT), Service de liaison et de promotion des migrants (SLPM), Répercussions des évènements; "Note d'information concernant l'état d'esprit des musulmans en résidence dans le département du Var à la suite des évènements du Moyen-Orient," 30 June 1967.

42. Ibid.; first quotation from "Devant l'aggression sioniste, l'émigration algérienne a retrouvé le sens du combat," *AE,* 30 June 1967; second quotation from "Violences raciales contre les maghrébins en France," *EM,* 9 June 1967.

43. Samir Kassir and Farouk Mardam-Bey, *Itinéraires de Paris à Jerusalem: La France et le conflit judéo-arabe*, vol. 2: *1958–1991* (Paris: Minuit, 1993), quotation from 140; Hajjat, "Aux origines"; Gastaut, "La guerre."

44. Le comité de liaison des étudiants juifs, "Tous les juifs ne sont pas sionistes," *AE*, 30 June 1967.

45. "Les émigrés algériens se tiennent prêts," *EM*, 6 June 1967.

46. "Devant l'aggression sioniste."

47. "Violences raciales contre les maghrébins en France," *EM*, 9 June 1967.

48. Ibid.

49. ADBR, MdI, DGSN, 709 D 133, reports of 19–30 June, 1967. On this confrontation with harkis, see report of 29 June 1967.

50. AN, F1a, 5025, note on "Etat d'esprit dans les milieux musulmans à la suite des évènements du Moyen-Orient," June 16, 1967.

51. The Khartoum conference of September 1967 famously issued the "three nos": no peace with Israel, no recognition of Israel, and no negotiation with Israel. While this delivered a rejectionist message as far as Israel was concerned, some have argued that in fact it constituted a relatively moderate position that opened the door to possible compromise.

52. AN, F1a, 5025, report on "activité des partis algériens de l'opposition réfugiée à l'étranger," 29 September 1967. On the OCRA, see David Ottaway and Marina Ottaway, *Algeria: The Politics of a Socialist Revolution* (Berkeley: University of California Press, 1970), 220–21. Regarding Algeria's position in the 1967 war and its aftermath, see Michael M. Laskier, "Israel and Algeria amid French Colonialism and the Arab-Israeli Conflict, 1954–1978," *Israel Studies* 6, no. 2 (1998): 21–26.

53. Drawn closely from Gilbert Cohen-Tanugi and Raphael Valensi, "Belleville après la guerre des six heures," *L'Arche*, special issue of June–July 1968, 46.

54. Interview with Simon Dahan, 17 May 2006.

55. As of 1969, with 414 North African Muslim students, Strasbourg had the fifth largest number of any university in France. See CAC, 19850087, 33, report on "Les étudiants nord-africains en France," July 22, 1969.

56. The two pamphlets are cited in Mandel, *Muslims and Jews*, 99; for the follow-up story, "Tract antisémite des étudiants arabes," *BNC*, June 2, 1967. For in-depth coverage of university interactions, see Mandel, chaps. 4–5.

57. "M. Gaston Defferre a accepté la présidence du Comité de soutien à Israël," *Provençal*, 2 June 1967. For greater discussion on this point, see Mandel, *Muslims and Jews*, 92–96.

58. ADBdR, 137 W 363, MdI, R-G report on Algerians and Middle East tension, 6 June 1967; AN, F1a, 5025, DGAPAT, SLPM, "Répercussions des évènements du Moyen-Orient sur la population algérienne et la communauté israélite de Marseille," 9 June 1967.

59. ADBdR, 137 W 363, MdI, R-G report on Algerians and Middle East tension; AN, F1a, 5025, DGAPAT, SLPM, "Répercussions des évènements." For

the importance of Defferre's support for Israel, I draw on the much more extended discussion of Mandel, *Muslims and Jews.*

60. AN, F1a, 5025, DGAPAT, SLPM, "Etat d'esprit dans les milieux musulmans."

61. See esp. Jay Berkovitz, *The Shaping of Jewish Identity in Nineteenth-Century France* (Detroit: Wayne State University Press, 1989); Lisa Moses Leff, *Sacred Bonds of Solidarity: The Rise of Jewish Internationalism in Nineteenth-Century France* (Stanford, CA: Stanford University Press, 2006).

62. Jacques Derogy and Georges Suffert, "La vieillesse d'un chef," *L'Arche,* December 1967–January 1968; "Après la conférence de presse du général de Gaulle," and "A la mutualité," *JDC,* 8 December 1967; CZA/S5/12536, report from the Zionist Federation of France to the Jewish Agency, 13 February 1968.

63. Wolf, *Harnessing the Holocaust.*

64. See Raymond Aron, *De Gaulle, Israël, et les juifs* (Paris: Plon, 1968), quoted in ibid., 46–47.

65. See Richard Vinen, "The End of an Ideology? Right-Wing Antisemitism in France, 1944–1970," *Historical Journal* 37, no. 1 (1994): 378–80.

66. William Cohen, "Legacy of Empire: The Algerian Connection," *Journal of Contemporary History* 15, no. 1 (January 1980): 113–14; Gastaut, "La guerre," 2–3; Winock, *La France,* 291.

67. Gastaut, "La guerre," 3, 6; Winock, *La France,* 291, 317–18.

68. See, in particular, "Au général de Gaulle," *EM,* 13 June 1967; "La France contre le fait accompli au moyen-orient," and "Accord algéro-français sur le gaz," *EM,* 16 June 1967; "La conférence presse de de Gaulle: Pour le général tout se tient," *EM,* 28 November 1967.

69. CAC, 0019850087, 033, memo on upcoming conference of the progressive parties of the Mediterranean basin, 16 January 1968.

70. CAC, 0019850087, 033, "Les affaires algériennes," 12 March 1968.

71. On Israeli celebration planning, for example, ADBdR, 135 W 57, Préfecture des Bouches-du-Rhône, Cabinet du préfet, communications téléphoniques, Consistoire israélite de Marseille, 5 June 1968; regarding the day of mourning, "5 June: Journée mondiale contre l'agression sioniste," *EM,* 2–3 June 1968.

72. Poster in cover photo, *La Tribune juive,* 21 June–4 July 1968.

73. See "An Eyewitness Account of the Anti-Jewish Riots in Tunis at the Outbreak of the Six-Day War," in Norman Stillman, ed., *The Jews of Arab Lands in Modern Times* (Philadelphia: Jewish Publication Society, 1991), 550–51.

74. In Algeria the situation remained calm, thus prompting few departures. Michael Laskier, *North African Jewry in the Twentieth Century: The Jews of Morocco, Tunisia, and Algeria* (New York: New York University Press, 1994). On Tunisia, 306; on Morocco, 246–48; on Algeria, 343.

75. American Joint Distribution Committee (AJDC) (Jerusalem), Geneva II, 234b, France, C-43.720, folder, "Movement of Refugees from North African and Egypt, June 1967–December 1970."

76. Interview with Gilles Taïeb, 6 June 2006.

77. AJDC, Geneva II, 234b, France, C-43.720, folder, "Movement of Refugees."

78. Figure from Cohen-Tanugi and Valensi, "Belleville après la guerre des six heures."

79. See the testimony of a participant cited in Simon and Tapia, *Le Belleville,* 173.

80. See Reine Silbert, "El Fatah à la Sorbonne," *L'Arche,* special issue of June—July 1968; cover photo and JG, "Juifs de France au moi de Mai," *La Tribune juive,* 21 June–4 July 1968; "El Fata'h à la Sorbonne," *CBL,* special issue of June–July 1968; "Les troubles."

81. The term Katangais referred to a group of nonstudent protestors inside the Sorbonne during the events of May '68 led by the self-named "Jackie the Katangais" (who claimed to have fought as a mercenary with the Katanga separatists in the Congo). They provided arms and acted as a security force during the student occupation of the university, but elicited complaints about intimidation and terror and finally provoked altercations with the leaders of the main student movement. This led to their expulsion from the Sorbonne in June 1968. The term Katangais appears to have quickly become a wider pejorative, both for those associated with ultra-radical politics and with thuggish tactics.

82. My arguments on the causes of the riots draw in part on Daniel Gordon, "Juifs et musulmans à Belleville (Paris 20e) entre tolérance et conflit," *Cahiers de la Méditerranée* 67 (December 2003), http://cdlm.revues.org/document.html ?id=135.

83. For example, R. Backman, "Belleville, la guerre des six heures," *L'Observateur,* 7 June 1968, cited in Simon and Tapia, *Le Belleville,*" 169.

84. See, for example, Lermon, Patri, and Nouailhac, "Les émeutes."

85. Ibid.

86. J.-P. Norbert, "Belleville."

87. Quoted in "Les affrontements."

88. Ibid.

89. CAC, 19850087, article 31, PP, Service d'assistance technique, Rapport Trimestriel, 13 August 1968.

90. "Les évènements de Belleville," *Union des étudiants algériens, Section de Paris: Bulletin intérieur,* June 1968, cited in "Troubles à Belleville," *JDC.*

91. Quotations cited in "Bagarres à Paris entre Algériens et groupes armés sionistes," *EM,* 4 June 1968. See also untitled editorial, *AE,* 15 June 1968.

92. HD, "Message de l'Association Algérie-France à M. Michelet, président de l'Association France-Algérie," *EM,* 6 June 1968. The Irgun was founded in

1931 as a breakaway from the main Jewish defense forces in Palestine. It became a right-wing paramilitary group, described by some as a terrorist organization, carrying out numerous attacks against Palestinian Arabs and British authorities in Palestine. After the founding of Israel in 1948, the Irgun was dissolved into the Israeli military.

93. For discussion of the riots far from Paris, see AN, F1a, 5025, DGAPAT, SLPM, report on the départements of the Var region, 25 June 1968; CAC, 0019850087, 033, "Les Algériens en France et les problèmes israélo-arabes," 14 June 1968.

94. Quoted in CAC, 0019850087, 031, Ministère des armes, SDECE, "Attitude de la main-d'œuvre algérienne en France," 7 June 1968.

95. "Troubles."

96. Archives du Consistoire Israélite Centrale de France (ACICF) (Paris), carton without code labeled "1967–1968," statement, "Le grand rabbin de France s'addresse aux populations israélite et musulmane du quartier de Belleville."

97. See Cohen-Tanugi and Valensi, "Belleville après."

98. CAC, 0019850087, 033, "Les algériens en France et les problèmes israélo-arabes," 14 June 1968.

99. AN, F1a, 5025, DGAPAT, SLPM, report on the départements of the Var region, 25 June 1968; CAC, 0019850087, 033, "Les algériens en France et les problèmes israélo-arabes."

100. ADBdR, 135 W 57, Préfecture des Bouches-du-Rhône, Cabinet du préfet, communications téléphoniques, Consistoire Israélite de Marseille, 5 June 1968.

101. CAC, 0019850087, 033, "Les algériens en France et les problèmes israélo-arabes."

102. Here I am indebted to Mandel, *Muslims and Jews,* esp. chap. 5.

103. On this component of May '68, largely ignored until recently by scholars, see esp. Daniel A. Gordon, *Immigrants and Intellectuals: May '68 and the Rise of Anti-Racism in France* (Pontypool, UK: Merlin Press, 2012).

104. See Mandel, *Muslims and Jews,* 100–101; Hajjat, "Aux origines," 9.

105. Mandel, *Muslims and Jews,* 105–6; Hajjat, "Aux origines," 6–7.

106. See Mandel, *Muslims and Jews,* 86, 106–9.

107. On this point, see Yaïr Auron, *Les juifs d'extrême gauche en mai 68* (Paris: Albin Michel, 1998).

108. To be sure, there were also North African–born Jews of the Left who took part in these circles such as the young Benjamin Stora.

109. Gordon, *Immigrants and Intellectuals,* 22–32.

110. Mandel, *Muslims and Jews,* 62–63.

111. Interview with Saïd Bouziri, July 24, 2006.

112. Mandel, *Muslims and Jews,* 219n77; CAC, 0019850087, 033, DCRG, "Monsieur M'Hamed YAZID," 2 October 1969; memo on "Les collectes et les

dons en faveur des combattants," in file dated 3 January 1970. On Yazid's role during the war, see Matthew Connelly, *A Diplomatic Revolution: Algeria's Fight for Independence and the Origins of the Post–Cold War Era* (Oxford: Oxford University Press, 2002), esp. 125–26, 129, 195.

113. Mandel, *Muslims and Jews,* 96.

114. This number comes from CAC, 0019850087, 033, "Les étudiants nord-africains en France," 22 July 1969. On reactions to Belleville, CAC, 0019850087, 033, "Les algériens en France et les problèmes israélo-arabes"; Archives génériques (AG) (Paris), Fonds Farouk Belkeddar, Carton 6, procès-verbaux of meeting of the Union nationale des étudiants algériens, 8 December 1968.

115. CAC, 0019850087, 033, DCRG, memo on appearance of AEMNA bulletin, 16 January 1970.

116. CAC, 0019850087, 033, DCRG, "L'action politique en France des nord-africains," March 1970. On the earlier stance, CAC, 0019850087, 033, "Les étudiants nord-africains en France," 22 July 1969.

117. CAC, 0019850087, 033, DCRG, "Les problèmes."

118. CAC, 0019850087, 033, DCRG, "Volontaires et mercenaires pour le moyen orient," September 1969; "Le recrutement de volontaires," in file dated 3 January 1970.

119. APP, BA 2315, untitled report of 14 January 1970; CAC, 0019850087, 033, DCRS, "Les problèmes."

120. CAC, 0019850087, 033, DCRG, "Attentats contre les bâtiments et les biens algériens en France," 8 December 1969.

121. Ibid.; Naomi Davidson, *Only Muslim: Embodying Islam in Twentieth-Century France* (Ithaca, NY: Cornell University Press), 192–95.

122. "La presse israélienne de France," *AE,* 16 January 1970.

123. Interview with Jacques Lazarus, 15 June 2006.

124. Jean Liberman, "Belleville juif d'aujourd'hui: Les 'Achkénazes' ont cédé la place," *PNH,* 21 May 1971.

125. Quoted in Joëlle Bahloul, *The Architecture of Memory: A Jewish-Muslim Household in Colonial Algeria, 1937–1962,* trans. Catherine du Peloux Ménagé (Cambridge: Cambridge University Press, 1996), 199.

126. APP, BA 2315, untitled report of 14 January 1970.

127. Regarding this incident and Betar's denial of involvement, Mandel, *Muslims and Jews,* 116, 222n134.

128. For higher numerical estimates on attacks, see "Nouvelle flambée de violence à Belleville," *JDC,* 26 June 1970. Chanting quotations from "Après les violences de Belleville: Qui tire les marrons du feu?" *PNH,* 26 June 1970; "Violence à Belleville," *IW,* 26 June 1970, the latter in CZA/C10/3947. For information on Jewish leaders' responses, "Après les incidents de Belleville," *JDC,* 10 July 1970. On the alleged origins of the riots, Bonnot, "La guerre"; "Vingt-huit magasins sont éventrés à Belleville après la nuit de bagarres entre Juifs et Arabes,"

France-Soir, 17 June 1970, in APP, DB 626; "Dans le quartier de Belleville: Violents affrontements entre israélites et musulmans: 33 personnes interpellées," *Le Monde,* 17 June 1970, in CZA/C10/3947; victim's name in CDJC, MDI-49, CRIF réunion du bureau of 24 June 1970.

129. "Nouvelle flambée."

130. FEJ tract, "Halte aux pogromistes arabes," in CZA/C10/3947.

131. "A Belleville, contre les division et la haine," *Droite et liberté,* July–August 1970, in CZA/C10/3947.

132. Cited in Mandel, *Muslims and Jews,* 104.

133. Quoted in "Après les incidents de Belleville," *Le Monde,* 20 June 1970, in CZA/C10/3947.

134. "Belleville: Escalade fasciste," *Lutte palestinienne: journal de soutien à la lutte du peuple palestinien,* June–July 1970, in AG, Fonds Bouziri, carton 1.

135. Alain Geismar, Serge July and Erlyn Morane, "Belleville ou le refus (du 2 au 5 juin 1968)," in Geismar, July, and Morane, *Vers la guerre civile* (Paris: Editions et publications premières, 1969), 339–43.

136. On previous treatments of North Africans as savage criminals in *L'Aurore,* see, for example, Neil MacMaster, *Colonial Migrants and Racism: Algerians in France, 1900–62* (New York: St. Martin's Press, 1997), 191.

137. "À Belleville: Israélites et Arabes ont continué à se battre"; "Les émeutes de Belleville: 'Les Arabes voulaient se venger de la victoire d'Israël sur l'Egypte' accusent les israélites dont les magasins ont été dévastés," in *L'Aurore,* 4 June 1968, in APP, DB 626.

138. CAC, 19850087, article 31, préfecture de police (PP), Service d'assistance technique, Rapport Trimestriel, 13 August 1968.

139. "Bagarres raciales à Belleville," *L'Aurore,* 16 June 1970; "Vingt-huit magasins sont éventrés à Belleville après la nuit de bagarres entre Juifs et Arabes," *France-Soir,* 17 June 1970, in APP, DB 626. On conventional conceptions of the Islamic city, see Emily Gottreich, *The Mellah of Marrakesh: Jewish and Muslim Space in Morocco's Red City* (Bloomington: Indiana University Press, 2007), introduction.

140. See, for instance, Gordon, *Immigrants and Intellectuals,* 124.

141. Silverstein, *Algeria in France,* 94–95.

142. Claude Tapia, *Les juifs sépharades en France (1965–1985): Études psychologiques et historiques* (Paris: L'Harmattan, 1986), 147–55.

143. Bonnot, "La guerre."

144. APP, BA 2315, untitled report of 14 January 1970.

145. See, for example, ADBR, 709 D 133, MdI, DGSN, memo of 12 August 1964.

146. APP, GA Br 50, PP, Direction R-G, "La communauté juive dans la région parisienne," undated, circa 1970.

147. Available at http://www.ina.fr/economie-et-societe/vie-sociale/video/I0427 1286/les-communautes-de-belleville.fr.html.

7. Jews as Jews and Muslims as Muslims

1. Romain Gary (Émile Ajar), *The Life before Us,* trans. Ralph Manheim (New York: New Directions, 1986), 1.

2. Figure from Ralph Schoolcraft, *Romain Gary: The Man Who Sold His Shadow* (Philadelphia: University of Pennsylvania Press, 2002), 16.

3. Gary, *The Life,* 131.

4. Schoolcraft, *Romain Gary,* 165.

5. Emma Garman, "Great Pretenders," *Tablet,* 31 October 2007, http://www.tabletmag.com/jewish-arts-and-culture/books/906/great-pretenders.

6. Gary, *The Life,* 3.

7. Ibid., 167.

8. Ibid., 148.

9. Such is in part the perspective of Maud Mandel, *Muslims and Jews in France: History of a Conflict* (Princeton, NJ: Princeton University Press, 2014), 122–23.

10. Ibid., 114–52.

11. Daniel A. Gordon, *Immigrants and Intellectuals: May '68 and the Rise of Anti-Racism in France* (Pontypool, UK: Merlin Press, 2012), 128–29, 148; Leah Haus, "Labor Unions and Immigration Policy in France," *International Migration Review* 33, no. 3 (1999): 698.

12. Quoted in James Shields, "Radical or Not So Radical? Tactical Variation in Core Policy Formation by the Front National," *French Politics Culture and Society* 29, no. 3 (2011): 82, 84.

13. On this broader shift, see Richard Vinen, "The End of an Ideology? Right-Wing Antisemitism in France, 1944–1970," *Historical Journal* 37, no. 2 (1994): 365–88. Regarding former collaborators and supporters of Vichy in the ranks of the FN in this period, see James Shields, *The Extreme Right in France: From Pétain to Le Pen* (New York: Routledge, 2007), 180; Henry Rousso, *The Vichy Syndrome: History and Memory in France since 1944,* trans. Arthur Goldhammer (Cambridge, MA: Harvard University Press, 1991), 190.

14. See Gordon, *Immigrants and Intellectuals,* esp. 66–70, 137–40, 150–58.

15. On the latter development's importance for Jews and Muslims, see Mandel, *Muslims and Jews,* chap. 6.

16. On the formation and affiliation of *Lutte palestinienne,* Abdellali Hajjat, "Aux origines du soutien à la cause palestinienne en France," *Europe solidaire sans frontières,* 1 February 2006, http://www.europe-solidaire.org/spip.php ?article3675, 10 (page numbers from online edition).

17. "Travailleurs français et immigrés tous unis!" *Lutte palestinienne (LP)*, June–July 1970, Archives Génériques (AG) (Paris), Fonds Bouziri, Carton 1. All issues of *Lutte palestinienne* cited are from this archival file.

18. Hajjat, "Aux origines."

19. Ibid., with the platform reprinted in full as an appendix.

20. Ibid., 1.

21. Ibid., 12–13; Gordon, *Immigrants and Intellectuals,* 110–11.

22. Hajjat, "Aux origines," 11–12; Gordon, *Immigrants and Intellectuals,* 109.

23. See, for example, *Fedai,* 25 November 1971, in AG, Fonds Bouziri, Carton 1. Unless otherwise stated, all cited issues of *Fedai* are from this archival file.

24. Quoted in Rabah Aissaoui, *Immigration and National Identity: North African Political Movements in Colonial and Postcolonial France* (London: Tauris Academic Studies, 2009), 186.

25. Hajjat, "Aux origines," 3.

26. Ibid., 13–16; Gordon, *Immigrants and Intellectuals,* 116–17, 121–26; Interview with Saïd Bouziri, 24 July 2006.

27. Aissaoui, *Immigration,* 156–57.

28. Mandel, *Muslims and Jews,* 118–19; Gordon, *Immigrants and Intellectuals,* 110.

29. Cited in Naomi Davidson, *Only Muslim: Embodying Islam in Twentieth-Century France* (Ithaca, NY: Cornell University Press, 2012), 94–95.

30. See, for example, "Le traitre Hussein vend Jérusalem à ses amis les sionistes," *Fedai,* undated issue.

31. See, for instance, "Le peuple palestinien défie les sionistes et donne un exemple de résistance," *Fedai,* 25 November 1971.

32. For a similar point, see Aissaoui, *Immigration,* 159, 179.

33. While I draw the historical accounts here from Gordon, *Immigrants and Intellectuals,* 127–30, much of the interpretation is my own.

34. Ibid., 141, 148.

35. Cited in ibid., 160.

36. Ibid., 168; Aissaoui, *Immigration,* 162.

37. Gordon, *Immigrants and Intellectuals,* 131–32.

38. Davidson, *Only Muslim,* 198–200.

39. Ibid., 172.

40. See ibid., 174–76. In Davidson's account, she emphasizes how such measures reflected long-standing equations on the part of the state between Islam and the culture of all individuals in France considered "Muslim." While this may be true, the government was also responding to a new kind of grassroots cultural politics on the part of Muslim workers in this era, a development largely ignored in the scholarship.

41. Gordon, *Immigrants and Intellectuals*, 176, 210.

42. Ibid., 137, makes a similar point.

43. Davidson, *Only Muslim*, 170–71, 178–82. SONACOTRA, founded in 1957 and originally called SONACOTRAL, was the widely used acronym for the Société nationale de construction de logements pour les travailleurs algériens. Despite the name and image of these hostels, by the mid-1970s, many of them actually housed more European than North African immigrant workers. See ibid., 178.

44. Aissaoui, *Immigration*, 166.

45. Cited in Mandel, *Muslims and Jews*, 120, 128.

46. My best count for total signatures is 779 (the frequent challenge of legibility makes arriving at an exact number rather difficult). AG, Fonds Bouziri, Carton 3, dossier entitled "56 petitions contre les expulsions, Lutte contre les expulsions," 1974.

47. "Belleville: au nom de nos frères victimes racisme: nous ferons la verité sur la mort d'Abdallah," *Fedai*, 23 February 1972, in AG, Fonds Bouziri, carton 2; several stories in *Fedai*, c. April 1972 (undated).

48. See, for example, AG, Fonds Bouziri, carton 1, tract, "15 May 1974: 26 années d'occupation israélienne, 26 années de lutte héroique du peuple palestinien"; Hajjat, "Aux origines," 5; Aissaoui, *Immigration*, 160.

49. Interview with Bouziri. Bouziri explained that in these discussions the movement made it a priority to avoid any kind of provocation.

50. In this discussion I am influenced by Patrick Simon and Claude Tapia, *Le Belleville des juifs tunisiens* (Paris: Éditions autrement, 1998), 172.

51. Claude Tapia, *Les juifs sépharades en France (1965–1985): Études psychologiques et historiques* (Paris: L'Harmattan, 1986), 134. Though published much later as part of this book in French, the study on which he based these observations originally appeared in English in 1974. See ibid., 109n.

52. Ibid., 136.

53. Ibid., 138, 153.

54. Ibid., 143–44, 147–53.

55. See a series of urgent reports and telegrams on the subject from March to October 1970 in Archives départementales des Bouches-du-Rhône (ADBdR) (Marseille), 135 W 57. The following year featured only one such memo, suggesting the threat had subsided.

56. ADBdR, 135 W 57, Commissariat central de Marseille, "Affichage nocturne," 3 May 1972; tract, "Halt . . . à l'oppression syrienne."

57. ADBdR, 135 W 57, Commissariat central de Marseille, "Affichage sur la Canebière," 12 January 1973; attached leaflet, "Golda Meir Assassin."

58. "En marge du conflit: A Marseille, juifs et arabes ont su éviter les pièges du racisme," *Le Monde*, 25 October 1973, in Centre de documentation juive contemporaine (CDJC) (Paris), MDI-159; ADBdR, 135 W 57, telegram from

the controller-general to the Ministry of the Interior, 8 October 1973; Commissariat central de Marseille, note of 8 October 1973 on rally in support of Israel.

59. ADBdR, 135 W 57, Prefect of Marseille and Commissariat central de Marseille, memos on Zionist demonstration against the sending of arms to Arab countries, both dated 12 October 1973; memos on the Comité de soutien Israel, October 1973; tract, "Le sang humain vaut plus que le petrol," unattributed, October 1973. Regarding French attitudes toward the Middle East conflict in this period, see Michel Winock, *La France et les juifs* (Paris: Seuil, 2004), 317–18.

60. "En Marge."

61. Ibid.

62. Cited in "Manifestation contre la politique française au Proche-Orient," *Lundi,* 4 November 1974, in CDJC, MDI-159.

63. On the first issue, see Rousso, *Vichy Syndrome.*

64. CDJC, MDI-159, "Appel du Comite de Marseille du conseil représentatif des institutions juives de France," 10 December 1974.

65. See Joan B. Wolf, *Harnessing the Holocaust: The Politics of Memory in France* (Stanford, CA: Stanford University Press, 2004), chap. 3. Quotations here from 57 and 61, respectively.

66. Quotation from CDJC, MDI-159, "La communauté Israélite de Marseille: 70,000 membres," article without publication name or date.

67. Wolf, *Harnessing,* 60.

68. First quotation from Judith E. Vichniac, "Jewish Identity Politics and the Scarf Affairs in France," *French Politics, Culture and Society* 26, no. 1 (2008): 112; second quotation from Phyllis Cohen Albert, "French Jewry and the Centrality of Israel: The Public Debate, 1968–1988," in Jacob Neusner, Ernest S. Frenchis, and Nahum M. Sarna, eds., *From Ancient Israel to Modern Judaism, Intellect in Quest of Understanding: Essays in Honor of Marvin Fox* (Providence, RI: Brown University Press, 1989), 210.

69. "Les associations juives de Marseille ont manifesté contre la reconnaissance de l'O.L.P. par la France," *Provençal,* 8 November 1974, in CDJC, MDI-159.

70. ADBdR, 135 W 57, "Entretien accorde le 5 novembre 1974 à une délégation du Comité de coordination des associations juives de Marseille."

71. Along similar lines, see William Safran, "Ethnoreligious Politics in France: Jews and Muslims," *West European Politics* 27, no. 3 (2004): 437; Mandel, *Muslims and Jews,* 124.

72. CDJC, MDI-159, F. de Muison, "Les juifs de Marseille: la 'révolution' des pieds noirs," article without publication name or date.

73. Wolf, *Harnessing.*

74. Michael Rothberg, *Multidirectional Memory: Remembering the Holocaust in the Age of Decolonization* (Stanford, CA: Stanford University Press, 2009), 3.

75. Gordon, *Immigrants and Intellectuals,* 147.

76. Quoted in Wolf, *Harnessing,* 73.

77. Ibid., 84–87.

78. Ibid., 94–95.

79. Gordon, *Immigrants and Intellectuals,* 176; Paul Silverstein, *Algeria in France: Transpolitics, Race, and Nation* (Bloomington: Indiana University Press, 2004), 163.

80. Gordon, *Immigrants and Intellectuals,* 210.

81. Ibid., chap. 6; Silverstein, *Algeria in France,* 160–64.

82. "Les feujs mettent la main à la pôte," *Libération,* 15–16 June 1985, in CDJC, MDI-207; "Le 'sabra et chatila tranquille' des 'beurs,'" *Le Matin,* 3–4 December 1982 in CDJC, MDI-206; Mandel, *Muslims and Jews,* 130–31, 135.

83. Mandel, *Muslims and Jews,* 130.

84. See Shields, "Radical or Not So Radical?" 84–86.

85. Shields, *Extreme Right,* 195.

86. Quoted in Rousso, *Vichy Syndrome,* 196.

87. Here I follow but seek to complicate chronologically the persuasive arguments of Mandel, *Muslims and Jews,* 125–28, 131–32.

88. Ibid., 132–33.

89. Ibid., 132; "Harlem Désir: cause à tes potes, leur tête est malade," *Libération,* 25 March 1985, in CDJC, MDI-207.

90. Ibid., 133–34.

91. "Dialogue d'en France," *Libération,* 15–16 June 1985, in CDJC, MDI-207.

92. "Débat cartes sur tables entre SOS Racisme et les beurs," *Libération,* 13 May 1985, in CDJC, MDI-207.

93. Cited in Mandel, *Muslims and Jews,* 137.

94. "Le dialogue de deux exils," *Libération,* 6 December 1985, in CDJC, MDI-207. Here I am drawing in part on the interpretation of Mandel, *Muslims and Jews,* 137, 145.

95. Shields, "Radical or Not So Radical?" 86–87.

96. Silverstein, *Algeria in France,* 167–69; Mandel, *Muslims and Jews,* 139–43.

97. Here I am partly influenced by Mandel, *Muslims and Jews,* 137–40 and Kimberly Arkin, *Rhinestones, Religion, and the Republic: Fashioning Jewishness in France* (Stanford, CA: Stanford University Press, 2012), 80–88.

98. Regarding Jews and the affair, I draw on Vichniac, "Jewish Identity Politics." On the broader meaning of this and subsequent headscarf affairs for the

place of Muslims in France, see esp. Joan Scott, *The Politics of the Veil* (Princeton, NJ: Princeton University Press, 2007).

99. Arkin, *Rhinestones,* 83.

100. Here I draw on John Western, *Cosmopolitan Europe: A Strasbourg Self-Portrait* (Burlington, VT: Ashgate, 2012); Laird Boswell, "The New Alsatian Malaise, 1984–2004," unpublished paper (2004).

101. Interview with Fouad Daoui, 24 April 2006; interview with Mohamed Latahy, 4 and 6 May, 2006.

102. Interview with Zoubida Tribak, 26 April 2006.

103. Ibid.; "Après St-Louis, Bischheim: Une mosquée pour les musulmans de la région strasbourgeoise," *Les Dernières Nouvelles d'Alsace,* 9 October 1977, in Archives de la ville et de la communauté urbaine de Strasbourg, 1001 W 9.

104. Interview with Mostafa Elqoch, 23 April 2006. All quotations from Elqoch come from this interview.

105. "Menora: la tour de Babel," press clipping without publication information, in A. S. Menora private archives.

106. Maud S. Mandel, "The War Comes Home: Muslim/Jewish Relations in Marseille during the 1991 Gulf War," in Nathalie Debrauwere-Miller, ed., *The Israeli-Palestinian Conflict in the Francophone World* (New York: Routledge, 2010).

107. Regarding the debates around the memory of 17 October 1961 and its relationship to Holocaust memory before and after the Papon trial, see Joshua Cole, "Remembering the Battle of Paris: 17 October 1961 in French and Algerian Memory," *French Politics, Culture and Society* 21, no. 3 (2003): 21–50.

108. Interview with René Guthman, 2 March 2006.

109. For instance, Farid Boudjellal, *Juif-Arabe* (Toulon: Soleil, 1990); on reception, Silverstein, *Algeria in France,* 168–69.

110. On the impact of the FN on the broader right, see Shields, "Radical or Not So Radical?"

Conclusion

1. For a useful, hour-by-hour account of events, see "Des attentats à la march républicaine: cinq jours en France," *Le Monde,* 13 January 2015, http://www.lemonde.fr/societe/visuel/2015/01/13/des-attentats-a-la-marche -republicaine-les-cinq-jours-de-charlie_4554716_3224.html.

2. "Valls: 'La France sans les juifs de France n'est plus France,'" *Paris Match,* 9 January 2015, http://www.parismatch.com/Actu/Societe/Le-premier -ministre-Manuel-Valls-la-France-sans-les-juifs-de-France-n-est-plus-la-France -686964; "Valls: 'Je ne veux pas que des juifs puissent avoir peur ou des mu-sulmans puissent avoir honte,'" *L'Obs,* 13 January 2015, http://tempsreel

.nouvelobs.com/charlie-hebdo/20150113.OBS9899/valls-je-ne-veux-pas-que
-des-juifs-puissent-avoir-peur-ou-des-musulmans-puissent-avoir-honte.html.

3. "Nétanyahu appelle les Juifs d'Europe à émigrer en Israël," *Le Figaro,*
15 February 2015, http://www.lefigaro.fr/international/2015/02/15/01003
-20150215ARTFIG00126-netanyahou-appelle-les-juifs-d-europe-a-emigrer-en
-israel.php; "Émigration des juifs: Valls et Hollande respondent une nouvelle
fois à Nétanyahu," *Le Figaro,* 16 February 2015, http://www.lefigaro.fr/politique
/le-scan/citations/2015/02/16/25002-20150216ARTFIG00119-emigration-des
-juifs-valls-et-hollande-repondent-une-nouvelle-fois-a-netanyahu.php.

4. These can be divided into slightly over 75 percent "threats" or "acts of
intimidation," and about 25 percent "violent actions."

5. For these statistics, I have drawn upon annual reports of the Commission Nationale Consultative des Droits de l'Homme (National Consultative Commission on Human Rights), on Racism, Anti-Semitism, and Xenophobia in
France, 2000–2011, http://lesrapports.ladocumentationfrancaise.fr/ (hereafter
CNCDH reports); and the reports of the Service de Protection de la Communauté Juive. While these reports catalogue numerous incidents in which the perpetrators have expressed motivations such as "solidarity with our Palestinian
brothers," or perceived loyalty to Islam, they do not offer precise assessments of
the number of Muslim or North African perpetrators.

6. "Les insultes anti-Semites de Coulibaly à ses victimes de l'Hyper Cacher,"
Libération, 26 February 2015, http://www.liberation.fr/societe/2015/02/26/les
-insultes-antisemites-de-coulibaly-a-ses-victimes-de-l-hyper-cacher_1210189.

7. See, for example, Marc Weitzmann, "'In the Beginning the Brothers,
They Told Me to Kill,'" *Tablet,* 29 July 2014, http://tabletmag.com/jewish-news
-and-politics/180009/france-toxic-hate-3-toulouse.

8. For the period from 2000 through 2007, forty-two anti-Muslim incidents (including both threats and violence) were attributed to Jewish individuals
or groups. These constituted 2.5 percent of the total recorded anti–North African or anti-Muslim incidents for this time frame. In the period from 2007
through 2011, no such incidents appear to have been recorded. All statistics here
from CNCDH reports, 2000–2011.

9. CNCDH report, 2001, 33–34.

10. CNCDH report, 2004, 39.

11. "Quand la justice oublie une aggression de la Ligue de défense juive," *Le
Monde,* 27 February 2015, http://www.lemonde.fr/police-justice/article/2015/02/27
/quand-la-justice-oublie-une-agression-de-la-ligue-de-defense-juive_4584595
_1653578.html.

12. See, for example, "La Ligue de défense juive, une micromilice extrémiste,"
Libération, 30 July 2014, http://www.liberation.fr/societe/2014/07/30/la-ligue-de
-defense-juive-une-micromilice-extremiste_1073085.

13. Interview with Michel Serfaty, 12 April 2007; Michel Serfaty, "Juifs et musulmans de France: une relation à construire" (unpublished paper, 2007).

14. Serfaty, "Juifs."

15. Interview with Serfaty.

16. Regarding broader European ideas about Muslims and the question of how such ideas relate to antisemitism, see esp. Matti Bunzl, *Anti-Semitism and Islamophobia: Hatreds Old and New in Europe* (Chicago: Prickly Paradigm Press, 2007).

17. In the early to mid-2000s, Jewish employment levels were just below those of the broader French population, and education levels were much higher, with proportionally higher Jewish representation in liberal professions and managerial positions. Muslims, meanwhile, had significantly higher unemployment and lower education levels than the rest of the French population, and Muslims with the same skills as their non-Muslim counterparts were statistically far less likely to get the same jobs. For Jews, Erik H. Cohen, *The Jews of France Today: Identity and Values* (Leiden: Brill, 2011), 67–74; for Muslims, Jonathan Laurence and Justin Vaisse, *Integrating Islam: Political and Religious Challenges in Contemporary France* (Washington, DC: Brookings Institution, 2006), 31–39.

18. See, for example, "Marine Le Pen: 'Nous sommes les seuls garants de la République,'" *Le Monde,* 30 November 2014, http://www.lemonde.fr/politique /article/2014/11/30/marine-le-pen-nous-sommes-les-seuls-garants-de-la-repub lique_4531718_823448.html.

19. On this issue from a Jewish perspective, see Kimberly Arkin, *Rhinestones, Religion, and the Republic: Fashioning Jewishness in France* (Stanford, CA: Stanford University Press, 2013). See also Cohen, *The Jews of France,* chap. 2. For Muslims, a good synthesis of recent studies appears in Laurence and Vaisse, *Integrating Islam,* chap. 3.

20. For a good synthesis of numerous studies showing anti-Muslim discrimination in the areas of employment, housing, health care, and other basic needs, as well as through incidents of police brutality, see *Muslims in the EU: Cities Report, Preliminary Research Report and Literature Survey—France* (Brussels: Open Society Institute, EU Monitoring and Advocacy Program, 2007), 45–64.

21. Michel Wieviorka, *La tentation antisémite: Haine des juifs dans la France d'aujourd'hui* (Paris: Robert Laffont, 2005); Vaisse and Laurence, *Integrating Islam,* 232–41.

22. See Arkin, *Rhinestones.*

23. Ibid.; Cohen, *The Jews of France,* chap. 2.

24. Interview with Simon Dahan, 17 May 2006; "Quand juifs et musulmans font équipe," *MCSInfo,* 20 September 2005, in private archive of A. S. Menora.

25. For prior results for Muslim attitudes, see *Muslims More Moderate: The Great Divide: How Westerners and Muslims View Each Other, The Pew Global Attitudes Project* (Washington, DC: Pew Research Center, 2006), 43–44; Lau-

rence and Vaisse, *Integrating Islam*, 236; and for earlier Jewish attitudes, Cohen, *The Jews of France*, 104–6.

26. Dominique Reynié, *L'antisémitisme dans l'opinion publique française: nouveaux éclairages* (Paris: Fondapol, 2014), 22, 24.

27. "Survey: Three-quarters of French Jews mulling emigration," *Haaretz*, 20 May 2014.

28. Ibid.; Reynié, *L'antisémitisme*, 24–26.

29. See Dominic Thomas, *Africa and France: Postcolonial Cultures, Migration, and Racism* (Bloomington: Indiana University Press, 2013), esp. chap. 7.

30. Eric Emmanuel-Schmitt, *Monsieur Ibrahim et les Fleurs du Coran* (Paris: Albin Michel, 2001); and *Monsieur Ibrahim et les fleurs du Coran*, film, directed by François Dupeyron (France 3 Cinema, 2003).

31. *La Petite Jérusalem*, film, directed by Karin Albou (Océans France, 2005).

32. *Le chant des mariées*, film, directed by Karin Albou (Gloria Films, 2008).

33. *Dans la vie*, film, directed by Philippe Faucon (Istiqlal Films, 2007).

34. For a good overview and analysis of many of these titles, Claire Eldridge, "Remembering the Other: Postcolonial Perspectives on Relationships Between Jews and Muslims in French Algeria," *Journal of Modern Jewish Studies* 11, no. 3 (2012): 1–19.

35. See Hisham D. Aidi, *Rebel Music: Race, Empire and the New Muslim Youth Culture* (New York: Pantheon Books, 2014), chap. 11.

36. Michael Herzfeld, "Time and the Oath in the Mountain Villages of Crete," *Man* n.s. 25, no. 2 (1990): 305.

37. Interview with Fouad Daoui, Strasbourg, 24 April 2006. All further quotations of Daoui from this interview.

38. Interview with Simon Dahan.

39. Interview with Zoubida Tribak, 24 April 2006. All further quotations of Tribak from this interview.

40. Interview with Patricia Jaïs, Paris, 5 April 2006. All further quotations of Patricia Jaïs from this interview.

41. Interview with Mohamed Latahy, Strasbourg, 4 and 6 April 2006.

42. Interview with Gilles Taïeb, Paris, 6 April 2006.

SELECTED BIBLIOGRAPHY

Interviews

Rabbi David Abergel, Meinau, 7 March 2006
Félix Amanou, correspondence and telephone conversation (from Biarritz), 11 June and 11 July 2006
Isidore Aragones, Marseille, 20 July 2006
Gabriel Attias, Strasbourg, 23 April and 3 May 2006
Nourredine Bakiz, Paris, 16 March 2006
Salah Bariki and Moulay Ghoul, Marseille, 10 July 2006
Farouk Belkeddar, Paris, 25 July 2006
Isaac Ben-David, Strasbourg, 30 April 2006
Derri Berkani, Paris, 10 May 2006
Dahlil Boubakeur, Paris, 30 May 2006
Saïd Bouziri, Paris, 24 July 2006
André Charbit, Paris, 16 June 2006
Pierre Chouissa, Strasbourg, 27 April 2006
Dr. Simon Dahan, Strasbourg, 17 April 2006
Fouad Douai, Strasbourg, 24 April 2006
Mostafa Elqoch, 23 April 2006
Robert Garcia, Strasbourg, 27 April 2006
Roger Gharbi, Paris, 6 April 2006
Gilbert Guigui and Claude Sabbah, Strasbourg, 2 May 2006
Rabbi René Gutman, Strasbourg, 2 March 2006
Habib Hihi and Evelyne Rueff-Hihi, Colmar, 3 May 2006
Gilbert Hostalier, Marseille, 10 July 2006
Patricia Jaïs, Paris, 5 April 2006
Louise Jaïs, née Fhal, Paris, 20 March 2006
Daniel Jaouis, Marseille, 7 June 2006
Jean-Marie Kutner, Strasbourg, 5 May 2006

Mohamed Latahy, Strasbourg, 4 and 6 April 2006
Jacques Lazarus, Paris, 5 April 2006
Pierre Lévy, Strasbourg, 15 December 2005
Dr. Jacques Leyris, Ris-Orangis, 19 June 2006
Ahmed Najar, Marseille, 17 July 2006
Dr. Léon and Laurette Nisand, Strasbourg, 20 April 2006
Pastor Michel de Passanal, Marseille, 3 February 2006
Larbi Saoudi, Marseille, 14 July 2006
Bernard Sberro, Marseille, 24 July 2006
Michel Serfaty, Ris-Orangis, 12 April 2007
Gilles Taïeb, Paris, 6 April 2006
Zoubida Tribak, Strasbourg, 24 April 2006
Clément Yana, Marseille, 17 July 2006

Public and Private Archival Collections

Archives of the American Joint Distribution Committee (Jerusalem)
Geneva II, Box 234B
Geneva II, Box 381C/382A
Geneva II, Box 382B
Geneva II, Box 383
Geneva II, Box 384

Archives de l'Alliance Israélite Universelle (Paris)
Fonds Jacques Lazarus
    Dossier I
    Dossier II
    Dossier III
    Dossier IV
    Dossier V
    Dossier XII
    Dossier XVI
    'Chemise Algérie'
Algérie
    IC-5
    IIC-1
    IIC-2
    IIC-3
    IIC-6

Archives de l'Association Génériques (Paris)
Fonds Farouk Belkeddar
   2
   6
   8
Fonds Bouziri
   1–3

Archives of the Association Sportive Menora (Strasbourg)
Private, uncatalogued collection of Simon Dahan

Archives de la Chambre de Commerce de Marseille (Marseille)
ML 42731, 01–03
Indicateur marseillais (1929, 1933, 1936)

Archives du Comité d'action sociale israélite de Paris-Comité juif d'action sociale et de reconstruction (CASIP-COJASOR) (Paris)
COJASOR. R. Egy. A
   Sous-série A, 1–3
   Sous-série B, 4
   Sous-série C, 1; 5
   Le Toit Familiale

Archives du Consistoire Israélite Centrale de France (Paris)
Fonds Jacques Lazarus, unnumbered dossiers of Algerian Jewry, 1947–1962
Fonds Jacques Lazarus, unnumbered dossiers of Association des Juifs Origi-
   naires d'Algérie (AJOA)
Unnumbered carton, "Guerre des 6 Jours—Troubles Belleville—May
   1968—Diverses affaires"

Archives du Consistoire Israélite de Paris (Paris)
B 129–130
Dossier 4f

Archives Départementales du Bas-Rhin (Strasbourg)
286 D 176
286 D 190
286 D 195
286 D 218
286 D 319
286 D 364
286 D 379

544 D 171–172
544 D 176
544 D 183
589 D 241–243
589 D 245
709 D 33
709 D 133

Archives Départementales des Bouches-du-Rhône (Marseille)

8 Fi 631/2
8 Fi 675/2
8 Fi 693/1
1 M 759
1 M 801
1 M 815
1 M 835
1 M 999
76 W 161–163
76 W 168
76 W 204–206
76 W 209
135 W 57
137 W 363
137 W 433–436
137 W 463–465
138 W 73–75
149 W 137
150 W 168
156 W 104

Archives du Ministère des Affaires Etrangères (Paris and La Courneuve)
Série Guerre 1939–1945 (SG39–45), M Vichy-Maroc, Mosquée de Paris
Inventaire Provisoire du fonds Levant 1944–65, 373, L. 72
148 W 85

Archives Municipales de Marseille (Marseille)
30 II 144
91 II 10

Archives Nationales (Paris)
AJ38, 6
AJ38, 152

AJ38, 154–156
AJ38, 162
AJ38, 170–172
AJ38, 176
AJ38, 3109
AJ38, 3185–3191
AJ40, 1593
F1a, 5012–5013
F1a, 5015
F1a, 5025
F1a, 5035

Archives de la Préfecture de Police (Paris)

BA 1793
BA 1811–1812
BA 1815
BA 1914
BA 1945–1950
BA 1954–1955
BA 1960
BA 2038
BA 2170–2172
BA 2314–2315
BA 2273
BA 2335
BS2/41
DA 768
DB 626
GA Br 50
GA, L19
HA 7–9
HA 15
HA 23
HA 25–26
HA 27
HA 29
HA 31

Archives de la Ville et de la Communauté Urbaine de Strasbourg (Strasbourg)

456 W 11–14
1001 W 9

Dossier Documentaire. Militaires tombes à la liberation de Strasbourg, 1944–1945

Archives de la Ville de Paris (Paris)
Recensements de population
  2 Mi LN 1926 / 7–8
  2 Mi LN 1936 / 5
  2 Mi LN 1936 / 7–8
  2 MI LN 1946 / 4

Central Zionist Archives (Jerusalem)
C10/3155
C10/3303
C10/3947
KKL5/13146
S25/1985
S5/12533
S5/12536
Z6/1558

Centre des Archives Contemporaines (Fontainebleau)
0019770346, 10–11
0019850087, 029
0019850087, 031
0019850087, 033
0019920172, 08, liasse 03
0019970239, 06

Centre des Archives Diplomatiques de Nantes (Nantes)
1TU/125/9
1TU/125/10
1TU/125/11
1TU/125/13
1TU/125/22
1TU/125/31
1TU/V/2793

Centre des Archives d'Outre-mer (Aix-en-Provence)
81 F 832–834
16 H 115
5 I 50

5 I 87
7 CAB 53
8 CAB 71
8 CAB 19
93/4298

Centre Culturel Algérien (Paris)
Dossiers of press clippings on musique judéo-arabe

Centre de Documentation Juive Contemporaine (Paris)
Collection Georges Epstein
CCXLV_249
CF161_6973
CDXL_37
CXV_164a
MXC_D4
MXC_D7
MXLV_A
XXXII_68
MDI-12–20
MDI-28
MDI-37
MDI-39–41
MDI-159
Fonds Kaplan
   20
   48–49
   53

Institute for Contemporary Jewry (Avraham Harman Institute) (Jerusalem)
Demography section
   FRO 4201

Private Collection of Derri Berkani, Paris
Material on histories of Muslim resistance during World War II

Private Collection of Martine Bernheim, Paris
Material on histories of resistance around the Grande Mosquée de Paris during
   World War II

Newspapers, Magazines, and Bulletins Consulted

French Jewish periodicals

Annuaire des Archives israélites (1912–1930)
L'Arche (Revue du FSJU) (1956–1968)
Les Archives israélites (1915–1935)
Le Bulletin de nos communautés (1954–1968)
Le Bulletin de l'union patriotique des français israélites (1934–1935)
Les Cahiers Bernard-Lazare (1957–1973)
Le Droit de Vivre (1932–1936)
L'Information juive (1954–1965)
Le Journal des communautés (1956–1972)
Kadimah (1953–1969)
Paix et droit (1934–1935)
La Presse nouvelle (1958–1972)
Samedi (1936–1939)
La Terre retrouvée (1928–1959)
La Tribune juive (1968)
L'Univers israélite (1913–1938)

French Muslim or Algerian periodicals

El Akhbar (1914–1934)
L'Algérien en Europe (1967–1970)
Le Fedai (1971–1972)
L'Ikdam (1919–1934)
L'Islam (1912–1914)
L'Entente franco-musulmane (1935–1942)
La Lutte sociale (1940–1943)
Lutte palestinienne (1968–1972)
El Moudjahid (1967–1968)
El Ouma (1934–1939)
Er Rachid (1943–1944)
La Voix du peuple algérien (1954–1962)

Other Primary Sources

Abdel-Kader, A. Razak. *Le conflit judéo-arabe.* Paris: François Maspero, 1961.

Abdoun, Mahmoud. *Témoignage d'un militant du mouvement nationaliste.* Algiers: Dahlab, 1990.

Adjoud, Rabah. "Les nord-africains aux côtés du peuple français: les faits d'armes des musulmans dans les combats de la capitale." *Liberté* (Algiers), 19 October 1944. Quoted nearly in full in Michel Renard, "Les nord-

africains aux côtés du peuple français." N.d. http://islamenfrance.canalblog
.com/archives/2007/02/16/4072472.html.

American Jewish Yearbook. 1960–1970.

Arnaud, Didier, and Jacky Durand. "Le 'cerveau des barbares' nouvel ennemi
public." *Libération,* 18 February 2006.

Assouline, Albert. "La paix sur lui." *Vae victis: Bulletin officiel d'information
de l'amicale libre du 22ᵉ B.M.N.A.* 27 (October 1984).

———. "Le racisme et non seulement l'antisémitisme durant la France libre."
*Vae victis: Bulletin officiel d'information d l'amicale libre du
22eme B.M.N.A.* 26 (August 1982): 27–31.

———. "Une vocation ignorée de la mosquée de Paris." In *Almanach du
combattant.* Paris: Comité National du Souvenir de Verdun, 1983.

Bachetarzi, Mahieddine. *Mémoires, 1919–1939.* Algiers: Éditions nationales
algériennes, 1968.

Barrès, Maurice. *Les diverses familles spirituelles de la France.* Paris, 1917.

Baruch, Jules. *Historique des corps des officiers interprètes de l'armée
d'Afrique.* Constantine: D. Braham, 1901.

Berkani, Derri. Untitled talk given before the Lion's Club. Paris, 8 February, 2005.

Chemouili, Henri. *Les juifs d'Algérie, une diaspora méconnue.* Paris, 1976.

Commission nationale consultative des droits de l'homme. Reports on Racism,
Anti-Semitism, and Xenophobia in France, 2000–2011. http://lesrapports
.ladocumentationfrancaise.fr.

"La communauté sefarade de Strasbourg." N.d. http://judaisme.sdv.fr/histoire
/villes/strasbrg/sefarade/index.htm.

"Les communautés de Belleville." 1973. http://www.ina.fr/econo.mie-et-societe
/vie-sociale/video/I04271286/les-communautes-de-belleville.fr.html.

Darville, Jacques, and Simon Wichené. *Drancy la juive ou la deuxième inquisition.* Cachan: A. Breger Frères, 1945.

"Le droit à l'insoumission." *Verité-liberté,* 6 September 1960.

Fédération de France du front de libération nationale algérien, ed. "Les juifs
d'Algérie dans le combat pour l'indépendence." *A l'adresse du peuple
français—FLN Documents.* No. 5. Paris: December 1959.

———, ed. *La question de la minorité européene et la révolution
algerienne.* N.d.

Gary, Romain (Émile Ajar). *The Life before Us.* Translated by Ralph Manheim.
New York: New Directions, 1986.

Hadj, Messali. *Mémoires.* Paris: J. C. Lattès, 1982.

Halff, Sylvain. "The Participation of the Jews of France in the Great War." In
The American Jewish Yearbook 21 (1919–1920): 2–97.

Kaddache, Mahfoud, and Mohamed Guenaneche, eds. *L'étoile nord-africaine,
1926–1937: Documents et témoignages pour servir à l'étude du nationalisme algérien.* Algiers: Office des Publications Universitaires, 1994.

Kateb, Yacine. *Nedjma*. Paris: Éditions du Seuil, 1956.

Lebjaoui, Mohamed. *Vérités sur la révolution algérienne*. Paris: Gallimard, 1970.

Le Livre d'or du Judaïsme Algérien (1914–1918). September 1919. New edition: Paris: Cercle de généalogie juive, with the collaboration of Georges Teboul and Jean-Pierre Bernard, 2000.

Maquet, Jean. "A Oran comme à Alger un passant invisible: La peur." *Paris Match,* 20 January 1962, 26–31.

Memmi, Albert. *The Colonizer and the Colonized*. Translated by Howard Greenfeld with a new introduction by the author. Preface by Jean-Paul Sartre. New York: Orion Press, 1965.

———. *The Pillar of Salt*. Translated by Edouard Roditi. Boston: Beacon Press, 1955.

Meiss, Homel. *Religion et patrie*. Paris: Librarie Durlacher, 1922.

Muslims in the EU: Cities Report: Preliminary research report and literature survey—France. Brussels: Open Society Institute, EU Monitoring and Advocacy Program, 2007.

Muslims More Moderate: The Great Divide—How Westerners and Muslims View Each Other, The Pew Global Attitudes Project. Washington, DC: Pew Research Center, 2006.

Niedermaier, Curt. "Union d'Etudiants . . . en France." *Communauté,* December 1959–January 1960.

Nogaro, B., and Lucien Weil. *La main-d'oeuvre étrangère et coloniale pendant la guerre*. Paris: Presses universitaires de France; New Haven, CT: Yale University Press, 1926.

Pétain, Philippe. *Discours au Français, 17 juin 1940–20 août 1944*. Edited by Jean-Claude Barabs. Preface by Antoine Prost. Paris: Albin Michel, 1989.

Serfaty, Michel. "Juifs et musulmans de France: une relation à construire." Unpublished paper, 2007.

"Strasbourg: la mosquée dans la cité." Dossier in *la Medina: le magazine des cultures musulmanes,* no. 6 (January–February 2001): 32–51.

Secondary Sources

Abdi, Nidam. "La chanson maghrébine orpheline." *Libération,* 13 July 2005.

Abitbol, Michel. "La cinquième république et l'accueil des juifs d'afrique du nord." In *Les juifs de France: de la révolution française à nos jours*. Edited by Jean-Jacques Becker and Annette Wieviorka. France: Liana Levi, 1998.

———. *The Jews of North Africa during the Second World War*. Translated by Catherine Tahanyi Zentelis. Detroit: Wayne State University Press, 1989.

Abulafia, David. The Mediterranean in History. London: Thames & Hudson, 2003.

Achcar, Gilbert. *The Arabs and the Holocaust: The Arab-Israeli War of Narratives*. Translated by G. M. Goshgarian. New York: Holt, 2009.

Ageron, Charles-Robert. *"L'Algérie algérienne" de Napoléon III à de Gaulle.* Paris: Sindbad, 1980.

———. "Une émeute anti-juive à Constantine (August 1934)." *Revue de l'occident musulman et de la Méditerranée* 13–14 (1973): 23–40.

———. "Les populations du Maghreb face à la propagande allemande." *Revue d'histoire de la deuxième guerre mondiale,* no. 114 (April 1979): 1–39.

Aidi, Hisham D. *Rebel Music: Race, Empire and the New Muslim Youth Culture.* New York: Pantheon Books, 2014.

Aissaoui, Rabah. *Immigration and National Identity: North African Political Movements in Colonial and Postcolonial France.* London: I. B. Tauris, 2009.

Albert, Phyllis Cohen. "Israelite and Jew: How Did Nineteenth-Century French Jews Understand Assimilation?" In *The Jews in Nineteenth-Century Europe.* Edited by Jonathan Frankel and Steven J. Zipperstein. Cambridge: Cambridge University Press, 1992.

Allouche-Benayoun, Joëlle, and Doris Bensimon. *Les Juifs d'Algérie: Mémoires et identités plurielles.* Paris: Éditions Stavit, 1998.

Aouate, Yves-Claude. "Les algériens musulmans et les mesures antijuives du gouvernement de Vichy (1940–1942)." *Pardes* 16 (1992): 189–202.

Arkin, Kimberly. *Rhinestones, Religion, and the Republic: Fashioning Jewishness in France.* Stanford, CA: Stanford University Press, 2013.

Attal, Robert. *Les émeutes de Constantine: 5 août 1934.* Paris: Romillat, 2002.

Ayoun, Richard. "Les juifs d'Algérie pendant la guerre d'indépendance (1954–1962)." *Archives juives* 29, no. 1 (1996): 15–29.

Bahloul, Joëlle. *The Architecture of Memory: A Jewish-Muslim Household in Colonial Algeria, 1937–1962.* Translated by Catherine du Peloux Ménagé. Cambridge: Cambridge University Press, 1996.

Bell, David. *The Cult of the Nation in France: Inventing Nationalism, 1680–1800.* Cambridge, MA: Harvard University Press, 2001.

Benbassa, Esther. *The Jews of France: A History from Antiquity to the Present.* Translated by M. B. DeBevoise. Princeton, NJ: Princeton University Press, 1999.

Bensimon-Donath, Doris. *L'intégration des juifs nord-africains en France.* Paris: Mouton, 1971.

Berceot, Florence. "Renouvellement socio-démographique des juifs de Marseille 1901–1937." *Provence historique* 175 (1994): 39–57.

Berkani, Derri. *Résistance oubliée . . . La Mosquée de Paris de 40 à 44.* Produced and directed by Berkani. 26 minutes. 1991. DVD.

Berkovitz, Jay. *Rites and Passages: The Beginnings of Modern Jewish Culture in France, 1650–1860.* Philadelphia: University of Pennsylvania Press, 2004.

———. *The Shaping of Jewish Identity in Nineteenth-Century France.* Detroit: Wayne State University Press, 1989.

Birnbaum, Pierre. *The Jews of the Republic: A Political History of State Jews in France from Gambetta to Vichy.* Translated by Jane Marie Todd. Stanford, CA: Stanford University Press, 1996.

Blanchard, Emmanuel. *La police parisienne et les algériens (1944–1962).* Paris: Nouveau Monde, 2011.

Blanchard, Pascal, and Gilles Boëtsch. "La France de Pétain et l'Afrique: Images et propagandes coloniales." *Canadian Journal of African Studies/ Revue canadienne des études africaines* 28, no. 1 (1994): 1–31.

Blanchard, Pascal, and Sandrine Lemaire, eds. *Culture impériale: Les colonies au coeur de la république, 1931–1961.* Paris: Éditions autrement, 2004.

Blévis, Laure. "Les avatars de la citoyenneté en Algérie coloniale ou les paradoxes d'une catégorisation." *Droit et Société* 48 (2001): 557–80.

Boittin, Jennifer. *Colonial Metropolis: The Urban Grounds of Anti-Imperialism and Feminism in Interwar Paris.* Lincoln: University of Nebraska Press, 2010.

Boukara, Philippe. "La gauche juive en France et la guerre d'Algérie." *Archives juives* 29, no. 1 (1996): 72–81.

Bouzeghrane, Nadjia. "Seconde guerre mondiale: Les FTP algériens et le sauvetage d'enfants juifs." *El Watan: Le quotidien independant,* 16 May 2005. http://www.elwatan.com/spip.php?page=article&id_article=19338.

Brubaker, Rogers. *Citizenship and Nationhood in France and Germany.* Cambridge, MA: Harvard University Press, 1992.

Burrin, Philippe. *France under the Germans: Collaboration and Compromise.* Translated by Janet Lloyd. New York: New Press, 1996.

Camiscioli, Elisa. "Reproducing the French Race: Immigration, Reproduction, and National Identity in France, 1900–1939." PhD dissertation, University of Chicago, 2000.

Carlier, Omar. "Le café maure. Sociabilité masculine et effervescence citoyenne (Algerie XVIIe–XXe siècles)." *Annales. Économies, Sociétés, Civilisations* 45, no. 4 (1990): 975–1003.

Caron, Vicki. *Uneasy Asylum: France and the Jewish Refugee Crisis, 1933– 1942.* Stanford, CA: Stanford University Press, 1999.

Centre nationale de la recherche scientifique. *Les relations entre juifs et musulmans en Afrique du Nord, XIXᵉ-XXᵉ siècles.* Marseille: Éditions du CNRS, 1980.

Clancy-Smith, Julia. *Mediterraneans: North Africa and Europe in an Age of Migration, c. 1800–1900.* Berkeley: University of California Press, 2011.

Clayton, Anthony. *France, Soldiers and Africa.* London: Brassey's Defence Publishers, 1988.

Cohen, David. "Le comité juif algérien d'études sociales dans le débat idéologique pendant la guerre d'Algérie (1954–1961)." *Archives juives* 29, no. 1 (1996): 30–50.

Cohen, Erik H. *The Jews of France Today: Identity and Values*. Leiden: Brill, 2011.

Cohen, Mark R. *Under Crescent and Cross: The Jews in the Middle Ages*. Princeton, NJ: Princeton University Press, 1994.

Cole, Joshua. "'A chacun son public': Le spectacle de la politique et de la culture en Algérie au temps du Front populaire." *Sociétés et représentations* 38 (2014): 21–51.

———. "Antisémitisme et situation coloniale pendant l'entre-deux-guerres en Algérie: Les émeutes antijuives de Constantine." *Vingtième siècle* 108, no. 4 (2012): 2–23.

———. "Remembering the Battle of Paris: 17 October 1961 in French and Algerian Memory." *French Politics, Culture and Society* 21, no. 3 (2003): 21–50.

Coller, Ian. *Arab France: Islam and the Making of Modern Europe, 1798–1831*. Berkeley: University of California Press, 2011.

Connelly, Matthew. *A Diplomatic Revolution: Algeria's Fight for Independence and the Origins of the Post–Cold War Era*. New York: Oxford University Press, 2002.

Cooper, Frederick. *Colonialism in Question: Theory, Knowledge, History*. Berkeley: University of California Press, 2005.

Cooper, Frederick, and Ann Stoler, eds. *Tensions of Empire: Colonial Cultures in a Bourgeois World*. Berkeley: University of California Press, 1997.

Crane, Sheila. *Mediterranean Crossroads: Marseille and Modern Architecture*. Minneapolis: University of Minnesota Press, 2011

Davidson, Naomi. *Only Muslim: Embodying Islam in Twentieth-Century France*. Ithaca, NY: Cornell University Press, 2012.

Davis, Natalie Zemon. *Fiction in the Archives: Pardon Tales and Their Tellers in Sixteenth-Century France*. Stanford, CA: Stanford University Press, 1987.

Debrauwere-Miller, Nathalie, ed. *The Israeli-Palestinian Conflict in the Francophone World*. New York: Routledge, 2010.

Dimier, Véronique. "For a Republic 'Diverse and Indivisible'? France's Experience from the Colonial Past." *Contemporary European History* 13, no. 1 (2004): 45–66.

———. "French Secularism in Debate: Old Wine in New Bottles." *French Politics, Culture and Society* 26, no. 1 (Spring 2008): 92–110.

Dubois, Laurent. *A Colony of Citizens: Revolution and Slave Emancipation in the French Caribbean, 1787–1804*. Chapel Hill: University of North Carolina Press, 2004.

Eisenbeth, Maurice. *Les juifs de l'Afrique du nord: Démographie et onomastique*. Algiers: Imprimerie du lycée, 1936.

Eldridge, Claire. "Remembering the Other: Postcolonial Perspectives on Relationships between Jews and Muslims in French Algeria." *Journal of Modern Jewish Studies* 11, no. 3 (2012): 1–19.

Fogarty, Richard. "Between Subjects and Citizens: Algerians, Islam and French National Identity during the Great War." In *Race and Nation: Ethnic Systems in the Modern World*. Edited by Paul Spickard. New York: Routledge, 2005.

———. "L'identité en question: l'islam, la captivité, et les soldats nord-africains pendant la grande guerre." *Migrance* 38, no. 2 (2011): 37–52.

———. *Race and War in France: Colonial Subjects in the French Army, 1914–1918*. Baltimore: Johns Hopkins University Press, 2008.

Friedman, Elizabeth. *Colonialism & After: An Algerian Jewish Community*. Boston: Bergin & Garvey, 1988.

Gastau, Yves. "La guerre des six jours et la question du racisme en France." *Cahiers de la Mediterranée* 71 (2005). http://cdlm.revues.org/930?lang=en.

Gildea, Robert. *Marianne in Chains: In Search of the German Occupation*. London: Macmillan, 2002.

Goldberg, Harvey E. "The Mimuna and the Minority Status of Moroccan Jews." *Ethnology* 17 (1978): 75–87.

Gordon, Bertram. *Collaborationism in France during the Second World War*. Ithaca, NY: Cornell University Press, 1980.

Gordon, Daniel A. *Immigrants and Intellectuals: May '68 and the Rise of Anti-Racism in France*. Pontypool, UK: Merlin Press, 2012.

———. "Juifs et musulmans à Belleville (Paris 20ᵉ) entre tolérance et conflit." *Cahiers de la Méditerranée* 67 (December 2003). http://cdlm.revues.org /document.html?id=135.

Gottreich, Emily. *The Mellah of Marrakesh: Jewish and Muslim Space in Morocco's Red City*. Bloomington: Indiana University Press, 2006.

Haine, W. Scott. *The World of the Paris Café: Sociability among the French Working Class, 1789–1914*. Baltimore: Johns Hopkins University Press, 1996.

Hajjat, Abdellali. "Aux origines du soutien à la cause palestinienne en France." *Europe solidaire sans frontières,* 1 February 2006. http://www.europe -solidaire.org/spip.php?article3675.

Hammerman, Jessica. "The Heart of the Diaspora: Algerian Jews during the War for Independence, 1954–1962." PhD dissertation, City University of New York, 2013.

Hazéra, Hélène. "La douce nostalgie des chants judéo-arabes." *Alger Info,* 10 May 1996.

Herf, Jeffrey. *Nazi Propaganda for the Arab World*. New Haven, CT: Yale University Press, 2009.

Horden, Peregrine, and Nicholas Purcell. *The Corrupting Sea: A Study of Mediterranean History.* Oxford: Wiley-Blackwell, 2000.

Hutchinson, John, and Anthony Smith, eds. *Ethnicity.* Oxford: Oxford University Press, 1996.

Hyman, Paula. *From Dreyfus to Vichy: The Remaking of French Jewry, 1906–1939.* New York: Columbia University Press, 1979.

Irvine, William. "Fascism in France and the Strange Case of the Croix-de-Feu." *Journal of Modern History* 63, no. 2 (1991): 271–95.

Jennings, Eric T. *Vichy in the Tropics: Pétain's National Revolution in Madagascar, Guadeloupe, and Indochina, 1940–1944.* Stanford, CA: Stanford University Press, 2001.

Jordi, Jean-Jacques, and Émile Temime, eds. *Marseille et le choc des décolonisations: Les rapatriements, 1954–1964.* Aix-en-Provence: Edisud, 1996.

Kalman, Samuel. *French Colonial Fascism: The Extreme Right in Algeria, 1919–1939.* New York: Palgrave Macmillan, 2013.

Katz, Ethan. "Did the Paris Mosque Save Jews? A Mystery and Its Memory." *Jewish Quarterly Review* 102, no. 2 (2012): 256–87.

Katz, Ethan, Maud Mandel, and Lisa Leff, eds. *Colonialism and the Jews.* Bloomington: Indiana University Press, forthcoming.

Katz, Jacob. *Exclusiveness and Tolerance: Jewish-Gentile Relations in Medieval and Modern Times.* New York: Oxford University Press, 1961; reprint, New York: Schocken, 1962.

Kupferstein, Daniel. *Les oubliés de l'histoire, les étrangers dans la résistance et la libération.* 56 minutes. 1992. Videocassette.

Laloum, Jean. "Des juifs d'Afrique du Nord au Pletzl? Une présence méconnue et des épreuves oubliées (1920–1945)." *Archives juives* 38, no. 2 (2005): 47–83.

———. "Portrait d'un Juif du FLN." *Archives juives* 29, no. 1 (1996): 65–71.

Landau, Philippe E. *Les juifs de France et la grande guerre: Un patriotisme républicain, 1914–1941.* Paris: Editions CNRS, 2000.

———. "Les juifs de Tunisie et la grande guerre." *Archives juives* 32, no. 1 (1999): 40–52.

Laskier, Michael M. "Israel and Algeria amid French Colonialism and the Arab-Israeli Conflict, 1954–1978." *Israel Studies* 6, no. 2 (1998): 1–32.

———. *North African Jewry in the Twentieth Century: The Jews of Morocco, Tunisia, and Algeria.* New York: New York University Press, 1994.

Laurence, Jonathan, and Justin Vaisse. *Integrating Islam: Political and Religious Challenges in Contemporary France.* Washington, DC: Brookings Institution, 2006.

Le Foll-Luciani, Pierre-Jean. "Des étudiants juifs algériens dans le mouvement national algérien à Paris (1948–1962)." In *La bienvenue et l'adieu: Migrants juifs et musulmans au Maghreb* (XVe–XXe siècle), vol. 3. Edited by

Frédéric Abécassis, Karima Dirèche, and Rita Aouad. Casablanca: Centre Jacques-Berque, 2012.

Le Pautremat, Pascal. *La politique musulmane de la France au XXᵉ siècle: De l'Hexagone aux terres d'Islam. Espoirs, réussites, échecs.* Paris: Maisonneuve & Larose, 2003.

Leff, Lisa Moses. *Sacred Bonds of Solidarity: The Rise of Jewish Internationalism in Nineteenth-Century France.* Stanford, CA: Stanford University Press, 2006.

Leveau, Rémy, and Dominique Schnapper. *Religion et politique: Juifs et musulmans maghrébins en France.* Paris: Association française de science politique, Centre d'études et de recherches internationales, 1987.

Lewis, Mary. *Boundaries of the Republic: Migrant Rights and the Limits of Universalism in France, 1918–1940.* Stanford, CA: Stanford University Press, 2007.

Lorcin, Patricia. *Imperial Identities: Stereotyping, Prejudice, and Race in Colonial Algeria.* New York: Saint Martin's Press, 1995.

MacMaster, Neil. *Colonial Migrants and Racism: Algerians in France, 1900–62.* New York: St. Martin's Press, 1997.

Mandel, Maud S. *In the Aftermath of Genocide: Armenians and Jews in Twentieth-Century France.* Durham, NC: Duke University Press, 2003.

———. *Muslims and Jews in France: History of a Conflict.* Princeton, NJ: Princeton University Press, 2014.

Mann, Gregory. *Native Sons: West African Veterans and France in the Twentieth Century.* Durham, NC: Duke University Press, 2006.

Marglin, Jessica M. "Mediterranean Modernity through Jewish Eyes: The Transimperial Life of Abraham Ankawa," *Jewish Social Studies* n.s. 20, no. 2 (Winter 2014): 34–68.

Marrus, Michael, and Robert Paxton. *Vichy France and the Jews.* New York: Basic Books, 1981; reprint with a new foreword by Stanley Hoffmann. Stanford, CA: Stanford University Press, 1995.

Mazower, Mark. *Salonica, City of Ghosts: Christians, Muslims and Jews, 1430–1950.* New York: Vintage Books, 2006.

McDougall, James. *History and the Culture of Nationalism in Algeria.* Cambridge: Cambridge University Press, 2006.

Meynier, Gilbert. *L'Algérie révelée, la guerre de 1914–1918 et le premier quart du siècle.* Geneva: Librairie Droz, 1981.

———. *Histoire intérieure du FLN, 1954–1962.* Paris: Fayard, 2002.

Nash, Manning. *The Cauldron of Ethnicity in the Modern World.* Chicago: University of Chicago Press, 1989.

Noiriel, Gérard. *The French Melting Pot: Immigration, Citizenship, and National Identity.* Edited by Charles Tilly. Translated by Geoffroy de Laforcade. Minneapolis: University of Minnesota Press, 1996.

Parks, Richard. "The Jewish Quarters of Interwar Paris and Tunis: Destruction, Creation, and French Urban Design." *Jewish Social Studies* n.s. 17, no. 1 (2010): 67–87.

Paxton, Robert. *Vichy France: Old Guard and New Order, 1940–1944*. New York: Knopf, 1972; reprint with a new introduction: New York: Columbia University Press, 1982.

Penslar, Derek J. *Jews in the Military: A History*. Princeton, NJ: Princeton University Press, 2013.

Poznanski, Renée. "French Apprehensions, Jewish Expectations: From a Social Imaginary to a Political Practice." In *The Jews Are Coming Back: The Return of the Jews to Their Countries of Origin after WWII*. Edited by David Bankier. New York: Berghahn Books, 2005.

———. *Jews in France during World War II*. Translated by Nathan Bracher. Hanover, NH: University Press of New England, 1997.

———. "Reflections on Jewish Resistance and Jewish Resistants in France." *Jewish Social Studies* n.s. 2, no. 1 (Autumn 1995): 124–58.

Recham, Belkacem. "Les musulmans algériens dans l'armée française (1919–1945)." PhD dissertation, University of Strasbourg, 1995.

———. "Les musulmans dans l'armée française, 1830–1945: Mercenaires ou citoyens?" *Migrance* 38, no. 2 (2011): 27–35.

Renard, Michel. "Aperçu sur l'histoire de l'islam à Marseille, 1813–1962. Pratiques religieuses et encadrements des nord-africains." *Revue française d'histoire d'outre-mer* 90 (2003): 269–96.

———. "Les chansons de Mahieddine en 1937." N.d. http://islamenfrance .canalblog.com/archives/2006/08/31/2598343.html.

———. "Si Kaddour ben Ghabrit: biographie." N.d. http://islamenfrance .canalblog.com/archives/2007/02/10/4057434.html.

Roblin, Michel. *Les juifs de Paris: Démographie—économie—culture*. Paris: Éditions A. et J. Picard, 1952.

Rodrigue, Aron. *French Jews, Turkish Jews: The Alliance Israélite Universelle and the Politics of Jewish Schooling in Turkey, 1860–1925*. Bloomington: Indiana University Press, 1990.

Rosen, Lawrence. *Bargaining for Reality: The Construction of Social Relations in a Muslim Community*. Chicago: University of Chicago Press, 1984.

Rosenberg, Clifford. *Policing Paris: The Origins of Modern Immigration Control between the Wars*. Ithaca, NY: Cornell University Press, 2006.

Rothberg, Michael. *Multidirectional Memory: Remembering the Holocaust in the Age of Decolonization*. Stanford, CA: Stanford University Press, 2009.

Satloff, Robert. *Among the Righteous: Lost Stories from the Holocaust's Long Reach into Arab Lands*. New York: Public Affairs Press, 2006.

Schechter, Ronald. *Obstinate Hebrews: Representations of Jews in France, 1715–1815*. Berkeley: University of California Press, 2003.

Scheck, Raffael. "Nazi Propaganda toward French Muslim Prisoners of War." *Holocaust and Genocide Studies* 26, no. 3 (2012): 447–77.

Schreier, Joshua. *Arabs of the Jewish Faith: The Civilizing Mission in Colonial Algeria*. New Brunswick, NJ: Rutgers University Press, 2010.

Scott, Joan. *Only Paradoxes to Offer*. Cambridge, MA: Harvard University Press, 1996.

———. *The Politics of the Veil*. Princeton, NJ: Princeton University Press, 2007.

Shepard, Todd. *The Invention of Decolonization: The Algerian War and the Remaking of France*. Ithaca, NY: Cornell University Press, 2006.

———. "Thinking between Metropole and Colony: The French Republic, 'Exceptional Promotion,' and the 'Integration' of Algerians, 1955–1962." In *The French Colonial Mind*, vol. 1. Edited by Martin Thomas. Lincoln: University of Nebraska Press, 2011.

Shields, James. *The Extreme Right in France: From Pétain to Le Pen*. New York: Routledge, 2007.

———. "Radical or Not So Radical? Tactical Variation in Core Policy Formation by the Front National." *French Politics, Culture and Society* 29, no. 3 (2011): 78–100.

Silverstein, Paul. *Algeria in France: Transpolitics, Race, and Nation*. Bloomington: Indiana University Press, 2004.

Simon, Patrick. "Les représentations des relations interethniques dans un quartier cosmopolite." *Recherches sociologiques* 28, no. 2 (1997): 5–37.

———. "La société partagée: Relations interethniques et interclasses dans un quartier en rénovation. Belleville, Paris XXᵉ." *Cahiers internationaux de sociologie* 98 (1995): 161–90.

Simon, Patrick, and Claude Tapia. *Le Belleville des juifs tunisiens*. Paris: Éditions autrement, 1998.

Soucy, Robert. *French Fascism: The Second Wave, 1933–1939*. New Haven, CT: Yale University Press, 1995.

Spire, Alexis. "Semblables et pourtants différents. La citoyenneté paradoxale des 'français musulmans d'Algérie' en métropole." *Genèses* 53 (2003): 48–68.

Stein, Sarah Abrevaya. "Protected Persons? The Baghdadi Jewish Diaspora, the British State, and the Persistence of Empire." *American Historical Review* 116, no. 1 (2011): 80–108.

———. *Saharan Jews and the Fate of French Algeria*. Chicago: University of Chicago Press, 2014.

Stillman, Norman, ed. *The Jews of Arab Lands in Modern Times*. Philadelphia: Jewish Publication Society, 1991.

Stoler, Ann Laura. *Along the Archival Grain: Epistemic Anxieties and Colonial Common Sense*. Princeton, NJ: Princeton University Press, 2009.

———. *Carnal Knowledge and Imperial Power: Race and the Intimate in Colonial Rule.* Berkeley: University of California Press, 2002.

Stora, Benjamin. *La gangrène et l'oubli: la mémoire de la guerre d'Algérie.* Paris: Éditions de la découverte, 1992.

———. *Histoire de l'Algérie coloniale (1830–1954).* Paris: Éditions de la découverte, 2004 (1991).

———. *Histoire de la guerre d'Algérie (1954–1962).* Paris: Éditions de la découverte, 2002 (1991).

———. *Ils venaient d'Algérie: l'immigration algérienne en France (1912–1992).* Paris: Fayard, 1992.

———. *Les trois exils: juifs d'Algérie.* Paris: Stock, 2006.

Stovall, Tyler. "The Color Line behind the Lines: Racial Violence in France during the Great War." *American Historical Review* 103, no. 3 (1998): 737–69.

Sussman, Sarah. "Changing Lands, Changing Identities: The Migration of Algerian Jewry to France, 1954–1967." PhD dissertation, Stanford University, 2003.

Tapia, Claude. *Les juifs sépharades en France, 1965–1985: études psychosociologiques et historiques.* Paris: L'Harmattan, 1986.

Temime, Émile. *Marseille transit: les passagers de Belsunce.* Paris: Éditions autrement, 1995.

Temime, Émile, and Nathalie Deguigné. *Le camp du Grand Arénas: Marseille, 1944–1966.* Paris: Éditions autrement, 2001.

Thomas, Dominic. *Africa and France: Postcolonial Cultures, Migration, and Racism.* Bloomington: Indiana University Press, 2013.

Turner, Victor. "Betwixt and Between: The Liminal Period in *Rites de passage.*" In *The Forest of Symbols: Aspects of Ndembu Ritual.* Ithaca, NY: Cornell University Press, 1967.

Van Rahden, Till. *Jews and Other Germans: Civil Society, Religious Diversity, and Urban Politics in Breslau, 1860–1925.* Translated by Marcus Brainard. Madison: University of Wisconsin Press, 2008.

Vichniac, Judith E. "Jewish Identity Politics and the Scarf Affairs in France." *French Politics, Culture and Society* 26, no. 1 (2008): 111–28.

Vinen, Richard. "The End of an Ideology? Right-Wing Antisemitism in France, 1944–1970." *Historical Journal* 37, no. 2 (1994): 365–88.

———. *The Unfree French: Life under the Occupation.* New Haven, CT: Yale University Press, 2006.

Weill, Patrick. *Qu'est-ce qu'un français? Histoire de la nationalité française depuis la révolution.* Paris: Grasset, 2002.

Weinberg, David H. *A Community on Trial: The Jews of Paris in the 1930s.* Chicago: University of Chicago Press, 1977.

Western, John. *Cosmopolitan Europe: A Strasbourg Self-Portrait.* Burlington, VT: Ashgate, 2012.

Wieviorka, Michel. *La tentation anti-Sémite: Haine des juifs dans la France d'aujourd'hui.* Paris: Ed. Robert Laffont, 2005.

Wilder, Gary. *The French Imperial Nation-State: Negritude and Colonial Humanism between the Two World Wars.* Chicago: University of Chicago Press, 2005.

Winock, Michel. *La France et les juifs.* Paris: Seuil, 2004.

Wolf, Joan. *Harnessing the Holocaust: The Politics of Memory in France.* Stanford, CA: Stanford University Press, 2004.

Zytnicki, Colette. "Du rapatrié au séfarade. L'intégration des juifs d'Afrique du Nord dans la société française: essai de bilan." *Archives juives* 38, no. 2 (2005): 84–102.

———, ed. *Terre d'exil, terre d'asile: Migrations juives en France aux XIXe et XXe siècles.* Villefranche-de-Roudergue: Éclat, 2010.

ACKNOWLEDGMENTS

This book has been ten years in the making. It is a true pleasure to recognize the many intellectual and personal debts I have accumulated along the way.

I have been blessed with remarkable educational opportunities and mentors, without which this book would not exist. At Amherst College, Ronald Rosbottom helped cultivate a fascination with French culture and history, Gordie Levin taught me to think about the history of Israel and Arab-Jewish relations in much more complicated ways, David Blight and Lawrence Douglas inspired me to explore history's lyrical side and to think harder about historical memory, and Catherine Epstein gave me critical practice in repeatedly rewriting and looking for the bigger picture. *The Burdens of Brotherhood* began to take shape at the University of Wisconsin–Madison, where an extraordinary group of teachers and fellow students powerfully influenced the ways I research, think, and write about the past. I was especially fortunate to have two exceptional PhD advisers, Laird Boswell and David Sorkin. Laird's unceasing red marks all over drafts (for which all of his graduate students develop a begrudging affection) made me a far more concise writer and thinker and called me out on my shortcuts. Laird has constantly pointed me toward broader questions and perspectives in French history. A gently exacting push from David—the only kind he gives—made me resituate the entire timeline of this book at the outset. I have benefited repeatedly from his careful attention both to how to write social, cultural, and political history together most effectively and to the larger implications of my story for modern Jewish history. Suzanne Desan and Lou Roberts each took me out of my intellectual comfort zone in highly productive (and supportive) ways on a number of occasions and helped me rethink critical aspects of this book. With much good humor along the way, Laird, David, Suzanne, and Lou have all remained true mentors and rocks of support. Among my fellow graduate students in Madison, Holly Grout, Adam Malka, Hunter Martin, Bill Meier, and Sarah Segev-Wobick were particularly supportive and generous with their friendship, time, and insights.

Two years of my research for this project were spent abroad, one in France and the other in Israel. During my year in France, I reconnected with my "French family," the Tahars, with whom I had lived as a visiting undergraduate years earlier. It was while sitting at their dining room table, eating dishes like couscous and tafina, and hearing their stories of Tunisia that I first began to formulate the questions that led to this book. In the intervening years, first with Danielle and Richard in Paris, later with their daughter Isabelle and her family in Philadelphia, I have always had a home away from home. My research year in France also introduced me to the Engel family in Strasbourg, who gave me not only a place to stay but also enriching insights about Jewish life in Alsace and contacts throughout the city. Also in Strasbourg, Dr. Simon Dahan shared his own stories and gave me access to the world—and the private archives—of the fascinating local sports association the A. S. Menora. In Marseille, Bernard Sperro offered me a place to crash after long research days that was comfortable and affordable, and he graciously shared stories and contacts.

In Paris, at the École pratique des hautes études, Esther Benbassa became a mentor, treating me like one of her own students. Jean Laloum facilitated interviews and offered helpful guidance on many occasions. While hosting me for ten days in their home, Gérard and Anne Chiffert took great interest in my work and became lifelong friends. Also in Paris, Jean-Paul Keane, Daniella Doron, and Naomi Davidson made work in the archives more enjoyable and provided valuable recommendations. Martine Bernheim and Derri Berkani generously shared research materials and insights about the history of the Grand Mosque of Paris. In Paris, Marseille, Strasbourg, and elsewhere, I had the remarkable opportunity to interview numerous Muslims, Jews, and Christians and hear their stories. These individuals, many of whose names appear in this book, gave me insight into their own fascinating lives as well as the broader texture of Jewish-Muslim encounters in the French Mediterranean.

During my year in Israel, my future family members Chaim, Iris, Adi (and Hagit) Caspi, along with their extended family, showed me extraordinary warmth and kindness. I owe a special debt to my wife's late grandparents Zvi and Halah Caspi, who invited me to their home weekly for Shabbat lunch, and Dov Zanutzki, who welcomed and encouraged me on a memorable visit to Haifa. At the Rothberg International School of the Hebrew University in Jerusalem, I learned a great deal from my ulpan teachers about not only Hebrew but also Israeli culture. My seminar at Rothberg with Jay Berkovitz gave me another valued mentor. Friends and colleagues Scott Ury and Ofer Ashkenazi helped me navigate my way in Israeli institutions, and our conversations regularly sharpened my analysis.

I was extremely fortunate to spend the 2009–2010 academic year as a postdoctoral fellow at the Katz Center for Advanced Judaic Studies at the University of Pennsylvania. I remain grateful to the center's director, David Ruderman, for inviting me to participate in that year's discussion, "Secularism and Its Discontents: The View from Jewish Studies," and for making my stay so enjoyable and stimulating. My conversations with the other fellows at the center opened new perspectives on Jewish history broadly and questions specific to this book. I am especially grateful for the advice, insights, and support of Annette Aronowicz, David Myers, Amnon Raz-Krakotzkin, and Yael Zerubavel. While coediting another book with Ari Joskowicz, I learned a great deal that pertains to this book, and Ari has provided invaluable feedback on parts of this manuscript. During my year at the University of Pennsylvania, I was exceedingly fortunate to make a wonderful friend and intellectual companion in Jonathan Gribetz. Inspiring me repeatedly to think in new ways about Jews and Muslims, Jonathan has read and reread parts of this manuscript with tremendous care and incisive feedback, offered wise counsel on numerous occasions, and given me support when I needed it most.

Since my arrival at the University of Cincinnati, I have benefited from the vibrant intellectual environment of the History Department. The book's fifth chapter was greatly improved by comments at our departmental research seminar. Numerous colleagues have discussed with me other parts of this book. Particularly valuable have been questions and suggestions from Lily Frierson, Maura O'Connor, Steve Porter, and Willard Sunderland. My fellow research fellows during my year at the Taft Center—Vanessa Carbonell, Sarah Jackson, Wendy Kline, and Adrian Parr—offered fresh insight on my analysis and writing. Shortly before this book entered the world, Susan Karr generously read the entire manuscript and provided numerous helpful suggestions and needed encouragement. Both of my research assistants, Yael Herskowitz in Jerusalem and Jordan Hager-Cuntz in Cincinnati, were hardworking and capable.

I have been invited to share work in numerous settings where I have received valuable feedback and encouragement. Particularly beneficial for this book were opportunities to present at the Jewish studies workshop of the University of Illinois at Urbana-Champaign run by Matti Bunzl; a conference on "Jews and Muslims at the Margins of French Nationhood" at Georgetown University organized by Sarah Fainberg; Works-in-Progress in Modern Jewish Studies at the AJS conference run by Julia Phillips Cohen and Claire Sufrin; a talk at the Frankel Center at the University of Michigan organized by Joshua Cole; the Jews in Modern Europe Study Group at the Center for European Studies at Harvard run by Phyllis Cohen Albert and Alex Sagan; and the Posen Seminar at Miami University organized by Sven-Erik Rose. At two conferences I co-organized—one, "Religion, Race, and the Secular in Jewish-Muslim Relations," with Jonathan Gribetz at the Katz Center at UPenn, and the other, "Jewish History after the Imperial Turn," with Lisa Moses Leff and Maud Mandel at Brown—I greatly benefited from the comments and papers of fellow participants.

A number of other colleagues and friends have given me crucial guidance along the way. Kimberly Arkin, Julia Clancy-Smith, Adam Malka, David Myers, Derek

Penslar, Joan Wallach Scott, Paul Silverstein, Moshe Sluhovsky, Sarah Abrevaya Stein, and Judith Zinsser all read sections of the manuscript and provided helpful critiques and suggestions. From the beginning, Sarah Sussman was generous with her time and insights. Todd Shepard, whose work has influenced my thinking substantially, gave valuable feedback on the Introduction. Paris Papamichos Chronakis generously read Chapter 2 and opened new perspectives from his expertise in Mediterranean history. Chris Silver kindly shared his expertise in Arabic music. Since this book began, Rena Lauer, Lisa Moses Leff, and Jessica Marglin have become dear friends and important interlocutors. Each read significant portions of the manuscript, provided valuable feedback, and offered crucial support. From early on, Daniel Sherman has been a wonderful mentor. His incisive feedback improved the Introduction, and his guidance proved crucial in helping this book find a home.

I'll always be glad that I hung onto an archival inventory booklet a bit too long one day in Aix-en-Provence, prompting Joshua Cole to come looking for it at the table where I was sitting. Ever since, what began as a conversation about the 1934 riots of Constantine has become a long-running discussion about many wider issues of mutual interest. Josh read the entire manuscript, much of it on multiple occasions, and taught me a great deal about how to think and write about colonial Algeria, race, ethnicity, and a range of challenging historical topics. Daniel Schroeter has become a guiding force in the later stages of this book. In particular, his incredibly detailed and insightful comments on the entire manuscript led me to make numerous improvements large and small. My discovery ten years ago that Maud Mandel was beginning her own book on Jews and Muslims in France has turned out to be luckier than I could ever have imagined. An extraordinarily generous colleague who has become an invaluable mentor and a cherished friend, Maud's collaboration from the start has made this a better book. She has read practically every word of the manuscript, shared generously her own drafts, sources, and insights, and partnered with me in several joint endeavors.

The assistance I have received in the editing and production of this book has been any author's dream. At Harvard University Press, my editor, Andrew Kinney, took an immediate interest in the project and supported it enthusiastically throughout. Along the way, he gave keen editorial advice, both substantive and stylistic. Katrina Vassallo kept me on track with my many images and permissions. In the final stages, Kimberly Giambattisto was a master production editor, and copyeditor Bev Miller saved me from countless errors. Andrew, Katrina, and Kimberly all showed great patience. Isabelle Lewis's mapmaking expertise produced images that should render far more accessible the urban spaces discussed in this book.

I have received generous financial support for *The Burdens of Brotherhood* from a number of institutions. During my graduate studies: the George L. Mosse fellowship at the University of Wisconsin–Madison and then the Hebrew University of Jerusalem; Bourse Chateaubriand from the French Foreign Ministry; a Vilas International Research Grant from the Graduate School of the University of Wisconsin; the John B. and Theta H. Wolf Prize of the Society for French Historical Studies; the Maurice and Marilyn Cohen Doctoral Dissertation Grant of the Foundation for Jewish Culture; and a Doctoral Fellowship of the Memorial Foundation for Jewish Culture (twice). Since receiving my PhD: the Katz Center for Advanced Judaic Studies at the University of Pennsylvania; at the University of Cincinnati, a Charles Phelps Taft Research Center yearlong fellowship; a Taft summer research fellowship; and a grant from the Faculty Development Council.

Numerous archivists and librarians went out of their way to help me navigate their filing systems, think through how their holdings might connect to my project (frequently a daunting task), and locate files for me. These included staff at the following locations: in and around Paris, the Archives of the Alliance Israélite Universelle (in particular Rose Levyne and Jean-Claude Kuperminc), Centre de Documentation Juive Contemporaine at the Mémorial de la Shoah (especially Lior Lalieu Smadja), Archives of the Consistoire Israélite Centrale (especially Jean-Marc Lévy), Archives de la Préfecture de Police, Archives de la Ministère des Affaires Étrangères, Archives of the Association Génériques, Archives Nationales, Bibliothèque Nationale, Archives de la Ville de Paris, Archives du CASIP-COJASOR (especially Laure Politis), Centre des Archives Contemporaines, and Centre Culturel Algérien; in Marseille, the Archives Départementales des Bouches-du-Rhône, Archives Municipales de Marseille, Archives de la Chambre de Commerce, and Bibliothèque de l'Arsenal; in Strasbourg, the Archives Départementales du Bas-Rhin, Archives du Consistoire du Bas-Rhin, Archives de la Ville et de la Communauté Urbaine de Strasbourg, and Bibliothèque Nationale et Universitaire de Strasbourg; in Aix-en-Provence, the Centre des Archives d'Outre-mer; in Nantes, the Centre des Archives Diplomatiques de Nantes; in Jerusalem, the Archives of the American Joint Distribution Committee, Central Zionist Archives, and National Library of the Hebrew University; in Madison, Memorial Library at the University of Wisconsin; and in Cincinnati, the Klau Library of the Hebrew Union College-Jewish Institute of Religion (particularly Dan Rettberg) and Langsam Library at the University of Cincinnati (especially Sally Moffitt). I am grateful to a number of these institutions for allowing me to reproduce images in this book. Every effort has been made to trace copyright holders and to obtain permission for the use of the copyrighted images. I apologize for any errors and would be grateful if notified of any corrections that should be incorporated in future reprints or editions of this book.

My discussion of the Constantine riots in Chapter 2 is informed by my earlier articles "Constantine Riots (1934)," in Norman Stillman, ed., *Encyclopedia of the Jews in the Islamic World* (Boston: Brill, 2010) and "Between Emancipation and Persecution: Algerian Jewish Memory in the *Longue Durée*," *Journal of North African Studies* 17, no. 5 (2012): 793–820. Some of the themes presented in Chapter 3 were developed in "Did the Paris Mosque Save Jews? A Mystery and Its Memory," *Jewish Quarterly Review* 102, no. 2 (2012): 256–87 (translated into French with minor revisions as "La Mosquée de Paris a-t-elle sauvé des juifs? Une énigme, sa mémoire, son histoire," *Diasporas: Histoire et Sociétés* 21 [2013]: 128–55) and "Secular French Nationhood and Its Discontents: Jews as Muslims and Religion as Race," in Ari Joskowicz and Ethan B. Katz, eds., *Secularism in Question: Jews and Judaism in Modern Times* (Philadelphia: University of Pennsylvania Press, 2015). Some of the analysis of Zionism and Arab nationalism in Chapters 1, 2, and 3 grew out of "Tracing the Shadow of Palestine: the Zionist-Arab Conflict and Jewish-Muslim Relations in France, 1914–1945," in Nathalie Debrauwere-Miller, ed., *The Israeli-Palestinian Conflict in the Francophone World* (New York: Routledge, 2010). Various ideas in the book receive brief attention in "In the Shadow of the Republic: A Century of Coexistence and Conflict," in Benjamin Stora and Abdelwahab Meddeb, eds., *A History of Jewish-Muslim Relations: From the Origins to the Present Day* (Princeton, NJ: Princeton University Press, 2013). This was published simultaneously (and originally commissioned) in French under the title "Dans l'ombre de la République française: un siècle de coexistence et de conflit," in Benjamin Stora and Abdelwahab Meddeb, eds., *Histoire des relations entre juifs et musulmans, du Qur'an à nos jours* (Paris: Albin Michel, 2013).

By far my greatest debts are the most deeply personal. So much of what I have achieved I owe to my family. My grandparents Floyd Cohn and Anne Cohn and Fred Katz, my aunt and uncle Florence and Hanley Cohn, and my aunts Joanne Katz and Michelle Bartlett have each supported me from the earliest age. Not only have they cheered me on through triumphs and setbacks, they have also kept me grounded. My brother, Matthew Katz, has been my best friend since before he could walk. We share an exceptionally tight bond, and he is always there for me. He has even promised to read this book—and knows that if he doesn't I won't love him any less.

My parents, Allan Katz and Nancy Cohn, imparted to their children values of kindness, compassion, hard work, and citizenship that remain a daily inspiration. Extended trips to France and Israel, deep conversations about politics, civic engagement, prejudice, and coexistence marked my childhood and adolescence; their imprint is, I hope, felt in these pages. By modeling lives of service, offering me countless opportunities, and providing unconditional love and support, they have made it possible for me not only to follow the path that led to this book but also to believe that doing so is worthwhile.

The person who has lived most deeply with this book for the longest is my lifelong companion, Hagit Caspi. *The Burdens of Brotherhood* has been written and rewritten in the shadow of first our transcontinental romance and then our marriage. The book's questions and characters have constantly crisscrossed our own lives. Sharing with me each stage along the way as only a true partner can, Hagit has offered far more useful suggestions, probing questions, and incisive commentaries than she knows. She has tolerated physical (and mental) absences with unparalleled patience and caring.

The final two years of this endeavor we were joined by Daniel Ephraim. His curiosity, sweetness, precociousness, and vocal chords peppered the revisions process with vitally necessary color, distraction, and perspective. If he reads this one day I hope he will be proud of his Abba.

In short, I have had a lot of help along the way. It goes without saying that any errors or misstatements that remain here are mine alone.

INDEX